SWNHS
C20070662
WM 33 BUT
STAFF LIBRARY
BODMIN HOSPITAL

Mental Health Tribunals
Law, Practice and Proce

Second Edition

Mental Health Tribunals
Law, Practice and Procedure

Second Edition

Jonathan Butler BA (Hons), MA, MEd
Barrister-at-Law

Contributing Editor: Helen Wilson LLB (Hons)
Barrister-at-Law

Published by
Jordan Publishing Limited
21 St Thomas Street
Bristol BS1 6JS

Whilst the publishers and the author have taken every care in preparing the material included in this work, any statements made as to the legal or other implications of particular transactions are made in good faith purely for general guidance and cannot be regarded as a substitute for professional advice. Consequently, no liability can be accepted for loss or expense incurred as a result of relying in particular circumstances on statements made in this work.

© Jordan Publishing Limited 2013

All rights reserved. No part of this publication may be reproduced, stored in a retrieval system, or transmitted in any way or by any means, including photocopying or recording, without the written permission of the copyright holder, application for which should be addressed to the publisher.

Crown Copyright material is reproduced with kind permission of the Controller of Her Majesty's Stationery Office.

British Library Cataloguing-in-Publication Data

A catalogue record for this book is available from the British Library.

ISBN 978 1 84661 602 0

Typeset by Letterpart Ltd, Reigate, Surrey

Printed in Great Britain by CPI Antony Rowe Limited, Chippenham and Eastbourne

FOREWORD

This new edition, first produced at a time of significant change in mental health law and practice, with the implementation of both the Mental Health Act 2007 and the Tribunals Courts and Enforcement Act 2007, remains a very welcome addition to the material available to those concerned in the field of mental health law. The author is an experienced practitioner and part-time Tribunal Judge in the Mental Health jurisdiction. He brings a wealth of knowledge and understanding to this work and is to be congratulated on his understanding of the legislation, Rules and Tribunal Structure.

This is a very worthwhile contribution to an important and sensitive subject and will be of real benefit to practitioners and others seeking an understanding of the law and practice.

His Honour Judge Phillip Sycamore
Chamber President of the First-Tier Tribunal
(Health Education and Social Care)
April 2013

PREFACE

In describing the rationale for this book, I am not able to improve upon the introduction to *Mental Health Review Tribunals – Essential Cases* (Kris Gledhill, Southside Legal Publishing Ltd, 2nd edn, 2011) where he states:

> 'The law relating to detention on the basis of mental disorder and the tribunal at the centre of applications for release should be settled and certain, given that it involves deprivation of liberty and a vulnerable population, two factors that make it important that the law be clear.'

The purpose of this book is to be of use to the entire spectrum of participants (from whichever perspective) who are involved in Mental Health Tribunals. It is intended to provide clear and practical assistance in respect of not only the long-established principles behind Mental Health Tribunals, but also to take the opportunity of covering the changes brought about by the Tribunals Courts and Enforcement Act 2007 and the amendments to the Mental Health Act 1983 (including the new Rules and the new Appellate Tier). If it contributes even in modest measure to clarity on the law and practice, then it will have achieved its objectives.

Jonathan Butler
Deans Court Chambers
24 St John Street
Manchester & Preston
March 2013

AUTHOR'S NOTE

Where appropriate, the citations to case-law incorporate references to both the *Mental Health Law Reports* and to *Essential Cases* (2nd edn, 2011), both published by Southside Legal Publishing Ltd and available at www.southsidepublishing.co.uk. The editor and author of both of these is Kris Gledhill (Barrister). The reader of this text will find that the case-law contained in *Essential Cases* is invaluable, and *Essential Cases* and *Mental Health Tribunals: Law, Practice and Procedure* should complement each other.

CONTENTS

Part B
Tribunal Procedure and Jurisdiction

Chapter 3

Part E
Supporting Materials

Part F
Statutory Materials (Including Tribunal Rules and Practice Direction)

ACKNOWLEDGMENTS

The author would like to acknowledge and thank the following individuals: Christopher Curran; Dr Sarah Davenport; Kris Gledhill; Tony Hawitt; the late Dr B Mahendra; HHJ Phillip Sycamore; Dr Geoffrey Van Der Linden and to all my long suffering clerks at Deans Court Chambers, but particularly to Martin Leech.

GLOSSARY OF MEDICAL TERMS (INCLUDING COMMON MEDICATIONS)

Addiction
An organism's psychological or physical dependence on a drug, characterised by tolerance and withdrawal.

Adjustment disorders
States of subjective distress and emotional disturbance, usually interfering with social functioning and performance, arising in the period of adaptation to a significant life change or a stressful life event. The manifestations vary and include depressed mood, anxiety or worry (or mixture of these), a feeling of inability to cope, plan ahead, or continue in the present situation, as well as some degree of disability in the performance of daily routine. Conduct disorders may be an associated feature, particularly in adolescents. The predominant feature may be a brief or prolonged depressive reaction, or a disturbance of other emotions and conduct.

Aetiology
Cause(s) of a disorder.

Affective disorders
Mood disorder, especially where mood is pathologically elevated or lowered as in mania or depressive illness. Examples would include Major Depressive Disorder, Dysthymia, Depressive Disorder, Bipolar Disorder.

Agoraphobia
A phobic anxiety disorder in which the patient has a pathological fear of venturing into situations where crowds of people may be met. Depressive and obsessional symptoms and social phobias are also commonly present as subsidiary features.

Alzheimer's disease
A dementing disorder due to degenerative processes taking place in the brain. Believed to be the commonest cause of both senile and pre-senile dementia.

Anorexia nervosa
A disorder characterised by deliberate weight loss, induced and sustained by the patient. It occurs most commonly in adolescent girls and young women, but adolescent boys and young men may also be affected, as may children approaching puberty and older women up to the menopause. There is usually malnutrition of varying severity with secondary endocrine and metabolic

changes and disturbances of bodily function. The symptoms include restricted dietary choice, excessive exercise, induced vomiting and purgation, and use of appetite suppressants and diuretics.

Anticholinergics
Anticholinergics or antimuscarinics are most often used to help control some of the common side-effects which can occur with some antipsychotic drugs (also called neuroleptics or major tranquillisers), for example, tremor or shaking, stiffness or movement problems. These side effects are known as the 'Extra-pyramidal side effects (EPSEs)' or 'Parkinsonian' side effects. Continuous administration may not be necessary as side effects tend to reduce in intensity over time. These drugs are also used to control the symptoms of Parkinson's Disease itself.

Commonly prescribed medications include Benzhexol, Benztropine, Biperidin, Orphenadrine and Procyclidine.

Anticholinesterases
Anticholinesterases help to treat the symptoms of mild or moderate Alzheimer's Disease. They do not help if the symptoms have become more severe.

Medications include Donepezil, Galantamine and Rivastigmine.

Anticonvulsants or Antiepileptics (First-line)
A group of drugs used to treat or prevent convulsions (as in epilepsy).

Medications include Carbamazepine, Lamotrigine, Oxcarbazepine, Phenobarbital, Phenytoin, Primidone and Sodium Valproate.

Some of these medications are also used to stabilise mood in affective disorders.

Antidepressants
Antidepressants are used to improve mood in people who are feeling low or depressed. Antidepressants may also be used to help the symptoms of anxiety, some phobias and obsessive compulsive disorder.

Medications include Citalopram, Sertraline, Fluoxetine, Doxepin, Mianserin, Mirtazapine, Reboxetine and Venlafaxine.

Antipsychotics (or Neuroleptics)
This group of drugs are usually used to help treat illnesses or conditions such as psychosis, schizophrenia and hypomania. They can also be used to help manage behaviour problems and personality disorders. They may also be used in smaller doses to help treat anxiety, tension and agitation (in confusion or dementia).

The pharmaceutical classes for this group of drugs include Phenothiazines, Thioxanthenes, Butyrophenones and others.

Medications include Amisulpride, Aripiprazole, Chlorpromazine, Clozapine, Flupenthixol, Fluphenazine, Haloperidol, Olanzapine, Pipothiazine, Promazine, Quetiapine, Risperidone, Sulpiride and Zuclopenthixol.

Anxiety
A disorder in which there is a pathological and disproportionate sense of fear in the presence of trivial or no stimuli. Usually categorised as generalised anxiety disorders and phobic anxiety disorders. Anxiety manifests through mental and somatic symptoms such as palpitations, dizziness, hyperventilation, and faintness.

Asperger's syndrome
A disorder placed within the higher end of autistic spectrum disorders due to a pervasive developmental disorder. It is characterised by mild autistic features involving impaired social functioning and stereotypical repetitive behaviour. There may be no impairment of intelligence.

Attention-deficit hyperactivity disorder (ADHD)
A disorder of childhood involving overactivity, distractibility and impulsive behaviour.

Autism
A pervasive developmental disorder of childhood within the severe end of the spectrum of autistic disorders. Intellectual impairment is usual.

Benzodiazepines
This is a pharmaceutical class name for a group of drugs also known as anxiolytics, and hypnotics. They are one of the common treatments for anxiety and insomnia, but lead to dependence if prescribed long term. Common medications include Diazepam, Lorazepam and Clonazepam.

Beta blockers
A drug that inhibits the action of beta-adrenergic receptors, which modulate cardiac functions, respiratory functions and the dilation of blood vessels. Beta-blockers are of value in the treatment of hypertension, cardiac arrhythmias and migraine. In psychiatry, they have been used in the treatment of aggression and violence, anxiety-related tremors and lithium-induced tremors, neuroleptic-induced akathisia, social phobias, panic states and alcohol withdrawal. Most common prescription is for Propranolol.

Bipolar affective disorder
A disorder of mood where episodes of mania (elation, increased energy and overactivity) and depression (lowering of mood, decreased energy and activity) both occur.

Bulimia nervosa
An eating disorder in which patients, usually women, display binge eating and preoccupation with weight which is regulated by vomiting, abuse of diuretics and laxatives and excessive dieting.

Chronic Schizophrenia
A disorder in which the symptoms of schizophrenia persist long term.

Cognitive
Pertaining to attention, concentration, orientation and memory. Cognitive disorders include dementia and delirium, and may follow brain injury.

Cognitive Behaviour Therapy
A form of psychological treatment used in dealing with maladaptive behaviours and abnormal mood states by attempting to change negative thought patterns of the patient.

Compulsion
The motor counterpart of obsessional thinking. The individual feels compelled to repeat a behaviour which has no immediate benefit beyond reducing the anxiety associated with the obsessional idea. For instance, a person obsessed by the idea that they are dirty may use repeated ritual handwashing to reduce anxiety.

CT Scanning (Computerised Tomography)
A technique using x-rays to produce serial images of interior parts of the body. Within the skull it can be used to view parts of the brain as an aid to diagnosis.

Delusion
An abnormal belief which is out of keeping with the person's cultural context, intelligence and social background and which is held with unshakeable conviction.

Delusional disorder
A disorder characterised by the development either of a single delusion or of a set of related delusions that are usually persistent and sometimes lifelong. The content of the delusions is very variable. Clear and persistent auditory hallucinations (voices), schizophrenic symptoms such as delusions of control and marked blunting of affect and definite evidence of brain disease are all incompatible with this diagnosis. However, the presence of occasional or transitory auditory hallucinations, particularly in elderly patients, does not rule out this diagnosis, provided that they are not typically schizophrenic and form only a small part of the overall clinical picture.

Dementia
An acquired global condition which leads to an impairment in functioning of

the intellect, memory, personality and social behaviour. The term is entirely descriptive and the causes may be various, for example, degenerative brain disease, endocrine disease etc.

Dependence syndrome
A cluster of behavioural, cognitive and physiological phenomena that develop after repeated substance use and that typically include a strong desire to take the drug, difficulties in controlling its use, persisting in its use despite harmful consequences and giving a higher priority to drug use than to other activities and obligations. It is associated with increased tolerance, and sometimes a physical withdrawal state.

Depot injection
A drug, usually an anti-psychotic agent, which is given periodically by intramuscular injection. Obviates the need for daily ingestion of oral medication and thereby improves compliance.

Depression
A pathological lowering of mood, which may be associated with somatic symptoms such as sleep and appetite disturbance and weight loss (see below).

Depressive episode
In typical mild, moderate or severe depressive episodes, the patient suffers from lowering of mood, reduction of energy and decrease in activity. Capacity for enjoyment, interest and concentration are reduced, and marked tiredness after even minimum effort is common. Sleep is usually disturbed and appetite diminished. Self-esteem and self-confidence are almost always reduced and, even in the mild form, some ideas of guilt or worthlessness are often present. The lowered mood varies little from day to day, is unresponsive to circumstances and may be accompanied by so-called 'somatic' symptoms, such as loss of interest and pleasurable feelings, waking in the morning several hours before the usual time, depression worst in the morning, marked psychomotor retardation, agitation, loss of appetite, weight loss and loss of libido. Depending upon the number and severity of the symptoms, a depressive episode may be specified as mild, moderate or severe. Symptoms persist over some weeks.

Detachment
A behavioural response characterised by general aloofness in interpersonal contact; may include intellectualisation, denial and superficiality.

Dissociative disorder
Formerly known as hysterical reactions. A disorder in which the integrity in the relationship between memory, identity, sensory perception and motor control appears lost as a result of unconscious mechanisms. Common manifestations include amnesia, fugue (wandering), stupor and motor disorders. An extreme variant is trance or possession states.

Electroconvulsive treatment (ECT)
A procedure by which seizures are induced by the passage of electricity through the brain. An effective treatment for severe depressive illness.

Euthymia
Indicates normal non-depressed, reasonably positive mood.

Functional Magnetic Resonance Imaging (MRI)
Technique for visualising the brain as an aid to diagnosis.

Functional disorder
A mental disorder in which no obvious adverse change in the structure and function of the brain can be discerned in the present state of knowledge.

Formal thought disorder
An inexact term referring to a disturbance in the form of thinking rather than to abnormality of content, where associations between ideas are lost or loosened.

Hallucination
An abnormal sensory experience that arises in the absence of a direct external stimulus, and which has the qualities of a normal percept. It is experienced as real and usually in external space. Hallucinations may occur in any sensory modality.

Their significance depends on the entirety of the clinical picture.

Huntington's chorea
Genetically determined pre-senile dementia characterised by abnormal movements and mental disorder including dementia.

Hypnotics
Medication to induce sleep; common prescriptions are for Zopiclone, nitrazepam and chloral.

Hypomania
A less severe form of mania (see below). A disorder characterised by a persistent mild-moderate elevation of mood, increased energy and activity. There are usually marked feelings of well-being and both physical and mental efficiency. Increased sociability, talkativeness, over-familiarity, increased sexual energy and a decreased need for sleep are often present but not to the extent that they lead to severe disruption of work or result in social rejection. Irritability, conceit and boorish behaviour may take the place of the more usual euphoric sociability. The disturbances of mood and behaviour are not accompanied by hallucinations or delusions.

Hypomanic or manic episodes in individuals who have had one or more previous affective episodes (depressive, hypomanic, manic or mixed) should be coded as bipolar affective disorder.

Insight
The awareness expressed by a patient, with regard to the mental condition from which he or she suffers. There are gradations through full, partial down to no insight.

Knights Move Thinking
A form of thought disorder characterised by non-understandable links between thoughts, but expressed by the patient as if they represented a special meaning.

Mania
Severe elevation of mood resulting in disruption of social functioning; may present a physical health risk (dehydration, exhaustion) and be associated with hallucinations or delusions.

Hypomanic or manic episodes in individuals who have had one or more previous affective episodes (depressive, hypomanic, manic or mixed) should be coded as bipolar affective disorder.

Major Depressive Disorder
A severe mental illness characterised by feelings of hopelessness, helplessness and worthlessness; often accompanied by suicidal thoughts and extreme lethargy

Mono-amine oxidase inhibitors or MAOIs
A class of antidepressant drugs used in treatment resistant depression where other drugs have failed. They have serious side effects and require a special diet to exclude tyramine (present in cheese etc).

The MAOIs may also be used to help the resistant symptoms of anxiety and a number of other symptoms.

Mood Stabilisers
Lithium salts or anticonvulsant drugs used to stabilise mood in bipolar disorder, recurrent depression and sometimes in Borderline Personality Disorder.

Common prescriptions are for Carbamazepine, Lamotrigine, Lithium carbonate, Lithium citrate, Sodium valproate, Valproate semisodium (depakote).

Negative symptoms (of schizophrenia)
Include lack of motivation, apathy, poverty of speech, social withdrawal, emotional unresponsiveness and self-neglect. May respond poorly to standard forms of treatment.

Neurosis
Minor psychiatric disorders in which insight and a sense of reality are preserved although the individual experiences some loss of function. There is a discernible contribution of the personality to 'colour' the disorder. Neurotic conditions include minor depressive illness, anxiety states, obsessive-compulsive disorder and hysterical reactions (dissociative/conversion disorders).

Obsession
An unpleasant or nonsensical thought which intrudes into a person's mind, despite a degree of resistance. The person recognises the thought as pointless or senseless, but nevertheless a product of their own mind. Obsessions may be accompanied by compulsive behaviours which serve to reduce the associated anxiety.

Obsessive-compulsive disorder
The essential feature is recurrent obsessional thoughts or compulsive acts. Obsessional thoughts are ideas, images or impulses that repeatedly enter the patient's mind in a stereotyped form. They are almost invariably distressing and the patient often tries, unsuccessfully, to resist them. They are, however, recognised as his or her own thoughts, even though they are involuntary and often repugnant. Compulsive acts or rituals are stereotyped behaviours that are repeated.

Organic
Refers to disorders where there is demonstrable structural or pathophysiological) disturbance of brain function.

Orientation
An individual's awareness of time, place and person. Disturbed in the dementias and delirium.

Panic attacks
Acute, episodic attacks of extreme anxiety, associated with physiological symptoms and avoidance behaviour.

Paranoia
A mental state that includes pervasive unreasonable suspiciousness of people and situations. A person who is paranoid may be suspicious, hostile and sensitive to perceived criticism or rejection by others.

Paranoid Schizophrenia
Commonest type of schizophrenia, characterised by relatively stable, often

paranoid, delusions, usually accompanied by auditory hallucinations and perceptual disturbances. Disturbances of affect, volition and speech are not prominent.

Parasuicide
Deliberate self-harm in which suicidal intent is absent from the behaviour leading to self-harm. May be understood as a maladaptive coping strategy and is often associated with reckless behaviour.

Persecutory delusion
Abnormal belief in which the patient believes that they are being attacked, harassed, cheated on, persecuted or conspired against.

Personality Disorder
These are severe disturbances in the personality and behavioural tendencies of the individual which are not the direct result of mental illness or brain disease. Several areas of the personality are involved (social and interpersonal function). Personality Disorder is nearly always associated with considerable personal distress and social disruption; it has usually been manifest since childhood or adolescence and continues throughout adulthood.

Positive symptoms (of schizophrenia)
These include symptoms such as delusions, hallucinations, speech and thought disorders. They are features of acute illness but may persist, unless they respond to antipsychotic medication.

Post-traumatic stress disorder (PTSD)
A delayed and/or protracted response to a stressful event of an exceptionally threatening nature likely to cause distress.

Clinical utility suspect as features may be subsumed within depressive illness and anxiety states.

Pre-morbid
Antedating illness; often used to characterise personality before onset of illness.

Pressure of speech
Increased speech rate, often associated with difficulty in interruption and override to the normal turn-taking in conversation.

Psychosis
Major mental disorder that involves changes in thinking, perception, behaviour and social function characterised by severity and loss of contact with reality. (Psychotic presentations usually include delusions and/or hallucinations.)

Psychotic disorder
A cluster of psychotic phenomena that can occur during or following

psychoactive substance use, but not explained by acute intoxication alone and not forming part of a withdrawal state. The disorder is characterised by hallucinations (typically auditory, but often in more than one sensory modality), perceptual distortions, delusions (often of a paranoid or persecutory nature), psychomotor disturbances (excitement or stupor) and an abnormal affect, which may range from intense fear to ecstasy. The sensorium is usually clear but some degree of clouding of consciousness, though not severe confusion, may be present.

Pseudohallucination
A hallucination, usually auditory, arising from within an individual's mind and not relating to the world outside. May be seen in states of grief and is less significant than true hallucinations.

Psychopathology
A study of abnormal mental states either in terms of their description (also called phenomenology) or as mode of causation (psychodynamic psychopathology).

Reversible inhibitors of monoamine oxidase type-A (RIMAs)
A class of psychiatric drugs and natural compounds that inhibit monoamine oxidase temporarily and reversibly. They are mostly used for alleviating depression and dysthymia. Their action is short-lived and selective.

Medications include Moclobemide.

Rehabilitation
Strategies to promote a patients strengths and social inclusion, by minimising or preventing secondary social disability due to mental disorder.

Schizoaffective Disorder
A condition that includes symptoms of both schizophrenia and affective (mood) disorder.

Schizoid
Socially isolated, withdrawn, having few friends and social relationships,

Schizophrenia
A common type of psychosis characterised by hallucinations and/or delusions, personality changes, withdrawal and serious thought and speech disturbances.

Schizophreniform
Used to describe the form of an illness as Schizophrenia-like; may be seen in cases involving drug abuse.

Senile dementia
Dementias occurring at the age of 65 or after. Pre-senile dementias occur before that age.

Separation anxiety disorder
A disorder (with onset before the age of 18) consisting of inappropriate anxiety concerning separation from home or from persons to whom the child is attached. Symptoms are unrealistic concern about harm befalling or loss of major attachment figures; refusal to go to school in order to stay at home and maintain contact with this figure; refusal to go to sleep unless close to this person; clinging; nightmares about the theme of separation; and development of physical symptoms or mood changes (apathy, depression) when separation occurs or is anticipated.

Somatic symptoms
Usually seen in cases of depressive illness. Involve symptoms such as sleep disturbance and changes in appetite, bowel habits, menstrual regularity and libido.

Specific serotonin reuptake inhibitors or SSRIs
SSRIs are antidepressants which are used to help to improve mood in people who are feeling low or depressed. Fluoxetine ('Prozac') may also be used to help treat the eating disorder 'Bulimia nervosa'. In addition to this, the SSRIs are now widely used to help a variety of other symptoms. These include anxiety (where a lower starting dose often helps), social phobia and social anxiety, obsessive-compulsive disorder, post-traumatic stress disorder, panic, pre-menstrual syndrome and agoraphobia.

Medications include Citalopram, Escitalopram, Fluoxetine, Fluvoxamine, Paroxetine and Sertraline.

Suicidal behaviour
Deliberate self-harming behaviour which involves an element of intent.

Tardive dyskinesia
Serious side-effect of antipsychotic medication, which includes involuntary movements of face, mouth, tongue, upper or lower limbs. Can occur on withdrawal from antipsychotic drugs and may be irreversible.

Tranquilizer
A medicine that produces a calming effect. The so-called major tranquilizers are used to treat serious mental disorders; the minor tranquilizers are often used to treat anxiety.

Tricyclic antidepressants
Used to improve mood in people who are feeling low or depressed. The tricyclics may also be used to help the symptoms of anxiety and a number of other symptoms. Medications include Amitriptyline, Amoxapine, Clomipramine, Desipramine, Doxepin, Imipramine, Lofepramine, Maprotiline, Nortriptyline, Protriptyline, Trazodone and Trimipramine.

Visual hallucination
A hallucination involving sight, which may consist of formed images, such as of people, or of unformed images, such as flashes of light. Visual hallucinations should be distinguished from illusions, which are misperceptions of real external stimuli.

Word salad
A form of thought disorder where the connexions between thoughts (as expressed in words) has completely broken down and appears random.

LIST OF COMMON MEDICATIONS

Name	Category of drug	Condition treated	Common side-effects
Alprazolam	Benzodiazepine	Anxiety and panic attacks	Drowsiness and confusion in the elderly
Amisulpride	Atypical antipsychotic	Schizophrenia	Restlessness stiffness on higher doses
			Insomnia, agitation, constipation
Amitriptyline	Tricyclic antidepressant	Depression	Dry mouth and constipation
Amoxapine	Tricyclic antidepressant	Depression	As above, menstrual irregularities and tardive dyskinesia
Aripiprazole	Atypical antipsychotic	Schizophrenia	Sleep disturbance
Benperidol	Antipsychotic	Antisocial sexual behaviour	Effectiveness for this condition NOT established
Benzhexol	Anticholinergic/ antimuscarinic	Counteracts common side effects of antipsychotic drugs, e g tremors, shaking, stiffness, known as Extrapyramidal side effects (EPSEs)	Memory difficulties and mood elevation on high doses
Benztropine	Anticholinergic/ antimuscarinic	As above	As above

Name	Category of drug	Condition treated	Common side-effects
Carbamazepine	Anticonvulsant, also acts as a mood stabiliser	Epilepsy, Bipolar Affective Disorder (BPAD), Schizoaffective Disorder, Borderline Personality Disorder	Nausea, vomiting, constipation, dizziness, drowsiness, ataxia, hyponatraemia on high doses
Cloral betaine (Welldorm)	Hypnotic	Now rarely used for insomnia	Gastrointestinal disturbances
Chloral hydrate	Sedative and hypnotic	Insomnia	Induces dependence if prescribed long term
Chlordiazepoxide	Benzodiazepine	Anxiety and acute alcohol withdrawal	Induces dependence if prescribed long term
Chlorpromazine	Typical antipsychotic	Schizophrenia, BPAD and other psychoses	Drowsiness, photo-sensitivity, raised serum prolactin leading to gynaecomastia, sexual problems, and osteoporosis
Citalopram	Selective serotonin re-uptake inhibitor (SSRI)	Depression or panic attacks	Gastro-intestinal effects, tachycardia and postural hypotension
Clobazam	Benzodiazepine	Severe anxiety, sleeping problems and adjuvant treatment of epilepsy	Drowsiness
Clomethiazole	Hypnotic	Insomnia, restlessness and agitation, and acute alcohol withdrawal	Dependence, nasal congestion and irritation
Clomipramine	Tricyclic antidepressant	Depression, phobic and obsessional states	Dry mouth, sedation, constipation

Name	Category of drug	Condition treated	Common side-effects
Clonazepam	Benzodiazepine	Severe anxiety and sleeping problems, status epilepticus	Drowsiness, coordination disturbances and muscle hypotonia
Clorazepate dipotassium	Benzodiazepine	Short-term use for anxiety, acute alcohol withdrawal and certain convulsive disorders such as epilepsy	Drowsiness
Clozapine	Atypical antipsychotic	Schizophrenia	Hypersalivation, constipation (cardiotoxicity, depression of white cell count)
Diazepam	Benzodiazepine	Anxiety, insomnia, seizures, muscle spasms and acute alcohol withdrawal	Drowsiness, confusion and ataxia (especially in the elderly) (paradoxical increase in aggression)
Donepezil	Acetylcholinesterase inhibitor	Mild or moderate Alzheimer's Disease	Gastrointestinal symptoms, headaches
Doxepin	Tricyclic antidepressant	Depression	Dry mouth and constipation
Escitalopram	Selective serotonin re-uptake inhibitor (SSRI)	Depression or panic attacks	Postural hypotension, yawning
Fluoxetine	Antidepressant	Depression, bulimia nervosa and obsessive-compulsive disorder (OCD)	Gastro-intestinal symptoms
Flupenthixol	Typical antipsychotic, oral or depot preparation	Schizophrenia and maintenance in depression	EPSEs
Fluphenazine	typical antipsychotic (DEPOT)	Maintenance treatment for schizophrenia	EPSEs
Fluvoxamine	Selective serotonin re-uptake inhibitor (SSRI)	Depression or panic attacks OCD	Nausea

Name	Category of drug	Condition treated	Common side-effects
Galantamine	Acetylcholinesterase inhibitor	Used to control mild or moderate Alzheimer's Disease	Gastro-intestinal disturbances
Haloperidol	Typical antipsychotic	Schizophrenia, acute psychotic states and delirium	EPSEs, akathisia
Imipramine	Tricyclic antidepressant	Depression, nocturnal enuresis in children	Dry mouth and constipation
Isocarboxazid	Antidepressant (monoamine-oxidase inhibitor which interacts with foods containing tyramine to cause dangerous hypertension)	Treatment Resistant Depression	Postural hypotension
Lamotrigine	Anticonvulsant and mood stabiliser	Epilepsy and bipolar disorder	Skin rashes and blood disorders, flu-like symptoms, photosensitivity, gastrointestinal disturbances
Levomepromazine	Antipsychotic	Schizophrenia	Drowsiness and postural hypotension
Lithium carbonate	Lithium salt	Treatment of mania and prophylaxis in bipolar disorder	Gastrointestinal disturbances, tremor and thirst
Lithium citrate	Lithium salt	Mood stabilizer in psychiatric treatment of manic states and bipolar disorde	As above
Lofepramine	Tricyclic antidepressant	Depression	Dry mouth and constipation
Lorazepam	Short acting benzodiazepine	Anxiety disorders and acute agitation	Induces dependence with prolonged administration
Maprotiline	Tetracyclic antidepressant	Depression	Skin rashes and convulsions in high dose

Name	Category of drug	Condition treated	Common side-effects
Mianserin	Tetracyclic antidepressant	Depression	Dry mouth and constipation (aplastic anaemia in the elderly)
Mirtazapine	Antidepressant	Depression	Increased appetite and weight gain
Moclobemide	Reversible monoamine-oxidase Inhibitor	Depression and phobias	Sleep disturbance and gastrointestinal upset
Nortriptyline	Tricyclic antidepressant	Depression	Dry mouth
Olanzapine	Atypical antipsychotic	Schizophrenia and bipolar disorder, Severe Borderline Personality Disorder	Weight gain, drowsiness, diabetes
Orphenadrine	Anticholinergic	Controls EPSEs induced by typical antipsychotics	Insomnia
Oxazepam	Benzodiazepine	Anxiety	Drowsiness
Paroxetine	Selective serotonin re-uptake inhibitor (SSRI)	Depression or panic attacks	Postural hypotension
Pericyazine	Antipsychotic	Schizophrenia, short-term management of severe anxiety or agitation	Cardiac arrythmias
Perphenazine	Typical antipsychotic	Schizophrenia, short-term management of severe anxiety or agitation	EPSEs
Phenelzine	Antidepressant (monoamine-oxidase inhibitor which interacts with foods containing tyramine to cause dangerous hypertension)	Treatment Resistant Depression	Postural hypotension and dizziness
Phenytoin	Antiepileptic	Epilepsy	Nausea, vomiting
Pipothiazine	Depot antipsychotic	Schizophrenia	EPSEs, akathisia

Name	Category of drug	Condition treated	Common side-effects
Primidone	Anticonvulsant	Epilepsy	Drowsiness, ataxia
Procyclidine	Anticholinergic/ antimuscarinic	EPSEs induced by antipsychotics	Memory impairment with high doses
Promazine	Antipsychotic	Short-term management of agitation	Drowsiness
Quetiapine	Atypical antipsychotic	Schizophrenia and bipolar disorder	Drowsiness, dyspepsia, metabolic effects
Reboxetine	Antidepressant	Depression	Insomnia, sweating
Risperidone	Atypical antipsychotic	Schizophrenia and bipolar disorder	Insomnia, agitation or drowsiness, constipation, (cardiac and metabolic abnormalities)
Rivastigmine	Acetylcholinesterase inhibitor	Control mild or moderate Alzheimer's Disease	Nausea, vomiting, drowsiness, tremor
Sertindole	Atypical antipsychotic	Schizophrenia	Prolongs cardiac conduction time, dry mouth, rhinitis and peripheral oedema
Sertraline	Selective serotonin re-uptake inhibitor (SSRI)	Depression, obsessive-compulsive disorder, PTSD, panic attacks	Tachycardia, confusion
Sodium valproate	Anticonvulsant and mood stabiliser	Epilepsy and bipolar affective disorder (BPAD)	Gastric irritation, ataxia, tremor, weight gain, hair loss, liver disorders
Semisodium Valproate Depakote	Mood stabiliser	Mania, BPAD	As above
Sulpiride	Typical antipsychotic	Schizophrenia and other psychotic disorders	Restlessness and tremor in high doses

Name	Category of drug	Condition treated	Common side-effects
Thioridazine	Typical antipsychotic, now withdrawn	Schizophrenia	Hypotension and prolonged cardiac conduction time, retinal pigmentation, sexual dysfunction
Tranylcypromine	Antidepressant (monoamine-oxidase inhibitor)	Treatment Resistant Depression	Insomnia if given in the evening, hypertensive crises and headache
Trazodone	Tetracyclic antidepressant	Depression	Constipation and dry mouth
Trifluoperazine	Antipsychotic	Schizophrenia	EPSEs (Blood dyscrasias, hyperpyrexia)
Trimipramine	Tricyclic antidepressant	Depression	Sedation
Tryptophan	Antidepressant RESTRICTED TO HOSPITAL USE	Treatment Resistant Depression	Interactions with other drugs and eosinophilia-myalgia
Venlafaxine	Serotonin and noradrenalin reuptake inhibitor SNRI antidepressant	Specialist treatment of resistant depression	Constipation, nausea, dizziness
Zaleplon	Hypnotic	short-term use for insomnia	Amnesia, parasthesia, dizziness
Zolpidem	Hypnotic	Insomnia	Diarrhea, nausea, vomiting, depression, ataxia and confusion
Zopiclone	Hypnotic	short-term use for insomnia	Aggression, irritability, confusion (particularly in the elderly), dependence
Zotepine	Atypical antipsychotic	Schizophrenia	Constipation, dry mouth, cardiac effects, sexual dysfunction

Name	Category of drug	Condition treated	Common side-effects
Zuclopenthixol	Typical antipsychotic in oral or injectable form	Schizophrenia, particularly if associated with hostility	Drowsiness, EPSE, weight gain, urinary frequency

LIST OF ABBREVIATIONS

AAC	Administrative Appeals Chamber
AC	Approved clinician
AMHP	Approved mental health professional
ACUS	After-care under supervision
AMPH	Approved mental health professional
ANH	Artificial nutrition and hydration
ASW	Approved social worker
CAMHS	Child and Adolescent Mental Health Services
CPR	Civil Procedure Rules 1998, SI 1998/3132
CTO	Community treatment order
ECHR	European Convention on Human Rights
ECT	Electro convulsive therapy
LSSA	Local social services authority
MAPPA	Multi-agency public protection arrangement
MCA 2005	Mental Capacity Act 2005
MHA 1983	Mental Health Act 1983
MHA 1989	Mental Health Act 1983
MHA 2007	Mental Health Act 2007
MHAC	Mental Health Act Commission
MHRT	Mental Health Review Tribunal
MHU	Mental Health Unit
NHS	National Health Service
NIMHE	National Institute for Mental Health in England
old rules	Mental Health Review Tribunal Rules 1983, SI 1983/942
PCT	Primary care trust
RA	Responsible authority
RC	Responsible clinician
RMO	Responsible medical officer
Rules	Tribunal Procedure (First-tier Tribunal) (Health, Education and Social Care Chamber) Rules 2008, SI 2008/2699
SCR	Social circumstances report
SCT	Supervised community treatment

SOAD	Second opinion appointed doctor
TCEA 2007	Tribunals, Courts and Enforcement Act 2007
TJ	Tribunal Judge
Tribunal	First-tier Tribunal (Health Education and Social Care) Mental Health
VLO	Victim liaison officer

TABLE OF CASES

References are to paragraph numbers.

TABLE OF STATUTES

References are to paragraph numbers.

TABLE OF STATUTORY INSTRUMENTS

References are to paragraph numbers.

TABLE OF EC AND INTERNATIONAL MATERIAL

References are to paragraph numbers.

Part A

TRIBUNAL ORGANISATION AND COMPOSITION

Chapter 1

ORIGINS, CONSTITUTION, ADMINISTRATION AND FUNCTION OF THE FIRST-TIER TRIBUNAL (MENTAL HEALTH)

ORIGINS

1.1 Concerns about the manner in which the mentally ill have been deprived of their liberty date back to at least 1815, with the *Parliamentary Inquiry into Madhouses* of that year. As the Chairman of the Mental Health Act Commission (MHAC) has observed in his foreword to the *Twelfth Biennial Report* of the MHAC, a number of the concerns expressed in the early nineteenth century are still apparent in the early twenty-first century.[1] Amongst those concerns were the 'Detention of persons the state of whose minds did not require confinement' and 'Restraint of persons much beyond what is necessary …'.[2] It is obvious that both of these matters are at the forefront of any consideration of the appropriacy and proportionality of detention under the Mental Health Act 1983 (MHA 1983) and by the First-tier Tribunal (Health Education and Social Care) Mental Health (the Tribunal). Although the term 'Mental Health Review Tribunal' (MHRT) is still in use, it should be noted that from 3 November 2008 it ceased to exist.[3] In order to minimise confusion in respect of terminology, the word 'Tribunal' is used throughout the commentary to refer to both the old regime and the new. Although the term 'Mental Health Review Tribunal' is still in use (including in the MHA 1983 itself), it should be noted that from 3 November 2008, it ceased to exist. In order to minimise confusion in respect of terminology, the word 'Tribunal' is used throughout the commentary to refer to both the old regime, and the new.

1.2 Within more modern legal and social history, the Tribunal was in part a product of the European Convention for the Protection of Human Rights and Fundamental Freedoms 1950 (ECHR). Specifically, under the regime of the Mental Health Act 1959, the access of a patient to an independent judicial body which had powers that were more than merely advisory were limited. Whilst this remains the case in some instances, MHA 1983 created a regime whereby the Tribunal is able to deal with the needs of a patient in a more extensive manner. The limitations on the powers of the Tribunal are still

---

1 Mental Health Act Commission *Risk, Rights, Recovery: Twelfth Biennial Report 2005–2007* (TSO, 2008) (MHAC Report).

2 Ibid, Foreword, at p 11.

3 See Transfer of Tribunal Functions Order 2008, SI 2008/2833.

circumscribed, however. The most recent developments have been as a result of the report of Sir Andrew Leggatt.[4] This was a review of *all* tribunals, and it has led to the current revisions to *all* tribunals, amongst which is the First-tier Tribunal (Health Education and Social Care) Mental Health. In respect of the First-tier Tribunal (Health Education and Social Care) Mental Health the Leggatt Report identified the following salient points:

- dual function of the medical member;
- problems of clerical and administrative support/resources;
- lack of powers of enforcement of orders; and
- appeal routes/judicial review.

1.3 More generally, the Leggatt Report reiterated the significance of the independence of tribunals as a method of adjudicating on issues, particularly when the issue is a dispute between the citizen and the state. It comments:[5] 'They [the tribunals] will keep the confidence of users only insofar as they are seen to demonstrate similar qualities of independence and impartiality to the courts.'

1.4 This in turn eventually caused the passing into legislation of the Tribunals, Courts and Enforcement Act 2007 (TCEA 2007), and the creation of the Tribunals Service (in April 2006). The Executive Summary to the Consultation Paper *Transforming Tribunals – Implementing Part 1 of the Tribunals Courts and Enforcement Act 2007*[6] produced by the Ministry of Justice reminds the reader that:[7]

> 'Fifty years ago a committee chaired by Sir Oliver Franks examined tribunals and inquiries and laid down the fundamental principle that tribunals perform a judicial role and should not be seen as part of the executive government.'

Thus, the significance of independence and impartiality and the status of the Tribunal has (implicitly) been reaffirmed. The restructuring of the Tribunal is considered at greater length below.

ADMINISTRATION

1.5 The administration of the Tribunal was the responsibility of the Mental Health Review Tribunal Secretariat. In 2006 (as a result of the creation of the Tribunals Service) the administration moved to a single office based in London.

---

4 Sir Andrew Leggatt *Tribunals for Users: One System, One Service – Report of the Review of Tribunals* (TSO, March 2001) (Leggatt Report).

5 Leggatt Report, at para 2.18.

6 CP 30/07, 28 November 2007 (*Transforming Tribunals*).

7 At p 5.

This was also coincidental with the abolition of the regional offices and distinct geographical regions (into simply the Northern and Southern Regions, each with a full-time Regional Chair). The London Office was subsequently closed in 2008, and is now based in Leicester. The Secretariat itself is divided into seven teams, which cover distinct geographical parts of England. Each of these teams has different responsibilities, which includes the listing of hearings, the selection of each member of the Tribunal to sit and the distribution of reports in advance of the hearings (where appropriate).

1.6 The Tribunals Service is an executive agency of the Department for Constitutional Affairs (the Ministry of Justice since 9 May 2007). When it was created, it was responsible for a number of tribunals (including the Tribunal). The changes to the arrangements will incorporate a still greater number of tribunals. There is also an intention to introduce greater flexibility, which is to encourage members of tribunals to sit on other tribunals, where appropriate.

CONSTITUTION

1.7 The arrangements for the constitution of the Tribunal have been substantially altered. It remains to be seen how much of an effect this will have on the day-to-day running of the Tribunal hearings themselves.

First-tier and Upper Tribunals

1.8 TCEA 2007 received Royal Assent on 19 July 2007. It contains provisions for a judicial and legal framework which is intended to complement the administrative arrangements summarised above. It creates a 'First-tier Tribunal' and an 'Upper Tribunal'. The Tribunal will function within the First-tier Tribunal. The old Mental Health Review Tribunal Rules ceased to exist, and have been replaced by rules of procedure that are common to *all* tribunals. These rules (the Tribunal Procedure (First-tier Tribunal) (Health, Education and Social Care Chamber) Rules 2008[8]) are considered at appropriate points below, and set out in full in Part F. There are separate Rules for Wales.[9] The new regime came into force on 3 November 2008. The creation of an Upper Tribunal is intended to cause there to be a common approach and consistency to all appeals from the First-tier Tribunal. It is within the First-tier Tribunal that all patients will appear in respect of challenges to detention under MHA 1983. It is to the Upper Tribunal that all appeals from the First-tier will proceed. This has largely replaced the current system of judicial review to the Administrative Court in respect of matters arising out of the discharge of functions by the Tribunal. The role of the Upper Tribunal, and its powers to use powers otherwise only available in the Administrative Court, are considered in Chapter 14. There are rules in respect of this tier as well (the Tribunal Procedure (Upper Tribunal) Rules 2008[10]), which are also considered in Part F.

8 SI 2008/2699.

9 Mental Health Review Tribunal for Wales Rules 2008, SI 2008/2705.

10 SI 2008/2698.

Permission to appeal to the Upper Tribunal is required. The Upper Tribunal is a superior Court of record, and its decisions are binding on lower tribunals and authoritative on the interpretation of the law. Appeal from the Upper Tribunal will be to the Court of Appeal (as is currently the case on appeal from the High Court in judicial review matters). Appeals will be confined to points of law only. The rules for both Tiers themselves will be supplemented by Practice Directions which will be specific to the individual jurisdictions. The first of these is set out in Part F. It is not retrospective.

1.9 The *Reference Guide to the Mental Health Act 1983* (Chapter 20) provides an accurate description of the new terminology in the following terms:

> 'The First-tier Tribunal is an independent judicial body ... The First-tier Tribunal's powers in these cases only apply to England. There is still an MHRT for Wales, established under section 65 of the Act.'

It continues:

> 'The First-tier tribunal does not review other people's decisions to detain patients or to make them subject to other forms of compulsory measures under the Act. It decides whether, at the time of the hearing, the patient should remain subject to the relevant parts of the Act.'

1.10 In respect of the *Upper Tribunal* it summarises its function thus:

> 'Its role in mental health cases is to determine appeals against decisions of the First-tier Tribunal. It also hears appeals against decisions of the MHRT in Wales ... Appeals to the Upper Tribunal may only be made on a point of law, and only with the permission of the First-tier Tribunal or the Upper Tribunal itself. Before deciding whether to grant permission to appeal, the First-tier Tribunal will first consider whether to review its own decision.'

The latter provisions were a real departure from previous practice, and are dealt with at greater length in Parts C and D of this book. The Upper Tribunal can make a new decision itself, or remit the matter back to the First-tier for a re-hearing.

Senior President

1.11 The office of Senior President is a free-standing senior judicial office, independent of the Executive and the Chief Justices responsible for the courts. The senior judiciary within the Chamber comprise a Chamber President, and a Deputy Chamber President.

Health, Education and Social Care Chamber

1.12 The alteration in terminology also applies to the creation of 'Chambers'. There are a number of these, and the Tribunal occupies the 'Health. Education and Social Care Chamber'. The largest part of the work within this Chamber will be the First-tier Tribunal (Health Education and Social Care) Mental Health, but it is shared by the Special Educational Needs and Disability Tribunal, the Care Standards Tribunal and by the Family Health Services Appeal Authority in the future. Each Chamber has a Chamber President. The Judicial Appointments Commission has also appointed a Deputy President. There are also a number of full-time salaried Tribunal Judges (STJs) of the First-tier Tribunal (Mental Health) based in London and Manchester.

Function

1.13 The function of the Tribunal is (broadly) confined to the following. It may uphold the detention of a patient or discharge a patient. It may make recommendations (but only in respect of limited matters). It may (in certain cases) attach conditions to a decision to discharge a patient. It can also adjourn cases and make orders/directions in respect of a number of issues, but usually for the obtaining of further evidence on issues that come within its jurisdiction. It can no longer re-classify the mental illness from which it is said that a patient suffers. However, even these apparently simple functions are fraught with traps for the unwary. The body of this book goes through each of these areas and powers, and limitations upon powers. However, as the MHAC has observed, its implicit function may be more subtle, even if no recommendations are made, or the patient is not discharged.[11] Neither legal representatives nor Tribunal members should overlook this important function that is ancillary to the main objective of a tribunal. It may well be the only opportunity that a patient (or indeed other professionals who participate) will have to present differing views in a formal environment.

Formality

1.14 Further, whilst the Tribunal will conduct itself in a manner which is not overly formal, all participants must remain aware that it is in effect a court, and not a meeting or a multi-disciplinary discussion. This is sometimes a problem with inexperienced social workers or psychiatrists who give evidence to the Tribunal. For example, the Tribunal does have the power to instigate proceedings for contempt of court (which can carry a sentence of imprisonment) if there is a failure to comply with its directions.

1.15 The new Rules (for both the First-tier and Upper Tribunal) and in particular r 2(2)(b) and (c)[12] make this explicit, in imposing as part of the 'overriding objective' an avoidance of unnecessary formality and the seeking of flexibility in proceedings, and also to ensure as far as possible that all the

---

11 'I have found MHRTs to be a very beneficial way of getting professionals to review my situation': Dawn Cutler-Nichol, S.37/41, Derbyshire, MHAC Report, at Chapter 4, p 170, para 4.70.

12 Tribunal Procedure (First-tier Tribunal) (Health, Education and Social Care Chamber) Rules 2008, SI 2008/2699, r 2(2)(b) and (c) and Tribunal Procedure (Upper Tribunal) Rules 2008, SI 2008/2698, r 2(2)(b) and (c).

parties participate in the proceedings. There is also an explicit encouragement for co-operation between parties and the Tribunal in order to achieve the overriding objectives (r 2(4)(b)).[13]

Context

1.16 According to Gostin and Fennell:[14]

> 'In 1982 there were 1,006 applications or references and 858 cases were dealt with. In 1988, there were 5,834 applications or references and 3,327 cases were disposed of during the year.'

At the time of the Leggatt Report, the Tribunal had received 18,806 references (1999). According the Mental Health Tribunal Secretariat, in 2005 the number of actual hearings was 9,522, and in 2006 it was 8,778. According to the same statistics, the number of patients discharged as a result of Tribunal hearings amounted to 14% in 2005 and 11% in 2006. This figure includes absolute discharge, delayed discharge, conditional discharge and deferred conditional discharge. The delay between an application and a hearing for those detained under MHA 1983, s 2 was 6 days (in 2005/06) and for s 3 it was 6 weeks. For restricted cases it took 18 weeks (in 2005/06) whereas in 2004/05 it had taken 16 weeks. In 2004/05, s 2 was used 21,000 times, but only 6,000 of these gave rise to an application to the Tribunal.[15] The Care Quality Commission (in its report for 2010–2011) stated that there had been a 5% increase in people detained under the Act (p 2) and that there were a total of 16,000 detained, in addition to 4,000 who were subject to CTOs (p 6). Specifically:

> 'In 2010/2011, the headline total number of formal detentions in hospital did not change significantly from the previous year. There were 45,248 admissions and detentions, compared with 45,755 in 2009/2010 … there was a total of 3,834 uses of CTO's across the NHS and independent sector, a 6.6% decrease from 4,103 in 2009/10. However, many of the CTO's still in place at the end of 2010/2011 were made in earlier years – of the CTO's made since November 2008, only 41% had ended by March 2011. The overall number of people subject to the Act rose by 5%, from 19,947 on 31 March 2010 to 20,938 on 31 March 2011. Almost all of this increase was due to the rise in the number of people subject to a CTO; this was 4,291, an increase of 29.1%'. (p 7)

The number of applications are also reported by the CQC to have risen, although the outcome remained the same in terms of 'successful appeals … accounted for 12% … the same as in 2009' (p 8). In 2010 the number of applications to the Tribunal was 23,533 (CQC Report, p 29) which represents a steady and significantly continuing increase in the workload of the Tribunal.

---

13 First-tier Tribunal (Health, Education and Social Care Chamber) Rules 2008, SI 2008/2699, r 2(4)(b) and Tribunal Procedure (Upper Tribunal) Rules 2008, SI 2008/2698, r 2(4)(b).

14 L Gostin and P Fennell *Mental Health: Tribunal Procedure* (1992, 2nd edn, Longman), preface.

15 *Hansard*, HL Deb, col 1459 (26 February 2007), Earl Howe.

Chapter 2

ROLE, FUNCTION AND POWERS OF MEMBERS OF THE TRIBUNAL

TRIBUNAL JUDGE

2.1 The designation was previously that of President, or Chair of the Tribunal. However, this changed to the title 'Tribunal Judge' (TJ). The TJ is always either a junior barrister or Queen's Counsel, or a circuit judge, or a solicitor. Restricted cases are limited to Queen's Counsel or a circuit judge, or those solicitors or barristers who have been approved, trained and appointed for the post, and who have been appointed as Recorders. The most commonly used form of address actually used was 'Sir/Madam'. There is no reason why this practice should not continue, unless addressing a circuit judge.

2.2 All but a small number of decisions have to be made by the Tribunal (which is comprised of three members, and cannot function as a tribunal unless quorate). However, it there is disagreement between the members then the TJ has the casting vote. Also, it is the TJ who will make decisions as to substantive law. It is also the responsibility of the TJ to draft the reasons for whatever decision is made (although these are formulated by the Tribunal as a whole). The TJ will regulate proceedings. In practice, the TJ will introduce the individual members, explain the purpose and function of the Tribunal, ensure that all parties have had sight of relevant reports or other documents (subject to any matters relating to non-disclosure) and identify any issues of concern to the Tribunal. This will include a summary of the results of the preliminary examination of the patient by the medical member. Generally, the function has been described as follows:[1]

> 'It will fall to them to identify gaps in the legal or factual content of the case put by either side, and to determine what steps should be taken to fill them … The chairmen will have to take the leading role in identifying those parties who are struggling with tribunal procedures, and in working out what can properly be done to assist them.'

POTENTIAL FOR BIAS

2.3 The MHAC expressed particular concerns over an aspect of the function of the legal member. It expressed the view that:[2]

---

1 Leggatt Report, at para 7.18.

2 MHAC Report, at para 4.84.

> '… we had made our views known to parties in a case[3] claiming a conflict of interest where a sentencing judge who had ordered a patient to hospital presided, fourteen months later, over his MHRT hearing. We had suggested that this should be deemed to present a "real danger of bias" and pointed to the Joint Committee on the Draft Mental Health Bill's recommendation that, under the revised Tribunal system proposed in the Mental Health Bill 2004, a member of a Tribunal system who has imposed an order should never hear the review or appeal that order.'

Again, generally, the same observation has been made elsewhere:[4]

> 'Demonstrating those qualities [independence and impartiality] to the individual user in a tribunal case will require establishing that those who are to decide the case adopt a properly impartial approach to it, and have no improper links to any of the parties … and that they will not feel beholden to the person who appointed or selected them, or fear adverse consequences, from the result of the case.'

The latter observation has caused problems, and led to case-law, in respect of the role of the medical member.

2.4 The specific case in which this point was considered (which does not expressly address the concerns of the MHAC) is reported at *R (M) v MHRT*.[5] It was held that in the circumstances, there was no real danger of bias.

> **Facts and outcome:** M was, in September 2003, sentenced by HHJ Walker to a hospital order with a restriction order (MHA 1983, ss 37 and 41). The judge also chaired a Tribunal in November 2004 which considered an application for discharge (on the basis that M's disorder had stabilised sufficiently to allow a conditional discharge. On advice, M did not apply that the judge recuse himself: however, the fact that he had sentenced M was raised, and the judge indicated that he had not remembered the case. The Tribunal decision not to discharge M was challenged on the basis of bias. The application was refused on the basis that the fair-minded and informed observer, having considered the relevant facts, would not conclude that there was a real possibility that the Tribunal was biased as, inter alia, the Tribunal was not concerned with whether the court sentence was correct, there was no basis for saying that the judge would be affected by information from the sentencing hearing, and in any event, there would be no reluctance to change his mind when a rational basis for so doing was put forward, as could be done in a Tribunal. (In any event, M had waived any right to object by not raising the matter.)
>
> **Bennett J**
>
> > '26. … neither the issues that the Tribunal had to consider, nor its decision, nor the reasons for its decision did in fact, or could have, cast any doubt upon the validity of the sentence passed by the judge in September 2003 …
> >
> > 46. … The decision of the judge and of a Tribunal exercising its powers under S.72, but particularly under S73 of the MHA, do directly affect the

---

3 *R (on the application of Brandenburg) v East London & the City Mental Health NHS Trust and Another* [2004] AC 280, at [3].

4 Leggatt Report, at para 2.19.

5 [2005] EWHC 2791 (Admin), [2006] MHLR 46; (*EC Ch 14*).

liberty/detention of the subject. It is, I agree, a material consideration that any fair minded and informed observer would have in mind; indeed very much to the forefront of his mind.

...

69. In my judgment the fair-minded and informed observer would take into account the following matters, which I list in no order of importance:

(a) the hearing in September 2003 was conducted completely in public. There was nothing which the judge knew the Claimant and the public did not know. The judge made his decision under ss37 and 41 of the MHA which required him to consider the facts and the evidence as they then stood.

(b) In November 2004, which I am prepared to accept in the context of the instant case is a comparatively short time after September 2003, the judge, as part of the Tribunal considering the Claimant's case, was required to consider the matters ... identified in ss 72 and 73 of the MHA. The Tribunal had no power at all to question the validity of the sentence passed in September 2003. Therefore, as a matter of logic and common sense there can be no question of the judge being swayed by a conscious or sub-conscious desire (even if one existed) to uphold the sentence he passed in September 2003 ...

(c) The decision the Tribunal had to make in November 2004, was not the same, or even substantially the same, as that made by the judge in September 2003. First, in November 2004 there was no issue or dispute that the Claimant was suffering from a requisite mental illness. Even if there had been a dispute on this issue it would have made no difference since the Tribunal had to consider the position as at November 2004. Second, the evidence before the Tribunal concerned how the Claimant had progressed (or not) since September 2003 and whether he could be safely released (conditionally) into the community ...

(d) there can be no basis for saying that the judge might have had information from September 2003 ... which may have affected his mind in November 2004.

(e) In any event the fair minded and informed observer would not attribute to the judge an inability or reluctance to change his mind when faced with a rational basis for doing so ... [The judge also noted that oral argument in front of a Tribunal has a role of promoting a change of mind in the members of the Tribunal.]'

MEDICAL MEMBER

2.5 The profession of the medical member is that of a consultant psychiatrist. However, it was an expressed intention of the Government (in *Transforming Tribunals*) to reconsider this professional status. There have been difficulties recruiting sufficient medical members (who are mainly culled from those who have retired from practice) and (perhaps) consequently the view was that:[6]

> 'Up to now medical membership has been limited to doctors. Some tribunals are used to all their medical members being consultants. In the changing world of health care, and with increasing demands from tribunals for some clinical specialisations, the government has it in mind to use a wider range of health care professionals in tribunals, according to the needs of the cases. This would be particularly appropriate if the role of the clinical expert member is more varied than simply sitting as a "wing" member with a judge. With an effective case management system in place and proper control of these different health care specialisations the government favours a "healthcare qualified professionals" member category which is not confined to doctors. An alternative would be to have a number of medical/clinical groupings, based on the different health care professions. That might include a separate category for psychiatrists in view of the particular demand for their services in cases of the type dealt with by the MHRT (although mental health cases form a significant proportion of the work of some other tribunals).'

According to the same document, there are currently 318 medical members of the Tribunal.[7] At the time of the Leggatt Report (2001) there were 144. If there is a change in the professional status of the medical member, then this would be in line with the alteration in the permitted professional status of those who can make recommendations for detention under MHA 1983. In practice, there has been no impact on the professional status of the medical member. There is now one full time medical member.

2.6 There is some disagreement as to whether the Tribunal process is adversarial, inquisitorial or some hybrid of the two. Within this debate, the role of the medical member is particularly problematic. The medical member is obliged to undertake an examination of the patient. The results of this examination are then reported to the TJ and lay member prior to the Tribunal commencing hearing evidence from witnesses. As indicated above, it is the task of the TJ to then report to the legal representative for the patient the outcome of the examination. The extent and purpose of the examination by the medical member is considered at greater length in Part C. The simple point is that once a medical member has examined the patient (in private) and reported to the Tribunal, it is arguable that this then achieves the status of evidence. It is *not* permissible to cross-examine the medical member. This in itself may not (practically) be a problem, unless the medical member either extends the scope of his or her investigation (eg by interviewing nursing staff, which is not uncommon), or the patient reveals information to the medical member which does not appear in the reports provided to the Tribunal, or which does not appear in any of the oral evidence provided to the Tribunal. There has been some case-law in respect of the role of the medical member, primarily to do with the slightly uncomfortable legal position that the medical member

---

6 *Transforming Tribunals*, at paras 235–236.

7 Ibid, at p 76.

occupies as both a potential arbiter and informant. Again, this problem was identified by Sir Andrew Leggatt as follows:[8]

> 'The medical member examines the applicant before the hearing, and discusses with the other members of the tribunal issues that are likely to arise at the hearing. There is therefore a dual role as a fact finder and a decision maker. This brings a clear risk of the tribunal acting on the basis of evidence known only to themselves. For that reason, guidance from the Regional Chairmen suggest that medical members should not give their opinion as to the patient's mental condition at the initial stage, and that it is essential that any differences between the medical member's and the RMO's assessment of mental condition should be made clear at the hearing … we are glad that the Government's latest proposals would seem likely to remove the problem by abolishing the dual function.'

Plainly, the latter function has not been abolished, and thus the problem remains. There is currently some discussion as to whether the requirement for the medical member to conduct a preliminary examination should be removed. If so, then this would solve this problem.

POTENTIAL FOR BIAS AND CONFLICT OF INTEREST

2.7 The potential for difficulties should be well known to practitioners, and there has been significant case-law on the point, both within the UK, and more widely. The Guidance given by the Regional Chairmen (April 2006) in respect of the old r 11 of the Mental Health Review Tribunal Rules 1983[9] encompasses these developments. The new r 34[10] has not had any impact upon the established principles. The old Guidance stated:

> 'The purpose of the medical examination is to assist the medical member, together with any other steps they deem appropriate, in forming an opinion as to the patient's mental state. Case law provides further guidance as follows:
>
> (a) the medical member must not form a concluded opinion, but can form a provisional opinion as to their current mental state.
> (b) All parties to the hearing should be given the opportunity to address and to comment upon any significant findings arising from the medical examination.
> (c) To assist in this process, the substance of the medical member's views, and in particular a summary of any significant findings, must be communicated to the parties at the outset of the case, unless exceptionally it is not practicable to do so.
>
> As a normal rule it shall be the President who takes responsibility for reporting a summary of the medical member's "significant findings" unless there are exceptional reasons for not doing so.'

---

8 Leggatt Report, at p 159.
9 SI 1983/942.
10 SI 2008/2699, r 34.

2.8 The case-law referred to above arises from *DN v Switzerland*[11] and *R (S) v MHRT*.[12] There is further specific case-law in respect of bias which is referred to separately below. The role of the medical member (where the doctor is also a member of the court) goes to the issue of judicial impartiality, and the significance of Art 5(4) of the ECHR. In effect, the substance of the authority (in terms of its effect on the way in which Tribunals must be conducted) is that the medical member must only form a preliminary view, and that view must be conveyed to the parties to the proceedings. In *DN v Switzerland* the issue of the dual role of a decision maker was considered. It was ruled that:[13]

> 'The Court has held that independence is one of the most important constitutive elements of the notion of a "court" ... In the court's opinion, it would be inconceivable that Article 5 (4) of the Convention, relating, inter alia, to such a sensitive issue as the deprivation of liberty of "persons of unsound mind" within the meaning of Article 5 (1) (e) should not equally envisage, as a fundamental requisite, the impartiality of that court ... an issue will arise as to the impartiality of the court under the objective test if it is called upon to assess evidence which had previously been given in the form of expert advice.'

On the facts in this particular case, there was found to have been a legitimate apprehension on the part of the litigant that the court had attached particular weight to the views of one of its constituent members, and therefore lacked the 'necessary impartiality'.

2.9 In respect of *R (S) v MHRT*, Stanley Burnton J analysed *DN* and held that the medical member was obliged to examine the patient, and was also obliged to form a preliminary opinion, but equally to keep an open mind until the end of the hearing and after all the evidence had been heard. It was also important that the medical member was seen to keep an open mind throughout. He held that:[14]

> 'Rule 11 [that which required the medical member to examine the patient prior to hearings] does not expressly require the medical member to form an opinion of the patient's mental condition; it requires him to take the steps necessary to form his opinion.'

That is to say, it is a part of the medical member's general 'fact gathering' function, in the same way that he or she may inspect the medical records, or discuss with other members of staff the presentation of the patient. Stanley Burnton J went on to hold:[15]

> '... it is obvious that the medical member must not form a concluded opinion until the conclusion of the hearing, since otherwise the outcome of the hearing would be prejudged ... the forming of an opinion before the hearing is normally

---

11 27154/95 (2001) ECHR 235, [2001] MHLR 117; (*EC Chs 7 and 9*).
12 [2002] EWHC 2522 (Admin), [2003] MHLR 118 (Admin); (*EC Chs 7 and 9*).
13 (2001) ECHR 235; [2001] MHLR 117, at [42] and [53]; (*EC Ch 9*).
14 [2003] MHLR 118, at [21]; (*EC Ch 9*).
15 Ibid, at [21], [22], [23], [32] and [34].

> objectionable only if it is not provisional, liable to be changed by the evidence adduced and the submissions of the parties, but is firm and concluded, in which case the hearing is an ineffective charade ... In my judgment "due impartiality" in the present context requires a member of a tribunal not to have a preconceived opinion on the merits of the applicant's case. The European Court did not suggest that a provisional view formed before the commencement of the hearing is objectionable ... if during the course of the hearing there is a factual conflict between the medical member and the patient, for example, as to what was said by the patient to the medical member, and that conflict may be material to the decision of the tribunal, the tribunal must consider whether it can properly continue to hear the patient's application.'

2.10 Whilst it would appear obvious that any preliminary findings should be passed on to the parties, this has not always been the practice, and has caused difficulties in the past. In *R v MHRT, London North and East ex parte H*, Crane J held that:[16]

> '... what is required ... as a matter of fairness and of natural justice at common law, is that if the medical member is taking into account or is drawing to the attention of the other members, either evidence or his views as an expert, the claimant and his advisers should be alerted to such evidence and such views in sufficient detail, and sufficiently early in the proceedings, to enable them to deal with them.'

A similar difficulty arose in *R (Ashworth Hospital Authority) v MHRT; R (H) v Ashworth Hospital*[17] where:[18]

> '... at no stage of the hearing before the Tribunal announced their decision were the parties before the Tribunal informed of the findings of [the medical member] as a result of his interview with [the patient].'

The Court of Appeal held that:[19]

> 'It seems to me both fair and sensible that, if the medical member of the Tribunal has formed any views on the basis of his or her interview with the patient, the substance of those views should be communicated to the patient and/or those who are representing him. I cannot think of any good reason why this should not be a requirement although I would not wish to rule out the possibility of exceptional cases where such a course may not be practicable.'

It follows that if a decision is made which rejects the view of the responsible clinician (RC), then the reasons for that rejection must be made clear in the reasons given by the Tribunal. The matter was re-considered on a similar basis in the case of *GB v South West London & St George's MH NHS Trust*.[20] In this

---

16 [2000] MHLR 242 (Admin Court), at [56]; (*EC Ch 9*).

17 [2002] MHLR 13 (Admin Court); upheld in part at [2002] MHLR 314, CA; (*EC Chs 1, 2, 9 and 15*).

18 [2002] MHLR 13 (Admin Court), at [86].

19 [2002] MHLR 314, CA, at [84]; (*EC Chs 1, 2, 9 and 15*).

20 [2013] UKUT 58 (AAC).

instance, it was argued that a comment made by the medical member during an early part of the Tribunal tended to suggest that he had reached a concluded view of the merits. If correct, then this would have been evidence of bias on the part of that member, with a consequent potential for a breach of the rules of natural justice. UTJ Wikeley considered the law summarised above, and in particular *S v MHRT* and also the subsequent case of *MB v BEH MH NHST & Secretary of State for Justice*[21] (and discussed in Chapter 3). The appeal was dismissed and it was held that 'A natural justice challenge has to be assessed in the light of all the circumstances of the case. It is fact and context specific. A tribunal hearing is not static – this was a case that went part-heard over three days over the course of a month'[22] and that 'My conclusion is that the fair minded and informed observer would not consider that there was a real possibility of bias'.

2.11 Finally, in *R (RD) v Mental Health Review Tribunal*[23] the issue again arose as to the status of the opinion of the medical member as to whether a patient was ready for transfer from high secure conditions. The opinion expressed by the medical member was summarised by the President as being 'a very preliminary view, subject to anything we hear today'.[24] The point taken was that a preliminary view as to mental state (which was permissible) was different to a preliminary view as to transfer. It was held that this was incorrect, and that the expression of a preliminary view was lawful.

2.12 Arguments have been raised regarding the situation where the medical member is also an employee of the hospital or trust that has been (in part) responsible for the detention of the patient. This in turn reflects upon the relatively small number of medical members available to sit on Tribunals and the almost inevitability of some medical members having worked at some stage for the larger trusts. The authority on the point is *R (PD) v West Midlands and North Mental Health Review Tribunal.*[25] In effect, it was held that the link between the medical member and the patient was sufficiently remote, and that the status of the member as an employee of the Trust also sufficiently disinterested from the outcome of the hearing (and that in any event would be guided by the best interests of the patient) that bias was not made out. The decision was made in respect of the old r 8(2)[26] which stated:

> 'A person shall not be qualified to serve as a member of a Tribunal for the purpose of any proceedings where … (b) he is a member or officer of a health authority which has the right to discharge the patient under section 23(3) of the [MHA 1983].'

---

21 [2011] UKUT 328 (AAC), [2011] MHLR 246.
22 Ibid, at [24].
23 [2007] EWHC 781 (Admin), [2007] MHLR 241.
24 [2007] EWHC 781 (Admin), at [13], [2007] MHLR 241, at 243.
25 [2004] EWCA Civ 311, [2004] MHLR 174.
26 SI 1983/942, r 8(2).

The situation would have been different if:[27]

> 'He had been employed at the Rathbone Hospital where D is detained, there might have been reasonable apprehension that he would have come into contact with those actually responsible for D's detention – the RMO, the social worker concerned and the hospital managers. In that event, there might also have been reasonable apprehension that, out of respect for, or friendship with, those concerned Dr I might have been reluctant to express a view which differed from that which they had reached ...'

2.13 From time to time it will become apparent that a patient has been treated by a medical member (in the past). If this is so, it is incumbent on the Tribunal to draw this to the attention of the parties (and in particular the legal representative of the patient). It is highly likely that if a patient were concerned about this, then the Tribunal would need to reconvene with a different medical member.

SPECIALIST LAY MEMBER

2.14 The professional background of what used to be termed the lay member (and who is now more usually called 'specialist member' or 'specialist tribunal member') is usually drawn from a social work, or mental health work milieu. The change in the terminology reflects the increasing level of professional expertise, knowledge and experience of this very important aspect of the Tribunal. It is common for this member to be asked by the TJ to ask questions of witnesses to the Tribunal that also derive their experience from this background. *Transforming Tribunals* observed that:[28]

> 'The Leggatt review concluded that all tribunal members should be appointed on the basis of the particular contribution which they have to make to the work of the tribunal, and that judicial managers should decide whether non-legal members should sit on particular cases or classes of cases, and what their role should be. Whatever the history behind the present use of non-legal members, the government believes that now is the time for a major re-assessment.'

Further, it observes: 'The government does not believe that there is a place for a purely lay category.' The conclusion set out at Appendix D, para 10 states:

> 'For those NLMs appointed by the Lord Chancellor there is a competence framework for each competition. The framework for MHRT lay members, for example, is:
>
> – professionalism (technical knowledge, expertise, showing authority, independence and integrity, developing knowledge and managing workload),
> – judgement (investigating and analysing and resolving and deciding, and
> – people skills (building positive relationships and communicating.'

---

27 [2004] EWCA Civ 311, [2004] MHLR 174, at [37].

28 At paras 225 and 226.

2.15 Thus the old expression 'lay member' was in fact somewhat misleading, since he or she usually had significant professional experience and/or qualifications to match the two other members in their respective fields of law and medicine.

DIFFERENTLY CONSTITUTED TRIBUNAL/JUDICIAL CONTINUITY

2.16 In *R (A) v (1) Secretary of State (2) Mental Health Review Tribunal*[29] the issue was whether the second hearing in an application to the Tribunal before a differently constituted Tribunal was fair. More precisely the issue turned upon the old rules.[30] Whether the principles arising out of these particular rules would have any relevance is debatable. However, the gravamen of the judgment was it was desirable for there to be continuity of the constitution of a tribunal wherever practicable. This must take into account undue delay in reconvening with the same members (who are likely to have other commitments). Stanley Burnton J held that:[31]

> 'Where a relatively short time has passed between the original decision and its reconsideration, the advantages and fairness involved in requiring the original constitution to reconsider the matter must be greater than when a considerable time has passed. One must bear in mind that the members of a Tribunal will have heard many other cases in the last 15 months ... neither of them can be expected to retain a clear recollection of the case as it was before them. Both of them will rely on the written decision of the Tribunal ... This is not a case in which adverse findings of credibility have been made by a Tribunal against anyone, where perhaps it is more important that there should be a continuity of constitution, where the decision has been favourable to the patient at least. In the circumstances of this case, it seems to me that the risk of any incorrect decision or any unfairness to the patient as a result of a change in constitution of the Tribunal is remote.'

MISCELLANEOUS

2.17 The powers of the individual members of the Tribunal are very limited (and where appropriate are identified at the relevant point in this book). The real power of the Tribunal only exists when it is quorate, and although there are some powers common to all the legal contexts in which the Tribunal sits, there is also considerable variation. Thus, the powers available are considered at each specific and relevant point in each section of the book.

---

29 [2003] EWHC 270 (Admin), [2005] MHLR 144.

30 SI 1983/942, rr 8 and 17(1).

31 [2003] EWHC 270 (Admin); [2005] MHLR 144, at [16].

ACCOMMODATION/RESOURCES

2.18 The Tribunal is unique in that its accommodation (and often its administrative support) is provided by the detaining authority. The Leggatt Report identified this problem thus:[32]

> 'It will be important that the new tribunal is adequately resourced, and is not subject to the shortcomings in clerical and IT support which have so obstructed the work of MHRTs ... we would wish to see greater efforts to ensure that the accommodation is suitable and properly prepared and equipped for its serious purpose.'

Sadly, this remains a particular problem. Rooms provided are very often airless, and far too small. Also, the abolition of dedicated clerks to the Tribunal leads to further delay, and sometimes confusion. If the difficulty is particularly acute in terms of the room or rooms provided, this should be drawn to the attention of the Tribunal.

2.19 The Code of Practice (Chapter 32) stresses the need for adequate accommodation (paras 32.33–32.35) not just for the Tribunal, but so that the legal representative has privacy to discuss the case with the patient. This has been supplemented by the Tribunal setting out minimum requirements for accommodation (March 2010). Neither the Code, nor the specific provisions set out in March 2010 have solved the problem. Appropriate accommodation does make a real difference to the proceedings, for all concerned.

---

[32] At p 161.

Part B

TRIBUNAL PROCEDURE AND JURISDICTION

Chapter 3

TRIBUNAL PROCEEDINGS: OVERVIEW AND PRE-HEARING PROCEDURES

OVERVIEW

3.1 An overview of the general function of the Tribunal has been given in Part A. In terms of the specific manner in which the Tribunal may operate, the chapters in Part B will consider those matters which the Tribunal can consider prior to a hearing (including consideration of who is a party to proceedings); matters relating to privacy (including disclosure and non-disclosure of documentary evidence); withdrawal of applications; the burden and standard of proof during Tribunals; and delays in convening Tribunals (including adjournments of hearings). The rules which govern the conduct of *all* Tribunals in the First-tier are now contained in the Tribunal Procedure (First-tier Tribunal) (Health, Education and Social Care Chamber) Rules 2008[1] ('the Rules', which replace the Mental Health Review Tribunal Rules 1983[2] ('the old rules')). Where appropriate, differences between the two will be indicated, since the case-law involving the old rules will still remain of significance. The Code of Practice has been rewritten (the last one having been revised in 1999), and all references are to the new format. The full text of both the Rules, and parts of the Code, are reproduced in Parts E and F.

JURISDICTION

Adversarial v inquisitorial

3.2 Insofar as the case-law is of assistance on this point, it tends towards the conclusion that the manner in which the Tribunal can conduct itself (by reference to the old rules) means that it is inquisitorial. In terms of its function, there is often a reference in papers supplied to the Tribunal of it being 'an appeal' against the decision by the detaining authority to detain a patient. This is not, strictly speaking, accurate. The Tribunal convenes in order to make a decision (amongst others) as to whether detention is required, or is not required. If the Tribunal reaches the conclusion that detention is not required, it may discharge the patient from detention under MHA 1983.

---

1 SI 2008/2699.
2 SI 1983/942.

3.3 In *R v London South and South West Region MHRT ex parte Moyle*[3] the following was held to be the case in respect of the jurisdiction of the Tribunal:[4]

> '... the mechanism that was adopted did not, in fact, give to the Tribunal a reviewing or appellate jurisdiction; its jurisdiction is an original jurisdiction. As the Tribunal includes a legally qualified Chairmen and a psychiatrist, it was clearly Parliament's intention that the Tribunal should come to its own conclusion as to whether or not in the case of restricted patients the criteria for discharge had been met ... The Tribunal ... have an original jurisdiction, in which they have to exercise their own judgment, based on the evidence before them. It is open to a Tribunal, provided they act rationally, to disagree with the views of any psychiatrists whose evidence is put before them.'

It follows that the same applies in respect of any evidence put before the Tribunal (ie not just that of psychiatrists). In other words, the Tribunal will be obliged to consider the quality and probative value of all of the evidence which it receives, and to ask questions (via all three of its members) of the witnesses that give evidence.

3.4 A further aspect of the distinctive jurisdiction of the Tribunal is the function of the medical member. This has been considered in Part A, but it is a part of that function to obtain information *for* the Tribunal. This also tends to indicate the inquisitorial nature of its jurisdiction.

3.5 Finally, the old rules themselves provided further powers to the Tribunal to adjourn hearings in order to gather further information, as long as that information related to its primary function (to consider whether detention was justified). This includes obtaining information that a party may have decided not to place before it (or simply omitted to provide). General observations on the above were made in *R (X) v MHRT*[5] when Collins J held that:[6]

> 'Scott J in *W v Egdell* [1990] Ch 359 375 ... stated that the nature of a hearing before a MHRT was inquisitorial, not adversarial, and he drew attention to the Rules, including rule 15 – but there are others – which pointed in that direction, for example one of the matters that occurs in proceedings before the Tribunal is that the medical member of the Tribunal examines the patient and takes such other steps as he considers necessary to form an opinion of the patient's mental condition and he has the right, if he thinks it necessary, to see the patient in private and to obtain medical records and investigate them. So he is, unusually perhaps, required by the Rules to form an independent view of the mental state of the patient. This is not on its face consistent with a purely adversarial process. In my view, it is not particularly helpful to label the proceedings one way or the other. The reality is that there is clearly a public interest involved in the exercise. The burden is of course on the authority to establish to the satisfaction of the Tribunal that the conditions for detention exist ... The Tribunal must clearly have to

---

3 [1999] MHLR 195 (Admin Court); (*EC Chs 5 and 14*).
4 [1999] MHLR 195 (Admin Court), at [9].
5 [2003] MHLR 299 (Admin Court); (*EC Chs 1, 7 and 14*).
6 Ibid, at [23], [24] and [27].

consider in every case whether there is a gap in the evidence which it requires to be filled in order to enable it to reach the right decision.'

3.6 The general purpose of the Tribunal is summarised at paras 32.2–32.4 of the Code (reproduced in Part E).

Extent of jurisdiction to consider validity of original detention/application

3.7 The question may arise as to the validity or otherwise of the original authority for detention (ie if this is invalid, then how can the Tribunal have any jurisdiction at all?). The issue is simply resolved. It is clear that the function of the Tribunal is to consider whether or not detention should be continued, upon the basis of the relevant statutory criteria. This does not extend to considering the validity or otherwise of the original basis or procedure for admission. The proper remedy for an unlawful initial detention would be challenged by way of a writ of habeas corpus.[7] Similarly, the Tribunal should not become embroiled in other issues ancillary to its statutory function (eg consent to treatment) (*SH v Cornwall Partnership NHS Trust*[8]). In *DP v Hywel DDA Health Board*[9] the issue of what a Tribunal should do when the legal basis of the application itself was in issue. In this instance, an application for a hearing had been made by someone who was not, in law, the nearest relative. This had already been detected as a result of the putative application by the same person to discharge the patient (and which had been barred). It was held that the basis of any applications are prescribed in the MHA 1983 (s 77) and that in this instance, as the opening words of s 72 make clear, the jurisdiction given to the Tribunal is limited to entertaining applications made by a person who is liable to be detained under the Act. The Tribunal's powers are thus confined to granting or refusing relief to persons liable to be detained. It has no power to consider the validity of the admission which gave rise to the liability to be detained.[10]

Private or public?

3.8 The old rule (at r 21) created a presumption of privacy, although hearings could be held in public in certain circumstances. The new Rule (at r 38) states that hearings 'must be held in private unless the Tribunal considers that it is in the interests of justice for the hearing to be held in public'. It also states that even if the hearing is in public, 'the Tribunal may give a direction that part of a hearing is to be held in private'. Although a public hearing is a rarity, this does mean that there is still the power to ensure certain parts are heard in private (ie without the public having access). This is a simpler test (in certain respects) than the old rule (which determined public hearings on the basis of the interests of the patient, not the interests of justice). There has been

---

7 *R (C) v South London and Maudsley NHS Trust and Mental Health Review Tribunal* [2003] EWHC 3467 (Admin), [2004] MHLR 280; (*EC Ch 1*).

8 [2012] UKUT 290 (AAC).

9 [2011] UKUT 381 (AAC), [2011] MHLR 394.

10 *Ex p Waldron* [1986] QB 824 at 826 per Ackner LJ at [9].

considerable debate in recent years over transparency in the court system (primarily in respect of litigation concerning children) and a move towards greater openness (including publication of anonymised judgments). The concept of a private hearing is often conflated with the perception that it is a 'secret' hearing. This is (of course) not the reason for the continued presumption of privacy. That exists to prevent prurience, and (in part) distribution of material which is confidential to the parties. It does not prevent those with a legitimate interest in the proceedings from participating. The case-law which considered the old rule is *R (Mersey Care NHS Trust) v MHRT*.[11] In essence (using the different test) the following matters needed to be considered before a Tribunal could be held in public:

(1) the Tribunal could exclude some people even if it was in public;

(2) it could control what information could be made public;

(3) a Tribunal sitting in private is covered by the Administration of Justice Act 1960, s 12 (whereby it is a contempt of court to publish information relating to a private hearing);

(4) a Tribunal sitting in public is covered by the Contempt of Court Act 1981, s 2 (which also permits fair and accurate reports of public proceedings);

(5) the issue of the interests of the patient was in part predicated by the controls that the Tribunal could exercise over publicity; and

(6) the Tribunal could also consider wider issues that that of the interests of the patient (including propriety, purpose, relevance and national security).

3.9 Rule 38(2), (3) and (4) explicitly retains the power to exclude particular individuals from the hearing (or part of it), or to permit particular individuals to attend the hearing (or part of it). Rule 38(4) specifically relates to exclusions (in part or as a whole) of those whose conduct is likely to disrupt the hearing. However, it is prohibited (in certain circumstances) from conducting a hearing in the absence of the patient (r 39(2)). This is mandatory, and is likely to cause problems unless the requirements of r 34 have been satisfied (which only requires an examination as far as is practicable), and the patient has either decided not to attend, or is unable to attend for reasons of ill-health. On the face of the Rules, there is no provision to exclude a patient whose behaviour is so disruptive that it will make conduct of the Tribunal impossible (ie there is a conflict between r 38(4)(a)–(d) and r 39(2)). It is rare for a patient to behave in this manner, but it does happen from time to time. It may be possible to argue that encompassed within the phrase 'ill-health' is the state of the mental health of the patient (which is usually, though not always, the source of the disruption).

---

11 [2004] MHLR 284 (Admin Court); (*EC Ch 14*).

3.10 The issue of public hearings has been addressed directly by the Upper Tribunal in two separate decisions made in respect of the same case. The first decision is *AH v West London MHT and Secretary of State for Justice*.[12] The patient requested a public hearing. The Upper Tribunal considered the implications of such a request, not only by reference to the old case-law, but also by reference to Article 6 and observed that 'Article 6 (1) of the Convention confers the right to a "fair and public hearing" in the determination of civil rights, subject to a power to exclude the press and public from all or part of the trial'[13] and 'At first sight R.38 which sets the presumption in favour of hearings in private, might be thought to conflict with this principle. However, the Strasbourg case law recognises that the presumption may be reversed for categories of case where this is justified under the exceptions ... It is true that mental health cases are not expressly mentioned as a special category under Article 6. However, it was not in dispute before us that similar principles should apply'.[14] It held that 'The underlying assumption is that the interests of justice will normally require a hearing in private. However, even under the new rule, in our view, having regard to the reasons for the exception under Art 6, the principal consideration remains the protection of the interests of the patient'.[15] It went on to summarise those matters that a Tribunal should consider which were listed as follows:

> '(a) Is it consistent with the subjective and informed wishes of the applicant (assuming he is competent to make an informed choice)?
> (b) Will it have an adverse effect on his mental health in the short or long term, taking account of the views of those treating him and any other expert views?
> (c) Are there any other special factors for or against a public hearing?
> (d) Can practical arrangements be made for an open hearing without disproportionate burden on the authority?'[16]

3.11 The ultimate decision (in *AH v West London MHT and Secretary of State for Justice (Final)*)[17] was that the hearing should be in public. However, this was by reference (in part) to the case being 'out of the ordinary'[18] and that once what is described as the 'threshold test'[19] listed above at (a)–(d) 'for establishing a right to a public hearing have been satisfied, Art 6 of the ECHR (reinforced by Art 13 of the CRPD) requires that a patient should have the same or substantially equivalent right of access to a public hearing as a non-disabled person who has been deprived of his or her liberty, if this Art 6 right to a public hearing is to be given proper effect'.[20] To put this in context, at the date of this decision, there had been '10 applications for tribunal hearings

---

12 [2010] UKUT 264 (AAC), [2010] MHLR 326.
13 Ibid, at [16].
14 Ibid, at [19]–[20].
15 Ibid, at [25].
16 Ibid, at [29].
17 [2011] UKUT 74 (AAC), [2011] MHLR 85.
18 Ibid, at [9].
19 Ibid, at [22].
20 Ibid.

in public (out of perhaps 100,000 hearings)'.[21] It is to be noted that similar debates and issues have been considered in the Court of Protection (eg *LB Hillingdon v Steven Neary and Mark Neary*;[22] *Independent News Media and Media Ltd and Others v A*[23]) where the media has requested access to proceedings where the rules also provide for all or part of the proceedings to be conducted in private, but where the court can also sit in public. The consequences for both jurisdictions is that more hearings have been made public, albeit with less of an impact on the Tribunal, than the Court of Protection thus far.

PARTIES TO PROCEEDINGS (INCLUDING APPLICANTS)

3.12 The new Rules provide more clarity on this than was previously the case, which were rather obscure. In Part 1, an applicant is defined (in part) as 'a person who starts Tribunal proceedings, whether by making an application … or a reference [or] is substituted as an appellant under rule 9(1)'. Rule 9 provides that substitution may be made where:

> '… the wrong person has been named as a party; or (b) the substitution has become necessary because of a change in circumstances since the start of proceedings. (2) The Tribunal may give a direction adding a person to the proceedings as a respondent.'

It would appear, therefore, that the Tribunal retains a fairly wide discretion to involve others in the hearing, where appropriate (as long as they can be said to have a genuine role to play in determining the statutory criteria). The specific listing of who is a party is set out at r 1(3) as:

(1) the patient (the person who is the subject of a mental health case);

(2) the responsible authority (the managers of a hospital within which the patient is detained, or the social services authority in relation to guardianship, or the managers of the responsible hospital in relation to a community patient);

(3) the Secretary of State (if the patient is a restricted patient);

(4) any other person who starts a mental health case by making an application.

Disclosure/non-disclosure of documents

3.13 Rule 14 governs the use of documents and information. It can prohibit publication and disclosure of documents, or any matter that would lead a

---

21 Ibid, at [10].

22 [2011] EWHC 413 (COP), [2011] MHLR 89.

23 [2010] EWCA Civ 343, [2010] MHLR 154.

member of the public to identify someone who should not be identified. The key phrase used in r 14(2)(a) is that of 'serious harm' which might be caused by disclosure, and 'the interests of justice'. Issues of confidentiality and privacy can be dealt with under the extensive case management powers created by r 5. In this context r 5(3)(d) is of relevance. This provides for a requirement to provide (whether a party or not) documents, information or submissions to the Tribunal or a party. A definition of 'document is to be found in r 1(3), and is comprehensive in scope. The issue of disclosure (in part pursuant to this rule, but also in respect of case management powers of the Tribunal generally) has been considered by the Upper Tribunal in *Dorset Healthcare NHS Foundation Trust v MH*.[24] In this particular case, the patient requested disclosure of his medical records, and the NHS Trust declined complete disclosure. Guidance on the issue has been given by the Upper Tribunal as follows: 'The starting point is that full disclosure of all relevant material should generally be given' (at [20]). If agreement cannot be reached, and the Tribunal is to be asked to make a determination of the matter, then regard should be given to r 14(2)–(6). However, it may be that the body which holds the records still has concerns about disclosure (which may, eg, relate to information provided by third parties). If so, then it should seek to obtain the consent of the third party, if possible. If this is not possible, then:[25]

> '… it should be possible for the responsible authority to disclose all such documents to the patient's solicitors subject to an undertaking from the solicitors not to disclose to the patient third-party documents specifically identified by the authority. The patient's solicitors can then take a view as to whether the third party rights override the rights of the patient, or vice-versa. Where they consider the documents ought to be disclosed to the patient, then they must make an application to the tribunal for disclosure.'

If the responsible authority does not even wish to take this step (and the Upper Tribunal held that this would only be in 'quite exceptional circumstances' (at [28])), then it would be obliged to provide a skeleton argument in support, and to identify the documents which it did not want to disclose. The patient's solicitors would then respond in kind. If, on the other hand, the patient's solicitors wished to disclose documents which had been provided to them by way of an undertaking, then the process would be reversed. If the exchange of such arguments still does not resolve the issue, then only at that stage should the Tribunal become involved. The Upper Tribunal suggests that such matters:[26]

> '… should be capable of being determined by the Tribunal on the day of the substantive hearing. However, there may be circumstances where the issue is more complicated, when it would be appropriate for the matter to be considered by a single judge in advance of the substantive hearing.'

---

24 [2009] UKUT 4 (AAC).

25 [2009] UKUT 4 (AAC), at [27].

26 Ibid, at [31].

The Upper Tribunal also pointed out that all the above steps can be taken by the use of the general case management powers available to it, and 'in particular rule 5(3)(d)' (at [33]). It also held that 'when this sort of decision is made without hearing both parties, to include a reference to the right to make an application under rule 6(5) if there is an objection to the direction' (at [35]). In terms of more general procedural points (for appeal) which are considered, see **14.2**.

3.14 Rule 14 should be considered alongside r 38 (public and private hearings). If a hearing is in public, there would be significant problems with r 14, for reasons that are self-evident.

Information or documents likely to cause serious harm

3.15 The principle equivalent to r 14 under the old rules was rr 6 and 12. Rule 12 permitted non-disclosure if it considered that disclosure would adversely affect the health or welfare of the patient *or others*. Even if such a document was withheld, nevertheless, it would be disclosed to a representative. Rule 14 refers to 'representatives' but not 'legal representatives'. Legal representatives are defined (r 1(3)) as 'an authorised advocate or authorised litigator as defined by section 119(1) of the Courts and Legal Services Act 1990'. This section defines such as:

> '… any person (including a barrister or solicitor) who has a right of audience granted by an authorised body in accordance with the provisions of this Act. "Authorised litigator" means any person (including a solicitor) who has the right to conduct litigation granted by an authorised body in accordance with the provisions of this Act.'

However, even this is subject to the caveat at r 14(5) and (6) which provides for disclosure of such documents or information to a party who has a representative if it is satisfied that 'disclosure to the representative would be in the interests of the party and (b) the representative will act in accordance with paragraph 6'. Paragraph 6 prevents the representative from disclosing the information 'either directly or indirectly to any other person without the Tribunal's consent'. This is likely to cause a representative formidable forensic (and ethical) difficulties if the information is vital to the case of his or her client. However, in practice, the commonest source of non-disclosure is where information has been received from a family member, and that information (if disclosed) would be likely to cause a breakdown in the relationship between the patient and that person. Usually, the information provided is (as a matter of fact) already known to at least one of the other professionals involved, and is contained (in one form or another) in documents that have already been disclosed (and therefore it is somewhat academic). In other instances, the information may not be essential or material in any event. Chapter 18 (Confidentiality and Information Sharing) and Chapter 2 (Information for patients, nearest relatives and others) of the Code contain further guidance on issues associated with privacy, fairness and confidentiality.

3.16 The test of 'serious harm' and 'the interests of justice' is a different test to the old rule, and appears to raise the criteria for non-disclosure to more extreme matters than the old test (health and welfare). The term 'serious harm' is not defined in the Rules. It is a qualitative term which the Tribunal will be obliged to evaluate, in all the circumstances. If there is a wish by a party for the Tribunal to prohibit disclosure, then that party:[27]

> '... must exclude the relevant document or information from any documents that will be provided to the second party and (b) provide to the Tribunal the excluded document or information, and the reasons for its exclusion, so that the Tribunal may decide whether the information should be disclosed to the second party or should be the subject of a direction under paragraph (2).'

3.17 As a matter of practice, parties often provide copies of an edited *and* unedited documents to the Tribunal, with no indication of which parts have been removed. This can make life very difficult. Adherence to the above rule will save much time. The issue has been considered at greater length in *RM v St Andrew's Healthcare*.[28] The stark nature of the dilemma was that the patient had been treated by way of covert medication. This had worked. He wished to be discharged. The RC did not wish the patient to know that he had been subject to covert medication. As it was put on behalf of the patient 'The patient's understanding of his present condition is central to the case he wants to present. As far as he is aware, he is largely free of symptoms without medication. The reality is the opposite: he is as free as he is from symptoms only by reason of his medication.'[29] The consequence (were there to be non-disclosure of the fact that he was being covertly medicated) would be 'The Tribunal may hold a hearing with the patient present. If it does, his legal team will not be able to present the real case. They cannot disclose the covert medication. Nor can the medical witnesses or the Tribunal. Everyone in the room will know what the patient does not. They will be reduced to performing a mere mummery. Justice will not be done at the end of the hearing; it will only seem to be done. The real proceedings will have to be conducted out of the patient's sight and knowledge.'[30] The longer term consequences would be 'a series of further non-disclosure orders. In total, they would exclude the claimant completely from knowing of the real process that was being followed and allow him to participate only in a pretence of a process. They would severely hamper his legal team in participating effectively in that process.'[31] The consequence was that there was no prohibition on the disclosure of the information that the patient was being covertly medicated.

---

27 Rule 14(5).

28 [2010] UKUT 119 (AAC), [2010] MHLR 176.

29 Ibid, at [24].

30 Ibid, at [26].

31 Ibid, at [31].

Victims

3.18 In certain circumstances the Domestic Violence, Crime and Victims Act 2004 governs the involvement of victims in the Tribunal. This extends to the provision of information by them to the Tribunal, and more significantly in the context of confidentiality and disclosure, notification to victims of decisions made by the Tribunal. This is considered in detail in Part D (Chapter 24). In addition, a document entitled 'Practice Guidance on Procedures Concerning Handling Representations from Victims in the First-tier Tribunal (Mental Health)' was issued on 1 July 2011, pursuant to Sch 4 of the Tribunals, Courts and Enforcement Act 2007 (TCEA 2007). This sets out in some detail the information to which parties and the Tribunal must have regard, and is also set out in its entirety in Part F.

3.19 The new Rules make no explicit provision for victims. Although unlikely to be appropriate in this context, r 33(e) (Notice of proceedings to interested persons) provides that 'any person' can be permitted (or requested) to 'attend and take part in a hearing to such extent as the Tribunal considers proper or (b) make written submissions in relation to a particular issue'. This is supplemented by r 36(2)(a) and (b), which allows for such a person to attend and take part to the extent the Tribunal feels is proper, and r 5(3)(d). The existing law on the involvement of victims tends to transfer fairly seamlessly into the new regime. In *R (T) v MHRT*,[32] Scott Baker J held that 'the interested party [a former partner of a restricted patient against whom she had obtained an injunction] could put her views before them very effectively by way of a written statement'. The old rule used for this purpose was r 14(2).

3.20 In *R (T) v MHRT*[33] the issue involved disclosure to a victim of that part of a decision which related to the conditions imposed on a conditional discharge. On the facts in that case Scott J held that there were a number of matters to which the victim was not entitled (where he was to live; what his medical treatment was to be) but that there was a legitimate interest if it was a condition that he should not (for example) live:[34]

> '... within a particular locality or perhaps to communicate or attempt to communicate with a particular individual. I see no reason why information of that nature should not be made public. No harm is done to the patient and the condition gives the victim some peace of mind.'

The mechanism for such disclosure would be via r 14 (as referred to above) or in certain circumstances via the Probation Service (see Part D).

3.21 The Code also provides specific guidance on the topic of victims at Chapter 18 (at paras 18.18–18.20). It draws attention to the Code of Practice for the Domestic Violence, Crime and Victims Act 2004 itself, and encourages

---

32 [2001] EWHC 602 (Admin); (*EC Ch 16*).
33 [2002] MHLR 275; (*EC Ch 16*).
34 [2002] MHLR 275, at [27].

professionals to persuade mentally disordered offenders to 'share information that will enable victims and victim's families to be informed of their progress'.

OTHER PRE-HEARING PROCEDURES

3.22 Some of these have been touched on above, but the remaining matters fall into fairly distinct categories unrelated to the issues of confidentiality or non-disclosure.

Examination by medical member

3.23 This topic has been dealt with from the perspective of (a) bias and (b) the requirements of natural justice above. This was governed by the old r 11, and is now governed by r 34. The main difference between the two is not great. Rule 11 required the medical member to examine the patient at any time prior to the hearing. Convention and guidance suggests that this should be a day or so before the hearing. This is more honoured in the breach than the observance. The new rule states:

> 'Before a hearing to consider the disposal of a mental health case an appropriate member of the Tribunal, must, so far as is practicable (a) examine the patient and (b) take such other steps as that member considers necessary to form an opinion of the patient's mental condition.'

This appears to remove the requirement that it should be specifically the medical member who carries out the examination, and indeed that an examination should take place at all, since the qualification that this should only be done *so far as is practicable* has been added. However, since it is unlikely that another suitably qualified member of the Tribunal would exist, this is a very remote possibility. Rule 34(2) provides that such an examination may be in private, and may include an examination of the records relating to detention or treatment of the patient and any after-care services, and take notes or copies of records for use in connection with the proceedings. If such documents were germane to the hearing, then, unless r 14 applied, they would be made available to the relevant parties (either by use of general case management powers, or r 15 (Evidence and submissions)).

Legal representative

3.24 The majority of patients elect to be represented. Some wish to conduct proceedings on their own. The old r 10 in respect of representation is now contained in r 11. In essence, this permits a party to appoint a representative (whether legally qualified or not) to represent him or her. It retains the prohibitions on certain categories of representatives (which previously related to those detained under the MHA 1983 or subject to guardianship, or receiving treatment for a mental disorder at the same hospital or nursing home as the patient) and are now set out in r 11(8)(a) and (b). The name and address of that representative must be provided by them to all other parties.

Appointment of legal representative

3.25 Under the old r 12, if a patient wished to represent him or herself, then, subject to the discretion of the Regional Chairman, if the *Mental Health Act Administrator* had doubts about (for example) the capacity of the patient to make any decisions, he or she was advised to refer the matter to the Regional Chair for a decision as to whether legal representation would be imposed or not. In practice, the problem often is not drawn to the attention of the Tribunal until the hearing itself. The new r 11 makes matters simpler. It covers parties appointing their own representative. However, if a *patient* has not appointed a representative, and they do not wish to conduct their own case, *or* they wish to be represented *or* they lack capacity but it is felt by the Tribunal that is in the patient's *best interests* to be represented, then the Tribunal can appoint one (r 11(7)(a) and (b)). It should be noted that many patients are perfectly able to represent themselves, albeit with assistance from the Tribunal. This is no different than the position of a litigant in person appearing before other courts or tribunals. There is also a retention of any party being accompanied by another person to help assist in presenting the case. In effect, this equates to the *McKenzie* friend in mainstream litigation (r 11(5)). The issue of whether or not the Official Solicitor could be appointed as a litigation friend was considered in *AA v Cheshire and Wirral Partnership NHS Trust and ZZ*.[35] It was held that the Tribunal had no power to appoint a litigation friend (whether the Official Solicitor, or any other suitable person). The point in issue was that whereas a litigation friend can act on behalf of a protected party, and will not be bound to follow instructions, a legal representative will be obliged to follow the instructions of the patient. The Upper Tribunal considered in some detail the practice note issue by the Law Society on this (and other points) dated 13 August 2009. In essence, it adopted the basis of this Guidance as being largely sufficient to obviate the requirement of a litigation friend, in any event. The conclusion was that:

> 'Rule 11(7)(b) plainly contemplates the possibility of a solicitor being appointed to represent a patient who does not have capacity to give any instructions at all. In such a case, the rule must, as the Law Society's guidance plainly expects, anticipate that the solicitor will ascertain any relevant wishes that the patient may be able to express, will inform the tribunal of such wishes, make such points in support of them as can properly be made and generally ensure that the tribunal has all the relevant material before it and does not overlook any statutory provision. However, in the absence of the patient's capacity to give valid instructions, the rule must, in my view, also anticipate that the solicitor will exercise his or her judgment and advance any argument that he or she considers to be in the patient's "best interests", which, as the Law Society's guidance recognises, will not necessarily involve arguing for the patient's discharge. In those circumstances, it seems to me that the solicitor has the same freedom of action as a litigation friend in the courts'. If the patient has capacity to give instructions on some matters but not others, the situation is not much different either than it would be in more mainstream litigation. The Law Society's guidance is unequivocal: a solicitor is

---

35 [2009] UKUT 195 (AAC), [2009] MHLR 308.

bound to act in accordance with the instructions that have been given. Therefore the more a patient has capacity to give detailed instructions, the less the solicitor has complete freedom of action.'[36]

Withdrawal of application

3.26 The old rule governing withdrawal of an application was r 19. An application could be withdrawn by the applicant, as long as it was in writing and the Tribunal agreed, or if the applicant ceased to be detained or subject to guardianship it was deemed to be withdrawn, or if the patient was subject to after-care under supervision but failed to undergo a medical examination without reasonable explanation, then the Tribunal could deem the application to be withdrawn.

3.27 Under r 17 of the new Rules, which is headed 'Withdrawal', a party may withdraw its case, at any time prior to the hearing for the disposal of the proceedings. This can be in writing, or orally *at* the hearing (r 17(1)(a) and (b)). The consent of the Tribunal is required, except with regard to cases under MHA 1983, s 67 or 71(1). It is not permissible for a party to withdraw its case if a reference has been made via MHA 1983, s 68, 71(2) or 75(1). These statutory provisions are given in Part D and F. If a patient withdraws, then a further application can still be made during the relevant specified period (MHA 1983, s 77(2)). It would also appear that such an application may now be made at any point up until the Tribunal has made its decision. This may have unfortunate results if a written application is not received (since this specifies that it should be before the hearing of the final determination), whereas there is no such caveat in respect of oral applications. The issue of withdrawing an application is considered in *KF v Birmingham and Solihull Mental Health Foundation Trust*.[37] If the application is no more than a tactical ploy then:

> 'In our view a First-tier Tribunal would certainly be justified in refusing consent to a withdrawal … However that should not be taken as meaning that a tribunal should only refuse its agreement in such a scenario. There is plainly no automatic right to withdraw, and we agree with counsel that the case for accepting a withdrawal will depend very much on the particular circumstance of the case (or cases). The 1983 Rules did not contain either the overriding objective or the extensive case management powers to which we have already made reference and the First-tier Tribunal should always have regard to those provisions when considering whether or not it is appropriate to consent to a withdrawal.'[38]

A decision to consent to withdrawal is an appealable decision in itself.[39] However, this particular appeal was in part predicated on the particular facts of the case. Finally, a party may apply for its case to be reinstated (r 17(4) and (5)) as long as the correct procedure is observed (r 17(6)). In respect of s 77(2), and

---

36 Ibid, at [18]–[19].

37 [2010] UKUT 185 (AAC), [2010] MHLR 201.

38 Ibid, at [37].

39 *MB v BEH MH NHST & Secretary of State for Justice* [2011] UKUT 328 (AAC); [2011] MHLR 246.

withdrawn applications, the Chamber President issued guidance on 8 December 2008. This is set out in full in Part F.

ADJOURNMENTS

3.28 As the function of the Tribunal is comparatively limited, and constrained, so it follows that the purposes for which a Tribunal may decide to adjourn a hearing are also comparatively limited and constrained. Many of the problems that have arisen in this area are where attempts have been made to do things which, as a matter of law, the Tribunal does not have the jurisdiction to control. The commonest purpose for which adjournments are used is to fill in gaps in the evidence in respect of those matters upon which the Tribunal is obliged to make a decision. For example, this may relate to those plans which would affect the patient, if he or she was to be discharged.

3.29 The basis of adjournments was usually pursuant to the old rr 13, 15 and 16. Rule 13 provided for 'such directions as it thinks fit to ensure the speedy and just determination of the application'. Rule 15 provided for the obtaining of further information or reports. Rule 16 provided for an adjournment 'for the purposes of obtaining further information or for such other purposes as it may think appropriate'. The ability of the Tribunal to give specific directions in respect of numerous issues is now more precise, but still provides great flexibility. Some of these are considered below, and some in Part F. In respect of the specific issues considered below, the existing case-law (which relates to the powers of the Tribunal) will still hold good.

After-care services

3.30 In *R (Ashworth Hospital Authority) v MHRT; R (H) v Ashworth Hospital Authority*[40] a part of the difficulty which the Tribunal encountered was that it had ordered an immediate discharge (of a patient detained under MHA 1983, s 3) when the care plan for him was very thin indeed. For example, he had no accommodation at all available to him. It would have been open to the Tribunal either to have deferred the discharge by a short period or to have adjourned the case until a fully fledged after-care plan was available. Moreover, on the facts of the case, the patient was likely to have required quite extensive and carefully planned support in the community. Dyson J held that:[41]

> 'H was a patient in respect of whom it was essential that the Tribunal considered the availability of suitable after-care services when deciding whether to order his immediate discharge from hospital. If the Tribunal had any doubt as to whether such services would be available, they should have adjourned to obtain any necessary information. I regard the deferral under s. 72 (2) as less satisfactory. Section 72 (3) authorises a tribunal to "direct the discharge of a patient on a future date specified in the direction" ... But if the Tribunal is in doubt as to

---

40 [2002] MHLR 314, CA; (*EC Chs 1, 2, 9 and 15*).

41 [2002] MHLR 314, at [68], CA.

whether suitable after-care arrangements will be made available, it is difficult to see how they can specify a particular date for discharge. In cases of doubt, the safer course is to adjourn …'

3.31 The matter was re-considered (in the context of a restricted patient) in *DC v Nottinghamshire Healthcare NHS Trust and the Secretary of State for Justice*.[42] The question posed was 'At what point in considering the possible discharge of a restricted patient is the tribunal no longer allowed to adjourn but obliged to defer a direction for a conditional discharge?'.[43] The problem faced by the Tribunal was that it did not have adequate information as to whether suitable aftercare could have been made available to the patient (and so it followed the dicta of Dyson J, as set out above). It was held that:

> 'The First-tier Tribunal has power to adjourn as one of its case management powers … the power must be exercised judicially and in accordance with the overriding objective in r.2. As a procedural power it cannot be exercised to override the provisions of the substantive legislation. In particular, a tribunal cannot adjourn if it is obliged to give a decision under s.73 of the 1983 Act'.'[44]

It went on to consider the conditions of s 73(1) and stated that:

> 'If and only if the tribunal is satisfied that the patient should not be detained but should be subject to recall, these 2 consequences follow. The first consequence is a duty – the tribunal must direct a conditional discharge under s. 73(2). The second consequence is a power – the tribunal may defer that direction under s. 73(7). The language of s. 73(7) is important. The tribunal does not defer the patient's conditional discharge. It defers the direction for a discharge. That is what s. 73(7) says and it is significant. That presupposes that there is a direction to discharge ready to take effect. Until there is, there is nothing to defer. That means that the conditions for discharge must be identified and included in the direction. The deferral allows time for the necessary arrangements to be made. That means the arrangements necessary for the conditional discharge. And it is impossible to make those arrangements without knowing what the conditions for the discharge are. Section 73(7), by its terms, operates until the tribunal is satisfied that the arrangements are in place. Once it is, there is nothing left for the tribunal to do except lift the deferral. In summary, the tribunal cannot exercise the power in s. 73(7) unless it finds that the patient should not be detained but should be subject to recall and it formulates a direction, including conditions for discharge, that can take effect if the necessary arrangements can be made. Until then, it is free to adjourn.'[45]

In other words, the only prohibition on adjournments in these circumstances is similar to that which applies to all applications (whether restricted patients or not) which is that s 73(7) must not be used as a method for obtaining evidence as to whether a conditional discharge may be appropriate or not, whether by reference to aftercare arrangements or other matters.

---

42 [2012] UKUT 92 (AAC), [2102] MHLR 238.

43 Ibid, at [A1].

44 Ibid, at [23].

45 Ibid, at [24]–[26].

3.32 In respect of adjournments generally where issues as to the provision of aftercare *may* be an issue, *AM v West London MH NHS Trust & Secretary of State for Justice*[46] provides guidance to the Tribunal as to when it may proceed with a hearing in the face of an application to adjourn based upon inadequacy of the reports provided on this issue. The issue in the case was stated to be 'when a tribunal is under a duty to adjourn to obtain information on possible aftercare available to a patient'.[47] The answer is that although by reference to r 32(6) (provision of relevant documents required by the Practice Direction) which is mandatory, this is qualified by r 7 (which permits a failure to comply to be waived) and paras 27.7–27.9 of the Code (aftercare). The consequence is that it is a matter for the Tribunal (with its own expertise and experience) to consider whether the hearing can still be effective without this information. Upper Tribunal Judge Jacobs held that:

> 'The witnesses for the detaining authority are familiar in general terms with the sort of aftercare that may be available and how effective it may be, and they know the patient. The panel hearing a mental health case is an expert one. It is entitled to use its own knowledge and expertise. Indeed, it is required to do so. It will form its own opinion of the patient and what is feasible for that patient. The Tribunal's decision including its approach to adjournments for further information, should be informed by its knowledge, expertise and assessment of the possibilities. In that context, I do not accept that it is essential for the tribunal to have specific information about aftercare in every case. It is an individual judgment to be made in the circumstances of the particular case.'[48]

It is to be noted that in this particular case, the decision not to adjourn was based on the following 'On the Tribunal's findings, Mr M had not yet progressed to the point where the issue of aftercare that was actually available would arise. Without some acceptance or insight, Mr M could not progress to the point where his management in the community could even be tested by unescorted leave, let alone where he could be conditionally discharged.'[49]

Natural justice

3.33 It should perhaps be self-evident that if the Tribunal is considering adjourning a case, then all the parties should be given an opportunity of responding to the suggestion.[50]

3.34 Similarly, in *R (X) v MHRT*[51] (where the parties were also not made aware of what the Tribunal was proposing to do in terms of adjourning to obtain further evidence after it appeared to have made a final determination of the issues) Collins J held that:[52]

---

46 [2012] UKUT 382 (AAC), [2012] MHLR 399.
47 Ibid, at [1].
48 Ibid, at [16].
49 Ibid, at [49].
50 *R (B) v MHRT and Home Secretary* [2003] MHLR 19; (*EC Chs 1, 7, 14 and 15*).
51 [2003] MHLR 299; (*EC Chs 1, 7 and 14*).
52 Ibid, at [53] and [60].

'… at all times, as I have sought to emphasise, the Tribunal must direct itself that it should only adjourn for that purpose [to hear from other witnesses] if it regards it as necessary to do so in order to reach a just decision … I emphasise that this will be a very exceptional case. It is obviously undesirable in the extreme that a decision of this sort is made after the submissions and evidence have been concluded and when the parties believe that the case is over but for the determination …'

3.35 On a different point, but related to the principles of natural justice, the position of a Tribunal that had expressed a concluded opinion prior to the conclusion of the hearing was considered in *MB v BEH MH NHST & Secretary of State for Justice*.[53] The patient was restricted. He applied for a discharge, and there was support from the RC for a conditional discharge, but the relevant conditions which might be appropriate were some way from being either found or tested. The TJ expressed an opinion that the application was unlikely to succeed and suggested that the application should be withdrawn. This was the subject of a successful appeal, on the basis that there had been a breach of the rules of natural justice. The judgment of Stanley Burton J was cited as follows:

'Useful guidance on how a tribunal panel should approach its task was given in … *R (S) v MHRT and Department of Health* [2003] MHLR 118

"22. … there can normally be no objection to members of a tribunal or court forming or discussing their provisional view of the case before the hearing. Judges and tribunal members are human and cannot be prevented from forming an initial view of a case when they read the papers. The forming of an opinion before the hearing is normally objectionable only if it is not provisional, liable to be challenged by the evidence produced and the submissions of the parties, but is firm and concluded: in which case the hearing is an ineffective charade. The business of multi-member courts could not be carried on efficiently if their members were not able to discuss the issues and exchange provisional views before the hearing …

32. In my judgment 'due impartiality' in the present context [as required by the ECHR] requires a member of a tribunal not to have a preconceived concluded opinion on the merits of the applicant's case. The [court] did not suggest that a provisional view formed before the commencement of the hearing is objectionable. If an otherwise impartial and independent member of a tribunal has a preconceived concluded opinion, or if he expresses himself in such a way as to give rise to a reasonable apprehension that he has a preconceived concluded opinion, he lacks the necessary impartiality, but not otherwise."'

3.36 A similar issue arose in *RN v Curo Care*,[54] where Upper Tribunal Judge Jacobs cited Megarry J as follows:

---

53 [2011] UKUT 328 (AAC), [2011] MHLR 246.

54 [2011] UKUT 263 (AAC), [2011] MHLR 337.

'What is not permissible is to reach firm conclusions and prevent the parties from arguing to the contrary. That is unwise, as Megarry J observed in *John v Rees* [1970] Ch 345 at 402:

> "As everybody who has anything to do with the law well knows, the path of the law is strewn with examples of open and shut cases which, somehow, were not; of unanswerable charges which, in the event, were completely answered; of inexplicable conduct which was fully explained; of fixed and unalterable determinations that, by discussion, suffered a change. Nor are those with any knowledge of human nature who pause to think for a moment likely to underestimate the feelings of resentment of those who find that a decision against them has been made without their being afforded any opportunity to influence events."

Not only is it unwise, it is a breach of natural justice and the Convention right to a fair hearing.'[55]

Recommendations

3.37 The patient in this instance was a restricted patient (in respect of whom the Tribunal has no power to make a recommendation for transfer to a less secure hospital). Such a recommendation was requested, and the Tribunal adjourned in order to obtain more evidence in respect of that issue. In *R (Home Secretary) v MHRT* the point was made as follows by Collins J:[56]

> '... the powers of the Tribunal are limited. First, it may discharge absolutely; second, it may discharge conditionally; and thirdly, it may decide that it is not appropriate to discharge. When one adds in the powers given by s 72 (5) it will be seen that the statutory powers of the Tribunal are thereby limited to four courses of action, because one adds in the power to reclassify.'

The fact that r 16 appears to give the power to adjourn for 'such other purposes as it may think appropriate' was dealt with as follows:[57]

> '... in considering whether or not to adjourn under r 16, the Tribunal must bear in mind that the only purpose for which they can adjourn is to enable them to carry out their statutory duties or powers.'

Those powers are listed above. Collins J concluded:[58]

> 'I would like to make it clear that nothing I have said is intended to inhibit the Tribunal from making recommendations if it considers it appropriate in any case so to do. Equally, there is nothing to prevent the Tribunal receiving or seeking evidence relevant to that issue, not can it be criticised if it chooses to do so. What it cannot do is to use its powers of adjournment solely for the purpose of obtaining such material. If it has reason to adjourn to obtain information material

---

55 Ibid, at [4].

56 [2000] MHLR 209, at [30]; (*EC Chs 1 and 12*).

57 Ibid, at [50].

58 Ibid, at [81].

to matters upon which it has to decide, that is to say discharge or classification, there is nothing to stop the Tribunal at the same time obtaining information which may be relevant to transfer.'

3.38 A further observation on non-statutory recommendations was made by Arden LJ in *Secretary of State for Justice v RB*[59] that 'A tribunal may be able to express some helpful non-statutory recommendations for a transfer in an appropriate case'.[60] However, in *RB v Nottinghamshire Healthcare NHS Trust (Merits)*[61] the issue of the purpose and procedure for statutory recommendations was considered. The patient had been detained pursuant to s 3, and a recommendation was made pursuant to s 72(3)(a). The Tribunal was requested to reconvene at a point where it appeared that the recommendation might not be capable of being implemented in accordance with the timescale that had been envisaged. However, the Upper Tribunal was unclear as to why (a) there had been a recommendation and (b) why there had been a refusal to reconvene, and this formed a part of the criticism of the absence of a clear judgment in support of two judicial decisions. Upper Tribunal Judge (UTJ) Jacobs held that:

> 'The power to make statutory recommendations is discretionary for the tribunal but it must be exercised, like all a tribunal's decisions, judicially. And once begun, it must be followed through fairly. It is obviously designed to assist in identifying the best way forward for the patient. But it operates by moral pressure and moral authority, not by order. The tribunal must be mindful of that limitation when deciding whether to make a recommendation in the first place. If it does so, it must carry the process through judicially, although the exercise of its powers will be tempered by the reality that it has no power to coerce [12] … It is surely undesirable to give a patient false hope. The first question is whether to make a recommendation at all. The more obvious the recommendation, the more likely it is that the authority will consider it anyway. So recommendations are likely to be made in this cases where the authority has not considered the possibility of would be unlikely to do so. If the Tribunal does not make a recommendation, it has to take account of the tenuous nature of its control. This makes it essential to consider very carefully the timescale and the directions that the tribunal might give in order (i) to apply its moral pressure on the authority and (ii) to be fully informed by the time it has to decide whether to reconvene. It may, for example, be appropriate for the tribunal to direct that a progress report be provided shortly before a specified date so that it can decide if there is any practical purpose in reconvening. Finally, the tribunal has to decide whether to reconvene. In making that decision, it has to decide what practical value this would serve. It has no power to enforce the recommendation and is not reconvening for that purpose. It has the power to embarrass the authority into explaining its thinking or, possibly, into compliance. But it has to make a judgment on what it can practically achieve, if anything. That is where the issue of proportionality comes in. It may be that that is what the tribunal had in mind by its references to proportionality.'[62]

---

59 [2011] EWCA Civ 1608, [2012] MHLR 131.

60 Ibid, at [66].

61 [2011] UKUT 73 (AAC), [2011] MHLR 296.

62 Ibid, at [16].

3.39 The matter of non-statutory recommendations was also considered in *EC v Birmingham and Solihull Mental Health NHS Trust*.[63] The appeal was based upon an alleged error of law when two Tribunals had not (in a different manner) made non-statutory recommendations. Both patients were subject to restriction orders, and therefore there was no statutory power for a Tribunal to make such recommendations in the first place. UTJ Rowland dismissed both appeals, and held that:

> 'there can be no right to an opportunity to invite a tribunal to act beyond its powers and it is sufficient explanation for not making a non-statutory recommendation that the patient is not entitled to one ... it has no **legal** power to make an extra-statutory recommendation and can never be compelled to do so ... while the making of a recommendation may confer an advantage, a refusal even to consider making a recommendation does not confer a corresponding disadvantage: it is neutral in its effect on the Secretary of State's decision making.'[64]

Consequently, there was no error of law by the Tribunal in refusing to hear argument on the subject, as patients had no right to advance such an argument. The judge acknowledged that a different tribunal might reach a different conclusion – it did not prevent an extra statutory recommendation being made if this was appropriate. However, he did hold that:

> '... if some panels are routinely spending a great deal of time considering issues not necessary for the exercise of their statutory functions for no better reason than that a party has asked them to do so, I would deprecate that practice.'[65]

3.40 Finally, in *RN v Curo Care*,[66] a decision **not** to make a recommendation was considered (for a transfer to a CTO). This case has been considered at **3.36** in the context of natural justice. Apart from the criticism that was made regarding reaching a firm opinion prior to the conclusion of the hearing in respect of the request by the patient for a recommendation, no judgment was given as to why the Tribunal would not make a recommendation, the reasons simply referring to the evidence of the RC who was opposed to the making of a CTO.

Monitoring of mental health of patient

3.41 In *R v Nottingham MHRT ex parte Home Secretary*[67] the Tribunal fell into error by adjourning in two instances to (in effect) determine the progress or otherwise that the patients might make, so that it could make its decision in due course. It was held that r 16 only permitted adjournments to obtain further information as to the present mental health of the patient (in this instance) and that 'for such other purposes as it might think appropriate' extended only to

---

63 [2012] UKUT 178 (AAC), [2012] MHLR 292.
64 Ibid, at [24]–[25].
65 Ibid, at [35].
66 [2011] UKUT 263, [2011] MHLR 337.
67 TLR, 12 October 1998; (*EC Chs 1 and 12*).

purposes ancillary to the powers conferred under MHA 1983. This did not include a supervisory jurisdiction, either to monitor treatment or to see if there was a general improvement. A similar issue was considered in *CNWL NHS Foundation Trust v H-JH*.[68] In this instance, the patient had the status of being on a community treatment order. The Tribunal ordered a deferred discharge from the CTO. In so doing it expressed the hope that prior to that discharge, the RC would consider reducing medication, and that if such a reduction had an adverse effect upon the patient then 'no doubt the appropriate action can be taken'.[69] The Trust queried what was meant by 'appropriate action' and the answer given was to the effect this was a matter for the RC, but amongst the possibilities was a further alteration in the medication, or recall under the existing s 3, or further sectioning after the date of the deferred discharge. In the judgment it was held that:

> 'It is well established that the tribunal has to decide whether the statutory conditions remain satisfied at the time of the hearing. In other words, it has to be satisfied that the patient is entitled to be discharged at that time. This applies whether the discharge is immediate or deferred. Deferral is a means of managing the discharge.'[70]

The reasons for the deferred discharge (and which incorporated time for the RC to alter medication if so decided) did *not* cross into the territory of trying to manage the treatment. Moreover, the answer given to the query raised by the Trust by the First-tier judge was correct in law. The CTO remained in force until the date of the deferred discharge. Up until then, the patient remained liable for recall, and to have medication changed. If a detention was required after discharge, that was another matter, but the possibility is permitted (if there is a change in circumstances) and by reference to *R (Von Brandenburg) v East London and the City Mental Health Trust*.[71]

Case management powers

3.42 Rule 1(3) defines the phrase 'dispose of proceedings' as including 'disposing of a part of proceedings'. Rule 42 defines 'Provisional decisions' as 'a decision with recommendations under section 72(3)(a) or (3A)(a) of the Mental Health Act 1983 or a deferred direction for conditional discharge under section 73(7) of that Act' which 'is a decision which disposes of the proceedings'. Anything else is therefore not a final disposal.

3.43 The Rules are all predicated by the overriding objective (r 2) and the obligation of the parties to co-operate with the Tribunal. This objective will be familiar to all practitioners from other areas of law, but it is the first time that it has been made explicit within the context of Tribunals. Within the context of adjournments, it states that the Tribunal (in dealing with the case fairly and

---

68 [2012] UKUT (AAC).

69 Ibid, at [6].

70 Ibid, at [17].

71 [2004] 2 AC 280.

justly) should avoid delay 'so far as is compatible with proper consideration of the issues'. Rule 5(3)(h) permits the Tribunal to 'adjourn or postpone a hearing' but adds no gloss as to the purpose of such a course of action (except by reference to the overriding objective and r 2(2)(e)). Rule 16 makes explicit the power to summons both witnesses and documents and r 5(3)(d) permits the Tribunal to 'permit or require a party or another person to provide documents, information or submissions to the Tribunal or a party'. In *TR v Ludlow Street Healthcare Ltd*[72] a case management decision was made prior to the actual Tribunal, which was to refuse disclosure. This decision itself was appealed. Although a case management decision could be appealed, permission depended upon a realistic prospect of success. In this instance, it was held that 'The President was entitled to decide that the hearing of the application should go ahead. I am sure she was aware of the possible risk to the patient if the hearing proved abortive, but she had to balance that risk against the possibility that the panel might be prepared to decide in favour of the nearest relative without the need for further evidence.'[73] In other words, case management decisions are by their very nature likely to be informed by those who have heard the case and it was not necessary to provide detailed reasons, when the case would in any event have been reconsidered by the actual full panel that would have heard the case.

Miscellaneous pre-hearing case management

3.44 Rule 5 lists the case management powers, all of which must surely be subject to the propositions in law outlined above as to the primary function of the Tribunal. For example, inviting though r 5(3)(f) might appear ('hold a hearing to consider any matter'), this will be constrained by the primary statutory powers peculiar to the Tribunal as adumbrated by Collins J. Rule 5(1) preserves the ability of the Tribunal to 'regulate its own procedure'.

Stays and suspensions

3.45 The most significant addition to the previous regime is that the Tribunal has the power to give directions to 'stay proceedings' (r 5(3)(j)) and, perhaps less controversially, to:[74]

> '... suspend the effect of its own decision pending the determination by the Tribunal or the Upper Tribunal of an application for permission to appeal against, and any appeal or review of, that decision.'

Procedure in mental health cases

3.46 Rule 32 sets out the specific procedure in mental health cases. Rule 33 provides the procedure for notifying interested persons. The expression

---

72 [2011] UKUT 152 (AAC), [2011] MHLR 190.

73 Ibid, at [12].

74 Rule 5(3)(l).

'interested person' is not defined. Rule 54.1(2)(f) of the Civil Procedure Rules 1998[75] (CPR) states that this is any other person who is 'directly affected by the claim'.

Delays

3.47 Delay and adjournments have been a particular problem over many years. Plainly, it is unlikely to be of benefit to a patient to have his or her Tribunal postponed for lengthy periods of time, and to some extent the old rules imposed time-limits. Rule 37 governs the time and place of hearings. Where a MHA 1983, s 2 case is concerned, the hearing must start within 7 days after the date upon which the Tribunal received the application notice. In respect of MHA 1983, s 75(1) (a restricted patient who has been conditionally discharged and then recalled) the period is between 5 and 8 weeks. There is a general inclusion in the overriding objective of a requirement to deal with cases so that delay is avoided (r 2(2)(e)).

3.48 In *R (C) v MHRT for the London and South West Region*[76] the policy of listing adopted in respect of admissions pursuant to MHA 1983, s 3 was considered by the Court of Appeal. That practice was to list all such hearings for a specified period after the request for a hearing had been received. This period was 8 weeks. Lord Phillips held that:[77]

> 'My conclusion is that the practice of fixing hearing dates 8 weeks after the date of application is bred of administrative convenience, not of administrative necessity. There is nothing inconsistent with Art 5 (4) of the ECHR in having a target date of 8 weeks maximum. The circumstances of some cases may well require 8 weeks' preparation for the hearing. In such cases an 8 week period will not conflict with the requirement of Art 5 (4) that the decision on the application must be obtained speedily.'

The imposition of a uniform period of 8 weeks was held to be unlawful.

3.49 The issue of delay (and the authority which led to an alteration in the organisation of listing procedures) was extensively considered in *R (KB, MK, JR, GM, LB, PD and TB) v Mental Health Review Tribunal and Secretary of State for Health*.[78] Insofar as it is relevant, the general principle of speedy access to a court (ECHR, Art 5(4)) within the specific context of detention of persons of unsound mind (ECHR, Art 5(1)(e)) was upheld in *Musial v Poland*.[79] In terms of more recent legislation (albeit within Scotland) where there had been a short-term detention order (which lasted for 28 days), the Tribunal was held to have acted unlawfully by not holding a hearing within the statutory time-limit.[80]

---

75 SI 1998/3132.

76 [2001] EWCA Civ 1110, [2001] MHLR 110, CA; (*EC Ch 14*).

77 [2001] EWCA Civ 1110, [2001] MHLR 110, at [64].

78 [2002] EWHC 639 (Admin), [2003] MHLR 1.

79 [1999] MHLR 35.

80 *In the Petition of John Smith (Mental Health Officer)* [2006] CSOH 44, [2007] MHLR 17.

Striking out

3.50 This is set out in r 8(3) and is a very limited power. It relates purely to a situation where the Tribunal has no jurisdiction, and does not transfer the case to another court or tribunal. It is unlikely to be used, given the very clear nature of a Tribunal. However, r 35 was changed in 2012 to permit a decision to be made without a hearing at all, in respect of references by way of s 68 where the patient was subject to a Community Treatment Order, and is over the age of 18. This is considered at greater length in Chapters 4 and 10.

Directions/failure to comply/summons

3.51 Either the Tribunal may make directions or it may do so upon application by one of the parties (r 6). A failure to comply with the Rules (which includes practice directions) leads to the options set out in r 7(2)(a)–(d). Rule 7(3) provides the opportunity to refer the matter to the Upper Tribunal in order to compel the production of individuals and documents (and to permit inspection of premises). However, it is difficult to see how this adds to the powers contained in r 16 (Summonsing of Witnesses and orders to answer questions or produce documents). The procedure contained in the latter direction simplifies the procedure of the Tribunal to compel evidence to be provided which had existed hitherto. In *CB v Suffolk County Council*,[81] a witness had failed to comply with a summons, the penalty for which was a fine of £500 (by usage[82]), and that if the payment was not made within 28 days, then a term of imprisonment would be imposed (by way of s 16(3) of the Contempt of Court Act 1981).

Costs

3.52 Rule 10 is an addition to the powers of the Tribunal, and an innovation within its jurisdiction. It is limited to wasted costs orders, and may be done on application or of its own volition. Such an order might (for example) be appropriate where a party has failed to comply with a direction, or practice direction, which has caused an adjournment to take place. The Tribunal is obliged to assess the amount of costs, either on the standard basis or on an indemnity basis. If the person paying the costs is an individual, then his or her financial means will be taken into account. In *RB v Nottinghamshire Healthcare NHS Trust (Costs)*[83] the issue as to whether a costs order could be made against the Tribunal itself was considered. It was held that the relevant UT Rules (r 10) provided that the UT could only make costs orders when the First-tier Tribunal could do so, and that power was confined to wasted costs orders against representatives only. It followed that there was no power for a costs order against the Tribunal.

---

81 [2010] UKUT 413 (AAC).

82 TCEA 2007, s 25.

83 [2011] UKUT 135 (AAC), [2011] MHLR 299.

Calculating time/sending and delivery of documents

3.53 Rules 12 and 13 are self-explanatory and deal respectively with the timing within which directions and practice directions must be given effect, and the method and format by which and in which documents must be delivered to or from the Tribunal.

Evidence and submissions

3.54 The substantive law on evidence in Tribunals is considered at greater length below. However, r 15 governs the arrangements, order and format in which evidence can be provided. It is all-encompassing, and for the first time there is a rule (r 15(1)(c)) which governs the provision of expert evidence. This is considered at greater length in Part C.

Notice of proceedings to interested persons

3.55 Rule 33 provides a specific list of those to whom notice must be given, and also 'to any other person who, in the opinion of the Tribunal, should have the opportunity of being heard'.

Disposal without a hearing

3.56 Rule 35 states that the Tribunal must not dispose of proceedings without a hearing. The definition of 'dispose of proceedings' is at r 1(3), and includes disposing of part of proceedings. A hearing is defined as 'an oral hearing ... or other means of instantaneous two-way electronic communication'. It would appear, therefore, that there is very little that may be done without a hearing in these terms, save for the provisions that relate to patients who are subject to a Community Treatment Order.

Participation in hearing

3.57 Rule 36 sets out the presumption that each party is entitled to attend a hearing (subject to the power to exclude a person from a hearing), together with a person who has been notified (r 33) at the discretion of the Tribunal. A hearing may take place in the absence of a party (either because of an exclusion) or if the party has failed to attend despite having been notified, or that reasonable steps have been taken to notify him or her, *and* it is in the interests of justice to proceed with the hearing (r 39(1)).

Allowances

3.58 Rule 40 permits the payment of allowances for travel, subsistence and loss of earnings. There are no guidelines as to amounts. The recipients may include applicants, witnesses, a patient who is neither an applicant nor a witness, a person who attends as the representative of the patient but who is not a legal representative. A similar provision already existed within the Scottish equivalent of the Rules, and a Tribunal was held to be in breach of Art 6 of the ECHR where there was a failure to pay the costs of attendance of a solicitor.[84]

Decisions and provisional decisions

3.59 Rule 41 governs the procedure for decisions. The substantive law on decisions is discussed in Part C. For MHA 1983, s 2, the written decision must be sent within 3 working days of the hearing, and in all other cases within 7 days (unless provided at the hearing). The decision must be provided to all parties (subject to r 14(2)). Rule 42 defines the term 'provisional decision'.

Burden of proof

3.60 There has been some discussion above as to whether the Tribunal is an inquisitorial or adversarial jurisdiction. The case-law tends towards the inquisitorial. Notwithstanding this, the significance of upon whom the legal and evidential burden of proof rests within a Tribunal is obviously very great. It was not until 2001 that there was a formal recognition of the requirement that the burden of proof (in certain cases) should rest upon the responsible authority,[85] which in turn arose directly out of the incorporation into domestic law of the Human Rights Act 1998 (and in particular ECHR, Art 5), and the authority of R (on the application of H) v Mental Health Review Tribunal, North and East London Region.[86] In the latter case, the Tribunal was concerned with a patient detained under MHA 1983, ss 37 and 41. The criteria that the Tribunal had to consider are contained in MHA 1983, s 73, and related to the power to discharge restricted patients. The remedial order revised both ss 72 and 73 of MHA 1983. Consequently, it is clear that the burden of proof lies upon the responsible authority. Some Tribunals deal with this in a pragmatic manner by simply dealing with the case as if the burden is on the responsible authority.

Restricted patients

3.61 A *restricted* patient still has to demonstrate that a discharge should be absolute rather than conditional.

Guardianship

3.62 A patient who is subject to an order pursuant to MHA 1983, s 7 (guardianship) still has to satisfy the Tribunal that the criteria for its imposition are not met.

---

84 *Duncan Hughes (Curatory ad Litem to PH) v Mental Health Review Tribunal* [2007] MHLR 29.

85 Mental Health Act 1983 (Remedial) Order 2001, SI 2001/3712.

86 [2001] EWCA Civ 415, [2001] MHLR 48; (*EC Chs 7, 8 and 14*).

Standard of proof

3.63 The standard of proof has been the subject of extensive litigation within the civil jurisdiction, and this is now in large part incorporated into the authorities in respect of Tribunals. The civil standard of proof is on a balance of probabilities. Practitioners will be aware that it is not infrequent for a fact that has remained in dispute to be adopted by a responsible authority (and by other professional witnesses) as an established fact. Tribunals will be alert to the difficulty that this can cause in evidential terms. It is not uncommon for professionals simply to assume that an event actually *did* occur, simply because this assertion is made in the documents. If the fact in issue is material to the decision to be made by the Tribunal, it follows that the question of burden and standard of proof has more than just academic importance. In *R (AN) v Mental Health Review Tribunal* Richard LJ held that:[87]

> '… the tribunal "is not … concerned so much with finding facts which are capable of exact demonstration but rather with a process of judgment, evaluation and assessment" … an opinion on the appropriateness or necessity of continuing detention may in principle be held with different degrees of certainty, and it may be important for the tribunal to know what degree of certainty is called for … we see no absurdity in a tribunal having some doubt as to the appropriateness or necessity of continuing detention, yet being satisfied on the balance of probability that it is appropriate and necessary. Accordingly, as it seems to us, the standard of proof has a potential part to play in the decision making process even in relation to issues that are the subject of judgment and evaluation. In practice, we would expect the tribunal generally either to form the requisite judgment or not to form it, without needing to have specific regard to any standard of proof. But the standard of proof provides a backdrop to the decision making process and may have an important role in some cases.'

Hearsay evidence

3.64 The same authority (in effect) adopted the judgment of Munby J in respect of the approach to be adopted by Tribunals in respect of hearsay evidence (of which there is often of necessity a great deal in these proceedings). Munby J held that:[88]

> 'The Tribunal must be appropriately cautious of relying upon assertions as to past events which are not securely recorded in contemporaneous notes, particularly if the only evidence is hearsay. The Tribunal must be alert to the well-known problem that the constant repetition in "official" reports or statements may, in the "official" mind, turn into established fact something which rigorous forensic investigation shows is in truth nothing more than "institutional folk-lore" with no secure foundation in either recorded or provable fact. The Tribunal must guard against too quickly jumping to conclusions adverse to the patient in relation to past events where the only direct evidence is that of the patient himself, particularly where there is no clear account in contemporaneous notes of what is alleged to have happened. In relation to past incidents which are centrally

87 [2005] EWCA Civ 1605, [2006] MHLR 59, at [98] and [99].

88 [2005] MHLR 56, at [129].

important to the decision it has to take the Tribunal must bear in mind the need for proof to the civil standard of proof; it must bear in mind the potential difficulties of relying upon second or third hand hearsay; and, if the incident is really fundamental to its decision, it must bear in mind that fairness may require the patient to be given the opportunity to cross-examine the relevant witnesses if their evidence is to be relied upon at all.'

Absent authors of reports

3.65 One of the further problems that the Tribunal encountered in *R (Ashworth Hospital Authority) v MHRT; R (H) v Ashworth Hospital Authority*[89] was that it was said not to have considered (of its own volition) making an adjournment to hear from psychiatrists whose reports were before it, but in respect of whom the responsible authority had made no provision to attend the hearing. In that instance, however, Dyson J held that:[90]

> 'I would not criticise them for failing to invite an application to adjourn so that Dr Heads and Dr Lomax or any of the other doctors could be called.'

3.66 Finally, in *MM v Nottinghamshire Healthcare NHS Trust*[91] UTJ Jacobs considered the situation when a Tribunal was aware that a patient had been visited by an independent doctor, but the results of that visit were not made available. The substance of the argument was that because the Tribunal was aware of this fact, and because no report from the independent doctor had been disclosed, the Tribunal might draw an inference that the report supported the continued detention of the patient, and so it ought to recuse itself. The appeal was dismissed. The UTJ adopted a pragmatic approach to a potentially complex and arcane argument in the following terms:

> 'The answer is that it would not be proper for the tribunal to draw inferences like those set out in counsel's argument ... the only thing known for certain is that Dr G visited Mr M ... But as a simple matter of reasoning it is not possible to infer that Dr G agreed with the diagnosis and conclusions of the clinical team. That is too precise an inference to be drawn from the earlier steps in the reasoning ... I cannot imagine any realistic circumstances in which a tribunal, having such evidence, could properly rely on the failure by a patient to produce a report as a basis for drawing inferences that would affect the outcome. The tribunal's duty, and the only proper course, would be to decide on the evidence available rather than speculate on possible explanations of why the report was not produced ... I begin with the proposition that it is a judicial skill that judges should be able to disregard things that they have heard.'[92]

---

89 [2002] MHLR 314, CA; (*EC Chs 1, 2, 9 and 15*).
90 Ibid, at [85].
91 [2013] UKUT 107 (AAC).
92 Ibid, at [7], [8], [10] and [12].

Chapter 4

APPLICATIONS AND REFERENCES

APPLICATIONS

4.1 Applications can only be made where authorised by MHA 1983. Those parts of the statute which are relevant are ss 66, 69, 70 and 75. Apart from s 75, these are all reproduced in Part F. An applicant is defined in r 1(3) as a person who starts proceedings (whether by application, appeal, claim or reference), or by way of permission to start such proceedings (which means an appeal), or a person who is substituted as a party pursuant to r 9(1) (where someone has been wrongly named as a party, or there has been a change in circumstances and substitution has become necessary as a result).

4.2 The old rr 3 and 30 governed the procedure for both applications and references. These are all now contained in rr 32 and 33.

4.3 There are some patients who have no right to apply to a Tribunal. These are those who are detained under the following sections of MHA 1983: s 4 (emergency); s 5 (doctor or nurses holding power); ss 135 and 136 (police powers to remove patients from premises or from a public place); s 35 (patient in a hospital for a report); s 36 (patients removed to hospital for treatment); and s 38 (interim hospital orders). None of these patients will be referred to a Tribunal.

4.4 All other patients (including those received into guardianship) may come before a Tribunal. The method and time within which such may occur is set out in the table reproduced below. This also includes referrals. However, in general terms, it will be the patient who makes an application, and in certain circumstances, the nearest relative. The table set out below is a helpful summary of the procedure.

Regional Chairmen's Manual, Issue 1, April 2006, Appendix 5, pp 50–51

APPLICATIONS TO THE MENTAL HEALTH REVIEW TRIBUNAL

Section of Mental Health Act 1983	**Patient**	**Nearest Relative**
2. Admission for assessment	Once in first 14 days 66(1)(a)	

3. Admission for treatment – 6 months then every 12 months	Once in the first 6 months 66(1)(b) and once in each subsequent renewal period 66(1)(f)	
7. Application for Guardianship – 6 months, renewed for 6 months then every 12 months	Once in first 6 months 6(1)(cc) [66(1)(c)] and once in each subsequent renewal period 66(1)(f)	
16. Reclassification report by RCO	Within 28 days of being informed of reclassification 66(1)(d)	Within 28 days of being informed of reclassification 66(1)(d)
25. RC bars nearest relative discharging		Within 28 days of being informed of RC's report barring discharge 66(1)(g)
29. Appointment by court of acting nearest relative		Once in each 12 month period 66(1)(h)
37. Hospital Order 6-months, renewed for six months then every 12 months	No right within first 6 months. Once in each renewal period 66(1)(f)	No right within first 6 months. Once in each renewal period 66(1)(a)
37. Guardianship Order	Once in the first 6 months 66(1)(b)(i). Once in each subsequent renewal period	Once in each 12 month period 69(1)(b)(ii)
37 'Notional' i.e. prisoner in hospital under ss47/49 becomes a 'notional' s 37 when his earliest date of release (EDR) occurs.	Unlike section 37 above, once in the first six months of the 'notional' s 37: s.69(2)(b) and at yearly intervals thereafter	No right within 6 months. Once in each renewal period s.69(1)(a)

(RESTRICTED)

37/41 – Hospital order with restriction order	No right within first 6 months. Once in second six months 70(a). Once in any subsequent period 70(b)	

CPIA	No right within first 6 months when court imposes section 37/41. The Domestic Violence, Crime and Victims Act 2004 has amended the Criminal Procedure (Insanity) Act 1964 and the Criminal Procedure (Insanity and Unfitness to Plead) Act 1991	
47/49 – removal to hospital from prison with restriction direction	Once in first 6 months 69(2)(b). Once in second 6 months 70(a) and in any subsequent 12 month period 70(b)	
Restricted patient Conditionally discharged	12–24 months after discharge 75(2)(a). Once in every subsequent period of 2 years 75(2)(b)	

AUTOMATIC REFERENCES TO THE MENTAL HEALTH REVIEW TRIBUNAL

Section of 1983 Mental Health Act under which reference is made	**Time of Reference**
67 – Reference by Secretary of State for Health	Any time
68(1) – Reference by Hospital Managers	Patients who have been detained under Section 3 and on renewal have not had a Tribunal within the previous six months
68(2) – Reference by Hospital Managers	Patients who have been detained under Section 3, or 37 and on renewal have not had a Tribunal within the previous three years

(RESTRICTED)

71(1) – Reference by the Home Secretary	Any time
71(2) – Reference by the Home Secretary	Restricted patient who has not had a Tribunal for three years will be automatically referred

71(5) – Reference by the Home Secretary	Repealed by Domestic Violence, Crime and Victims Act 2004 as from 31 March 2005
75(1) – Reference by the Home Secretary	Conditionally discharged patient recalled to Hospital – automatically referred within 1 month

COMMUNITY TREATMENT ORDERS

4.5 To this must be added the system for community treatment orders. The relevant tables from the *Reference Guide to the Mental Health Act 1983* are set out below. It is to be noted that r 35 has been amended so that in certain circumstances, a CTO can be considered on paper and without a hearing at all. This is considered in greater detail in Chapter 10.

Table 22.8: Applications by Part 2 SCT patients [section 66]

Applies to SCT patients who, immediately before becoming SCT patients, were:

- detained on the basis of an application for admission for treatment under section 3; or
- treated as if detained on the basis of such an application, following transfer from guardianship or from outside England or Wales

If	**the patient may apply once during**	**Notes**
the patient becomes an SCT patient	the period of six months starting with the day the CTO is made (or treated as made).	In the case of patients transferred from outside England or Wales, they are treated as if their CTO was made on the day of their arrival at the place they are to reside in England or Wales.
the patient's CTO is revoked	the period of six months starting with the day the CTO is revoked.	The hospital managers must also refer the patient's case to the Tribunal as soon as possible after the CTO is revoked.
the patient's CTO is extended (section 20A or 21B)	the period for which the CTO is extended.	The first extension period is six months. Subsequent periods are 12 months. The right to apply begins when the new period begins, not when the extension report is made. A section 21B report only triggers a right to apply if it also serves as a section 20A extension report.

Table 22.9: Applications by Part 3 SCT patients and their nearest relatives [section 66 as applied by Part 1 of Schedule 1 and modified by section 69(3) to (5)]

Applies to SCT patients who, immediately before becoming SCT patients, were:

- detained on the basis of a hospital order, unrestricted hospital direction or unrestricted transfer direction under Part 3; or
- treated as if detained on the basis of such an order or direction, following transfer from outside England or Wales, or for any other reason.

It also applies to the nearest relatives of such patients.

If	**the patient and the nearest relative may each apply once during**	**Notes**
a patient is discharged onto SCT from an unrestricted hospital order which was given by a court within the previous six months	the period between the end of the six months starting with the day the hospital order was given and the six months starting with the day the CTO was made.	This only applies to patients who are actually given an unrestricted hospital order by a court. It does not apply to patients who are treated as having been given such an unrestricted hospital order and who therefore have the right to apply to the Tribunal before that order is first renewed (see table 22.3). Example: A patient given an unrestricted hospital order on 1 January and a CTO on 1 March can apply only from 1 July.
a patient becomes detained again under an unrestricted hospital order which was given by a court within the previous six months because the patient's CTO is revoked	the period between the end of the six months starting with the day the hospital order was given and the six months starting with the day the CTO is revoked.	
any other Part 3 patient becomes an SCT patient	the period of six months starting with the day the CTO is made.	This applies to patients who, before becoming SCT patients, were detained under unrestricted transfer directions or hospital directions, as well as unrestricted hospital order patients not covered by the rules above.
any other Part 3 patient's CTO is revoked	the period of six months starting with the day the CTO is revoked.	

the patient's CTO is extended (section 20A or 21B)	the period for which the CTO is extended.	The first extension period is six months. Subsequent periods are 12 months. The right to apply begins when the new period begins, not when the extension report is made. A section 21B report only triggers a right to apply if it also serves as a section 20A extension report.

Note: when an SCT patient's CTO is revoked, the hospital managers must also refer the patient's case to the Tribunal as soon as possible, even if the patient is not permitted to apply at that point.

Table 22.14: Applications by nearest relatives of Part 2 SCT patients [section 66(1)(g)]

Applies to SCT patients who, immediately before becoming SCT patients, were:

- detained on the basis of an application for admission for treatment under section 3; or
- who are treated as such following their transfer from guardianship or from outside England and Wales.

If	**the nearest relative may apply once during**
a responsible clinician bars a nearest relative's order for the discharge of a patient from SCT	the period of 28 days starting with the day on which they are informed of the report by the responsible clinician which bars discharge.

This is the only case in which a nearest relative may apply for the discharge of a Part 2 SCT patient.

For applications by nearest relatives of Part 3 SCT patients, see table 22.9.

WITHDRAWAL (R 17)

4.6 There can be only one application in the relevant period, unless there has been a withdrawal in accordance with r 17.

REFERRALS

4.7 This system (in part) is designed to ensure that even where an application has not been made on the volition of the patient (or a nearest relative) that nonetheless there is oversight by the Tribunal as to the need for detention. It is sometimes the case that this will not be apparent to the Tribunal which hears the matter (due to deficient paperwork), but it is in itself is an important piece of information of which the Tribunal should be made aware, particularly in respect of MHA 1983, Part II patients. This is for the simple reason that it is helpful if the Tribunal knows whether the patient is positively applying in order for the relevant section to be discharged, or whether he or she has been brought before a Tribunal due to the obligations imposed by MHA 1983 (and may not, in fact, wish to be discharged at all, or may take the opportunity to be discharged if the Tribunal considers this to be appropriate). According to the status of the patient, a referral will be by the hospital managers, the Ministry of Justice or the Department of Health.

4.8 The relevant statutory provisions are MHA 1983, ss 67, 68, 71, 75 and 77, all of which are set out in Part F (except s 75, which is set out in Part D).

4.9 In respect of MHA 1983, s 68 (duty of hospital managers to refer cases to Tribunals), the categories of patient to whom this is relevant are those detained for treatment, or where there has been a move from guardianship to detention in a hospital. If a reference has been made, this does not prevent the patient making an application during the period of detention when the hearing in respect of the reference took place. A reference is not an application, and therefore not subject to the prohibition on applications set out at MHA 1983, s 77(2).

4.10 From the perspective of the patient, it is important that a representative is aware of the provisions in order to (a) maximise opportunities to apply to a Tribunal (if it is appropriate so to do) and (b) so as not to lose or forfeit the right to apply.

4.11 The Department of Health has also published information regarding references 'References by the Secretary of State for Health to the First-tier Tribunal – s 67 of the Mental Health Act 1983'.

Chapter 5

INTERACTION BETWEEN MENTAL HEALTH ACT 1983 AND MENTAL CAPACITY ACT 2005

5.1 The interaction between MHA 1983 and the Mental Capacity Act 2005 (MCA 2005) is an area which should still not directly have an effect upon the actual proceedings before a mental health review tribunal. If a patient has been detained, then it follows that at the point of detention the statutory criteria were made out, and the function of the Tribunal is to consider and evaluate the evidence placed before it when the hearing takes place. However, it is important that the issue of individuals (or patients) who may lack capacity is considered at this point, since it may have a bearing on some aspects of the Tribunal itself, or be raised as an issue. In addition, issues relating to deprivation of liberty have sometimes arisen at Tribunals, and it is important to know the extent to which this can be taken into account, or considered by a Tribunal. The cases set out below illustrate the type of matters that have been considered by UKUT, the High Court, and the Court of Appeal.

MENTAL CAPACITY ACT 2005: CODE OF PRACTICE

'Bournewood'[1]

5.2 This Code (issued on 23 April 2007) has been supplemented by 'Deprivation of Liberty Safeguards' (to supplement the main Code of Practice) which was issued on 26 August 2008. The problem that gave rise to this area of law is summarised in the supplemental Code of Practice thus:[2]

> 'The deprivation of liberty safeguards were introduced to provide a legal framework around the deprivation of liberty. Specifically, they were introduced to prevent breaches of the European Convention on Human Rights such as the one identified in the case of *HL v the United Kingdom* ((2004) Application No 00045508/99) (commonly referred to as the 'Bournewood' judgment). The case concerned an autistic man (HL) with a learning disability, who lacked the capacity to decide whether he should be admitted to hospital for specific treatment. He was admitted on an informal basis under common law in his best interests, but this decision was challenged by HL's carers. In its judgment, the ECtHR held that this admission constituted a deprivation of HL's liberty and further, that:

---

1 *HL v the United Kingdom* App No 45508/99 (2005) 40 EHRR 761, 5 October 2004 (*'Bournewood'*), [2004] MHLR 236; (*EC Chs 3 and 7*).

2 Chapter 1, at p 9.

- the deprivation of liberty had not been in accordance with 'a procedure prescribed by law' and was, therefore, in breach of Article 5 (1) of the ECHR and
- there had been a contravention of Article 5 (4) of the ECHR because HL had no means of applying quickly to a court to see if the deprivation of liberty was lawful.

To prevent further similar breaches of the ECHR, the Mental Capacity Act 2005 has been specifically amended to provide safeguards for people who lack capacity specifically to consent to treatment or care in either a hospital or care home that, in their own best interests, can only be provided in circumstances that amount to a deprivation of liberty, and where detention under the Mental Health Act 1983 is not appropriate for that person at that time.'

5.3 In terms of admission to hospital (either as an informal patient, or one who is subject to detention) the Code of Practice for MHA 1983 refers (at paras 4.13–4.24) to this category of patient, and the need for detention or not. The Code suggests that MHA 1983 may be more likely to be used for detention if either:[3]

> '... providing appropriate care or treatment for the patient will unavoidably involve depriving of their liberty and the MCA deprivation of liberty safeguards cannot be used; or for any other reason, the assessment or treatment the patient needs cannot be safely or effectively delivered by relying on the MCA alone.'

It goes on the suggest that MHA 1983 may not be appropriate where the safeguards cannot be used, and these are if:[4]

> '... the patient is under 18; the patient has made a valid and applicable advance decision refusing a necessary element of the treatment for which they are to be admitted to hospital; the use of the safeguards would conflict with a decision of the person's attorney or deputy or of the Court of Protection or the patient meets the criteria in section 2 or section 3 of the Mental Health Act and is objecting to being admitted to (or remaining in) hospital for mental health treatment (unless an attorney or deputy consents on their behalf).'

5.4 The Code of Practice for MCA 2005 adds that detention under MHA 1983 is 'not an option if the patient's mental disorder does not justify detention in hospital, or the patient's needs treatment only for a physical illness or disability'.[5] It reminds the reader that:[6]

> 'Most of the MHA does not distinguish between people who have the capacity to make decisions, and those who do not. Many people who are covered by the MHA have the capacity to make decisions for themselves.'

---

3 Chapter 4, at para 4.16.
4 Chapter 4, at para 4.18.
5 Chapter 13, Summary.
6 At para 13.2.

It states that MHA 1983 rather than MCA 2005 might be preferred if:[7]

> '... it is not possible to give the person the care and treatment they need without carrying out an action that might deprive them of their liberty; the person needs treatment that cannot be given under the MCA (for example, because the person has made a valid and applicable advance decision to refuse all or part of that treatment); the person may need to be restrained in a way that is not allowed under the MCA; it is not possible to assess or treat the person safely or effectively without treatment being compulsory (perhaps because the person is expected to regain capacity to consent, but might then refuse to give consent); the person lacks capacity to decide on some elements of the treatment but has the capacity to refuse a vital part of it – and they have done so, or there is some other reason why the person might not get the treatment they need, and they or somebody else might suffer harm as a result.'

GUARDIANSHIP

5.5 If a guardianship order is in existence, MCA 2005 cannot be used to make a decision as to where the patient lives, or to require the patient to attend at set times and places for treatment, occupation, education or training. MCA 2005 could be used to address matters that were not in conflict with the powers of a guardian under MHA 1983, or where such powers did not exist (eg treatment). It is worth briefly considering the interaction between the Mental Capacity Act 2005 and the provisions of MHA 1983. When an application is considered under MHA 1983 it is always appropriate to consider the least restrictive regime for the patient. If a patient lacked capacity, it may be that the Mental Capacity Act 2005 is the more appropriate route. However, much will turn on whether or not it is felt by the professionals involved that it would be preferable that the compulsory aspects of s 7 are appropriate. Those powers of compulsion are contained at s 8 of the MHA 1983 and commented upon in the Code of Practice (MHA 1983). The Mental Capacity Act 2005 may not be used as a way of challenging decisions made by a guardian appointed under MHA 1983. Useful guidance on the distinction between the two jurisdictions are given at paras 13.16–13.21 of the Code of Practice (Mental Capacity Act 2005). However, the Mental Health Act 2007 has extended the ambit of guardianship to anyone who suffers from 'any disorder or disability of mind' and also (via Sch 3, para 3(5)) which 'broadens the power of the guardian by introducing a new power to take and convey a person to their required place of residence under guardianship alongside the power which already exists to return a guardianship patient who has absconded to their place of residence'.[8] Together with the developing jurisprudence of the Mental Capacity Act 2005, and in particular the effect of the Deprivation of Liberty Safeguards there is an ongoing debate about certain aspects of the extent to which guardianship can be used. The Code of Practice (MCA 2005) (para 13.16) asserts that guardianship cannot be used to deprive someone of

---

7 At para 13.12.

8 See Professor Philip Fennell, *Mental Health – The New Law* (Jordan Publishing, 2007) at para 8.19.

their liberty. However, as a matter of law the powers conferred on a Guardian are the power to remove and place elsewhere; power to force residence at a specific place; power to return if the person 'absents' themselves; power to take the person to a place for purposes of receiving medical treatment. There is an explicit power to enable a local authority to remove a patient from his home (if it is necessary for this to happen) in order to impose upon him the requirement of residence. Once so placed, if the subject of the guardianship order leaves without the consent of the guardian, he may be taken into custody and returned.[9] Once an order is in place it confers upon the guardian 'to the exclusion of any other person' decisions on a number of matters (the most significant of which is the issue of where the individual shall live). This section, and the interrelationship that guardianship has with the jurisdiction of the Court of Protection, has been considered in *C v Blackburn with Darwen Borough Council & A Care Home & Blackburn with Darwen Teaching Care Trust*[10] where it was argued on behalf of C that the word 'person' could not extend to preventing a judge of the Court of Protection deciding where an individual should live, where that issue was before the Court, and P was also subject to an order pursuant to s 7 of the MHA 1983. The local authority and the Trust argued that:

(a) in the particular circumstances of the case C was not deprived of his liberty (there being a secondary issue as to whether he either could be, or needed to be, subject to a standard authorisation via 'DOLS') and was also ineligible for this scheme; and

(b) that s 8 prevents any court from exercising a jurisdiction that would have the effect of emasculating the MHA 1983.

In respect of the matter of s 8, and its legal effect, Mr Justice Peter Jackson relied upon *GJ v Foundation Trust*[11] to the effect that in general the MHA 1983, where it applies, has primacy over the MCA 2005. He also held that 'there are good reasons why the provisions of the MHA should prevail where they apply. It is a self-contained system with inbuilt checks and balances and it is well understood by professionals working in that field. It is cheaper than the Court of Protection.'[12] However, it is important to note the following caveat:

> 'On the other hand, it is not in my view appropriate for genuinely contested issues about the place of residence of a resisting incapacitated person to be determined either under the guardianship regime or by means of a standard authorisation under the DOLS regime. Substantial decisions of that kind ought properly to be made by the Court of Protection, using its power to make welfare decisions under s.16 MCA.'[13]

---

9 Mental Capacity Act 2005, s 18(4).
10 [2011] EWHC 3321 (Fam), [2012] MHLR 202, COP.
11 [2009] EWHC 2972 (Fam).
12 [2011] EWHC 3321 (Fam), [2012] MHLR 202, COP, at [34] and [35].
13 Ibid, at [37].

In other words, local authorities may well conclude that in cases where there is a dispute about residence, and as to whether that is in the best interests of P or not, the correct court within which to determine that point (assuming a lack of capacity) is not by using ss 7 and 8 at all, but by way of an application to the Court of Protection instead. However, the issues to be determined by a Tribunal relate purely to the statutory criteria (which are considered in Chapter 9) and not to whether the Mental Capacity Act 2005 is the preferable regime. It has no power to do anything other than discharge the order for guardianship or not. It might be able to discharge the guardianship using its residual discretion if it reached the conclusion that the manner in which the regime of guardianship was being used was so inimical to the welfare of the patient that this was required (and in turn might contrast this with what the powers of the Court of Protection are, as opposed to that of the First-tier Tribunal). What is clear, on the current law, is that guardianship itself (and the powers it confers listed above) do not amount to a deprivation of liberty in themselves, however contrary to instincts this might appear to be. Guardianship, however, can only be used for the purposes listed above, and no more. If there is a regime that goes beyond the powers legally conferred upon the guardian, that might persuade the Tribunal that the entire order should be discharged, but equally, the matter could be brought before the Court of Protection by the patient, or if there is a suggestion of unlawfulness in the execution of the powers, then judicial review would be another possible remedy. It remains to be seen how Tribunals deal with such issues.

INTERPLAY BETWEEN MHA 1983/MCA 2005 AND DEPRIVATION OF LIBERTY SAFEGUARDS

5.6 This issue was specifically considered by the UKUT in *DN v Northumberland Tyne and Wear NHS Foundation Trust.*[14] The case turns on whether a Tribunal is obliged to address the law on the respective regimes for depriving someone of their liberty under both the MHA 1983 and the MCA 2005. The short answer is that it is required to address the law, and although the decision of the Tribunal is described in glowing terms, nevertheless it was remitted for a re-hearing, on the basis that the legal issues were not directly addressed. As will be apparent from elsewhere in this text, the purpose of the MHA is to deal with those who have a mental disorder, and there are specific statutory criteria that are required for detention, and discharge of that detention. The MCA 2005 can only concern itself with those who lack capacity. This is the pre-requisite for any consideration of such arguments. The MCA 2005 also has its own provisions for depriving a person of their liberty, and in this case by way of the Deprivation of Liberty Safeguards (DOLS) created by Sch A1 of that Act. However, *treatment* for a mental disorder is not possible under the MCA 2005 at all.[15] The DOLS regime (which was the source of the complexity in this case) can only apply to hospitals or care homes. A 'standard

---

14 [2011] UKUT 327 (AAC), [2011] MHLR 249.

15 MCA 2005, s 28.

authorisation' under DOLS can oblige someone to live in a particular place, and impose other restrictions upon their movements. A standard authorisation is granted (usually) by a local authority social services officer after certain procedures have been followed. It can last for up to one year. The argument before the Tribunal was that it was expected to consider the minimum method of restraint required, and that if the MCA 2005 regime was available, then this should be the preferred option. It was argued that the 'treatment' that the patient required was not that which came within the meaning of s 145 of the MHA 1983 (being a distraction technique to prevent the use of alcohol) and thus would not in itself mean that the MCA 2005 could not be used, due to the prohibition on treatment for a mental disorder imposed by s 28. Schedule A1 sets out those persons who may be *ineligible* to be deprived of their liberty under the MCA 2005. In the circumstances of this case, he was not ineligible to be deprived of his liberty under the MCA 2005 (ie it could apply to him). It was held that the patient did not meet the criteria for detention under s 2 of the MHA 1983 (his actual status was under s 3) as his condition had already been assessed. The crucial issue of whether that disorder warranted his detention in a hospital turned on whether or not there was a *less* restrictive regime under the MCA 2005. Paragraph 12(5) of Sch A1 required there to be an assumption that treatment for a mental disorder could not be provided (and of course there is a prohibition to that effect at s 28 of the MCA 2005). However, as indicated, the argument was on the facts of this case that 'treatment' was not required. So, the necessity of detention would depend upon what regime could be provided by way of a standard authorisation (within DOLS). On the facts of this case, there was a genuine alternative. If there was a genuine alternative, and as this went to the specific criteria that the Tribunal is obliged to consider (does the disorder warrant detention?) then the Tribunal would be required to consider the matter. As ever, much of this case was based upon the very particular facts, and as UTJ Jacobs comments:

> 'I note that, on the evidence before me at the oral hearing, it was doubtful whether Mr N could be prevented from obtaining alcohol. He managed to obtain alcohol even when detained on an acute ward … I assume that there was tight security and supervision on that ward and that alcohol was not allowed. That may indicate that the success of an arrangement under the MCA is not as clear cut as Ms Rickard argued. That will be a matter for the First-tier Tribunal at the rehearing. No doubt Mr N's lawyers will present the necessary evidence for the tribunal to decide the issue.'[16]

In other words, if, on the evidence before a Tribunal, the less draconian regime of the MCA does not as a matter of fact provide the environment that is required, then the grounds for warranting detention may be made out.

5.7 The third case which addressed deprivation of liberty generally (as opposed to deprivation of liberty within the meaning of the DOLS regime) is *Secretary of State for Justice v B*.[17] The legal status of the patient was that he

---

16 [2011] UKUT 327 (AAC), [2011] MHLR 249, at [27].
17 [2011] EWCA Civ 1608, [2012] MHLR 131.

was subject to ss 37 and 41 of the MHA 1983 (a restricted patient). A point had been reached where it was considered that he could be treated in conditions of lesser security, and the RC had accepted that a conditional discharge would be appropriate. The issue (as a matter of fact) was that one of the conditions would be that he would require escorted access to the community. It was said that such a condition would inevitably amount to a deprivation of liberty (although this issue was not argued before the Court of Appeal). The appeal was by the Secretary of State against the decision of the First-tier Tribunal to order a conditional discharge to a care home, with the condition of an escort at all times in the community, on the basis that there was no power to make an order of that kind. For reasons that are considered in detail in Chapter 18, the argument of the Secretary of State prevailed. The Court of Appeal addressed one of the problems which might face a Tribunal, which is whether or not someone is or would be deprived of their liberty, as a matter of fact and law. Arden LJ held that:

> 'I respectfully venture that it is unlikely to be a difficult issue in every case and in any event tribunals often need to determine complex questions of fact. It is established by authority that it is only necessary to determine whether the deprivation of liberty will be the inevitable result of the order, so that the inquiry need not fully explore every possible outcome.'[18]

However, the assertion that the issue of deciding whether there is a deprivation of liberty or not is far from straightforward. It is beyond the scope of this book to consider the law fully on this point.[19] The threshold for establishing deprivation of liberty is currently very high, and only in particular and extreme circumstances will it exist. Nevertheless, the Supreme Court will be reconsidering the two Court of Appeal decisions that have attempted to address this matter in the autumn of 2013, which may resolve matters or at least clarify them.

TREATMENT

5.8 Part IV of MHA 1983 (which permits treatment without consent) does not apply to those detained under s 4(4)(a) of MHA 1983 (an emergency); s 5 (temporary detention); remanded by a court to hospital under s 35; detained in a place of safety pursuant to s 37(4), 135 or 136; or who have been conditionally discharged by the Tribunal, and not recalled to hospital. In each of these situations, MCA 2005 could apply (even if the treatment is for a mental disorder). Section 28 of MCA 2005 specifically limits its own jurisdiction where Part IV of MHA 1983 applies.

---

18 Ibid, at [67].

19 For a full consideration the reader is directed either to Ashton et al, *Court of Protection Practice 2013* (Jordan Publishing, 2013) or Butler, *Community Care Law and Local Authority Handbook* (2nd edn, Jordan Publishing, 2012).

Chapter 6

TREATMENT AND TREATABILITY

MENTAL DISORDER

6.1 A part of the criteria for detention under the Act hitherto has been that the patient has either a mental disorder, a mental illness, a mental impairment or a psychopathic disorder. However, with the amendments to MHA 1983 that have been made by the Mental Health Act 2007 (MHA 2007), these four categories have been removed and replaced with a single category which is 'any disorder or disability of the mind'. Before looking at the implications for the new provision contained within MHA 1983, s 1(2), it is worth examining the previous case-law in respect of the old categories. The new section, however, is set out below.

> '1 Application of Act: "mental disorder"
>
> (1) The provisions of this Act shall have effect with respect to the reception, care and treatment of mentally disordered patients, the management of their property and other related matters.
>
> (2) In this Act –
> "mental disorder" means any disorder or disability of the mind; and
> "mentally disordered" shall be construed accordingly;
>
> and other expressions shall have the meanings assigned to them in section 145 below.
>
> (2A) But a person with learning disability shall not be considered by reason of that disability to be –
>
> (a) suffering from mental disorder for the purposes of the provisions mentioned in subsection (2B) below; or
> (b) requiring treatment in hospital for mental disorder for the purposes of sections 17E and 50 to 53 below,
>
> unless that disability is associated with abnormally aggressive or seriously irresponsible conduct on his part.
>
> (2B) The provisions are –
>
> (a) sections 3, 7, 17A, 20 and 20A below;
> (b) sections 35 to 38, 45A, 47, 48 and 51 below; and
> (c) section 72(1)(b) and (c) and (4) below.

(3) Dependence on alcohol or drugs is not considered to be a disorder or disability of the mind for the purposes of subsection (2) above.

(4) In subsection (2A) above, "learning disability" means a state of arrested or incomplete development of the mind which includes significant impairment of intelligence and social functioning.'

6.2 The term *mental disorder* remains in MHA 1983 (and is defined as above, ie any disorder or disability of the mind). A mental disorder does not equate to irrational or bizarre thinking processes. In *R v Collins, Pathfinder Mental Health Services NHS Trust and St George's Healthcare NHS Trust ex parte S*,[1] an adult woman was detained under MHA 1983. She was pregnant and wished to give birth naturally. The social worker (an approved social worker (ASW)) applied for the woman to be admitted for assessment pursuant to MHA 1983, s 2, as there were concerns about her mental health and the risk that might be posed to both her and her unborn child. It was held that if an adult of sound mind rejected treatment then no power of compulsion existed. MHA 1983 could not be used to compel treatment unconnected with the reasons for detention. Merely illogical or bizarre thought processes would be insufficient in any event. The sequence of events set in train by the ASW was vitiated by unlawfulness, and the declaration made ex parte was set aside. Guidelines were set down for situations when surgical or invasive treatment may be needed by a male or female patient who does not consent to that treatment. Those guidelines are set out below.

'*R v Collins, Pathfinder Mental Health Services NHS Trust and St George's Healthcare NHS Trust ex p S*

The case highlighted some major problems which could arise for hospital authorities when a pregnant woman presented at hospital, the possible need for Caesarean surgery was diagnosed, and there was serious doubt about the patient's capacity to accept or decline treatment. To avoid any recurrence of the unsatisfactory events recorded in this judgment, and after consultation with the President of the Family Division and the Official Solicitor, and in the light of written submissions from Mr Havers and Mr Gordon, we shall attempt to repeat and expand the advice given in *Re MB (Medical Treatment)* [1997] 2 FLR 426. This advice also applies to any cases involving capacity when surgical or invasive treatment may be needed by a patient, whether female or male. References to "she" and "he" should be read accordingly. It also extends, where relevant, to medical practitioners and health practitioners generally as well as to hospital authorities.

The guidelines depend upon basic legal principles which we can summarise:

(i) They have no application where the patient is competent to accept or refuse treatment. In principle a patient may remain competent notwithstanding detention under the Mental Health Act.

1 [1998] 1 CCLR 410, [1998] 2 FLR 728.

(ii) If the patient is competent and refuses consent to the treatment an application to the High Court for a declaration would be pointless. In this situation the advice given to the patient should be recorded. For their own protection hospital authorities should seek unequivocal assurances from the patient (to be recorded in writing) that the refusal represents an informed decision: that is, that she understands the nature of and reasons for the proposed treatment, and the risks and likely prognosis involved in the decision to refuse or accept it. If the patient is unwilling to sign a written indication of this refusal, this too should be noted in writing. Such a written indication is merely a record for evidential purposes. It should not be confused with or regarded as a disclaimer.

(iii) If the patient is incapable of giving or refusing consent, either in the long term or temporarily (eg due to unconsciousness), the patient must be cared for according to the authority's judgment of the patient's best interests. Where the patient has given an advance directive, before becoming incapable, treatment and care should normally be subject to the advance directive. However, if there is reason to doubt the reliability of the advance directive, (for example it may sensibly be thought not to apply to the circumstances which have arisen) then an application for a declaration may be made.

Concern over capacity

(iv) The authority should identify as soon as possible whether there is concern about a patient's competence to consent to or refuse treatment.

(v) If the capacity of the patient is seriously in doubt it should be assessed as a matter of priority. In many such cases the patient's general practitioner or other responsible doctor may be sufficiently qualified to make the necessary assessment, but in serious or complex cases involving difficult issues about the future health and well-being or even life of the patient, the issue of capacity should be examined by an independent psychiatrist, ideally one approved under s 12(2) of the Mental Health Act. If following this assessment there remains a serious doubt about the patient's competence, and the seriousness or complexity of the issues in the particular case may require the involvement of the court, the psychiatrist should further consider whether the patient is incapable by reason of mental disorder of managing her property or affairs. If so the patient may be unable to instruct a solicitor and will require a guardian ad litem in any court proceedings. The authority should seek legal advice as quickly as possible. If a declaration is to be sought the patient's solicitors should be informed immediately and if practicable they should have a proper opportunity to take instructions and apply for legal aid where necessary. Potential witnesses for the authority should be made aware of the criteria laid down in *Re MB* and this case, together with any guidance issued by the Department of Health, and the British Medical Association.

(vi) If the patient is unwilling to instruct solicitors, or is believed to be incapable of doing so, the authority or its legal advisors must notify the Official Solicitor and invite him to act as guardian ad litem. If the Official Solicitor agrees he will no doubt wish, if possible, to arrange for the patient to be interviewed to ascertain her wishes and to explore the reasons for any refusal of treatment. The Official Solicitor can be contacted through the Urgent Court Business Officer out of office hours on 0171 936 6000.

The hearing

(vii) The hearing before the judge should be inter partes. As the order made in her absence will not be binding on the patient unless she is represented either by a guardian ad litem (if incapable of giving instructions) or (if capable) by counsel or solicitor, a declaration granted ex parte is of no assistance to the authority. Although the Official Solicitor will not act for a patient if she is capable of instructing a solicitor, the court may in any event call on the Official Solicitor (who has considerable expertise in these matters) to assist as an amicus curiae.

(viii) It is axiomatic that the judge must be provided with accurate and all the relevant information. This should include the reasons for the proposed treatment, the risks involved in the proposed treatment, and in not proceeding with it, whether any alternative treatment exists, and the reason, if ascertainable, why the patient is refusing the proposed treatment. The judge will need sufficient information to reach informed conclusion about the patient's capacity, and, where it arises, the issue of best interest.

(ix) The precise terms of any order should be recorded and approved by the judge before its terms are transmitted to the authority. The patient should be accurately informed of the precise terms.

(x) Applicants for emergency orders from the High Court made without first issuing and serving the relevant applications and evidence in support have a duty to comply with the procedural requirements (and pay the court fees) as soon as possible after the emergency hearing.

Conclusion

There may be occasions when, assuming a serious question arises about the competence of the patient, the situation facing the authority may be so urgent and the consequences so desperate that is impracticable to attempt to comply with these guidelines. The guidelines should be approached for what they are, that is, guidelines. Where delay may itself cause serious damage to the patient's health or put her life at risk then formulaic compliance with these guidelines would be inappropriate.'

CODE OF PRACTICE

6.3 The MHA 1983 Code of Practice (Chapter 3) adds little to the case-law but does provide a list of mental disorders which are recognised and clinically defined (see Part E). It stresses that:

'... difference should not be confused with disorder ... Beliefs, behaviours or actions which do not result from a disorder or disability of the mind are not a basis for compulsory measures under the Act, even if they appear unusual or cause other people alarm, distress or danger.'

ALCOHOL OR DRUGS

6.4 MHA 1983, s 1(3) specifically *excludes* dependence upon either of the above as a basis for detention. However, either or both of these may cause a mental disorder, or be associated with a disorder which does come within the definition provided by the Act. Further, it is permissible to provide treatment for either drug or alcohol dependence alongside the treatment for a mental disorder. The *Reference Guide to the Mental Health Act 1983* ('the *Reference Guide*') (published September 2008) makes similar observations (at paras 1.8–1.11). ECHR, Art 5(e) does refer to 'alcoholics' and an interpretation of this term can be found in *Litwa v Poland*.[2]

LEARNING DISABILITIES

6.5 Similarly, someone with a learning disability is not to be considered as suffering from a mental disorder, unless associated with abnormally aggressive or seriously irresponsible conduct. The term 'learning disability' is also defined (see above). Autistic spectrum disorders also come within the terms of MHA 1983. However, this aspect of a mental disorder does *not* apply to admission via MHA 1983, s 2 (for assessment). It does apply in respect of detention for treatment (s 3); guardianship; SCT; detention in hospital by the courts; transfer from prison to detention and vice versa; criteria for detention by Tribunal from detention in hospital for treatment, from SCT and from guardianship. According to the Code, the qualification of abnormally aggressive or seriously irresponsible conduct does not attach to autistic spectrum disorders (including Asperger's syndrome). In other words, it is within the compass of the statutory definition in its unadorned form, and may in itself be sufficient to warrant detention. The Code (Chapter 34) gives further guidance on the learning disability qualification. This will be of particular significance in determining what constitutes abnormally aggressive and irresponsible behaviour, since neither of these terms are defined in the Act, although they existed in the old Act (as a part of the definition of psychopathic disorder). Plainly, this will be a qualitative assessment, with the Code suggesting that it may depend upon persistence and severity; the triggers for such behaviour; the harm or distress caused to others, or damage to property; the likelihood of recurrence if the behaviour has not been recent; and how common such behaviour is in the general population. Irresponsibility may include factors such as disregard or inadequate regard for serious or dangerous consequences; persistence and frequency of such behaviour; seriousness of consequence to the patient or to other people; or the potential consequences of the same to either the patient, other people, or property. It also draws attention to the danger of using IQ as a basis for determining a learning disability at an arbitrary level (ie 70), or making assumptions in respect of capacity. The complete list can be found at para 34.12 of the Code.

---

2 [2000] MHLR 226; (*EC Ch 7*).

PERSONALITY DISORDERS

6.6 There is no distinction at all between different types of disorder (apart from learning disabilities) and therefore personality disorders of any type can come within the overall statutory definition. The Code (Chapter 35) gives further guidance on this aspect. Treatment is considered below, but it will not meet the criteria for treatment unless it is for the purpose of alleviating or preventing a worsening of the disorder, its symptoms or manifestations. Treatment for personality disorders is a notoriously controversial area of medical and psychological science (including the setting for such treatment).

MENTAL ILLNESS

6.7 Although this term is no longer in MHA 1983, the long-established law is that the phrase must be given its natural meaning.[3] Lawton LJ held that the phrase contained:[4]

> '... ordinary words of the English language. They have no particular medical significance. They have no particular legal significance ... ordinary words of the English language should be construed in the way that ordinary sensible people would construe them. That being, in my judgment, the right test, then I ask myself, what would the ordinary sensible person have said about the patient's condition in this case if he had been informed of his behaviour to the dogs, the cat and his wife?'

MENTAL IMPAIRMENT

6.8 This expression is in part retained by virtue of MHA 1983, s 1(4), which defines a learning disability as a state of arrested or incomplete development of the mind which includes significant impairment of intelligence and social functioning. The old provision at s 1(2) is indistinguishable from this definition, and also included the phrase abnormally aggressive and seriously irresponsible conduct. The matter of 'seriously irresponsible conduct' was considered in *Re F (A Child)*,[5] where there was an attempt to construe the wishes of a child to return home as seriously irresponsible conduct. It was held that the urge of children to return home 'is almost universal'. There were other complexities in the case unrelated to MHA 1983.

PSYCHOPATHIC DISORDER

6.9 The previous definition included the qualification of 'abnormally aggressive or seriously irresponsible behaviour', which is now imported into the learning disability qualification. The Code of Practice provides a gloss on this

---

3 *W v L* [1974] QB 711, CA.

4 Ibid.

5 [1999] MHLR 175, CA, [2000] 1 FLR 192.

expression (Chapter 34). In the case of *R (P) v MHRT*[6] the issue as to whether there was a requirement for the disability of mind which caused the abnormally aggressive or seriously irresponsible behaviour to be extant at the time of the Tribunal was considered. The Court of Appeal held that:[7]

> 'The judge's conclusion was at paragraph 27 "In my judgment, the definition of psychopathic disorder requires that the disability of mind should be one which is either liable or capable of resulting in abnormally aggressive or seriously irresponsible conduct. It is then a matter for medical judgment, of the judgment of a Tribunal, whether, if those conditions are satisfied, it is necessary for the patient to be detained by reason of the nature or degree of his illness and in accordance with the statutory questions reflected in the pro-forma decision of the Tribunal" … The task of the Tribunal is to decide on the evidence, not what has resulted from the condition, but whether the condition exists at the material time.'

The Code of Practice (Chapter 34) reflects the frequency of the behaviour as a factor in the qualitative analysis as to whether or not the disability is such that detention is necessary.

RECEPTION, CARE AND TREATMENT OF MENTALLY DISORDERED PATIENTS

6.10 MHA 1983, s 1(1) should make its overall purpose clear enough. The meaning of 'treatment' for the purposes of treating a mental disorder is set out at MHA 1983, s 145(1) and (4):

> '(1) … "medical treatment" includes nursing, and also includes psychological intervention and specialist mental health habilitation, rehabilitation and care (but see also subsection (4) below);
>
> …
>
> (4) Any reference in this Act to medical treatment, in relation to mental disorder, shall be construed as a reference to medical treatment the purpose of which is to alleviate, or prevent a worsening of, the disorder or one or more of its symptoms or manifestations.'

Section 145(4) has been amended by MHA 2007. It should also be noted that for the purposes of s 72(2)(a) (which applies to discharge from detention other than that under s 2) there is to be a consideration by the Tribunal 'that appropriate medical treatment is available to him'. Thus, this test is now a part of the basis for both detention (s 3(2)(d)) and discharge. Chapter 6 of the Code of Practice for MHA 1983 sets out in detail the practical implications for patients in terms of what should be available by way of appropriate medical treatment. The substance of the Code is confirmation that such treatment must be more than just detention (or 'mere containment'), cf **6.11**. It should also be

---

6 [2002] EWCA Civ 697, [2002] MHLR 253, CA.

7 Ibid, at [21] and [24].

noted that s 72(2)(a) and (b) of MHA 1983 has now been repealed. The latter (in part) provided for the Tribunal to have regard to the 'likelihood of medical treatment alleviating or preventing a deterioration of the patient's condition'. Whilst the test has altered, the case in law in respect of what constitutes 'medical treatment' and treatability remains valid and is set out below.

6.11 The treatment itself is such that it will alleviate or prevent the worsening of the disorder, or one or more of its manifestations. The *Reference Guide* (para 1.20) states that symptoms and manifestations 'include the way a disorder is experienced by the individual concerned and the way in which the disorder manifests itself in the person's thoughts, emotions, behaviour and actions'. *Reid v Secretary of State for Scotland* reiterates the broad nature of treatment which:[8]

> '... includes nursing ... care and training under medical supervision ... medication or other psychiatric treatment which is designed to alleviate or to prevent a deterioration of the mental disorder plainly falls within the scope of the expression ... It is also wide enough to include treatment which alleviates or prevents a deterioration of the symptoms of the mental disorder, not the order itself which gives rise to them ...'

Similarly, in *R v Canon's Park MHRT ex parte A* it was held that:[9]

> '... there was evidence before the Tribunal from which the tribunal was entitled to conclude that over a prolonged period treatment, consisting at first of no more than nursing, care and gradual persuasion to accept group therapy itself was likely to alleviate or prevent deterioration of her condition, even if at first some deterioration could not be avoided.'

The theme was developed in *South West London and St George's Mental Health NHS Trust v 'W'* where Crane J held that:[10]

> 'It is to be noted, however, that a conclusion that certain treatment amounts to medical treatment does not necessarily mean that such treatment will be likely to alleviate or prevent deterioration of the patient's condition. That is a separate matter ... It is clear also that treatment includes monitoring and assessment, although not assessment in isolation ... transfer to hospital involving admission, nursing, medical, and here psychological supervision, and staged discharge under medical supervision, is capable of amounting to "treatment" and if, in a particular case, it is likely to "alleviate or prevent a deterioration of the condition" then the medical conditions of s 47 are fulfilled.'

---

8 [1999] 2 AC 512; (*EC Chs 5 and 6*).

9 [1995] QB 60.

10 [2002] EWHC 1770 (Admin), [2002] MHLR 392, at [17] and [24]; (*EC Ch 5*).

6.12 Significantly, for the purposes of the jurisdiction of the Tribunal he also held, 'The location of the patient, in the sense of his location in a particular hospital is not a matter for the Court or for the MHRT', although Sullivan J held that:[11]

> '... treatment includes rehabilitation (see s 145(1)) and I can envisage cases where transfer to a particular institution because of the particular form of therapy available there would be a necessary step in the patient's rehabilitation.'

Crane J also held that 'the detention must not become mere containment'. These issues were revisited in two cases, the first of which is *MD v Nottinghamshire Health Care NHS Trust*.[12] The argument on behalf of the patient amounted to a suggestion that the detention was unlawful, since it amounted to mere containment, as there was no possibility of the reduction of risk, and no possibility of a progression beyond milieu therapy as he had no capacity to engage in treatment. This proposition was rejected, comprehensively. UTJ Jacobs started with a consideration of s 145(1) and (4) and observed that it was not an exhaustive definition or list (but that it '*includes*' the matters referred to in the Act). He reiterated that:

> 'Treatment must be given for the purpose of alleviating or preventing the worsening of the patient's disorder, symptoms or manifestations. Treatment is not to be defined by reference to its likely effect ...'.[13]

> 'Those provisions only define "medical treatment". They do not define the circumstances in which medical treatment is either available or appropriate. It is possible that medical treatment may be available without being appropriate, appropriate without being available, both or neither...'[14]

> 'Appropriateness is an important additional criterion for detention: it is not surplus verbiage. There may come a point (I put it no higher) at which continuing treatment, even viewed in the long term, would no longer be appropriate.'[15]

The judgment also quotes from Chapter 6 of the Code at great length, and comments that its function is not to 'give an answer, only the way to reach an answer' [19].[16] In respect of containment versus treatment, it held that 'This distinction is fundamental in our law. Containment is essentially a matter for the criminal courts and prisons ... Treatment is a matter for hospitals with oversight by the First-tier Tribunal ...'.[17] In respect of risk, it was held that this was *not* an element of treatment – just that it had to be appropriate.[18] It was, UTJ Jacobs held 'sufficient if it will alleviate but one of the symptoms or

---

11 *R (F) v (1) Oxfordshire Mental Healthcare NHS Trust (2) Oxfordshire NHS Health Authority* [2001] EWHC 535 (Admin); [2001] MHLR 140, at [68]; (*EC Ch 5*).

12 [2010] UKUT 59 (AAC), [2010] MHLR 93.

13 Ibid, at [14].

14 Ibid, at [15].

15 Ibid, at [31].

16 Ibid, at [19].

17 Ibid, at [30].

18 Ibid, at [34].

manifestations, regardless of the impact on the risk posed by the patient'.[19] The judge conceded that *if* it became the case that there was no progression beyond milieu then it might be that the stage had been reached of mere containment. On the facts of this case, the Tribunal had found that this was not so, and that there was a benefit to the patient. Finally, UTJ Jacobs held that:

> 'I have not given a definition of either "available" or "appropriate". Nor have I drawn the boundary between containment and treatment. Those are matters of fact and judgment for the tribunal. It is an expert body and it has to use that expertise to make its findings and exercise its judgment. In doing so, it has to grapple with difficult issues of evidence and principle that affect the liberty of the subject. That can only be done, as the tribunal did in this case, on the evidence before the tribunal and in the circumstances of a particular patient's case at the time of the hearing before the First-tier Tribunal.'[20]

The second case is connected with treatment outside hospital, and is considered at **6.13**.

TREATMENT OUTSIDE HOSPITAL

6.13 Patients who are granted leave (MHA 1983, s 17) are still liable to detention and can be compelled to take medication (for example). The granting of leave is in itself a form of treatment. In *R v Barking, Havering and Brentwood Community Healthcare NHS Trust ex parte B*[21] leave was granted 7 days per week to a patient detained under MHA 1983, s 3. There was a challenge to her continued detention upon the basis that it was not predicated by sufficient in-patient treatment to fulfil the test at MHA 1983, s 20(4)(c) that medical treatment in hospital 'cannot be provided unless he continues to be detained'. Lord Woolf MR held that:[22]

> 'The requirement that the patient has to return to hospital and be monitored and is liable to be recalled and from time to time is subjected to the discipline of being treated in hospital as an inpatient under direct supervision with urine and other tests is an essential part of the treatments. They enable the patient to attempt the process of rehabilitation in the wider community which would be more precarious otherwise. This appears to be just the type of treatment contemplated by the second half of the definition of treatment contained in s 145 of the Act … the fact that an assessment by itself cannot amount to treatment for s 3 does not mean that assessment cannot be a legitimate treatment under s 3 and s 20.'

A similar conclusion was reached in *R (DR) v Merseycare NHS Trust*,[23] save that the patient was on permanent leave of absence, and where an essential

---

19 Ibid.
20 Ibid, at [48].
21 [1999] 1 FLR 106, CA; (*EC Ch 5*).
22 Ibid, at 113C and 114E.
23 [2002] EWHC 1810 (Admin), [2002] MHLR 386.

ingredient of the treatment was the power to compulsorily administer medication if required. Wilson J (as he then was) held that:[24]

> '… the compulsory administration of medication to a patient can be secured only by making him liable to be detained or renewing such liability … such may be achieved only if a significant component of the plan is for treatment in hospital; and … in such an enquiry, the difference between in-patient and out-patient treatment is irrelevant.'

In *R (CS) v MHRT*[25] the in-patient treatment for a patient detained under s 3 amounted to attendance at a ward round once in 4 weeks and a weekly session with a psychologist. She also (by preference) received her medication at the hospital. The Tribunal did not discharge the section upon the basis that that was a sufficient lack of insight, combined with past and recent lack of engagement, and that without the remaining element of compulsion, a lack of compliance with taking medication (which would in turn lead to a relapse). The challenge to the Tribunal failed, it being held that it had 'acted lawfully and rationally upon the evidential material available'. In *KL v Somerset Partnership NHS Foundation Trust*[26] a patient had been given leave (s 17) and had been receiving medication for his disorder at a local community mental health treatment base. Both of the authorities cited above are referred to in this judgment. The relevant part of the appeal was based on the contention that as he was detained under s 3 (although the same would apply to s 2) then the hospital treatment (as defined in part in s 145) required this to be in a hospital. UTJ Rowland held that:

> 'It is important to note that s.145 of the 1983 Act defines "hospital" so that it includes "any health service hospital within the meaning of the National Health Service Act 2006". which in turn includes "any institution for the reception and treatment of persons suffering from illness" and "any clinics, dispensaries and out-patient departments maintained in connection with any such … institution".'[27]

Consequently, applying this part of the legislation, and given that the attendance was in conjunction with a community health nurse who in turn liaised with the RC, it was 'accurate to regard the Appellant as receiving "outpatient" treatment, and therefore hospital treatment'.[28] Consequently, the appeal was dismissed. However, it was noted that the Tribunal had recommended that a CTO should be used (and this recommendation was duly accepted and acted upon). UTJ Rowland commented that:

> '… one might expect community treatment orders to be made in many of the circumstances in which reliance was previously placed on extended leave. The implication … appears to be that, if the First-tier Tribunal considers a community

---

24 Ibid, at [34].

25 [2004] EWHC 2958 (Admin), [2004] MHLR 355.

26 [2011] UKUT 233 (AAC), [2011] MHLR 194.

27 Ibid, at [9].

28 Ibid.

treatment order to be appropriate and makes a recommendation to that effect, it may discharge the patient if the recommendation is not followed and the responsible clinician does not give a persuasive reason for not following it.'[29]

6.14 In respect of leave of absence Chapter 21 of the Code (*Reference Guide*, at paras 12.39–12.56) (see Part E), confirms that 'leave of absence can be an important part of a detained person's care plan', but also adds that:

> 'When considering whether to grant leave of absence for more than seven consecutive days, or extending leave so that the total period is more than seven consecutive days responsible clinicians must first consider whether the patient should go onto supervised community treatment instead.'

Unrestricted Part 3 patients may be subject to this regime, as can restricted patients if the Secretary of State for Justice consents.

6.15 In *R (Epsom & St Helier NHS Trust) v MHRT*[30] the Tribunal discharged a patient upon the basis that there was no inpatient treatment for her at the hospital in which she was being detained. Sullivan J held that:[31]

> 'The matter has to be looked at in the round, including the prospect of future in-patient treatment, but there will come a time when, even though it is certain that treatment will be required at some stage in the future, the timing of that treatment is so uncertain that it is no longer "appropriate" for the patient to continue to be liable to detention. It is the Tribunal's function to use its expertise to decide whether the certainty, or the possibility, of the need for in-patient treatment at some future date makes it "appropriate" that the patient's liability to detention shall continue … The Tribunal should look at the reality of the situation in deciding whether it is appropriate that a patient should be liable to be detained in hospital for medical treatment. Artificial cut-offs should not be applied. It follows that there will be a broad spectrum between the *Hallstrom* type of case at one end, where no in-patient treatment is, or is proposed to be, provided, and the *Barking* case at the other, where in-patient treatment forms an "essential ingredient" of the overall treatment programme.'

CLASSIFICATION

6.16 The powers relating to reclassification of mental disorder (which used to form one function of the Tribunal) have now been rendered otiose by the amendments set out above. However, the issue of a mismatch between the mental disorder from which the patient may be suffering and the treatment he or she is being given, or the environment in which he or she is being detained, may still be of more than historical interest. *R (B) v Ashworth Hospital Authority*[32] considered the situation when a patient who had been detained as suffering from one form of mental disorder (that of psychopathy) was in fact

---

29 Ibid, at [11].

30 [2001] EWHC 101 (Admin), [2001] MHLR 8; (*EC Ch 5*).

31 Ibid, at [52] and [61].

32 [2005] UKHL 20, [2005] MHLR 47; (*EC Ch 5*).

being treated for a personality disorder. The House of Lords relied upon MHA 1983, s 63 (now amended slightly by MHA 2007) for the proposition that it authorised treatment for any mental disorder, and not the one that had originally justified detention. Consequently, it was lawful for a different course of treatment to be given. The Code of Practice (Chapter 6) elaborates upon this proposition, and also provides further examples of what may constitute treatment generally. In terms of the appropriacy of treatment, paras 6.10, 6.12, 6.13 and 6.16 are particularly significant in this context.

TREATABILITY

6.17 It follows from the above that some of the same issues as to what constitutes treatment will overlap with the concept of what is amenable to treatment itself (treatability) and which has been considered in more recent decisions referred to at para 6.12 above. For example, in *Reid v Secretary of State for Scotland*[33] it was held that the fact that '... in the structured setting of the State Hospital in a supervised environment ... the petitioner's anger management improves, resulting in his being less physically aggressive' even if 'the treatment does not cure the disorder itself'.

6.18 Similarly, in *R v Canon's Park MHRT ex parte A* Roch LJ held as follows:[34]

> 'I would suggest the following principles. First, if a tribunal were to be satisfied that the patient's detention in hospital was simply and attempt to coerce the patient into participating in group therapy, then the tribunal would be under a duty to direct discharge. Second, "treatment in hospital" will satisfy the "treatability" test although it is unlikely to alleviate the patient's condition, provided that it is likely to prevent a deterioration. Third "treatment in hospital" will satisfy the "treatability test" although it will not immediately alleviate or prevent deterioration in the patient's condition, provided that alleviation or stabilisation is likely in due course. Fourth, the "treatability" test can still be met although initially there may be some deterioration in the patient's condition, due for example to the patient's initial anger at being detained. Fifth, it must be remembered that medical treatment in hospital covers "nursing and also includes care, habilitation and rehabilitation under medical supervision". Sixth, the "treatability" test is satisfied if nursing care etc are likely to lead to an alleviation of the patient's condition in that the patient is likely to gain an insight into his problem or cease to be unco-operative in his attitude towards treatment which would have a lasting benefit.'

6.19 In *R (Wheldon) v Rampton Hospital Authority* Elias J held that:[35]

---

33 [1992] 2 AC 512.

34 [1995] QB 60.

35 [2001] EWHC 134 (Admin); [2001] MHLR 19, at [14].

'It is plain that the concept [of treatability] is a very wide one, and that the responsible medical officer making the assessment can look to the future and consider whether the treatment is likely, in the future, to achieve beneficial results.'

6.20 In *Noel Ruddle v Secretary of State for Scotland* is was held that:[36]

'In the absence of any primary, focused therapeutic or other treatment, the only treatment to which the applicant has been subject in the State Hospital has been the structured environment and nursing care under medical supervision. While this structured environment and nursing care in the regime of the State hospital is medical treatment in the widest sense, it is not clinical treatment; while it may sometimes alleviate or prevent deterioration of condition, it has not done so in the recent past for the applicant and is not so doing at the present. Accordingly, since the medical treatment which the applicant has received and is at present receiving has not alleviated or prevented and is not likely to alleviate or prevent a deterioration of his condition, he does not meet the "treatability test" and it is not appropriate for him to be liable to be detained in a hospital for medical treatment, nor to remain liable to be recalled to hospital for further treatment.'

6.21 Although not strictly of relevance within the above context, it has been held that force feeding of a detained patient (with a personality disorder) amounts to treatment, within the meaning of MHA 1983.[37]

6.22 Finally, in *SH v Cornwall Partnership NHS Trust* ,[38] the issue of whether or not the Tribunal had jurisdiction to consider issues relating to consent to medical treatment or not was considered. The appeal was dismissed. The Tribunal only had power to consider the statutory criteria for discharge (in this instance from a CTO). None of these criteria related to whether the patient consented to treatment, or not. If the Tribunal did have jurisdiction to consider issues of consent to treatment, it would logically have powers to consider treatment as well, and it had no power to do that, either.

---

36 [1999] MHLR 159, at [10.5] and [10.6].

37 *R v Dr James Collins and Ashworth Special Hospital ex parte Ian Stewart Brady* [2000] MHLR 17.

38 [2012] UKUT 290 (AAC), [2012] MHLR 383.

Part C

NON-OFFENDER PATIENTS

Chapter 7

DETENTION AND DISCHARGE (MENTAL HEALTH ACT 1983, S 2)

TERMINOLOGY

7.1 Common to all the procedures within MHA 1983 is a set of descriptions of various professionals. A full set of the abbreviations is set out at the beginning of this text. The responsible medical officer (RMO) has been replaced with the responsible clinician (RC). The approved social worker (ASW) is now an approved mental health professional (AHMP). Each of these professionals (but particularly the RC and AHMP) have important roles to play, and their status and origins are set out in Chapters 11 and 12. All non-offender patients are sometimes referred to as 'Part II' patients, as this is the Part of MHA 1983 which governs that category of patient. In respect of the initial application for admission this will be to the hospital managers and, if the application is accepted, will be followed by the substantive detention.

ADMISSION CRITERIA

7.2 These are contained in MHA 1983, s 2, and are set out below:

> '2 Admission for assessment
>
> (1) A patient may be admitted to a hospital and detained there for the period allowed by subsection (4) below in pursuance of an application (in this Act referred to as "an application for admission for assessment") made in accordance with subsections (2) and (3) below.
>
> (2) An application for admission for assessment may be made in respect of a patient on the grounds that –
>
> (a) he is suffering from mental disorder of a nature or degree which warrants the detention of the patient in a hospital for assessment (or for assessment followed by medical treatment) for at least a limited period; and
> (b) he ought to be so detained in the interests of his own health or safety or with a view to the protection of other persons.
>
> (3) An application for admission for assessment shall be founded on the written recommendations in the prescribed form of two registered medical practitioners, including in each case a statement that in the opinion of the practitioner the conditions set out in subsection (2) above are complied with.

(4) Subject to the provisions of section 29(4) below, a patient admitted to hospital in pursuance of an application for admission for assessment may be detained for a period not exceeding 28 days beginning with the day on which he is admitted, but shall not be detained after the expiration of that period unless before it has expired he has become liable to be detained by virtue of a subsequent application, order or direction under the following provisions of this Act.'

7.3 The limit of the period under which detention can be made (without the use of another order) is 28 days from the date upon which the patient was admitted. The most common order that is made if further detention is required is under MHA 1983, s 3. In order for such an application to succeed, it will need to be supported by two registered medical practitioners. The application for admission will be made to a hospital is in itself lawful authority to convey the patient to that hospital (MHA 1983, s 6(1)). If the application for admission appears to be 'duly made and to be founded on the necessary medical recommendations' it may be acted upon by the admitting hospital without further proof (s 6(3)).[1] Section 6 covers the effect of an application for admission and is set out below.

'6 Effect of application for admission

(1) An application for the admission of a patient to a hospital under this Part of this Act, duly completed in accordance with the provisions of this Part of this Act, shall be sufficient authority for the applicant, or any person authorised by the applicant, to take the patient and convey him to the hospital at any time within the following period, that is to say –

(a) in the case of an application other than an emergency application, the period of 14 days beginning with the date on which the patient was last examined by a registered medical practitioner before giving a medical recommendation for the purposes of the application;
(b) in the case of an emergency application, the period of 24 hours beginning at the time when the patient was examined by the practitioner giving the medical recommendation which is referred to in section 4(3) above, or at the time when the application is made, whichever is the earlier.

(2) Where a patient is admitted within the said period to the hospital specified in such an application as is mentioned in subsection (1) above, or, being within that hospital, is treated by virtue of section 5 above as if he had been so admitted, the application shall be sufficient authority for the managers to detain the patient in the hospital in accordance with the provisions of this Act.

(3) Any application for the admission of a patient under this part of this Act which appears to be duly made and to be founded on the necessary medical recommendations may be acted on without further proof of the signature or qualification of the person by whom the application or any such medical recommendation is made or given or of any matter of fact or opinion stated in it.

---

1 *Re S-C (Mental Patient: Habeas Corpus)* [1996] 1 All ER 532, CA.

(4) Where a patient is admitted to a hospital in pursuance of an application under this Part of this Act by virtue of which he was liable to be detained in a hospital or subject to a guardianship shall cease to have effect.'

7.4 The grounds for admission are set out at MHA 1983, s 2(2)(a) and (b) (see **7.2**). They are almost identical to the grounds which the Tribunal considers during a hearing. The threshold for admission in respect of a prerequisite that the patient 'is suffering' from a mental illness appears to be fairly low, and certainly does not need to be a finally concluded diagnosis.[2]

7.5 By the time the matter comes before a Tribunal, the evidence in support of the criteria will be primarily in the report of the RC and a social work and nursing report (of some description). It is possible that the RC will have limited knowledge of the patient. Sometimes the author of a social report will have greater knowledge, but this is not always the case. A member of the nursing staff will usually attend a Tribunal, and it is very often from that professional that the best evidence is obtained (in terms of direct observation of the demeanour of the patient since detention). The original recommendation for admission will have been by an AMHP.

7.6 In summary, the Tribunal may be faced with a patient whose contact with the mental health system prior to detention has been little or none. The evidence may also be very scant (simply through lack of knowledge). The Tribunal will be faced with evaluating (in part) the question of risk upon the basis of limited information, and therefore may prefer to err on the side of caution. It is often said that the greatest difficulty in assessing risk lies in the evaluation of patients detained under MHA 1983, s 2 rather than (for example) with a restricted patient (who will have been the subject of many reports, and will have a well-documented forensic history). Representatives should not underestimate the task that a Tribunal faces in such cases. Representatives should also be aware that (apart from the examination by the medical member) the Tribunal is unlikely to have examined the records compiled by the hospital since admission in detail (or at all). There is often useful information contained in these documents. The representative is also faced with a complex and difficult task, in that he or she may never have met the patient before and will only have access to the reports at the very last minute. Advocacy before a Tribunal can be extremely demanding, and requires a high degree of specialist knowledge of both the law and the subject matter itself (ie mental illness).

MENTAL DISORDER

7.7 This has been considered above (at **6.1–6.9**). It is very unlikely that this ground will not be made out by the RA. It is also very likely that the patient will not accept that he or she suffers from a mental disorder. The reasons for this could be either a lack of insight or the stigma attached to such a label, or

---

2 *R v Kirklees MBC ex parte C* [1993] 2 FLR 187; *St George's Healthcare NHS Trust v S* [1998] 3 All ER 673.

both. However, in extremely rare cases, it may be that (in fact) there *is* no mental illness. Evidentially, the legal representative will be faced with a difficult task in challenging a diagnosis without an alternative psychiatric opinion. If there is no mental disorder, then obviously there will be no continuation of the order. Also, dependence on drugs or alcohol alone is not considered to be a mental disorder. The tense used is the present continuous (*is suffering*), i e present at the time of the assessment of the mental disorder. This extends to the duration of the Tribunal itself.

'Of a nature'

7.8 This is a term of art, and requires definition. Generally, nature refers to the history of the illness (e g how long the patient has suffered from it, whether it has a tendency to relapse, and in what conditions and how rapidly), whether there are long or short interludes in recurrence, or whether it is of a cyclic nature. This list is very far from exhaustive. It is also not always possible to distinguish precisely where nature ends and degree begins since the two may be aspects of the same problem. In *R v London and South West Region Mental Health Review Tribunal ex parte Moyle*[3] the problem was illustrated by example in the evidence provided by Dr Eastman and Dr Humphrey as follows:[4]

> '… for the moment assuming that only "nature" is required as the basis for the "appropriateness" test it will be clear from our description of [the] illness that it both relapses very rapidly on cessation of medication and is then substantially more difficult to control on re-commencement of medication …'

Latham J relied upon citation from Anselm Eldergill *Mental Health Review Tribunals, Law and Practice*,[5] which in turn had been cited with approval in *R v MHRT for the South Thames Region ex parte Smith* as follows:[6]

> 'Practitioners and Tribunals commonly confine their consideration of a patient's mental state to the degree of mental disorder present, seemingly interpreting the words "nature" and "degree" as essentially interchangeable. Accordingly a patient is considered not to be detainable if his condition has responded to medication and is no longer acute. This approach takes no real account of the nature of the particular disorder and mistakenly quotes [sic] its "degree" with its "severity". As such there is a failure to give due weight to the chronicity of the disorder and prognosis … "*Nature*" … The Tribunal does not, however, oblige to discharge unless it is also satisfied that the nature of the patient's disorder, evidenced by his medical history or the outcome usually associated with such condition, also makes liability to detention inappropriate. Similarly, where the degree of disorder apparently at the time of the hearing is quite low but the patient's recent mental state has been subject to marked fluctuations, the nature of the disorder may mean that the Tribunal cannot be satisfied that the first of the grounds for discharge is made out.'

---

3 [1999] MHLR 195, Administrative Court CO/1977/99; (*EC Chs 5 and 14*).
4 [1999] MHLR 195, at [21].
5 Sweet & Maxwell, 1997.
6 Unreported, 4 August 1998, Admin Ct; (*EC Ch 5*).

In *Smith* itself Popplewell J held that:

> 'In my judgment there is a reason for this distinction [between nature and degree] of which this case is perhaps a good example. If one had simply to look at the degree it would have been right for the discharge to take place, but the nature of the condition was such that it was clear that he should not be discharged. It may well be that in a great number of cases that nature and degree involve much the same questions ... and it may be that Tribunals will be wise, if they have any doubts about it, to include them both.'

7.9 In the context of detention using MHA 1983, s 2 (as indicated above), the evidence in respect of nature may be fairly thin if the patient is new to mental health services. Further, since the purpose of the order is for assessment, there is no requirement for a confirmed diagnosis. In practice, the symptoms which presented at the time of detention will readily fit into some form of psychiatric classification for the purposes of a working diagnosis, which in turn is likely to inform (generally) the nature of such illnesses.

7.10 The MHA 1983 Code of Practice summarises the position thus: 'Nature refers to the particular disorder from which the patient is suffering, its chronicity, its prognosis, and the patients previous response to receiving treatment for the disorder' (Chapter 4, para 4.3).

'Or degree'

7.11 The disjunctive '*or*' is significant, as will be apparent from the above exposition on *nature*. It is not necessary for both criteria to be made out in order for detention to be required. The degree of the illness is 'the current manifestation of the patient's disorder' (ibid), that is to say, the symptoms that are demonstrated at the time of the detention (or during the Tribunal itself). Again, as should be evident from the above, it may well be the case that the symptoms have diminished considerably by the time that a Tribunal convenes, at which point the significance of the phrase 'which warrants detention' becomes of greater significance. This area of law was revisited in *CM V DHNHSFT and Secretary of State for Justice*.[7] The patient in this instance was detained on a restricted basis, and had a history of schizophrenia, and had been conditionally discharged, but recalled at various times. UTJ Levenson cited *ex p Smith* for the proposition set out at **7.8**, and added 'If the nature of a patient's illness is such that it will relapse in the absence of medication, then whether the nature is such as to make it appropriate for him to be liable to be detained in hospital for medical treatment depends on an assessment of the probability that he will relapse in the near future if he were free in the community and on whether the evidence is that without being detained in hospital he will not take the medication *(Smirek v Williams* [2000] MHLR 38, CA; *R v MHRT ex p Moyle* [1999] MHLR 195).'[8] The Tribunal had concluded that the patient might *eventually* relapse if discharged, through a

7 [2011] UKUT 129 (AAC), [2011] MHLR 153.

8 Ibid, at [12].

combination of his past chaotic lifestyle and non-compliance. The evidence before the Tribunal was that the degree of the illness did not warrant detention – so this was not in issue. The Tribunal also accepted that he was a model patient, but that if returned to the community, then within six months or so 'it is almost inevitable that he will revert to his dysfunctional and chaotic lifestyle'.[9] The appeal was upheld on the basis that liability to detention (in this instance) depended on an assessment of the probability of relapse. The speculative relapse was 6 months. There was no evidence of a failure to comply with medication. A Tribunal is not permitted to detain a patient due to a lifestyle of drug taking. The combination of all of these factors led to the UT quashing the decision not to discharge, and remitting the case to a fresh Tribunal. Whilst this case is peculiar to its facts, the scenario that it describes is not uncommon, albeit not within the context of the short life span of detention by way of s 2.

'Which warrants the detention of the patient in a hospital for assessment (or for assessment followed by medical treatment) for at least a limited period'

7.12 The simple question that this begs is whether the extent of either the nature or degree is so serious that deprivation of liberty is required within a hospital. The Code (for example) suggests that prior to admission 'consideration must be given to whether there are alternative means of providing the care and treatment which the patient requires' (ibid). In other words, the deprivation of liberty in order to achieve either assessment or assessment followed by treatment must be a last resort, and must be a proportionate response to the problem, and must be a prerequisite to achieving that aim.

7.13 Although 'treatment' is not the primary focus of admission via MHA 1983, s 2 (whereas it is the sole function of MHA 1983, s 3) the law in respect of the availability of treatment (and by analogy the appropriate nature of that treatment), and whether or not it actually is in the hospital, is of some relevance. This is set out at **6.10–6.20**. However, the relatively new test of appropriate medical treatment being available does not explicitly apply in respect of s 2. The short-term nature of detention using s 2 means that it is unlikely that some of the arguments in respect of treatment will be relevant. However, it is still possible that a patient may (by way of example only) have sufficient insight into the nature of his or her illness, and the degree may either be sufficiently abated or absent, which, coupled with sufficient support within the community (either from professionals or family, or both) could combine to defeat the assertion that detention in hospital is required. In principle (and in fact) there is no reason (in the absence of other factors) why a patient cannot be assessed and treated in the community, even if after only a short time after having been detained. The above two provisions in the statute were further considered (albeit on a highly technical and slightly academic footing) in *MS v*

---

9 Ibid, at [18].

North East London Foundation Trust.[10] UTJ Jacobs was concerned with an apparent error in the reasons given by the Tribunal, but this involved a consideration of the relevant statutory criteria, in the following terms. First, it is noted that the criteria for admission with s 2 uses the word 'ought to be so detained'. This is in contrast with the criteria for s 3 which states that the admission should be both necessary and appropriate (see Chapter 8). The criteria for discharge by the Tribunal are that it has to be satisfied that the detention is justified (in respect of s 2). The UTJ held:

> 'The most significant factor … is the purpose of sections 2 and 3. Detention, for whatever purpose, involves a deprivation of liberty. As such, it must be strictly justified … detention for assessment must, of necessity, be less exacting, since the need for treatment is not then known. Assessment under section 2 may, as an essential preliminary to establishing the need for treatment, be necessary in order to render section 3 effective for some patients. To that extent, it plays an important role in protecting the health and safety of those patients and the protection of others. This does, of course, reduce the protection for the patient, but this is balanced by the fact that, unlike section 3, detention under section 2 is limited by the need for an assessment and for a period of 28 days.[11]
>
> The difference in the language of the sections reflects the difference in purpose. For the purposes of this case, the key difference is that under section 2 the mental disorder must warrant detention and the patient ought to be detained for health, safety or protection, whereas under section 3 the mental disorder must make detention appropriate and necessary for health, safety and protection. The terms relevant to section 2 are less exactly on their own and in their context. The context is related to their purpose …'[12]
>
> 'This is not to say that the conditions for detention under section 2 are not demanding. Just that they are less demanding than for section 3. It would not be appropriate for me to try and define the differences between those sections. The language is everyday language that merely has to be applied. But it has to be applied in a context that requires detention to be strictly justified.'[13]

'And he ought to be so detained in the interests of his own health or safety'

7.14 The next part of MHA 1983 is conjunctive with the preceding s 2(2)(a) (ie both limbs require to be made out). Whether there is a requirement to do so in the interests of his or her own health *or* safety (which is disjunctive) will depend upon all the circumstances of the case. The term 'health' can be construed widely, and will include both mental and physical health. The commonest practical examples are where a patient is unlikely to comply with an assessment or treatment if not detained (mental health), and/or where there has been physical neglect (as a result of the mental illness). Similarly, in respect of

---

10 [2013] UKUT 92 (AAC).

11 Ibid, at [9].

12 Ibid, at [10].

13 Ibid, at [13].

safety this is likely to be relevant where the patient has involved him or herself (or been involved by others) in behaviour that is dangerous or risky, and is causally linked to the mental illness. Another example may be where the patient is liable to sexual or financial exploitation by others by virtue of his or her mental illness.

'Or with a view to the protection of other persons'

7.15 It is more usual for a patient to be a risk to themselves, than to others. However, it is also the case that the symptoms of an illness may lead to a need for the protection of others (either by way of direct physical harm or otherwise). If this is relied upon as a basis for detention, then both the Tribunal and practitioners need to be aware of the importance of the sound evidential basis for such assertions (see paras 3.59 and 3.62–3.64 of the Code of Practice). However, it must be remembered that this is only one limb of the test, and may not be particularly significant within the overall context of the admission. The Code sets out some the relevant considerations in respect of this part of the statutory criteria (paras 4.7 and 4.8).

DISCHARGE

7.16 In terms of the evidence available to the Tribunal, this has been summarised at **7.5**. The AMHP (who will be employed by the relevant local authority social services authority) may also be available. The statutory test for *discharge* (as opposed to *admission*) is set out at MHA 1983, s 72(1)(a)(i) and (ii).

> '72 Powers of tribunals
>
> (1) Where application is made to the appropriate tribunal by or in respect of a patient who is liable to be detained under this Act or is a community patient, the tribunal may in any case direct that the patient be discharged, and –
>
> (a) the tribunal shall direct the discharge of a patient liable to be detained under section 2 above if it is not satisfied –
> (i) that he is then suffering from mental disorder or from mental disorder of a nature or degree which warrants his detention in a hospital for assessment (or for assessment followed by medical treatment) for at least a limited period; or
> (ii) that his detention as aforesaid is justified in the interests of his own health or safety or with a view to the protection of other persons.'

7.17 The criteria for discharge therefore mirror the criteria for admission, and each of them need to be considered by a Tribunal. The formulation that is used by the Tribunal is phrased in a slightly different manner. All decisions made by Tribunals are in typed form on 'Form 2'. The formulation is as follows:

'(a) The Tribunal is/is not satisfied that the patient is suffering from mental disorder or from mental disorder of a nature or degree which warrants the patient's detention in a hospital for assessment (or for assessment followed by medical treatment) for at least a limited period.

(b) The Tribunal is/is not satisfied that the patient's detention as aforesaid is justified in the interests of the patient's own health or safety, or with a view to the protection of other persons.

(c) The Tribunal does/does not consider that it is appropriate to discharge the patient under its discretionary powers.'

The same form provides for a recommendation to be made. These are for leave of absence, or transfer to another hospital. It is to be noted that a CTO is not available to a patient detained under s 2, but that transfer into guardianship can also form a lawful recommendation.

7.18 The law in respect of each of the statutory criteria set out in Form 2 has been set out above (paras **7.7–7.15**). However, there still remain a number of matters to be considered.

Discretion to discharge

7.19 MHA 1983, s 72(1) makes it clear that the Tribunal 'may in any case direct that the patient be discharged'. This therefore confers upon it a discretion to discharge irrespective of the statutory criteria. It is difficult to imagine how circumstances might arise where a reasonable Tribunal would exercise this power, given that it is obliged to consider the precise statutory criteria as the basis for its decision.

Health or safety of the patient or the protection of other persons

7.20 In *R v London and South West Region Mental Health Review Tribunal ex parte Moyle*, Latham J held that:[14]

'... the Tribunal failed to deal adequately with the question of whether or not it was necessary for the health or safety of the patient or for the protection of other persons that he should receive hospital treatment. The Tribunal was obliged to consider this as a discrete question.'

The terminology considered in this case did not relate to MHA 1983, s 2 (as can be seen by reference to the word 'necessary'). Whether much turns on the difference between 'necessary' and 'justified' is arguable (in the context of s 2). However, the principles outlined by Latham J (as set out in full at **8.16**) must surely be of significance. Finally, in *R v North West London Mental Health*

---

[14] [1999] MHLR 195, at [40].

NHS Trust ex parte S,[15] Harrison J held that the phrase 'other persons' does not need to relate to society as a whole, but can relate to an individual.

Deferred discharge and recommendations

7.21 The Tribunal has the power to make recommendations (MHA 1983, s 72(3)) as set out below.

> '(3) A tribunal may under subsection (1) above direct the discharge of a patient on a future date specified in the direction; and where a tribunal does not direct the discharge of a patient under that subsection the tribunal may –
>
> (a) with a view to facilitating his discharge on a future date, recommend that he be granted leave of absence or transferred to another hospital or into guardianship; and
> (b) further consider his case in the event of any such recommendation not being complied with.'

Deferred/delayed discharge

7.22 The relevance of this provision is of greater significance in respect of more long term detentions, and is considered at greater length below at **8.21**. Although precisely the same principles apply to delaying a discharge, it is clear that given the lifespan of an admission via MHA 1983, s 2 (which will have shortened considerably by the time a Tribunal is listed), any such delay would in itself be very short.

Recommendations

7.23 Similarly, it is unlikely that any of the recommendations available will be of much significance when a Tribunal is considering detention under MHA 1983, s 2. The range and status of such recommendations are considered at **8.22–8.29** and also at **3.32**.

THE HEARING

7.24 Some of the practical aspects of the actual hearing have been dealt with in Part A (eg at **1.14**, **1.15**, **2.1–2.2**, **2.5–2.7**, **2.14**, **2.17** and **2.18**). All matters referred to in Part B (Pre-hearing Procedures) have included applications which could lead to an adjournment of the substantive hearing. Matters may be raised by either the Tribunal itself or by the legal representative. It is usually acceptable for a legal representative to address the Tribunal on his or her own (or with the RC present) on such preliminary points.

7.25 The Code (Chapter 32, paras 32.26–32.32) gives guidelines as to who should be present during a hearing, and for what duration of the hearing itself.

---

15 (1996) 39 BMLR 105.

As can be seen from the Rules, there is an almost infinite flexibility in terms of who is present and in which order the evidence is given. In as much as it is possible to give an account of the 'normal' procedure, it will be as follows. Assuming that the Tribunal is to proceed, the legal representative is not expected to make an 'opening' of the case. The TJ will introduce the panel and explain briefly the role of each member and the independent status of the Tribunal. This is usually addressed to the patient, who may have little or no experience of being in a court or a Tribunal. The TJ will also ensure that the RC and the legal representative (and any other parties) have all the relevant documentation. The RC will usually give evidence first, and then be asked questions by the medical member, followed by the other Tribunal members. Finally, the legal representative will ask questions. It is not uncommon for the RC to leave at this point, but to be available by telephone within the hospital if required. The relevant personnel from a social services department will then follow, with the specialist member asking questions, followed by the other Tribunal members, and concluding with the legal representative. Other professional witnesses will follow in a similar order of questioning. When the patient comes to give his or her evidence, some legal representatives prefer to elicit evidence from their client. Others are content for the Tribunal to ask questions first (which are usually led by the TJ). In theory, where the burden of proof is upon the responsible authority, it is open to the patient not to give evidence at all, but this would be a risky strategy. Finally, the legal representative makes his or her submissions on the law and the evidence, and then the Tribunal will consider its decision in private. It should be stressed that the above procedure is not fixed, and is open to an almost infinite number of variations. The duration of a Tribunal for a straightforward case is likely to be not less than approximately 2 hours. This excludes the time that will be taken to formulate the reasons for the decision, albeit the usual practice is for this to be done separately.

7.26 Some Tribunals will compile reasons for the decision in full at the conclusion of the hearing. Others will provide a brief summary of the reasons for the decision. The decision itself is always announced upon conclusion of the deliberations of the Tribunal. If the decision is to discharge, it is the *section* which is being discharged, and not the patient. In other words, the lawful authority upon which the hospital relied to deprive the patient of his or her liberty no longer exists as at that precise time. It is permissible for the patient to remain as an informal patient (although probably unwise if the discharge is from a secure hospital). Form P6 should be completed to record the outcome (whichever decision is made). As before, there is a good deal of flexibility in the manner in which this is done, although the format for reasons is more complex. These are also governed by rr 41 and 42. All matters in respect of decisions are considered at **14.57–14.59**.

USE OF INTERPRETERS FOR THE DEAF

7.27 If a patient is deaf, then adequate provision must have been made for this in advance (including a considerably extended period of time for the hearing itself, and sufficient room to accommodate a relay interpreter in addition to a CACDP qualified or ASLI licensed British sign language interpreter).

RECORD KEEPING

7.28 The Regional Chairmen's Manual suggests that Presidents must take a full note of the proceedings in an appropriate notebook, and keep these in a secure place for a minimum period of 6 months from the date of final determination. This also applies to any notes taken by other Tribunal members.

7.29 A patient who wishes to tape-record the proceedings must first obtain leave of the Tribunal, which will determine the matter by considering the Contempt of Court Act 1981, s 9. If permission is granted, then the Secretariat will make the necessary technical arrangements. The status of a tape-recording, and its use in appeals, was considered in *A-G v MHRT for Scotland.*[16] However, this merely considers whether or not it is proportionate for a transcription to take place. A recording of a Tribunal would be very unusual (the purpose might be questionable) and would be governed by r 14.

7.30 All other documents received by the Tribunal should be shredded.

TRIBUNAL ASSISTANT

7.31 Tribunal assistants have a number of functions, which include ensuring that the room allocated is appropriate, that papers are available and distributed in advance, that the clinical records are available if requested and to be present during the hearing, or close by. However, it is by no means certain that a tribunal assistant dedicated to this task will be available at all. More often than not the Mental Health Act Administrator will fulfil the role, although he or she will be doing this in addition to discharging his or her responsibilities to the hospital. On the whole, the system in this respect is still far from satisfactory.

HUMAN RIGHTS ARGUMENTS

7.32 In common with mainstream litigation, it is expected that if a substantial point is to be made in respect of the Human Rights Act 1998, then a skeleton argument should be provided in advance. Any authorities relied upon should be complete and in an authorised format. Copies must be provided 3 days prior to the hearing (and to all parties, as well as to the Tribunal).

---

16 [2007] MHLR 1.

Chapter 8

DETENTION AND DISCHARGE (MENTAL HEALTH ACT 1983, S 3)

ADMISSION CRITERIA

8.1 The admission criteria are contained in MHA 1983, s 3, and are set out below:

> '3 Admission for treatment
>
> (1) A patient may be admitted to a hospital and detained there for the period allowed by the following provisions of this Act in pursuance of an application (in this Act referred to as "an application for admission for treatment") made in accordance with this section.
>
> (2) An application for admission for treatment may be made in respect of a patient on the grounds that –
>
> (a) he is suffering from mental disorder of a nature or degree which makes it appropriate for him to receive medical treatment in a hospital; and
> (b) (*repealed*);
> (c) it is necessary for the health or safety of the patient or for the protection of other persons that he should receive such treatment and it cannot be provided unless he is detained under this section; and
> (d) appropriate medical treatment is available for him.
>
> (3) An application for admission for treatment shall be founded on the written recommendations in the prescribed form of two registered medical practitioners, including in each case a statement that in the opinion of the practitioner the conditions set out in subsection (2) above are complied with; and each such recommendation shall include –
>
> (a) such particulars as may be prescribed of the grounds for that opinion so far as it relates to the conditions set out in paragraphs (a) and (d) of that subsection; and
> (b) a statement of the reasons for that opinion so far as it relates to the conditions set out in paragraph (c) of that subsection, specifying whether other methods of dealing with the patient are available and, if so, why they are not appropriate.
>
> (4) In this Act, references to appropriate medical treatment, in relation to a person suffering from mental disorder, are references to medical treatment which is

> appropriate in his case, taking into account the nature and degree of the mental disorder and all other circumstances of his case.'

8.2 Initial detention using s 3 is up to a period of 6 months, although it may be renewed. The statutory procedure for application for admission is similar to that set out at **7.3**, except that the consequence of admission for *treatment* means that any previous application (including guardianship) will cease to have effect.

8.3 In terms of the situation that might arise by the time a Tribunal is convened, it is possible that the information available will be limited. However, more often than not, if detention for treatment has been authorised there is likely to have been a history of past involvement with mental health services.

SECTION 2 OR S 3?

8.4 The function of the Tribunal is confined to the statutory criteria (or its discretion) in respect of discharge or otherwise. It is not the function of the Tribunal to consider the lawfulness or otherwise of the original admission to hospital. However, there are a number of situations that can arise in respect of MHA 1983, ss 2 and 3 which need to be addressed. For a discussion on some of the differences of the language used for admission and discharge, refer to **7.14** and the exegesis on the relevant sections by UTJ Jacobs in *MS v North East London Foundation Trust*.[1]

8.5 The Code (Chapter 4, paras 4.25–4.27) gives some guidance as to the basis upon which professionals should make a decision as to whether s 2 or s 3 is the more appropriate route to detention.

8.6 Detention under s 2 cannot be renewed or extended. In other words, if the assessment period is ended, or about to end, and the criteria are likely to be made out and, in particular, if it is unlikely that the treatment plan will be complied with upon a voluntary basis, then s 3 is the most common avenue used. The *Reference Guide* at para 2.11 summarises the matter thus (and refers to *R v Wilson ex parte Williamson*[2]):

> 'The conditions for section 2 admissions are not quite so stringent as those for section 3 admissions because assessment may well be used for the purpose of determining whether the more stringent conditions apply. However, the powers under section 2 can only be used for the limited purpose for which they were intended. They cannot be used to further detain patients for the purposes of assessment beyond the 28 day period. Nor can they be used as a temporary alternative to detention under section 3 merely to allow an application to be made to the County Court under Section 29 for an order appointing an acting nearest relative in place of a nearest relative who objects to the use of section 3.'

---

1 [2013] UKUT 92 (AAC).

2 [1996] CoD 42; (*EC Ch 6*).

If detention using s 3 is (as a matter of fact) *only* being used for assessment in order to determine a course of treatment, then that is the function of s 2, and not a permissible use of s 3.[3] However, in *Barker v Barking, Havering and Brentwood Community Healthcare NHS Trust and Taylor*,[4] it was held that detention under s 3 can be renewed, even where the patient is on leave from the hospital and the only 'treatment' which he or she is receiving in the hospital is assessment. The justification for this was that the assessment was part of the process of medical treatment, which in turn prevented a deterioration in the condition of the mental health of the patient. The same factual basis can be used for either s 2 or s 3.[5]

8.7 It is not infrequently the case that the legal authority for detention of the patient will have changed from s 2 to s 3 by the time that the Tribunal hears the case. If this is so, then the Tribunal should proceed with the application, and use the criteria relating to s 3. The practical effect of this is that the patient does not lose the right to re-apply for discharge from s 3. Collins J referred to the issue by reference to s 66(1) in the following terms:[6]

> 'Section 66 (1) does not refer to detention, merely to the admission, as the foundation for the right of application to the Tribunal ... "admission" is something which happens at a moment in time ... it is not a continuing state of affairs ... If one goes to s 72 ... there is nothing in that which suggests that the change in circumstances (that is to say the change in the nature of the detention from s 2 to s 3) affects the validity of the application, nor is there any reason why it should. The powers of the Tribunal under s 72 are ... to be exercised on consideration of the state of affairs before the Tribunal ... Accordingly when the matter comes before the Tribunal, if there has been a change from s 2 to s 3, then the Tribunal must exercise its powers in relation to a patient who is liable to be detained otherwise than under s 2 above and therefore must consider what are loosely described as the s 3 criteria in determining the case before them.'

Mental disorder

8.8 This is referred to at **6.1–6.9** and **7.7**.

'Of a nature or degree which makes it appropriate for him to receive medical treatment in hospital'

8.9 Save that the caveat the admission should be for a limited period, and is for treatment only this phrase is considered at **7.8–7.13**.

---

3 *R v Riverside Mental Health Trust ex parte Hussey* (1998) 43 BMLR 167; (*EC Ch 5*).

4 [1999] 2 CCLR 5, [1999] 1 FLR 106.

5 *C v South London and the Maudsley Hospital NHS Trust and LB Lambeth* [2001] MHLR 269; (*EC Ch 5*).

6 *R v South Thames MHRT ex parte M* (*EC Ch 5*).

'And it is necessary for the health or safety of the patient or for the protection of other persons that he should receive such treatment and it cannot be provided unless he is detained under this section'

8.10 The phrase is different from the admission criteria for s 2 by virtue of the use of the word 'necessary' (rather than 'ought'). Consequently, reference should be made to **7.14–7.15**.

'And appropriate medical treatment is available to him'

8.11 The 'treatability' test which existed at MHA 1983, s 3(2)(b) and which applied to psychopathic disorder and mental impairment has been repealed. Treatment is defined at s 3(4), and medical treatment at MHA 1983, s 145. The concept of treatment as it has been interpreted by the courts is set out at **6.1–6.3** and **6.10–6.20**. Chapter 6 of the Code considers the appropriate medical treatment test. The relevance of the significance of the amendment to s 72 (Powers of Tribunals) in respect of the discharge criteria is considered at **8.17**. It has also been determined that a patient detained for treatment can be treated without his or her consent for any disorder from which he or she is suffering.[7]

DISCHARGE

8.12 The statutory test for *discharge* from detention under MHA 1983, s 3 (as opposed to *admission*) is set out at MHA 1983, s 72(1)(b)(i)–(iia):

> '72 Powers of tribunals
>
> (1) Where application is made to a Mental Health Review Tribunal by or in respect of a patient who is liable to be detained under this Act or is a community patient, the tribunal may in any case direct that the patient be discharged, and –
>
> ...
>
> (b) the tribunal shall direct the discharge of a patient liable to be detained otherwise than under section 2 above if they are not satisfied –
>
> (i) that he is then suffering from mental disorder or from mental disorder of a nature or degree which makes it appropriate for him to be liable to be detained in a hospital for medical treatment; or
>
> (ii) that it is necessary for the health of safety of the patient or for the protection of other persons that he should receive such treatment; or
>
> (iia) that appropriate medical treatment is available for him; ...'

---

7 *R v Ashworth Hospital and another ex parte B* [2005] UKHL 20, [2005] 8 CCLR, [2005] MHLR 47; (*EC Ch 5*).

8.13 There are different forms used by the Tribunal. Where a nearest relative makes an application, Form 4 is used (and different criteria apply). For non offender patients Form 3 is used (and this incorporates ss 37.47 and 48). The formulation used is as follows:

> '(a) The Tribunal is/is not satisfied that the patient is suffering from mental disorder or from mental disorder of a nature or degree which makes it appropriate for the patient to be liable to be detained in a hospital for medical treatment.
>
> (b) The Tribunal is/is not satisfied that it is necessary for the health or safety of the patient or for the protection of other persons that he/she should receive such treatment.
>
> (c) The Tribunal is/is not satisfied that appropriate medical treatment is available for the patient.
>
> (d) The Tribunal considers that it is/is not appropriate to discharge the patient under its discretionary powers.'

Discretion to discharge

8.14 This has been referred to at **7.19**.

Nearest relative application

8.15 If an application has been made by the nearest relative, then MHA 1983, s 72(1)(b)(iii) applies (in the case of an application by virtue of MHA 1983, s 66(1)(g), that the patient, if released, 'would be likely to act in a manner dangerous to other persons or himself') and the additional criteria for the Tribunal to consider will be whether the Tribunal is or is not satisfied that the patient, if released, would be likely to act in a manner dangerous to other persons or to him or herself. The form used is Form 4. The criterion is considered at **8.33–8.35**.

Necessary for the health or safety of the patient or for the protection of other persons that he should receive such treatment

8.16 This has been (in part) referred to at **7.14** and **7.20**. A fuller exposition is contained in the judgment of Latham J in *R v London and South West Region Mental Health Review Tribunal ex parte Moyle*:[8]

> 'The test of "necessity" is different from the test of "appropriateness". It may well be that the facts found by the Tribunal to support the conclusion that the patient does not satisfy the criteria relating to "appropriateness" may determine the question of whether or not he or she has satisfied the criteria in relation to "necessity". But that will not inevitably be the case. However, it is fair to say, that if the test that I have formulated as the test in relation to "appropriateness" cannot

8 [1999] MHLR 195, at [40]; (*EC Ch 5*).

be met by a patient whose mental illness is of a nature which, untreated, may result in danger to himself or others, that is likely to be sufficient to justify the conclusion that he cannot meet the "necessity" test; nonetheless, the statute requires that both issues be resolved.'

A similar point is made in *R (Home Secretary) v MHRT*:[9]

> 'Such treatment [MHA 1983, s 72(1)(b)(ii)] refers back to the treatment which, given the nature or degree of his disorder, makes it appropriate for him to be liable to be detained. Accordingly, separate consideration is needed.'

Appropriate medical treatment

8.17 Matters relating to medical treatment (and treatments which correspond to the mental disorder from which the patient is said to have been suffering) have been considered at **6.1–6.21** and **7.7**. Specifically the issue of treatment outside hospital (but whilst still detained under MHA 1983) has been considered at **6.13–6.15**. A Tribunal is now obliged to address the issue of appropriate treatment directly, whereas previously, it did not. It will be recalled that the limits of the jurisdiction of the Tribunal are quite tightly defined (Part B). This certainly included a prohibition upon the Tribunal investigating treatment options. However, as Gledhill has trenchantly observed:[10]

> 'How to apply the appropriate treatment test has the potential to give rise to legal argument. First, the deference that arises in relation to purely clinical matters from the treating team's longer-term knowledge of most patients has less force in relation to non-clinical considerations. Secondly, the test is supplemental to the appropriateness and necessity tests, and so there will be cases when the latter tests are met but the appropriate test is not met. A further point may then arise, namely whether the response should be immediate discharge or adjournments to allow changes to treatment (e g by recommending transfer, which is formal power in a non-restricted case and an accepted practice in restricted cases) … the previously understood position that the tribunal is concerned with the propriety of detention rather than the propriety of the treatment being given – see Lord Phillips CJ in *R (B) v (1) Dr SS (2) Dr G (3) Secretary of State for Health* [2006] MHLR 131 CA [65] … must be revisited, given the need for appropriate treatment.

RCs should therefore be prepared to justify the treatment that is being made available to the patient, and that this accords with the (wide) principles set out in Chapter 6.

Risk assessment

8.18 The Tribunal is concerned in all hearings (irrespective of the statutory configuration of the detention) with an assessment of risk. As has been indicated, the less information available, the more difficult becomes the task of

---

9 [2003] EWHC 2864 (Admin), at [59], [2004] MHLR 91, per Beatson J.

10 Kris Gledhill *Mental Health Tribunals – Essential Cases* (3rd edn, 2011, Southside Legal Publishing Ltd) Chapter 5, paras 5.16–5.17.

evaluation. This is particularly so with detentions under MHA 1983, s 2. At the opposite end of the spectrum will be offender patients, who may have a very extensive forensic history, and may have been detained in conditions of high security for many years. As a consequence of the latter, those patients will have had their lives examined minutely by a range of professionals whose specific task is to consider the issue of risk. However, those detained under MHA 1983, s 3 may also have a significant history (and sometimes are to be found detained within high security hospitals). Whichever section has been used, the Tribunal (and the detaining authority) will be carrying out an exercise that is (necessarily) one of speculation. The commonest adage employed by mental health professionals in this field is that the best predictor of future behaviour is to look at past behaviour.

8.19 One of the crucial features which arises in all Tribunals will be the question of the degree of insight that the patient has into his or her own mental illness, and the behaviour which is associated with that illness. It should also be noted that it does not necessarily follow that there is any risk associated with the mental illness which has led to the initial detention. However, the rock upon which most applications to the Tribunal founder is the lack of insight of the patient into the very reason why he or she was detained in the first place. In specific terms, this tends to lead to a typical situation where medication will not be taken if there is a lack of compulsion (since the patient does not regard him or herself as ill, there would be no point in taking medicine for a non-existent illness). This in turn is likely to lead to a deterioration in the mental health of the patient, and a consequent elevation of the risk that is posed both to the patient and to others. Representatives should also not underestimate the side effects of some of the commonest medications (see Glossary) which can be very unpleasant, and which add a further disincentive to compliance.

8.20 A scenario which reflected in part the question of insight and risk was considered in *R (On the Application of N) v Mental Health Review Tribunal.*[11] The patient had been detained under the category of psychopathic disorder, and his original offences were three counts of manslaughter. These offences had been committed some 20 years prior to the Tribunal. Consequently, substantial information was made available to the Tribunal via the RC, which contained comprehensive information about concerns of risk, and in particular the remaining work that was required in respect of insight. The patient himself had shown no disposition towards violence for many years, although other concerns were expressed about his behaviour. The specific issue was whether the patient could be transferred to conditions of lesser security for this work to be carried out. The Tribunal declined either to discharge the section or to make a recommendation for transfer. The main focus of the claim by way of judicial

---

11 [2001] EWHC 1133 (Admin), [2002] MHLR 70; (*EC Chs 5 and 13*).

review was that the issue of risk had been 'vaguely expressed and had pointed to the fact that the risk had been said to range from nil to maximum risk'.[12] It was held that:[13]

> 'The medical evidence [was] careful and detailed [and] was not rebutted by any expert evidence on behalf of the claimant … I have come to the view … that it was open to the Tribunal to conclude, and at the very least it was not unreasonable for it to conclude, that there was a substantial, if unquantifiable, risk in this case; and whilst that risk was uncertain in its degree it was sufficiently grave to fulfil the statutory test.'

Further, Gibbs J continued:[14]

> 'To be blunt, the risk in this case is a horrific one … I accept … that there may arise a stage at which a Tribunal must reasonably be required to quantify a risk. It depends upon the context. If it was clear that all available evidence was there for it to consider but that the Tribunal simply walked away from its responsibility and sat on the fence, then there would be justice in the criticism. I acknowledge also that even where the medical evidence before it does not enable it to quantify the risk there must come, or may come, a point where continuous deferment of quantification is unreasonable … It is, in my judgment, unreasonable … to say that the Tribunal should attempt the impossible and reach some kind of assessment of risk which would be in danger of amounting to purely arbitrary speculation. Instead, in my judgment, they were, as I have said, entitled to accept [the RC's] views.'

Deferred discharge

8.21 This is not to be confused with conditional discharge and/or deferred conditional discharge (which is considered in Part D). It is concerned purely with the circumstances in which a Tribunal has reached a conclusion that the grounds for detention are not made out, but that nevertheless a discharge should not be immediate. This is a permissible course of action in (a) a limited number of situations and (b) for a limited period of time. In respect of the first aspect, the case of *R (On the Application of Ashworth Hospital Authority) v MHRT; R (On the Application of H) v Ashworth Hospital Authority*[15] illustrates the function of a deferred discharge perfectly. Although the court considered a number of issues (including rationality of reasons) one of the criticisms levelled at the Tribunal by Ashworth Hospital was that it had opted to discharge the patient with immediate effect. The basic facts of the case involved a patient (detained under MHA 1983, s 3) who had an extensive history which remained of concern to the hospital. He had no real access to support in the community and, in particular, he had no accommodation available to him. The Tribunal had not been provided with an effective

---

12 [2001] EWHC 1133 (Admin), at [26].

13 Ibid, at [49].

14 Ibid, at [53]–[54].

15 [2001] EWHC 901 (Admin), [2002] MHLR 13; [2002] EWCA Civ 923, [2002] MHLR 314; (*EC Chs 1, 2, 9 and 15*).

after-care plan (see Chapter 11) which would have addressed this issue. It was held that:[16] 'This was a case in which ... it was obvious that suitable after-care should be available.' It should be noted that the Court of Appeal (and the High Court) were both concerned that it had been unreasonable for the Tribunal not to have *adjourned* the case in order to obtain further information which would have enabled it to consider whether the criteria for detention were made out or not. Neither an adjournment nor a deferred discharge can be for the purpose of monitoring treatment (for example), and where a decision has actually been made that discharge is appropriate, then the period of deferral should be quite short. The commonest factual example is that which occurred in *R (On the Application of H)* above, or something of a similar nature. It may be that the after-care plan has not been precisely finalised (eg specific details of accommodation) but that this will be available in the foreseeable future. If that is the case, then a Tribunal may wish to defer discharge for a matter of days or weeks in order for that to be available. It should not be a matter for those who are responsible for ensuring that such services are available to dictate to the Tribunal when such discharge should be effective (since this might lead to detention for indefinite periods of time in the absence of any justification other than a shortage of resources on the part of the relevant social services authority, which in turn could lead to an ever-receding horizon for discharge of the patient). In *MP v Mersey Care NHS Trust*[17] a Tribunal made an order deferring discharge to 6 April 2010. However, on 31 March 2010, the RC made the patient subject to a CTO. There appears to have been some confusion thereafter on the part of the STJ who 'reviewed' the original decision. HHJ Pearl held that 'It is common ground that a deferred discharge brings to an end a community treatment order made before the deferred discharge date'.[18] In other words, if the decision of the original Tribunal was upheld, then because the order for detention ended on 6 April 2010, so would the CTO put in place on 31 March 2010. The decisions of the STJ made after the decision of the FTT were quashed as being unlawful. The original decision of the Tribunal was upheld. The consequence of that was that the CTO did not survive beyond 6 April 2010. Any acts taken pursuant to a non-existent order, would, of course, be unlawful.

RECOMMENDATIONS

8.22 The provision for a Tribunal to make recommendations in set out at MHA 1983, ss 3 and 3A. This is set out below. The law in respect of supervision applications and community treatment orders is considered separately at Chapter 10 et seq and recommendations are also considered at **3.32**. This has direct relevance to any recommendation that a Tribunal might make pursuant to s 3A.

---

16 [2002] EWCA Civ 923, at [67].

17 [2011] UKUT 107 (AAC), [2011] MHLR 146.

18 Ibid, at [32].

'(3) A tribunal may under subsection (1) above direct the discharge of a patient on a future date specified in the direction; and where a tribunal do not direct the discharge of a patient under that subsection the tribunal may –

(a) with a view to facilitating his discharge on a future date, recommend that he be granted leave of absence or transferred to another hospital or into guardianship; and
(b) further consider his case in the event of any such recommendation not being complied with.

(3A) Subsection (1) above does not require a tribunal to direct the discharge of a patient just because they think it might be appropriate for the patient to be discharged (subject to the possibility of recall) under a community treatment order; and a tribunal –

(a) may recommend that the responsible clinician consider whether to make a community treatment order; and
(b) may (but need not) further consider the patient's case if the responsible clinician does not make an order.'

'With a view to facilitating his discharge on a future date'

8.23 This is the key phrase in respect of the function of recommendations. What a recommendation cannot do is stray into the territory of supervising, controlling or directing treatment. This remains within the discretion of the hospital. It is a fine line between the purpose of a recommendation (which is with a view to facilitating discharge on a future date) and the supervision of treatment. Moreover, it is very often the case that the RC will have already considered the potential way forward (in relation to the limited number of recommendations which the Tribunal can make) and either accepted that they are appropriate, or not. If the RC has accepted that they are appropriate, it may be argued that there is nothing to be gained by a formal recommendation being included in the judgment of the Tribunal (since this would be otiose).

8.24 In practical terms, the recommendations are limited to (a) granting of leave of absence; (b) transfer to another hospital; (c) transfer to guardianship; (d) whether a supervision application should be made; (e) whether a community treatment order should be made. Rule 42 states that a decision with recommendations is a decision 'which finally disposes of the proceedings'. This does not prevent the Tribunal from reconvening if the date by which it is intended the recommendation should be complied with is not met, since this power is retained in the Act as set out above (MHA 1983, s 72(3)(b)). It may, in certain circumstances, be the preferred option on the part of the Tribunal to set a horizon for recommendations to be either complied with by the relevant party, or not. If the recommendations are complied with by that date, then the Tribunal has no further jurisdiction. If they have not been, then the provisions of MHA 1983 permit a reconsideration of the issue (notwithstanding the definition in r 42 of a provisional decision). This issue was considered in *R v MHRT ex parte Hemstock*.[19] It was held that the phrase:[20]

> '… "his case" … would seem to suggest that the tribunal can consider the whole matter again. "His case" must, in my judgment, mean his application for discharge. That is the case that has been considered and therefore the case that is to be further considered. If it had been the intention of Parliament to restrict the further consideration to the recommendations made by the tribunal, the subsection could very readily have been worded "further consider such recommendation".'

Consequently, a Tribunal that reconvenes to consider implementation of recommendations has all the powers available to it, which include discharge.

Failure to follow recommendation

8.25 Thus, although a recommendations remain just that – a recommendation – if the detaining hospital were unable to provide good reason for failing to comply with recommendations, it would be open to the Tribunal to discharge, rather than permit an indefinite refusal to comply. Obviously, this will not be the preferred option of the Tribunal, and it would not be able to take such a course of action unless the primary criteria for detention were not made out. In the absence of power to order transfer, the only remedy on the part of the patient would be to apply for permission to judicially review the decision of the detaining authority (or other party) not to comply with the recommendation made by the Tribunal. This cumbersome process would be assisted by full reasons being provided by the Tribunal as to the basis for its recommendations, and details of the reasons given as to why such a recommendation has not been followed.

8.26 In *R (P) v (1) Mersey Care NHS Trust (2) Dr Mulligan (3) Home Secretary*[21] a recommendation was made for trial leave in less secure conditions. The case was in respect of a restricted patient (although this makes no difference to the general legal principle established, it should be noted that there is no power to make recommendations for transfer where the patient is restricted). The RC opposed such a course of action, and a claim by way of judicial review of his decision was commenced (as indicated at **8.25**). Accompanying the claim for judicial review was an assertion that the ECHR, Art 8 rights of the patient were being infringed. Richards J held that:[22]

> 'In my judgment the central question in this case is whether the risk posed by the claimant is sufficiently low to make it appropriate for him to be accommodated in medium security rather than high security … who is to decide that question of risk?'

---

19 (1998) 39 BMLR 123 (Admin Ct); (*EC Ch 12*).

20 Ibid, at 125–126.

21 [2003] EWHC 994 (Admin), [2004] MHLR 107.

22 Ibid, at [25]–[26].

He found that the answer to this question lay with those to whom Parliament had entrusted such a decision to be made (which in this instance was the Secretary of State), and that the role of the court was to ensure that such a decision was made in a proper fashion, and whether 'the judgment reached is one reasonably open on the evidence'.[23] In respect of the status of the recommendation he held that: 'It is an important input but it is not determinative.'[24]

Failure to make recommendation and status of extra-statutory recommendations

8.27 A similar point was taken (but from the reverse legal position) in *R (On the Application of H) v (1) Mental Health Review Tribunal (2) Secretary of State for Health*[25] and *R (LH) v (1) MHRT (2) Secretary of State for Health*.[26]

8.28 In the first case, the patient had been detained under MHA 1983, s 3. One issue was whether a transfer to conditions of lesser security was appropriate. The Tribunal declined to make such a recommendation. There were two limbs upon which the claim was mounted. The first was inadequacy of reasons, and the second ECHR, Art 8. There was no suggestion that the transfer to conditions of lesser security was in order to facilitate discharge on a future date (on the facts, it was to enable him to be closer to his family). Thus, the authority confirms the limited function that it must serve. However, it also held that where a recommendation was made which fell outside the statutory jurisdiction, it had no legal effect at all (and therefore, could not be susceptible to judicial review in the first place). However:[27]

> '... it does not follow ... that a failure by an MHRT to give reasons for failing to make a recommendation within the scope of s 72(3) [of MHA 1983] would not be susceptible to judicial review in circumstances where the contentions and material before the Tribunal justified its consideration of such a recommendation.'

In other words, such a decision would have to be made in accordance with the normal principles of adjudication. Adequacy of reasons is considered in Chapter 14. The case also turns upon the absence of the power of the Tribunal to order transfer.

8.29 In the second case, there is no mention of whether the patient was restricted or not. The claim was in part against the Secretary of State and was a similar argument as to the statutory lacuna referred to above. This aspect of the claim failed upon the basis (in part) that the evidence indicated that there was no hospital with conditions of lesser security, and that therefore the Secretary

---

23 Ibid, at [27].

24 Ibid, at [29].

25 [2002] EWHC 1522 (Admin), [2002] MHLR 362; (*EC Ch 12*).

26 [2002] EWHC 170 (Admin), [2002] MHLR 130; (*EC Ch 12*).

27 [2002] EWHC 1522 (Admin); [2002] MHLR 130, at [24]; (*EC Ch 12*).

of State could not be in breach of any duty he might owe to the patient (via of the National Health Service Act 1977, s 3(1)). A similar reasoning led to the failure of the claim as against the Tribunal (ie it had provided the same justification for not making a recommendation, since there was no hospital available as a matter of fact to which the patient could be transferred).

8.30 Aside from the recommendations that the Tribunal can make, there is a power for hospital managers to transfer patients between hospitals (MHA 1973, s 19), but the consent of the Secretary of State is required if the patient is restricted (MHA 1983, s 41). The Secretary of State had the power to transfer patients from high security hospitals to less secure environments (MHA 1983, s 123, removed when it was repealed by way of the Health and Social Care Act 2012, s 42(1)). However, the author of this text had never come across this power being used by the Secretary of State in any event.

LEAVE OF ABSENCE

8.31 MHA 1983, s 17 is set out in Part F. This can be a very flexible regime, and is a useful tool in determining whether a patient is ready for discharge. Some RCs can be slow to arrange such leave, and it is an important function of the Tribunal to consider this aspect of the detention of a patient. Section 17A (which considers the use of community treatment orders) is dealt with in Chapter 10. The Code of Practice deals with this in Chapter 21 (see Part E). The latter suggests that where leave is for more than 7 consecutive days, an order for SCT must first be considered (para 21.9 of the Code). Leave cannot be granted to restricted patients without the agreement of the Secretary of State for the Ministry of Justice. A patient who is on leave is still liable to be detained, and the rules in Part 4 of MHA 1983 apply to treatment. A patient can be recalled at any time from leave by the RC, and the reasons for that recall must be explained to the patient (paras 21.23 and 21.31 of the Code).

RECLASSIFICATION

8.32 Now that the provision for different categories which existed has been repealed, plainly the Tribunal is no longer obliged to consider this issue.

APPLICATIONS BY NEAREST RELATIVES/BARRING ORDERS

8.33 The significance of the effect of the use of barring orders has, however, arisen in respect of Tribunal proceedings themselves. A nearest relative may make an application to discharge a patient (MHA 1983, s 23), the response to which will almost certainly be a 'barring order' by the RC (using MHA 1983, s 25). If the patient is detained under MHA 1983, s 3 (and has been barred) then he or she can still make an application to the Tribunal for discharge (MHA 1983, s 66(1)(g)). MHA 1983, s 25 is set out in Part F.

8.34 In *R (B) v MHRT*[28] the nearest relative had made such an application, and had been barred. The nearest relative then made an application to the Tribunal, which discharged the patient, but deferred in order that a suitable after-care package was in place. Where an application has been made by a nearest relative, the Tribunal is obliged to consider the criteria at MHA 1983, s 72(1)(b)(iii) ('that the patient, if released, would be likely to act in a manner dangerous to other persons or to himself'). It follows that if a Tribunal takes place after a barring order, it is necessary, if the patient is not to be discharged, for the Tribunal to be satisfied that the patient would, if released, be likely to act in a manner dangerous to other persons or to him or herself. It was argued that an order for deferred discharge cannot be made in these circumstances. Burnton J held that:[29]

> '... it is quite clear that s 72(1)(b)(iii) and s 72(3) must be read together. The phrase "if released" in s 72(1)(b)(iii) does not necessarily refer to immediate release, that is to say a release on a future date as envisaged by s 72(3). If a Tribunal ... comes to the conclusion that a patient, if released immediately, would be likely to act in a manner dangerous to other persons, or to himself or herself, but that if proper aftercare arrangements are put in place that will not be the position, in my judgment, it is clear that the Tribunal may make an order for deferred discharge to a date when it is reasonably assured that the appropriate aftercare arrangements will be in place.'

8.35 In *R (MH) v (1) Secretary of State for Health (2) Mental Health Review Tribunal*[30] the same test was applied, except in relation to detention under MHA 1983, s 2. The assertion that s 2 should also include a requirement to consider dangerousness was rejected absolutely and thoroughly.

DISPLACEMENT ORDERS

8.36 The problem of extended detention and the interplay of the different sections was considered in *R (MH) v Secretary for State of Health*.[31] The factual background to the case was that the patient herself lacked capacity. She was detained pursuant to MHA 1983, s 2 (for assessment). Her mother (who was her nearest relative) tried to discharge her from this section. The result was a 'barring order'. The local authority wished to make the patient subject to a guardianship order (MHA 1983, s 7). The mother objected, and consequently an application was made pursuant to MHA 1983, s 29(1). The consequence of such an application was to automatically extend the duration of detention under s 2 (s 29(4)). Since the patient herself lacked capacity, she had not applied to a Tribunal within the 14-day period required by MHA 1983, s 66(2)(a). The solicitors acting for the patient subsequently requested the Secretary of State to make a referral to the Tribunal using powers under MHA 1983, s 67. This was done, and the matter came before a Tribunal. The county

28 [2003] EWHC 815 (Admin), [2003] MHLR 218.
29 Ibid, at [8].
30 [2004] EWHC 56 (Admin), [2004] MHLR 155; (*EC Ch 5*).
31 [2005] UKHL 60, [2005] MHLR 302; (*EC Chs 3, 5, 8 and 14*).

court made an interim order in due course, and the patient was duly admitted into guardianship. Baroness Hale gave the leading judgment, and it rewards close reading. In general, the judgment held that:[32]

> 'It must have been originally contemplated that county courts would deal with these cases very quickly. In practice, however, they may drag on for a considerable time: the county court order in this case was made after a 3 day trial in July 2004 and the application not "finally disposed of" until the Court of Appeal dismissed the mother's appeal in May 2005, more than two years after the proceedings had begun.'

It comments on upon the effect of s 29(4) thus:[33]

> 'Section 29(4) of the 1983 Act places the patient in a most unsatisfactory legal position. She has been compulsorily admitted to hospital under a power which is meant to last for 28 days at most before either lapsing or being replaced with a longer term power for which the procedure and criteria are more stringent.'

The judgment then lists the protection conferred upon the patient in terms of access to a Tribunal where s 29(4) does not operate. However:[34]

> 'None of these rights to a review arises if the patient is kept waiting under section 29(4). Yet the timetable for proceedings under section 29 has nothing to do with the patient's needs and is not under her control … nor does the nearest relative have any right to apply to a Tribunal instead.'

What remains in this interregnum is 'a discretionary power in the Secretary of State for Health at any time to refer the case of any patient who is liable to be detained (whether or not she is actually in hospital) or is subject to guardianship'.[35] The issue before the court was whether or not the situation created by virtue of the effect of s 29(4) was compatible with the rights of the patient under Art 5(4) of the ECHR. The House of Lords held that it was compatible. The court relied upon the existing safeguards that exist (even with patients who lack capacity) in the following terms. First, the managers of the hospital have an obligation to take such steps as are practical to ensure that the patient understands the effect of the provisions of detention, and the right to apply to a Tribunal (MHA 1983, s 132). Secondly, a referral is treated in the same manner as if the patient herself had made an application (r 29). An application can be signed by any person authorised by the patient so to do and even where a patient's capacity is compromised:[36]

> 'The common law presumes that every person has capacity until the contrary is shown and the threshold for capacity is not a demanding one. These principles have recently been confirmed by Parliament in the Mental Capacity Act 2005.'

---

32 [2005] MHLR 302, at 305.
33 Ibid, at 305, [11].
34 Ibid, at 305, [14].
35 Ibid, at 306, [15].
36 Ibid, at 308, [26].

Thirdly, as in this case, the nearest relative stimulated the reference by the Secretary of State. Fourthly, in respect of s 29(4) itself:[37]

> 'The system is obviously *capable* of being operated compatibly … the county court proceedings may produce a swift displacement order, whether interim or final, after which the patient is admitted under section 3 … alternatively, a displacement order may be refused … the problem arises when the county court proceedings drag on and the patient is detained indefinitely without recourse to a Tribunal … Hence there may well come a time when her Article 5(4) rights will be violated unless some means of taking proceedings is available to her.'

The judgment then returns to the facts of the case, in which the Secretary of State did act swiftly to refer the case to a Tribunal. Had this not been the case, then 'judicial review would be swiftly available to oblige her to do so'. Finally the remedy of judicial review/habeas corpus remains available to challenge the lawfulness of the detention of the patient, although this remedy was not felt to be the most appropriate.

RE-DETENTION AFTER DISCHARGE

8.37 There are circumstances in which a patient will be discharged by a Tribunal (either from MHA 1983, s 2 or 3) and a re-detention will follow fairly swiftly upon the heels of such a decision. It is impermissible for either an RC, or any other professional (eg an AMHP), to re-detain a patient on the basis that there is a disagreement with the decision of the Tribunal. The proper course in that event is set out at Chapter 14. The leading case on this is *R (Von B) v (1) East London and the City Mental Health NHS Trust and (2) Snazell.*[38] However, there is also an analysis of similar issues in the Court of Appeal in *R (Ashworth Hospital Authority) v MHRT; R (H) v Ashworth Hospital Authority.*[39] In summary, the principles are that the process of applying for readmission is not lawful where a Tribunal has discharged the section, unless there is a reasonable and bona fide opinion that there is information available that had not been available to the Tribunal, and which 'puts a significantly different complexion on the case as compared with that which was before the Tribunal'.[40] The court gave three examples of such a situation (but stressed that it was neither possible nor desirable to give an exhaustive description of the circumstances that might give rise to such an opinion). The first example is where information comes to light after the hearing that a patient has made an attempt on his or her own life, and the Tribunal has (in the absence of such information) determined as the salient issue in the case that such risk did not exist. The second example is where a patient is stabilised on medication, and assures the Tribunal that he or she will continue to take it, then, either before the actual discharge or shortly afterwards, the patient reneges on this assurance

---

37 Ibid, at 308, [28].

38 [2003] UKHL 58, [2004] MHLR 44; (*EC Ch 5*).

39 [2002] EWCA Civ 923, [2002] MHLR 314, at [49]–[60], commenting on *Von Brandenburg* in the Court of Appeal.

40 Ibid, at [10].

and (based upon medical opinion) it is adjudged that he or she then poses a risk to him or herself and others. The third example is where there is a significant deterioration in the mental health of the patient (either before or shortly after discharge) and this was neither apparent nor anticipated at the hearing. In *R (Care Principles Ltd) v Mental Health Review Tribunal; R (AL) v Care Principles Ltd and Julie Bartlett (ASW)*[41] the above principles were affirmed, in that a social worker may only apply for a readmission if there is new information. This could be as a result of events after the Tribunal, or material that the Tribunal had not taken into account. Also, it was not open to the hospital managers to accept uncritically the admission of a patient where they were aware of a recent discharge by the Tribunal.

APPLICATIONS FOR DISCHARGE (S 3) AND CTO

8.38 In *AA v Cheshire and Wirral Partnership NHS Trust and ZZ*[42] the question arose as to 'whether an application to the First-tier Tribunal made whilst a patient is detained under s.3 of the Mental Health Act 1983 … lapses if the patient is made subject to a community treatment order under s.17A of that Act before the application is heard'.[43] A decision had been made that it did, and that therefore the FTT had no jurisdiction.[44] UTJ Rowland held that:

> 'there are no reasons for giving s.72(1) of the 1983 Act anything other than a literal construction. A tribunal has the power – or, if the conditions of s.72(1)(c) are satisfied, a duty – to direct that a person subject to a community treatment order be discharged notwithstanding that that person made the application to the tribunal while liable to be detained under s.2 or s.3. Therefore, an application to the First-tier Tribunal made by or on behalf of a person detained under s.2 or 3 of the Act does not lapse if a community treatment order is made in respect of that person before the application is determined.'[45]

---

41 [2006] EWHC 3194 (Admin), [2006] MHLR 365.

42 [2009] UKUT 195 (AAC), [2009] MHLR 308.

43 Ibid, at [2].

44 Ibid, at [39].

45 Ibid, at [60].

Chapter 9

DETENTION AND DISCHARGE (MENTAL HEALTH ACT 1983, S 7)

GUARDIANSHIP

Admission criteria

9.1 The criteria for admission appear at MHA 1983, s 7, as set out below. There is a separate route to admission (via MHA 1983, s 37 in respect of Part III patients) which is dealt with at **9.13**. The technical aspects of preparation for a guardianship order are slightly more complex than for either MHA 1983, s 2 or 3, and should provide (to a certain extent) a greater source of information as to the rationale for the use of guardianship.

'7 Application for guardianship

(1) A patient who has attained the age of 16 years may be received into guardianship, for the period allowed by the following provisions of this Act, in pursuance of an application (in this Act referred to as "a guardianship application") made in accordance with this section.

(2) A guardianship application may be made in respect of a patient on the grounds that –

(a) he is suffering from mental disorder, of a nature or degree which warrants his reception into guardianship under this section; and
(b) it is necessary in the interests of the welfare of the patient or for the protection of other persons that the patient should be so received.

(3) A guardianship application shall be founded on the written recommendations in the prescribed form of two registered medical practitioners, including in each case a statement that in the opinion of the practitioner the conditions set out in subsection (2) above are complied with; and each such recommendation shall include –

(a) such particulars as may be prescribed of the grounds for that opinion so far as it relates to the conditions set out in paragraph (a) of that subsection; and
(b) a statement of the reasons for that opinion so far as it relates to the conditions set out in paragraph (b) of that subsection.

(4) A guardianship application shall state the age of the patient or, if his exact age is not known to the applicant, shall state (if it be the fact) that the patient is believed to have attained the age of 16 years.

(5) The person named as guardian in a guardianship application may be either a local social services authority or any other person (including the applicant himself); but a guardianship application in which a person other than a local social services authority is named as guardian shall be of no effect unless it is accepted on behalf of that person by the local social services authority for the area in which he resides, and shall be accompanied by a statement in writing by that person that he is willing to act as guardian.'

'Is suffering from a mental disorder of a nature or degree which warrants his reception into guardianship'

9.2 As is self-evident from the wording of the statute, the criteria are essentially no different from those set out above in respect of s 2 and s 3. However, it must be noted that a reception into guardianship is not tantamount to the deprivation of the liberty of the patient, and (in theory) there is no reason why (for example) the patient could not be able to live in his or her own home. A further difference is that although s 2 and s 3 may be used to detain someone of any age, there must be evidence that the subject of a guardianship application has attained the age of 16.

'In the interests of the welfare of the patient or for the protection of other persons'

9.3 The expression 'the welfare of the patient', although differing from the criteria in either s 2 or s 3, has precisely the same effect in practice, when recommendations are being made for this course of action. However, the concept of 'welfare of the patient' is an important one, and must not be overlooked, for reasons that are set out below.

Purpose and basis for guardianship

9.4 In practice it is the local authority which will most commonly be responsible for making an application for guardianship (via an AMHP), although the nearest relative may also make an application (MHA 1983, s 11(1)). Also, a nearest relative may require an AHMP to take the patient's case into consideration with a view to making an application for guardianship (MHA 1983, s 13(4)). The typical scenario in which circumstances arise where a local authority may intervene are likely to be where an elderly patient has a mental impairment caused by some form of dementia, which in turn may have compromised his or her ability to care for him or herself. This is sometimes coupled with concerns regarding vulnerability to financial and/or emotional abuse. It may be the case that the nearest relative is suspected of being involved in such activities, in which case consideration would have to be given to an application to displace. Very frequently, the aim of the local authority will be to remove the patient from his or her own home, and to place him or her in a setting such as a care home (of some description). However, it is worth noting that this is not the intention of the statute, and a patient may be maintained in his or her own home if sufficient and appropriate support can be provided by the local authority, and other agencies (such as health authorities). Also, this section does not trigger MHA 1983, s 117. However, by way of example, a patient may be subject to s 3 of the Act who could equally as easily have been made subject to MHA 1983, s 7. If made subject to s 3, then the consequences for funding and service provision pursuant to s 117 will follow. If made subject to s 7, then there are no such consequences (or benefits for the patient). Clearly, the use of s 7 may be of considerable importance in terms of the financial impact upon a patient (and a local authority). Financial considerations should not, of course, form any part of the basis for such an application.

9.5 Chapter 26 of the Code of Practice gives very helpful further guidance, as does Chapter 19 of the *Reference Guide*. In essence, there may be situations when the use of MCA 2005, s 5 is more appropriate, particularly where the patient lacks capacity. Distinctions between the two jurisdictions are also considered in the Code of Practice to MCA 2005 (Chapter 13).

EFFECT OF GUARDIANSHIP

9.6 The format in which an application should be made is self-explanatory, although the requirement that such an order is required as being necessary for the welfare of the patient is often given less attention by the AMHP and the recommendations of the medical practitioners than it should be, and there may be an inadequate analysis of the needs of the patient in any subsequent care plan provided for the patient.

9.7 Guardianship lasts for 6 months in the first instance, and can be renewed for a further 6 months and then for periods of one year at a time. The RC must examine the patient within 2 months of the date of expiry of the order. If the RC is satisfied that the order should continue, then he or she must report in writing to the local authority (if it is the local authority that has responsibility). Once this is done, there is an automatic renewal of the order (subject to the appropriate forms having been completed (Parts I and II of Form 31) and unless the local authority decides to discharge the patient). The order itself can be brought to an end in various ways other than via the Tribunal. The most obvious is that the responsible local social services authority can discharge the order. However, the RC also has this power, as does the nearest relative. The consequences for a nearest relative in taking such a course of action is likely to be an application to displace them (see **8.36** et seq). All such discharges have to be in writing. There is no barring order that can be made if the nearest relative does discharge.

9.8 MHA 1983 sets out the explicit statutory effect of an application, and the relevant sections are reproduced in Part F. It is important to note that these are the *only* powers conferred upon a guardian. If a guardian is acting beyond his or her legal powers, then in the absence of any lawful authority for the same, it follows that the guardian will be acting unlawfully. It is possible (*if* there is unlawful activity) that this might amount to sufficient in itself for the Tribunal to reach a conclusion that it was not necessary in the interests of the welfare of the patient to remain subject to guardianship, or to use its residual discretion to discharge the order. The concept of guardianship itself was introduced into UK law with the enactment of the Mental Health Act 1959. Mrs Justice Hale (as she then was) held that 'the ancient power derived from the royal prerogative to make orders relating to the person, as opposed to the property and affairs, of people unable to look after themselves was revoked when the new system of guardianship was introduced by the Mental Health Act 1959, designed to place all the necessary features of the prerogative jurisdiction on a statutory footing'.[1] The ancient power referred to is that of *parens patriae* which had been given statutory recognition in 1339. It is important to note that the emphasis and purpose of the *parens patriae* jurisdiction was (and still is) directed to that of *the person as opposed to property and affairs*. The MHA 1983 imported into it the concept of guardianship in an almost unaltered form from the Mental Health Act 1959. The reader is referred to **5.6–5.7** for further information about the potential implications for the concepts of 'welfare' and where these might overlap with the MCA 2005. There is no power for compulsory treatment via s 7.

9.9 MHA 2007, Sch 3, para 3(5) provides a power to take and convey a person to the required place of residence. However, this power has (in effect) always been implicit, as without such power the provisions of both a condition of residence and for the person to attend at places and at times specified for the purposes of medical treatment, occupation, education or training would be rendered useless. Once so placed, if the subject of the guardianship order leaves without the consent of the guardian, he or she may be taken into custody and returned (MHA 1983, s 18(4)). In addition, the order permits access to the patient. The *Reference Guide* (at para 19.3) summarises the purpose and effect thus:

> 'In most cases it should be possible for patients who need care, but do not need to be in hospital, to receive that care without being subject to the control of guardianship. However, in a minority of cases, the powers which may be exercised by the guardian, and the structure imposed by guardianship, may assist relatives, friends and professionals to help a mentally disordered person manage in the community.'

THE NEAREST RELATIVE AND GUARDIANSHIP

9.10 MHA 1983, s 11(1) means that a nearest relative can make an application for guardianship. There may be circumstances where this method is to be preferred by the family of the patient, or where a local authority is proving dilatory. Similarly, there may be circumstances in which those who are not the nearest relative (but who are members of the family, or others) may have concerns about the probity of the de jure nearest relative achieving the degree of control over the patient which a guardianship order confers. The nearest

---

1 *Cambridgeshire County Council v R (An Adult)* [1995] 1 FLR 50.

relative can also make a request that the authority consider whether a guardianship order is appropriate, and if a decision is made not to make such an application, it shall notify the nearest relative of the reasons for not making such an application in writing (MHA 1983, s 13(4)). If the nearest relative does make an application and the patient is admitted as a result, then the managers of the hospital are in any event obliged to give notice of that fact to the local social services authority for the area in which the patient resided immediately before his or her admission (MHA 1983, s 14). The significance of this section is twofold. First, a local authority will be notified of (and involved in) all guardianship orders to a greater or lesser degree. Secondly, the provision as to the relevant responsible local authority mirrors the provision as to residence (and therefore the case-law upon the point) should there be any argument on this aspect.

9.11 If it is the local authority that makes the application, then the nearest relative still retains considerable power (MHA 1983, s 23(2)(a) and (b)). In any event, there is a prohibition upon such application being made if the nearest relative has notified the social worker who has recommended that such an order should be made that he or she objects to such an application. There is also a requirement that whomsoever makes the application must have seen the patient personally within 14 days ending with the date of the application. The provision for personal examination also applies to the medical recommendations (albeit with different timescales) (MHA 1983, s 12(1)). If the local authority is the guardian, then it is a party to the proceedings (Rule 1(3)(a) defined a party as including the Responsible Authority, and 'responsible authority' is defined (within this context) as 'in relation to a patient subject to guardianship, the responsible local social services authority, as defined by section 34(3) of the Mental Health Act 1983' (ibid). It follows that the guardian would be entitled to legal representation at a Tribunal (Rule 11(1) but subject to Rule 11(2) of the Tribunal Procedure (First-tier Tribunal) (Health, Education and Social Care Chamber) Rules 2008[2]).

9.12 A nearest relative has no statutory right to apply to a Tribunal on behalf of the patient, but if displaced can apply on his or her own behalf once within every 12-month period after a court order replacing him or her (MHA 1983, ss 29(6), 66(1)(h) and (i) and (2)(g)).

ORDERS OF COURT IN RESPECT OF GUARDIANSHIP

9.13 An order of the court (a 'hospital order') can also be made, without an application having been made by anybody. This may be to a local authority, or such other person approved by a local authority. The evidential preconditions are identical to other hospital orders save for MHA 1983, s 37(2)(ii), which specifically refers to guardianship orders as being appropriate where the mental disorder is of a nature or degree which warrants reception into guardianship.

---

2 SI 2008/2699.

An order cannot be made unless the local authority or approved person is willing to receive the patient into guardianship, and the court must be satisfied that such is the case before the order can be made. If the court is considering making an order for guardianship, then it may request the local social services authority for the area in which the offender either resides, or last resided *or any other local social services that appears to the court to be appropriate* to inform the court of those matters set out at MHA 1983, s 39A. In respect of the italicised words above, this provides the court with apparent discretion to override any considerations of ordinary residence in considering which local authority should be responsible for providing information (but not which local authority would be responsible for the order itself).

DISCHARGE FROM GUARDIANSHIP

9.14 It should be noted that once a guardianship application has been accepted, the effect on all other orders made for detention is that they have no effect (apart from a restricted hospital order, hospital and limitation directions or a restricted transfer direction). This includes any order or direction in respect of a patient who is subject to SCT. For a full review of the procedural details of guardianship orders (which is outside the scope of this book) the reader is referred to Chapter 19 of the *Reference Guide*.

9.15 The powers of the Tribunal to discharge are contained in MHA 1983, s 72(4) as follows:

> '(4) Where application is made to the appropriate tribunal by or in respect of a patient who is subject to guardianship under this Act, the tribunal may in any case direct that the patient be discharged, and shall so direct if it is satisfied –
>
> (a) that he is not then suffering from mental disorder; or
> (b) that it is not necessary in the interests of the welfare of the patient, or for the protection of other persons, that the patient should remain under such guardianship.'

9.16 Thus, the Tribunal will be required to determine (a) whether or not it is satisfied that the patient is suffering from a mental disorder; (b) whether it is or is not satisfied that it is in the interests of the welfare of the patient or for the protection of other persons that the patient should remain under guardianship; and (c) that it either is, or is not, appropriate to discharge the patient under its discretionary powers. The law in respect of each of these has already been set out at Chapters 7 and 8. The pro forma used by the Tribunal is 'Form 7. The wording is as follows:

> 'The tribunal is/is not satisfied that the patient is suffering from a mental disorder;
>
> The tribunal is/is not satisfied that it is necessary in the interests of the welfare of the patient, or for the protection of other persons, that the patient should remain under Guardianship;

The tribunal does/does not consider that it is appropriate to discharge the patient under its discretionary powers.'

In addition to the concept of 'welfare' which has been referred to above, there is no reference to the mental disorder having to be of a nature or degree. Consequently, on a strict legal interpretation, none of the law in respect of these terms is relevant. This could be where the broader concept of 'welfare' comes into play, and the *necessity* of the patient remaining under guardianship.

BURDEN OF PROOF

9.17 However, there are two other anomalies which exist in respect of discharge from reception into guardianship. The first is that the phrasing of MHA 1983, s 72(4) places the burden of proof upon the patient to demonstrate that the order is *not* required. It is a moot point as to whether in practice this makes any difference to the way in which a Tribunal is conducted. It is likely that alternative sources of evidence will be of greater assistance in guardianship cases. In particular, the evidence of specialists in psychogeriatrics, and from social workers with similar experience, may be helpful in persuading a Tribunal that a less restrictive regime would be more appropriate.

ADJOURNMENTS AND AFTER-CARE

9.18 The second is that in addition to there being no requirement for MHA 1983, s 117 after-care (see Chapters 11 and 12) there is no power to defer the discharge of the order. However, there is an obligation (under the Code – see paras 26.19–26.21) to develop a care plan, and it would be a legitimate use of the case management powers to adjourn the application in order for more information about details of such a care plan to be made available. It is also very important for practitioners to be aware of the other statutory obligations that a local authority may well owe towards a patient who has been received into guardianship (eg National Health Service and Community Care Act 1990, s 47). These are also considered below, and a separate care plan may have been produced as a result of such obligations (or, at the very least, an assessment for the purposes of establishing what the needs of the patient are).

Chapter 10

DETENTION AND DISCHARGE (SUPERVISED COMMUNITY TREATMENT ORDERS: MENTAL HEALTH ACT 1983, S 17A–17G)

TRANSITIONAL PROVISIONS

10.1 Every detention under MHA 1983, s 25A disappeared between 3 November 2008 and 3 May 2009 and MHA 1983, ss 25A–25J have been repealed. The primary focus for community treatment is now to be found at MHA 1983, ss 17A–17G. There are several useful sources of information in respect of the operation of this new aspect of MHA 1983, which include the Code of Practice, the *Reference Guide* and *Supervised Community Treatment: A Guide for Practitioners*[1] (the *Guide for Practitioners*).

SUPERVISED COMMUNITY TREATMENT ORDERS

Eligibility for detention

10.2 A patient may become subject to SCT if they are already detained by virtue of MHA 1983, s 3, 37, 51, 45A, 47 or 48. A patient may *not* become subject to a CTO if detained by virtue of MHA 1983, s 2 or 4 or if they are restricted patients. The expressions 'mental disorder' and 'appropriate medical treatment' have the same meaning as used in s 3 (see Chapter 8).

Criteria for CTO

10.3 These are contained at MHA 1983, s 17A(5)(a)–(e). This is set out below in part. The remaining sections are to be found in Part F.

> '17A Community treatment orders
>
> ...
>
> (5) The relevant criteria are –
>
> (a) the patient is suffering from mental disorder of a nature or degree which makes it appropriate for him to receive medical treatment;

---

1 National Institute for Mental Health in England, October 2008.

(b) it is necessary for his health or safety or for the protection of other persons that he should receive such treatment;
(c) subject to his being liable to be recalled as mentioned in paragraph (d) below, such treatment can be provided without his continuing to be detained in a hospital;
(d) it is necessary that the responsible clinician should be able to exercise the power under section 17E(1) below to recall the patient to hospital; and
(e) appropriate medical treatment is available for him.

(6) In determining whether the criterion in subsection (5)(d) above is met, the responsible clinician shall, in particular, consider, having regard to the patient's history of mental disorder and any other relevant factors, what risk there would be of a deterioration of the patient's condition if he were not detained in a hospital (as a result, for example, of his refusing or neglecting to receive the medical treatment he requires for his mental disorder).'

10.4 The criteria at (a), (b) and (e) are not substantially different from the criteria considered and discussed elsewhere. The matters referred to at s 17A(6) plainly refer to the problem associated with a failure to take medication. The criteria at (c) and (d) are fact specific, and again will be considered as against the biography of the patient. For example, as the *Guide for Practitioners* observes, 'SCT is particularly designed to support people with a history of non-compliance, relapse and re-admission cycles' (Section A, p 10). Both an RC and an AMHP must agree that a CTO is appropriate.

Conditions to CTO

10.5 First, there are two conditions that *must* be contained in the CTO. These are that (a) the patient must make him or herself available to the RC in order to decide whether the CTO should be extended and (b) that the patient must do the same in respect of any decision made regarding certain types of treatment. The types of treatment to which this applies are set out in Chapter 17 of the *Reference Guide*.

10.6 Other conditions that can be included (all of which require the agreement of the AMHP) *must* be for the purposes of ensuring that (a) the patient receives treatment; (b) preventing the risk of harm to the patient's own health and safety; or (c) protecting others. The Code (at para 25.33) suggests that such conditions should be kept to a minimum. They should also seek to restrict the patient's liberty as little as possible. The Code further suggests examples such as where and when treatment is to be given, where the patient is to live and avoidance of known risk factors or high-risk situations relevant to the mental disorder. It is easy to envisage conditions being applied which amount to a form of injunctive relief, or a prohibition on activities which would seriously compromise the liberty of the patient. There is no power directly to enforce these conditions, but the RC can take a breach of conditions into account if considering a recall to hospital. Even a breach of the mandatory conditions does not automatically trigger a recall, although it is highly likely to do so, but still should only be used as a last resort (cf Code, at para 25.49). Breach of other conditions where the criteria for recall are not met must not lead to the recall of the patient. The conditions may be varied, without the agreement of an AMHP, by the RC.

Duration of CTO

10.7 A CTO expires at the end of 6 months starting on the day it is made (in most circumstances). It can be extended for a further 6 months, and after that for one year at a time. The criteria for extension are the same as those for the initial order. It can be brought to an end prior to those periods in a variety of ways, the only relevant mechanism for the purposes of this text being via a Tribunal.

Effect of a CTO

10.8 A CTO discharges the patient from detention in a hospital (subject to the power of recall). Whilst it is in force, the original basis for detention still exists, but the authority upon which the hospital managers can rely to authorise such detention is suspended. This authority (in effect) lies dormant and there is no requirement for it to be extended. It is awoken only if the CTO ends by way of revocation by the RC following the exercise of his or her power to recall. At this point, the original authority comes into operation (MHA 1983, s 17F(4)) and the patient will be treated as if their first detention was on the day of revocation. The managers must then refer the case to the Tribunal as soon as possible. In certain circumstances (where an ACUS started just before 3 November 2008) some patients may move seamlessly from one regime to the next without having been detained again in the interim. If this is the case, and the CTO is revoked, the Reference Guide suggests that 'they are treated as if they were liable to be detained on the basis of an application under section 3, regardless of the actual authority under which they were detained before becoming ACUS patients'.

10.9 However, when a CTO comes to an end other than by way of revocation as a result of a recall, so does any underlying authority for detention. This means that when a Tribunal discharges a CTO, the discharge is absolute. There will be no power to recall or detain. A Tribunal *can* discharge a CTO in respect of a patient who has been recalled to hospital via s 17E (if the statutory criteria are not met, of course). Patients may be recalled when in hospital (eg to receive treatment). The technical procedure for recall varies slightly in Wales. The consequence of recall permits detention in hospital for 72 hours only, unless the CTO is revoked (and then the original authority is revived).

Medical treatment

10.10 Apart from a variety of exceptions, (contained in Chapter 17 of the *Reference Guide*) it is not permissible to administer medical treatment to a patient who is subject to a CTO without the patient's consent, unless he or she has been recalled to hospital.

Discharge from CTO

10.11 The criteria for discharge mirror the criteria for detention. The relevant sections of MHA 1983, s 72 are set out below.

> '(1) …
>
> (c) the tribunal shall direct the discharge of a community patient if it is not satisfied –
>   (i) that he is then suffering from mental disorder or mental disorder of a nature or degree which makes it appropriate for him to receive medical treatment; or
>   (ii) that it is necessary for his health or safety or for the protection of other persons that he should receive such treatment; or
>   (iii) that it is necessary that the responsible clinician should be able to exercise the power under section 17E(1) above to recall the patient to hospital; or
>   (iv) that appropriate medical treatment is available for him; or
>   (v) in the case of an application by virtue of paragraph (g) of section 66(1) above, that the patient, if discharged, would be likely to act in a manner dangerous to other persons or to himself.
>
> (1A) In determining whether the criterion in subsection (1)(c)(iii) above is met, the tribunal shall, in particular, consider, having regard to the patient's history of mental disorder and any other relevant factors, what risk there would be of a deterioration of the patient's condition if he were to continue not to be detained in a hospital (as a result, for example, of his refusing or neglecting to receive the medical treatment he requires for his mental disorder).
>
> …
>
> (3) A tribunal may under subsection (1) above direct the discharge of a patient on a future date specified in the direction; and where a tribunal does not direct the discharge of a patient under that subsection the tribunal may –
>
> (a) with a view to facilitating his discharge on a future date, recommend that he be granted leave of absence or transferred to another hospital or into guardianship; and
> (b) further consider his case in the event of any such recommendation not being complied with.
>
> (3A) Subsection (1) above does not require a tribunal to direct the discharge of a patient just because it thinks it might be appropriate for the patient to be discharged (subject to the possibility of recall) under a community treatment order; and a tribunal –
>
> (a) may recommend that the responsible clinician consider whether to make a community treatment order; and
> (b) may (but need not) further consider the patient's case if the responsible clinician does not make an order.'

10.12 Form 5 is used by the Tribunal. The statutory framework is rendered thus:

> '(a) The Tribunal is/is not satisfied that the patient is suffering from mental disorder or from mental disorder of a nature or degree which makes it appropriate for the patient to receive medical treatment.
>
> (b) The Tribunal is/is not satisfied that it is necessary for the patient's health or safety or for the protection of other persons that the patient should receive such treatment.
>
> (c) The Tribunal is/is not satisfied that it is necessary that the responsible clinician should be able to exercise the power under s 17E(1) to recall the patient to hospital.
>
> (d) The Tribunal is/is not satisfied that appropriate medical treatment is available to him/her.
>
> (e) The Tribunal considers that it is/is not appropriate to discharge the patient from the Order under its discretionary powers.'

The 'appropriate treatment' test has been considered at **8.17**. In respect of the case-law that has developed on other matters arising from CTOs, these have all been considered hitherto (in Part B). However, for the sake of convenience, that case-law is summarised below, and cross-referenced to the relevant earlier parts of the text.

Developments in case-law (2008–2013)

Change in status

10.13 There have been three cases specifically concerned with this aspect of CTOs. The first significant case was *AA v Cheshire v Wirral Partnership NHS Trust*[2] (and referred to at **3.24** and **8.38**). For the purposes of this chapter, the key question was whether an application made by a patient (detained either by way of s 2 or s 3) lapsed if the patient was then placed on a CTO. The simple answer was held to be as follows '... an application made by or on behalf of a person detained under s.2 or 3 of the 1983 Act does not lapse if a community treatment order is made in respect of that person before the application is determined'.[3] Consequently, the FTT *does* have jurisdiction to consider a s 2 or s 3 application. This is of more than academic significance, as if either s 2 or s 3 were to be discharged, then the legal substratum for a CTO also disappears, which would leave the patient without any restrictions on his or her liberty. A similar issue was also considered in *KF, MO and FF v Birmingham & Solihull Mental Health NHS Foundation Trust*[4] (and referred to at **3.26**). In this instance, the UKUT considered the effect of placement on a CTO of a s3

---

2 [2009] UKUT 195 (AAC), [2009] MHLR 308.

3 Ibid, at [60].

4 [2010] UKUT 185 (AAC), [2010] MHLR 201.

patient whose case had been *referred* to the FTT. The distinction on the facts from *AA* was merely between a *referral* and an *application* and whether this could lead to a different conclusion. It was held that it made no difference, and that the outcome as held in *AA* was still correct. It was held that 'we agree that there is no reason to hold that references to the First-tier Tribunal should be treated any differently to applications in this regard … This analysis is consistent with the approach taken by Collins J in *R v South Thames Mental Health Tribunal ex P M*, namely that the patient's right to make an application to a tribunal is founded on the fact of admission, rather than the detention'.[5] The Court concluded that 'any movement from s 2 to s 3 or to community patient status does not affect the continuing validity of an extant and undetermined application or reference to the First-tier Tribunal. The application of reference still falls to be determined in accordance with the patient's status at the time of the actual hearing and subject to the relevant criteria under s.72(1)(a)–(c)'.[6] Finally, in *PS v Camden and Islington NHS Foundation Trust*,[7] UTJ Jacobs considered the issue 'does a reference made when a patient's community treatment order is revoked lapse when a new community treatment order is made?'.[8] The legislative structure of a CTO is set out in the judgment, and it is a helpful and succinct analysis of the law:

> 'Community treatment orders are governed by ss.17A to 17G of the Act. They are available only for patients who have been detained for treatment under s.3 of that Act (s.17A(1) and (2)). While an order is in force, the authority to detain the patient under s.3 is suspended (s.17D(1) and (2)(a)). The responsible clinician may recall the patient to hospital without revoking the order (s.17E), as was initially done in this case, and may revoke the order (s.17F(4)) as was later done. If an order is not revoked after a patient has been recalled for 72 hours, the patient must be released (s.17F(6)). Once an order is revoked, the position is as if the patient had never been discharged from hospital under the order (s.17G(2)) and the Act applies accordingly (s.17G(3)). The managers of the hospital responsible for the patient's detention must refer the patient's case to the First-tier Tribunal 'as soon as possible after the order is revoked (s.68(7)). Once a reference has been made, the tribunal's duties are the same as on any other application or reference (s.72).'[9]

UTJ Jacobs applied the reasoning in the two previous decisions to reach the same conclusion in answering the question posed. He held that:

> 'Whether or not the reference has lapsed depends upon the nature of the reference, which is a matter of statutory interpretation … the subject matter of a reference under s.68(7) is not related to the circumstances that trigger it. The reference is not a review of the patient's recall to hospital or the revocation of the community treatment order. Those events triggered the duty on the hospital managers to make the reference. However, the tribunal had to exercise its powers under s.72. The reference is not limited to a review of the events that led to the patient being recalled and her community treatment order revoked. So, the subject matter of the

---

5 Ibid, at [54], [55].
6 Ibid, at [59].
7 [2011] UKUT 143 (AAC), [2011] MHLR 159.
8 Ibid, at [1].
9 Ibid, at [9].

reference does not cease to exist when a new order is made. The statutory conditions of detention must be satisfied whether the patient is detained in hospital or released under a new order. Accordingly, the subject matter of the reference survives and in line with *AA* and *KF* it requires the tribunal to consider the position as at the date of the hearing ... Section 68(1) sets out some events that trigger a reference. One of those triggers applies to a community patient, who is by definition the subject of a community treatment order. Section 68(3)(c) provides that they do not apply if "a reference has been made in respect of the patient under subsection (7) below". The obvious purpose of that provision is to prevent duplication of proceedings. It envisages that a s.68(7) reference would otherwise be triggered for the same patient who has since become a community patient. Such provision would not be necessary if the s.68(7) reference had lapsed by the making of the later order.'[10]

Deferred discharges

10.14 There have been other cases where (in essence) the CTO has been incidental to the issue to be determined. For example, the case of *MP v Mersey Care NHS Trust*[11] has already been considered at **8.21**. The FTT itself (ie the original Tribunal) did not fall into error in this case (which had decided to defer discharge from detention) but the subsequent two decisions by an STJ did amount to errors of law. The issue arose out of a decision by the RC to implement a CTO *after* the decision by the FTT to discharge, but *before* the discharge became effective. The decision to defer was to enable after-care provisions to be put into place (which is a conventional and fairly straightforward, and appropriate decision to make). The Tribunal which heard the case decided that the original basis for detention no longer existed, and that the patient should be discharged.

10.15 A similar issue was considered in *CNWL NHS Foundation Trust v H-JH*[12] (and set out and considered at **3.33**). In this instance, the patient had the status of being on a community treatment order. The Tribunal ordered a deferred discharge from the CTO. The CTO remained in force until the date of the deferred discharge. Up until then, the patient remained liable for recall, and to have medication changed. If a detention was required after discharge, that was another matter, but the possibility is permitted (if there is a change in circumstances) and by reference to *R (Von Brandenburg) v East London and the City Mental Health Trust*.[13]

Recommendations

10.16 In *RN v Curo Care*[14] the issue of recommendations was considered in relation to a CTO (see **3.32**) to the effect that as with any other decision of the Tribunal, reasons were required for that decision.

---

10 Ibid, at [15]–[17].

11 [2011] UKUT 107 (AAC), [2011] MHLR 146.

12 [2012] UKUT (AAC), [2012] MHLR 305.

13 [2004] 2 AC 280.

14 [2011] UKUT 263 (AAC), [2011] MHLR 337.

Treatment and consent

10.17 In *KL v Somerset Partnership NHS Foundation Trust*[15] (referred to at **6.13**) the issue of **treatment** as a part of the criteria was considered, albeit that this related to a s 3 case, and where extensive s 17 leave had been used. However, the extent to which treatment could include outpatient reviews in an NHS facility is still helpful.

10.18 The role of the Tribunal in addressing matters of consent (in the context of a CTO) is referred to at **3.7** and **6.22** and *SH v Cornwall Partnership NHS*.[16] The specific question was whether treatment given without the consent of the patient amounted to it being both available and appropriate. The answer is that issues of consent fall outside the remit of the Tribunal, which is confined to the statutory criteria. Whether the patient consents or not does not govern whether it is either available or appropriate.

Application by nearest relative

10.19 The role of the 'nearest relative' is considered in Chapter 13. There is a right of a nearest relative to apply to discharge from a community treatment order. The basis of the decision is set out in Form 6, and is identical to that set out at **10.12**, save that in addition, the Tribunal has to consider the following:

> 'The tribunal is/is not satisfied that the patient, if discharged, would be likely to act in a manner dangerous to themselves or to other persons.'

This criteria is common to all applications by a nearest relative, and is considered in Chapter 13.

AFTER-CARE

10.20 This is explored in more detail in Chapters 11 and 12, but it will be clear from the above that a care plan of some detail will be necessary for the successful working of a CTO. A patient who is subject to such an order comes within the scope of MHA 1983, s 117. The *Guide for Practitioners* provides a care plan checklist (at Section D, pp 26–28) which includes the following subject areas for inclusion: supervision and monitoring; accommodation; occupational therapy services; day time activities; personal support, counselling and advocacy; carer and family support; welfare rights and other financial assistance; cultural requirements; crisis support; physical health needs. The Practice Direction (Health, Education and Social Care Chamber Mental Health Cases) is reproduced in Part F. Section H specifically deals with the contents of the reports required for SCT.

---

15 [2011] UKUT 233 (AAC), [2011] MHLR 194.
16 [2012] UKUT 290 (AAC), [2012] MHLR 383.

GUARDIANSHIP/CTO/SECTION 17 LEAVE

10.21 The Code of Practice (Chapter 28) provides a very useful list of specific situations in which one or the other of the above may be the preferred option. This is reproduced in Part E.

CONSIDERATION OF CTO WITHOUT A HEARING

10.22 Reference to the alteration to r 35 in respect of CTOs has already been made at **3.50**. Not only does the alteration permit a single judge to strike out an application where the Tribunal has no jurisdiction, but where a reference has been made, then if the patient is over 18, and the Tribunal can be satisfied that that patient has confirmed in writing that he does not wish to attend a hearing, and the Tribunal is satisfied that he has the requisite capacity to make such a decision, or his legal representative has stated that he neither wishes to attend or be represented, then the matter can be considered on the papers (ie administratively). It is not clear whether the RC (who would be making an assessment of capacity on this issue) could be considered either sufficiently independent to make such an assessment, or whether the RC has the sufficient knowledge and expertise to apply the principles for making such an assessment (cf Mental Capacity Act 2005, ss 1–3). The amendment to the Rules does not include those who are under the age of 18.

Chapter 11

THE RESPONSIBLE CLINICIAN: ROLE, FUNCTION AND POWERS (INCLUDING AFTER-CARE)

ROLE, FUNCTION AND POWERS

Professional status

11.1 From the perspective of a Tribunal, the RC is likely to be the most significant witness. Formerly the title 'Responsible Medical Officer' (RMO) was used, and it was a consultant psychiatrist who would have overall responsibility for the patient (although in evidential terms more often than not the actual RMO would not be present for the Tribunal). The term RC encompasses the possibility that this role may no longer be limited to a psychiatrist. The *Reference Guide* makes this clear:[1]

> 'The responsible clinician is the approved clinician who has overall responsibility for the patient's case. Having overall responsibility for the patient's case does not mean that the responsible clinician must personally supervise all the medical treatment provided to the person under the Act. Indeed, because they may come from a number of different professions, responsible clinicians may not be professionally qualified to take personal responsibility for each particular type of treatment their patient is receiving.'

The Code adds:[2]

> 'For example, where psychological therapies are central to the patient's treatment, it may be appropriate for a professional with particular expertise in this area to act as a responsible clinician.'

The National Institute for Mental Health in England (NIMHE) adds:[3]

> 'The RC will have overall responsibility for the patient, and will be an approved clinician (AC), but might belong to any of the following professions: nurse, psychiatrist, psychologist, occupational therapist or social worker.'

NIMHE has also provided guidance in *Mental Health Act 2007 – New Roles* (October 2008) which sets out the new regime very clearly. It specifies that

---

1 At para 12.37, p 94.

2 Chapter 14, para 14.5, reproduced in Part E.

3 *Guide for Practitioners*, at p 13.

approved clinicians (ACs) may be 'registered medical practitioners; chartered psychologists; first level nurses whose field of practice is mental health or learning disabilities; registered occupational therapists; registered social workers'.[4] MHA 1983, s 145(1) defines an AC as 'a person approved by the appropriate national authority to act as an approved clinician'. NIMHE comments that:[5]

> 'An RC is the AC who has been given overall responsibility for a patient's case. ACs who are allocated as RCs will undertake the majority of functions previously performed by Responsible Medical Officers, whose role will end on the implementation date of the Act.'

Evidence to Tribunal

11.2 The best individual to give evidence in respect of the medical aspects of the criteria to the Tribunal should be the RC (although very often the most illuminating evidence will be obtained from nursing staff, who are more likely to have had daily contact with the patient, and also will be able to provide very up-to-date information). The content of the report must comply with the Practice Direction (Health Education and Social Care Chamber Mental Health Cases (reproduced in Part F). The legal status of Practice Directions (PDs) is as follows. A PD is defined as a direction given under TCEA 2007, s 23 (r 1(3)[6]). It is the Senior President of the Chamber who has the power to make such directions. Such power has been conferred upon the Senior President by Parliament. Consequently, the force of the PD is (in effect) that of a primary statute, and the responsible authority (RA) may not depart from it contents. The most recent PD is dated 6 April 2012, and is considered in greater detail in Chapter 16.

11.3 As indicated above, the Tribunal may not actually have the RC present, and the PD permits latitude in any event ('Unless it is not reasonably practicable, the report must be written or countersigned by the patient's responsible clinician'). The report must also be 'up to date'. The latter phrase is a moveable feast, and will vary according to the section relevant to the patient. Plainly, with MHA 1983, s 2 the report will be fresh, whereas with MHA 1983, s 7 (by way of example only) it may be older. As a rule of thumb, if a report from any professional is more than a couple of weeks old, it is likely to require considerable updating at the Tribunal. This is due to the fluctuating nature of the mental state of a patient, and the rapidity with which recovery can be made or, in the alternative, the rapidity with which a relapse can occur. It is sometimes the case that reports are provided which are months out of date. These will only be of use in terms of historical information about the patient. In practice, however, whether the RC is present or not, the Tribunal will wish to know if there have been any developments since the report was written, and

---

4 At p 19.

5 Ibid, at p 17.

6 References to rules in this chapter are to the Tribunal Procedure (First-tier Tribunal) (Health, Education and Social Care Chamber) Rules 2008, SI 2008/2699.

also how much professional contact the RC has had with the patient (either since admission or in the past if there have been previous admissions). Sometimes an RC will have an historical knowledge of the patient, and will have seen the patient for a reasonable amount of time since admission. However, at the other end of the spectrum (and according to the circumstances), the RC may have very little direct knowledge. This is why the evidence of nurses and other professionals can be of such great significance.

11.4 Although not explicitly stated in the PD, it is helpful to a Tribunal (and to the patient) if the RC sets out (specifically) the basis upon which the relevant statutory criteria are made out, with concrete examples. It is surprisingly rare for this simple (yet effective) approach to be taken in reports.

Role within Tribunal

11.5 It is very common for the RC to give evidence first (although this may depend upon a number of factors). Also, although it is preferable for the RC to remain until the conclusion of the hearing, it is also common (and acceptable) for the RC to leave after having given evidence, but to remain contactable within the confines of the hospital until the Tribunal has made its decision.

11.6 The significance of the RC in contributing to the evidence in respect of after-care is considered at **11.10–11.16** and in respect of after-care generally at **11.17–11.28**.

11.7 If the RC is not available and it is apparent that the professional delegated to give evidence by the RA is lacking in the necessary knowledge, then it is very likely that an adjournment will follow. In *R v MHRT ex parte Manns*[7] the concern expressed was not whether the actual RC was present, but that whichever professional was present had thought 'of the relevant issues independently and carefully when giving his view in support of [the RC] … [and] … were up-to-date' (para 28).

11.8 There is only one authority which addresses the issue of the ability of the RC actually to participate in the hearing in any other capacity than that of a professional witness, *R (Mersey Care NHS Trust) v Mental Health Review Tribunal*.[8] It would appear that the RC attempted to interrupt cross-examination by the solicitor for the patient. The Tribunal itself was constituted by a very experienced and competent panel. The complaint (in part) on behalf of the RC was that he was not permitted to cross-examine a social worker (who was also giving evidence on behalf of the RA), nor to sum up the case on behalf of the RA. It was held that if an RC did wish to represent the RA (rather than appear as a witness) then notice of this intention should be given at the outset. It is the view of the author of this text that if such a course of

---

7 [1999] MHLR 101; (*EC Ch 14*).

8 [2003] EWHC 1182 (Admin), [2003] MHLR 354.

action is to be taken, then suitable legal representation should be obtained, rather than an RC acting as an advocate in his or her own case.

11.9 In terms of procedure, the following avenues are open in the above circumstances. First, the RA is a party to proceedings (r 1(3)). Secondly, as a party it may appoint a representative (whether legal or not) (r 11(1)), and if it does so, then it must (in effect) notify the Tribunal (r 11(2)). It is a matter for the Tribunal as to how the proceedings themselves are conducted, but r 15 (specifically) enables it to give directions as to the manner in which submissions and evidence may be heard.

Role prior to Tribunal (after-care)

11.10 The RC has the power to discharge a non-restricted patient (MHA 1983, s 23) in any event. Thus, if a Tribunal occurs, it will be self-evident that the RC has considered the case afresh, and decided that this is not the appropriate way forward. This part of the text considers the significance of the role of the RC in respect of after-care, and the law in relation to after-care generally.

11.11 The statutory origin of a requirement for after-care is MHA 1983, s 117 (see below) and it applies to all patients who have been the subject of the following sections of MHA 1983: s 3; s 37; s 45A; s 47; and s 48. It includes patients who have been given leave (MHA 1983, s 17) or who have moved onto CTOs (MHA 1983, s 17A et seq). The position in relation to those who have been subject to s 2 and s 7 is that they do not come within the terms of s 117. However, this does not mean that they may not come within the ambit of other statutory obligations in certain circumstances. This is considered separately at **11.28**.

11.12 The Code emphasises that it is the RC who 'should ensure that the patient's needs for after-care have been fully assessed, discussed with the patient and addressed in their care plan'.[9] It also adds that 'the planning of after-care needs to start as soon as the patient is admitted to hospital'.[10] Paragraph 27.13 sets out 16 separate areas which might require consideration for assessment for after-care. An additional summary of the law can be found at Chapter 24 of the *Reference Guide*.

> 'Mental Health Act 1983, s 117 "After-Care"
>
> (1) This section applies to persons who are detained under section 3 above, or admitted to hospital in pursuance of a hospital order made under section 37 above, or transferred to a hospital in pursuance of a hospital direction made under section 45A above or a transfer direction made under section 47 or 48 above, and then cease to be detained and (whether or not immediately after so ceasing) leave hospital.

---

9 Chapter 27, para 27.10.

10 Chapter 27, para 27.8.

(2) It shall be the duty of the Primary Care Trust or Local Health Board and of the local social services authority to provide, in co-operation with relevant voluntary agencies, after-care services for any person to whom this section applies until such time as the Primary Care Trust or Local Health Board and the local social services authority are satisfied that the person concerned is no longer in need of such services ; but they shall not be so satisfied in the case of a community patient while he remains such a patient.

(2A) *repealed*

(2B) Section 32 above shall apply for the purposes of this section as it applies for the purposes of Part II of this Act.

(3) In this section "the Primary Care Trust or Local Health Board" means the Primary Care Trust or Local Health Board, and 'the local social services authority' means the local social services authority, for the area in which the person concerned is resident or to which he is sent on discharge by the hospital in which he was detained.'

Persons who are detained

11.13 MHA 1983, s 117 applies only to those who have been detained under the relevant sections of MHA 1983, and the provision of *after-care services* to them. The guidance issued by the Secretary of State in the form of the Code of Practice is reproduced in Part E.

After-care and care plans

11.14 There is no definition of what constitutes after-care services, but the key elements of any plan should include an assessment of the health and social care needs of the patient, a plan which reflects those needs, the appointment of a key worker to keep in touch with the patient and regular reviews and/or changes to the plan. It is clear that there is an obligation to provide appropriate accommodation (including ordinary housing, if appropriate (cf *R (on the application of Lambeth LBC)* at **11.15**)). What the nature of that accommodation might be will plainly depend upon each case, and all aspects of the care plan need to be clearly set out.

11.15 Whilst the duty to provide such services generally does not apply until a patient has actually been discharged,[11] it is important to note a plan should be considered prior to discharge. This is more than a mere technicality when the necessity for detention is being considered not by the detaining authority, but by the Tribunal or a hospital managers meeting. As indicated above, it is the responsibility of the RC to ensure that the needs of the patient for health and social care are fully assessed, and that the care plan addresses those needs. This plan should be devised in consultation with all the professionals concerned with the patient. A list of 13 separate professionals is provided at para 27.12 of

---

11 *R (on the application of B) v Camden LBC and Camden and Islington Mental Health and Social Care Trust* [2005] EWHC 1366 (Admin), [2005] MHLR 258; (*EC Ch 2*).

the Code. In order for health authorities and local authority social services to fulfil their obligations, they must take 'reasonable steps to identify appropriate after-care facilities for a patient before his or her actual discharge from hospital'.[12] The extent of such preparation does not need to be any greater than discussion, and a failure to do no more than this within the context of a contested hearing before a Tribunal does not mean that there is a breach of any duty arising from MHA 1983, s 117.[13] Within the context of the Tribunal, it is appropriate for there to be an adjournment if the care plan is undeveloped or lacking in specificity, so that the burden is passed to the health authority and local authority to prepare and implement the plan within a reasonable period of time.[14] It is not a breach of the duty imposed by s 117 where a health authority is unable to provide psychiatric supervision of a patient simply because no doctor could be found to provide such supervision.[15] However, a local authority was found to be in breach of its duty of care when it failed to provide alternative accommodation to a patient who was subject to possession proceedings based upon her behaviour (which was in turn caused by her mental illness).[16] Should a health authority fail to comply with its obligations pursuant to s 117(2), it will not found an action for breach of statutory care, nor an action for breach of a common law duty of care. The appropriate remedy would be via the default powers of the Secretary of State,[17] or by way of judicial review.[18]

Persons who cease to be detained

11.16 Where a patient is the subject of a provisional decision of the Tribunal to conditionally discharge him or her, then the patient is still detained under MHA 1983, and the actual duty to provide him or her with after-care services does not arise.[19] The same case held that a local authority was not under a parallel obligation (in such circumstances) under the National Health Service and Community Care Act 1990, s 47.

Health care needs v social care needs

11.17 Once a patient ceases to be detained, then the duty of service provision arises. Again, guidance as to the purpose and extent of such provision is included in Chapter 27 of the Code. There may be an argument as between the

---

12 *R v Ealing District Health Authority ex parte Fox* [1993] 3 All ER 170.

13 *R (on the application of W) v Doncaster MBC* [2004] EWCA Civ 378, [2004] MHLR 201; (*EC Chs 2 and 6*).

14 *R v Mental Health Review Tribunal, Torfaen County BC and Gwent Health Authority ex parte Hall* [1999] 2 CCLR 383, [1999] MHLR 49; (*EC Ch 2*).

15 *R (on the application of K) v Camden and Islington Health Authority* [2001] EWCA Civ 240, [2001] 4 CCLR 170, [2001] MHLR 24; (*EC Ch 2*).

16 *R (on the application of B) v Lambeth LBC* [2006] EWHC 2362 (Admin), [2007] 10 CCLR 84.

17 MHA 1983, s 124.

18 *Clunis (Christopher) by his next friend Christopher Prince v Camden and Islington Health Authority* [1998] 1 CCLR 215.

19 *R (B) v (1) Camden LBC (2) Camden & Islington Health and Social Care Trust* [2005] EWHC 1366 (Admin); [2005] MHLR 258; (*EC Ch 2*).

providers of health services and social services as to who should provide which, and what constitutes a health need, and what constitutes a social care need. In *Special Report NHS Funding for Long-Term Care – investigation into Complaints Nos E208/99-00*[20] an attempt was made to identify criteria which might differentiate the two areas of responsibility. Within the report the guidance of the Department of Health (in 1995) was cited as suggesting that the NHS should be responsible:

> '… where the complexity or intensity of their medical, nursing or other care or the need for frequent not easily predictable interventions requires the regular … supervision of a consultant, specialist nurse or other NHS member of the multidisciplinary team … who routinely use specialist health care equipment or treatments which require the supervision of specialist NHS staff … who have a rapidly degenerating or unstable condition which means that they will require specialist medical or nursing supervision [and] the in patient care might be provided in a hospital or nursing home.'

This dispute is likely to be particularly acute where the condition from which the patient suffers is chronic and deteriorating, such as with forms of dementia. In the First-tier of decisions that culminated in *R v Manchester CC ex parte Stennett and two other actions*,[21] Sullivan J observed:[22]

> 'There may be cases where in due course there will be no need for after care services for the persons mental condition, but he or she will still need social services provision for other needs eg physical disability. Such cases will have to be examined individually on their facts … in such a case as Mrs W, where the illness is dementia, it is difficult to see how such a situation could arise in practice.'

The Law Commission (Law Com No 326) *Adult Social Care* (May 2011) has also made observations on this area of law, together with recommendations. These are as follows:

> 'Section 117 is a joint duty placed on health and social service authorities but it is not clear from the statute whether the duty falls jointly and severally on health and social services authorities, in that both are responsible for the entire duty, or whether the duty falls primarily on health authorities to provide **healthcare after-care** and social services to provide **social care after-care**. In the consultation paper we argued that it is unlikely that a court would regard a health body as being accountable for the provision of **social care after-care**, or a social services authority as being accountable for **healthcare after-care.** However, the position is not clear in law and this could cause difficulties. We therefore proposed that section 117 should be amended to state expressly that the duty falls on health authorities to provide **healthcare after-care** and on social services authorities to provide **social care after-care** … Since consultation, the Health and Social Care Bill 2011 has been introduced to Parliament and, amongst other matters, proposes

---

20 Health Service Ombudsman, February 2003.

21 [2002] 5 CCLR 500; [2002] UKHL 34.

22 *R v Richmond LBC ex parte Watson; R v Redcar and Cleveland BC ex parte Armstrong; R v Manchester CC ex parte Stennett; R v Harrow LBC ex parte Cobham* [1999] 2 CCLR 402, at 416J–416K.

to amend section 117 to make clear that in England the commissioning consortia are responsible only for the health (rather than social) services provided under section 117. It also proposes to split the termination of the section 117 duty. The section 117 duty on the consortia in question continues until it (rather than it and the local social services authority together) is satisfied that the after-care is no longer required. Likewise, the duty on the local social services authority continues until it (rather than it and the consortia) is satisfied that after-care is no longer required. These amendments would apply in England, but not in Wales.'
(Chapter 11, paras 11.93 and 11.94)

Extent of duties of local authority

11.18 The extent of the duties of a local authority were also considered at length in *Investigation into Complaint Nos 97/0177 and 97/0755 against the former Clwyd CC and Conwy County BC*.[23] The complaint arose out of circumstances where the services to be provided ceased. There was no consultation and the complainant was required to pay for her own residential accommodation. The complaint was upheld and the Local Government Ombudsman concluded that the local authority had a duty to provide after-care until it was satisfied (as a social services authority and irrespective of the views of the district *health* authority) that the complainant was no longer in need of such services. It was also concluded that the local authority had taken into account irrelevant matters in deciding not to provide after-care services, and had failed to consult at all with the complainant herself. It was also concluded that she had been wrongly charged for the services and that there had been further maladministration by virtue of a decision to register a caution upon her property. It stressed the need to conform to the Code. In *R (on the application of Michael Mwanza) v Greenwich LBC and Bromley LBC*[24] it was held that the services which needed to be referred to were 'restricting its scope to services necessary to meet a need arising from a mental disorder'.[25] In other words, if the service was not primarily causally connected with the disorder, then it falls outside the range of duties under s 117.

Relevant local authority

11.19 The relevant after-care bodies responsible for arranging the after-care, and providing it are those in which the patient was resident at the time that he was detained.[26] Those bodies will continue to be responsible until the patient is no longer in need of such services. A decision that such after-care services are not required should be formally recorded together with the reasons for discontinuance and include the same generic professionals as those who were involved in formulating the original plan. The decision in *Hall* was subject to Department of Health Guidance[27] which alerted local authorities to their

---

23 [1998] 1 CCLR 546.
24 [2010] EWHC 1462 (Admin), [2010] MHLR 226.
25 Ibid, at [68].
26 *R v Mental Health Review Tribunal ex parte Hall* [1999] 3 All ER 131, [1999] MHLR 63; (*EC Chs 1, 2 and 6*).
27 Circular No LAC (2000) 3; HSC 2000/3, 10 February 2000.

obligations including that if the patient had no ordinary residence when admitted, the authorities where the patient must reside as a part of his or her conditional discharge have responsibility for providing after-care.

Continuation of after-care services

11.20 Whilst it is clear that after-care services do not have to continue indefinitely, a retrospective decision by a responsible body that MHA 1983, s 117 no longer applied to the services provided (which might result in charging for the services under the National Assistance Act 1948) is likely to be susceptible to remedy by way of judicial review. The caution that should be used in considering the use of retrospective assessments was the basis of complaints made to the Local Government Ombudsman, which resulted in the *Special Report (The Local Government Ombudsmen) Advice and Guidance on the funding of AfterCare under Section 117 of the Mental Health Act 1983*. This was published in July 2003. It stated:[28]

> 'We see very little scope under the Code for a retrospective decision to be made – in default of consultation, review and a formal decision communicated to all relevant parties – that a patient's status as a recipient of Section 117 after-care can have changed. It is difficult to see how such a retrospective assessment could operate fairly. If a decision had been taken at the right time and upon the right assumptions, that is that aftercare had to be provided free until the authorities no longer considered it to be required, a patient or relative could, in the event of a decision to discontinue section 117 after-care, then decide whether or not to have the aftercare at his own expense. If the effect of a retrospective decision is to disentitle a patient or relative to reimbursement of charges until after the date of the notional decision to discontinue (on the grounds of the absence of need) this would deprive those persons of the opportunity, which they otherwise would have had, not to continue with the aftercare and not to incur the cost of its provision. For all those reasons a retrospective assessment may be found to be maladministration, subject always to the facts of each case.'

Ordinary residence

11.21 The issue of residence is touched upon in *Hall* (above) and is a much traversed route in respect of virtually all areas of litigation where a subsidiary branch of the state (that is to say local authority or health care provider) may be obliged to pay for services to a citizen who comes within its geographic jurisdiction. It tends to involve somewhat sterile and technical arguments designed to ensure that someone else pays, or so that an authority is able to manage its budget effectively in a predictable fashion. Almost all such arguments are likely to be determined upon the facts peculiar to the case, but a number of principles have emerged within the context of community care law generally which it is worth considering at this point. With specific reference to MHA 1983, s 117(3) it is enough that the service user is 'resident' in the area of the local authority.

---

[28] At Section D, para 4.

11.22 With specific reference to s 117(3) it is enough that the service user is 'resident' in the area of the local authority. However, the issue has been re-visited both in terms of case law, and guidance provided by the Department of Health. In *R on the application of Hertfordshire County Council v London Borough of Hammersmith and Fulham and JM (interested party)*[29] [2011] EWCA Civ 77, [2011] 14 CCLR 224 the provisions of s 21 of the National Assistance Act 1948 (NAA 1948) and s 117 of the MHA 1983 were considered. In effect, the problem that both local authorities wished to have considered arose out of what happened when (as a matter of fact) it could be argued that the provisions of s 117 were incompatible with the provisions of s 21. JM himself had lived within the jurisdiction of the London Borough of Hammersmith and Fulham for a considerable number of years. His accommodation had been provided by way of s 21 of the NAA 1948. However, he was then placed in another local authority area, following an assessment of his mental health. Ultimately, he was detained under s 3 of the MHA 1983 (after having been detained under s 2), and reached a stage where he was able to be discharged. By this time, the original local authority had decided that it would not be responsible for his after care. Section 24(1) provides that responsibility lies with the local authority in whose area the person was ordinarily resident and s 24(5) deems that the ordinary residence of that person remains where the person had been provided with accommodation under Part 3 of the NAA 1948. Thus, it was argued that the London Borough of Hammersmith and Fulham should have responsibility for him, as he was (on that construction) ordinarily resident in their area. However, s 117 has no such 'deeming' provision, and simply places the responsibility for after-care services on the local authority for the area in which the person was resident, or to which the hospital sent him on discharge. The court held that (following *Stennett*) s 117 was a free-standing provision which was not dependent on the NAA 1948. It also held that the period of detention could not be considered as pointing towards residence. The provisions of s 117(3) in respect of residence could not be taken to mean that period when the person was compulsorily detained by virtue of s 2 or 3 of the MHA 1983. The consequence of the decision, therefore, tends to re-affirm the existing law as to the separate status of s 117 in terms of the issue of residence. The Law Commission, in *Adult Social Care*[30] also commented on this case, and this same issue. It was concerned about the distinction between the NAA and the MHA on this point and commented:

> 'In our view, extending the concept of ordinary residence to apply to section 117 after-care services would bring greater clarity and consistency. As pointed out in the consultation paper, it would also ensure that section 117 service users would benefit from having access to the dispute resolution procedures that apply to ordinary residence … the decision in *R (M) v London Borough of Hammersmith and Fulham* raises serious questions about the efficacy of current policy …

---

29 [2011] EWCA Civ 77, [2011] 14 CCLR 224.

30 Law Com 326 (May 2011).

> Recommendation 63: The concept of ordinary residence should be extended to apply to after-care services provided under section 117 of the Mental Health Act 1983. The issue of how ordinary residence rules should be applied to section 117 should be taken forward as a general review of the policy of the Government and Welsh Assembly Government.'
> (Chapter 11, paras 11.89, 11.90, 11.92)

Consequently, it would appear that the tide is changing, and that in the reasonably near future, the law on ordinary residence will be harmonious as between different areas of law. The Law Commission have also recommended that s 117 should no longer be a free-standing duty.[31] Nevertheless, for the present, disputes between local authorities, based upon the interpretation of what is meant by the term 'ordinary residence' continue. In *R (on the application of Sunderland City Council) v South Tyneside Council*[32] two councils were in dispute over the residence of a patient, and as to which one of them was responsible for the provision of s 117 after-care services. As ever, the facts on each case will be of particular relevance, but in this instance the patient had been informally admitted to hospital in one area, prior to moving to the other area, where she was subsequently detained under s 3 of the MHA. The judgment sets out a clear and helpful summary of the law in this area (concluding, inter alia, that an unavoidable voluntary stay in a hospital did not make the patient's case to be a resident in the area where she had been previously resident). The attention of the court did not seem to have been drawn to the new Guidance (referred to below).

11.23 Guidance to local authorities on the issue of ordinary residence had existed for many years in the form of Circular No LAC (93) 7 (issued in March 1993 by the Department of Health). This was long overdue for a replacement, which was duly provided in April 2010, and then in an amended form on 15 April 2011. It is called '*Ordinary Residence: Guidance on the identification of the ordinary residence of people in need of community care services, England*'. The basic principles remain those as set out in *Shah v Barnet LBC*.[33] It means:

> '[343G–343H] a man's abode in a particular place or country which he has adopted *voluntarily and for settled purposes as part of the regular order of his life for the time being, whether of long or short duration*.' (emphasis added)

It is an essential component of this test that the move must be voluntary, thus excluding prisoners, those detained under the MHA 1983, and (surely) those who lack capacity to make a decision as to where they reside or wish to reside. Similarly, ordinary residence can be lost in a day, if there is a move with an intention not to return. Where new ordinary residence is concerned, this may also be acquired with some rapidity, but as with all these cases, the determination is likely to be fact specific. The substance of the authorities is that it takes longer to acquire a new ordinary residence than it does to lose it,

---

31 Ibid, Recommendation 66, Chapter 11, para 11.111.

32 [2011] EWHC 2355 (Admin).

33 [1983] 2 AC 309.

but there is no time limit which exists. Another complexity which may arise is where a service user has dual residence (or a primary and secondary residence). The relevant parts of the Guidance are set out at appropriate parts of this book where they relate to the law to which it refers, apart from the general test, which is produced below. The Guidance itself is a much more substantial document than its predecessor, and it is to be hoped that it may be amended with greater regularity (ie on an annual basis).

'ORDINARY RESIDENCE

Meaning of ordinary residence

18. Responsibility for the provision of accommodation and community care services under sections 21 and 29 of the 1948 Act is largely based on the concept of "ordinary residence". However, there is no definition of "ordinary residence" in the 1948 Act. Therefore, the term should be given its ordinary and natural meaning subject to any interpretation by the courts.

19. In many cases, establishing a person's ordinary residence is a straightforward matter. However, this is not always the case and where uncertainties arise, local authorities should consider each case on its own merits, taking relevant court judgments and Secretary of State determinations (see paragraphs 67–71) into account. The concept of ordinary residence involves questions of fact and degree. Factors such as time, intention and continuity (each of which may be given different weight according to the context) have to be taken into account.

20. The courts have considered the meaning of "ordinary residence" and the leading case is that of *Shah v London Borough of Barnet* (1983) 1 All ER 226. In this case, Lord Scarman stated that:

> "unless … it can be shown that the statutory framework or the legal context in which the words are used requires a different meaning I unhesitatingly subscribe to the view that 'ordinarily resident' refers to a man's abode in a particular place or country which he has adopted voluntarily and for settled purposes as part of the regular order of his life for the time being, whether of short or long duration."

21. Local authorities should always have regard to this case when determining the ordinary residence of people who have capacity to make their own decisions about where they wish to live (for people who lack capacity to make decisions about their accommodation, one of the alternative tests set out in *R v Waltham Forest London Borough Council, ex Parte Vale* (1985) *The Times* 25 February (the "Vale case", see paragraphs 27–34 below) should be used). The starting presumption is that a person does have such capacity unless it is shown otherwise.

22. Particular attention should be paid to Lord Scarman's statement that ordinary residence is the place a person has voluntarily adopted for a settled purpose for **short or long duration**. Ordinary residence can be acquired as soon as a person moves to an area if their move is voluntary and for settled purposes, irrespective of whether they own, or have an interest in, a property in another local authority area. **There is no minimum period in which a person has to be living in a particular**

place for them to be considered ordinarily resident there, because it depends on the nature and quality of the connection with the new place.

Temporary absences

23. Local authorities should have regard to the case of *Levene v Inland Revenue Commissioners* (1928) AC 217. This case is particularly useful for considering the effect of temporary absences on a person's ordinary residence or when assessing whether someone has lost their ordinary residence in a particular place. In this case, Viscount Cave stated:

> "It [ordinary residence] connotes residence in a place with some degree of continuity and apart from accidental or temporary absences."

24. Viscount Cave went on to give examples of temporary absence as being absences for the purpose of business or pleasure, such as a fisherman going away to sea. This issue of absence and its effect on ordinary residence was further considered in the case of *Fox v Stirk* 1970 2 QB 463. In this case, Lord Denning MR set out the principle that temporary absence does not deprive a person of their ordinary residence:

> "If he happens to be away for a holiday or away for the weekend or in hospital, he does not lose his residence on that account."

Urgent need during temporary absences

25. The fact that a person may be temporarily away from the local authority in which they are ordinarily resident does not preclude them from receiving accommodation and/or services from another local authority if they become in urgent need (see paragraphs 47–50).

More than one place of residence

26. Although in general terms it would be possible for a person to have more than one ordinary residence (for example, a person who divides their time equally between two homes), this is not possible for the purposes of the 1948 Act. The purpose of the ordinary residence test in the 1948 Act is to determine which single local authority has responsibility for meeting a person's eligible social care needs, and this purpose would be defeated if a person could have more than one ordinary residence. If a person appears genuinely to divide their time equally between two homes, it would be necessary to establish (from all of the circumstances) to which of the two homes the person has the stronger link. Where this is the case, it would be the responsibility of the local authority in which the person is ordinarily resident to provide or arrange services during the time the person is temporarily away at their second home. Scenario 4 on page 53 provides further guidance on how the ordinary residence provisions operate where a person lives in two different local authority areas.

...

After-care services under section 117 of the Mental Health Act 1983

182. Under section 117 of the Mental Health Act 1983 ("the 1983 Act"), local authorities, together with Primary Care Trusts (PCTs), have a duty to provide after-care services to people who have been detained in hospital under certain provisions of the 1983 Act. This duty stands by itself and is not a "gateway" to the provision of services under other legislation, such as the 1948 Act.

183. Section 117 of the 1983 Act sets out that the duty falls on the authorities "for the area in which the person concerned is resident or to which the person is sent on discharge by the hospital in which the person was detained."

184. The term "resident" in the 1983 Act is not the same as "ordinarily resident" in the 1948 Act and therefore the deeming provisions (and other rules about ordinary residence explained in this guidance) do not apply.

185. Guidance on section 117 of the 1983 Act was given in the case of *R v Mental Health Review Tribunal Ex p. Hall* (1999) 4 All ER 883. This case made clear that responsibility for the provision of such services falls to the local authority and PCT for the area in which the person was resident before being detained in hospital, even if the person does not return to that area on discharge. If no such residence can be established, the duty falls on the authority where the person is to go on discharge from hospital.

186. For example, the Local Government Ombudsman's investigation into the provision of after-care services by Medway Council (06/B/12248) and Wigan Metropolitan Borough Council (06/B12247) considered the case of a man who was detained under section 3 of the 1983 Act and required section 117 after-care following his discharge. He was discharged to a specialist care facility in Wigan Metropolitan Borough Council but had been living in Medway Council prior to his detention. Both local authorities refused to meet the cost of providing after-care services. The Ombudsman considered the man to have been 'resident' in Medway prior to his compulsory admission and therefore found Medway Council to be responsible for the provision of the after-care services.

187. The term "resident" is not defined in the 1983 Act, and so, like "ordinarily resident" the term should be given its ordinary and natural meaning subject to any interpretation by the courts.

188. The duty to provide after-care services remains with the same local authority even if the person subsequently becomes resident in another area, unless they are then re-detained under a provision of the 1983 Act which again entitles them to section 117 after-care. In this situation, the rules would need to be applied again from scratch, to decide which authority has responsibility for any after-care once the person leaves hospital again.

189. Disputes arising in connection with section 117 of the 1983 Act cannot be referred to the Secretary of State or Welsh Ministers for determination under section 32(3) of the 1948 Act. If such a dispute could not be resolved locally, it would be necessary to involve the courts.'

It is to be noted that despite the anomalies identified by the Law Commission, the current state of the law in respect of s 117 and ordinary residence is summarised at para 188. In particular, where the patient is discharged and then re-detained, the law is re-applied 'from scratch'. There is no formal method of resolving a dispute between local authorities apart from recourse to the Courts (which would be by way of judicial review). The scenario set out at para 189 is clearly based upon *R (on the application of Hertfordshire County Council) v London Borough of Hammersmith and Fulham and JM (interested party).*[34]

Definition of services

11.24 In *Clunis v Camden & Islington Health Authority*[35] after-care services were held to include residential facilities. If there was any doubt as to this, it has been confirmed in *R v Manchester CC ex parte Stennett.*[36] Also, in *Clunis* it was held that after-care services would include social work support, support in helping the discharged patient with problems of employment, accommodation or family relationships, provision of domiciliary services and the use of day centres and residential facilities. In *R v North East Devon Health Authority ex parte Coughlan*[37] it was held that nursing care could in appropriate cases be provided by a local authority as a social service. As observed above, the Code contains no guidance as to what actually constitutes an after-care service, and neither did its predecessors. However, the old Codes did include a statement that purpose of after-care is 'to enable a patient to return to his home or accommodation other than a hospital or nursing home, and to minimise the chances of him needing any future in-patient hospital care'. The revised version (effective from April 1999) states 'a central purpose of all treatment and care is to equip patients to cope with life outside hospital and function there without danger to themselves or other people'.

Charges for services

11.25 None of those responsible for providing services are able to charge for them.[38] The series of decisions that ended in this judgment started on 28 July 1999. It also gave rise to Circular No LAC (2000) 3: HSC 2000/3 in which local authorities were alerted to the consequences of the developments and instructed them to cease charging for s 117 after-care services immediately (even prior to the decision in the House of Lords). Thus, no local authority can have any justification for having levied charges since (at least) 10 February 2000. The Circular also states that:

> 'The Court did not address the question of charging for non-residential services provided under Section 117 but there is a strong implication that the responsible authorities may not charge for such services.'

---

34 [2011] EWCA Civ 77, [2011] 14 CCLR 224.

35 [1998] QB 978.

36 [2002] UKHL 34.

37 [2000] 2 WLR 622, [1999] 2 CCLR 285.

38 *R v Manchester CC ex parte Stennett* [2002] UKHL 34, [2002] 5 CCLR 500.

It also advises that:

> 'Social Services and Health Authorities should jointly agree local policies on providing section 117 after-care. Policies should set out clearly the criteria for deciding which services fall under section 117 and which authorities should finance them. The section 117 after-care plan should indicate which services are provided as a part of the plan.'

In Circular LAC (2002) 15 (14 October 2002) this advice was confirmed in the light of the judgment in the House of Lords, and added that 'those authorities that have made such a charge will no doubt wish to address that issue and will each wish to seek their own advice as to the extent of their liability'.

Deficient information/defective reports

11.26 The significance of full information being made available when a Tribunal is intending to discharge a patient has been considered at **8.21**, and in particular the significance of *R (On the Application of Ashworth Hospital Authority) v MHRT; R (On the Application of H) v Ashworth Hospital Authority*.[39]

11.27 In addition to the PD in respect of reports by RCs the Rules provide a plethora of powers to obtain additional information. Rule 5(3)(d) allows the Tribunal to require either a party (or another person) to provide either documents or other information. If there is a failure to comply with either the Rules, a PD or a direction, then r 7 sets out the potential consequences for such default. Rule 10 includes a power (in limited circumstances) to make an order for costs (pursuant to MHA 2007, s 29(4)). Rule 15 contains all the specific provisions as to directions for obtaining evidence. Rule 16 contains the provisions for compelling witnesses to give evidence, the issuing of a summons to give evidence and the consequences of a failure so to do (which might amount to a contempt of court, which in turn can lead to a fine or a term of imprisonment up to a maximum period of 2 years).

Independent evidence

11.28 The evidence presented to a Tribunal may include evidence from professionals who have no links with the RA or the local social services authority (LSSA). Prior to the new Rules coming into force, a patient was under no obligation to seek directions in respect of independent evidence, nor to disclose adverse reports. In practice, it usually became obvious that independent evidence had been obtained (and if it was not then disclosed, it became equally obvious that it was not favourable to the patient). For a discussion as to this, please refer to Chapter 3. Alternative sources of evidence may be vital to a patient if the RA or LSSA is to be challenged. Rule 15(1)(c) considers the issue for the first time, and in particular whether or not joint

---

39 [2001] EWHC 901 (Admin), [2002] MHLR 13, [2002] EWCA Civ 923, [2002] MHLR 314; (*EC Chs 1, 2, 9 and 15*).

instruction of an expert or experts is appropriate. This has been a feature of nearly all other areas of litigation for many years. It does not contain any specific prohibition on the continuation of the practice of obtaining expert reports without reference to the Tribunal, but it would be wise to assume that this is the proper convention, particularly in the context of r 2(1) and (4)(a) and (b).

Care planning and local authority obligations

11.29 For those who fall outside MHA 1983, s 117, there may be an obligation to assess patients pursuant to the National Health Service and Community Care Act 1990, s 47. Community care services are defined within the Act as including 'services which a local authority may provide or arrange to be provided under … section 117 of the Mental Health Act 1983'. However, this does not exclude a local authority considering the community care needs of a patient who falls *outside* the range of s 117. If this proposition is correct, then it may be that the full panoply of community care legislation is available to (for example) those who have been received into guardianship, and consequently to the remedies available resulting from that legislation. A full consideration of that area of law is outside the scope of this book.[40]

Nursing reports

11.30 Although not part of the role of the RC, it is worth considering the function of the evidence of nursing staff at this point in the text. Over recent years it has become more and more common for nursing staff to formalise their observations of the patient in the form of a report. It is less common for the author of the report to attend the Tribunal (usually due to the shift patterns worked by nurses). The quality of the reports, and of the evidence given, is variable. However, good evidence from a member of nursing staff can give a very clear and more up-to-date picture of the progress or otherwise of a patient than that provided by the RC. For example, it is often the case that a nurse will have either been involved in previous admissions (and thus can compare and contrast the state of the patient over months or sometimes years), or will have been involved with the patient on a daily basis since a recent admission.

11.31 For the first time, the significance of evidence from nurses has been recognised by virtue of having been incorporated into a PD (reproduced in Part F). It also states that a copy of the nursing plan must be attached to the report. The information that it must contain only relates to those who are in-patients, and each of the areas that should be covered are at Section 11(a)–(e) of the PD. Practitioners will be aware that it has long been the habit of medical members to include into their pre-hearing investigations an examination of nursing notes and discussions with nursing staff, in any event.

---

40 See Jonathan Butler *Community Care Law and Local Authority Handbook* (Jordan Publishing, 2012).

Chapter 12

APPROVED MENTAL HEALTH PROFESSIONAL: ROLE, FUNCTION AND POWERS

DEFINITION AND RELEVANCE TO THE TRIBUNAL

12.1 The title approved mental health professional (AMHP) replaces the approved social worker (ASW). Generally, AMHPs will be acting on behalf of a local social services authority (LSSA). The *Reference Guide* considers the approval and function of all practitioners at Chapter 32. AMHPs have (broadly) the same functions as an ASW did, and for the purposes of this text, these cover the following categories and functions: applications for admission for assessment and/or treatment; power to convey to hospital; applications for admission for treatment; applications for guardianship; provision of social circumstances report if application made for admission by a nearest relative; confirmation that CTO/SCT are appropriate and agreeing conditions to be attached with RC; approving extension and revocation of CTOs. LSSAs have the power to approve people to act as AMHPs if 'they are satisfied that they have appropriate competence in dealing with people who are suffering from mental disorder'.[1] An AMHP may be a social worker; a registered first level nurse whose field of practice is mental health nursing or learning disabilities nursing; a registered occupational therapist; or a chartered psychologist who holds a relevant practising certificate issued by the BPS. A doctor cannot be an AMHP (MHA 1983, s 114(2)). The process of approval is outside the scope of this book. There are transitional provisions for those who became ASWs immediately prior to 3 November 2008. NIMHE also provides further information on the same topic.[2] The specific statutory provisions are contained in MHA 1983, ss 114 and 114A (reproduced in Part F). It should be noted that the AMHP has additional responsibilities within the context of a CTO (see Chapter 10).

ROLE WITHIN THE TRIBUNAL

12.2 The AMHP may be responsible for providing the social circumstances report (SCR), but this is not necessarily the case. In the PD there are various different requirements as to the contents of a report. The following sections are often the most important, and equally often the information that is missing:

---

1 *Reference Guide*, at para 32.8.

2 *Mental Health Act 2007 – New Roles*, Section 1.

home and family circumstances; the view of anyone playing a substantial part in caring for the patient (other than a professional); the opportunities for work and housing; community support and its effectiveness; the financial circumstances of the patient. In addition, it has been suggested that the SCR should contain the following specific information: ward (or community address if a CTO); legal status (eg married or single); MHA status; date of detention; referral or application date; address at time of admission; SCR author; professional relationship with patient; RC; care coordinator; RA/PCT; index offence; introduction (with MHA history in chronological order); sources of information relied upon; events leading up to current admission; s 17 leave; brief psychiatric history; age, gender, race, culture, class, disability; safeguarding issues (eg protection of children or vulnerable adults); conclusion and recommendations; dating and signing of report. The mandatory requirements for the content of a report are set out in the Practice Direction (Part F). For a fuller account of this topic, see *Social Circumstances Reports for Mental Health Tribunals*[3] and *Responsible Authority Statements for Mental Health Tribunals*.[4]

12.3 Accommodation is the commonest source of difficulties, and authors of SCRs will often seek to avoid responsibility for failing to provide specific information as to dates by which accommodation will be available. This is sometimes done by attempting to persuade the Tribunal that it is beyond their specific professional capacity to give any assurances. This is almost certainly incorrect, but in any event it belies the fact that a Tribunal may decide to discharge a patient, and any delay in such discharge cannot be justified for very long – certainly not as a result of a failure by the LSSA to ensure that information is available.

12.4 A further problem may occur where the patient is detained in a hospital some distance from his or her 'home' local authority. Frequently, in these circumstances, there is no attendance by the author of the SCR at all. This leads to delay, and can be remedied by the Tribunal using the same rules referred to at **11.27**.

12.5 As with the RC, there may be a need for an independent report in respect of the social circumstances of the patient.

AFTER-CARE

12.6 It follows from the comments above that one of the most significant aspects of the contents of the report will relate to after-care provision. This information is vital. The law (and practice) is set out at **11.14–11.24**, and the observations about recourse to statutes other than MHA 1983 also hold good.

---

3 Legal Action Group, June 2010, pp 30–32, Curran, Golightley and Fennell.

4 Legal Action Group, March 2012, pp 15–19, Curran, Fennell and Burrows.

Chapter 13

NEAREST RELATIVE: ROLE, FUNCTION AND POWERS

13.1 A consideration of the role of the nearest relative is only given to that which is directly relevant to the Tribunal. Chapter 8 of the Code provides some information in respect of the nearest relative, but principally in respect of applications to the county court, not the Tribunal. It is reproduced in Part E. The role of the nearest relative is extensive and significant, and has been the subject of some modification where there has been a conflict between the powers of the nearest relative and the rights of the patient. However, the involvement of the nearest relative remains great, and its main implications are as follows:

(1) the nearest relative may make an application for admission for assessment (MHA 1983, s 2);

(2) the nearest relative may make an application for an emergency admission for assessment (MHA 1983, s 4);

(3) the nearest relative may make an application for admission for treatment (MHA 1983, s 3) or for guardianship (MHA 1983, ss 7 and 11(1));

(4) an AHMP is required to consult with the nearest relative prior to making an application for admission pursuant to either MHA 1983, s 3 or s 7 unless the social worker considers that such consultation is not reasonably practicable or would involve unreasonable delay (MHA 1983, s 11(4));

(5) the managers of a hospital in which the patient is detained are obliged to inform the nearest relative on the right to apply to a Tribunal, the right to be discharged, the right to receive and send correspondence and the right to consent to or refuse treatment (MHA 1983, s 132(4));

(6) the nearest relative can order the discharge of a patient who is detained under either s. 2, s 3 or s 7 (MHA 1983, s 23(3));

(7) the nearest relative can arrange an assessment of the patient by a doctor, who can in turn require the production of the medical records of the patient (MHA 1983, s 24);

(8) where a patient is to be discharged (other than by the nearest relative), the detaining authority is required to notify the nearest relative of this. The

only way in which the patient can prevent this is by making a request that no such information is supplied (MHA 1983, s 133(2));

(9) the nearest relative can make an application for a local authority to consider making an application into hospital or guardianship (MHA 1983, s 13(4));

(10) the nearest relative may make an application to a Tribunal for the discharge of the patient (MHA 1983, s 66(1)(g) and (h));

(11) the nearest relative is entitled to be informed of the progress of the Tribunal, to be represented at the hearing and to take such part in proceedings as the Tribunal thinks proper;

(12) the nearest relative is entitled to receive a copy of the decision and the reasons for the decision;

(13) if the nearest relative has made an application for discharge he or she can appoint a doctor to examine the patient and the records in respect of detention (MHA 1983, s 76(1));

(14) if the nearest relative is the applicant, he or she can attend the hearing, call witnesses and cross-examine witnesses;

(15) if the nearest relative is an applicant, he or she should receive all the documentation that the Tribunal receives; and

(16) the nearest relative can seek to discharge a CTO (s 23).

For a full consideration of the role of the nearest relative, the reader is directed to *The Nearest Relative Handbook*.[1]

13.2 Using the current rules, the nearest relative will be a party to proceedings only if (a) he or she has made an application or (b) he or she has been either an applicant or a respondent in previous proceedings (r 1(3)[2]). The Tribunal may in any event add the nearest relative as a party (respondent) if appropriate (r 9(2)). Rule 33(c) (Notice of proceedings to Interested Persons) provides that unless a patient with capacity to do otherwise has requested otherwise, and where any other person than the applicant is named as the nearest relative, notice of proceedings must be sent to that person. If the nearest relative is notified then they may attend and take part in a hearing to the extent that the Tribunal considers proper, or provide written submissions to the Tribunal. In practice, nearest relatives have attended Tribunals, albeit often as impromptu witnesses. The full text of MHA 1983, s 26 is set out in Part F.

---

1 D Hewitt (2009, 2nd edn, Jessica Kingsley Publishers).

2 References to rules in this chapter are to the Tribunal Procedure (First-tier Tribunal) (Health, Education and Social Care Chamber) Rules 2008, SI 2008/2699.

NEAREST RELATIVE AND RESTRICTED PATIENTS

13.3 If a patient has been remanded to hospital under MHA 1983, s 35, 36 or 38, there is no nearest relative for the purposes of MHA 1983.

13.4 A patient who is a restricted patient, or who is conditionally discharged, does not have a nearest relative.

13.5 However, if a patient is the subject of an unrestricted hospital order, or hospital directions to which limitation directions do not apply, or unrestricted transfer directions, then the patient will have a nearest relative.

13.6 In the case of *R (on the application of H) v Mental Health Review Tribunal*[3] it was held (in the context of a restricted patient and the old rules) that a nearest relative was not an automatic party to proceedings. This would also be the case under the new Rules (cf the definition of 'party' at r 1(3)). However, as with the old rules, a direction may be given adding a person as a party if necessary (r 9(2)). A similar method is to be found in r 33(e) (notice of proceedings to interested persons).

NEAREST RELATIVES AND APPLICATIONS TO DISCHARGE

13.7 There are some additional complexities that may arise when a nearest relative is an applicant (although these are relatively rare in themselves, and are said to number approximately 75 per annum). The same criteria for considering discharge exist as for any other applicant, unless a 'barring' order is in place. The additional criteria is contained in s 72(1)(b)(iii) which reads 'in the case of an application by virtue of paragraph (g) of section 66(1) above, that the patient, if released, would be likely to act in a manner dangerous to other persons or himself'. Section 66(1)(g) concerns applications to Tribunals, and reads as follows 'a report furnished under section 25 above in respect of a patient who is detained for treatment or a community patient'. Section 25 itself places restrictions on the power of the nearest relative to order a discharge of a patient liable to be detained in hospital, which enables the RC to respond to such an application by the nearest relative to provide a report stating that the patient, if discharged '*would be likely to act in a manner dangerous to other persons or himself*' (s 25 (1)). The consequence of such a report is that any order for discharge by the nearest relative shall be of no effect, and the nearest relative is prevented from making any further applications within 6 months of the date of the report. A further consequence (albeit not of direct relevance to the Tribunal) may well be an application to the county court for displacement of the nearest relative entirely (by way of s 29 of the Mental Health Act 1983). There is no equivalent procedure for guardianship. Once a report has been made, this does prevent the nearest relative from making an application, but it

---

3 [2000] MHLR 203; (*EC Chs 11 and 14*).

does add the additional criteria which have been referred to above. The relevant pro-formas used by the Tribunal in such circumstances are Form 4 (Section 3); Form 6 (CTO) and Form 10.

13.8 There is little specific authority as to what is meant by the term 'likely to act in a manner dangerous to other persons or himself'. The Code of Practice states that 'This question focuses on the probability of dangerous acts, such as causing serious physical injury or lasting psychological harm, not merely on the patient's general need for safety and others general need for protection' (para 29.21). This tends to suggest a higher threshold on the part of the authors of the Code as having been imported into the statutory criteria.

13.9 There have been two cases which have considered the interaction between the status of nearest relatives, and Tribunals. The first is *DP v Hywel DDA Health Board* [2011] UKUT 381 (AAC).[4] The facts are somewhat unusual, in that a barring report was made by the RC, in respect of a person who was thought to have been the nearest relative. As a matter of law, this individual was *not* the nearest relative. However, the putative nearest relative had made an application (by virtue of s 66(1)(g)) which met with the response that as he was not the nearest relative, the Tribunal had no jurisdiction. Since the effect of the barring report had been accepted as having no force or effect, s 66(1)(g) was of no relevance either, and UTJ Jacobs held that:

> 'The effect of those provisions [s 66(1)(g)] in the circumstances of this case is that the Tribunal only had jurisdiction if the application was made at a time when there was a report under section 25. However, that report had been withdrawn before the application was sent to or received by the Tribunal. Accordingly, the tribunal had no jurisdiction to deal with the application and was right to rule that it was outside its jurisdiction.'[5]

13.10 The second case is *MA v Secretary of State for Health*.[6] In this instance, the patient had been admitted pursuant to s 2. He made his own application to the Tribunal. However, his nearest relative also exercised her right to discharge the patient. A Tribunal considered the application by the patient, and upheld his detention. On the same day, the RC issued a barring report (s 25(1)). Shortly after this, an application was made to the county court to displace the nearest relative. The legal consequence of this is to extend the 28-day period of a section 2 order, until the county court had decided upon whether or not to displace the nearest relative. The nearest relative then made an application by way of s 66(1)(g). The Tribunal refused to hear the application. There was no dispute but that in the circumstances of the case, the nearest relative did **not** have a right to apply to the Tribunal (as it does not encompass s 2). The argument on behalf of the nearest relative was that since this was correct, it contravened the ECHR Rights of the nearest relative. The conclusion of UTJ Levenson was that:

---

4 [2011] UKUT 381 (AAC), [2011] MHLR 394.

5 Ibid, at [8].

6 [2012] UKUT 474 (AAC).

> 'the bundle of civil rights of a nearest relative conferred by the 1983 Act, and in particular the right to discharge, are a civil right for the purposes of Article 6 of the Convention. As I said above, being a nearest relative is a status clearly defined and conferred by law. Although the rights do not involve economic rights, they do involve the protection of liberty, albeit that of the patient rather than that of the nearest relative. The fact that the status is conferred on a relative and that the hierarchy begins with the spouse or civil partner means that the nearest relative will usually have a close and intimate interest in the patient's liberty ... the nearest relative can request the Secretary of State to refer the matter to the tribunal, and the patient can also make an application ... However, in the current proceedings [the] county court proceedings have the knock on effect of extending the 28 day period, perhaps for a very long period. This raises the question of whether in these circumstances the absence of a right of the nearest relative to apply to the First-tier Tribunal breaches the provisions of Article 6. In my view, in the present case, it does not. The nearest relative is a party to the county court proceedings ... if the county court does not displace the nearest relative, that relative's rights are preserved. If there is any subsequent failure by the hospital authorities or by the Secretary of State ... judicial review is an adequate remedy.[7]

The principle thrust of the decision is in respect of Article 6 (right to a fair trial) which includes access to a fair and public hearing before an independent and impartial tribunal within a reasonable time. On the facts in this case, therefore, there was no such breach, and the Tribunal had been correct to determine that it had no jurisdiction to consider the application by the nearest relative.

7 Ibid, at [31]–[32].

Chapter 14

REMEDIES

14.1 The most significant procedural alteration in respect of the Tribunal is the creation of a dedicated appellate body (Upper Tribunal) governed by the Tribunal Procedure (Upper Tribunal) Rules 2008.[1] Appeals to the Upper Tribunal are also governed by the First-tier Tribunal Rules.[2] Both sets of Rules are reproduced in Part F. Prior to the existence of the Upper Tribunal, all matters arising from Tribunals proceeded by way of judicial review, to the Administrative Court. However, of equal significance is the new procedure available for the Tribunal to reconsider its own decisions. This chapter therefore deals with (a) the procedure in respect of the First-tier; (b) the procedure in respect of the Upper Tribunal; and (c) the relevance of judicial review. In respect of (b) and (c) there is an overlap between the two.

FIRST-TIER AND PROCEDURE

14.2 The rules in respect of correcting, setting aside, reviewing and appealing Tribunal decisions are contained in Part 5 of the Rules[3] (see Part F). An appeal is defined as the exercise of the right of appeal on a point of law (Tribunals, Courts and Enforcement Act 2007, s 11), and a review means the review of a decision of the Tribunal (Tribunals, Courts and Enforcement Act 2007, s 9). The former statutory provision has been considered in *Dorset Healthcare NHS Foundation Trust v MH*.[4] The overall context of the case considered the disclosure of materials supplied by or referring to third parties (which has been discussed at **3.12**). It also raised a number of procedural points which go beyond the issue of disclosure. The first issue was whether or not the Upper Tribunal had jurisdiction to hear the appeal (within the meaning of s 11) at all. The Upper Tribunal did accept that the (interlocutory) decision came within the meaning of s 11, and, moreover, that even if it did not then:[5]

> '... we could treat the appeal as an application for judicial review and waive the requirement to serve the First-tier Tribunal (such challenges having been transferred from the Administrative Court to this Tribunal: Lord Chief Justice's

---

1 SI 2008/2698.

2 Tribunal Procedure (First-tier Tribunal) (Health, Education and Social Care Chamber) Rules 2008, SI 2008/2699.

3 References to rules in this section (**14.2–14.16**) are to the Tribunal Procedure (First-tier Tribunal) (Health, Education and Social Care Chamber) Rules 2008, SI 2008/2699.

4 [2009] UKUT 4 (AAC).

5 Ibid, at [8].

Practice Direction: Classes of Cases Specified under s. 18 (6) of the Tribunals, Courts and Enforcement Act 2007, 31 October 2008).'

This is dealt with a greater length at **14.20–14.35**. The second issue was the procedure by which the Tribunal deal with the matter of disclosure in the first place. This has largely been considered at **3.12**, but the Upper Tribunal deprecated the need for the First-tier Tribunal having give permission to appeal at all on the point. The NHS Trust could have used r 6(5) to have challenged the decision made (at [16]), but did not do so. The Tribunal decided to refer the matter to the Upper Tribunal, and in the interim stayed the proceedings. The Upper Tribunal held that:[6]

> 'With respect, we do not consider that the Tribunal ought to have been as timid as it was. At the hearing the Tribunal was properly placed to reconsider the issue of disclosure under rule 5 (2), if no application had been made by any party under rule 6 (5) … the case management powers under rule 5 are wide ranging and provide Tribunals with a powerful armoury to further the overriding objective of dealing with cases fairly and justly under rule 2 … The Tribunal ought to have taken these procedural matters in hand and not, at least at that stage before it had reached a proper conclusion and been challenged, have simply referred the matter to the Upper Tribunal by way of permission to appeal.'

The extent of the ambit of a review, and r 49 (review of a decision) is set out in greater detail in **14.14**.

Minor errors

14.3 Minor amendments may be made to a decision (clerical errors, accidental slips and omissions) (r 44). This is akin to the 'slip rule' in mainstream litigation.

Setting aside decisions (r 45)

14.4 More substantive matters may be dealt with *without* the need for an appeal, in that a Tribunal can set aside its own decision (if that decision has disposed of the proceedings – ie it is a final decision). This is a complete departure from the procedure which existed prior to 3 November 2008. It relates to procedural irregularities alone. The Tribunal may set aside a part of its decision. The basis upon which this may be done is either if it is in the interests of justice so to do (which confers a very wide discretion) or on the basis of specific points. Those specific points (in effect) exemplify when it may be in the interests of justice to set aside a decision. They are as follows:

(1) Documents were either not sent or not sent at the appropriate time to a party or their representative. One must assume that the missing documents were of basic significance to the case of that party, and not merely incidental to it.

---

6 Ibid, at [19].

(2) A document was not sent to the Tribunal itself at an appropriate time. It is again assumed that this document was of significance, and that by 'appropriate time' it is meant that it was not made available to the Tribunal at the stage before which the Tribunal had made its decision.

(3) Either a party or a party's representative was not present at a hearing related to the proceedings. Again, it must be assumed that the decision made had a direct and adverse effect upon that party.

(4) There had been some other procedural irregularity. It is assumed that this irregularity must be more than merely trifling.

14.5 The time-limit for such an application is 28 days from the date upon which the Tribunal sent notice of its decision to the party.

14.6 The pro forma to be used is P9. It is very similar in format to the type of forms used within judicial review. It requires the applicant to:

(1) specify which of the above criteria are relied upon;

(2) provide a detailed statement of grounds;

(3) state what outcome is sought;

(4) provide a statement of facts to be relied upon;

(5) provide any written evidence relied upon;

(6) provide a copy of the Tribunal's decision; and

(7) provide copies of any other documents relied upon.

14.7 Established practice would suggest that the pleadings should follow the format for judicial review (or appeals) that is to say a clear and focused statement of the basis upon which the application is made by reference to the Rules and the facts of the case.

Permission to appeal (to the Upper Tribunal) (r 46)

14.8 A request for permission to appeal must be made in writing and sent or delivered within 28 days of the latest of the dates that the Tribunal sent to the applicant either (a) written reasons; (b) amended reasons or correction following a review; or (c) notification that the decision to set aside a decision has been unsuccessful. This rule deals with the more substantive area of errors of law.

14.9 There is a provision for time to be extended, which would be decided by reference to r 5(3)(a) (Case Management).

14.10 The content of such an application is set out at r 46(5), and requires:

(1) identification of the decision (or implicitly part of decision) to which the appeal relates;

(2) identification of errors of law; and

(3) specification of the relief required.

14.11 The pro forma supplied in this instance is 'P10'. It requests the applicant to specify (in addition to the above):

(1) whether or not there is to be an application to extend time;

(2) a detailed statement of grounds;

(3) the outcome required;

(4) whether there is an application pursuant to r 5(3)(l) (a suspension of the effect of the decision);

(5) a statement of facts to be relied upon; and

(6) a list of appropriate other documents (including any directions requested and case-law relied upon).

Consideration of application for permission to appeal to Upper Tribunal

14.12 When such an application for permission to appeal is considered, the Tribunal must first consider whether to *review* its decision (and take into account the overriding objective at r 2 in making that decision). Again, this is a departure in the procedure which existed hitherto, and permits the Tribunal to alter its own original decision. A review of a decision is governed by r 49. If the decision is either *not* to review the decision, or any part of it, *or* the Tribunal reviews its decision and decides not to take any action in respect of the decision, the Tribunal must still consider whether permission to appeal will be granted or not. If there is a refusal of permission to appeal, then it the Tribunal must send with the record of refusal a statement of reasons for such refusal, together with the notification of the right to appeal to the Upper Tribunal.

14.13 It seems unlikely that if a review is not thought to be appropriate, the Tribunal would then grant permission to appeal. A decision must be sent 'as soon as is practicable'. It is assumed that the format for such a decision would follow the current practice of the Administrative Court and Court of Appeal (that is to say, fairly brief comments).

Review of a decision (r 49)

14.14 There is a precondition that a review may only take place if the Tribunal is satisfied that it has made an error of law. An error of law might, for example, encompass a situation where it had not followed case-law, or had misinterpreted legislative provisions. Reasons for refusal to refuse permission must be provided. The complexities of what might appear to be a simple procedure were considered at length in the case of *R (RB) v First-tier Tribunal (Review)*.[7] The Secretary of State had applied for permission to appeal against a decision. However, the Regional Tribunal Judge used the power of review, and set aside the judgment. The patient had not had the opportunity to make any representations, and was entitled to do so (r 49(3)). However, this application was refused. The decision nevertheless was considered at length by the Upper Tribunal. First, it held that the purpose of r 49 was to provide an alternative remedy to an appeal. It was not intended to usurp the appellate function of the Upper Tribunal, where there was a contentious point of law. A review should only set aside an original decision where there was an error of law, when that error was clear. Secondly, when considering whether to invite representations, and whether a decision should be set aside, or whether permission to appeal should be granted to the UT, it was essential to consider whether the case could be dealt with fairly and justly in the absence of such representations. This would include a number of factors, including the significance of any error of law and whether consideration of the point by the UT would lead to an authoritative decision on the point. The substance of a decision where a review was appropriate was likely to be a short decision. The more involved the decision, the less likely it would be for it to be suitable for a review. In this particular case, there were further errors of procedure in the manner in which it reached the UT (on the part of the patient's representatives) but which were resolved by the UT treating the application as if it were an application for judicial review. The analysis of the relevant procedure is complex, and the judgment of Carnwath LJ, Walker J and UTJ Rowland is set out below in its entirety.

> **'Reviews – the legislation**
>
> 16. Part 5 of the HESC Rules makes procedural provision in respect of, among other things, applications to the First-tier Tribunal for permission to appeal to the Upper Tribunal under s.11 of the 2007 Act and reviews under s.9.
>
> 17 Rule 47 (1) and 2 provides
>
>> "(1) On receiving an application for permission to appeal the Tribunal must first consider, taking into account the overriding objective in rule 2, whether to review the decision in accordance with rule 49 (review of a decision).

7 [2010] UKUT 160 (AAC), [2010] MHLR 192.

(2) If the Tribunal decides not to review the decision, or reviews the decision and decides to take no action in relation to the decision, or part of it, the Tribunal must consider whether to give permission to appeal in relation to the decision or that part of it."

18. The power to review decisions is conferred by s.9(1) of the 2007 Act which provides

"9(1) The First-tier Tribunal may review a decision made by it on a matter in a case, other than a decision that is an excluded decision for the purposes of section 11(1) (but see subsection (9))."

19. Rule 49 (1) of the Rules, made under s.9(3), cuts down the width of that power

"(1) The Tribunal may only undertake a review of a decision –

(a) pursuant to rule 47(1) (review on an application for permission to appeal) if it is satisfied that there was an error of law in the decision;"

20. Section 9(4) to 6 of the 2007 Act makes provision as to the action that may be taken following a review.

"(4) Where the First-tier Tribunal has under subsection (1) reviewed a decision, the First-tier Tribunal may in the light of the review do any of the following –

(a) correct accidental errors in the decision or in a record of the decision;

(b) amend reasons given for the decision;

(c) set the decision aside.

(5) Where under subsection (4)(c) the First-tier Tribunal sets a decision aside, the First-tier Tribunal must either –

(a) re-decide the matter concerned, or

(b) refer that matter to the Upper Tribunal.

(6) Where a matter is referred to the Upper Tribunal under subsection (5)(b), the Upper Tribunal must re-decide the matter."

21. Rule 49 (2) and (3) then makes further procedural provision

"(2) The Tribunal must notify the parties in writing of the outcome of any review, and of any right of appeal in relation to the outcome.

(3) If the Tribunal takes any action in relation to a decision following a review without first giving every party an opportunity to make representations, the notice under paragraph (2) must state that any party

that did not have an opportunity to make representations may apply for such action to be set aside and for the decision to be reviewed again."

The exercise of the power to review a decision

22. The power to review decisions is an important and valuable one. It is common ground that the power of review on a point of law is intended, among other things, to provide an alternative remedy to an appeal. In a case where the appeal would be bound to proceed, a review will enable appropriate corrective action to be taken without delay.

23. In this regard para 100 of the explanatory notes to the 2007 Act states

> "Sections 9 and 10 provide powers for the First-tier and Upper Tribunals to review their own decisions without the need for a full onward appeal and, where the tribunal concludes that an error was made, to re-decide the matter. This is intended to capture decisions that are clearly wrong, so avoiding the need for an appeal. The power has been provided in the form of a discretionary power for the Tribunal so that only appropriate decisions are reviewed. This contrasts with cases where an appeal on a point of law is made, because, for instance, it is important to have an authoritative ruling."

24. It cannot have been intended that the power of review should enable the First-tier Tribunal to usurp the Upper Tribunal's function of determining appeals on contentious points of law. Nor can it have been intended to enable a later First-tier Tribunal Judge or panel, or the original First-tier Tribunal judge or panel on a later occasion, to take a different view of the law from that previously reached, when both views are tenable. Both these considerations demonstrate that if a power of review is to be exercised to set aside the original decision because of a perceived error of law, this should only be done in clear cases.

25. There are, of course, degrees of clarity and there are practical reasons for taking a flexible approach. An important consideration may be the likelihood of the party in whose favour the original decision was made objecting to the review. In the event of an objection, the review may well cause delay rather than reducing it.

26. Rule 49(3) enables the First-tier Tribunal to take a robust approach when it first receives an application for permission to appeal – for it enables it to take a decision without calling for representations by the other side, on the basis that if the other side objects there can be an application to set aside. However, if the tribunal receives an application to set aside the action that it has taken following a review, it must consider afresh whether that action was appropriate, in the knowledge that it is contentious. Moreover, the tribunal is not obliged to take the robust approach permitted by r 49(3) and in many cases it will be preferable to invite representations before concluding that an original decision should be set aside.

27. We agree with Mr Barnes that consideration whether or not to review a decision involves a large element of judgment or discretion. Indeed, even if the First-tier Tribunal is satisfied that there is a clear error of law, it may decide not to review a decision but instead to give permission to appeal. The error may be a

> common one and, for that or other reasons, it may be helpful to have an authoritative decision on the point of the Upper Tribunal on the point.
>
> 28. We also agree with Mr Barnes' suggestion that there are occasions when it is desirable for a case to be reconsidered by the First-tier Tribunal so that further findings may be made even if it is likely to go to the Upper Tribunal eventually. The key question is what, in all the circumstances of the case including the degree of delay that may arise from alternative courses of action, will best advance the overriding objective of dealing with the case fairly and justly – see r.2 of the HESC Rules. The answer will depend on a large number of factors, to some but not all of which we have drawn attention.
>
> ...
>
> **Challenges to review decisions**
>
> 30. The substantial element of discretion is no doubt a reason for review decisions not being appealable and it is also a reason for expecting that the Upper Tribunal will seldom interfere with review decisions when judicial review proceedings are brought. Moreover, the Upper Tribunal might in an appropriate case refuse permission to apply for judicial review on the ground that the applicant should wait for the case to be re-decided and then, if less successful than before, consider appealing on the ground that the review was unlawful.
>
> 31. In the present case the question we ask ourselves is whether the reviewing judge properly directed himself as to the law governing the power of review. In particular, did he focus upon the need to make sure that the review did not usurp the Upper Tribunal's function of determining appeals on contentious points of law? This was a case where the law had to be particularly clear if a review was to be justified ...
>
> 32. One indication that it is not clear that the original decision was erroneous in point of law is the length of the review decision. If an error of law is clear it should be possible to give reasons in a couple of paragraphs. Often a single sentence is sufficient ... as review decisions are appropriate only where an authoritative decision is not necessary – because permission to appeal to the Upper Tribunal should be given when an authoritative decision is considered desirable ....'

Finally, it may be worth noting that the *actual* procedure adopted is that it is STJs who consider all applications in respect of the original FTT decisions (and most of these decisions are still made by fee-paid (ie part time) TJs). Thus, the original decision makers will not be involved in deciding whether there should be an appeal, or a review, or any other aspect of the case. In effect, therefore, as STJs are appointed at the same level as non-STJs, the effect of this procedure is that a judge of the same seniority has the power to overrule a decision by another judge of the same level of seniority.

General power (r 50)

14.15 Finally, whichever application is made (to set aside, to correct, to review, or for permission to appeal) the Tribunal can treat the application as an application for any of those things.

14.16 Thus, there exists a filtering exercise which has the potential to be quite extensive, and might avoid the necessity for extensive delay caused (hitherto) by an application for judicial review in the Administrative Court. In particular, the Tribunal has the power to stay its own decisions. However, in so doing, it may wish to consider the ratio of Dyson J (see **14.60**).

OVERVIEW OF ROLE OF UPPER TRIBUNAL

Administrative Appeals Chamber

14.17 The appellate structure is intended to replace the Administrative Court in certain respects. It is intended that the AAC should be led by a High Court judge with experience of the Administrative Court. This is currently Mr Justice Charles.

14.18 The AAC will only hear appeals on points of law. Permission is required for such an appeal. Relevant AAC decisions are published, with a neutral citation number (e g [2008] UKUT 123 (AAC)).

14.19 The new Rules have applied to appeals received after 3 November 2008.

Judicial review and AAC

14.20 The AAC will have all the powers available with judicial review, either by way of category or if transferred to it by the Administrative Court.

Appeals

14.21 Plainly, if permission is granted, then the matter will go straight to the Upper Tribunal. Many of the rules are similar to those which govern the First-tier. These are set out at in Part F. In *DL-H v Devon Partnership NHS Trust and Secretary of State for Justice*[8] the issue of what arguments might be heard over and above those considered when permission was granted was considered. It was held by UTJ Jacobs that first, the appeal may be granted on limited grounds (r 47(5)) by the First-tier Tribunal itself. Secondly, once the appeal is before the UT, it can control the issues on which it requires submissions (r 15(1)(a) Upper Tribunal Rules) and which can extend to striking out (r 8(3)). Finally, having regard to the overriding objective, it was (in this case) not proper to limit the grounds upon which the original permission had been granted. In *KF, MO and FF v Birmingham & Solihull Mental Health NHS*

---

8 [2010] UKUT 102 (AAC), [2010] MHLR 162.

Foundation Trust[9] the issue of an appeal where the substantive subject matter had become academic was considered. If (in a public law case) there remained an important point of principal to be considered, and where guidance could be provided, then as this was a legitimate function of the UT, such appeals could be heard.

14.22 Parts 1 and 2 of the Rules[10] deal with various matters that are similar to the equivalent within the rules which govern the First-tier (see Part F). It is not likely that oral evidence would be heard on a point of law (as is currently the practice within judicial review and other appeals), although there is a provision for this (r 16). Part 3 deals with appeals and references. Part 4 deals with judicial review proceedings within the Upper Tribunal. For this purpose the person who is attempting judicial review is 'an applicant' (r 1(3)). For all other purposes, he or she is an 'appellant' (r 1(3)). Part 5 deals with the hearing itself. Part 6 deals with decisions. Part 7 deals with appeals from the Upper Tribunal, and correcting, setting aside and reviewing its decisions.

Permission to appeal (Upper Tribunal) (r 21)

14.23 This applies to *any* decision made by the Tribunal. It can only be considered if the First-tier Tribunal has refused permission to appeal, and then an application may be made to the Upper Tribunal. The time-limit is much shorter than that for judicial review (3 months), and is one month from the date which the Tribunal *sent* the notice of refusal of permission to appeal to the putative appellant. The contents of the application are specified at r 21(4)(a)–(f) and (5)(a)–(c). Again, those who are familiar with appeals in other jurisdictions, or specifically with judicial review, will find nothing of surprise. The reader is also referred to **14.4–14.11**.

Decision in relation to permission to appeal (r 22)

14.24 The application is determined on paper, but there is a provision for the application for permission to appeal to be the subject of an oral hearing (r 22(4)). As in judicial review (or an appeal) some aspects of the application may be refused, whilst others are not.

Response to notice of appeal (r 24)

14.25 A respondent *may* provide a response to the notice of appeal no later than one month after the date on which the Upper Tribunal sent the notice that it had granted permission to appeal. The balance of the rule provides for the formalities with which the response must comply.

---

9 [2010] UKUT 185 (AAC), [2010] MHLR 201.

10 Unless otherwise stated, references to rules in this section (**14.17–14.43**) are to the Tribunal Procedure (Upper Tribunal) Rules 2008, SI 2008/2698.

Appellant's reply (r 25)

14.26 The appellant may provide a reply to the response.

Judicial review (within the Upper Tribunal)

14.27 Rule 27 deals with judicial review proceedings which have been transferred to the AAC. This would appear to envisage a situation whereby a judicial review has started in the Administrative Court, but which should be determined in the AAC.

14.28 In any event, the extent of the judicial review jurisdiction within the Upper Tribunal is set out at TCEA 2007, s 15 and reproduced in Part F. It permits the Upper Tribunal to make orders for relief that are identical to those available within judicial review. These powers may be exercised if the conditions at s 18 are made out. There are four conditions (and if these are not met, then the matter will be transferred to the High Court and treated as if commenced in the High Court). Condition 1 simply encompasses the extent of the relief required (ie it must not exceed that which the Upper Tribunal may order). Condition 2 is that it does not call into question anything done in the Crown Court (which will have a bearing on offender patients). Condition 3 specifies certain classes, and is very general. Condition 4 requires a High Court judge or equivalent to hear the application.

14.29 The relief which may be granted is conditional upon permission having been obtained from the Tribunal. If a quashing order is made, then the Tribunal can remit the matter to the First-tier Tribunal, and reconsider the matter, and reach a decision in accordance with the findings of the Upper Tribunal (TCEA 2007, s 17).

Transfer to Upper Tribunal

14.30 TCEA 2007, s 19 governs transfer, by inserting a new s 31A into the Supreme Court Act 1981. As long as conditions 1, 2 and 4 are met, the matter may be transferred if it appears to be 'just and convenient to do so'. The conditions are slightly different from those referred to at **14.28**, but will not in most cases make any difference. There are separate but similar provisions for transfer from Northern Ireland and from the Court of Sessions.

Commencement of judicial review within AAC

14.31 This is governed by r 28, and cross refers to TCEA 2007, s 16. The test is essentially the same as the test for permission if an application were to be made to the High Court. It also sets out the basis upon which an appeal against refusal to grant permission to appeal may be made to the Court of Appeal. The time-limit for making an application for permission to bring judicial review within the AAC is 3 months, save that if it is to challenge a decision of the First-tier Tribunal it may be at a later date if it is made within one month after the date on which written reasons for the decision were sent, or that notification that an application for the decision to be set aside had been unsuccessful. It will be noted that judicial review within the AAC is not limited (therefore) simply to decisions made by the Tribunal. The balance of r 28 deals with the content of any application and the documents with which it must be accompanied.

14.32 Rule 29 is almost identical to the CPR provision for acknowledgment of service[11] (and the time-limit of 21 days to file such a document from the date that the Upper Tribunal sent the application).

14.33 Once a decision is made, then r 30 governs the procedure by which the Upper Tribunal must notify the parties (and any other relevant bodies or individuals involved) of (a) the decision and (b) the reasons, together with any conditions or limitations. Whatever decision is made, the applicant may apply for an oral hearing for the decision to be reconsidered. The time-limit for such an application is 14 days.

14.34 If any person who has received notification of the grant of permission wishes to either support or oppose the substantive claim, then the grounds must be supplied within 35 days after the notice of permission was sent (r 31). If further grounds in support or opposition are required, then the permission of the Upper Tribunal is required (r 32).

14.35 Within the substantive hearing itself, each party may submit evidence, make representations (either orally at the hearing, or in writing if there is no hearing) (r 33). A decision may be made without a hearing, after the Upper Tribunal has taken into account the views of the parties (r 34). Each party is entitled to attend a hearing (r 35), unless r 37(4) applies. The extent of this rule is identical to r 39 of the First-tier Tribunal Rules.[12] Reasonable notice must be given of the time and date of the hearing. This must be at least 14 days, unless it relates to an application for permission, in which case it is 2 days. The period can be shortened with either the consent of the parties or in urgent or exceptional cases (r 36).

Public v private

14.36 All hearings must be in public, save for the provisions pursuant to r 37 referred to above (ie that parts of it may be in private and that there is a power to exclude individuals if necessary).

---

11 CPR, rr 54.1(2)(f), 54.8, 58.8(4).

12 Tribunal Procedure (First-tier Tribunal) (Health, Education and Social Care Chamber) Rules 2008, SI 2008/2699, r 39.

Non-attendance of party

14.37 If a party fails to attend, as long as the Upper Tribunal is satisfied that he has been notified and that it is in the interests of justice to proceed, it will proceed (r 38).

Decisions

14.38 A consent order may be made (r 39), and the Upper Tribunal may also deliver a decision orally and must do so in writing in any event (unless the parties have agreed that a written decision is not required). Also, any decision may be subject to the provisions of r 14(2) (withholding of harmful information) (r 40).

Correction, setting aside, reviews, appeals

14.39 The statutory basis for this part of the Rules may be found in TCEA 2007, ss 10, 13 and 14. Sections 13 and 14 concern appeals from the Upper Tribunal to the Court of Appeal, which may only be on a point of law.

Correction

14.40 Rule 41 is interpretative. Rule 42 deals with clerical errors, accidental slips and omissions.

Setting aside

14.41 If the Upper Tribunal considers it in the interests of justice so to do, and the conditions set out at r 43(2) are made out, it may set aside its own decision. The conditions are the same as those that apply to setting aside decisions by the First-tier Tribunal. The time-limit for such an application is one month from the date that the decision was sent to the party.

Appeals and reviews

14.42 Appeals must be in writing and within one month of the date upon which the decision was sent to the party (r 44). It is the Upper Tribunal that first considers whether such an appeal should be allowed, and it may at that stage review its own decision, but only if when making its decision it overlooked either an authority or legislative provision that could have had an effect on the outcome of the hearing, or if since the decision was made another court has made a binding decision which, had it been before the Upper Tribunal, could have effected the decision (rr 45 and 46). A review can only be made upon application for permission to appeal. If there is either no review, or a review and decides to take no action, then there must be a consideration of whether to permit an appeal to the Court of Appeal. The right of appeal to the Court of Appeal is at TCEA 2007, s 13 (which is confined to a point of law, or if some important point of principle or practice is raised or if there is some other compelling reason to hear the appeal (s 13(1) and (6)(a) and (b)).

Court of Appeal

14.43 The powers of the Court of Appeal are set out at TCEA 2007, s 14. These are that the decision may be set aside, remitted to the Upper Tribunal or remade. In *RH v South London and Maudsley NHS Foundation Trust*[13] the issue of the approach to the granting of permission to appeal from the Upper Tribunal was considered. In this instance, the Upper Tribunal (having been satisfied that the basis of the original appeal was without merit, granted permission to appeal to the Court of Appeal on the basis of a written argument which raised additional matters. This was considered by the Court of Appeal, but dismissed. The basis for permission by the UT to appeal was considered thus 'permission to appeal should not be granted for such appeals unless the UT or the Court of Appeal is satisfied that the appeal raises an important point of principle or practice, or there is some other compelling reason for this Court to consider the appeal ... If the UT does consider it appropriate to grant permission to appeal ... it should carefully consider whether the grant of permission should be limited to that ground or grounds'.[14] On the law in this case, the Court of Appeal regarded the grounds as without merit, and was particularly concerned that the UT did not know what the response from the other parties were, prior to deciding to give its permission to appeal to the Court of Appeal.

JUDICIAL REVIEW (ADMINISTRATIVE DIVISION OF THE HIGH COURT)

14.44 This part of the text is not a substitute for a text on administrative law. Its purpose is to illustrate the way in which the new regime may work, and the difference between the previous regime and the new regime (where such exist). A table which compares the CPR with the Tribunal Rules is given in Part F. Furthermore, there are very obvious similarities between the manner in which conventional applications to issue a writ of judicial review has operated hitherto and the procedures described above.

14.45 Hitherto, there have been a number of specific areas arising out of Tribunals which have been the subject of judicial review. In effect, when judicial review was used, it was as an appeal against a decision of a Tribunal. The creation of the Upper Tribunal should see a substantial decrease in the use of judicial review applications. However, there may still be situations where it is required (eg when judicial review is required in respect of an issue which is outside the scope of the Tribunal, but connected to the manner in which another public body has acted, or where the person who is trying to make an

---

13 [2010] EWCA Civ 1273, [2010] MHLR 341.

14 Ibid, at [36].

application does not have the requisite locus standi within the Rules). Moreover, there has been consideration given as to whether a decision by the UT can itself be subject to a judicial review within the Administrative Division of the High Court. In *R (Cart) v Upper Tribunal; R (MR (Pakistan) v Upper Tribunal*[15] it was held that where a decision of the UT could not itself be appealed, the TCEA 2007 did not specifically exclude the remedy of judicial review. The case was determined on the basis that the test to be applied should be that judicial review should be available upon the same basis as the criteria which apply for the granting of appeal from the UT to the Court of Appeal (see **14.43**), that is to say, some important point of principle or practice or some other compelling reason.

Scope and purpose of judicial review

14.46 This is set out at CPR, r 54.1(a) (see Part F). Its function is to permit the Administrative Court to exercise a supervisory function over any public body and, within the context of this book, an inferior court or tribunal (that is to say, the First-tier Tribunal). CPR, r 54.1(2) identifies this as being 'the lawfulness of … a decision'. Generally, it was that lawfulness and that part of a judicial review which was linked to the function of the Tribunal. The Administrative Court concerns itself with the lawfulness of the decision-making process, not the merits of the decision that was made.

Grounds for judicial review

14.47 The grounds upon which a claim might rely are as follows:

(1) error of law;

(2) procedural impropriety/breach of natural justice;

(3) irrationality; and

(4) abuse of power.

14.48 It can be seen from the body of case-law referred to in this text that those grounds set out at (1), (2) and (3) above have all been used to examine the jurisdiction of the Tribunal, and to formulate the common law in those respects.

Remedies within judicial review

14.49 The power of the Administrative Court is in the following terms:

(1) a quashing order (this brings up the decision of the tribunal for it to be set aside);

---

15 [2011] UKSC 28, [2011] MHLR 196.

(2) a mandatory order (this compels a tribunal to carry out its statutory obligations, for example, to hear a case where it determined that it had no jurisdiction);

(3) a prohibiting order (this compels a tribunal to refrain from acting outside its jurisdiction);

(4) a declaration;

(5) a stay on the decision of the inferior court;

(6) interim orders for (1) to (4).

All of the above remedies are at the discretion of the court.

PROCEDURE (JUDICIAL REVIEW)

Permission stage

14.50 A claimant must first seek permission from the court (CPR, r 54.4), which will then conduct an exercise on the papers presented to it as to whether or not such permission will be granted. The parties (if permission is granted) will be the claimant, the defendant and any interested parties. An interested party is an individual or body who is directly affected by the outcome of the relief sought. If permission to issue a writ of judicial review is refused, then the claimant can request an oral hearing (CPR, r 54.12(2) and (3)). If this does not succeed then an application can be made to the Court of Appeal. If this succeeds, then permission will be granted for the Administrative Court to hear the application. There is no further appeal if the Court of Appeal does not so direct. The purpose of the above procedure is to filter out unmeritorious claims in an expeditious manner. If there is demonstrated to be an arguable case, then the matter will proceed to a full hearing.

Limitation (judicial review)

14.51 In the context of a Tribunal, this will be 3 months from the date of the decision that was made by the Tribunal, and/or when the written decision was provided (although an extension of time is permissible: CPR, r 3.1(2)(a)).

Acknowledgment of service

14.52 A brief statement of the summary of grounds for challenging the claim should be provided within 21 days after service of the claim form (CPR, r 54.8 et seq). This may be accompanied by a statement or statements of evidence, although is not usually.

Substantive response

14.53 If the claim is to be contested, then within 35 days of the claim form having been served all evidence and augmented grounds must be provided (CPR, r 54.14). Bundles and skeleton arguments must be provided not less than 21 days before the final hearing.

Appeals

14.54 If the claim fails, then permission may be sought to appeal to the Court of Appeal.

Transfer

14.55 CPR, r 54.20 permits the court to order a claim to continue as if it had not been started under CPR Part 54, and to give directions about its future management. As set out **14.30**, there is now a new s 31A of the Supreme Court Act 1981 which permits a transfer to the Upper Tribunal.

Specific case-law

14.56 In some circumstances it may be necessary for a patient to judicially review (within the scope of the UT to consider such an application, for example) a decision made by a responsible authority, an RC, an AMHP, or the Secretary of State. An example of this would be where a decision has been made to re-detain a patient who has been discharged by a Tribunal. The patient would have no cause of action as against the Tribunal, but instead would have to move against the professionals who made a decision in the face of a discharge (and which therefore would be unconnected directly with the Upper Tribunal). In any event, whether by way of judicial review or by way of the Upper Tribunal, the arguments are likely to constellate around (a) the rationality of the decision-making process; (b) making an error of law; and (c) breaching the requirements of natural justice. Each of these is illustrated by way of the case-law referred to in the body of this text. Set out below are some of the more general areas which have been considered by the Administrative Court. However, these would (and have) been considered as part of the basis of an appeal to the Upper Tribunal, without the need for judicial review. The majority of case-law in the UT has turned on the provision of inadequate reasons for the decision that has been made.

Inadequate reasons

14.57 The reasons given for the decision of the Tribunal are a composite of the deliberations of each of the Tribunal members. They should amount to a lucid judgment, in which it is clearly possible to understand why some evidence has been accepted and some rejected. However, the reasons are directed towards a specialist audience. At the very minimum, reasons should contain (a) a brief summary of the oral evidence heard; (b) a statement of the issues upon which the Tribunal has to deliberate (these may be the statutory criteria in their entirety, or a discrete point, for example, an adjournment); (c) the decision on each of the issues, and the specific rationale for reaching that decision based upon the evidence. All of this sounds very straightforward and obvious, but nevertheless it is an area which still causes problems.

14.58 *R (Ashworth Hospital) v MHRT; R (H) v Ashworth Hospital*[16] is a perfect example of the interaction between a number of procedural and substantive issues. The facts of the case are significant in that the patient (H) had been detained pursuant to MHA 1983, s 3, and had been transferred to Ashworth Hospital. A Tribunal heard evidence from a number of witnesses, including the RMO and an independent psychiatrist. The Tribunal preferred the evidence of the independent psychiatrist and discharged the patient with immediate effect. It was common ground that arrangements for his after-care were almost non-existent, and that his main need was for accommodation. The RA (via the RMO) made arrangements for an ASW to assess H within a few days of the decision to discharge. This led to a recommendation that he be readmitted for treatment (and this is what happened). Plainly, this had the appearance of a dissatisfied RMO deciding to overrule the decision of the Tribunal. Very shortly after this step was taken, the RA obtained leave to judicially review the Tribunal (and based its claim largely on the inadequacy of the reasons and on the decision to discharge immediately). The patient (H) was obliged to judicially review the RA, the RMO (and second opinion psychiatrist) and the ASW for the decision to make a recommendation readmit him. There was also an issue as to whether the High Court had the power to stay the decision of a Tribunal pending the outcome of the claim for judicial review. Thus, the case involved (a) rationality of reasons for discharge of a patient by a Tribunal; (b) rationality of reasons for re-detention of the patient in the face of such discharge; and (c) the procedural issue of whether a stay of a decision was a power available to the High Court. The judgment itself contains a thorough analysis of all of the areas of law, and rewards close reading.

Elucidation of reasons

14.59 The Tribunal panel provided witness statements in respect of the reasons for discharging H. It should be self-evident that cogent reasons would not require elucidation. It is not permissible for there to be an ex post facto justification of a decision reached, again for reasons which are self-evident (ie it is comparatively easy to justify a decision reached after the event). Stanley Burnton J considered this issue at first instance and concluded:[17]

> 'It appears from a number of cases cited to me that it used to be the common practice on applications for the judicial review of their decisions for Mental Health Review Tribunals to supplement the reasons for their decisions in affidavits or witness statements. However, that practice must now be reconsidered in the

16 [2002] EWCA Civ 923, [2002] MHLR 314, CA; (*EC Chs 1, 2, 9 and 15*).

17 Reported at [2002] MHLR 13, at [56]–[59].

> light of the decision in the Court of Appeal in *R v Westminster City Council v Ermakov* [1996] 2 All ER 302 … the general rule [is] as stated in *Ermakov*, permitting the admission of evidence that merely elucidates original written reasons.'

It is, of course, possibly a fine line between elucidation and justifying a decision after the event with additional reasons (which is impermissible).

Stay on decision

14.60 The Court of Appeal held that there was jurisdiction to stay the decision of a Tribunal to discharge a patient (by reference to CPR, r 54.10, the full text of which is set out in Part F). However, Dyson J added the following caveat which is of importance within the context of this specific area of law:[18]

> '… the grant of permission to apply for judicial review is a necessary condition of a stay. But, in the special context of orders for discharge by Mental Health Review Tribunals, it is in my view not a sufficient condition. The mere fact that an arguable case for judicial review has been demonstrated is not a sufficient reason for granting a stay. It is important to bear in mind that the consequence of granting a stay is that the patient once again becomes subject to the regime of the Act and is deprived of his liberty. That is because the effect of the stay is to suspend the tribunal's order, and temporarily to treat it as being of no effect … This is a particularly grave consequence in the light of the fact that he has only recently been given his liberty by the specialist tribunal designated by Parliament to determine these matters. This is an important consideration that has to be weighed against the public interest in seeing that patients who may be a danger to themselves as well as to other members of the public are deprived of their liberty, and given the treatment that they need. In striking that balance, it seems to me that the Court should usually refuse to grant a stay unless satisfied that there is a strong, and not merely arguable, case that the tribunal's decision was unlawful. Even in such a case, the court should not grant a stay in the absence of cogent evidence of risk and dangerousness.'

The case management powers of the Upper Tribunal[19] confer this power on the Upper Tribunal pending resolution of the outcome of the hearing.

Lawfulness of re-detention

14.61 On the particular facts in this case, it was held that:[20]

> 'It was not open to them [Ashworth; the RMO; the second opinion doctor; the ASW] to act as they did simply because they disagreed with the decision of the Tribunal, whether or not they had been advised and believed that the decision was arguably unlawful.'

Consequently the decision to readmit H was quashed.

---

18 [2002] EWCA Civ 923, [2002] MHLR 314, at [47].

19 Tribunal Procedure (Upper Tribunal) Rules 2008, SI 2008/2698, r 5(3)(j).

20 [2002] EWCA Civ 923, [2002] MHLR 314, at [62].

Adequate reasons

14.62 The main authority relied upon by the Court of Appeal was that of *English v Emery Reimbold & Strick Ltd*[21] ('justice will not be done if it is not apparent to the parties why one has won and the other has lost'). In particular, where expert evidence was in conflict (as it was in *H*) there is a requirement for:[22]

> '... a coherent reasoned opinion expressed by a suitably qualified expert should be the subject of a coherent reasoned rebuttal ... [the judge] ... should simply provide an explanation as to why he has accepted the evidence of one expert and rejected that of another.'

The authority of *R v Mental Health Review Tribunal ex parte Booth*[23] was also relied upon to the following extent:[24]

> 'It has to be remembered ... that the quality of reasons required of a Mental Health Review Tribunal has to be looked at in the light of the fact that the decision is addressed to an informed audience.'

14.63 Where there was a dispute as to facts, the matter was clearer, and the court adopted the ratio in *Flannery v Halifax Estate Agents Ltd*[25] to the effect that:[26]

> 'Where there is a straightforward factual dispute whose resolution depends simply on which witness is telling the truth about events which he claims to recall, it is likely to be enough for the judge (having, no doubt, summarised the evidence) to indicate simply that he believes X rather than Y ... But where there is something of in the nature of an intellectual exchange, with reasons and analysis advanced on either side, the judge must enter into the issues canvassed before him and explain why he prefers one case over the other.'

14.64 Since the UT began to consider appeals in the manner which would have otherwise have been by way of judicial review, the following refinements of the above test have been provided. The first of many of these was *BB v South London & Maudsley NHS Trust and the Ministry of Justice*.[27] This covered much of the same principles summarised above. First, notes of the oral evidence heard are required for such an appeal. Secondly, the reasons themselves must enable the parties, and any appellate tribunal, to be able to analyse the essential reasoning, and to explain how and why it had accepted the evidence of one expert, and rejected that of another. In reaching this conclusion, it specifically considered *English v Emery Reimbold & Strick Ltd* and *R (Ashworth Hospital) v MHRT; R (H) v Ashworth Hospital*. In *DL-H v*

---

21 [2002] 1 WLR 2409.
22 [2002] EWCA Civ 923, [2002] MHLR 314, at [72].
23 [1997] EWHC 816 (Admin).
24 [2002] EWCA Civ 923, [2002] MHLR 314, at [73].
25 [2000] 1 WLR 377, at 381G–382D.
26 [2002] EWCA Civ 923, [2002] MHLR 314, at [80].
27 [2009] UKUT 157 (AAC), [2009] MHLR 302.

Devon Partnership NHS Trust and Secretary of State for Justice[28] the Tribunal failed to provide adequate reasons for the criteria in respect of whether appropriate treatment was available or not, and did not address the evidence upon which the patient relied on this key issue. In *RH v South London and Maudsley NHS Foundation Trust*[29] the sole issue (in respect of reasons) was whether or not the Tribunal had dealt adequately with disagreeing with the conclusions of all the expert witnesses before it, and it was held that it had done so, and had given clear and cogent reasons for the basis of that disagreement. In *DL v South London & Maudsley NHS Trust Foundation & Secretary of State for Justice*,[30] a decision was made not to absolutely discharge the patient. On the facts of the case, it was held that the decision was inadequate. It had not explained why the recent date of the index offence was significant, nor the short time between a previous conditional discharge and the application for absolute discharge. There were two experts who supported an absolute discharge, but no consideration was given to this evidence in the reasons. The reports themselves were clearly reasoned, but the decision was not, and was based on remote possibilities, without weighing up the actual risks that it perceived and the problems that might occur as a result of those risks. In *JLG v Managers of Llanarth Court and Secretary of State for Justice*[31] the issue was not one of fact, but of law. The appeal itself was so comprehensive in its attack upon the reasons that UTJ Jacobs observed 'If the tribunal had indeed committed so many and such egregious errors, it would have been astonishingly incompetent'.[32] These criticisms included an alleged lack of the burden and standard of proof. He stated that 'the Upper Tribunal is entitled to make, and does make assumptions. It assumes that members understand the basic legal concepts that they apply' [6].[33] He added 'The issue is whether there is anything to indicate that they have exceptionally failed to apply the basic tools of their craft'.[34] The criticism on these basic points was rejected, as was the suggestion that the Tribunal had been selective in its citing of evidence in support of its conclusions and held that 'What it has been is selective in its references to evidence in its reasons. That is permissible'.[35] Selection of evidence does not equate to having ignored the other evidence. It also referred to the concept of proportionality, which is 'amply covered by the terms of the legislation and the allocation of the burden of proof'[36] and was not a separate issue.

---

28 [2010] UKUT 102 (AAC), [2010] MHLR 162.
29 [2010] EWCA Civ 1273, [2010] MHLR 341.
30 Justice [2010] UKUT 455 (AAC), [2010] MHLR 43.
31 [2011] UKUT 62 (AAC), [2011] MHLR 74.
32 Ibid, at [4].
33 Ibid, at [6].
34 Ibid.
35 Ibid, at [14].
36 Ibid, at [15].

Chapter 15

ROUTES TO DETENTION AND DISCHARGE OUTSIDE THE JURISDICTION OF THE TRIBUNAL

15.1 The Tribunal is only one way in which a patient may be discharged from detention under MHA 1983. There are a number of methods by which a patient may be detained, and which have no remedy for discharge via a Tribunal. As (by definition) none of these will ever come before a Tribunal, they are set out below by way of reference only, and for the sake of completeness.

AHMP AND POLICE (MHA 1983, SS 135 AND 136)

15.2 An order pursuant to MHA 1983, s 135 can be made by a Justice of the Peace on information on oath from an AMHP. This provides authority for the patient to be taken to a place of safety and detained for no more than 72 hours.

15.3 MHA 1983, s 136 enables a constable to do the same, but without the need for a warrant, if the patient is in a public place.

EMERGENCY APPLICATIONS (MHA 1983, S 4)

15.4 Emergency applications are governed by MHA 1983, s 4. They can be made by an AMHP or a nearest relative and last for 72 hours. Emergency applications are intended to be for exceptional cases only, and in the absence of a second medical recommendation. If a second opinion is obtained during that 72-hour period then the detention may be 'converted' to a s 2 detention. If this does happen, then time for the 28-day period runs from the time of the original detention under s 4. Also, there is no reason why an application for treatment (MHA 1983, s 3) cannot be made during the 72-hour period, assuming that two *new* medical recommendations are available to support this course of action and the statutory criteria are fulfilled.

HOLDING POWERS (MHA 1983, S 5(2) AND (4))

15.5 This covers a situation in which a registered medical practitioner is of the opinion that an application for admission ought to be made and makes a report to that effect available to the hospital managers. This confers authority for detention for 72-hours.

15.6 MHA 1983, s 5(4) confers the same authority upon a nurse, except that the period of detention is for 6 hours only. The nurse has to be of 'a prescribed class'. The period of detention starts from the time that the nurse records an opinion that the relevant criteria are met (on Form H2).

15.7 The *Reference Guide* provides a glossary on each of the above (with the exception of MHA 1983, ss 135 and 136). In respect of the latter, the Royal College of Psychiatrists has published a paper on its use.[1] The statutory provisions are presented separately in Part F.

DISCHARGE BY NEAREST RELATIVE

15.8 The implications for a nearest relative in exercising this power have been considered at **8.33**. A nearest relative can only exercise this power in respect of a patient detained under MHA 1983, Pt 2. Notice of this must be given 72 hours prior to it being exercised. The notice has to be in writing, but there is no specific format. The only authority on this point is *Re GK (Patient: Habeas Corpus)*.[2] If the RC considers it inappropriate for there to be a discharge, then a 'barring report' will be written which will nullify the effect of the application by the nearest relative. It also prevents any further attempts to discharge being made within the next 6 months.

DISCHARGE BY RESPONSIBLE CLINICIAN

15.9 The RC can discharge any Part 2 or unrestricted Part 3 patient. The order to this effect must be made available to the hospital managers as soon as possible.

15.10 It is not uncommon for this method of discharge to be used shortly before a Tribunal.

DISCHARGE BY HOSPITAL MANAGERS

15.11 Hospital managers also have the power to discharge Part 2 and unrestricted Part 3 patients. There is a positive obligation to consider discharge

---

1 CR149 *Standards on the use of Section 136 of the Mental Health Act 1983 (2007)*, September 2008.

2 [1999] MHLR 128.

when an RC makes a report renewing authority for the detention of a patient. There must always be three managers (or the equivalent) to make a decision, and all three must agree that this is the correct course of action.

15.12 Once a patient is discharged (by whatever means) he or she may remain in hospital as a voluntary patient. This is not a recommended course of action in respect of special hospitals.

Chapter 16

SPECIAL PROVISION FOR CHILDREN AND ADOLESCENTS

16.1 The Tribunal has established a specialist panel in respect of Child and Adolescent Mental Health Services (CAMHS). Training is provided on an annual basis to the members of the Panel, and the purpose of the panel is to:[1]

> '… ensure that where a child who is either detained under the Mental Health Act 1983 or subject to another order under the Act applies, or has their case referred to a Tribunal, at least one of the MHRT members appointed to deal with the case has special expertise in dealing with cases of this nature.'

This chapter attempts to summarise the separate statutory provisions that exist in respect of children (those under the age of 18). As a part of the process of ensuring that not only the Tribunal members have the expertise for these types of cases, but also the RC and AMHPs are alert to the legal aspects, a Practice Direction was produced. This has been in effect since 6 April 2012. It is included in Part F. Section E of Part F sets out what is a **compulsory** requirement for the contents of reports prepared in respect of children who are detained in hospital. In the experience of the author, it is still the case that the understanding of the legal context of this area is more often than not lamentable on the part of professionals involved in the treatment of a child. The most common problem is a lack of liaison between adult and children's social services departments. The consequence is delay, including the adjournment of hearings.

16.2 Within MHA 1983 itself, the relevant provisions are ss 27, 28, 33, 64E, 64F, 116 and 131A. The relevant sections are reproduced in Part F, and Chapter 36 of the Code, which is devoted to the subject, is reproduced in Part E.

CHILDREN AND YOUNG PERSONS IN CARE) (NEAREST RELATIVE) (MHA 1983, S 27)

16.3 If a child is subject to a care order (pursuant to the Children Act 1989) then the local authority is the nearest relative, unless the child has a husband, wife or civil partner.

---

1 Tribunals Service *Mental Health Review Tribunal* (July 2008).

NEAREST RELATIVE OF MINOR UNDER GUARDIANSHIP (MHA 1983, S 28)

16.4 It will be recalled that an order for guardianship cannot be made in respect of someone under the age of 16. Where a guardian has been appointed for someone between 16 and 18, or there is a residence order in force (Children Act 1989, s 8), then the guardian or guardians named in the residence order will be deemed to be his or her nearest relative. This also includes the term 'special guardian' (used in the Children Act 1989 and the Adoption and Children Act 2002).

WARDS OF COURT (MHA 1983, S 33)

16.5 With the advent of the Children Act 1989, the use of wardship has declined. However, were there to be any application for a child who is a ward of court, then permission of the High Court would be required. The full text of this section is reproduced in Part F. If the ward is subject to detention, then the powers of the nearest relative can only be exercised with the permission of the High Court. This also applies to MHA 1983, s 17A (Community Treatment Orders), but not MHA 1983, s 17E (recall to hospital). The NIMHE *Guide for Practitioners* has a specific section (Section G) devoted to children and adolescents who are the subject of CTOs. A parent, or other person with parental responsibility, may not consent (or refuse to consent) to medical treatment for a mental disorder on behalf of a child who is subject to SCT. A ward of court may not be subject to a guardianship order (MHA 1983, s 7), nor transferred from hospital to guardianship.

CHILD COMMUNITY PATIENTS (MHA 1983, SS 64E, 64F, 64G, 64J AND 64K)

16.6 If a child is under the age of 16, and is not recalled to hospital (MHA 1983, s 17E), then he or she cannot be given treatment without (a) authority to treat and (b) if it is MHA 1983, s 58 or 58A, unless MHA 1983, s 64G applies (a child community patient who lacks competence) or the treatment is immediately necessary. No patient under the age of 18 (whether detained or not) may be given either electro-convulsive therapy (ECT) or any other treatment to which s 58A applies without a second opinion approved doctor (SOAD). A child who is subject to a CTO cannot be the subject of a 'paper' consideration where there has been a referral.[2]

16.7 MHA 1983, s 64F sets out the preconditions for treatment where a child community patient lacks capacity. The remaining sections set out similar factors in considering issues related to capacity and objections to treatment.

---

2 Tribunal Procedure (First-tier Tribunal) (Health, Education and Social Care Chamber) Rules 2008, SI 2008/2699, r 35(3).

DUTY OF HOSPITAL MANAGERS TO REFER CASES TO THE TRIBUNAL (MHA 1983, S 68(6))

16.8 If a patient is under the age of 18, then hospital managers are obliged to refer the case to the Tribunal if more than one year has elapsed since the patient's case was last considered by a Tribunal (as opposed to the normal 3-year period with an adult).

WELFARE OF CERTAIN HOSPITAL PATIENTS (MHA 1983, S 116)

16.9 MHA 1983, s 116 provides that a local authority shall make arrangements to visit a child who is detained under the Act if either (a) the child is subject to a care order in favour of the local authority; (b) the child is subject to a guardianship order in favour of the local authority; (c) the local authority is the nearest relative. It will be likely that the self-same local authority will be obliged to consider the implications for discharge, and MHA 1983, s 117, or other statutory obligations. It is equally likely that the Children's Services Department (which will be dealing with the child) will be inadequately informed about the extent of their obligations towards the child under the Mental Health Acts.

INFORMAL ADMISSION OF PATIENTS 16+ (MHA 1983, S 131)

16.10 If a patient is aged 16 or 17 and has the capacity to consent to being admitted as an informal patient, then arrangements may be made on the basis of that consent even though there may be others who have parental responsibility for him or her. It is unclear whether this includes the case where a local authority has parental responsibility via a care order. Even if the patient has capacity to consent to admission (but does not do so), then the same applies (ie that the person or persons with parental responsibility cannot consent to that course of action upon the patient's behalf).

ACCOMMODATION ETC FOR CHILDREN (MHA 1983, S 131A)

16.11 Where a patient is under the age of 18, and is either liable to be detained in hospital, or is admitted to hospital, then arrangements *shall* ensure that the environment in which he or she is detained is *suitable*. There is no definition of what is meant by this adjective, but there is a further mandatory obligation to consult someone who has the appropriate knowledge and experience to assist them in making these arrangements. This is likely to be someone from Child and Adolescent Mental Health Services. Also, the Code (at para 36.68) provides illustrative examples of what is meant by suitable. Hospital managers should have taken steps to ensure that such facilities are available from April 2010 onwards, which is when MHA 1983, s 131A came into force.

INFORMATION AS TO HOSPITALS (MHA 1983, S 39(1A) AND (1B))

16.12 A similar example of appropriate accommodation being available comes via the Crown Court (which may make a request as to suitability of facilities for those under the age of 18).

PARENTAL RESPONSIBILITY

Scope

16.13 This is a much misunderstood concept. The Children Act 1989, s 3(1) defines parental responsibility as 'all the rights, duties, powers, responsibilities and authority which by law a parent of a child has in relation to the child and his property'. There is no definitive list as to what those 'rights, duties, powers, responsibilities and authority' might be. However, from the abundance of case-law on the subject, it is possible to list what they include. Some examples are as follows: providing a home; having contact and living with the child; protecting and maintaining the child; disciplining the child; choosing and providing for the education of the child; determining the religion of the child; consenting to medical treatment on behalf of the child; naming the child and changing the name; leaving the UK with the child and agreeing to the emigration of the child; being responsible for the property of the child; appointing a guardian for the child; allowing confidential information about the child to be disclosed.

Acquisition

16.14 If a child was born before 1 December 2003 (in England and Wales), or 15 April 2002 (Northern Ireland) or 4 May 2006 (Scotland), the mother would automatically acquire parental responsibility upon birth of the child, and a father would acquire it if he were married to the mother. In the case of unmarried parents a father could only acquire parental responsibility through the making of a parental responsibility agreement or a parental responsibility order made by a court. If a court is asked to make an order it will take a number of factors into account, including the degree of commitment that the applicant has shown towards the child, the degree of attachment that exists between them and the motivation of the application itself.

16.15 In the case of a child born after the above dates, and where both parents' names are registered on the child's birth certificate, they both have parental responsibility. Where a child is adopted, the adoptive parents become the child's legal parents and both automatically acquire parental responsibility. A person other than a child's biological parents can acquire parental responsibility by being appointed as a child's guardian (usually upon the death of a parent or parents), or by having a residence order in their favour. In the latter case, parental responsibility lasts for as long as the residence order does. If a care order is in force (under Part IV of the Children Act 1989) a local authority acquires parental responsibility (which is shared with whoever else has parental responsibility). However, when a care order is in existence the local authority may limit the extent to which the parent can exercise parental responsibility. A special guardian also obtains parental responsibility, which remains shared with whoever else has it. In theory, there is no limit to the number of people who can share parental responsibility for the same child, although it is usually shared between two parents. If there is a dispute between those with parental responsibility in relation to an issue regarding its use, the court can be asked to adjudicate. Also, it must be noted that any power in respect of parental responsibility must not generally be exercised unilaterally, if it is shared. However, the Children Act 1989, s 2(7) states:

> 'Where more than one person has parental responsibility for a child, each of them may act alone and without the other (or others) in meeting that responsibility; but nothing in this Part shall be taken to affect the operation of any enactment which requires the consent of more than one person in a matter affecting the child.'

In England, Wales and Northern Ireland, parental responsibilities may be exercised until a child reaches the age of 18. In Scotland, only the aspect of parental responsibilities concerned with the giving of 'guidance' endures until 18 years. 'Guidance' means the giving of advice. The rest is lost when the child reaches the age of 16.

The Code

16.16 Chapter 36 of the Code sets out very fully the rationale and law in respect of children who are involved with the Mental Health Act. It states that professionals in this area will need to be familiar with a number of statutes (the most significant being the Children Act 1989 and MCA 2005).

16.17 Notwithstanding the legislation adumbrated below, if decisions about treatment are being made, then professionals will have to find out who has parental responsibility for a child (either by order of the court or otherwise), and the consequences of those orders. In addition, NIMHE produced guidance in respect of children (*The Legal Aspects of the Care and Treatment of Children and Young People with Mental Disorder: A Guide for Professionals*) in January 2009 which practitioners will find helpful, together with *Children with Mental Disorder and the Law*[3] and *Young Minds in Transition in Mental Health Care*.[4]

---

3 Anthony Harbour (Jessica Kingsley Publishers, 2008).

4 National Mental Health Development Unit.

Care orders

16.18 In particular, it should be noted that where a care order is in force 'it shall be the duty of the local authority designated by the order to receive the child into their care and to keep him in their care while the order remains in force' (Children Act 1989, s 33(1)). This does not prevent a local authority from agreeing that a child should be detained in a hospital or elsewhere. Section 33(3)(b) states that the local authority 'shall have the power … to determine the extent to which a parent or guardian of the child may meet his parental responsibility for him'. If a child is subject to a care order, and is older than 16, and is leaving care, then that child will come within the scope of the Children (Leaving Care) Act 2000. This came into force in October 2001. This statute is accompanied by the Care Leavers (England) Regulations 2010[5] and (in part) the Care Planning, Placement and Case Review (England) Regulations 2010.[6] These came into force on 1 April 2011. These entitle the child to be the subject of a pathway plan, the extent of which will depend upon the precise status of the child in terms of the various statutory regimes. Details of the latter can be found in Chapter 5 of *Community Care Law and Local Authority Handbook*. The differing regimes are fairly complex, but the significance for a child who is both subject to a care order and detained under the Act is that the local authority retains a significant level of direct responsibility for the child, extending in some cases up to the age of 24. The pathway plan itself must be quite precise and must contain more than vague aspirations.[7] A failure to provide a pathway plan is unlawful.[8] The provision of services must be specific, and should include (amongst other matters) a strategy for the child, provision of appropriate accommodation, provision of education, training and employment. The advantages for a child from provision of these services should be self-evident, and may act as a significant augmentation to other obligations (eg MHA 1983, s 117 or s 47 of the National Health Service and Community Care Act 1990).

Residence orders

16.19 This is an order which settles the living arrangements for a child until the age of 18. As mentioned at **16.15**, there will be an order for parental responsibility which accompanies this order, in favour of the person or persons who have the residence order.

Guardian (private)

16.20 Section 5(1) of the Children Act 1989 states that:

---

5 SI 2010/2571.

6 SI 2010/959.

7 *R (on the Application of J) (by his litigation friend MW) v Caerphilly CBC* [2005] EWHC 586 (Admin), [2005] 2 FLR 860.

8 *R (on the application of P) v Newham LBC* [2004] EWHC 2210 (Admin).

'... where an application with respect to a child is made to the Court by any individual. The court may by order appoint that individual to be the child's guardian if (a) the child has no parent with parental responsibility for him or (b) a residence order has been made with respect to the child in favour of a parent or guardian of his who has died while the order is in force.'

That individual will then have parental responsibility.

Looked after children and children in need

16.21 Section 17 of the Children Act 1989 requires a local authority to consider whether or not a child is 'in need' and included in the definition of what amounts to being in need is whether he 'suffers from mental disorder of any kind' (s 17(11)). In addition, s 28A of the Chronically Sick and Disabled Persons Act 1970 imposes upon a local authority an obligation to comply with the requirements of this Act, insofar as it applies to disabled children. As the definition set out amounts to a child being disabled, and as s 28A incorporates into the Children Act 1989 the effect of the Chronically Sick and Disabled Persons Act 1970 this is an important additional level of mandatory support for a child with a mental disorder, and is more than merely nugatory. Section 22 of the Children Act 1989 refers to a category known as 'looked after children'. These are looked after by the local authority and it will be the local authority's duty to 'promote his welfare and (b) to make such use of services available for children cared for by their own parents as appears to the authority to be reasonable in his case' (s 22(3)). A local authority does not share parental responsibility in this situation.

Secure accommodation orders

16.22 This is an order pursuant to the Children Act 1989, s 25. It is arguably more draconian in effect than any orders for detention under MHA 1983 (for non-offender patients), and is less governed by safeguards concerning review of the necessity for deprivation of liberty. It states that:

'... a child who is looked after by a local authority may not be placed, and if placed, may not be kept, in accommodation provided for the purpose of restricting liberty ... unless it appears (a) that (i) he has a history of absconding and is likely to abscond from any other description of accommodation; and (ii) if he absconds, he is likely to suffer significant harm; or (b) that if he is kept in any other description of accommodation he is likely to injure himself or other persons.'

Paragraph 36.17 of the Code refers to secure accommodation where a child with a mental disorder needs to be detained, but not for the purposes of treatment for the mental disorder. It should also be added that as a consequence of reg 5(1) of the Children (Secure Accommodation) Regulations 1991[9] 'Section 25 of the Act shall not apply to a child who is

---

9 SI 1991/1505.

detained under any provision of the Mental Health Act 1983 …'. However, if a child has been detained by way of s 25 there is likely to be a lot of information available about the biography of the child, and the extent and treatment of any mental disorder.

Family Reform Act 1969, s 8 and consent

16.23 Paragraph 36.27 of the Code makes reference to this statute. It states that:

> 'The consent of a minor who has attained the age of sixteen years to any surgical, medical or dental treatment which, in the absence of consent, would constitute a trespass to his person, shall be effective as it would be if he were of full age; and where a minor has by virtue of this section given an effective consent to any treatment it shall not be necessary to obtain any consent to it from his parent or guardian.'

Looked after children and contact, visits and welfare when apart from parents; children accommodated by health authorities or in care homes or independent hospitals

16.24 If a child is looked after, but is not visited by a parent regularly, then the local authority is under an obligation to arrange for independent visitors to visit and befriend the child (Children Act 1989, Sch 2, para 17(1)). In addition Sch 2, para 10(b) states that:

> 'Every local authority shall take such steps as are reasonably practicable, where any child within their area who is in need and whom they are not looking after is living apart from his family … (b) to promote contact between him and his family, if, in their opinion, it is necessary to do so in order to safeguard or promote his welfare.'

Similarly, Sch 2, para 15(1) states:

> 'Where a child is being looked after by a local authority, the authority shall, unless it is not reasonably practicable or consistent with his welfare, endeavour to promote contact between the child and (a) his parents; (b) any person who is not a parent of his but who has parental responsibility for him; and (c) any relative, friend or other person connected with him.'

Section 85 of the Children Act 1989 applies where a child has been accommodated by a health authority or a local education authority for a consecutive period of more than 3 months or with the intention of accommodating him for such a period (s 85(1)(a) and (b)). If so, then the accommodating authority must notify the relevant local authority, and that local authority must then 'take such steps as are reasonably practicable to enable them to determine whether the child's welfare is adequately safeguarded and promoted while he is accommodated by the accommodating authority and … consider the extent to which (if at all) they should exercise any of their functions under this Act with respect to the child' (s 85(4)(a) and (b)). The range of powers relevant to a child with a mental disorder have been summarised above. Finally, s 86 of the Children Act 1989 (children accommodated in care homes or independent hospitals) applies in the same circumstances as s 85 save that it concerns care homes and hospitals, and has exactly the same consequences for the notification to a local authority, and the exercising of any of its powers (s 86(1)(a) and (b); s 86(3)(a) and (b)). If a notification is given, under either section, then the local authority is obliged to ensure that an independent visitor sees the child and then to provide the local authority with advice on the performance of its duties, which may include the frequency of visiting arrangements, circumstances in which visiting arrangements must require a child to be visited and additional functions of a representative (s 86A(1)–(6)).

16.25 It should be clear from the above that where a local authority is involved with a child, there will be obligations owed to the child over and above the provisions of MHA 1983 which may make a significant difference to the quality of life of the child whilst detained. If there are deficiencies in the care plan for the child, it may be incumbent upon the Tribunal to draw attention to these deficits.

16.26 There is no lower age limit for detention under MHA 1983. If this is to happen, then expertise is required from CAMHS. Gillick competence is plainly relevant to admission and treatment and, whilst it relates to children, the overall consideration of competence is indistinguishable from that which falls to be considered in respect of adults (eg there may be competence to consent to some things, but not others, and competence may fluctuate). Emergency treatment should not await a determination of any of the above.

16.27 In certain circumstances (eg where neither MHA 1983 nor MCA 2005 can be applied) it may be necessary to apply to the High Court to exercise its inherent jurisdiction. Paragraph 36.66 of the Code provides examples.

16.28 Children have the same entitlement to apply to a Tribunal as other patients. They should also have facilities for education if they are below school leaving age.

Part D

OFFENDER PATIENTS

Chapter 17

OFFENDER PATIENTS – INTRODUCTION

17.1 The routes *into* hospital for mentally disordered offenders are manifold, and fairly complex. For a detailed consideration of those routes, a textbook from the criminal jurisdiction must be consulted. An outline of the procedures is set out in Chapter 20. The criteria for discharge *via* the Tribunal are all to be found in MHA 1983, s 72(7); s 73 (power to discharge restricted patients); s 74 (discharge of restricted patients subject to restriction directions); and s 75 (conditionally discharged restricted patients).

DEFINITIONS AND TERMINOLOGY

17.2 A 'hospital order' or 'guardianship order' can be made as a result of MHA 1983, s 37. An 'interim hospital order' can be made as a result of MHA 1983, s 38. These orders can be made as 'unrestricted orders' or 'restricted orders'. MHA 1983, s 41 enables the court to restrict the discharge of those who are subject to hospital (or guardianship) orders from hospital. The order will be without limit of time. There is no longer a provision for time-limited restriction orders (MHA 2007, s 40(1)). The only way of being discharged will be as a result of a decision by the Secretary of State for Justice, or the Tribunal. The Tribunal can discharge either *absolutely* or *conditionally* in respect of a patient who is subject to a hospital order with a restriction. If an absolute discharge is given, then both the hospital order and the restriction come to an end. If a conditional discharge is given, then it is dependent upon compliance with the conditions.

17.3 A prisoner who has been sentenced can be transferred from prison to hospital. This will be done by the Secretary of State, and may in addition be subject to restrictions. This is a 'restriction direction'. This class of patient is sometimes referred to as 'a restricted transfer direction patient'.

17.4 An *unsentenced* prisoner can also be transferred in a similar manner to that set out above at **17.3**.

17.5 A hospital order may be made (with or without restrictions) the purpose of which is treatment (and not punishment). A sentenced prisoner may be transferred to hospital (for treatment) whilst serving out his or her term of imprisonment. An unsentenced prisoner falls into a similar category. MHA 1983, s 45A enables both to happen (eg punishment by way of a sentence *and* hospital order for treatment). His or her status remains that of a prisoner. If the prisoner gets better, he or she will go back to prison.

17.6 All patients who have been moved to hospital (via one method or another), and who are subject to restriction orders, restriction directions or limitation directions, are referred to as 'restricted patients'.

17.7 All patients who are concerned with criminal proceedings or are under sentence are commonly referred to as 'Part III' patients. The most directly relevant specific statutory provisions (together with a brief explanation) are set out below. Most of Part C has direct relevance to Part D, and where appropriate references are made to the appropriate paragraphs or chapters within those parts of the text.

17.8 The Code of Practice (Chapter 33, reproduced in Part E) sets out in broad terms the guidance for those who 'arrange treatment for mentally disordered people who come into contact with the criminal justice system' (para 33.1).

REMAND TO HOSPITAL FOR REPORT AND ASSESSMENT

17.9 The process of entry into hospital from prison may start at this stage. The Tribunal has no involvement with this part of the detention process. MHA 1983, ss 35 and 36 govern the regime whereby an accused person may be remanded to hospital for a report on his or her mental condition, or for treatment for his or her mental condition (see Part F). In respect of s 35, the process will start where there is evidence (oral or written) from a doctor that there is reason to suspect that the accused is suffering from a mental disorder, The maximum period is 28 days at a time, and not for more than 12 weeks in all. The accused is entitled to obtain his or her own independent report as to his or her mental state. In respect of s 36, the process will start where two doctors provide evidence (written or oral) that the accused is suffering from a mental disorder of a nature or degree which makes it appropriate for him or her to be detained in a hospital for medical treatment, and that appropriate medical treatment is available for him or her. The balance of the provision matches those for s 35. Those remanded under these sections do not have a nearest relative for the purpose of the MHA 1983.

Chapter 18

DETENTION AND DISCHARGE

DETENTION AND DISCHARGE UNDER THE MENTAL HEALTH ACT 1983, S 37

Admission criteria

18.1 Admission criteria are contained in MHA 1983, s 37. Specifically, the criteria for an order for either hospital admission or guardianship are set out in s 37(2)(a)(i)–(ii) and (b):

> '37 Powers of courts to order hospital admission or guardianship
>
> …
>
> (2) The conditions referred to in subsection (1) above are that –
>
> (a) the court is satisfied, on the written or oral evidence of two registered medical practitioners, that the offender is suffering from mental disorder and that either –
> (i) the mental disorder from which the offender is suffering is of a nature or degree which makes it appropriate for him to be detained in a hospital for medical treatment and appropriate medical treatment is available for him; or
> (ii) in the case of an offender who has attained the age of 16 years, the mental disorder is of a nature or degree which warrants his reception into guardianship under this Act; and
>
> (b) the court is of the opinion, having regard to all the circumstances including the nature of the offence and the character and antecedents of the offender, and to the other available methods of dealing with him, that the most suitable method of disposing of the case is by means of an order under this section.'

18.2 These expressions used in the statute have been considered at **6.1–6.3**, **6.10–6.20**, **7.7**, **7.8**, **7.10**, **7.11**, **9.1**, **9.2**, **9.4–9.9** and **9.15**. There is also a power to make interim hospital orders (MHA 1983, s 38) (see Part F).

Effect of hospital orders, guardianship orders and interim hospital orders

18.3 These are set out at MHA 1983, s 40 (see Part F). If a guardianship order is made, then it has the same effect as one made via Part II (see **9.4** and **9.6–9.9**). The hospital order lasts for a maximum of 6 months, and can be renewed. This runs from the day upon which the court made the order. The nearest relative has no power to discharge the patient. A patient may not apply for discharge by a Tribunal until after the initial 6-month period has expired, and nor do hospital managers have an obligation to refer the case to the Tribunal for the same period. An unrestricted order brings all other existing authority to detain to an end.

Discharge

Hospital order

18.4 If no restriction order or limitation direction is made, then the law in respect of all of aspects discharge is as set out at Chapter 8 (ie it is the same as for MHA 1983, s 3). A hospital order (whether with or without restrictions) 'diverts the offender from punishment to treatment' (Code, para 33.22). This principle has also been set out (in greater detail) in *R v Birch*.[1]

Guardianship

18.5 If an order that the patient should be received into guardianship has been made then the law is as set out at Chapter 9 (ie it is the same as for MHA 1983, s 7).

18.6 As a general rule, those who are subject to either of the above are likely to have been convicted of relatively minor offences. The opposite will be the case for those who are subject to restriction orders.

DETENTION AND DISCHARGE UNDER MHA 1983, SS 37 AND 41

Restriction and detention

18.7 The regime for restriction orders is different to that set out in Part C. MHA 1983, s 41 is set out in Part F. A restriction order may be made at the same time as a hospital order.

18.8 The patient will remain subject to the order irrespective of any time-limits imposed by MHA 1983, Part II. CTOs and community patients are not a part of this regime at all. Neither MHA 1983, s 66 nor s 69(1) (see Part F) apply to patients detained pursuant to a restriction order. Leave of absence, transfer elsewhere, discharge via MHA 1983, s 23 and recall from leave granted can only be granted with the permission of the Secretary of State for the Ministry of Justice. There may be an order that the patient is detained in a specific facility. The order itself can be terminated by the Secretary of State, or if the patient is absolutely discharged by the RC, by the hospital managers (if

---

1 (1989) 11 Cr App R (S) 202.

they have the consent of the Secretary of State) or by the Tribunal. While the restriction order remains in force, so does the hospital order.

18.9 It should be noted that prior to October 2007 a restriction order could be made for a fixed period, and these will expire through effluxion of time. It is no longer possible for the court to impose a restriction order for a specific period.

Discharge

18.10 The criteria for discharge of a restricted patient are contained in MHA 1983, s 73. (It should be noted that the residual discretion to discharge a Part II patient contained in MHA 1983, s 72(1) is specifically disapplied in respect of this category of patient by s 72(7).)

> **'73 Power to discharge restricted patients**
>
> (1) Where an application to the appropriate tribunal is made by a restricted patient who is subject to a restriction order, or where the case of such a patient is referred to the appropriate tribunal, the tribunal shall direct the absolute discharge of the patient if –
>
> (a) the tribunal is not satisfied as to the matters mentioned in paragraph (b)(i) or (ii) or (iia) of section 72(1) above; and
> (b) the tribunal is satisfied that it is not appropriate for the patient to remain liable to be recalled to hospital for further treatment.
>
> (2) Where in the case of any such patient as is mentioned in subsection (1) above –
>
> (a) paragraph (a) of that subsection applies; but
> (b) paragraph (b) of that subsection does not apply,
>
> the tribunal shall direct the conditional discharge of the patient.
>
> (3) Where a patient is absolutely discharged under this section he shall thereupon cease to be liable to be detained by virtue of the relevant hospital order, and the restriction order shall cease to have effect accordingly.
>
> (4) Where a patient is conditionally discharged under this section –
>
> (a) he may be recalled by the Secretary of State under subsection (3) of section 42 above as if he had been conditionally discharged under subsection (2) of that section; and
> (b) the patient shall comply with such conditions (if any) as may be imposed at the time of discharge by the tribunal or at any subsequent time by the Secretary of State.
>
> (5) The Secretary of State may from time to time vary any condition imposed (whether by the tribunal or by him) under subsection (4) above.

(6) Where a restriction order in respect of a patient ceases to have effect after he has been conditionally discharged under this section the patient shall, unless previously recalled, be deemed to be absolutely discharged on the date when the order ceases to have effect and shall cease to be liable to be detained by virtue of the relevant hospital order.

(7) A tribunal may defer a direction for the conditional discharge of a patient until such arrangements as appear to the tribunal to be necessary for that purpose have been made to its satisfaction; and where by virtue of any such deferment no direction has been given on an application or reference before the time when the patient's case comes before the tribunal on a subsequent application or reference, the previous application or reference shall be treated as one on which no direction under this section can be given.

(8) This section is without prejudice to section 42 above.'

It should be noted that the residual discretion to discharge a Part II patient contained in s 72(1) is specifically disapplied in respect of this category of patient by s 72(7).

18.11 The pro forma for the Tribunal (Form 15 Restricted) sets out the criteria in the following format:

'The Tribunal is/is not satisfied that the patient is suffering from mental disorder or from mental disorder of a nature or degree which makes it appropriate for the patient to be detained in a hospital for medical treatment.

The Tribunal is/is not satisfied that it is necessary for the health or safety of the patient or for the protection of other persons that the patient should receive such treatment.

The Tribunal is/is not satisfied that appropriate medical treatment is available for the patient.

The Tribunal is/is not satisfied that it is appropriate for the patient to remain liable to be recalled to hospital for further treatment.

The Tribunal considers that conditions are not required.'

18.12 The options available to the Tribunal are set out in the same pro-forma as being:

'The patient shall NOT be discharged from liability in hospital for medical treatment.

The patient shall be CONDITIONALLY discharged from liability to be detained in hospital for medical treatment, BUT the patient will remain liable to be recalled to hospital for further treatment should it become necessary. The tribunal also imposes the CONDITION(S) set out below.

> The patient shall be ABSOLUTELY discharged from liability to be detained in hospital for medical treatment.
>
> The tribunal is currently of the view that a Conditional Discharge should be directed but it is not satisfied that the conditions now proposed (set out below) can be implemented immediately. Consequently the tribunal DEFERS a final decision.
>
> The tribunal directs that, by no later than [insert date] it must be advised as to the progress of the arrangements necessary for the proposed Conditional Discharge to be implemented, after which time it will decide whether to direct an immediate Conditional Discharge, or, alternatively, whether to reconvene.'

Thus, the options are actually (a) to adjourn; (b) not to discharge; (c) to discharge absolutely; (d) to discharge conditionally; (e) to discharge conditionally but to defer the discharge until it is satisfied that the necessary arrangements have been made to meet those conditions, and the Tribunal will reconvene to review the decision and its implementation. It can also, of course, make appropriate case management directions.

18.13 All of the phrases used above, save for that at relating to whether or not the Tribunal can be satisfied as to it being appropriate for the patient to remain liable to be recalled to hospital for further treatment, have been discussed at various points in Chapters 6, 7 and 8.

18.14 If the Tribunal is *not* satisfied that the criteria for continued detention for treatment under a hospital order are made out, then it must discharge. However, unless the Tribunal is *also* satisfied that the patient does not need to remain liable to recall for further treatment, then such a discharge must be conditional. This type of decision has been recently considered in two cases. The first is *DC v Nottinghamshire Healthcare Trust and the Secretary of State for Justice*.[2] On the facts, a Tribunal considered the application, but adjourned it to allow aftercare arrangements to be made, but also concluded that none of the criteria for detention in hospital for treatment were made out. It also held that he should be subject to recall. When the Tribunal reconvened, it was argued that it should have made an order for a deferred discharge at the earlier hearing. It then adjourned again, on the basis of a lack of time to hear evidence as to after-care arrangements, and also as it wished further evidence as to any risk of a recurrence of the conduct which had led to the original offence. The appeal was heard by UTJ Jacobs, and reached the following conclusions. First, where a Tribunal is satisfied that a patient should not be detained, but should be subject to a recall, then MHA 1983, s 73 imposes a duty to discharge, subject to deferring the direction by reason of s 73(7) (in order to ensure that the arrangements can be put in place). The power to *adjourn* cannot be used if there is an obligation to make a specific decision under s 73 (as there was in this case). As a direction will include any conditions required on discharge, the Tribunal should use s 73 when it is able to find that a patient should *not* be detained, and *should* be subject to recall. Thus, s 73(7) will continue to operate

---

2 [2012] UKUT 92 (AAC), [2012] MHLR 238.

until all is in place, and the sole function of the Tribunal is to lift the deferred discharge, and the specified conditions can be put in place (assuming that this has been done, of course). UTJ Jacobs held that s 73(7) is not the mechanism for gathering information as to whether *in principle* a conditional discharge might be appropriate or not, or what the conditions might be, or whether aftercare is available and if so in which form. However, an adjournment itself might be an appropriate mechanism for obtaining information such as that listed. Thus, although the decision sheds light on the respective function of s 73(7) and the procedure to be adopted, the appeal was dismissed upon the basis that 'the choice on the facts may be difficult'. The second case is *Secretary of State v MP and Nottinghamshire Healthcare NHS Trust*.[3] On the facts in this case, the patient was given a conditional discharge, but then recalled, and then discharged by the Tribunal with no conditions at all attached. UTJ Jacobs considered the appeal, and concluded that the task of the Tribunal was (a) to consider whether the patient should be discharged on the day of the hearing and (b) to use the evidence it had to make that decision. The Tribunal had found that there was no mental disorder, and that the substance abuse had not led to any recurrence of his psychotic symptoms. The UT pointed out that:

> 'A tribunal has power to make a patient's discharge conditional even if the patient does not have a mental disorder *(R v Merseyside Mental Health Review Tribunal ex parte K* [1990] 1 All ER 694 at 699–700). It is permissible to direct a conditional discharge without imposing any further conditions, as envisaged by section 73(4)(b). A tribunal is under a duty to explain its decision, including a decision not to impose further conditions … the tribunal found that Mr P had a drug induced psychosis and that he continued to use drugs. Indeed, he said that he would do if he were discharged. The tribunal found that that involved a risk of self-neglect. In those circumstances, the tribunal was under a duty to explain why it did not impose conditions.'[4]

Due to the circumstances of the case that were peculiar to it, the decision was not set aside, but constituted declarations of the errors made. In effect, these amounted to a failure to provide adequate reasons for the conclusions that it had reached in respect of the cause of the mental disorder, and the absence of conditions.

ABSOLUTE DISCHARGE

18.15 The subject of *treatability* has been considered at **6.1–6.20**. If the mental disorder is not amenable to treatment (and this is a very broad concept) and is therefore untreatable, there must be an absolute discharge. The authority for this proposition is to be found in *Reid v Secretary of State for Scotland*.[5] If a Tribunal finds that a patient is not mentally disordered at the time of the Tribunal, then it must direct a conditional discharge unless satisfied that it is appropriate for the patient to remain liable to recall to hospital. If this is the

3 [2013] UKUT 25 (AAC).

4 Ibid, at [20].

5 [1999] 2 AC 512, HL; (*EC Chs 5 and 6*).

decision of the Tribunal (either that it is or is not appropriate), it must address this issue in its decision. In *R (Home Secretary) v Mental Health Review Tribunal (BR as Interested Party*[6] issues arose as to (a) the rationality of decision to absolutely discharge and (b) reclassification. The latter is no longer relevant. In respect of the former, the Tribunal determined that it was not appropriate for the patient to remain liable for recall, and that he did not suffer from a (psychopathic) disorder and nor was there an enduring mental disorder. The court held that the decisions for reaching such a decision were adequate. In *DL v South London & Maudsley NHS Trust Foundation & Secretary of State for Justice*[7] the issue of adequate reasoning was considered when a decision was made not to grant an absolute discharge. The patient had applied for an absolute discharge under s 75(3) of the MHA 1983. UTJ Lane held that although s 75(3) had no criteria for the exercise of discretion to grant a conditional discharge, the Tribunal was obliged to consider such matters as the nature, gravity and circumstances of the offence, the nature and gravity of his mental disorder, past, present and future, the risk of likelihood of reoffending and the degree of harm possible, the risk and likelihood of a recurrence of exacerbation of any mental disorder, the risk and likelihood of the need for recall for hospital and the reasons for the conditional discharge. All of this, of course, is included in the case of *R (SC) v (1) Mental Health Tribunal (2) Secretary of State for Health (3) Home Secretary* as set out in **18.36**.

Prohibition on deferred absolute discharge

18.16 An absolute discharge is just that – it takes place immediately, and it is not possible for the Tribunal to defer it for any period. It also brings the authority imposed by the restriction order and the hospital order to an end. In *R v Home Secretary v MHRT (VW as Interested Party)*[8] the court considered the regime for both absolute discharge and conditional discharge. In respect of absolute discharge, Moses J held that:[9]

> 'It is plain from the structure of the statute that the Tribunal is only required to direct an absolute discharge where it is both not satisfied as to the matters referred to in s.72 (1) (b) (i) or (ii), and where it is satisfied that it is not appropriate for the patient to remain liable to be recalled to hospital for further treatment … There is no power in the Tribunal to defer an absolute discharge. It must either absolutely discharge the patient where the conditions are not met, or it must not.'

Whether appropriate for the patient to remain liable to be recalled to hospital for further treatment

18.17 The same authority went on to consider the statutory regime in respect of the appropriacy of the patient for recall for treatment. It also queried the evidential basis upon which the Tribunal had determined that the mental

6 [2005] EWHC 2468 (Admin), [2006] MHLR 168.
7 [2010] UKUT 455 (AAC), [2011] MHLR 34.
8 [2004] EWHC 1029 (Admin), [2004] MHLR 184; (*EC Ch 6*).
9 Ibid, at [18], [20].

disorder from which the patient suffered was deemed by the Tribunal to be untreatable. However, Moses J held that:[10]

> 'It is plain to me, even when the Tribunal conclude that a patient is not suffering from a [mental disorder] … it is incumbent upon the Tribunal in cases of restricted patients to go on to consider whether it is satisfied that it is not appropriate for the patient to be recalled for further treatment. That is clear from the words of s 73(1)(b) … I conclude that it was incumbent on the Tribunal to consider the question of a conditional discharge.'

In effect, the Tribunal was wrong to consider the mental disorder to be untreatable, since it appeared on the evidence that treatment was being carried out which 'alleviates or prevents a deterioration of the symptoms of mental disorder, not the disorder itself which gives rise to them'[11] and the proper course of action would possibly have been to order a conditional discharge.

18.18 The importance of the Tribunal considering MHA 1983, s 73(1)(b) was affirmed in *R (On the Application of the Home Secretary) v MHRT: G as Interested Party*.[12] An absolute discharge had been made in that case, as well, and it was held that the Tribunal had failed to consider this part of the statutory criteria. Pill LJ held that:[13]

> 'The requirement of this paragraph must be satisfied before an absolute discharge can be directed … The possible consequences for the safety of members of the public and the patient, when an order of absolute discharge is made, are such that the question of liability to be recalled must be dealt with expressly … The importance of the factor of public safety, where restriction orders have been made, has recently been affirmed by the House of Lords *Anderson and Others v Scottish Ministers* [2001] MHLR 192. An order of absolute discharge has the effect of determining finally the s 37 and s 41 orders. The failure to deal with the requirement of s 73(1)(b) is a flaw fatal to the tribunal's decision.'

CONDITIONAL DISCHARGE

Deferred conditional discharge

18.19 If the Tribunal does discharge a patient subject to conditions, it is permissible for that discharge to be deferred in order for it to be satisfied that arrangements have been made for those conditions to be fulfilled. However, the case-law cited at **7.22**, **8.21** and **8.23** prevents such a deferral being for the purposes of monitoring the progress of the patient pending that discharge. Also, where a restricted patient is concerned, the deferred discharge does not become effective *until* the conditions have been fulfilled. It must only be to achieve the (limited) function of the Tribunal. This has been confirmed

---

10 Ibid, at [21], [26].

11 *Reid v Secretary of State for Scotland*, cited at [15].

12 [2001] EWHC 849 (Admin), [2002] MHLR 260; (*EC Ch 6*).

13 Ibid, at [24], [25].

(additionally) in the authorities referred to below. Pending discharge, decisions as to (for example) leave still fall to be considered by the RC, and permission granted not by the Tribunal, but by the Secretary of State. This issue arose in *R (RA) v Home Secretary*,[14] where it was held that the Secretary of State has an obligation to respond with reasonable promptness to the recommendations of a Tribunal, and not in a fashion that obstructs or frustrates the overall purpose of its order (which was for a deferred conditional discharge).

18.20 In *R (Home Secretary) v MHRT (PG as Interested Party)*[15] a decision was made to defer discharge pending various incomplete assessments of the patient. Newman J held that this amounted to a:[16]

> '... "wait and see" decision; not for the proper objective of seeing whether the nature of the accommodation was to be available or for other matters in connection with arrangements ...'

Since this is not a permissible function of the Tribunal the decision was quashed. A similar matter was considered in *R (on the application of the Secretary of State for the Home Department) v MHRT*[17] (see also **3.37**). A restricted patient was the subject of an extra-statutory recommendation for consideration of transfer to conditions of lesser security. This is outside the statutory powers of the Tribunal within this context. The Tribunal adjourned in order for further investigations to be made on this issue, and the Secretary of State made a (successful) application to judicially review that decision. It succeeded upon the basis that the Tribunal had acted in excess of its jurisdiction. A very similar situation arose in *MP v Nottinghamshire Healthcare NHS Trust*,[18] with similar results. In *LC v DHIC(CHL) Secretary of State for Justice, CUK*[19] the circumstances in which a decision to make a deferred conditional discharge could be set aside was considered. The facts of the case involved a Tribunal making a decision to grant a deferred conditional discharge, but with a date set to reconvene to review the implementation of the decision. At the subsequent hearing the Tribunal decided that there should not be a discharge. It cited various matters as being the basis of its decision. UTJ Levenson accepted that it was lawful for a Tribunal to monitor progress, and change its decision if it could not be implemented within a reasonable time; in this instance there was no evidence of a change in the behaviour of the patient that would justify such a decision. The decision was inadequate by reason of a lack of justification for the decision, and was remitted to a fresh Tribunal.

---

14 [2002] EWHC 1618 (Admin), [2003] MHLR 54.
15 [2002] EWHC 2043 (Admin), [2002] MHLR 381; (*EC Ch 6*).
16 Ibid, at [32].
17 [2000] MHLR 209.
18 [2003] EWHC 1782 (Admin), [2003] MHLR 381.
19 [2010] UKUT 319 (AAC), [2010] MHLR 337.

Legal status of deferred conditional discharge

18.21 The issue of deferred conditional discharge and the conditions that a Tribunal might wish to impose have been considered comprehensively in *R (IH) v (1) Home Secretary (2) Secretary of State for Health)*.[20] The substance of the claim of the patient was essentially that the Tribunal had no power to ensure that conditions which it had imposed were implemented either within a reasonable time or at all. The House of Lords upheld the decision in the Court of Appeal, and confirmed that the decision in *R v Oxford Regional MHRT ex parte Secretary of State for the Home Department*[21] should no longer be followed. In so doing, it relied upon the judgment of Lord Phillips MR, which in itself was summarised thus:[22]

> '(i) the tribunal can, at the outset, adjourn the hearing to investigate the possibility of imposing conditions. (ii) The tribunal can make a provisional decision to make a conditional discharge on specified conditions, including submitting to psychiatric supervision, but defer directing a conditional discharge while the authorities responsible for after-care under s 117 of the Act make the necessary arrangements to enable the patient to meet those conditions. (iii) The tribunal should meet after an appropriate interval to monitor progress in making these arrangements if they have not by then been put in place. (iv) Once the arrangements have been made, the tribunal can direct a conditional discharge without holding a further hearing. (v) If problems arise with making arrangements to meet the conditions, the tribunal has a number of options, depending upon the circumstances; (a) it can defer for a further period, perhaps with suggestions as to how any problems can be overcome; (b) it can amend or vary the proposed conditions to seek to overcome the difficulties that have been encountered; (c) it can order a conditional discharge without specific conditions, thereby making the patient subject to recall; (d) it can decide that the patient must remain detained in hospital for treatment. (vi) It will not normally be appropriate for a tribunal to direct a conditional discharge on conditions with which the patient will be unable to comply because it has not proved possible to make the necessary arrangements.'

The matter was taken to the European Court of Human Rights, but was dismissed as 'manifestly ill-founded'.[23]

18.22 Therefore, deferred conditional discharges must be treated as a provisional decision. This is (in part) to ensure that a patient is not left in limbo, with uncertainty as to his or her future. The options adumbrated above are open to the Tribunal whilst the decision remains provisional, which ranges across the entire spectrum of intermediate and final decisions available to it, and which remain within its powers. Ultimately, however, it may not be possible for conditions initially attached to a decision to be met. If this was the case, then according the individual facts of the case, and the risks associated with the patient (or lack of risk) this would then inform that final decision. It should be

---

20 [2003] UKHL 59, [2004] MHLR 51; (*EC Chs 1 and 6*).
21 [1988] AC 120.
22 [2003] EWHC 1782 (Admin), [2003] MHLR 381, at [24].
23 *IH v UK* [2005] MHLR 252.

noted that there is no absolute imposition on health authorities of an obligation to fulfil conditions imposed by a Tribunal (which might, for example, be impossible to perform).[24] Where a conditional discharge has been ordered and there is a substantial delay before such a discharge takes place, there is likely to be a breach of Art 5(4) of the ECHR, from which will flow an award of damages.[25] In that instance, there had been a delay of over one year.

Scope, purpose and effect of conditions

18.23 However, as cited in *R (SC) v (1) Mental Health Review Tribunal (2) Secretary of State for Health (3) Home Secretary* (see **18.33** and **18.35**):[26]

> 'What is for present purposes the important aspect of the legislative scheme has been recognised by the Court of Appeal in *R v Merseyside Mental Health Review Tribunal ex P K* [1990] 1 All ER 694 per Butler-Sloss LJ at 699 "Section 73 gives to the tribunal power to impose a conditional discharge and retain residual control over patients not then suffering from mental disorder or not to a degree requiring continued detention in hospital. This would appear to be a provision designed both for the support of the patient in the community and the protection of the public, and is an important discretionary power vested in an independent tribunal." As Moses J commented in *R (Home Secretary) v MHRT* [25] "It might very well be in such a case that, whilst a Tribunal would not be satisfied at one particular moment that someone was suffering from a [mental disorder] later on symptoms might emerge which would make it highly appropriate and indeed necessary for such a patient to be recalled to hospital".'

18.24 Munby J continued thus:[27]

> 'These cases show that the purpose of conditional discharge is not necessarily to impose a requirement for ongoing treatment for a [mental disorder]. It may be no more … than to ensure monitoring … it makes no sense to demand a link between the mental disorder from which the patient … is suffering and the grounds for believing, within the meaning of s 73 (1) (b) that "it is appropriate for the patient to remain liable to be recalled to hospital for further treatment". It follows … quite clearly from the language of s.73 itself, that there is no necessary link between the disorder from which a restricted patient was previously classified as suffering and the grounds for the conditional discharge in accordance with s 73.'

18.25 Finally, in *R (IH) v Nottinghamshire Healthcare NHS Trust and Others* it was held that:[28]

> '… the conditional discharge regime, properly used, is of great benefit to the patients and the public, and conducive to the Convention object of restricting the curtailment of personal liberty to the maximum, because it enables tribunals to

---

24 *R (On the Application of K) v Camden and Islington Health Authority* [2001] EWCA Civ 240, [2001] MHLR 24; (*EC Ch 2*).

25 *Kolanis v UK* (2006) 42 EHRR 12, [2006] CCLR 297, [2005] MHLR 238; (*EC Ch 6*).

26 [2005] EWHC 17 (Admin), [2005] MHLR 31, at [33].

27 Ibid, at [36]–[37].

28 [2003] UKHL 59, [2004] MHLR 51, at [26]; (*EC Chs 1 and 6*).

ensure that restricted patients compulsorily detained in hospital represent the hardcore of those who suffer from mental illness … If there is any possibility of treating and supervising a patient in the community, the imposition of conditions permits that possibility to be explored and, it may be, tried.'

The relevant primary care trust (PCT) and LSSA must then make arrangements to implement arrangements for after-care in order to permit the patient to be discharged in accordance with those conditions (see Chapters 11, 12, 24 and 25).

18.26 The type of conditions which either the Tribunal or the Secretary of State are likely to impose are similar to those for a CTO (see **10.18** and **10.19**), and will include staying in contact with mental health professionals (eg social worker, psychiatrist), probation officer, and so on. Conditions of residence are also very common, as are conditions to remain away from certain places. The Secretary of State can vary the conditions imposed by the Tribunal. Where a patient has been discharged, those in charge of supervision are obliged to report to the Secretary of State on the degree of compliance with the conditions. The issues referred to above have been revisited to some extent in the Court of Appeal (*Secretary of State for Justice v RB*).[29] The case had a tortuous journey prior to reaching the Court of Appeal, but the substance of the matter was the objection by the Secretary of State for Justice to what (it was argued) amounted to a decision of the Tribunal that was in excess of its powers. The patient had been granted a deferred conditional discharge to a care home, and the condition was that she must not leave the care home without an escort. This case should be considered alongside those referred to at **18.28** and **18.29** below. The appeal by the Secretary of State was predicated by the established law that a Tribunal could not direct a conditional discharge if the actual effect of such was that the conditions meant that the patient remained in detention, and that it also permitted the Tribunal to transfer a patient from one state of detention to another (and of course, the Tribunal has no power at all to do this). Arden LJ set out the law in great detail (by reference to the statute) and in this context held that:

'… a person who is conditionally discharged remains liable to recall … sections 42 and 73 make no reference to detention otherwise than in a hospital, and this would indicate that Parliament did not contemplate that on discharge a patient should be detained in an institution which was not a hospital.'[30]

Further, it was held that:

'… the core issue in this case is whether there is any statutory authority for a deprivation of liberty once an order for a conditional discharge has been made. The Strasbourg Court has made it clear that such an important matter must be "prescribed by law" … and that includes a requirement that the grounds on which a person may be deprived of his liberty when an order for conditional discharge is

---

29 [2011] EWCA Civ 1608, [2012] MHLR 131.

30 Ibid, at [27].

> to be made and the grounds upon which he is entitled to be released from the conditions imposing a deprivation of liberty must be found in the legislation.'[31]

Arden LJ characterised this as the 'prescribed by law' issue, and went on to consider other matters which are not of direct relevance for tribunals, given the decision in respect of the 'prescribed by law' issue. The Court held that the initial order of the Court related to a hospital only. There was no power in MHA 1983 that permitted a Tribunal to continue the detention in another form (a care home, in this instance). Detention (in a care home, not a hospital) would be counter to the scheme of MHA 1983. Transfers of restricted patients between forms of detention were a matter for the hospital and the Secretary of State (and not the Tribunal). The effect of the decision is that a Tribunal cannot order a conditional discharge that involves a continuing deprivation of liberty, outside hospital.

18.27 It is also worth noting that MHA 1983, s 42(1), (2) and (3) (see Part F) provides the Secretary of State with the power to direct that conditions and restrictions cease, as well as recalling the patient if there is non-compliance.

Escort

18.28 In *R (Home Secretary) v MHRT (PH as interested party)*[32] a Tribunal had discharged a patient with a condition attached that he did not leave his hostel without an escort. The Home Secretary sought to argue that this exceeded the power of the Tribunal in that it amounted to a transfer to a condition of lower security, within which detention still formed a part of the life of the patient (since, it was argued, when there was no escort, the patient would be obliged to remain in the hostel). The court dismissed the application (in part based upon the particular facts of the case, and the function of hostel accommodation and an escort in supporting the patient in the community, rather than depriving him of his liberty), but also based upon an extensive analysis of Strasbourg jurisprudence. In summary, Keene LJ enunciated the principles thus:[33]

> 'First, a basic distinction is to be drawn between mere restrictions on liberty of movement and the deprivation of liberty … Secondly, the distinction is one merely of degree or intensity of restrictions, not of nature or substance. Thirdly, the court must start with the concrete or actual situation of the individual concerned and take account of the range of criteria, such as the type, duration and effects and manner of implementation of the measure in question. Fourthly, account must be taken of the cumulative effect of the various restrictions … Fifthly, the purpose of any measures of restriction is a relevant consideration. If the measures are taken principally in the interests of the individual who is being restricted, they may well be regarded as not amounting to a deprivation of liberty and so no breach of

---

31 Ibid, at [48].

32 [2002] EWCA Civ 1868, [2003] MHLR 202; (*EC Ch 6*).

33 Ibid, at [14]–[16], [24].

> Article 5 (1) would arise … I cannot accept that [the] conditions [imposed] *inevitably* mean that this man would be in a regime so restrictive that he would be deprived of his liberty.'

This enunciation of the principle distinction between *deprivation* of liberty and *restriction* upon liberty has distinct similarities with the same principles used in guidance and case-law arising out of deprivation of liberty safeguards (MHA 2007, s 50, amending MCA 2005, in force April 2009).

18.29 In *R (Home Secretary) v MHRT (MP as interested party)*[34] similar conditions imposed by the Tribunal led the court to precisely the opposite conclusion. In large part that conclusion was predicated by the facts of the case and the effect of the conditions. The patient was a risk to young children (by virtue of his paedophilia, amongst other matters), and the conditions imposed were that he reside in a hostel with 24-hour staffing (who were to be experienced in dealing with violent sexual offenders) and must not leave his accommodation at any time, or go anywhere at any time, without an escort. Collins J held that this amounted to a deprivation of the patient's liberty, and the application by the Home Secretary was allowed.

Residence in hospital

18.30 In *R (G) v MHRT*[35] a condition was imposed that required the patient to live in a named hospital (but the decision was deferred until this condition could be met). It could not be met, and the Tribunal declined to vary the putative condition in accordance with the wishes of the patient (which were that he should reside in a flat within the secure part of the hospital). The Tribunal so declined on the basis that this would not amount to a discharge at all. Collins J agreed, in that such a condition would amount to a deprivation of liberty.

Medication

18.31 In *R (SH) v Mental Health Review Tribunal*[36] the principle issue was a condition imposed by the Tribunal that a condition of discharge was that the patient comply with taking his medication. However, the Tribunal also considered the scope and purpose of conditions generally, and to that extent amplifies the conclusions reached in that respect and referred to above. On a factual basis, the patient had been the subject of three conditions. The first was that he should comply with depot (injection) medication; the second was that he reside in a named hostel; and the third was that he should receive visits and attend appointments as required by his RC and social supervisor. His claim for judicial review of a decision by the Tribunal not to order an absolute discharge

---

34 [2004] EWHC 2194 (Admin), [2004] MHLR 273; (*EC Ch 6*).

35 [2004] EWHC 2193 (Admin), [2004] MHLR 265; (*EC Ch 6*).

36 [2007] EWHC 884 (Admin), [2007] MHLR 234; (*EC Ch 6*).

(and which had formed a part of his original application to the Tribunal) was that he would agree to take his medication without compulsion in any event. Holman J held (generally) that:[37]

> 'The critical difference between absolute and conditional discharge is that if the patient is only conditionally discharged, he may be recalled by the Secretary of State. The tribunal themselves do not necessarily have to impose any actual condition (see words "(if any)" in subs 4 (b)) but may do so. The Secretary of State has a wide power himself to impose conditions at any subsequent time, and from time to time vary any condition whether imposed by the tribunal or by himself … The references to conditions are entirely general and open ended and there are no express words in s.73, 75 or elsewhere limiting the scope or effect of any condition which may be attached. Clearly, however, the law imports or requires some limitations. A condition could not lawfully be capricious and must be relevant and for a proper purpose within the scope of the statute. It is not suggested that condition 1 is not relevant and for a proper purpose.'

In terms of the practical effect of a failure to comply with a condition, the court referred to the impact of *R (B) v MHRT and Home Secretary*[38]) and added:[39]

> 'The Secretary of State has a general power of recall under s 73(4)(a) but there is nothing to make recall and automatic sanction for non-compliance as such with a specific condition.'

Specifically, (in terms of the condition to accept medication) he held that:[40]

> 'The condition must be read as respecting and being subject to his own final choice, which must be his real or true choice … This approach no doubt requires that a Tribunal should not attach a condition in, or similar to, the terms of condition 1 unless there is a proper basis for anticipating that the patient does, and will, consent to the treatment … it would be better if there were added to condition 1 some such words as "subject always to his right to give or withhold consent to treatment or medication on any given occasion".'

Conditions/after-care

18.32 In *R v MHRT ex parte Russell Hall*[41] there were substantial delays in implementing the conditions imposed by the Tribunal (which in themselves were unremarkable), but it was held that those conditions should be capable of implementation within a reasonable time. It was also held, however, that a Tribunal (in the circumstances of this case) should have called for further evidence, including a care plan.

---

37 Ibid, at [17]–[18].

38 [2003] MHLR 19; (*EC Chs 1, 7 14 and 15*).

39 [2007] EWHC 884 (Admin), [2007] MHLR 234, at [36].

40 Ibid, at [37]–[41].

41 [1999] MHLR 63; (*EC Chs 1, 2 and 6*).

Recall

18.33 The effect of non-compliance can be a recall to hospital. This is done by a warrant being issued. Once recalled, the patient will be obliged to apply to the Tribunal for discharge, and the Secretary of State must in any event refer the case to the Tribunal within one month of such a recall. The recall itself has an impact on the right to apply to a Tribunal, in that it has the effect of permitting the patient to be treated as if he or she had first been admitted to hospital (and therefore not until 6 months has elapsed from recall). However, this in itself may be academic given the obligation of the Secretary of State to refer the case to the Tribunal in any event. The issue of delays inherent within this procedure, and the system itself, was considered in *Rayner and Marsh v (1) Secretary of State for the Home Department (2) MHRT (3) West Kent NHS and Social Care Trust (4) Secretary of State for Health (5) Attorney General (6) Mental Health Review Tribunal Office*.[42] It was held that it was compliant with Art 5 of the ECHR, although delays caused by administrative oversight (amounting to 14 weeks) could lead to an award of damages.

18.34 The power of the Secretary of State to issue a warrant is not unfettered. Munby J held that:[43]

> 'In recalling a restricted patient, the Secretary of State has to act compatibly with the patient's right under the [ECHR] … This means that the Secretary of State must have up to date medical evidence that the patient is, at the time of the recall, suffering from a true mental disorder, and that evidence must show that the criteria for detention are met.'

The same issue was considered in *B v MHRT and Secretary of State for the Home Department* where Scott Baker J held that:[44]

> 'Since *Kay v UK* 40 BMLR 20 it has been necessary for the Secretary of State, in order to justify recall, to have up to date medical evidence showing that the criteria for detention are met.'

Discharge of conditions (MHA 1983, s 75)

18.35 It is open to a patient to apply to discharge or vary the conditions that have been imposed. This may happen (in addition) where a referral has been made to the Tribunal (after a recall) in any event.

> '75 Applications and references concerning conditionally discharged restricted patients
>
> (1) Where a restricted patient has been conditionally discharged under section 42(2), 73 or 74 above and is subsequently recalled to hospital –

---

[42] [2007] EWHC 1028 (Admin), [2007] 10 CCLR 464, [2008] MHLR 115; (*EC Ch 14*).

[43] *R (SC) v (1) Mental Health Review Tribunal (2) Secretary of State for Health (3) Home Secretary* [2005] EWHC 17 (Admin), [2005] MHLR 31, at [7].

[44] [2002] EWHC 1553 (Admin), [2003] MHLR 19, at [31].

(a) the Secretary of State shall, within one month of the day on which the patient returns or is returned to hospital, refer his case to the appropriate tribunal; and
(b) section 70 above shall apply to the patient as if the relevant hospital order, hospital direction or transfer direction had been made on that day.

(2) Where a restricted patient has been conditionally discharged as aforesaid but has not been recalled to hospital he may apply to the appropriate tribunal –

(a) in the period between the expiration of 12 months and the expiration of two years beginning with the date on which he was conditionally discharged; and
(b) in any subsequent period of two years.

(3) Sections 73 and 74 above shall not apply to an application under subsection (2) above but on any such application the tribunal may –

(a) vary any condition to which the patient is subject in connection with his discharge or impose any condition which might have been imposed in connection therewith; or
(b) direct that the restriction order, limitation direction or restriction direction to which he is subject shall cease to have effect;

and if the tribunal gives a direction under paragraph (b) above the patient shall cease to be liable to be detained by virtue of the relevant hospital order, hospital direction or transfer direction.

Criteria for discharge of conditions

18.36 The significance of s 75(3) was considered extensively in *R (SC) v (1) Mental Health Review Tribunal (2) Secretary of State for Health (3) Home Secretary*[45] (see **18.33**). The issue was whether or not this section provides the patient with sufficient foreseeability in respect of any such application. Munby J held that a number of factors did provide sufficient foreseeability. First, there was the statutory context in which the law was framed. On the facts in the case (and by extrapolation to restricted patients generally) he held:[46]

'Any patient applying under s 75(3) will, by definition, have been, just as SC was:

(i) convicted of a criminal offence sufficiently grave as to merit a possible sentence of imprisonment (s 37(1));
(ii) found to be suffering from a mental disorder meriting his detention in hospital for treatment (s 37(2)(a)(i));
(iii) found to be someone whose risk of re-offending is such that a restriction order is "necessary for the protection of the public from serious harm" (s 41(1)); and
(iv) found by the Tribunal (unless previously discharged by the Secretary of State under s 42 (2)) to be someone who, although not requiring for the time being

---

45 [2005] EWHC 17 (Admin), [2005] MHLR 31.
46 Ibid, at [56]–[59].

> to be detained in hospital for medical treatment (ss 72(1)(b), s 73(1)(a), s 73(2)(a)) should nonetheless remain liable to be recalled to hospital for further treatment s.73 (2) (b)).
>
> ...
>
> It is against this background that the exercise by the Tribunal of its powers under s 75(3) takes place. Accordingly the Tribunal when exercising these powers will need to consider such matters as the nature, gravity and circumstances of the patient's offence, the nature and gravity of his mental disorder, past, present and future, the risk and likelihood of the patient re-offending, the degree of harm to which the public may be exposed if he re-offends, the risk and recurrence or exacerbation of any mental disorder, and the risk and likelihood of his needing to be recalled in the future for further treatment in hospital. The Tribunal will also need to consider the nature of any conditions previously imposed ... the reasons why they were imposed and the extent to which it is desirable to continue, vary or add to them ... the existence of the broad discretion which is conferred by s.75 (3) ... serves to ensure that the Tribunal can respond flexibly and appropriately to the varied and potentially complex situations which may arise when a restricted patient has been conditionally discharged ... such an exercise is fact-intensive and strongly dependant upon the clinical details of each particular case ... He also held that 'one of the key questions that the Tribunal will wish to ask itself when considering how to exercise its powers under s 75(3) is whether it is – as s 73(1)(b) puts it – "satisfied that it is not appropriate for the patient to remain liable to be recalled to hospital for further treatment". If the Tribunal is not so satisfied, then it is difficult to see that is could be appropriate for it to make an order under s 75(3)(b).'

The pro-forma for this type of application is Form 18. The options are clear: either to order that the conditional discharge continues as before and/or to remove or vary conditions, or to order that the relevant parts of the order shall cease to have effect. In the body of the pro-forma itself there is included almost verbatim the ratio of Munby LJ (as he now is) in the case cited above.

Restricted patients subject to restriction directions (MHA 1983, s 74)

18.37 A summary of the provisions in respect of a patient who falls into this category is as follows. There is no distinction to be made between a patient subject to a restriction direction and a restricted hospital order in terms of the criteria for discharge. However, if a Tribunal decides that such a patient is entitled to be either discharged absolutely or subject to conditions, then it is obliged to notify the Secretary of State.

18.38 The pro formas used by the Tribunal are Form 19 and Form 20 which set out the basis for its decision thus:

'Form 19

If the patient had been subject to a Restriction Order under section 41 the patient would NOT have been entitled to be discharged from liability to be detained in hospital for medical treatment.

The patient would have been entitled to be CONDITIONALLY discharged from liability to be detained in hospital for medical treatment (whilst remaining liable to be recalled to hospital for further medical treatment should it become necessary) without any conditions/with the conditions set out below.

In the event of the patient (who would have been entitled to a Conditional Discharge If subject to a restriction order) not being so discharged (or being a s.48/49 patient) the Tribunal makes NO RECOMMENDATION.

The tribunal RECOMMENDS under s.74(1)(b) that the patient should continue to be detained in hospital.

The patient would have been entitled to be ABSOLUTELY discharged from liability to be detained in hospital for medical treatment.

The Tribunal is/is not satisfied that the patient is suffering from mental disorder or from mental disorder of a nature or degree which makes it appropriate for the patient to be detained in a hospital for medical treatment.

The Tribunal is/is not satisfied that it is necessary for the health or safety of the patient or for the protection of other persons that the patient should receive such treatment.

The Tribunal is/is not satisfied that appropriate medical treatment is available for the patient.

The Tribunal is/is not satisfied that it is appropriate for the patient to remain liable to be recalled to hospital for further treatment.

The tribunal considers that conditions are not required.'

Form 20

By a notification dated [insert date] the tribunal notified the Secretary of State that, if the patient had been subject to a restriction order under section 41, the patient would have been entitled to be ABSOLUTELY discharged from liability to be detained in hospital for medical treatment.

The patient would have been entitled to be CONDITIONALLY discharged from liability to be detained in hospital for medical treatment (whilst remaining liable to be recalled to hospital for further treatment should it become necessary) but without conditions.

In accordance with s.74(2) the tribunal therefore directs the ABSOLUTE/ CONDITIONAL Discharge of the patient and the patient shall be subject to the CONDITION (S) set out below.'

18.39 The Tribunal then may follow any of the courses open to it as set out above. This includes a recommendation that the patient remain in hospital (rather than be transferred elsewhere) if he or she is not discharged. If a sentenced prisoner does so remain in hospital by virtue of such a recommendation, then he or she make may an application to a parole board for release, once he or she has reached that stage of their sentence which amounts to the minimum period.

'74 Restricted patients subject to restriction directions

(1) Where an application to the appropriate tribunal is made by a restricted patient who is subject to a limitation direction or restriction direction, or where the case of such a patient is referred to the appropriate tribunal the tribunal –

(a) shall notify the Secretary of State whether, in its opinion, the patient would, if subject to a restriction order, be entitled to be absolutely or conditionally discharged under section 73 above; and
(b) if they notify him that the patient would be entitled to be conditionally discharged, may recommend that in the event of his not being discharged under this section he should continue to be detained in hospital.

(2) If in the case of a patient not falling within subsection (4) below –

(a) the tribunal notifies the Secretary of State that the patient would be entitled to be absolutely or conditionally discharged; and
(b) within the period of 90 days beginning with the date of that notification the Secretary of State gives notice to the tribunal that the patient may be so discharged,

the tribunal shall direct the absolute or, as the case may be, the conditional discharge of the patient.

(3) Where a patient continues to be liable to be detained in a hospital at the end of the period referred to in subsection (2)(b) above because the Secretary of State has not given the notice there mentioned, the managers of the hospital shall, unless the tribunal has made a recommendation under subsection (1)(b) above, transfer the patient to a prison or other institution in which he might have been detained if he had not been removed to hospital, there to be dealt with as if he had not been so removed.

(4) If, in the case of a patient who is subject to a transfer direction under section 48 above, the tribunal notifies the Secretary of State that the patient would be entitled to be absolutely or conditionally discharged, the Secretary of State shall, unless the tribunal has made a recommendation under subsection (1)(b) above, by warrant direct that the patient be remitted to a prison or other institution in which he might have been detained if he had not been removed to hospital, there to be dealt with as if he had not been so removed.

(5) Where a patient is transferred or remitted under subsection (3) or (4) above the relevant hospital direction and the limitation direction or, as the case may be, the relevant transfer direction and the restriction direction shall cease to have effect on his arrival in the prison or other institution.

(5A) Where the tribunal has made a recommendation under subsection (1)(b) above in the case of a patient who is subject to a restriction direction or a limitation direction –

(a) the fact that the restriction direction or limitation direction remains in force does not prevent the making of any application or reference to the Parole Board by or in respect of him or the exercise by him of any power to require the Secretary of State to refer his case to the Parole Board, and
(b) if the Parole Board make a direction or recommendation by virtue of which the patient would become entitled to be released (whether unconditionally or on licence) from any prison or other institution in which he might have been detained if he had not been removed to hospital, the restriction direction or limitation direction shall cease to have effect at the time when he would become entitled to be so released.

(6) Subsections (3) to (8) of section 73 above shall have effect in relation to this section as they have effect in relation to that section, taking references to the relevant hospital order and the restriction order as references to the hospital direction and the limitation direction or, as the case may be, to the transfer direction and the restriction direction.

(7) This section is without prejudice to sections 50 to 53 above in their application to patients who are not discharged under this section.'

18.40 Finally, there are two cases which considered the test for lifting of a restriction order and the status of an application to the Tribunal when there was a change in the status of the patient at the end of a restriction order, respectively. In *RH v South London and Maudsley NHS Foundation Trust*,[47] the Court of Appeal affirmed the test as set out by Munby J (see above at **18.36**) and that the First-tier Tribunal had properly applied the test. In the second case, *R (MN) v Mental Health Review Tribunal*[48] a restricted patient (MHA 1983, ss 47 and 49) had applied to a Tribunal by way of s 70. However, before the Tribunal convened, his restriction order came to an end. This meant that he was (functionally) treated as if detained pursuant to s 37 of MHA 1983. The Tribunal declined to hear his application as he was no longer a restricted patient and would be required to make a further application under MHa 1983, s 69. It was held that the Tribunal was correct in law to conclude that the application had lapsed, by virtue of the change in status.

47 [2010] EWCA Civ 1273, [2010] MHLR 341.
48 [2008] EWHC 3383, [2009] MHLR 98.

Chapter 19

HOSPITAL TREATMENT

POWER OF COURTS TO DIRECT HOSPITAL ADMISSION (MHA 1983, S 45A)

19.1 MHA 1983, s 45A permits the Crown Court to make hospital orders and limitation directions at the same time as imposing a prison sentence. The order is that the patient is detained in a hospital, and the limitation directions are the restrictions imposed in accordance with s 41. A hospital *direction* accompanies a prison sentence, and 'means that the offender will be managed in hospital in the same way as a prisoner who has been transferred to hospital subject to special restrictions under sections 47 and 49' (Code, para 33.23). The court also has the power to order admission to a specific hospital unit (Crime (Sentences) Act 1997, s 47).

EFFECT OF HOSPITAL AND LIMITATION DIRECTIONS (MHA 1983, S 45B)

19.2 A limitation direction ends on the release date of the patient. However, the hospital direction does not end in that manner. The patient remains liable to be detained. The patient is detained primarily upon the basis of a prison sentence, and for the duration of the limitation direction can be removed to prison, or released on licence (but only by direction from the Secretary of State for Justice). This may only occur where the Secretary of State has been notified (by the RC, AC or Tribunal) that the patient no longer requires treatment for mental disorder in a hospital, or there is no effective treatment available for the disorder within the hospital where he or she is detained. The legislative basis for the former is in MHA 1983, s 50(1) and (5).

19.3 When a limitation direction is in force, the patient cannot be discharged without the permission of the Secretary of State. If the Tribunal does conclude that the patient is entitled to be discharged, and the Secretary of State does not consent, then the patient will be returned to prison. MHA 1983, ss 45A, 45B, 50(1) and (5) are reproduced in Part F. The criteria for admission under s 45A are that the offender is suffering from a mental disorder, that it is of a nature or degree which makes it appropriate for him or her to be detained in hospital for medical treatment and that appropriate medical treatment is available to him or her. Each of these criteria has been considered elsewhere in the text and will be familiar to the reader.

TRANSFER OF SENTENCED PRISONERS TO HOSPITAL (MHA 1983, S 47)

19.4 The Secretary of State may make a transfer direction that the sentenced prisoner is taken to a specific hospital and detained in that hospital. This is known as a 'transfer direction'. The Secretary of State must be satisfied (upon the basis of the written reports of two doctors, one of whom must be approved pursuant to MHA 1983, s 12) that (a) the prisoner is suffering from a mental disorder, (b) the disorder is of a nature or degree which makes it appropriate for the prisoner to be detained in a hospital for medical treatment and (c) appropriate medical treatment is available. The Secretary of State has also to be of the opinion that having regard to the public interest and all the circumstances, it is expedient to direct the transfer of the prisoner. Once the Secretary of State are aware of such a need for a transfer, he or she is obliged to act expeditiously in ensuring that such a transfer does take place.[1]

19.5 The Secretary of State can also give a restriction direction (MHA 1983, s 49) which is then termed a 'restricted transfer direction', which imposes restrictions on discharge from hospital. If no restriction direction is given, then the prisoner will be within the same regime as applies for unrestricted hospital orders. The phraseology contained in MHA 1983, s 47(1)(a)–(c) has been considered in Parts B and C. MHA 1983, ss 47 and 49 are reproduced in Part F.

19.6 If there is no restriction direction, then detention lasts for a maximum of 6 months. If a restriction direction is made, this will expire on the earliest release date for the prisoner. If the prisoner remains after that date, then he or she achieves the status of a s 37 patient and falls within the ambit of MHA 1983, s 72. Restricted transfer direction patients can only be discharged by the Tribunal if the Secretary of State agrees. The restricted direction keeps the powers of the Tribunal within those set out in MHA 1983, s 74. If the Tribunal determines that the patient should not be detained in hospital, if his or her sentence of imprisonment remains, then he or she will be returned to prison.

REMOVAL TO HOSPITAL OF OTHER PRISONERS (MHA 1983, S 48)

19.7 This provision relates to unsentenced prisoners and others on remand. The same provisions as set out in MHA 1983, s 47 apply, except for the additional criterion that the prisoner is in urgent need of treatment. The Secretary of State may impose a restriction direction (as above) using MHA 1983, s 49. If a patient is transferred without a restriction direction, then his or her status is that of a patient with an unrestricted hospital order. If a restriction direction is made, then the prisoner will be treated in a similar manner to those with a restricted hospital order. The effect of a transfer direction is to extinguish any previous applications for admission, guardianship, unrestricted

---

1 *R (on the application of D) v Secretary of State for the Home Department and National Assembly for Wales* [2004] EWHC 2857 (Admin), [2005] MHLR 17.

hospital order or direction or for guardianship. It does not have this effect on a restricted hospital order. In respect of unsentenced prisoners, there is an automatic expiry of the transfer directions (MHA 1983, ss 51, 52(1) and 53(1)). Section 48 is reproduced in Part F.

19.8 In *R (Abu-Rideh) v MHRT* a summary of the procedures which arise from s 48 are set out (using the skeleton argument provided by counsel) as follows:[2]

> 'The effect in the case of a restricted patient subject to a restriction direction made under s 48 is firstly: (i) The tribunal must, if not satisfied *either* that the patient is suffering from a mental disorder of a nature or degree which makes it appropriate for him to be liable to be detained in a hospital for medical treatment *or* that it is necessary for the health and safety of the patient or for the protection of others that he continue to receive medical treatment in hospital, make a recommendation for discharge under s 74(1)(a). Secondly: (ii) If the tribunal is satisfied that it is not appropriate for the patient to remain liable to be recalled to hospital, they must recommend the patient's absolute discharge; if they are not so satisfied, they must recommend the patient's conditional discharge (s 73(1)(b) and 73(2)). Thirdly: (iii) If the tribunal recommends the patient's conditional discharge then it may also make a recommendation under s 74(1)(b) that, in the event of his not being discharged under s 74, the patient should continue to be detained in hospital. If the Secretary of State accepts that recommendation the patient remains in hospital notwithstanding he no longer satisfies the criteria for detention under the Act (or under Art 5(1)(e)). Fourthly: (iv) by virtue of s 74(4) a patient subject to a transfer direction under s 48 *cannot* be discharged by the Secretary of State under s 74, either absolutely or conditionally. His discharge powers under s 74(2) only apply to serving prisoners transferred under s 47. The patient will automatically be remitted back to the place of his former detention if the recommendation is for absolute discharge *or* if a recommendation for conditional discharge has been made but without a recommendation under s 74(1)(b). If a recommendation has been made under s 74(1)(b) the patient is not automatically remitted back to their former place of detention and he will remain detained until remitted back to prison by the Secretary of State under s 53, discharged by the Secretary of State under s 42 (2) or the justification for his underlying detention expires.'

19.9 The pro forma used by the Tribunal (Form 19) contains a formulation of the statutory criteria that have been considered already throughout this book. It is set out in the preceding chapter (at **18.38**).

Summary of discharge by the Tribunal (restriction directions and hospital directions with limitation directions)

19.10 Any patient transferred from a prison to a hospital may apply to a Tribunal. By virtue of MHA 1983, s 74, if an unsentenced prisoner is subject to transfer directions, he or she can apply to a Tribunal. If discharged, and unrestricted, then the prisoner will be free to leave hospital. However, if the patient is restricted, then different considerations apply. If there is a restriction

---

2 [2004] EWHC 1999 (Admin), [2004] MHLR 308, at [19]–[22]; (*EC Ch 13*).

direction, or a hospital *direction* (either by way of transfer or detention via the court), then the Tribunal does not have the power of discharge. The final arbiter is the Minister for Justice. The decision that the minister can make will lead either to a return to prison or discharge from detention. All that the Tribunal may do is notify the Ministry of Justice that had the patient been subject of a restriction *order*, then whether or not if he or she had had been subject to a restriction order, whether he or she would have been entitled to either a condition or absolute discharge. The statutory criteria that the Tribunal considers are therefore obviously the same as those which apply to a patient who actually *is* subject to a restriction order. The issue of whether a patient detained under ss 47 and 49 has a right to apply to the Tribunal during the first 6 months of such detention is the subject of guidance provided by the Chamber President.[3] The conclusion is that:

> '... a patient transferred to hospital under s.47, with or without a restriction direction under s.49, has the right to apply to the Tribunal in the period of six months beginning with the date of the transfer direction. S. 69 (2) (b) is not incompatible with s.70 but additional to it ...The right so to apply is compatible with Art 5 (4) of the ECHR. Detention in hospital ordered by the court eg under s.37 has been authorised by the court, as an independent judicial body, and there is no imperative for an immediate further review. A transfer direction, by contrast, is made by the Executive and should attract immediate access to an independent review by the Tribunal. S. 69 (2) (b) provides the means of access to the Tribunal.'

19.11 If the Tribunal reaches the conclusion that an absolute discharge would have been appropriate, then once the Ministry of Justice has been notified, it has a period of 90 days within which to respond. If it agrees that an absolute discharge is appropriate, then the Tribunal will discharge the patient. If the Ministry of Justice does not consent, the patient will be transferred back to the place from whence he or she was originally taken (which in most cases will be prison), where he or she will serve the remainder of his or her sentence.

19.12 If the Tribunal reaches the conclusion that the patient would have been entitled to a conditional discharge (because of the same consideration referred to above) it will also be obliged to notify the Ministry of Justice. It may also add a recommendation that the patient remain in hospital, should the Ministry of Justice not approve the course of conditional discharge. Again, the Ministry of Justice has 90 days within which to agree or not. If there is agreement, then a conditional discharge will follow. This may be deferred in accordance with the procedure described above for ordinary deferred conditional discharges for patients subject to restriction orders. If there is neither consent nor recommendation, then the patient will follow the same course as above.

19.13 As Gledhill has observed, the practical outcome of the above provisions in respect of the above are that:[4]

---

3 Guidance of Chamber President, 15 December 2008.

4 *EC Ch 13*.

> '(i) transfer to hospital without a restriction direction does not bring a prison sentence to an end; (ii) in deciding whether or not to recommend release, the tribunal should assess the realistic alternative, which may be return to prison rather than release to the community.'

19.14 In respect of MHA 1983, s 49 (see Part F), in the case of *R (T) v Home Secretary*[5] the issue of whether or not it was proper to impose a restriction direction using s 49 on a prisoner transferred from prison via MHA 1983, s 47 was considered. It was held that this was a permissible course of action for the Home Secretary to take.

---

5 [2003] EWHC 538 (Admin), [2003] MHLR 239; (*EC Ch 13*).

Chapter 20

CRIMINAL JURISDICTION

20.1 Mention has been made (at **17.1**) of the routes into hospital via the court process. What follows is a short account of some of those processes. Fennell has provided an admirable summary of the philosophy behind the systems for disposing of a mentally disordered offender. He states:[1]

> 'Mentally disordered offenders have traditionally been exempt from ordinary penal measures on the grounds that they are not criminally responsible for their behaviour (not guilty by reason of insanity), that their responsibility for doing or being a party to a homicide is diminished by abnormality of mind (diminished responsibility), or that they are unable to understand the course of the proceedings at their trial and contribute to their defence (unfit to plead). Each of these may lead to a psychiatric rather than a penal disposal.'

INSANITY AT TIME OF OFFENCE

20.2 The Trial of Lunatics Act 1883 provides for a special verdict of not guilty by reason of insanity. The powers of the court in respect of such a verdict having been given are set out in the Criminal Procedure (Insanity) Act 1964, s 5 et seq. Evidence as to the issue of the state of mind of the defendant is admissible in the form of two registered medical practitioners, one of whom must be approved for such a purpose pursuant to MHA 1983, s 12(2) (Criminal Procedure (Insanity and Unfitness to Plead) Act 1991, ss 1(1) and 6(1)).

DOMESTIC VIOLENCE, CRIME AND VICTIMS ACT 2004

20.3 The Domestic Violence, Crime and Victims Act 2004 amended the Criminal Procedure (Insanity) Act 1964 in respect of proceedings after 31 March 2005. This is set out in the MHA 1983, ss 4 and 4A. The question of fitness to plead is determined by a court without a jury. If the court determines that the defendant is unfit to plead, then the trial proceeds on the limited basis that a jury will decide that either the act or omission charged against him or her as the offence was committed by the defendant (ie that the actus reus of the offence was as a result of the activities of the defendant). If it is determined that the accused did the act or made the omission, the court must make an order in accordance with the Criminal Procedure (Insanity) Act 1964, ss 5 and 5A.

---

1 P Fennell *Mental Health: The New Law* (Jordans, 2007), at para 7.41, p 176.

20.4 If the jury decides that the act or omission was attributable to the defendant, the judge has three options. The first is that there may be a hospital order (either with or without restriction). The second is that there shall be a supervision order. The third is that there shall be an absolute discharge. If the offence carries a sentence fixed by law, and the court has the power to make a hospital order, then it will be accompanied by a restriction order. For a fuller discussion of MHA 1983, s 37 (hospital orders) and s 41 (restriction orders) see Chapters 18 and 19.

20.5 There is an alternative procedure which operates in the magistrates' court (which has no method of determining the matter of fitness to plead) which may lead to an order pursuant to MHA 1983, s 37 without a conviction of the defendant. The case of *R (P) v Barking Youth Court*[2] states that MHA 1983, s 37(3), combined with the Powers of Criminal Courts (Sentencing) Act 2000, s 11(1), provides a complete statutory framework for the manner in which summary only offences are dealt with, and where the defendant has or might have a mental disorder.

20.6 If s 5 applies, but there has been no disposal by way of a hospital order, a supervision order, or an absolute discharge, then orders may be made by way of MHA 1983, s 35, 36 or 38 (interim hospital orders) (see **17.9**).

20.7 If both the criteria for an order pursuant to s 37 and for a discretionary life sentence were made out, then the court is still obliged to consider 'having regard to all the circumstances including the nature of the offence and the character and antecedents of the offender' whether as a matter of fact a disposal by way of a hospital order was 'the most suitable method of disposing of the case'. The focus of a Tribunal is different from that of a parole board. In *R v IA*[3] it was held that on the basis of the evidence in that case, the hospital regime was better suited to offering protection to the public, particularly where the risks were associated with a need for medical treatment. A hospital order may be made without a requirement for a link between the offence committed and the mental disorder from which the offender suffers.[4]

20.8 It must be remembered that the issue at the time of disposal (ie sentencing) is whether the defendant is suffering from a mental disorder at that point. If a hospital order is made, it is because it is appropriate in the particular circumstances of the case (as illustrated above) and not the seriousness or otherwise of the offence itself. It is not uncommon for hospital orders to be made for quite minor offences (although it is unlikely that these would be accompanied with a restriction order).

---

2 [2002] 2 Cr App R 294, [2002] MHLR 304.

3 [2006] 1 Cr App R (S) 91, CA.

4 *R v McBride* [1972] Crim LR 322, CA.

Chapter 21

ROLE OF MINISTRY OF JUSTICE

21.1 The function of the Secretary of State for the Ministry of Justice is largely as set out above. Insofar as the role is concerned with regard to the Tribunal, this is also largely self-evident. The Ministry is obliged to provide its opinion and report to the Tribunal wherever there is an issue in which it is involved. From April 2007, the Home Office Mental Health Unit became the responsibility of the Ministry of Justice (MoJ). It is now known as the Mental Health Casework Section. It has published guidance on working with offenders with personality disorders, for clinical and social supervisors (see Chapters 22 and 23), the recall of conditionally discharged patients, section 17 leave, remand and sentencing powers of the Crown Court for mentally disordered offenders, foreign national restricted patients and repatriation, clinicians and duties to victims under the Domestic Violence, Crime and Victims Act 2004 (see Chapter 24), and on working with MAPPA and mentally disordered offenders. The information that is provided to the Tribunal by the MoJ is vital to its decision making, and it is rarely the case that there will be legal representation on behalf of the Secretary of State at the hearing. The purpose of early receipt of all documentation by the MoJ is to respond to all matters that the Tribunal will have to consider. The commonest problem is late receipt of such documents, and upon which there is no comment by the MoJ. If there has been a failure to do this, the information contained in the documents is of sufficient significance and the Tribunal has proceeded and made a decision with which the Secretary of State disagrees, then it is open to the Secretary of State to challenge the decision by way of Rule 45. However, as there is no specific obligation on the part of the MoJ to comment on each report, a Tribunal may proceed, as long as it is satisfied that the MoJ actually *has* received such reports. It may also be the case that during the Tribunal, oral evidence from a professional source is given which contradicts the opinion of written evidence (eg an opinion expressed by an RC). The Tribunal will have to deal with this as it sees fit, with the Secretary of State having access to the same basis of appeal, or review of the decision, if not satisfied, as any other party to the proceedings.

21.2 In *R (Home Secretary) v MHRT*[1] the role and significance of the (then) Home Office was considered. A Tribunal had discharged a patient detained pursuant to MHA 1983, ss 37 and 41, on the basis of a deferred conditional discharge. The patient subsequently made an application (via MHA 1983, s 75) and was granted an absolute discharge. It transpired that the Home Office had not been given notice of the proceedings, and consequently had not been able

---

1 [2004] EWHC 650 (Admin), [2004] MHLR 170.

to make its views known. It was argued on behalf of the patient that these views would have made no difference to the outcome of the Tribunal. The new Practice Directions (see Part F) set out what the contents of the statement from the Secretary of State should contain. It was held that the absence of the views of the Home Secretary vitiated the decision, which was quashed and remitted to a different Tribunal. The ratio for the decision was (citing Lord Bridge in *R v Oxford Regional Mental Health Review Tribunal ex parte Secretary of State for the Home Department*[2]):[3]

> 'What is more important here is that there was a breach of the most fundamental rule of natural justice, in that the Secretary of State, as a vitally interested party, was denied a hearing.'

Owen J also held that:[4]

> 'Thus where, as in this case, the patient has been conditionally discharged, not only is there a duty on the Secretary of State to give the Tribunal his views on the suitability of the patient for absolute discharge, but it is only the Secretary of State who is subject to that duty. He is the only party capable of representing any interest that the public may have in opposing an application for an absolute discharge. His role is therefore of central importance.'

Thus, if the Ministry of Justice is not given an opportunity to make its views known, then this may vitiate any decision made by the Tribunal.

21.3 According to the now defunct MHAC, the Mental Health Unit (MHU) has 'indicated to care teams that it is keen to work with them to increase the number of conditional discharges granted by the Secretary of State'.[5] It continues by expressing a number of concerns about the manner in which the MHU functions in the following terms:[6]

> '... we are concerned that decisions about risk and mental disorder may be taken by the MHU at a purely administrative level, without benefit of independent clinical advice. We also believe that a more complete judicial check on the political administration of deprivation of liberty for reasons of mental disorder would be provided were the MHRT to have, at the very least, the same range of powers as the Secretary of State in whose name the MHU operates, so that it could direct transfer or community leave. A more complete separation of powers could be achieved were the MHU to act in a purely advisory capacity to the MHRT, with the latter body alone empowered to discharge restricted patients.'

The Care Quality Commission (which has taken over the monitoring of the Mental Health Act) is silent on this aspect.

---

2 [1988] AC 120.

3 [2004] EWHC 650 (Admin), [2004] MHLR 170, at [7].

4 Ibid, at [24].

5 Mental Health Act Commission *Risk, Rights, Recovery: Twelfth Biennial Report 2005–2007* (TSO, 2008) (MHAC Report), at para 7.54.

6 Ibid.

21.4 The MHAC Report also cites the report into the care and treatment of George Leigers, and the conclusions reached by that report. They are worth setting out in full, together with the commentary provided by the MHAC:[7]

> '[The report] asked that consideration be given at government level to two issues: (i) "Whether patients who have committed very serious offences and who have received restriction orders under s.41 of the MHA should remain under supervision for the rest of their lives" … (ii) Alternatively, if such patients are to be absolutely discharged, whether this would be undertaken only by the MHRT rather than by administrative action taken by the MHU on behalf of the Secretary of State. The panel pointed out that the MHU decisions over absolute discharge "are usually wholly reliant on reports prepared by the team caring for the patient, and as such is dependent upon the quality of their assessments and conclusions. In contrast, the MHRT is able to carry out a much more extensive, and independent review of a case, including information obtained from interviews carried out by its own medical member" … The MHU's consistently oppositional stance towards discharge at any MHRT hearing has led to accusations that it is selective in its presentation of information about patients to the MHRT, and to the danger that its representation are therefore seen as partial and given less weight than they deserve. In this sense, the effectiveness of the MHU might be enhanced, rather than diminished, were it to have a purely advisory role to the MHRT over discharge decisions.'

21.5 The Mental Health Casework Section itself has described its own function as being:[8]

> 'The Mental Health Casework Section in the Ministry of Justice employs nearly 60 officers whose sole concern is to carry out the Secretary of State's responsibilities under the Mental Health Act 1983 and related legislation. Among their duties, they authorise the admission to hospital of patients transferred from prison. They consider recommendations from responsible clinicians for the leave, transfer or discharge of restricted patients from hospital, seeking the personal authority of a Ministry of Justice Minister in some instances. They prepare the Secretary of State's statement to tribunal panels hearing restricted panel cases, as required under the First-tier Tribunal – Mental Health Rules 2008. After the conditional discharge of a patient by authority of either the Secretary of State or the tribunal, they monitor the patient's progress and give consideration to the variations of conditions, recall to hospital or absolute discharge as circumstances require.'

---

7 Ibid, at paras 7.55–7.56.

8 *Guidance for Clinical Supervisors*, Section 3, 18 March 2009.

Chapter 22

RESPONSIBLE CLINICIAN AND CLINICAL SUPERVISORS (ROLE, FUNCTION AND POWERS)

22.1 For the role of the RC whilst the patient is detained, refer generally to Chapter 11. There are specific additional obligations and/or powers and limitations on powers that an RC has within the context of restricted patients. A supervising psychiatrist will be involved where a patient subject to the restrictions set out in MHA 1983, s 41 is conditionally discharged from hospital either with the agreement of the Secretary of State, or by the Tribunal (MHA 1983, ss 42(2) and 73(2)).

LEAVE

22.2 If a patient is subject to restrictions, an RC may not grant leave without the consent of the Secretary of State. This applies even if there is a move between units in the same hospital, if the hospital order specifies residence in a particular unit.

22.3 Leave cannot be granted to a patient detained under MHA 1983, s 35, 36 or 38.

22.4 An RC cannot recall the patient if he or she has been absent on leave for more than 12 months. In all other circumstances, the RC does have this power.

DISCHARGE

22.5 An RC can discharge an unrestricted patient at any time, but not without the consent of the Secretary of State where the patient is restricted.

CONDITIONAL DISCHARGE

22.6 The Ministry of Justice has prepared several documents to assist clinical supervisors (and others). The first is *Guidance for Clinical Supervisors* (18 March 2009). The second is *The Recall of Conditionally Discharged Restricted Patients* (4 February 2009). The third is *Guidance for Working with MAPPA and Mentally Disordered Offenders* (undated). The notes in respect of the first say it is intended to be:

> '... for the guidance of clinicians who take on the role of clinical supervisors for a restricted patient subject to a conditional discharge ... the notes cover the procedures which should take place before the patient leaves hospital, the responsibilities of those involved with the patient after discharge from hospital and the action to be taken in some of the circumstances which may arise while the patient is in the community.'[1]

It adds, 'the notes refer throughout to the "clinical supervisor"'.[2]

22.7 The main points are set out in this chapter, and will not be repeated in respect of the role of the social supervisor (Chapter 23) except where there are material differences.

PURPOSE OF CONDITIONS

22.8 The Ministry of Justice describes the purpose of the conditions as:[3]

> '... designed to operate for the protection of the discharged patient and others and to enable the patient's safe management in the community. They are not measures for social control, or even for crime prevention ... the purpose is to prevent the public from further serious harm ... the Secretary of State's ability to exercise his statutory powers to protect the public is dependent on the reports he receives from the supervisors about the patient's condition and behaviour in the community.'[4]

22.9 In respect of the initial admission, the Secretary of State comments that:

> 'The aim will be to understand what led to the dangerous behaviour which resulted in the patient's detention, and, as the mental disorder is treated in hospital, to assess the extent to which that treatment is likely to reduce the risk of the patient behaving in a dangerous manner if returned to the community.'[5]

Preparation for discharge should commence before any authority for discharge is sought. This includes preparation prior to a Tribunal in case such a discharge is ordered. It adds that these should be 'choice of suitable accommodation, employment or other day-time occupation, a social supervisor and a supervising consultant psychiatrist'.

DOCUMENTATION TO BE PROVIDED BY THE DISCHARGING HOSPITAL

22.10 The documentation provided by the discharging hospital should include full information about the patient, including social, offending and medical

---

1 *Guidance for Clinical Supervisors*, Section 1, para 1.

2 Ibid.

3 Ibid, Section 4, paras 16 and 17.

4 Ibid, Section 4, paras 7 and 8.

5 Ibid, Section 5, para 9.

history; progress in hospital; insight; compliance; warning signs of relapse; information about groups or individuals who might be at risk; home circumstances; and all after-care and supervision arrangements.

REPORTS TO THE SECRETARY OF STATE

22.11 The supervising psychiatrist (that is, the consultant who will be responsible for the mental health of the patient whilst the patient is in the community) is obliged to report to the Secretary of State one month after discharge, and every 3 months after that. He or she will also be responsible for making all arrangements in respect of medication and any additional outpatient or inpatient treatment. The latter can be done voluntarily. If this is done, the Secretary of State must be notified.

22.12 The psychiatrist should ensure continuity, and should not (if possible) permit the role to be filled by junior doctors or other consultants.

22.13 An observation made by the Secretary of State is that:

> '… the reluctance of supervisors to send reports … that showed clients in an unfavourable light … reports should never overlook or minimise problems for fear of jeopardising the patient's progress.'[6]

MULTI-AGENCY PUBLIC PROTECTION ARRANGEMENTS (MAPPAS)

22.14 MAPPAs apply to certain sexual and violent offenders and to those who pose a risk of serious harm to others. The RC and the supervising psychiatrist should liaise in respect of a decision to refer the patient to MAPPA or not. In order for this to happen, there should be information upon which to base the referral, which would be whether the patient poses a high or a very high risk of serious harm to others, and where risk management could not be achieved using the Care Programme Approach (CPA), but needed other agencies to be involved. Lower-risk patients may also be referred if there are 'local notoriety/threats to the offender/difficult victim issues'. If absolute discharge is a possibility, and there remain serious concerns about risk, there should also be consideration of a referral to MAPPA. The Secretary of State asks that it is made aware of any such referrals. Separate guidance is available on this aspect (see **22.6**).

DETERIORATION IN CONDITION OF PATIENT

22.15 If there is information about the deterioration in the condition of a patient, then the supervising psychiatrist should consider admission without

---

6 Ibid, Section 12, para 58.

delay. An example given of warning signs is where a patient has refused to comply with testing for substance abuse (and where this has been indentified as connected with a deterioration in his or her mental health). This may well have been a condition of discharge in any event.

22.16 The MoJ encourages supervisors to contact them as soon as possible if there is perceived to be a deterioration or lack of co-operation and immediately if there is a need to readmit a conditionally discharged patient. The Secretary of State states that:

> '... If a clinical supervisor is concerned about a conditionally discharged patient's mental state or behaviour, the concern should first be discussed with the other professionals involved in the case, particularly the social supervisor. In addition, an early telephone call must be made to alert the Mental Health Casework Section.'[7]

ABSCONDING

22.17 If the patient breaks off contact with the supervising psychiatrist (or social supervisor), then the Ministry of Justice must be contacted immediately.[8]

CRITERIA FOR ABSOLUTE DISCHARGE

22.18 The Ministry of Justice suggests that:

> 'The decision on absolute discharge will turn on the extent to which the maintenance of conditions and supervision is seen to be contributing to public safety. For example, where a patient's offence is assessed as directly linked to his disorder, and he is entirely compliant with the treatment that controls the disorder, restrictions may not need to persist for long even when the offence was serious.'[9]

22.19 Annex A of the *Guidance for Clinical Supervisors* sets out 21 key points which a supervising psychiatrist should consider at the discharging hospital. The previous Guidance set out 16 points (and these remain a useful checklist). These are as follows:

(1) discussion with MHU;

(2) get to know the patient and attend at least one multi-disciplinary conference;

(3) get hold of written details from the discharging hospital;

---

7 Ibid, Section 12, para 55.
8 Ibid, Section 12, para 66.
9 Ibid, Section 13, para 72.

(4) the supervising psychiatrist is responsible for monitoring the mental health of the patient;

(5) the frequency, manner and type of treatment is determined by the supervising psychiatrist;

(6) the supervising psychiatrist should be directly involved in rehabilitation into the community;

(7) medication must be kept under review, and discussed with the social supervisor;

(8) there should be close liaison with the social supervisor, and any clinical personnel;

(9) there should be a meeting at least once per year with the social supervisor, followed by a report to the MHU;

(10) there should be consideration given to the use of MAPPA;

(11) the Ministry of Justice will ask for reports one month after discharge, and every 3 months after that;

(12) all reports should be copied to the social supervisor;

(13) if the patient wishes to go on holiday, and there is agreement over this, there should be consideration given as to whether special arrangements need to be made for medication;

(14) if there are concerns about a patient, the social supervisor should be contacted first. If that concern amounts to a fear of safety of the patient or others, there may be a need for immediate admission to hospital. Whatever action is or is not taken, the Ministry of Justice must be contacted;

(15) if no further supervision is required, there should be liaison with the social supervisor, and then the Ministry of Justice should be approached with evidence of stability; and

(16) a supervising psychiatrist is obliged to provide a report to the Tribunal. The content of this should be as stipulated in the Practice Direction (see Part F).

22.20 In respect of the recall of conditionally discharged restricted patients the Ministry of Justice has produced guidance (see **22.6**) and reminds practitioners that:

> 'There is no statutory requirement for the Justice Secretary to obtain the agreement of the hospital doctors to re-admit a recalled patient. The Justice Secretary is entitled to take a different view to that of the supervising psychiatrist, provided there are sufficient grounds/evidence to justify this and satisfy the Secretary of State that the criteria for detention under the Mental Health Act are met ... There is no need for the patient's mental health to have necessarily deteriorated in order to justify recall.'[10]

It sets out the policy of the Mental Health Casework Section,[11] which includes reference to alcohol and substance misuse and defaulting on medication. The overall purpose of the policy is:

> 'patients will be recalled where it is necessary to protect the public from the actual or potential risk posed by that patient **and** that risk is linked to the patient's mental disorder. It is not possible to specify all the circumstances when recall will be appropriate but **public safety will always be the most important factor**.'[12]

---

10 *The Recall of Conditionally Discharged Restricted Patients*, para 4.

11 Ibid, para 5.

12 Ibid.

Chapter 23

APPROVED MENTAL HEALTH PRACTITIONERS AND SOCIAL SUPERVISOR (ROLE, FUNCTION AND POWERS)

23.1 The role of the AMHP is no different from that set out in Chapter 12. The term 'social supervisor' is used in respect of conditionally discharged patients, and the duties of that supervisor are in many ways very similar to that of the clinical supervisor set out in Chapter 22.

23.2 The document prepared by the Ministry of Justice is *Guidance for Social Supervisors* (18 March 2009). It largely complements and replicates the *Guidance for Clinical Supervisors* referred to in Chapter 22.

23.3 The social supervisor should become involved in the pre-discharge contact and this:

> 'should include at least two visits to the hospital by the social supervisor to meet the patient and participation in at least one multi-disciplinary case conference at which the prospective social supervisor can discuss the case and the plans for discharge with the responsible clinician, and the staff of all the disciplines who know the patient.'[1]

23.4 After discharge, meetings should take place at least once per week for the first month, then once per fortnight and then once per month as the supervisor judges suitable. This is regarded as the *minimum*. These meetings should 'usually take place on the patient's home territory but some meetings away from the home, perhaps in the supervisor's office, may also prove valuable'.[2] There should be continuity of supervision and, if on leave, the supervisor should transfer responsibility to a colleague.

23.5 The supervisor may also have to decide what information can be disclosed, and to whom. This should be done with the full knowledge and consent of the patient, and the patient's wishes should only be disregarded if there are strong reasons for so doing.[3]

---

1 *Guidance for Social Supervisors*, Section 5, para 21.

2 Ibid, Section 7, para 35.

3 Ibid, Section 8, paras 39 and 40.

23.6 If there is a change of address by the patient, or he or she wishes to be away even for a short period, and the supervisor agrees, then the Ministry of Justice must be contacted in order for the Secretary of State to agree to this change in condition.

23.7 The details of what is required in a report by a social supervisor are now contained in the Practice Direction (see Part F). It is more than likely that a Tribunal would want the author of the report to attend the Tribunal.

23.8 Social Supervisors are reminded of their obligations towards victims (paras 22–24) and in respect of MAPPA (paras 51–55). A request will be made to the supervisor for a report one month after discharge, and every 3 months thereafter (para 56). It sets out in some detail what a social supervisor should do if there is a deterioration in the condition of the patient, which is similar in all respects to the guidance given to clinical supervisors (paras 67–70). Annex A contains a summary of all that is required, and contains 16 different points. Annex B contains a summary of good practice in respect of staff at the discharging hospital.

Chapter 24

VICTIMS' RIGHTS

24.1 There has been an increase in the standing of victims of offences committed by mentally disordered offenders. This started with the Domestic Violence (Crime and Victims) Act 2004. It applies to the following categories:

- conviction for violent or sexual offence;
- hospital order with restrictions;
- hospital direction and limitation direction (MHA 1983, s 45A);
- transfer direction and restriction direction (MHA 1983, s 47);
- conditional discharge of the above;
- discharge to SCT; and
- hospital order following being found not guilty of an offence by reason of insanity.

The complete (very extensive) list of offences is to be found in Sch 15 to the Criminal Justice Act 2003.

24.2 If the patient comes within these categories, the victim may receive the opportunity to make representations about conditions to be imposed upon the patient if discharged, or just to receive information about conditions that may be imposed. It only applies where a disposal was made on or after 1 July 2005. The obligation for organisation of this falls upon the victim liaison officer (VLO) of the Probation Board. The Domestic Violence (Crime and Victims) Act 2004 requires the Tribunal (and the Ministry for Justice) to notify the probation service of certain information, which includes when a discharge from hospital is being considered.

24.3 The Domestic Violence, Crime and Victims Act 2004 is modified by MHA 2007, s 48, which adds to the above the categories that of a patient who is subject to a hospital order without restrictions, or transfer direction without restrictions, or who may be the subject of a CTO/SCT. This came into force on 3 November 2008 and is set out (in the category 'unrestricted chapter 2 patients' – see **24.9**). These arrangements are not retrospective. The Ministry of

Justice has no involvement with such patients, and the obligation for liaison falls upon the hospital managers (together with the VLO).

24.4 The practical effect upon the Tribunal (in terms of information provided to it) is that the victim is entitled to make representations and to receive information about discharge and conditions. When a Tribunal is considering a discharge, notification of this will be made (via the hospital manager to the Probation Board). The Tribunal must then consider these representations.

24.5 The MHAC commented upon the progress and effect of the legislation in the following terms:[1]

> 'In our last report we expressed concern at the suggestion that victims should have an expectation of access and representation to the patient's care team through arrangements with their VLO. We believe that the new duties should not detract from the offender's status as a patient rather than a prisoner. Patients to whom the new rules apply may have been determined by a court to have reduced or negated legal culpability for the actions that made "victims", and we would not want an assumption made that the status of victim provides a person with particular insight into clinical care of the mentally disordered offender.'

24.6 Further, the MHAC observed that:[2]

> '... the new powers in the DVCV Act replicate that Act's general powers and allows that hospital managers may provide "such other information as [they] consider appropriate in all the circumstances of the case". Whilst it would seem appropriate for the VLO to act as a conduit (and gatekeeper) for such information, there is nothing in the law that would prevent direct access to hospital managers by victims.'

The substance of the concerns expressed by the MHAC is the potential for revenge upon a discharged patient by victims if the information given out is mishandled. It refers to *R (on the application of OS) v Secretary of State for the Home Department*[3] as a source of its concerns (where the Home Office argued successfully that it was factor in refusing to agree to unescorted leave that the patient might be exposed to reprisals).

GUIDANCE

24.7 The Ministry of Justice has published *Duties to Victims under the Domestic Violence, Crime and Victims Act 2004*.[4] A far more comprehensive document, *Practice Guidance on Procedures Concerning Handling Representations from Victims in the First-tier Tribunal (Mental Health)* was issued by the

---

1 Mental Health Act Commission *Risk, Rights, Recovery: Twelfth Biennial Report 2005–2007* (TSO, 2008), at para 7.82.

2 Ibid, at para 7.86.

3 [2006] EWHC 1903 (Admin).

4 26 March 2009.

Chamber President (HHJ Sycamore) pursuant to Sch 4 to the Tribunals, Courts and Enforcement Act 2007, and is dated 1 July 2011. The full text of this is contained in Part F.

Victim

24.8 A victim is any person who appears to be, or to act for, the victim of a specified offence, which includes the family of a victim who has died as a result of the offence, or who has been rendered incapable, or who is a child, or any circumstances which might make it appropriate for a family member to act instead of the victim.

Rights of victim

24.9 The rights of victims are divided into two categories. The first are 'Restricted Chapter 2 patients'. These are subject to restricted hospital orders, limitation directions, or a restricted transfer direction, and includes conditionally discharged patients. The second are 'unrestricted Chapter 2 patients'. These are unrestricted hospital orders, hospital directions whose limitation direction is no longer in force and unrestricted transfer directions. In respect of unrestricted patients, obligations are imposed on hospital managers, RCs, AMHPs and NHS bodies responsible for NHS patients detained in independent hospitals. Generally, they are entitled to receive the following information:

- if patients are discharged subject to conditions;
- details of conditions that relate to contact with the victim or family;
- if there is an unconditional discharge;
- if a restricted patient ceases to be restricted; and
- of any other information that the relevant authority thinks is appropriate (para 1.13).

24.10 The probation board must inform the victim whether the patient is to be subject to any conditions if discharged, provide details of conditions relating to contact with the victim or his/her family, notify the victim of the date when a restriction order ceases to have effect and provide such information to the victim as the board considers appropriate in all the circumstances. When the Justice Secretary is considering discharge, he must inform the probation board whether a discharge is to be made, and if so, whether absolute or conditional, and what the conditions are. If the Secretary of State varies the discharge conditions or recalls the patient to hospital, or lifts the restriction order, then this information must be communicated to the probation board, and a date of recall must be provided.

Tribunal

24.11 The Guidance contains very little in respect of Tribunals, and for that reason the attention of the reader is directed to Part F and the full text of *Practice Guidance on Procedures Concerning Handling Representations from Victims in the First-tier Tribunal (Mental Health)* which is the definitive document on this point, and upon procedure. In particular it deals with matters such as to how representations might be heard, imposition of conditions on discharge which are relevant to the victim, notice of hearings to a victim of a tribunal hearing, the extent or otherwise of the participation of a victim in the tribunal process, disclosure of evidence from a victim to the patient, disclosure of the decision of the Tribunal to the victim, and the extent to which the Tribunal should consider those who fall outside the Domestic Violence, Crime and Victims Act 2004.

Part E

SUPPORTING MATERIALS

E1

E1

MENTAL HEALTH ACT 1983 CODE OF PRACTICE

STATUS OF CODE

The status of the Code of Practice has been definitively considered in *R (Munjaz) v Merseycare NHS Trust*.[1] It is issued pursuant to s 118 of MHA 1983. Sections 2A–2D have been inserted by MHA 2007, which incorporate a slight alteration of its purpose in that there are additional matters to which the Code must address itself (s 118(2B)), all of which should 'inform decisions under this Act'. The general proposition arising from *Munjaz* was that the Code is for guidance, not instruction. However, it was guidance to which great weight should be given. The dissenting judgments of Lord Steyn and Lord Brown are of particular interest in this context. Lord Steyn held that:

> 'The Code of Practice is a special type of soft law which derives its status from the legislative context and the vulnerability of the patients that it serves to protect; it is designed to ensure that some minimum safeguards and a modicum of centralised protection are in place. Accordingly, it should be observed by all hospitals unless they have a very good reason for departing from it in relation to an individual patient; departure from the Code as a matter of policy is not permitted, since a dilution of the minimum centrally imposed safeguards, by pragmatic policy decisions from hospital to hospital is not appropriate.'

Lord Brown went further '... the Code must be given a status akin to law, which disentitles individual hospitals to depart from it on policy grounds'. However, despite the small amendments now in force as a result of MHA 2007, it remains guidance only.

ENGLISH CODE/WELSH CODE

There is a separate Code for Wales and for England. The difference between the two is very slight indeed. The Welsh Code provides more detail on the role of the RC (Chapter 12). The Welsh Code does not deal with the privacy of patients, nor with confidentiality and information sharing (Chapters 21 and 18 respectively, English Code). There is more detail on after-care planning in the English Code (Chapter 31). There is no mention of the distinction between guardianship, leave and SCT in the Welsh Code (Chapter 28). There is no mention in the Welsh Code for the requirement of

---

1 [2005] UKHL 58, [2005] MHLR 276.

the Tribunal to provide written reasons (Chapter 26). There is no reference to personality disorders in the Welsh Code (Chapter 35). There is more detail on care planning in the Welsh Code (Chapter 14).

KEY EXTRACTS FROM THE CODE OF PRACTICE

Chapters 3, 4, 6, 8, 20, 21, 25–28 and 32–36 are reproduced below.

CHAPTER 3
MENTAL DISORDER

3.1 This chapter gives guidance on the definition of mental disorder for the purposes of the Act.

Definition of mental disorder

3.2 Mental disorder is defined for the purposes of the Act as "any disorder or disability of the mind". [Section 1(2)]. Relevant professionals should determine whether a patient has a disorder or disability of the mind in accordance with good clinical practice and accepted standards of what constitutes such a disorder or disability.

3.3 Examples of clinically recognised conditions which could fall within this definition are given in the following box.

Clinically recognised conditions which could fall within the Act's definition of mental disorder

- affective disorders, such as depression and bipolar disorder
- schizophrenia and delusional disorders
- neurotic, stress-related and somatoform disorders, such as anxiety, phobic disorders, obsessive compulsive disorders, post-traumatic stress disorder and hypochondriacal disorders
- organic mental disorders such as dementia and delirium (however caused)
- personality and behavioural changes caused by brain injury or damage (however acquired)
- personality disorders
- mental and behavioural disorders caused by psychoactive substance use (but see paragraphs 3.8–3.12)
- eating disorders, non-organic sleep disorders and non-organic sexual disorders
- learning disabilities (but see paragraphs 3.13–3.15)

- autistic spectrum disorders (including Asperger's syndrome) (but see paragraphs 3.16–3.17)
- behavioural and emotional disorders of children and adolescents

(Note: this list is not exhaustive.)

3.4 The fact that someone has a mental disorder is never sufficient grounds for any compulsory measure to be taken under the Act. Compulsory measures are permitted only where specific criteria about the potential consequences of a person's mental disorder are met. There are many forms of mental disorder which are unlikely ever to call for compulsory measures.

3.5 Care must always be taken to avoid diagnosing, or failing to diagnose, mental disorder on the basis of preconceptions about people or failure to appreciate cultural and social differences. What may be indicative of mental disorder in one person, given their background and individual circumstances, may be nothing of the sort in another person.

3.6 Difference should not be confused with disorder. No-one may be considered to be mentally disordered solely because of their political, religious or cultural beliefs, values or opinions, unless there are proper clinical grounds to believe that they are the symptoms or manifestations of a disability or disorder of the mind. The same is true of a person's involvement, or likely involvement, in illegal, anti-social or "immoral" behaviour. Beliefs, behaviours or actions which do not result from a disorder or disability of the mind are not a basis for compulsory measures under the Act, even if they appear unusual or cause other people alarm, distress or danger.

3.7 A person's sexual orientation towards people of the same gender (or both the same and the other gender) is not a mental disorder for any purpose.

Dependence on alcohol or drugs

3.8 Section 1(3) of the Act states that dependence on alcohol or drugs is not considered to be a disorder or disability of the mind for the purposes of the definition of mental disorder in the Act.

3.9 This means that there are no grounds under the Act for detaining a person in hospital (or using other compulsory measures) on the basis of alcohol or drug dependence alone. Drugs for these purposes may be taken to include solvents and similar substances with a psychoactive effect.

3.10 Alcohol or drug dependence may be accompanied by, or associated with, a mental disorder which does fall within the Act's definition. If the relevant criteria are met, it is therefore possible (for example) to detain people who are suffering from mental disorder, even though they are also dependent on alcohol or drugs. This is true even if the mental disorder in question results from the person's alcohol or drug dependence.

3.11 The Act does not exclude other disorders or disabilities of the mind related to the use of alcohol or drugs. These disorders – for example, withdrawal state with delirium or associated psychotic disorder, acute intoxication and organic mental disorders associated with prolonged abuse of drugs or alcohol – remain mental disorders for the purposes of the Act.

3.12 Medical treatment for mental disorder under the Act (including treatment with consent) can include measures to address alcohol or drug dependence if that is an appropriate part of treating the mental disorder which is the primary focus of the treatment.

Learning disabilities and autistic spectrum disorders [Reference Guide 1.12-1.15]

3.13 Learning disabilities and autistic spectrum disorders are forms of mental disorder as defined in the Act.

3.14 However, someone with a learning disability and no other form of mental disorder may not be detained for treatment or made subject to guardianship or supervised community treatment unless their learning disability is accompanied by abnormally aggressive or seriously irresponsible conduct on their part.

3.15 This "learning disability qualification" applies only to specific sections of the Act [Section 1(2A) and (2B)]. In particular, it does not apply to detention for assessment under section 2 of the Act.

3.16 The learning disability qualification does not apply to autistic spectrum disorders (including Asperger's syndrome). It is possible for someone with an autistic spectrum disorder to meet the criteria for compulsory measures under the Act without having any other form of mental disorder, even if their autistic spectrum disorder is not associated with abnormally aggressive or seriously irresponsible behaviour. While experience suggests that this is likely to be necessary only very rarely, the possibility should never automatically be discounted.

3.17 For further guidance on particular issues relating to people with learning disabilities or autistic spectrum disorders (including further guidance on the learning disability qualification), see **chapter 34**.

Personality disorders

3.18 Apart from the learning disability qualification described above, the Act does not distinguish between different forms of mental disorder. The Act therefore applies to personality disorders (of all types) in exactly the same way as it applies to mental illness and other mental disorders.

3.19 No assumptions should be made about the suitability of using the Act – or indeed providing services without using the Act – in respect of personality disorders or the people who have them. The factors which should inform decisions are the needs of the individual patient, the risks posed by their disorder and what can be done to address those needs and risks, in both the short and longer term (see **chapter 35** for further guidance on personality disorders).

CHAPTER 4
APPLICATIONS FOR DETENTION IN HOSPITAL

4.1 This chapter gives guidance on the making of applications for detention in hospital under Part 2 of the Act. [Reference Guide chapter 2].

Grounds for making an application for detention

4.2 An application for detention may only be made where the grounds in either section 2 or section 3 of the Act are met (see box below).

Criteria for applications

A person can be detained for assessment under section 2 only if both the following criteria apply:

- the person is suffering from a mental disorder of a nature or degree which warrants their detention in hospital for assessment (or for assessment followed by treatment) for at least a limited period; and
- the person ought to be so detained in the interests of their own health or safety or with a view to the protection of others.

A person can be detained for treatment under section 3 only if all the following criteria apply:

- the person is suffering from a mental disorder of a nature or degree which makes it appropriate for them to receive medical treatment in hospital;
- it is necessary for the health or safety of the person or for the protection of other persons that they should receive such treatment and it cannot be provided unless the patient is detained under this section; and
- appropriate medical treatment is available.

4.3 The criteria require consideration of both the nature and degree of a patient's mental disorder. Nature refers to the particular mental disorder from which the patient is suffering, its chronicity, its prognosis, and the patient's previous response to receiving treatment for the disorder. Degree refers to the current manifestation of the patient's disorder.

4.4 Before it is decided that admission to hospital is necessary, consideration must be given to whether there are alternative means of providing the care and treatment which the patient requires. This includes consideration of whether there might be other effective forms of care or treatment which the patient would be willing to accept, and of whether guardianship would be appropriate instead.

4.5 In all cases, consideration must be given to:

- the patient's wishes and view of their own needs;

- the patient's age and physical health;
- any past wishes or feelings expressed by the patient;
- the patient's cultural background;
- the patient's social and family circumstances;
- the impact that any future deterioration or lack of improvement in the patient's condition would have on their children, other relatives or carers, especially those living with the patient, including an assessment of these people's ability and willingness to cope; and
- the effect on the patient, and those close to the patient, of a decision to admit or not to admit under the Act.

Factors to consider – the health or safety of the patient

4.6 Factors to be considered in deciding whether patients should be detained for their own health or safety include:

- the evidence suggesting that patients are at risk of:
  - suicide;
  - self-harm;
  - self-neglect or being unable to look after their own health or safety; or
  - jeopardising their own health or safety accidentally, recklessly or unintentionally; or that their mental disorder is otherwise putting their health or safety at risk;
- any evidence suggesting that the patient's mental health will deteriorate if they do not receive treatment;
- the reliability of such evidence, including what is known of the history of the patient's mental disorder;
- the views of the patient and of any carers, relatives or close friends, especially those living with the patient, about the likely course of the disorder and the possibility of it improving;
- the patient's own skills and experience in managing their condition;
- the potential benefits of treatment, which should be weighed against any adverse effects that being detained might have on the patient's wellbeing; and
- whether other methods of managing the risk are available.

Factors to consider – protection of others

4.7 In considering whether detention is necessary for the protection of other people, the factors to consider are the nature of the risk to other people arising from the patient's mental disorder, the likelihood that harm will result and the severity of any potential harm, taking into account:

- that it is not always possible to differentiate risk of harm to the patient from the risk of harm to others;
- the reliability of the available evidence, including any relevant details of the patient's clinical history and past behaviour, such as contact with other agencies and (where relevant) criminal convictions and cautions;
- the willingness and ability of those who live with the patient and those who provide care and support to the patient to cope with and manage the risk; and
- whether other methods of managing the risk are available.

4.8 Harm to other people includes psychological as well as physical harm.

Alternatives to detention – patients with capacity to consent to admission

4.9 When a patient needs to be in hospital, informal admission is usually appropriate when a patient who has the capacity to do so consents to admission. (See **chapter 36** for guidance on when parents might consent to admission on behalf of children and young people.)

4.10 However, this should not be regarded as an absolute rule, especially if the reason for considering admission is that the patient presents a clear danger to themselves or others because of their mental disorder.

4.11 Compulsory admission should, in particular, be considered where a patient's current mental state, together with reliable evidence of past experience, indicates a strong likelihood that they will have a change of mind about informal admission, either before or after they are admitted, with a resulting risk to their health or safety or to the safety of other people.

4.12 The threat of detention must not be used to induce a patient to consent to admission to hospital or to treatment (and is likely to invalidate any apparent consent).

Alternatives to detention – patients who lack capacity to consent to admission or treatment

4.13 In deciding whether it is necessary to detain-patients, doctors and approved mental health professionals (AMHPs) must always consider the alternative ways of providing the treatment or care they need.

4.14 The fact that patients cannot consent to the treatment they need, or to being admitted to hospital, does not automatically mean that the Act must be used. It may be possible to rely instead on the provisions of the Mental Capacity Act 2005 (MCA) to provide treatment in the best interests of patients who are aged 16 or over and who lack capacity to consent to treatment.

4.15 This may be possible even if the provision of treatment unavoidably involves depriving patients of their liberty. Deprivation of liberty for the purposes of care or treatment in a hospital or care home can be authorised in a person's best interests under the deprivation of liberty safeguards in the MCA if the person is aged 18 or over.[2]

4.16 If admission to hospital for assessment or treatment for mental disorder is necessary for a patient who lacks capacity to consent to it, an application under the Mental Health Act should be made if:

- providing appropriate care or treatment for the patient will unavoidably involve depriving them of their liberty and the MCA deprivation of liberty safeguards cannot be used; or[3]

- for any other reason, the assessment or treatment the patient needs cannot be safely or effectively delivered by relying on the MCA alone.

4.17 The MCA deprivation of liberty safeguards can be used only if the six qualifying requirements summarised in the table below are met.

Summary of qualifying requirements in the MCA's deprivation of liberty safeguards

Age requirement	The person is at least 18 years old.
Mental health requirement	The person has a mental disorder.
Mental capacity requirement	The person lacks capacity to decide whether to be in a hospital or care home for the proposed treatment or care.
Best interests requirement	The proposed deprivation of liberty is in the person's best interests and it is a necessary and proportionate response to the risk of them suffering harm.
Eligibility requirement	The person is not subject, or potentially subject, to specified provisions of the Mental Health Act in a way that makes them ineligible.

[2] The deprivation of liberty safeguards have been in force from April 2009. It is also possible for the Court of Protection to authorise deprivation of liberty under the MCA, but doctors and AMHPs are not required to apply to the Court before considering whether the use of the Mental Health Act is necessary.

[3] The version of the Code presented to Parliament also included the words "there is no attorney or deputy willing to consent to admission and treatment on their behalf" – but, in fact, those words are redundant because attorneys or deputies may not consent to deprivation of liberty.

No refusals requirement	There is no advance decision, or decision of an attorney or deputy which makes the proposed deprivation of liberty impossible.

4.18 The key points when considering whether an application for detention should be made under the Mental Health Act instead of relying on the MCA's deprivation of liberty safeguards are that those safeguards cannot be used if:

- the patient is aged under 18;
- the patient has made a valid and applicable advance decision refusing a necessary element of the treatment for which they are to be admitted to hospital (see chapter 17);
- the use of the safeguards would conflict with a decision of the person's attorney or deputy or of the Court of Protection; or
- the patient meets the criteria in section 2 or section 3 of the Mental Health Act and is objecting to being admitted to (or remaining in) hospital for mental health treatment (unless an attorney or deputy consents on their behalf).[4]

4.19 In that last case, whether a patient is objecting has to be considered in the round, taking into account all the circumstances, so far as they are reasonably ascertainable. The decision to be made is whether the patient objects to treatment – the reasonableness of that objection is not the issue. In many cases the patient will be perfectly able to state their objection. But in other cases doctors and AMHPs will need to consider the patient's behaviour, wishes, feelings, views, beliefs and values, both present and past, so far as they can be ascertained. If there is reason to think that a patient would object, if able to do so, then the patient should be taken to be objecting.

4.20 Even if providing appropriate care or treatment will not unavoidably involve a deprivation of liberty, it may be necessary to detain a patient under the Mental Health Act rather than relying on the MCA because:

- the patient has, by means of a valid and applicable advance decision, refused a necessary element of the treatment required; or
- the patient lacks capacity to make decisions on some elements of the care and treatment they need, but has capacity to decide about a vital element – eg admission to hospital – and either has already refused it or is likely to do so.

4.21 Whether or not the deprivation of liberty safeguards could be used, other reasons why it may not be possible to rely on the MCA alone include the following:

- the patient's lack of capacity to consent is fluctuating or temporary and the patient is not expected to consent when they regain capacity. This may be particularly relevant to patients having acute psychotic, manic or depressive episodes;

---

4 The final words in brackets were omitted by mistake from the version of the Code presented to Parliament.

- a degree of restraint needs to be used which is justified by the risk to other people but which is not permissible under the MCA because, exceptionally, it cannot be said to be proportionate to the risk to the patient personally; and
- there is some other specific identifiable risk that the person might not receive the treatment they need if the MCA is relied on and that either the person or others might potentially suffer harm as a result.

4.22 Otherwise, if the MCA can be used safely and effectively to assess or treat a patient, it is likely to be difficult to demonstrate that the criteria for detaining the patient under the Mental Health Act are met.

4.23 For further information on the MCA deprivation of liberty safeguards, see the addendum to the MCA Code of Practice.

4.24 For the different considerations which apply to children and young people, see **chapter 36**.

Section 2 or section 3

4.25 An application for detention can be made under either section 2 or section 3 of the Mental Health Act.

4.26 Section 2 should be used if:

- the full extent of the nature and degree of a patient's condition is unclear;
- there is a need to carry out an initial in-patient assessment in order to formulate a treatment plan, or to reach a judgement about whether the patient will accept treatment on a voluntary basis following admission; or
- there is a need to carry out a new in-patient assessment in order to re-formulate a treatment plan, or to reach a judgement about whether the patient will accept treatment on a voluntary basis.

4.27 Section 3 should be used if:

- the patient is already detained under section 2 (detention under section 2 cannot be renewed by a new section 2 application); or
- the nature and current degree of the patient's mental disorder, the essential elements of the treatment plan to be followed and the likelihood of the patient accepting treatment on a voluntary basis are already established.

The assessment process

4.28 An application for detention may be made by an AMHP or the patient's nearest relative. An AMHP is usually a more appropriate applicant than a patient's nearest relative, given an AMHP's professional training and knowledge of the legislation and local resources, together with the potential adverse effect that an application by the nearest relative might have on their relationship with the patient.

4.29 An application must be supported by two medical recommendations given in accordance with the Act.

4.30 Doctors who are approached directly by a nearest relative about making an application should advise the nearest relative that it is preferable for an AMHP to consider the need for a patient to be admitted under the Act and for the AMHP to make any consequent application. Doctors should also advise the nearest relative of their right to require a local social services authority (LSSA) to arrange for an AMHP to consider the patient's case. Doctors should never advise a nearest relative to make an application themselves in order to avoid involving an AMHP in an assessment.

Objective of the assessment

4.31 The objective of the assessment is to determine whether the criteria for detention are met and, if so, whether an application for detention should be made.

4.32 Because a proper assessment cannot be carried out without considering alternative means of providing care and treatment, AMHPs and doctors should, as far as possible in the circumstances, identify and liaise with services which may potentially be able to provide alternatives to admission to hospital. That could include crisis and home treatment teams.

Responsibilities of local social services authorities

4.33 LSSAs are responsible for ensuring that sufficient AMHPs are available to carry out their roles under the Act, including assessing patients to decide whether an application for detention should be made. To fulfil their statutory duty, LSSAs must have arrangements in place in their area to provide a 24-hour service that can respond to patients' needs.

4.34 Section 13 of the Act places a specific duty on LSSAs to arrange for an AMHP to consider the case of any patient who is within their area if they have reason to believe that an application for detention in hospital may need to be made in respect of the patient. LSSAs must make such arrangements if asked to do so by (or on behalf of) the nearest relative.

4.35 If a patient is already detained under section 2 as the result of an application made by an AMHP, the LSSA on whose behalf that AMHP was acting is responsible for arranging for an AMHP to consider the patient's case again if the LSSA has reason to believe that an application under section 3 may be necessary. This applies even if the patient has been detained outside that LSSA's area.

4.36 These duties do not prevent any other LSSA from arranging for an AMHP to consider a patient's case if that is more appropriate.

Setting up the assessment

4.37 Local arrangements should, as far as possible, ensure that assessments are carried out by the most appropriate AMHP and doctors in the particular circumstances.

4.38 Where a patient is known to belong to a group for which particular expertise is desirable (eg they are aged under 18 or have a learning disability), at least one of the professionals involved in their assessment should have expertise in working with people from that group, wherever possible.

4.39 If this is not possible, at least one of the professionals involved in the person's assessment should, if at all possible, consult with one or more professionals who do have relevant expertise and involve them as closely as the circumstances of the case allow.

4.40 Unless different arrangements have been agreed locally between the relevant authorities, AMHPs who assess patients for possible detention under the Act have overall responsibility for co-ordinating the process of assessment. In doing so, they should be sensitive to the patient's age, gender (and gender identity), social, cultural, racial and religious background and sexual orientation. They should also consider how any disability the patient has may affect the way the assessment needs to be carried out.

4.41 Given the importance of good communication, it is essential that those professionals who assess patients are able to communicate with the patient effectively and reliably to prevent potential misunderstandings. AMHPs should establish, as far as possible, whether patients have particular communication needs or difficulties and take steps to meet them, for example by arranging a signer or a professional interpreter. AMHPs should also be in a position, where appropriate, to supply suitable equipment to make communication easier with patients who have impaired hearing, but who do not have their own hearing aid.

4.42 See **paragraphs 4.106–4.110** for specific guidance in relation to the assessment of people who are deaf. For further guidance on specific issues that may arise when assessing people who have a learning disability or an autistic spectrum disorder, or who have a personality disorder, see **chapter 34** and **chapter 35** respectively.

4.43 Doctors and AMHPs undertaking assessments need to apply professional judgement and reach decisions independently of each other, but in a framework of co-operation and mutual support.

4.44 Unless there is good reason for undertaking separate assessments, patients should, where possible, be seen jointly by the AMHP and at least one of the two doctors involved in the assessment.

4.45 While it may not always be feasible for the patient to be examined by both doctors at the same time, they should both discuss the patient's case with the person considering making an application for the patient's detention.

4.46 Everyone involved in an assessment should be alert to the need to provide support for colleagues, especially where there is a risk of the patient causing physical harm. People carrying out assessments should be aware of circumstances in which the police should be asked to provide assistance, in accordance with arrangements agreed locally with the police, and of how to use that assistance to maximise the safety of everyone involved in the assessment.

4.47 Locally agreed arrangements on the involvement of the police should include a joint risk assessment tool to help determine the level of risk, what (if any) police assistance may be required and how quickly it is needed. In cases where no warrant for the police to enter premises under section 135 of the Act is being applied for (see **chapter 10**), the risk assessment should indicate the reasons for this and explain why police assistance is nonetheless necessary.

The role of approved mental health professionals

4.48 AMHPs may make an application for detention only if they: [Section 13(1A) and (2)].

- have interviewed the patient in a suitable manner;
- are satisfied that the statutory criteria for detention are met; and
- are satisfied that, in all the circumstances of the case, detention in hospital is the most appropriate way of providing the care and medical treatment the patient needs.

4.49 Once AMHPs have decided that an application should be made, they must then decide whether it is necessary or proper for them to make the application themselves. If they decide it is, having considered any views expressed by the patient's relatives and all the other relevant circumstances, AMHPs must make the application.

4.50 At the start of an assessment, AMHPs should identify themselves to the person being assessed, members of the person's family, carers or friends and the other professionals present. AMHPs should ensure that the purpose of the visit, their role and that of the other professionals are explained. They should carry documents with them at all times which identify them as AMHPs and which specify both the LSSA which approved them and the LSSA on whose behalf they are acting.

4.51 Although AMHPs act on behalf of a LSSA, they cannot be told by the LSSA or anyone else whether or not to make an application. They must exercise their own judgement, based on social and medical evidence, when deciding whether to apply for a patient to be detained under the Act. The role of AMHPs is to provide an independent decision about whether or not there are alternatives to detention under the Act, bringing a social perspective to bear on their decision.

4.52 If patients want someone else (e g a familiar person or an advocate) to be present during the assessment and any subsequent action that may be taken, then ordinarily AMHPs should assist in securing that person's attendance, unless the urgency of the case makes it inappropriate to do so. Patients may feel safer or more confident with a friend or other person they know well in attendance. Equally, an advocate can help to reassure patients. Some patients may already be receiving help from an advocate.

4.53 Patients should usually be given the opportunity of speaking to the AMHP alone. However, if AMHPs have reason to fear physical harm, they should insist that another professional is present.

4.54 It is not desirable for patients to be interviewed through a closed door or window, and this should be considered only where other people are at serious risk. Where direct access to the patient is not possible, but there is no immediate risk of physical danger to the patient or to anyone else, AMHPs should consider applying for a warrant under section 135 of the Act, allowing the police to enter the premises (see **chapter 10**).

4.55 Where patients are subject to the short-term effects of alcohol or drugs (whether prescribed or self-administered) which make interviewing them difficult, the AMHP should either wait until the effects have abated before interviewing the patient or arrange to return later. If it is not realistic to wait, because of the patient's disturbed behaviour and the urgency of the case, the assessment will have to be based on whatever information the AMHP can obtain from reliable sources. This should be made clear in the AMHP's record of the assessment.

The AMHP and the nearest relative

4.56 AMHPs are required by the Act to attempt to identify the patient's nearest relative as defined in section 26 of the Act.

4.57 When AMHPs make an application for detention under section 2, they must take such steps as are practicable to inform the nearest relative that the application is to be (or has been) made and of the nearest relative's power to discharge the patient. [Section 11(3)].

4.58 Before making an application for detention under section 3, AMHPs must consult the nearest relative, unless it is not reasonably practicable or would involve unreasonable delay. [Section 11(4)].

4.59 Circumstances in which the nearest relative need not be informed or consulted include those where:

- it is not practicable for the AMHP to obtain sufficient information to establish the identity or location of the nearest relative, or where to do so would require an excessive amount of investigation involving unreasonable delay; and

- consultation is not possible because of the nearest relative's own health or mental incapacity.

4.60 There may also be cases where, although physically possible, it would not be reasonably practicable to inform or consult the nearest relative because there would be a detrimental impact on the patient which would result in infringement of the patient's right to respect for their privacy and family life under article 8 of the European Convention on Human Rights and which could not be justified by the benefit of the involvement of the nearest relative.[5] Detrimental impact may include cases where patients are likely to suffer emotional distress, deterioration in their mental health, physical harm, or financial or other exploitation as a result of the consultation.

4.61 Consulting and notifying the nearest relative is a significant safeguard for patients. Therefore decisions not to do so on these grounds should not be taken lightly. AMHPs should consider all the circumstances of the case, including:

- the benefit to the patient of the involvement of their nearest relative;

---

5 See in particular *R (on the application of E) v Bristol City Council* [2005] EWHC 74 (Admin).

- the patient's wishes (taking into account whether they have the capacity to decide whether they would want their nearest relative involved and any statement of their wishes they have made in advance);
- any detrimental effect that involving the nearest relative would have on the patient's health and wellbeing; and
- whether there is any good reason to think that the patient's objection may be intended to prevent information relevant to the assessment being discovered.

4.62 AMHPs may also consider the degree to which the nearest relative has been willing to be involved on previous occasions, but unwillingness to act previously should not automatically be taken to imply current unwillingness.

4.63 If they do not consult or inform the nearest relative, AMHPs should record their reasons. Consultation must not be avoided purely because it is thought that the nearest relative might object to the application.

4.64 When consulting nearest relatives AMHPs should, where possible:

- ascertain the nearest relative's views about both the patient's needs and the nearest relative's own needs in relation to the patient;
- inform the nearest relative of the reasons for considering an application for detention and what the effects of such an application would be; and
- inform the nearest relative of their role and rights under the Act.

4.65 If the nearest relative objects to an application being made for admission for treatment under section 3, the application cannot be made. If it is thought necessary to proceed with the application to ensure the patient's safety and the nearest relative cannot be persuaded to agree, the AMHP will need to consider applying to the county court for the nearest relative's displacement under section 29 of the Act (see **chapter 8**).

Consultation with other people

4.66 Although there are specific requirements to consult the nearest relative, it is important to recognise the value of involving other people, particularly the patient's carers and family, in the decision-making process as well. Carers and family members are often able to provide a particular perspective on the patient's circumstances. Insofar as the urgency of the case allows, AMHPs should consider consulting with other relevant relatives, carers or friends and should take their views into account.

4.67 Where patients are under 18, AMHPs should in particular consider consulting with the patient's parents (or other people who have parental responsibility for the patient), assuming they are not the patient's nearest relative anyway.

4.68 In deciding whether it is appropriate to consult carers and other family members, AMHPs should consider:

- the patient's wishes;

- the nature of the relationship between the patient and the person in question, including how long the relationship has existed; and
- whether the patient has referred to any hostility between them and the person in question, or there is other evidence of hostility, abuse or exploitation.

4.69 AMHPs should also consult wherever possible with other people who have been involved with the patient's care. These could include people working for statutory, voluntary or independent mental health services and other service providers who do not specialise in mental health services but have contact with the patient. For example, the patient may be known to services for older people or substance misuse services.

4.70 Some patients may have an attorney or deputy appointed under the MCA who has authority to make decisions about their personal welfare. Where such a person is known to exist, AMHPs should take reasonable steps to contact them and seek their opinion. Where attorneys or deputies have the power to consent or refuse treatment for mental disorder on the patient's behalf, they should also be given the opportunity to talk directly to the doctors assessing the patient, where practicable.

Medical examination by doctors as part of the assessment

4.71 A medical examination must involve:

- direct personal examination of the patient and their mental state; and
- consideration of all available relevant clinical information, including that in the possession of others, professional or non-professional.

4.72 If direct physical access to the patient is not immediately possible and it is not desirable to postpone the examination in order to negotiate access, consideration should be given to requesting that an AMHP apply for a warrant under section 135 of the Act (see **paragraph 4.54**).

4.73 Where practicable, at least one of the medical recommendations must be provided by a doctor with previous acquaintance with the patient. Preferably, this should be a doctor who has personally treated the patient. But it is sufficient for the doctor to have had some previous knowledge of the patient's case.

4.74 It is preferable that a doctor who does not have previous acquaintance with the patient be approved under section 12 of the Act. The Act requires that at least one of the doctors must be so approved.

4.75 If the doctors reach the opinion that the patient needs to be admitted to hospital, it is their responsibility to take the necessary steps to secure a suitable hospital bed. It is not the responsibility of the applicant, unless it has been agreed locally between the LSSA and the relevant NHS bodies that this will be done by any AMHP involved in the assessment. Primary care trusts are responsible for commissioning mental health services to meet the needs of their areas. They should ensure that procedures are in place through which beds can be identified where required.

4.76 Doctors must give reasons for the opinions stated in their recommendations. When giving a clinical description of the patient's mental disorder as part of these reasons, doctors should include a description of the patient's symptoms and behaviour, not merely a diagnostic classification.

4.77 When making recommendations for detention under section 3, doctors are required to state that appropriate medical treatment is available for the patient (see **chapter 6**). Preferably, they should know in advance of making the recommendation the name of the hospital to which the patient is to be admitted. But, if that is not possible, their recommendation may state that appropriate medical treatment will be available if the patient is admitted to one or more specific hospitals (or units within a hospital).

Communicating the outcome of the assessment

4.78 Having decided whether or not to make an application for detention, AMHPs should inform the patient, giving their reasons. Subject to the normal considerations of patient confidentiality, AMHPs should also give their decision and the reasons for it to:

- the patient's nearest relative;
- the doctors involved in the assessment;
- the patient's care co-ordinator (if they have one); and
- the patient's GP, if they were not one of the doctors involved in the assessment.

4.79 An AMHP should, when informing the nearest relative that they not do intend to make an application, advise the nearest relative of their right to do so instead. If the nearest relative wishes to pursue this, the AMHP should suggest that they consult with the doctors involved in the assessment to see if they would be prepared to provide recommendations anyway.

4.80 Where the AMHP has considered a patient's case at the request of the nearest relative, the reasons for not applying for the patient's detention must be given to the nearest relative in writing. [Section 13(4)]. Such a letter should contain, as far as possible, sufficient details to enable the nearest relative to understand the decision while at the same time preserving the patient's right to confidentiality.

Action when it is decided not to apply for detention

4.81 There is no obligation on an AMHP or nearest relative to make an application for detention just because the statutory criteria are met.

4.82 Where AMHPs decide not to apply for a patient's detention they should record the reasons for their decision. The decision should be supported, where necessary, by an alternative framework of care and treatment. AMHPs must decide how to pursue any actions which their assessment indicates are necessary to meet the needs of the patient. That might include, for example, referring the patient to social, health or other services.

4.83 The steps to be taken to put in place any new arrangements for the patient's care and treatment, and any plans for reviewing them, should be recorded in writing and copies made available to all those who need them (subject to the normal considerations of patient confidentiality).

4.84 It is particularly important that the patient's care co-ordinator (if they have one) is fully involved in decisions about meeting the patient's needs.

4.85 Arrangements should be made to ensure that information about assessments and their outcome is passed to professional colleagues where appropriate, for example where an application for detention is not immediately necessary but might be in the future. This information will need to be available at short notice at any time of day or night.

4.86 More generally, making out-of-hours services aware of situations that are ongoing – such as when there is concern over an individual but no assessment has begun, or when a person has absconded before an assessment could start or be completed – assists out-of-hours services in responding accordingly.

Action when it is decided to make an application

4.87 Most compulsory admissions require prompt action. [Sections 6(1) and 11(5)]. However, applicants have up to 14 days (depending on when the patient was last examined by a doctor as part of the assessment) in which to decide whether to make the application, starting with the day they personally last saw the patient. There may be cases where AMHPs conclude that they should delay taking a final decision, in order to see whether the patient's condition changes, or whether successful alternatives to detention can be put in place in the interim.

4.88 Before making an application, AMHPs should ensure that appropriate arrangements are in place for the immediate care of any dependent children the patient may have and any adults who rely on the patient for care. Their needs should already have been considered as part of the assessment.

4.89 Where relevant, AMHPs should also ensure that practical arrangements are made for the care of any pets and for the LSSA to carry out its other duties under the National Assistance Act 1948 to secure the patient's home and protect their property.

4.90 Applications for detention must be addressed to the managers of the hospital where the patient is to be detained. An application must state a specific hospital. An application cannot, for example, be made to an NHS trust without specifying which of the trust's hospitals the patient is to be admitted to.

4.91 Where units under the management of different bodies exist on the same site (or even in the same building), they will be separate hospitals for the purposes of the Act, because one hospital cannot be under the control of two sets of managers. Where there is potential for confusion, the respective hospital managers should ensure that there are distinct names for the units. In collaboration with LSSAs, they should take steps to ensure that information is available to AMHPs who are likely to be making relevant applications to enable them effectively to distinguish the different hospitals on the site and to describe them correctly in applications.

4.92 Once an application has been completed, the patient should be conveyed to the hospital as soon as possible, if they are not already in the hospital. But patients should not be moved until it is known that the hospital is willing to accept them.

4.93 A properly completed application supported by the necessary medical recommendations provides the applicant with the authority to convey the patient to hospital even if the patient does not wish to go. [Section 6(1)]. That authority lasts for 14 days from the date when the patient was last examined by one of the doctors with a view to making a recommendation to support the application. See **chapter 11** for further guidance on conveyance.

4.94 The AMHP should provide an outline report for the hospital at the time the patient is first admitted or detained, giving reasons for the application and details of any practical matters about the patient's circumstances which the hospital should know. Where possible, the report should include the name and telephone number of the AMHP or a care co-ordinator who can give further information. LSSAs should consider the use of a standard form on which AMHPs can make this outline report.

4.95 Where it is not realistic for the AMHP to accompany the patient to the hospital – for example, where the admitting hospital is some distance from the area in which the AMHP operates – it is acceptable for them to provide the information outlined above by telephone or fax or other means compatible with transferring confidential information. If providing the information by telephone, the AMHP should ensure that a written report is sent to the admitting hospital as soon as possible.

4.96 An outline report does not take the place of the full report which AMHPs are expected to complete for their employer or the LSSA on whose behalf they are acting (if different).

4.97 If the patient is a restricted patient, the AMHP should ensure that the Mental Health Unit of the Ministry of Justice is notified of the detention as soon as possible. A duty officer is available at all times to receive this information, which should not be left until office hours.[6]

4.98 An application cannot be used to admit a patient to any hospital other than the one stated in the application (although once admitted a patient may be transferred to another hospital – see **chapter 30**).

4.99 In exceptional circumstances, if patients are conveyed to a hospital which has agreed to accept them, but there is no longer a bed available, the managers and staff of that hospital should assist in finding a suitable alternative for the patient. This may involve making a new application to a different hospital. If the application is under section 3, new medical recommendations will be required, unless the original recommendations already state that appropriate medical treatment is available in the proposed new hospital. The hospital to which the original application was made should assist in securing new medical recommendations if they are needed. A situation of this sort should be considered a serious failure and should be recorded and investigated accordingly.

---

6 At the time of publication the telephone number is 020 7035 4848.

Resolving disagreements

4.100 Sometimes there will be differences of opinion between professionals involved in the assessment. There is nothing wrong with disagreements: handled properly they offer an opportunity to safeguard the interests of the patient by widening the discussion on the best way of meeting their needs. Doctors and AMHPs should be ready to consult other professionals (especially care co-ordinators and others involved with the patient's current care), while themselves retaining the final responsibility for their decision. Where disagreements do occur, professionals should ensure that they discuss these with each other.

4.101 Where there is an unresolved dispute about an application for detention, it is essential that the professionals do not abandon the patient. Instead, they should explore and agree an alternative plan – if necessary on a temporary basis. Such a plan should include a risk assessment and identification of the arrangements for managing the risks. The alternative plan should be recorded in writing, as should the arrangements for reviewing it. Copies should be made available to all those who need them (subject to the normal considerations of patient confidentiality).

Responsibilities of strategic health authorities for doctors approved under section 12 [Reference Guide chapter 32]

4.102 The Secretary of State has delegated to strategic health authorities (SHAs) the task of approving medical practitioners under section 12(2) of the Act. Medical practitioners who are approved clinicians under the Act are automatically treated as being approved under section 12 as well.

4.103 SHAs should:

- take active steps to encourage sufficient doctors, including GPs and those working in prison health services and the police service, to apply for approval;
- ensure that arrangements are in place for 24-hour on-call rotas of approved doctors (or an equivalent arrangement) sufficient to cover each area for which they are responsible;
- ensure that regularly updated lists of approved doctors are maintained which indicate how they can be contacted and the hours that each is available; and
- ensure that the up-to-date list of approved doctors and details of 24-hour on-call rotas (or the equivalent arrangement) are available to all those who may need them, including GPs, providers of hospital and community mental health services and social services.

Co-operation between local agencies

4.104 NHS bodies and LSSAs should co-operate in ensuring that there are opportunities for regular communication between professionals involved in mental health assessments, in order to promote understanding and to provide a forum for clarification of their respective roles and responsibilities. NHS bodies and LSSAs should also keep in mind the interface with the criminal justice agencies, including the probation service and the police.

4.105 Opportunities should also be sought to involve and learn directly from people with experience of being assessed.

Patients who are deaf

4.106 AMHPs and doctors assessing a deaf person should, wherever possible, have had deaf awareness training, including basic training in issues relating to mental health and deafness. Where required, they should also seek assistance from specialists with appropriate expertise in mental health and deafness. This may be available from one of the specialist hospital units for deafness and mental health. Contact with such units may, in particular, help to prevent deaf people being wrongly assessed as having a learning disability or another mental disorder.

4.107 Unless different arrangements have been agreed locally, the AMHP involved in the assessment should be responsible for booking and using registered qualified interpreters with expertise in mental health interpreting, bearing in mind that the interpretation of thought-disordered language requires particular expertise. Relay interpreters (interpreters who relay British Sign Language (BSL) to hands-on BSL or visual frame signing or close signing) may be necessary, such as when the deaf person has a visual impairment, does not use BSL to sign or has minimal language skills or a learning disability.

4.108 Reliance on unqualified interpreters or health professionals with only limited signing skills should be avoided. Family members may (subject to the normal considerations about patient confidentiality) occasionally be able to assist a professional interpreter in understanding a patient's idiosyncratic use of language. However, family members should not be relied upon in place of a professional interpreter, even if the patient is willing for them to be involved.

4.109 Pre-lingual deafness may cause delayed language acquisition, which may in turn influence social behaviour. People carrying out assessments of deaf people under the Act should have an awareness and knowledge of how mental health problems present in pre-lingually deaf people.

4.110 Cultural issues need to be taken into account, for instance in people who are pre-lingually deaf, as they have a visual perspective of the world and may consider themselves to be part of a cultural and linguistic minority. This means that they may behave in ways which are misperceived as evidence of mental disorder. For example, animated signing may be misunderstood as aggression, while touching a hearing person to talk to them may be misunderstood as an assault. Deaf people's spoken or written English may be poor, giving rise to a false assumption of thought disorder.

Related material

- Mental Capacity Act 2005.
- *Mental Capacity Act 2005 Code of Practice,* TSO, 2007.

- *Deprivation of Liberty Safeguards,* Addendum to the *Mental Capacity Act 2005 Code of Practice.*
- National Assistance Act 1948.

This material does not form part of the Code. It is provided for assistance only.

CHAPTER 6
THE APPROPRIATE MEDICAL TREATMENT TEST

6.1 This chapter gives guidance on the application of the appropriate medical treatment test in the criteria for detention and supervised community treatment (SCT) under the Act.

Purpose of medical treatment for mental disorder

6.2 For the purposes of the Act, medical treatment also includes nursing, psychological intervention and specialist mental health habilitation, rehabilitation and care. [Section 145(1)]. Habilitation means equipping someone with skills and abilities they have never had, whereas rehabilitation means helping them recover skills and abilities they have lost.

6.3 In the Act, medical treatment for mental disorder means medical treatment which is for the purpose of alleviating, or preventing a worsening of, a mental disorder or one or more of its symptoms or manifestations. [Section 145(4)].

6.4 Purpose is not the same as likelihood. Medical treatment may be for the purpose of alleviating, or preventing a worsening of, a mental disorder even though it cannot be shown in advance that any particular effect is likely to be achieved.

6.5 Symptoms and manifestations include the way a disorder is experienced by the individual concerned and the way in which the disorder manifests itself in the person's thoughts, emotions, communication, behaviour and actions. But it should be remembered that not every thought or emotion, or every aspect of the behaviour, of a patient suffering from a mental disorder will be a manifestation of that disorder.

6.6 Even if particular mental disorders are likely to persist or get worse despite treatment, there may well be a range of interventions which would represent appropriate medical treatment. It should never be assumed that any disorders, or any patients, are inherently or inevitably untreatable. Nor should it be assumed that likely difficulties in achieving long-term and sustainable change in a person's underlying disorder make medical treatment to help manage their condition and the behaviours arising from it either inappropriate or unnecessary.

Appropriate medical treatment test

6.7 The purpose of the appropriate medical treatment test is to ensure that no-one is detained (or remains detained) for treatment, or is an SCT patient, unless they are actually to be offered medical treatment for their mental disorder.

6.8 This medical treatment must be appropriate, taking into account the nature and degree of the person's mental disorder and all their particular circumstances, including cultural, ethnic and religious considerations. By definition, it must be treatment which is for the purpose of alleviating or preventing a worsening of the patient's mental disorder or its symptoms or manifestations.

6.9 The appropriate medical treatment test requires a judgement about whether an appropriate package of treatment for mental disorder is available for the individual in question. Where the appropriate medical treatment test forms part of the criteria for detention, the medical treatment in question is treatment for mental disorder in the hospital in which the patient is to be detained. Where it is part of the criteria for SCT it refers to the treatment for mental disorder that the person will be offered while on SCT.

Applying the appropriate medical treatment test

6.10 The test requires a judgement about whether, when looked at in the round, appropriate medical treatment is available to the patient, given:

- the nature and degree of the patient's mental disorder; and
- all the other circumstances of the patient's case.

In other words, both the clinical appropriateness of the treatment and its appropriateness more generally must be considered.

6.11 The other circumstances of a patient's case might include factors such as:

- the patient's physical health – how this might impact on the effectiveness of the available medical treatment for the patient's mental disorder and the impact that the treatment might have in return;
- any physical disabilities the patient has;
- the patient's culture and ethnicity;
- the patient's age;
- the patient's gender, gender identity and sexual orientation;
- the location of the available treatment;
- the implications of the treatment for the patient's family and social relationships, including their role as a parent;
- its implications for the patient's education or work; and
- the consequences for the patient, and other people, if the patient does not receive the treatment available. (For mentally disordered offenders about to be sentenced for an offence, the consequence will sometimes be a prison sentence.)

6.12 Medical treatment need not be the most appropriate treatment that could ideally be made available. Nor does it need to address every aspect of the person's disorder. But the medical treatment available at any time must be an appropriate response to the patient's condition and situation.

6.13 Medical treatment must actually be available to the patient. It is not sufficient that appropriate treatment could theoretically be provided.

6.14 What is appropriate will vary greatly between patients. It will depend, in part, on what might reasonably be expected to be achieved given the nature and degree of the patient's disorder.

6.15 Medical treatment which aims merely to prevent a disorder worsening is unlikely, in general, to be appropriate in cases where normal treatment approaches would aim (and be expected) to alleviate the patient's condition significantly. For some patients with persistent mental disorders, however, management of the undesirable effects of their disorder may be all that can realistically be hoped for.

6.16 Appropriate medical treatment does not have to involve medication or individual or group psychological therapy – although it very often will. There may be patients whose particular circumstances mean that treatment may be appropriate even though it consists only of nursing and specialist day-to-day care under the clinical supervision of an approved clinician, in a safe and secure therapeutic environment with a structured regime.

6.17 Simply detaining someone – even in a hospital – does not constitute medical treatment.

6.18 A patient's attitude towards the proposed treatment may be relevant in determining whether the appropriate medical treatment test is met. But an indication of unwillingness to co-operate with treatment generally, or with a specific aspect of treatment, does not make such treatment inappropriate.

6.19 In particular, psychological therapies and other forms of medical treatments which, to be effective, require the patient's co-operation are not automatically inappropriate simply because a patient does not currently wish to engage with them. Such treatments can potentially remain appropriate and available as long as it continues to be clinically suitable to offer them and they would be provided if the patient agreed to engage.

6.20 People called on to make a judgement about whether the appropriate medical treatment test is met do not have to be satisfied that appropriate treatment will be available for the whole course of the patient's detention or SCT. What is appropriate may change over time, as the patient's condition changes or clinicians obtain a greater understanding of the patient's case. But they must satisfy themselves that appropriate medical treatment is available for the time being, given the patient's condition and circumstances as they are currently understood.

CHAPTER 8
THE NEAREST RELATIVE

8.1 This chapter gives guidance on the identification, appointment and displacement of nearest relatives under the Act. [Reference Guide chapter 33.]

Identification of the nearest relative

8.2 Section 26 of the Act defines 'relative' and 'nearest relative' for the purposes of the Act. It is important to remember that the nearest relative for the purposes of the Act may not be the same person as the patient's next of kin. The identity of the nearest relative may also change with the passage of time (eg if the patient enters into a marriage or civil partnership). (See **paragraphs 4.56–4.65**.)

8.3 Patients remanded to hospital under sections 35 and 36 of the Act and people subject to interim hospital orders under section 38 do not have nearest relatives (as defined by the Act). Nor do patients subject to special restrictions under Part 3 of the Act (restricted patients).

Delegation of nearest relative functions

8.4 A nearest relative is not obliged to act as such. They can authorise, in writing, another person to perform the functions of the nearest relative on their behalf. The procedure for doing this is set out in the Mental Health (Hospital, Guardianship and Treatment) (England) Regulations 2008.

Where there is no nearest relative

8.5 Where an approved mental health professional (AMHP) discovers, when assessing a patient for possible detention or guardianship under the Act (or at any other time), that the patient appears to have no nearest relative, the AMHP should advise the patient of their right to apply to the county court for the appointment of a person to act as their nearest relative.

Displacement of nearest relatives and appointment of acting nearest relatives by the county court [Sections 29 and 30]

Grounds for displacement and appointment

8.6 An acting nearest relative can be appointed by the county court on the grounds that:

- the nearest relative is incapable of acting as such because of illness or mental disorder;
- the nearest relative has objected unreasonably to an application for admission for treatment or a guardianship application;
- the nearest relative has exercised the power to discharge a patient without due regard to the patient's health or wellbeing or the safety of the public;

- the nearest relative is otherwise not a suitable person to act as such; or
- the patient has no nearest relative within the meaning of the Act, or it is not reasonably practicable to ascertain whether the patient has a nearest relative or who that nearest relative is.

8.7 The effect of a court order appointing an acting nearest relative is to displace the person who would otherwise be the patient's nearest relative.

8.8 However, as an alternative to an order by the court, it may sometimes be enough for the actual nearest relative to delegate their role to someone else (see **paragraph 8.4**).

Who can make an application to the court?

8.9 An application to displace the nearest relative may be made by any of the following people:

- the patient;
- any relative of the patient;
- anyone with whom the patient is residing (or was residing prior to admission); or
- an AMHP.

Applications to the court by AMHPs

8.10 AMHPs will need to consider making an application for displacement or appointment if:

- they believe that a patient should be detained in hospital under section 3 of the Act, or should become a guardianship patient, but the nearest relative objects; or
- they believe that the nearest relative is likely to discharge a patient from detention or guardianship unwisely.

8.11 They should also consider doing so if they think that:

- a patient has no identifiable nearest relative or their nearest relative is incapable of acting as such; or
- they have good reasons to think that a patient considers their nearest relative unsuitable and would like them to be replaced;

and it would not be reasonable in the circumstances to expect the patient, or anyone else, to make an application.

8.12 AMHPs should bear in mind that some patients may wish to apply to displace their nearest relative but may be deterred from doing so by the need to apply to the county court.

8.13 It is entirely a matter for the court to decide what constitutes "suitability" of a person to be a nearest relative. But factors which an AMHP might wish to consider when deciding whether to make an application to displace a nearest relative on grounds of unsuitability, and when providing evidence in connection with an application, could include:

- any reason to think that the patient has suffered, or is suspected to have suffered, abuse at the hands of the nearest relative (or someone with whom the nearest relative is in a relationship), or is at risk of suffering such abuse;
- any evidence that the patient is afraid of the nearest relative or seriously distressed by the possibility of the nearest relative being involved in their life or their care; and
- a situation where the patient and nearest relative are unknown to each other, there is only a distant relationship between them, or their relationship has broken down irretrievably.

This is not an exhaustive list.

8.14 In all cases, the decision to make an application lies with the AMHP personally.

8.15 Before making an application for displacement, AMHPs should consider other ways of achieving the same end, including:

- whether the nearest relative will agree to delegate their role as the patient's nearest relative to someone else; or
- providing or arranging support for the patient (or someone else) to make an application themselves. This could include support from an independent mental health advocate.[7]

8.16 Local social services authorities (LSSAs) should provide clear practical guidance to help AMHPs decide whether to make an application and how to proceed. Before producing such guidance, LSSAs should consult with the county court. LSSAs should ensure that they have access to the necessary legal advice and support.

Making an application

8.17 People making an application to the county court will need to provide the court with the facts that will help it make a decision on the application. Exactly what will be required will depend on the type of application and the specific circumstances of the case.

8.18 When applying to displace a nearest relative, AMHPs should nominate someone to become the acting nearest relative in the event that the application is successful. Wherever practicable, they should first consult the patient about the patient's own preferences and any concerns they have about the person the AMHP proposes to nominate. AMHPs should also seek the agreement of the proposed nominee prior to an application being made, although this is not a legal requirement.

---

7 Independent mental health advocacy services under the Act were introduced in April 2009.

8.19 LSSAs should provide clear practical guidance to help the AMHP decide who it is appropriate to nominate when making an application to displace a nearest relative.

8.20 If the patient has any concerns that any information given to the court on their views on the suitability of the nearest relative may have implications for their own safety, an application can be made to the court seeking its permission not to make the current nearest relative a party to the proceedings. The reasons for the patient's concerns should be set out clearly in the application.

8.21 Hospital managers should provide support to detained patients to enable them to attend the court, if they wish, subject to the patient being granted leave under section 17 for this purpose.

8.22 If, exceptionally, the court decides to interview the patient (as the applicant), the court has the discretion to decide where and how this interview may take place and whether it should take place in the presence of, or separate from, other parties.

8.23 If the court decides that the nearest relative should be displaced and finds the proposed replacement to be suitable, and that person is willing to act as nearest relative, then the court will appoint them.

CHAPTER 20
INDEPENDENT MENTAL HEALTH ADVOCATES

20.1 This chapter explains the role of independent mental health advocates (IMHAs) under the Act.

Purpose of independent mental health advocacy services

20.2 Independent mental health advocacy services provide an additional safeguard for patients who are subject to the Act. IMHAs are specialist advocates who are trained specifically to work within the framework of the Act to meet the needs of patients.[8]

20.3 Independent mental health advocacy services do not replace any other advocacy and support services that are available to patients, but are intended to operate in conjunction with those services.

Patients who are eligible for independent mental health advocacy services (qualifying patients)

20.4 Patients are eligible for support from an IMHA if they are:

- detained under the Act (even if they are currently on leave of absence from hospital);
- conditionally discharged restricted patients;

---

[8] Independent mental health advocacy services under the Act were introduced in April 2009.

- subject to guardianship; or
- supervised community treatment (SCT) patients.

20.5 For these purposes, detention does not include being detained:

- on the basis of an emergency application (section 4) until the second medical recommendation is received (see **chapter 5**);
- under the holding powers in section 5; or
- in a place of safety under section 135 or 136.

20.6 Other patients ("informal patients") are eligible if they are:

- being considered for a treatment to which section 57 applies ("a section 57 treatment"); or
- under 18 and being considered for electro-convulsive therapy or any other treatment to which section 58A applies ("a section 58A treatment").

20.7 The Act calls patients who are eligible for the support of an IMHA "qualifying patients".

The role of independent mental health advocates

20.8 The Act says that the support which IMHAs provide must include helping patients to obtain information about and understand the following:

- their rights under the Act;
- the rights which other people (eg nearest relatives) have in relation to them under the Act;
- the particular parts of the Act which apply to them (eg the basis on which they are detained) and which therefore make them eligible for advocacy;
- any conditions or restrictions to which they are subject (eg as a condition of leave of absence from hospital, as a condition of a community treatment order, or as a condition of conditional discharge);
- any medical treatment that they are receiving or might be given;
- the reasons for that treatment (or proposed treatment); and
- the legal authority for providing that treatment, and the safeguards and other requirements of the Act which would apply to that treatment.

20.9 It also includes helping patients to exercise their rights, which can include representing them and speaking on their behalf.

20.10 IMHAs may also support patients in a range of other ways to ensure they can participate in the decisions that are made about their care and treatment.

20.11 The involvement of an IMHA does not affect a patient's right (nor the right of their nearest relative) to seek advice from a lawyer. Nor does it affect any entitlement to legal aid.

Duty to inform patients about the availability of independent mental health advocacy services

20.12 Certain people have a duty to take whatever steps are practicable to ensure that patients understand that help is available to them from IMHA services and how they can obtain that help, as set out in the following table. This must include giving the relevant information both orally and in writing.

Duty to provide patients with information about advocacy services

Type of patient	Steps to be taken by	As soon as practicable after
Detained patient	The managers of the hospital in which the patient is liable to be detained	The patient becomes liable to be detained
Guardianship patient	The responsible local social services authority	The patient becomes subject to guardianship
SCT patient	The managers of the responsible hospital	The patient becomes an SCT patient
Conditionally discharged patient	The patient's responsible clinician	The patient is conditionally discharged
Informal patient	The doctor or approved clinician who first discusses with the patient the possibility of them being given the section 57 or 58A treatment in question	That discussion (or during it)

20.13 The relevant person must also take whatever steps are practicable to give a copy of the written information to the patient's nearest relative, unless the patient requests otherwise (and subject to the normal considerations about involving nearest relatives – see **paragraphs 2.27–2.33**).

20.14 However, any information about independent mental health advocacy services should make clear that the services are for patients and are not advocacy services for nearest relatives themselves.

20.15 The duty to give information to nearest relatives does not apply to informal patients, nor to patients detained in hospital under Part 3 of the Act (although it does apply to those patients if they subsequently become SCT patients).

Seeking help from an independent mental health advocate

20.16 A qualifying patient may request the support of an IMHA at any time after they become a qualifying patient. Patients have the right to access the independent mental health advocacy service itself, rather than the services of a particular IMHA, though where possible it would normally be good practice for the same IMHA to remain involved while the person's case stays open.

20.17 A patient may choose to end the support they are receiving from an IMHA at any time.

20.18 IMHAs must also comply with any reasonable request to visit and interview a qualifying patient, if the request is made by the patient's nearest relative, an approved mental health professional (AMHP) or the patient's responsible clinician (if they have one). But patients may refuse to be interviewed and do not have to accept help from an IMHA if they do not want it.

20.19 AMHPs and responsible clinicians should consider requesting an IMHA to visit a qualifying patient if they think that the patient might benefit from an IMHA's visit but is unable or unlikely for whatever reason to request an IMHA's help themselves.

20.20 Before requesting an IMHA to visit a patient, they should, wherever practicable, first discuss the idea with the patient, and give the patient the opportunity to decide for themselves whether to request an IMHA's help. AMHPs and responsible clinicians should not request an IMHA to visit where they know, or strongly suspect, that the patient does not want an IMHA's help, or the help of the particular IMHA in question.

Independent mental health advocates' access to patients and professionals

20.21 Patients should have access to a telephone on which they can contact the independent mental health advocacy service and talk to them in private.

20.22 IMHAs should:

- have access to wards and units on which patients are resident;
- be able to meet with the patients they are helping in private, where they think it appropriate; and
- be able to attend meetings between patients and the professionals involved in their care and treatment when asked to do so by patients.

20.23 When instructed by a patient, the nearest relative, an AMHP or the responsible clinician, an IMHA has the right to meet the patient in private. IMHAs also have a right to visit and speak to any person who is currently professionally concerned with a patient's medical treatment, provided it is for the purpose of supporting that patient in their capacity as an IMHA.

20.24 Professionals should remember that the normal rules on patient confidentiality apply to conversations with IMHAs, even when the conversation is at the patient's request. IMHAs have a right of access to patients' records in certain cases (described below), but otherwise professionals should be careful not to share confidential information with IMHAs, unless the patient has consented to the disclosure or the disclosure is justified on the normal grounds (see **chapter 18**).

CHAPTER 21
LEAVE OF ABSENCE

21.1 This chapter provides guidance on leave of absence for detained patients under section 17 of the Act. [Reference Guide 12.39–12.56.]

General points

21.2 In general, while patients are detained in a hospital they can leave lawfully – even for a very short period – only if they are given leave of absence by their responsible clinician under section 17 of the Act.[9]

21.3 Responsible clinicians cannot grant leave of absence from hospital to patients who have been remanded to hospital under sections 35 or 36 of the Act or who are subject to interim hospital orders under section 38.

21.4 Except for certain restricted patients (see **paragraph 21.14**), no formal procedure is required to allow patients to move within a hospital or its grounds. Such "ground leave" within a hospital may be encouraged or, where necessary, restricted, as part of each patient's care plan.

21.5 What constitutes a particular hospital for the purpose of leave is a matter of fact which can be determined only in the light of the particular case. Where one building, or set of buildings, includes accommodation under the management of different bodies (eg two different NHS trusts), the accommodation used by each body should be treated as forming separate hospitals. Facilities and grounds shared by both can be regarded as part of both hospitals.

Power to grant leave

21.6 Only the patient's responsible clinician can grant leave of absence to a patient detained under the Act. Responsible clinicians cannot delegate the decision to grant leave of absence to anyone else. In the absence of the usual responsible clinician (eg if

9 Patients will also lawfully be absent from hospital if they are being transferred or taken to another place under the Act, or under another piece of legislation. This would include, for example, patients being transferred to another hospital under section 19 of the Act, or patients who are required to attend court.

they are on leave), permission can be granted only by the approved clinician who is for the time being acting as the patient's responsible clinician.

21.7 Responsible clinicians may grant leave for specific occasions or for specific or indefinite periods of time. They may make leave subject to any conditions which they consider necessary in the interests of the patient or for the protection of other people.

21.8 Leave of absence can be an important part of a detained patient's care plan, but can also be a time of risk. When considering and planning leave of absence, responsible clinicians should:

- consider the potential benefits and any risks to the patient's health and safety of granting or refusing leave;
- consider the potential benefits of granting leave for facilitating the patient's recovery;
- balance these benefits against any risks that the leave may pose in terms of the protection of other people (either generally or particular people);
- consider any conditions which should be attached to the leave, e g requiring the patient not to visit particular places or persons;
- be aware of any child protection and child welfare issues in granting leave;
- take account of the patient's wishes, and those of carers, friends and others who may be involved in any planned leave of absence;
- consider what support the patient would require during their leave of absence and whether it can be provided;
- ensure that any community services which will need to provide support for the patient during the leave are involved in the planning of the leave, and that they know the leave dates and times and any conditions placed on the patient during their leave;
- ensure that the patient is aware of any contingency plans put in place for their support, including what they should do if they think they need to return to hospital early; and
- (in the case of mentally disordered offender patients) consider whether there are any issues relating to victims which impact on whether leave should be granted and the conditions to which it should be subject.

21.9 When considering whether to grant leave of absence for more than seven consecutive days, or extending leave so that the total period is more than seven consecutive days, responsible clinicians must first consider whether the patient should go onto supervised community treatment (SCT) instead. [Section 17(2A)]. This does not apply to restricted patients, nor, in practice, to patients detained for assessment under section 2 of the Act, as they are not eligible for SCT.

21.10 The requirement to consider SCT does not mean that the responsible clinician cannot use longer-term leave if that is the more suitable option, but the responsible clinician will need to be able to show that both options have been duly considered. The decision, and the reasons for it, should be recorded in the patient's notes.

21.11 One use of leave for more than seven days may be to assess a patient's suitability for discharge from detention. Guidance on factors to be considered when deciding between leave of absence and SCT is given in **chapter 28**.

21.12 Hospital managers cannot overrule a responsible clinician's decision to grant leave. However, the fact that a responsible clinician grants leave subject to certain conditions, e g residence at a hostel, does not oblige the hospital managers or anyone else to arrange or fund the particular placement or services the clinician has in mind. Responsible clinicians should not grant leave on such a basis without first taking steps to establish that the necessary services or accommodation (or both) are available.

Restricted patients

21.13 Any proposal to grant leave to a restricted patient has to be approved by the Secretary of State for Justice, who should be given as much notice as possible and full details of the proposed leave. [Section 41(3).]

21.14 Where the courts or the Secretary of State have decided that restricted patients are to be detained in a particular unit of a hospital, those patients require leave of absence to go to any other part of that hospital as well as outside the hospital.

21.15 Restricted patients are not eligible for SCT. The Secretary of State would normally consider any request for section 17 leave for a restricted patient to be in the community for more than a few consecutive nights as an application for conditional discharge.

Short-term leave

21.16 Subject to the agreement of the Secretary of State for Justice in the case of restricted patients, responsible clinicians may decide to authorise short-term local leave, which may be managed by other staff. For example, patients may be given leave for a shopping trip of two hours every week to a specific destination, with the decision on which particular two hours to be left to the discretion of the responsible nursing staff.

21.17 The parameters within which this discretion may be exercised must be clearly set out by the responsible clinician, e g the particular places to be visited, any restrictions on the time of day the leave can take place, and any circumstances in which the leave should not go ahead.

21.18 Responsible clinicians should regularly review any short-term leave they authorise on this basis and amend it as necessary.

Longer periods of leave

21.19 Longer-term leave should be planned properly and, where possible, well in advance. Patients should be fully involved in the decision and responsible clinicians should be satisfied that patients are likely to be able to manage outside the hospital. Subject to the normal considerations of patient confidentiality, carers and other relevant people should be consulted before leave is granted (especially where the patient is to reside with them). Relevant community services should also be consulted.

21.20 If patients do not consent to carers or other people who would normally be involved in their care being consulted about their leave, responsible clinicians should reconsider whether or not it is safe and appropriate to grant leave.

Recording leave

21.21 Hospital managers should establish a standardised system by which responsible clinicians can record the leave they authorise and specify the conditions attached to it. Copies of the authorisation should be given to the patient and to any carers, professionals and other people in the community who need to know. A copy should also be kept in the patient's notes. In case they fail to return from leave, an up-to-date description of the patient should be available in their notes.

21.22 The outcome of leave – whether or not it went well, particular problems encountered, concerns raised or benefits achieved – should also be recorded in patients' notes to inform future decision-making. Patients should be encouraged to contribute by giving their own views on their leave; some hospitals provide leave records specifically for this purpose.

Care and treatment while on leave

21.23 Responsible clinicians' responsibilities for their patients remain the same while the patients are on leave.

21.24 A patient who is granted leave under section 17 remains liable to be detained, and the rules in Part 4 of the Act about their medical treatment continue to apply (see **chapter 23**). If it becomes necessary to administer treatment without the patient's consent, consideration should be given to whether it would be more appropriate to recall the patient to hospital (see **paragraphs 21.31–21.34**), although recall is not a legal requirement.

21.25 The duty on local social services authorities and primary care trusts to provide after-care under section 117 of the Act for certain patients who have been discharged from detention also applies to those patients while they are on leave of absence (see **chapter 27**).

Escorted leave [Section 17(3)]

21.26 A responsible clinician may direct that their patient remains in custody while on leave of absence, either in the patient's own interests or for the protection of other people. Patients may be kept in the custody of any officer on the staff of the hospital or any person authorised in writing by the hospital managers. Such an arrangement is often useful, for example, to enable patients to participate in escorted trips or to have compassionate home leave.

21.27 While it may often be appropriate to authorise leave subject to the condition that a patient is accompanied by a friend or relative (eg on a pre-arranged day out from the hospital), responsible clinicians should specify that the patient is to be in the legal custody of a friend or relative only if it is appropriate for that person to be legally responsible for the patient, and if that person understands and accepts the consequent responsibility.

21.28 Escorted leave to Scotland, Northern Ireland or any of the Channel Islands can only be granted if the local legislation allows patients to be kept in custody while in that jurisdiction.[10]

Leave to reside in other hospitals

21.29 Responsible clinicians may also require patients, as a condition of leave, to reside at another hospital in England or Wales, and they may then be kept in the custody of staff of that hospital. However, before authorising leave on this basis, responsible clinicians should consider whether it would be more appropriate to transfer the patient to the other hospital instead (see **chapter 30**).

21.30 Where a patient is granted leave of absence to another hospital, the responsible clinician at the first hospital should remain in overall charge of the patient's case. If it is thought that a clinician at the other hospital should become the responsible clinician, the patient should instead be transferred to that hospital. An approved clinician in charge of any particular aspect of the patient's treatment may be from either hospital. (For further guidance on allocating responsible clinicians see **chapter 14**.)

Recall from leave [Section 17(4)]

21.31 A responsible clinician may revoke their patient's leave at any time if they consider it necessary in the interests of the patient's health or safety or for the protection of other people. Responsible clinicians must be satisfied that these criteria are met and should consider what effect being recalled may have on the patient. A refusal to take medication would not on its own be a reason for revocation, although it would almost always be a reason to consider revocation.

21.32 The responsible clinician must arrange for a notice in writing revoking the leave to be served on the patient or on the person who is for the time being in charge of the patient. Hospitals should always know the address of patients who are on leave of absence.

21.33 The reasons for recall should be fully explained to the patient and a record of the explanation included in the patient's notes. A restricted patient's leave may be revoked either by the responsible clinician or by the Secretary of State for Justice.

---

10 When this edition of the Code ccame into force, it was expected that escorted leave to Scotland would be possible – but that is subject to the Scottish Parliament.

21.34 It is essential that carers (especially where the patient is residing with them while on leave) and professionals who support the patient while on leave should have easy access to the patient's responsible clinician if they feel consideration should be given to return of the patient before their leave is due to end.

Renewal of authority to detain

21.35 It is possible to renew a patient's detention while they are on leave if the criteria in section 20 of the Act are met (see **chapter 29**). But leave should not be used as an alternative to discharging the patient either completely or onto SCT where that is appropriate. **Chapter 28** gives further guidance on factors to consider when deciding between leave of absence and SCT.

Patients who are in hospital but not detained

21.36 Patients who are not legally detained in hospital have the right to leave at any time. They cannot be required to ask permission to do so, but may be asked to inform staff when they wish to leave the ward.

Related material

- Guidance for Responsible Medical Officers – Leave of Absence for Patients Subject to Restrictions, Ministry of Justice Mental Health Unit.

This material does not form part of the Code. It is provided for assistance only.

CHAPTER 25
SUPERVISED COMMUNITY TREATMENT

25.1 This chapter gives guidance on supervised community treatment (SCT). [Reference Guide chapter 15.]

Purpose of SCT

25.2 The purpose of SCT is to allow suitable patients to be safely treated in the community rather than under detention in hospital, and to provide a way to help prevent relapse and any harm – to the patient or to others – that this might cause. It is intended to help patients to maintain stable mental health outside hospital and to promote recovery.

25.3 SCT provides a framework for the management of patient care in the community and gives the responsible clinician the power to recall the patient to hospital for treatment if necessary.

Who can be discharged onto SCT? [Section 17A]

25.4 Only patients who are detained in hospital for treatment under section 3 of the Act, or are unrestricted Part 3 patients, can be considered for SCT. Patients detained in hospital for assessment under section 2 of the Act are not eligible. (See also **paragraphs 36.64–36.65** on children and young people.)

25.5 SCT is an option only for patients who meet the criteria set out in the Act, which are that:

- the patient is suffering from a mental disorder of a nature or degree which makes it appropriate for them to receive medical treatment;
- it is necessary for the patient's health or safety or for the protection of others that the patient should receive such treatment;
- subject to the patient being liable to be recalled as mentioned below, such treatment can be provided without the patient continuing to be detained in a hospital;
- it is necessary that the responsible clinician should be able to exercise the power under section 17E(1) of the Act to recall the patient to hospital; and
- appropriate medical treatment is available for the patient.

Assessment for SCT

25.6 The decision as to whether SCT is the right option for any patient is taken by the responsible clinician and requires the agreement of an approved mental health professional (AMHP). SCT may be used only if it would not be possible to achieve the desired objectives for the patient's care and treatment without it. Consultation at an early stage with the patient and those involved in the patient's care will be important.

25.7 In assessing the patient's suitability for SCT, the responsible clinician must be satisfied that the patient requires medical treatment for mental disorder for their own health or safety or for the protection of others, and that appropriate treatment is, or would be, available for the patient in the community. The key factor in the decision is whether the patient can safely be treated for mental disorder in the community only if the responsible clinician can exercise the power to recall the patient to hospital for treatment if that becomes necessary (see **paragraphs 25.47–25.53**).

25.8 In making that decision the responsible clinician must assess what risk there would be of the patient's condition deteriorating after discharge, for example as a result of refusing or neglecting to receive treatment.

25.9 In assessing that risk the responsible clinician must take into consideration:

- the patient's history of mental disorder; and
- any other relevant factors.

25.10 Whether or not a patient has previously had repeated admissions, the patient's history may be relevant to the decision. For example, a tendency to fail to follow a treatment plan or to discontinue medication in the community, making relapse more likely, may suggest a risk justifying use of SCT.

25.11 Other relevant factors will vary but are likely to include the patient's current mental state, the patient's insight and attitude to treatment, and the circumstances into which the patient would be discharged.

25.12 Taken together, all these factors should help the responsible clinician to assess the risk of the patient's condition deteriorating after discharge, and inform the decision as to whether continued detention, SCT or discharge would be the right option for the patient at that particular time.

25.13 A risk that the patient's condition will deteriorate is a significant consideration, but does not necessarily mean that the patient should be discharged onto SCT. The responsible clinician must be satisfied that the risk of harm arising from the patient's disorder is sufficiently serious to justify the power to recall the patient to hospital for treatment.

25.14 Patients do not have to consent formally to SCT. But in practice, patients will need to be involved in decisions about the treatment to be provided in the community and how and where it is to be given, and be prepared to co-operate with the proposed treatment.

Action upon Tribunal recommendation [Section 72(3A)]

25.15 When a detained patient makes an application to the Tribunal for discharge, the Tribunal may decide not to order discharge, but to recommend that the responsible clinician should consider whether the patient should go onto SCT. In that event, the responsible clinician should carry out the assessment of the patient's suitability for SCT in the usual way. It will be for the responsible clinician to decide whether or not SCT is appropriate for that patient.

Care planning, treatment and support in the community

25.16 Good care planning, in line with the Care Programme Approach (CPA) (or its equivalent) will be essential to the success of SCT. A care co-ordinator will need to be identified. This is likely to be a different person from the responsible clinician, but need not be.

25.17 The care plan should be prepared in the light of consultation with the patient and (subject to the normal considerations of patient confidentiality):

- the nearest relative;
- any carers;
- anyone with authority under the Mental Capacity Act 2005 (MCA) to act on the patient's behalf;

- the multi-disciplinary team involved in the patient's care; and
- the patient's GP (if there is one). It is important that the patient's GP should be aware that the patient is to go onto SCT. A patient who does not have a GP should be encouraged and helped to register with a practice.

25.18 If a different responsible clinician is to take over responsibility for the patient, it will be essential to liaise with that clinician, and the community team, at an early stage. Where needed, arrangements should be made for a second opinion appointed doctor (SOAD) to provide the Part 4A certificate to enable treatment to be given (see **paragraphs 24.25–24.27**).

25.19 The care plan should set out the practicalities of how the patient will receive treatment, care and support from day to day, and should not place undue reliance on carers or members of the patient's family. If the patient so wishes, help should be given to access independent advocacy[11] or other support where this is available (see also **chapter 20**).

25.20 The care plan should take account of the patient's age. Where the patient is under the age of 18 the responsible clinician and the AMHP should bear in mind that the most age-appropriate treatment will normally be that provided by child and adolescent mental health services (CAMHS). It may also be necessary to involve the patient's parent, or whoever will be responsible for looking after the patient, to ensure that they will be ready and able to provide the assistance and support which the patient may need.

25.21 Similarly, specialist services for older people may have a role in the delivery of services for older SCT patients.

25.22 Patients on SCT are entitled to after-care services under section 117 of the Act. The after-care arrangements should be drawn up as part of the normal care planning arrangements. The Primary Care Trust and local social services authority (LSSA) must continue to provide after-care services under section 117 for as long as the patient remains on SCT. (See also **chapter 27**.)

25.23 The care plan should be reviewed regularly, and the services required may vary should the patient's needs change.

Role of the AMHP [Section 17A(4)]

25.24 The AMHP must decide whether to agree with the patient's responsible clinician that the patient meets the criteria for SCT, and (if so) whether SCT is appropriate. Even if the criteria for SCT are met, it does not mean that the patient must be discharged onto SCT. In making that decision, the AMHP should consider the wider social context for the patient. Relevant factors may include any support networks the patient may have, the potential impact on the rest of the patient's family, and employment issues.

25.25 The AMHP should consider how the patient's social and cultural background may influence the family environment in which they will be living and the support

---

11 Independent mental health advocacy services under the Act were introduced in April 2009.

structures potentially available. But no assumptions should be made simply on the basis of the patient's ethnicity or social or cultural background.

25.26 The Act does not specify who this AMHP should be. It may (but need not) be an AMHP who is already involved in the patient's care and treatment as part of the multi-disciplinary team. It can be an AMHP acting on behalf of any willing LSSA, and LSSAs may agree with each other and with hospital managers the arrangements that are likely to be most convenient and best for patients. But if no other LSSA is willing, responsibility for ensuring that an AMHP considers the case should lie with the LSSA which would become responsible under section 117 for the patient's after-care if the patient were discharged.

25.27 If the AMHP does not agree with the responsible clinician that the patient should go onto SCT, then SCT cannot go ahead. A record of the AMHP's decision and the full reasons for it should be kept in the patient's notes. It would not be appropriate for the responsible clinician to approach another AMHP for an alternative view.

Making the community treatment order

25.28 If the responsible clinician and AMHP agree that the patient should be discharged onto SCT, they should complete the relevant statutory form and send it to the hospital managers. The responsible clinician must specify on the form the date that the community treatment order (CTO) is to be made. This date is the authority for SCT to begin, and may be a short while after the date on which the form is signed, to allow time for arrangements to be put in place for the patient's discharge.

Conditions to be attached to the community treatment order [Section 17B]

25.29 The CTO must include the conditions with which the patient is required to comply while on SCT. There are two conditions which must be included in all cases. Patients are required to make themselves available for medical examination:

- when needed for consideration of extension of the CTO; and
- if necessary, to allow a SOAD to provide a Part 4A certificate authorising treatment.

25.30 Responsible clinicians may also, with the AMHP's agreement, set other conditions which they think are necessary or appropriate to:

- ensure that the patient receives medical treatment for mental disorder;
- prevent a risk of harm to the patient's health or safety;
- protect other people.

25.31 Conditions may be set for any or all of these purposes, but not for any other reason. The AMHP's agreement to the proposed conditions must be obtained before the CTO can be made.

25.32 In considering what conditions might be necessary or appropriate, the responsible clinician should always keep in view the patient's specific cultural needs and background. The patient, and (subject to the normal considerations of patient confidentiality) any others with an interest such as a parent or carer, should be consulted.

25.33 The conditions should:

- be kept to a minimum number consistent with achieving their purpose;
- restrict the patient's liberty as little as possible while being consistent with achieving their purpose;
- have a clear rationale, linked to one or more of the purposes in paragraph 25.30; and
- be clearly and precisely expressed, so that the patient can readily understand what is expected.

25.34 The nature of the conditions will depend on the patient's individual circumstances. Subject to **paragraph 25.33**, they might cover matters such as where and when the patient is to receive treatment in the community; where the patient is to live; and avoidance of known risk factors or high-risk situations relevant to the patient's mental disorder.

25.35 The reasons for any conditions should be explained to the patient and others, as appropriate, and recorded in the patient's notes. It will be important, if SCT is to be successful, that the patient agrees to keep to the conditions, or to try to do so, and that patients have access to the help they need to be able to comply.

Information for SCT patients and others

25.36 As soon as the decision is made to discharge a patient onto SCT, the responsible clinician should inform the patient and others consulted of the decision, the conditions to be applied to the CTO, and the services which will be available for the patient in the community.

25.37 There is a duty on hospital managers to take steps to ensure that patients understand what SCT means for them and their rights to apply for discharge. [Section 132A]. This includes giving patients information both orally and in writing and must be done as soon as practicable after the patient goes onto SCT. Hospital managers' information policies should set out whether this information is to be provided by the responsible clinician, by another member of the professional team or by someone else. A copy of this information must also be provided to the nearest relative (subject to the normal considerations about involving nearest relatives – see **paragraphs 2.27–2.33**). (See also **paragraphs 18.18–18.20** and **30.29** on information to be given to the victims of certain Part 3 patients.)

Monitoring SCT patients

25.38 It will be important to maintain close contact with a patient on SCT and to monitor their mental health and wellbeing after they leave hospital. The type and scope of the arrangements will vary depending on the patient's needs and individual circumstances and the way in which local services are organised. All those involved will need to agree to the arrangements. Respective responsibilities should be clearly set out in the patient's care plan. The care co-ordinator will normally be responsible for co-ordinating the care plan, working with the responsible clinician (if they are different people), the team responsible for the patient's care and any others with an interest.

25.39 Appropriate action will need to be taken if the patient becomes unwell, engages in high-risk behaviour as a result of mental disorder or withdraws consent to treatment (or begins to object to it). The responsible clinician should consider, with the patient (and others where appropriate), the reasons for this and what the next steps should be. If the patient refuses crucial treatment, an urgent review of the situation will be needed, and recalling the patient to hospital will be an option if the risk justifies it. If suitable alternative treatment is available which would allow SCT to continue safely and which the patient would accept, the responsible clinician should consider such treatment if this can be offered. If so, the treatment plan, and if necessary the conditions of the CTO, should be varied accordingly (note that a revised Part 4A certificate may be required).

25.40 If the patient is not complying with any condition of the CTO the reasons for this will need to be properly investigated. Recall to hospital may need to be considered if it is no longer safe and appropriate for the patient to remain in the community. The conditions may need to be reviewed – for example, if the patient's health has improved a particular condition may no longer be relevant or necessary. The responsible clinician may vary conditions as appropriate (see **paragraphs 25.41–25.45**). Changes may also be needed to the patient's care or treatment plan.

Varying and suspending conditions [Section 17B]

25.41 The responsible clinician has the power to vary the conditions of the patient's CTO, or to suspend any of them. The responsible clinician does not need to agree any variation or suspension with the AMHP. However, it would not be good practice to vary conditions which had recently been agreed with an AMHP without discussion with that AMHP.

25.42 Suspension of one or more of the conditions may be appropriate to allow for a temporary change in circumstances, for example, the patient's temporary absence or a change in treatment regime. The responsible clinician should record any decision to suspend conditions in the patient's notes, with reasons.

25.43 A variation of the conditions might be appropriate where the patient's treatment needs or living circumstances have changed. Any condition no longer required should be removed.

25.44 It will be important to discuss any proposed changes to the conditions with the patient and to ensure that the patient, and anyone else affected by the changes (subject to the patient's right to confidentiality), knows that they are being considered, and why. As when the conditions were first set, the patient will need to agree to try to keep to any new or varied conditions if SCT is to work successfully, and any help the patient needs to comply with them should be made available. (See also **paragraphs 18.10–18.13**.)

25.45 Any variation in the conditions must be recorded on the relevant statutory form, which should be sent to the hospital managers.

Responding to concerns raised by the patient's carer or relatives

25.46 Particular attention should be paid to carers and relatives when they raise a concern that the patient is not complying with the conditions or that the patient's mental health appears to be deteriorating. The team responsible for the patient needs to give due weight to those concerns and any requests made by the carers or relatives in deciding what action to take. Carers and relatives are typically in much more frequent contact with the patient than professionals, even under well-run care plans. Their concerns may prompt a review of how SCT is working for that patient and whether the criteria for recall to hospital might be met. The managers of responsible hospitals should ensure that local protocols are in place to cover how concerns raised should be addressed and taken forward. (See also **paragraphs 18.2–18.5**.)

Recall to hospital [Section 17E]

25.47 The recall power is intended to provide a means to respond to evidence of relapse or high-risk behaviour relating to mental disorder before the situation becomes critical and leads to the patient or other people being harmed. The need for recall might arise as a result of relapse, or through a change in the patient's circumstances giving rise to increased risk.

25.48 The responsible clinician may recall a patient on SCT to hospital for treatment if:

- the patient needs to receive treatment for mental disorder in hospital (either as an in-patient or as an out-patient); and
- there would be a risk of harm to the health or safety of the patient or to other people if the patient were not recalled.

25.49 A patient may also be recalled to hospital if they break either of the two mandatory conditions which must be included in all CTOs – that is, by failing to make themselves available for medical examination to allow consideration of extension of the CTO or to enable a SOAD to complete a Part 4A certificate. The patient must always be given the opportunity to comply with the condition before recall is considered. Before exercising the recall power for this reason, the responsible clinician should consider whether the patient has a valid reason for failing to comply, and should take any further action accordingly.

25.50 The responsible clinician must be satisfied that the criteria are met before using the recall power. Any action should be proportionate to the level of risk. For some patients, the risk arising from a failure to comply with treatment could indicate an immediate need for recall. In other cases, negotiation with the patient – and with the nearest relative and any carer (unless the patient objects or it is not reasonably practicable) – may resolve the problem and so avert the need for recall.

25.51 The responsible clinician should consider in each case whether recalling the patient to hospital is justified in all the circumstances. For example, it might be sufficient to monitor a patient who has failed to comply with a condition to attend for treatment, before deciding whether the lack of treatment means that recall is necessary. A patient may also agree to admission to hospital on a voluntary basis. Failure to comply with a condition (apart from those relating to availability for medical examination, as above) does not in itself trigger recall. Only if the breach of a condition results in an increased risk of harm to the patient or to anyone else will recall be justified.

25.52 However, it may be necessary to recall a patient whose condition is deteriorating despite compliance with treatment, if the risk cannot be managed otherwise.

25.53 Recall to hospital for treatment should not become a regular or normal event for any patient on SCT. If recall is being used frequently, the responsible clinician should review the patient's treatment plan to consider whether it could be made more acceptable to the patient, or whether, in the individual circumstances of the case, SCT continues to be appropriate.

Procedure for recall to hospital

25.54 The responsible clinician has responsibility for co-ordinating the recall process, unless it has been agreed locally that someone else will do this. It will be important to ensure that the practical impact of recalling the patient on the patient's domestic circumstances is considered and managed.

25.55 The responsible clinician must complete a written notice of recall to hospital, which is effective only when served on the patient. It is important that, wherever possible, the notice should be handed to the patient personally. Otherwise, the notice is served by delivery to the patient's usual or last known address. (See **paragraphs 25.57–25.58**.)

25.56 Once the recall notice has been served, the patient can, if necessary, be treated as absent without leave, and taken and conveyed to hospital (and a patient who leaves the hospital without permission can be returned there). The time at which the notice is deemed to be served will vary according to the method of delivery.

25.57 It will not usually be appropriate to post a notice of recall to the patient. This may, however, be an option if the patient has failed to attend for medical examination as required by the conditions of the CTO, despite having been requested to do so, when the need for the examination is not urgent (see **paragraph 25.49**). First class post should be used. The notice is deemed to be served on the second working day after posting, and it will be important to allow sufficient time for the patient to receive the notice before any action is taken to ensure compliance.

25.58 Where the need for recall is urgent, as will usually be the case, it will be important that there is certainty as to the timing of delivery of the notice. A notice handed to the patient is effective immediately. However, it may not be possible to achieve this if the patient's whereabouts are unknown, or if the patient is unavailable or simply refuses to accept the notice. In that event the notice should be delivered by hand to the patient's usual or last known address. The notice is then deemed to be served (even though it may not actually be received by the patient) on the day after it is delivered – that is, the day (which does not have to be a working day) beginning immediately after midnight following delivery.

25.59 If the patient's whereabouts are known but access to the patient cannot be obtained, it may be necessary to consider whether a warrant issued under section 135(2) is needed (see **chapter 10**).

25.60 The patient should be conveyed to hospital in the least restrictive manner possible. If appropriate, the patient may be accompanied by a family member, carer or friend. (See also **chapter 11**.)

25.61 The responsible clinician should ensure that the hospital to which the patient is recalled is ready to receive the patient and to provide treatment. While recall must be to a hospital, the required treatment may then be given on an out-patient basis, if appropriate.

25.62 The hospital need not be the patient's responsible hospital (that is, the hospital where the patient was detained immediately before going onto SCT) or under the same management as that hospital. A copy of the notice of recall, which provides the authority to detain the patient, should be sent to the managers of the hospital to which the patient is being recalled.

25.63 When the patient arrives at hospital after recall, the clinical team will need to assess the patient's condition, provide the necessary treatment and determine the next steps. The patient may be well enough to return to the community once treatment has been given, or may need a longer period of assessment or treatment in hospital. The patient may be detained in hospital for a maximum of 72 hours after recall to allow the responsible clinician to determine what should happen next. During this period the patient remains an SCT patient, even if they remain in hospital for one or more nights. The responsible clinician may allow the patient to leave the hospital at any time within the 72-hour period. Once 72 hours from the time of admission have elapsed, the patient must be allowed to leave if the responsible clinician has not revoked the CTO (see **paragraphs 25.65–25.70**). On leaving hospital the patient will remain on SCT as before.

25.64 In considering the options, the responsible clinician and the clinical team will need to consider the reasons why it was necessary to exercise the recall power and whether SCT remains the right option for that patient. They will also need to consider, with the patient, the nearest relative (subject to the normal considerations about involving nearest relatives), and any carers, what changes might be needed to help to prevent the circumstances that led to recall from recurring. It may be that a variation in the conditions is required, or a change in the care plan (or both).

Revoking the CTO [Section 17F]

25.65 If the patient requires in-patient treatment for longer than 72 hours after arrival at the hospital, the responsible clinician should consider revoking the CTO. The effect of revoking the CTO is that the patient will again be detained under the powers of the Act.

25.66 The CTO may be revoked if:

- the responsible clinician considers that the patient again needs to be admitted to hospital for medical treatment under the Act; and
- an AMHP agrees with that assessment, and also believes that it is appropriate to revoke the CTO.

25.67 In making the decision as to whether it is appropriate to revoke a CTO, the AMHP should consider the wider social context for the patient, in the same way as when making decisions about applications for admissions under the Act (see **chapter 4**).

25.68 As before, the AMHP carrying out this role may (but need not) be already involved in the patient's care and treatment, or can be an AMHP acting on behalf of any willing LSSA. If no other LSSA is willing, responsibility for ensuring that an AMHP considers the case should lie with the LSSA which has been responsible for the patient's after-care.

25.69 If the AMHP does not agree that the CTO should be revoked, then the patient cannot be detained in hospital after the end of the maximum recall period of 72 hours. The patient will therefore remain on SCT. A record of the AMHP's decision and the full reasons for it should be kept in the patient's notes. It would not be appropriate for the responsible clinician to approach another AMHP for an alternative view.

25.70 If the responsible clinician and the AMHP agree that the CTO should be revoked, they must complete the relevant statutory form for the revocation to take legal effect, and send it to the hospital managers. The patient is then detained again under the powers of the Act exactly as before going onto SCT, except that a new detention period of six months begins for the purposes of review and applications to the Tribunal (see also **paragraph 24.31**).

Hospital managers' responsibilities

25.71 It is the responsibility of the hospital managers to ensure that no patient is detained following recall for longer than 72 hours unless the CTO is revoked. The relevant statutory form must be completed on the patient's arrival at hospital. Hospital managers should ensure that arrangements are in place to monitor the patient's length of stay following the time of detention after recall, as recorded on the form, so that the maximum period of detention is not exceeded. (See also **paragraphs 2.8–2.15** on information for patients.)

25.72 The hospital managers should also ensure that arrangements are in place to cover any necessary transfers of responsibility between responsible clinicians in the community and in hospital.

25.73 If a patient's CTO is revoked and the patient is detained in a hospital other than the one which was the responsible hospital at the time of recall, the hospital managers of the new hospital must send a copy of the revocation form to the managers of the original hospital.

25.74 The hospital managers have a duty to ensure that a patient whose CTO is revoked is referred to the Tribunal without delay.

Review of SCT

25.75 In addition to the statutory requirements in the Act for review of SCT, it is good practice to review the patient's progress on SCT as part of all reviews of the CPA care plan or its equivalent.

25.76 Reviews should cover whether SCT is meeting the patient's treatment needs and, if not, what action is necessary to address this. A patient who no longer satisfies all the criteria for SCT must be discharged without delay.

Discharge from SCT [Sections 23 and 72]

25.77 SCT patients may be discharged in the same way as detained patients, by the Tribunal, the hospital managers, or (for Part 2 patients) the nearest relative. The responsible clinician may also discharge an SCT patient at any time and must do so if the patient no longer meets the criteria for SCT. A patient's CTO should not simply be allowed to lapse.

25.78 The reasons for discharge should be explained to the patient, and any concerns on the part of the patient, the nearest relative or any carer should be considered and dealt with as far as possible. On discharge from SCT, the team should ensure that any after-care services the patient continues to need under section 117 of the Act will be available.

25.79 If guardianship is considered the better option for a patient on SCT, an application may be made in the usual way.

Related material

- *Refocusing the Care Programme Approach,* Care Programme Approach guidance, March 2008.

This material does not form part of the Code. It is provided for assistance only.

Applying the principles

This scenario is not intended to provide a template for decisions in applying the principles in similar situations. The scenario itself is only illustrative and does not form part of the Code itself.

Recall of a supervised community treatment patient to hospital

Mary has a long-standing bipolar disorder. She has been on SCT for the past 12 months following an initial two months' detention in hospital.

Mary's condition has been managed successfully by a care plan which includes oral medication. However, it has transpired that Mary has missed taking a significant amount of her medication over the past couple of weeks. ➡

One of the conditions of Mary's CTO is that she regularly attends a named clinic to review her treatment and progress. For the first time since her discharge from hospital, she fails to attend.

The responsible clinician meets with members of the multi-disciplinary team to decide whether Mary needs to be recalled to hospital for treatment.

When the multi-disciplinary team members meet, they are required to consider the principles. Among the questions they might wish to consider in making a decision in these circumstances are the following.

Purpose principle

- What are the risks to Mary and others if she does not receive her medication? How soon might those risks arise and in what circumstances?
- What will be best for Mary's wellbeing overall?

Least restriction principle

- What are the possible alternatives for managing Mary's care? For example, the multi-disciplinary team contacting Mary, or arranging a home visit to see her.
- Would varying the conditions of the CTO assist Mary to comply with her treatment programme?
- Might Mary be prepared to accept another treatment regime if there is an alternative which would be as clinically effective?
- Have alternative options been explored with Mary before?

Respect principle

- What is Mary's view of why she has stopped taking her medication?
- Is Mary's failure to attend clinic anything to do with a conscious decision to refuse medication, or is there some other reason? Have all possible reasons been considered?
- Are there any social, cultural or family-related factors, which may have led Mary to miss her appointment?
- Taking into account Mary's history and known past and present wishes, are there any particular reasons why Mary may not have presented at the clinic?
- Has Mary expressed any views about what she would like to happen if she stopped taking her medication?

Participation principle

- Is Mary willing to discuss what is going on?

➡

- What might be the best way of approaching Mary to discuss the current situation?
- Are Mary's family or carers involved in her day-to-day care aware that she is on SCT, and if so should their views be sought on the best way to help Mary to re-establish contact with services?
- What is Mary's view about her family being contacted?
- Have Mary's family or carers expressed any views about what they think may help Mary?
- Does Mary's GP have any ideas about engaging Mary?

Effectiveness, efficiency and equity principle

- Mary has said in the past that she enjoys her contact with the team's community psychiatric nurse (CPN) – would giving her more time with the CPN be an effective way of tackling the current situation? Could it be done without other patients with the same or greater clinical needs being disadvantaged?

CHAPTER 26
GUARDIANSHIP

26.1 This chapter gives guidance on guardianship under the Act. [Reference Guide chapter 19.]

Purpose of guardianship

26.2 The purpose of guardianship is to enable patients to receive care outside hospital when it cannot be provided without the use of compulsory powers. Such care may or may not include specialist medical treatment for mental disorder.

26.3 A guardian may be a local social services authority (LSSA) or someone else approved by an LSSA (a "private guardian"). [Section 8.] Guardians have three specific powers as follows:

- they have the exclusive right to decide where a patient should live, taking precedence even over an attorney or deputy appointed under the Mental Capacity Act 2005 (MCA);
- they can require the patient to attend for treatment, work, training or education at specific times and places (but they cannot use force to take the patient there);
- they can demand that a doctor, approved mental health professional (AMHP) or another relevant person has access to the patient at the place where the patient lives.

26.4 Guardianship therefore provides an authoritative framework for working with a patient, with a minimum of constraint, to achieve as independent a life as possible within the community. Where it is used, it should be part of the patient's overall care plan.

26.5 Guardianship does not give anyone the right to treat the patient without their permission or to consent to treatment on their behalf.

26.6 While the reception of a patient into guardianship does not affect the continued authority of an attorney or deputy appointed under the MCA, such attorneys and deputies will not be able to take decisions about where a guardianship patient is to reside, or take any other decisions which conflict with those of the guardian.

Assessment for guardianship [Section 7]

26.7 An application for guardianship may be made on the grounds that:

- the patient is suffering from mental disorder of a nature or degree which warrants their reception into guardianship; and
- it is necessary, in the interests of the welfare of the patient or for the protection of other persons, that the patient should be so received.

26.8 Guardianship is most likely to be appropriate where:

- the patient is thought to be likely to respond well to the authority and attention of a guardian and so be more willing to comply with necessary treatment and care for their mental disorder; or
- there is a particular need for someone to have the authority to decide where the patient should live or to insist that doctors, AMHPs or other people be given access to the patient.

26.9 As with applications for detention in hospital, AMHPs and doctors making recommendations should consider whether the objectives of the proposed application could be achieved in another, less restrictive, way, without the use of guardianship.

26.10 Where patients lack capacity to make some or all important decisions concerning their own welfare, one potential alternative to guardianship will be to rely solely on the MCA – especially the protection from liability for actions taken in connection with care or treatment provided by section 5 of the MCA. While this is a factor to be taken into account, it will not by itself determine whether guardianship is necessary or unnecessary. AMHPs and doctors need to consider all the circumstances of the particular case.

26.11 Where an adult is assessed as requiring residential care but lacks the capacity to make a decision about whether they wish to be placed there, guardianship is unlikely to be necessary where the move can properly, quickly and efficiently be carried out on the basis of:

- section 5 of the MCA or the decision of an attorney or deputy; or

- (where relevant) the MCA's deprivation of liberty safeguards.[12]

26.12 But guardianship may still be appropriate in such cases if:

- there are other reasons – unconnected to the move to residential care – to think that the patient might benefit from the attention and authority of a guardian;
- there is a particular need to have explicit statutory authority for the patient to be returned to the place where the patient is to live should they go absent; or
- it is thought to be important that decisions about where the patient is to live are placed in the hands of a single person or authority – for example, where there have been long-running or particularly difficult disputes about where the person should live.

26.13 However, it will not always be best to use guardianship as the way of deciding where patients who lack capacity to decide for themselves must live. In cases which raise unusual issues, or where guardianship is being considered in the interests of the patient's welfare and there are finely balanced arguments about where the patient should live, it may be preferable instead to seek a best interests decision from the Court of Protection under the MCA.

26.14 Where the relevant criteria are met, guardianship may be considered in respect of a patient who is to be discharged from detention under the Mental Health Act. However, if it is thought that the patient needs to remain liable to be recalled to hospital (and the patient is eligible), supervised community treatment is likely to be more appropriate (see **chapter 28**).

Responsibilities of local social services authorities

26.15 Each LSSA should have a policy setting out the arrangements for:

- receiving, scrutinising and accepting or refusing applications for guardianship. Such arrangements should ensure that applications are properly but quickly dealt with;
- monitoring the progress of each patient's guardianship, including steps to be taken to fulfil the authority's statutory obligations in relation to private guardians and to arrange visits to the patient;
- ensuring the suitability of any proposed private guardian, and that they are able to understand and carry out their duties under the Act;
- ensuring that patients under guardianship receive, both orally and in writing, information in accordance with regulations under the Act;
- ensuring that patients are aware of their right to apply to the Tribunal and that they are given the name of someone who will give them the necessary assistance, on behalf of the LSSA, in making such an application;

---

12 The deprivation of liberty safeguards have been in force since April 2009.

- authorising an approved clinician to be the patient's responsible clinician;
- maintaining detailed records relating to guardianship patients;
- ensuring that the need to continue guardianship is reviewed in the last two months of each period of guardianship in accordance with the Act; and
- discharging patients from guardianship as soon as it is no longer required.

26.16 Patients may be discharged from guardianship at any time by the LSSA, the responsible clinician authorised by the LSSA, or (in most cases) the patient's nearest relative. [Section 23.]

26.17 Discharge decisions by LSSAs may be taken only by the LSSA itself, or by three or more members of the LSSA or of a committee or sub-committee of the LSSA authorised for that purpose. Where decisions are taken by three or more members of the LSSA (or a committee or sub-committee), all three people (or at least three of them, if there are more) must agree.

26.18 LSSAs may consider discharging patients from guardianship at any time, but must consider doing so when they receive a report from the patient's nominated medical attendant or responsible clinician renewing their guardianship under section 20 of the Act.

Components of effective guardianship

Care planning

26.19 An application for guardianship should be accompanied by a comprehensive care plan established on the basis of multi-disciplinary discussions in accordance with the Care Programme Approach (or its equivalent).

26.20 The plan should identify the services needed by the patient and who will provide them. It should also indicate which of the powers that guardians have under the Act are necessary to achieve the plan. If none of the powers are required, guardianship should not be used.

26.21 Key elements of the plan are likely to be:

- suitable accommodation to help meet the patient's needs;
- access to day care, education and training facilities, as appropriate;
- effective co-operation and communication between all those concerned in implementing the plan; and
- (if there is to be a private guardian) support from the LSSA for the guardian.

26.22 A private guardian should be prepared to advocate on behalf of the patient in relation to those agencies whose services are needed to carry out the care plan. So should an LSSA which is itself the guardian.

26.23 A private guardian should be a person who can appreciate any special disabilities and needs of a mentally disordered person and who will look after the patient in an appropriate and sympathetic way. The guardian should display an interest in promoting the patient's physical and mental health and in providing for their occupation, training, employment, recreation and general welfare in a suitable way. The LSSA must satisfy itself that a proposed private guardian is capable of carrying out their functions and it should assist them with advice and other forms of support.

26.24 Regulations require private guardians to appoint a doctor as the patient's nominated medical attendant. It is the nominated medical attendant who must examine the patient during the last two months of each period of guardianship and decide whether to make a report extending the patient's guardianship. (Where the patient's guardian is the LSSA itself, this is done by the responsible clinician authorised by the LSSA.)

26.25 It is for private guardians themselves to decide whom to appoint as the nominated medical attendant, but they should first consult the LSSA. The nominated medical attendant may be the patient's GP, if the GP agrees.

Power to require a patient to live in a particular place

26.26 Guardians have the power to decide where patients should live. If patients leave the place where they are required to live without the guardian's permission, they can be taken into legal custody and brought back there (see **chapter 22**). [Section 18(3).]

26.27 This power can also be used to take patients for the first time to the place they are required to live, if patients do not (or, in practice, cannot) go there by themselves. [Section 18(7).]

26.28 Patients should always be consulted first about where they are to be required to live, unless their mental state makes that impossible. Guardians should not use this power to make a patient move without warning.

26.29 The power to take or return patients to the place they are required to live may be used, for example, to discourage them from:

- living somewhere the guardian considers unsuitable;
- breaking off contact with services;
- leaving the area before proper arrangements can be made; or
- sleeping rough.

But it may not be used to restrict their freedom to come and go so much that they are effectively being detained.

26.30 The power to require patients to reside in a particular place may not be used to require them to live in a situation in which they are deprived of liberty, unless that is authorised separately under the MCA. That authorisation will only be possible if the patient lacks capacity to decide where to live. If deprivation of liberty is authorised under the MCA, the LSSA should consider whether guardianship remains necessary, bearing in mind the guidance earlier in this chapter.

Guardianship and hospital care

26.31 Guardianship does not restrict patients' access to hospital services on an informal basis. Patients who require treatment but do not need to be detained may be admitted informally in the same way as any other patient. This applies to both physical and mental healthcare.

26.32 Nor does guardianship prevent an authorisation being granted under the deprivation of liberty safeguards[13] in the MCA, if the person needs to be detained in a hospital in their best interests in order to receive care and treatment, so long as it would not be inconsistent with the guardian's decision about where the patient should live.

26.33 Otherwise, guardianship should not be used to require a patient to reside in a hospital except where it is necessary for a very short time in order to provide shelter while accommodation in the community is being arranged.

26.34 Guardianship can remain in force if the patient is detained in hospital under section 2 or 4 of the Mental Health Act for assessment, but it ends automatically if a patient is detained for treatment as a result of an application under section 3. [Section 6.] Regulations also allow a patient to be transferred from guardianship to detention in hospital under section 3. The normal requirements for an application and medical recommendations must be met, and the transfer must be agreed by the LSSA.

Patients who resist the authority of the guardian

26.35 If a patient consistently resists exercise by the guardian of any of their powers, it can normally be concluded that guardianship is not the most appropriate form of care for that person, and the guardianship should be discharged. However, the LSSA should first consider whether a change of guardian – or change in the person who, in practice, exercises the LSSA's powers as guardian – might be appropriate instead.

Guardianship orders under section 37 [Reference Guide 19.60-19.66]

26.36 Guardianship may be used by courts as an alternative to hospital orders for offenders with mental disorders where the criteria set out in the Act are met. The court must first be satisfied that the LSSA or named person is willing to act as guardian. In considering the appropriateness of the patient being received into their guardianship, LSSAs should be guided by the same considerations as apply to applications for guardianship under Part 2 of the Act.

26.37 The guidance in this chapter on components of effective guardianship applies to guardianship order patients in the same way as it applies to other guardianship patients. The main difference between applications for guardianship under Part 2 of the Act and guardianship orders is that nearest relatives may not discharge patients from guardianship orders. Nearest relatives have rights to apply to the Tribunal instead.

---

13 The deprivation of liberty safeguards have been in force since April 2009.

Related material

- Mental Capacity Act 2005.

- *Mental Capacity Act 2005 Code of Practice*, TSO, 2007.

- *Deprivation of Liberty Safeguards*, Addendum to the *Mental Capacity Act 2005 Code of Practice*.

This material does not form part of the Code. It is provided for assistance only.

CHAPTER 27
AFTER-CARE

27.1 This chapter gives guidance on the duty to provide after-care for patients under section 117 of the Act. [Reference Guide chapter 24.]

Section 117 after-care

27.2 Section 117 of the Act requires primary care trusts (PCTs) and local social services authorities (LSSAs), in co-operation with voluntary agencies, to provide after-care to patients detained in hospital for treatment under section 3, 37, 45A, 47 or 48 of the Act who then cease to be detained. This includes patients granted leave of absence under section 17 and patients going onto supervised community treatment (SCT).

27.3 The duty to provide after-care services continues as long as the patient is in need of such services. In the case of a patient on SCT, after-care must be provided for the entire period they are on SCT, but this does not mean that the patient's need for after-care will necessarily cease as soon as they are no longer on SCT.

27.4 Services provided under section 117 can include services provided directly by PCTs or LSSAs as well as services they commission from other providers.

27.5 After-care is a vital component in patients' overall treatment and care. As well as meeting their immediate needs for health and social care, after-care should aim to support them in regaining or enhancing their skills, or learning new skills, in order to cope with life outside hospital.

27.6 Where eligible patients have remained in hospital informally after ceasing to be detained under the Act, they are still entitled to after-care under section 117 once they leave hospital. This also applies when patients are released from prison, having spent part of their sentence detained in hospital under a relevant section of the Act.

After-care planning

27.7 When considering relevant patients' cases, the Tribunal and hospital managers will expect to be provided with information from the professionals concerned on what after-care arrangements might be made for them under section 117 if they were to be discharged. Some discussion of after-care needs, involving LSSAs and other relevant agencies, should take place in advance of the hearing.

27.8 Although the duty to provide after-care begins when the patient leaves hospital, the planning of after-care needs to start as soon as the patient is admitted to hospital. PCTs and LSSAs should take reasonable steps to identify appropriate after-care services for patients before their actual discharge from hospital.

27.9 Where a Tribunal or hospital managers' hearing has been arranged for a patient who might be entitled to after-care under section 117 of the Act, the hospital managers should ensure that the relevant PCT and LSSA have been informed. The PCT and LSSA should consider putting practical preparations in hand for after-care in every case, but should in particular consider doing so where there is a strong possibility that the patient will be discharged if appropriate after-care can be arranged. Where the Tribunal has provisionally decided to give a restricted patient a conditional discharge, the PCT and LSSA must do their best to put after-care in place which would allow that discharge to take place.

27.10 Before deciding to discharge, or grant more than very short-term leave of absence to, a patient, or to place a patient onto SCT, the responsible clinician should ensure that the patient's needs for after-care have been fully assessed, discussed with the patient and addressed in their care plan. If the patient is being given leave for only a short period, a less comprehensive review may be sufficient, but the arrangements for the patient's care should still be properly recorded.

27.11 After-care for all patients admitted to hospital for treatment for mental disorder should be planned within the framework of the Care Programme Approach (or its equivalent), whether or not they are detained or will be entitled to receive after-care under section 117 of the Act. But because of the specific statutory obligation it is important that all patients who are entitled to after-care under section 117 are identified and that records are kept of what after-care is provided to them under that section.

27.12 In order to ensure that the after-care plan reflects the needs of each patient, it is important to consider who needs to be involved, in addition to patients themselves. This may include:

- the patient's responsible clinician;
- nurses and other professionals involved in caring for the patient in hospital;
- a clinical psychologist, community mental health nurse and other members of the community team;
- the patient's GP and primary care team;
- subject to the patient's views, any carer who will be involved in looking after them outside hospital, the patient's nearest relative or other family members;
- a representative of any relevant voluntary organisations;
- in the case of a restricted patient, the probation service;

- a representative of housing authorities, if accommodation is an issue;
- an employment expert, if employment is an issue;
- an independent mental health advocate,[14] if the patient has one;
- an independent mental capacity advocate, if the patient has one;
- the patient's attorney or deputy, if the patient has one; and
- any other representative nominated by the patient.

27.13 A thorough assessment is likely to involve consideration of:

- continuing mental healthcare, whether in the community or on an out-patient basis;
- the psychological needs of the patient and, where appropriate, of their family and carers;
- physical healthcare;
- daytime activities or employment;
- appropriate accommodation;
- identified risks and safety issues;
- any specific needs arising from, for example, co-existing physical disability, sensory impairment, learning disability or autistic spectrum disorder;
- any specific needs arising from drug, alcohol or substance misuse (if relevant);
- any parenting or caring needs;
- social, cultural or spiritual needs;
- counselling and personal support;
- assistance in welfare rights and managing finances;
- the involvement of authorities and agencies in a different area, if the patient is not going to live locally;
- the involvement of other agencies, for example the probation service or voluntary organisations;
- for a restricted patient, the conditions which the Secretary of State for Justice or the Tribunal has imposed or is likely to impose on their conditional discharge; and

---

14 Independent mental health advocacy services under the Act were introduced in April 2009.

- contingency plans (should the patient's mental health deteriorate) and crisis contact details.

27.14 The professionals concerned should, in discussion with the patient, establish an agreed outline of the patient's needs and agree a timescale for the implementation of the various aspects of the after-care plan. All key people with specific responsibilities with regard to the patient should be properly identified.

27.15 It is important that those who are involved are able to take decisions regarding their own involvement and, as far as possible, that of their agency. If approval for plans needs to be obtained from more senior levels, it is important that this causes no delay to the implementation of the after-care plan.

27.16 If accommodation is to be offered as part of the after-care plan to patients who are offenders, the circumstances of any victims of the patient's offence(s) and their families should be taken into account when deciding where the accommodation should be offered. Where the patient is to live may be one of the conditions imposed by the Secretary of State for Justice or the Tribunal when conditionally discharging a restricted patient.

27.17 The after-care plan should be recorded in writing. Once the plan is agreed, it is essential that any changes are discussed with the patient as well as others involved with the patient before being implemented.

27.18 The after-care plan should be regularly reviewed. It will be the responsibility of the care co-ordinator (or other officer responsible for its review) to arrange reviews of the plan until it is agreed that it is no longer necessary.

Ending section 117 after-care services

27.19 The duty to provide after-care services exists until both the PCT and the LSSA are satisfied that the patient no longer requires them. The circumstances in which it is appropriate to end section 117 after-care will vary from person to person and according to the nature of the services being provided. The most clear-cut circumstance in which after-care will end is where the person's mental health has improved to a point where they no longer need services because of their mental disorder. But if these services include, for example, care in a specialist residential setting, the arrangements for their move to more appropriate accommodation will need to be in place before support under section 117 is finally withdrawn. Fully involving the patient in the decision-making process will play an important part in the successful ending of after-care.

27.20 After-care services under section 117 should not be withdrawn solely on the grounds that:

- the patient has been discharged from the care of specialist mental health services;
- an arbitrary period has passed since the care was first provided;
- the patient is deprived of their liberty under the Mental Capacity Act 2005;
- the patient may return to hospital informally or under section 2; or

- the patient is no longer on SCT or section 17 leave.

27.21 Even when the provision of after-care has been successful in that the patient is now well settled in the community, the patient may still continue to need after-care services, for example to prevent a relapse or further deterioration in their condition.

27.22 Patients are under no obligation to accept the after-care services they are offered, but any decisions they may make to decline them should be fully informed. An unwillingness to accept services does not mean that patients have no need to receive services, nor should it preclude them from receiving them under section 117 should they change their minds.

Related material

- *Refocusing the Care Programme Approach: Policy and Positive Practice Guidance*, March 2008.

This material does not form part of the Code. It is provided for assistance only.

CHAPTER 28
GUARDIANSHIP, LEAVE OF ABSENCE OR SCT?

28.1 This chapter gives advice on deciding between guardianship, leave of absence and supervised community treatment (SCT) as ways of supporting patients once it is safe for them to leave hospital.

Deciding between guardianship, leave of absence and SCT

28.2 There are three ways in which an unrestricted patient may be subject to the powers of the Act while living in the community: guardianship, leave of absence and SCT.

28.3 **Guardianship** (section 7 of the Act) is social care-led and is primarily focused on patients with welfare needs. Its purpose is to enable patients to receive care in the community where it cannot be provided without the use of compulsory powers. (See **chapter 26**.)

28.4 **Leave of absence** (section 17) is primarily intended to allow a patient detained under the Act to be temporarily absent from hospital where further in-patient treatment as a detained patient is still thought to be necessary. It is clearly suitable for short-term absences, to allow visits to family and so on. It may also be useful in the longer term, where the clinical team wish to see how the patient manages outside hospital before making the decision to discharge. However, for a number of patients, SCT may be a better option than longer-term leave for the ongoing management of their care. [Section 17(2A).] Reflecting this, whenever considering longer-term leave for a patient (that is, for more than seven consecutive days), the responsible clinician must first consider whether the patient should be discharged onto SCT instead. (See **chapter 21**.)

28.5 **SCT** (section 17A) is principally aimed at preventing the "revolving door" scenario and the prevention of harm which could arise from relapse. It is a more structured system than leave of absence and has more safeguards for patients. A key feature of SCT is that it is suitable only where there is no reason to think that the patient will need further treatment as a detained in-patient for the time being, but the responsible clinician needs to be able to recall the patient to hospital. (See **chapter 25**.)

28.6 Some pointers to the use of the three options are given in the following boxes.

SCT or longer-term leave of absence: relevant factors to consider

Factors suggesting longer-term leave	Factors suggesting SCT
• Discharge from hospital is for a specific purpose or a fixed period.	• There is confidence that the patient is ready for discharge from hospital on an indefinite basis.
• The patient's discharge from hospital is deliberately on a "trial" basis.	• There are good reasons to expect that the patient will not need to be detained for the treatment they need to be given.
• The patient is likely to need further in-patient treatment without their consent or compliance.	• The patient appears prepared to consent or comply with the treatment they need – but risks as below mean that recall may be necessary.
• There is a serious risk of arrangements in the community breaking down or being unsatisfactory – more so than for SCT.	• The risk of arrangements in the community breaking down, or of the patient needing to be recalled to hospital for treatment, is sufficiently serious to justify SCT, but not to the extent that it is very likely to happen.

SCT or guardianship: relevant factors to consider

Factors suggesting guardianship	Factors suggesting SCT
• The focus is on the patient's general welfare, rather than specifically on medical treatment.	• The main focus is on ensuring that the patient continues to receive necessary medical treatment for mental disorder, without having to be detained again.
• There is little risk of the patient needing to be admitted compulsorily and quickly to hospital.	• Compulsory recall may well be necessary, and speed is likely to be important.
• There is a need for enforceable power to require the patient to reside at a particular place.	

Deprivation of liberty[15] while on SCT, on leave or subject to guardianship

28.7 Patients who are on SCT or on leave, and who lack capacity to consent to the arrangements required for their care or treatment, may occasionally need to be detained in a care home for further care or treatment for their mental disorder in circumstances in which recall to hospital for this purpose is not considered necessary. The same might apply to admission to a care home or hospital because of physical health problems.

28.8 If so, the procedures for the deprivation of liberty safeguards in the Mental Capacity Act 2005 (MCA) should be followed. Deprivation of liberty under the MCA can exist alongside SCT or leave of absence, provided that there is no conflict with the conditions of SCT or leave of absence set by the patient's responsible clinician.

28.9 Where patients on SCT or on leave who lack capacity to consent to the arrangements required for their care or treatment need to be detained in hospital for further treatment for mental disorder, they should be recalled under the Mental Health Act itself. The MCA deprivation of liberty safeguards cannot be used instead.

28.10 For guidance on the interface between guardianship and the deprivation of liberty safeguards, see **chapter 26** on guardianship.

CHAPTER 32
THE TRIBUNAL

32.1 This chapter provides guidance on the role of the Tribunal[16] and related duties on hospital managers and others.

Purpose of the Tribunal [Reference Guide chapters 20 and 21]

32.2 The Tribunal is an independent judicial body. Its main purpose is to review the cases of detained, conditionally discharged, and supervised community treatment (SCT) patients under the Act and to direct the discharge of any patients where it thinks it appropriate. It also considers applications for discharge from guardianship.

32.3 The Tribunal provides a significant safeguard for patients who have had their liberty curtailed under the Act. Those giving evidence at hearings should do what they can to help enable Tribunal hearings to be conducted in a professional manner, which includes having regard to the patient's wishes and feelings and ensuring that the patient feels as comfortable with the proceedings as possible.

32.4 It is for those who believe that a patient should continue to be detained or remain an SCT patient to prove their case, not for the patient to disprove it. They will therefore need to present the Tribunal with sufficient evidence to support continuing liability to

---

15 The deprivation of liberty safeguards are in force from April 2009.

16 At the time of publication, the Tribunal was the Mental Health Review Tribunal (MHRT). However, the MHRT has been replaced in England by a new First-Tier Tribunal established under the Tribunals, Courts and Enforcement Act 2007. There is also a right of appeal, on a point of law, from that Tribunal to the Upper Tribunal.

detention or SCT. Clinical and social reports form the backbone of this evidence. Care should be given to ensure that all information is as up to date as possible to avoid adjournment. In order to support the Tribunal in making its decision all information should be clear and concise.

Informing the patient and nearest relative of rights to apply to the Tribunal

32.5 Hospital managers and the local social services authority (LSSA) are under a duty to take steps to ensure that patients understand their rights to apply for a Tribunal hearing. Hospital managers and the LSSA should also advise patients of their entitlement to free legal advice and representation. They should do both whenever:

- patients are first detained in hospital, received into guardianship or discharged to SCT;
- their detention or guardianship is renewed or SCT is extended; and
- their status under the Act changes – for example, if they move from detention under section 2 to detention under section 3 or if their community treatment order is revoked.

32.6 Unless the patient requests otherwise, the information should normally also be given to their nearest relative (subject to the normal considerations about involving nearest relatives see – **paragraphs 2.27–2.33**).

32.7 Hospital managers and professionals should enable detained patients to be visited by their legal representatives at any reasonable time. This is particularly important where visits are necessary to discuss a Tribunal application. Where the patient consents, legal representatives and independent doctors should be given prompt access to the patient's medical records. Delays in providing access can hold up Tribunal proceedings and should be avoided.

32.8 In connection with an application (or a reference) to the Tribunal, an independent doctor or approved clinician authorised by (or on behalf of) a patient has a right to visit and examine the patient in private. [Sections 67 and 76.] Those doctors and approved clinicians also have a right to inspect any records relating to the patient's detention, treatment and (where relevant) after-care under section 117. Where nearest relatives have a right to apply to the Tribunal, they too may authorise independent doctors or approved clinicians in the same way. The patient's consent is not required for authorised doctors or approved clinicians to see their records, and they should be given prompt access to the records they wish to see.

Hospital managers' duty to refer cases to the Tribunal

32.9 The hospital managers have various duties to refer patients to the Tribunal. They may also request the Secretary of State to refer a patient, and there are certain circumstances where they should always consider doing so. (See **chapter 31**.)

Reports – general

32.10 Responsible authorities (that is the managers of the relevant hospital or the LSSA responsible for a guardianship patient) should be familiar with the Tribunal's rules and procedures. The rules place a statutory duty on the responsible authority to provide the Tribunal with a statement of relevant facts together with certain reports.

32.11 It is important that documents and information are provided in accordance with the Tribunal's rules and procedures in good time for any Tribunal hearing. Missing, out-of-date or inadequate reports can lead to adjournments or unnecessarily long hearings. Where responsible clinicians, social workers or other professionals are required to provide reports, they should do this promptly and within the statutory timescale.

32.12 In the case of a restricted patient, if the opinion of the responsible clinician or other professional changes from what was recorded in the original Tribunal report(s), it is vital that this is communicated in writing, prior to the hearing, to the Tribunal office and the Mental Health Unit of the Ministry of Justice to allow them the opportunity to prepare a supplementary statement.

32.13 If a Tribunal panel feels that it needs more information on any report, it may request it, either in the form of a supplementary report or by questioning a witness at the hearing itself.

32.14 In some circumstances, the Tribunal will not sit immediately after receiving the report. In these cases, the report writers should consider whether anything in the patient's circumstances have changed and should produce a concise update to the report. This is especially important if the patient's status changes – for example, if a patient becomes an SCT patient or moves from detention under section 2 to section 3.

32.15 In those cases, the application will need to be considered under the new circumstances, and the report will need to provide a justification for continued detention or liability to recall under the new circumstances. The Tribunal may ask the author of the report to talk through it, so it is good practice for the authors to re-familiarise themselves with the content of any report before the hearing. If the author of the report is unable to attend, it is important that anyone attending in their place should, wherever possible, also have a good knowledge of the patient's case.

32.16 Hospital managers (or LSSAs in guardianship cases) should ensure that the Tribunal is notified immediately of any events or changes that might have a bearing on Tribunal proceedings – for example, where a patient is discharged or one of the parties is unavailable.

32.17 If the author of a report prepared for the Tribunal is aware of information they do not think the patient should see, they should follow the Tribunal's procedure for the submission of such information. Ultimately, it is for the Tribunal to decide what should be disclosed to the patient.

32.18 Reports should be sent to the appropriate Tribunal office, preferably by secure e-mail, otherwise by post.

32.19 The responsible authority must ensure that up-to-date reports prepared specifically for the Tribunal are provided in accordance with the Tribunal's rules and procedures. In practice, this will normally include a report completed by the patient's responsible clinician. Where the patient is under the age of 18 and the responsible clinician is not a child and adolescent mental health service (CAMHS) specialist, hospital managers should ensure that a report is prepared by a CAMHS specialist.

32.20 Where possible, reports should be written by the professionals with the best overall knowledge of the patient's situation.

32.21 The reports should be submitted in good time to enable all parties, including the Secretary of State in restricted cases, to fulfil their responsibilities.

Medical examination

32.22 A medical member of the Tribunal may want to examine the patient at any time before the hearing. Hospital managers must ensure that the medical member can see patients who are in hospital in private and examine their medical records. It is important that the patient is told of the visit in advance so that they can be available when the medical member visits.

Withdrawing the application

32.23 A request to withdraw an application may be made by the applicant in accordance with the Tribunal rules. The applicant may not withdraw a reference made by the Secretary of State.

32.24 An application will also be considered to be withdrawn if the patient is discharged. If this happens outside office hours, someone acting on behalf of the hospital managers (or the LSSA, if it is a guardianship case) should contact the Tribunal office as soon as possible, to inform them. For detained patients, this could be done by a member of the ward staff.

Representation

32.25 Hospital managers (or LSSAs, as the case may be) should inform patients of their right to present their own case to the Tribunal and their right to be represented by someone else. Staff should be available to help patients make an application. This is especially important for SCT patients who may not have daily contact with professionals.

The hearing

Attendance at hearings

32.26 Normally, a patient will be present throughout their Tribunal hearing. Patients do not need to attend their hearing, but professionals should encourage them to attend unless they judge that it would be detrimental to their health or wellbeing.

32.27 It is important that the patient's responsible clinician attends the Tribunal, supported by other staff involved in the patient's care where appropriate, as their evidence is crucial for making the case for the patient's continued detention or SCT under the Act. Wherever possible, the responsible clinician, and other relevant staff, should attend for the full hearing so that they are aware of all the evidence made available to the Tribunal and of the Tribunal's decision and reasons.

32.28 A responsible clinician can attend the hearing solely as a witness or as the nominated representative of the responsible authority. As a representative of the responsible authority, the responsible clinician has the ability to call and cross-examine witnesses and to make submissions to the Tribunal. However, this may not always be desirable where it is envisaged that the responsible clinician will have to continue working closely with a patient.

32.29 Responsible authorities should therefore consider whether they want to send an additional person to represent their interests, allowing the responsible clinician to appear solely as a witness. Responsible clinicians should be clear in what capacity they are attending the Tribunal, as they may well be asked this by the panel.

32.30 It is important that other people who prepare reports submitted by the responsible authority attend the hearing to provide further up-to-date information about the patient, including (where relevant) their home circumstances and the after-care available in the event of a decision to discharge the patient.

32.31 Increasingly, Tribunal hearings find it helpful to speak to a nurse, particularly a nurse who knows the patient. It is often helpful for a nurse who knows the patient to accompany them to the hearing.

32.32 Hospital managers should ensure that all professionals who attend Tribunal hearings are adequately prepared.

Accommodation for hearings

32.33 The managers of a hospital in which a Tribunal hearing is to be held should provide suitable accommodation for that purpose. The hearing room should be private, quiet, clean and adequately sized and furnished. It should not contain confidential information about other patients. If the room is also used for other purposes, care should be taken to ensure that any equipment (such as a video camera or a two-way mirror) would not have a disturbing effect on the patient.

32.34 The patient should have access to a separate room in which to hold any private discussions that are necessary – for example, with their representative – as should the Tribunal members, so that they can discuss their decision.

32.35 Where a patient is being treated in the community, the hospital managers should consider whether a hospital venue is appropriate. They may wish to discuss alternatives with the Tribunal office.

Interpretation

32.36 Where necessary, the Tribunal will provide, free of charge, interpretation services for patients and their representatives. Where patients or their representatives are hard of hearing or have speech difficulties (or both), the Tribunal will provide such services of sign language interpreters, lip speakers or palantypists as may be necessary. Hospital managers and LSSAs should inform the Tribunal well in advance if they think any such services might be necessary.

Communication of the decision

32.37 The Tribunal will normally communicate its decision to all parties orally at the end of the hearing. Provided it is feasible to do so, and the patient wishes it, the Tribunal will speak to them personally. Otherwise, the decision will be given to the patient's representative (if they have one). If the patient is unrepresented, and it is not feasible to discuss matters with them after the hearing, the hospital managers or LSSA should ensure that they are told the decision as soon as possible. Copies of the decision can be left at a hospital on the day of the hearing. All parties to the hearing should receive a written copy of the reasons for the decision.

Complaints

32.38 Complaints from users about the Tribunal should be sent to the Tribunal office. The Tribunal has procedures in place to deal with complaints promptly.

Further information on the Tribunal

32.39 The Tribunal itself publishes further information and guidance about its procedures and operations.

CHAPTER 33
PATIENTS CONCERNED WITH CRIMINAL PROCEEDINGS

33.1 This chapter offers guidance on the use of the Act to arrange treatment for mentally disordered people who come into contact with the criminal justice system. [Reference Guide chapters 3–11.]

Assessment for potential admission to hospital

33.2 People who are subject to criminal proceedings have the same rights to psychiatric assessment and treatment as anyone else. Any person who is in police or prison custody or before the courts charged with a criminal offence and who is in need of medical treatment for mental disorder should be considered for admission to hospital.

33.3 Wherever possible, people who appear to the court to be mentally disordered should have their treatment needs considered at the earliest possible opportunity, by the court mental health assessment scheme where there is one. Such people may be at greatest risk of self-harm while in custody. Prompt access to specialist treatment may prevent significant deterioration in their condition and is likely to assist in a speedier trial process, helping to avoid longer-term harm or detention in an unsuitable environment.

33.4 If criminal proceedings are discontinued, it may be appropriate for the relevant local social services authority (LSSA) to arrange for an approved mental health professional (AMHP) to consider making an application for admission under Part 2 of the Act.

33.5 A prison healthcare centre is not a hospital within the meaning of the Act. The rules in Part 4 of the Act about medical treatment of detained patients do not apply and treatment cannot be given there under the Act without the patient's consent (see **chapter 23**).

Agency responsibilities

33.6 Primary care trusts (PCTs) should:

- provide the courts, in response to a request under section 39 of the Act, with comprehensive information on the range of facilities available for the admission of patients subject to the criminal justice process. In particular, PCTs should provide the courts with comprehensive information regarding child and adolescent mental health service (CAMHS) beds that are (or could be made) available for patients;
- appoint a named person to respond to requests for information; and
- ensure that prompt medical assessment of defendants is provided to assist in the speedy completion of the trial process and the most suitable disposal for the offender.

33.7 Section 39A requires an LSSA to inform the court, if requested, whether it, or any person approved by it, is willing to receive an offender into guardianship and how the guardian's powers would be exercised. LSSAs should appoint a named person to respond to requests from the courts about mental health services provided in the community, including under guardianship.

Assessment by a doctor

33.8 A doctor who is asked to provide evidence in relation to a possible admission under Part 3 of the Act should bear in mind that the request is not for a general report on the defendant's condition but for advice on whether or not the patient should be diverted from prison by way of a hospital order (or a community order with a mental health treatment requirement under criminal justice legislation).

33.9 Doctors should:

- identify themselves to the person being assessed, explain who has requested the report and make clear the limits of confidentiality in relation to the report. They should explain that any information disclosed, and the medical opinion, could be relevant not only to medical disposal by the court but also to the imposition of a punitive sentence, or to its length; and

- request relevant pre-sentence reports, the Inmate Medical Record, if there is one, and previous psychiatric reports, as well as relevant documentation regarding the alleged offence. If any of this information is not available, the doctor's report should say so clearly.

33.10 The doctor, or one of them if two doctors are preparing reports, should have access to a bed, or take responsibility for referring the case to another clinician who does, if they propose to recommend admission to hospital. In the case of a defendant under the age of 18, the doctor should ideally have specialist knowledge of CAMHS and the needs of young people.

33.11 The doctor should, where possible, identify and access other independent sources of information about the person's previous history (including convictions). This should include information from GP records, previous psychiatric treatment and patterns of behaviour.

33.12 Assessment for admission of the patient is the responsibility of the doctor, but other members of the clinical team who would be involved with the person's care and treatment should also be consulted. A multi-disciplinary assessment should usually be undertaken if admission to hospital is likely to be recommended. The doctor should also contact the person who is preparing a pre-sentence report, especially if psychiatric treatment is recommended as a condition of a community order.

33.13 In cases where the doctor cannot state with confidence at the time of sentencing whether a hospital order will be appropriate, they should consider recommending an interim hospital order under section 38 of the Act. This order provides for the person to be admitted to hospital for up to 12 weeks (which may be extended for further periods of up to 28 days to a maximum total period of 12 months) so that the court can reach a conclusion on the most appropriate and effective disposal.

Independent medical assessment

33.14 A patient who is remanded to hospital for a report (section 35) or for treatment (section 36) is entitled to obtain, at their own expense, or where applicable through legal aid, an independent report on their mental condition from a doctor or other clinician of their choosing, for the purpose of applying to court for the termination of the remand. The hospital managers should help in the exercise of this right by enabling the patient to contact a suitably qualified and experienced solicitor or other adviser.

Reports to the court

33.15 Clinical opinion is particularly important in helping courts to determine the sentence to be passed. In particular, it will help to inform the decision whether to divert the offender from punishment by way of a hospital order, or whether a prison sentence is the most suitable disposal.

33.16 A medical report for the court should set out:

- the material on which the report is based;

- how that material relates to the opinion given;

- where relevant, how the opinion may relate to any other trial issue;
- factors relating to the presence of mental disorder that may affect the risk that the patient poses to themselves or to others, including the risk of re-offending; and
- if admission to hospital is recommended, what, if any, special treatment or security is recommended and whether the doctor represents an organisation that is able to provide what is required.

The report should not speculate about guilt or innocence.

33.17 Section 157 of the Criminal Justice Act 2003 requires the court to obtain a medical report before passing a custodial sentence other than one fixed by law. Before passing such a sentence, the court must consider any information before it which relates to the offender's mental condition and the likely effect of such a sentence on that condition and on any treatment that may be available for it.

33.18 It may, therefore, be appropriate to include recommendations on the disposal of the case. In making recommendations for disposal, the doctor should consider the longer-term, as well as immediate, consequences. Factors to be taken into account include:

- whether the court may wish to make a hospital order subject to special restrictions;
- whether, for restricted patients, the order should designate admission to a named unit within the hospital;
- whether, in the event of the court concluding that a prison sentence is appropriate, the offender should initially be admitted to hospital by way of a hospital direction under section 45A; and
- whether a community order with a mental health treatment requirement may be appropriate.

33.19 Where an offender is made subject to special restrictions ("restricted patients"), the court, or the Secretary of State for Justice in some circumstances, may specify that the person be detained in a named unit within a hospital. This is to ensure an appropriate level of security.

33.20 A named hospital unit can be any part of a hospital which is treated as a separate unit. It will be for the court (or the Secretary of State, as the case may be) to define what is meant in each case where it makes use of the power. Admission to a named unit will mean that the consent of the Secretary of State will be required for any leave of absence or transfer from the named unit, whether the transfer is to another part of the same hospital or to another hospital.

33.21 The need to consider the longer-term implications of a recommended disposal is particularly important where an extended or indeterminate sentence for public protection is indicated under the Criminal Justice Act 2003. Either a hospital order under section 37 or attachment of a hospital direction to the prison sentence under section 45A is available to the court. Discretion lies with the court.

33.22 A hospital order, with or without restrictions, diverts the offender from punishment to treatment. There is no tariff to serve, and the period of detention will be determined by the disorder and the risk of harm which attaches to it.

33.23 A hospital direction, by contrast, accompanies a prison sentence and means that, from the start of the sentence, the offender will be managed in hospital in the same way as a prisoner who has been transferred to hospital subject to special restrictions under sections 47 and 49 of the Act (see **paragraph 33.34**). The responsible clinician can propose transfer to prison to the Secretary of State for Justice at any time before the prisoner's release date if, in their opinion, no further treatment is necessary or likely to be effective.

Availability of places

33.24 If the medical evidence is that the person needs treatment in hospital, but the medical witness cannot identify a suitable facility where the person could be admitted immediately, they should seek advice from the PCT for the person's home area. If the person has no permanent address, responsibility lies with the PCT for the area where they are registered with a GP or, if they are not registered with a GP, where the offence was committed for which sentence is being passed.

Transport to and from court

33.25 For patients remanded to hospital under sections 35 or 36 of the Act, or subject to a hospital order or an interim hospital order, the court has the power to direct who is to be responsible for conveying the defendant from the court to the receiving hospital. In practice, when remand orders are first made, patients are usually returned to the holding prison, and arrangements are then made to admit them to hospital within the statutory period.

33.26 When a patient has been admitted on remand or is subject to an interim hospital order, it is the responsibility of the hospital to return the patient to court as required. The court should give adequate notice of hearings. The hospital should liaise with the court in plenty of time to confirm the arrangements for escorting the patient to and from the court. The hospital will be responsible for providing a suitable escort for the patient when travelling from the hospital to the court and should plan for the provision of necessary staff to do this. The assistance of the police may be requested, if necessary. If possible, and having regard to the needs of the patient, medical or nursing staff should remain with the patient on court premises, even though legal accountability while the patient is detained for hearings remains with the court.

33.27 For further guidance on conveyance of patients under the Act, see **chapter 11**.

Treatment without consent – patients remanded for report [Section 56]

33.28 The rules in Part 4 of the Act about medical treatment of detained patients do not apply to patients remanded to hospital under section 35 for a report on their mental condition. As a result, treatment can be administered only with their consent, or, in the case of a patient aged 16 or over who lacks capacity to consent, in accordance with the Mental Capacity Act 2005 (see **chapter 23**).

33.29 Where a patient remanded under section 35 is thought to be in need of medical treatment for mental disorder which cannot otherwise be given, the patient should be referred back to court by the clinician in charge of their care as soon as possible, with an appropriate recommendation and with an assessment of whether they are in a fit state to attend court.

33.30 If there is a delay in securing a court date, consideration should be given to whether the patient meets the criteria for detention under Part 2 of the Act to enable compulsory treatment to be given. This will be concurrent with, and not a replacement for, the remand made by the court.

Transfer of prisoners to hospital

33.31 The need for in-patient treatment for a prisoner should be identified and acted upon quickly, and prison healthcare staff should make contact immediately with the responsible PCT. Responsible NHS commissioners should aim to ensure that transfers of prisoners with mental disorders are carried out within a timeframe equivalent to levels of care experienced by patients who are admitted to mental healthcare services from the community. Any unacceptable delays in transfer after identification of need should be actively monitored and investigated.

33.32 Prisoners with a diagnosis of severe and enduring mental disorder who have given informed consent to treatment should also be considered for transfer to hospital for treatment if the prison environment is considered to be contributing to their disorder. An assessment of need and regular review should consider whether the prison healthcare centre is capable of providing for the prisoner's care if they are considered to be too unwell or vulnerable to return to residential wings.

33.33 Prisoners transferred to hospital under sections 47 or 48 should not be remitted to prison unless clinical staff from the hospital and prison have met to plan the prisoner's future care. This is often called a "section 117 meeting". Appropriate staff from the receiving prison should be invited to attend the review meeting prior to the prisoner's discharge back to prison.

Patients transferred from prison subject to special restrictions

33.34 When a person is transferred from prison to hospital under sections 47 or 48 as a restricted patient, it is the responsibility of the hospital managers and the responsible clinician to ensure that the patient has received, and as far as possible has understood, the letter from the Ministry of Justice explaining the roles of hospital managers and responsible clinicians in relation to restricted patients.

33.35 When prisoners have been transferred under section 47 and remain detained in hospital after their release date, they cease to be restricted patients but remain detained as if on a hospital order without restrictions. The responsible clinician's options under the Act are modified accordingly, and the patient may, for example, be discharged onto supervised community treatment (SCT).

Further guidance on the management of restricted patients

33.36 Professionals should approach the Mental Health Unit of the Ministry of Justice for more detailed guidance about the management of restricted patients.

Related material

- *Notes for the Guidance of Social Supervisors – Supervision and After-care of Conditionally Discharged Restricted Patients*, Home Office, 2007.
- *Mental Health Act 2007 – Guidance for the Courts and Sentencing Powers for Mentally Disordered Offenders*, March 2008.
- Prison Service Instruction 3/2006, which gives comprehensive guidance on the transfer process, professional roles and timescales.
- Criminal Justice Act 2003.
- *Guidance for Supervising Psychiatrists – Supervision and After-care of Conditionally Discharged Restricted Patients*, Home Office, June 2006.

This material does not form part of the Code. It is provided for assistance only.

CHAPTER 34
PEOPLE WITH LEARNING DISABILITIES OR AUTISTIC SPECTRUM DISORDERS

34.1 This chapter deals with issues of particular relevance to patients with learning disabilities, autistic spectrum disorders or both.

Learning disabilities

34.2 For the purposes of the Act, a learning disability is defined as "a state of arrested or incomplete development of the mind which includes significant impairment of intelligence and social functioning". [Section 1(4).]

34.3 Although defined as a mental disorder in this way, learning disability shares few features with the serious mental illnesses that are the most common reason for using the Act. Relatively few people with learning disabilities are detained under the Act, and where they are, it is not usually solely because of their learning disability itself.

34.4 The identification of an individual with a learning disability is a matter for clinical judgement, guided by current professional practice. Those assessing the patient must be satisfied that they display a number of characteristics. The following is general guidance in relation to the key factors in the definition of learning disability for the purposes of the Act.

> *Arrested or incomplete development of mind:* An adult with arrested or incomplete development of mind is one who has experienced a significant impairment of the normal

process of maturation of intellectual and social development that occurs during childhood and adolescence. By using these words in its definition of learning disability, the Act embraces the general understanding that features which qualify as a learning disability are present prior to adulthood. For the purposes of the Act, learning disability does not include people whose intellectual disorder derives from accident, injury or illness occurring after they completed normal maturation (although such conditions do fall within the definition of mental disorder in the Act).

Significant impairment of intelligence: The judgement as to the presence of this particular characteristic must be made on the basis of reliable and careful assessment. It is not defined rigidly by the application of an arbitrary cut-off point such as an IQ of 70.

Significant impairment of social functioning: Reliable and recent observations will be helpful in determining the nature and extent of social competence, preferably from a number of sources who have experience of interacting with the person in social situations, including social workers, nurses, speech and language and occupational therapists, and psychologists. Social functioning assessment tests can be a valuable tool in determining this aspect of learning disability.

34.5 It is important to assess the person as a whole. It may be appropriate to identify learning disability in someone with an IQ somewhat higher than 70 if their social functioning is severely impaired. A person with a low IQ may be correctly diagnosed as having a learning disability even if their social functioning is relatively good.

Abnormally aggressive and seriously irresponsible behaviour

34.6 An application for detention for treatment, or for reception into guardianship, on the basis of a learning disability without another concomitant mental disorder may be made only where it is associated with one or both of the following further features [Section 1(2A) and (2B) Reference Guide 1.12–1.15]:

- abnormally aggressive behaviour; or
- seriously irresponsible conduct.

34.7 Neither term is defined in the Act, and it is not possible to state with any precision exactly what type of conduct could be considered to fall into either category. It will, inevitably, depend not only on the nature of the behaviour and the circumstances in which it is exhibited, but also on the extent to which that conduct gives rise to a serious risk to the health or safety of the patient or to the health or safety of other people, or both.

34.8 In assessing whether a patient's learning disability is associated with conduct that could not only be categorised as aggressive but as abnormally so, relevant factors may include:

- when such aggressive behaviour has been observed, and how persistent and severe it has been;
- whether it has occurred without a specific trigger or seems out of proportion to the circumstances that triggered it;

- whether, and to what degree, it has in fact resulted in harm or distress to other people, or actual damage to property;
- how likely, if it has not been observed recently, it is to recur; and
- how common similar behaviour is in the population generally.

34.9 Similarly, in assessing whether a patient's learning disability is associated with conduct that is not only irresponsible but seriously so, relevant factors may include:

- whether behaviour has been observed that suggests a disregard or an inadequate regard for its serious or dangerous consequences;
- how recently such behaviour has been observed and, when it has been observed, how persistent it has been;
- how seriously detrimental to the patient, or to other people, the consequences of the behaviour were or might have been;
- whether, and to what degree, the behaviour has actually resulted in harm to the patient or the patient's interests, or in harm to other people or to damage to property; and
- if it has not been observed recently, how likely it is to recur.

34.10 When assessing whether a patient with a learning disability should be detained for treatment under the Act, it is important to establish whether any abnormally aggressive or seriously irresponsible conduct identified stems from difficulties in communication. If, for example, the patient is displaying such conduct as their only way of drawing attention to an underlying physical health problem, it would be wrong to interpret the behaviour as an indication of a worsening of their mental disorder, and treatment under the Act would not be an appropriate response.

Practice considerations

34.11 Unless urgent action is required, it would not be good practice to diagnose a patient who has a learning disability as meeting either of these additional conditions without an assessment by a consultant psychiatrist in learning disabilities and a formal psychological assessment. Ideally, this would be part of a complete appraisal by medical, nursing, social work, speech and language therapy, occupational therapy and psychology professionals with experience in learning disabilities, in consultation with a relative, friend or supporter of the patient. Wherever possible, an approved mental health professional (AMHP) who assesses a patient with a learning disability under the Act should have training and experience in working with people with learning disabilities. The patient's person-centred plan and health action plan may also inform the assessment process.

34.12 All those involved in examining, assessing, treating or taking other decisions in relation to people with learning disabilities should bear in mind that there are particular issues that people with learning disabilities may face. These include:

- incorrect assumptions that they do not have capacity to make decisions for themselves and a tendency to be over-protective;

- over-reliance on family members, both for support and for decision-making. Although the considerable expertise that family members often have should be acknowledged, this may put them in the difficult position of having to take decisions inappropriately on behalf of the patient;

- a lack of appreciation of the potential abilities of people with learning disabilities, including their potential to speak up for themselves;

- being denied access to decision-making processes, not being included in meetings about them, information made inaccessible to them, and decisions being made in their absence;

- limited life experiences to draw on when making choices; and

- their learning disability being seen as the explanation for all their physical and behavioural attributes when there may, in fact, be an underlying cause relating to a separate issue of physical or mental health (diagnostic overshadowing).

34.13 Those working under the Act with people with learning disabilities should bear in mind the following general points:

- people with learning disabilities may use non-verbal communication rather than spoken language. This non-verbal communication may include behaviour, gestures, posture and body language, ways of moving, signing, noises and pointing. It is important to recognise people's communication in all its forms and to avoid assuming that people's behaviour is a symptom of their mental disorder, when it may be an attempt to communicate feelings or physical pain or discomfort.

- people with learning disabilities may find new environments, such as a medical setting, frightening. All "reasonable adjustments" (as required by the Disability Discrimination Act 1995) need to be made to adapt and respond to each individual's needs. This may mean offering a quiet space, for example, or having one link person assigned who speaks with the person.

- the most appropriate method of communication for each person with learning disabilities should be identified as soon as possible, and the help of a speech and language therapist should be sought wherever appropriate. It is helpful to identify a specific person who will undertake this task.

- some people with learning disabilities may prefer to have written material in simple language with images or symbols to assist, and this could be reinforced orally, through personal contact or other means. It can be helpful to repeat information and leave a record of the information that has been passed on, so that the person can consult it and ask others to clarify anything that is difficult to understand.

- it is important to set aside sufficient time for preparation of suitable information and for preparation before meetings. Meetings should be held in an environment that is not intimidating, in order to allow the patient every chance to understand the information given.

34.14 People with learning disabilities may also encounter problems in:

- understanding what is being explained to them and communicating their views (in situations that increase their levels of anxiety they may find it even more difficult to understand what is said to them); and
- in being understood, particularly where lack of spoken language makes it hard for them to provide explanations of pain or other symptoms that might aid diagnosis of physical or mental illness.

34.15 Where information relates to their right to have their case reviewed by the Tribunal, the information will need to be designed to help people with learning disabilities understand the Tribunal's role. They may well need support to make an informed decision about whether and when to make an application.

34.16 Where professionals taking decisions under the Act have limited expertise with people with learning disabilities, it is good practice to seek advice from the local specialist service, which can provide details of alternatives to compulsory treatment and give advice on good communication. But any problem with availability of such services should not be allowed to delay action that is immediately necessary. It is desirable that, during examination or assessment, people with learning disabilities have someone with them whom they know well and with whom they have good communication (subject to the normal considerations of patient confidentiality).

34.17 The potential of co-morbidity with mental illness and personality disorder should also be kept in mind, in order that the skills of clinicians and others with appropriate expertise can be brought into play at all points in the assessment, treatment and care pathway. The possibility of physical health problems underlying the presentation of abnormally aggressive or seriously irresponsible behaviour should similarly always be kept in mind.

Autistic spectrum disorders

34.18 The Act's definition of mental disorder includes the full range of autistic spectrum disorders, including those existing alongside a learning disability or any other kind of mental disorder. While it is possible for someone on the autistic spectrum to meet the conditions for treatment under the Act without having any other form of mental disorder, even if it is not associated with abnormally aggressive or seriously irresponsible behaviour, this is likely to happen only very rarely. Compulsory treatment in a hospital setting is rarely likely to be helpful for a person with autism, who may be very distressed by even minor changes in routine and is likely to find detention in hospital anxiety provoking. Sensitive, person-centred support in a familiar setting will usually be more helpful. Wherever possible, less restrictive alternative ways of providing the treatment or support a person needs should be found.

34.19 Autistic spectrum disorders are disorders occurring from early stages in development in which the person shows marked difficulties with social communication, social interaction and social imagination. They may be preoccupied with a particular subject of interest.

34.20 These disorders are developmental in nature and are not mental illnesses in themselves. However, people with an autistic spectrum disorder may have additional or related problems, which frequently include anxiety. These may be related to social factors associated with frustration or communication problems or to patterns of thought and behaviour that are rigid or literal in nature. As with people with learning disabilities, it should be borne in mind that people with autistic spectrum disorders may also have co-morbid mental disorders, including mood disorders and, occasionally, personality disorders.

34.21 A person with an autistic spectrum disorder may have additional sensory and motor difficulties that make them behave in an unusual manner and that might be interpreted as a mental illness but are in fact a coping mechanism. These include sensitivity to light, sound, touch and balance and may result in a range of regulatory behaviours, including rocking, self-injury and avoidance, such as running away.

34.22 A person with an autistic spectrum disorder is likely to behave in ways that seem odd to other people. But mere eccentricity, in anyone, is not in itself a reason for compulsory measures under the Act.

34.23 There can also be a repetitive or compulsive element to much of the behaviour of people with autistic spectrum disorders. The person may appear to be choosing to act in a particular way, but their behaviour may be distressing even to themselves. It may be driven or made worse by anxiety and could lead to harm to self or others. Repetitive behaviour does not in itself constitute a mental disorder.

34.24 The examination or assessment of someone with an autistic spectrum disorder requires special consideration of how to communicate effectively with the person being assessed. Whenever possible, the people carrying out assessments should have experience and training in working with people with these disorders. If this is not possible, they should seek assistance from specialists with appropriate expertise, but this should not be allowed to delay action that is immediately necessary. Assessment should ideally be part of a complete appraisal – a multi-disciplinary process involving medical, nursing, social work, occupational therapy, speech and language therapy and psychology professionals (as necessary) with relevant specialist experience.

34.25 Where appropriate, someone who knows the person with an autistic spectrum disorder should be present at an initial examination and assessment (subject to the normal considerations of patient confidentiality). Knowledge of the person's early developmental history and usual pattern of behaviour will help prevent someone with an autistic spectrum disorder from being wrongly made subject to compulsory measures under the Act, or treated inappropriately with psychopharmacological agents.

34.26 A person with an autistic spectrum disorder may show a marked difference between their intellectual and their emotional development, associated on occasion with aggressive or seriously irresponsible behaviour. They may be able to discuss an action intellectually and express a desire to do it (or not, as the case may be) but not have the instinctive social empathy to keep to their intentions. This should be understood and responded to by professionals, who should recognise that the nature of the communication problems may require specialist structured approaches to communication. However, when the person is unable to prevent themselves from causing severe harm to themselves or others, compulsory measures under the Act may become necessary.

34.27 If people with autistic spectrum disorders do need to be detained under the Act, it is important that they are treated in a setting that can accommodate their social and communication needs as well as being able to treat their mental disorder.

Related material

- *Valuing People – A New Strategy for the 21st Century* (Cm 5086), The Stationery Office, March 2001.
- *Valuing People: A New Strategy for Learning Disability for the 21st Century: Planning with People towards Person Centred Approaches – Guidance for Partnership Boards*, Department of Health, 28 January 2002.
- *Action for Health, Health Action Plans and Health Facilitation Detailed Good Practice Guidance on Implementation for Learning Disability Partnership Boards*, Department of Health, 6 August 2002.

This material does not form part of the Code. It is provided for assistance only.

Applying the principles

This scenario is not intended to provide a template for decisions in applying the principles in similar situations. The scenario itself is only illustrative and does not form part of the Code itself.

Autism and learning disability

Albert is a 22 year old man with profound and multiple learning disabilities. He is six feet four inches tall and very powerfully built. As a child, he was also diagnosed with Kanner syndrome – a severe form of autistic spectrum disorder. He is unable to speak.

Albert lives in a residential care home. Following the recent death of a close friend, Albert became withdrawn and uncommunicative. His GP diagnosed depression and prescribed medication.

After a few weeks on this medication, Albert's mood changed. He was no longer withdrawn but began to display aggressive behaviour and, in particular, began banging the side of his head against the door handle. Staff at the group house felt he was becoming a risk to himself and to other people who came into contact with him and asked for a Mental Health Act assessment.

In considering whether admission to hospital under the Act is appropriate for Albert, the doctors and the AMHP should consider the principles and how they might be applied.

Among the things they might wish to consider in making a decision in these circumstances are the following. ➡

Purpose principle

- What factors need to be considered in assessing for Albert's safety and wellbeing?
- Have any physical health factors been considered?
- Are there any social, occupational, psychological or sensory issues that may be influencing Albert's behaviour?
- Are there any issues of risk? If so, is the risk to Albert or to other people? Or both?
- If Albert were to be detained, how may the resultant change of environment impact on his condition?

Least restriction principle

- What are the possible alternatives to admission under the Act? Additional support to Albert in the residential care home? Further assessment, including investigation of possible underlying physical health problems?

Respect principle

- Is any aspect of Albert's behaviour an attempt to communicate what is wrong or express any views about what he would want to happen?
- How has he communicated his views in the past?
- Given that Albert is young and strong, are any assumptions being made about the risk his behaviour poses and, if so, how might they be affecting the options being considered?

Participation principle

- What methods have been employed to try to ascertain Albert's view about his care and treatment?
- Have Albert's family been contacted?
- What do they know about Albert that might inform an evaluation of his condition and the likely effectiveness of the various possible responses?
- What do they want and what do they know about him that might inform what he might want?
- Have the staff at the residential care home been asked what they think Albert's behaviour might mean and whether they have any information that might inform an evaluation of his condition and the likely effectiveness of the various possible responses?
- Do the staff know what Albert might want?

➡

- Does Albert have access to an advocate or other support mechanism that can help interpret his behaviour?

- Has Albert's GP been contacted? What is the GP's view about Albert's condition and what is their view about what Albert might want?

Effectiveness, efficiency and equity principle

- Is there someone with specialist knowledge of learning disability and autism available to be involved in the assessment? If so, given the circumstances, can the assessment wait until they can attend?

CHAPTER 35
PEOPLE WITH PERSONALITY DISORDERS

This chapter deals with issues of particular relevance to people with a personality disorder.

Personality disorders – general points

35.1 The Act applies equally to all people with mental disorders, including those with either primary or secondary diagnoses of personality disorder.

35.2 Generally, people who have personality disorders present a complex range of mental health and other problems:

- many people may have a diagnosis of more than one personality disorder, and they may also have other mental health problems such as depression, anxiety or post-traumatic stress syndrome;

- suicidality, self-harm, substance misuse problems and eating disorders are also common in people with personality disorders;

- some individuals experience very severe, periodic emotional distress in response to stressful circumstances and crisis, particularly people with borderline personality disorder;

- some individuals can at times display a form of psychosis that is qualitatively different from that displayed by people with a diagnosis of mental illness;

- people with personality disorders usually have long-standing and recurrent relationship difficulties;

- people with personality disorders are more likely than other population groups to experience housing problems and long-term unemployment;

- a very small subgroup of people with personality disorders may be anti-social and dangerous;

- anti-social personality disorder is strongly associated with offending, and it is estimated that personality disorders have a high prevalence within offender populations.

Personality disorders and mental health legislation

35.3 People with personality disorders who are subject to compulsory measures under the Act may include individuals who:

- have a primary diagnosis of personality disorder and present a serious risk to themselves or others (or both);
- have complex mental disorders, including personality disorder, and present a serious risk to themselves or to others (or both);
- have a primary diagnosis of personality disorder or complex disorders including personality disorder and are transferred from prison for treatment in secure psychiatric or personality disorder in patient services;
- are transferred from prison or other secure settings for treatment within designated dangerous and severe personality disorder (DSPD) units in hospitals; and
- are personality disordered offenders who have completed in-patient treatment in DSPD units, or other secure settings, but who may need further treatment in the community.

Practice considerations

Assessment

35.4 People with personality disorders may present and behave in very different ways from those with other mental disorders. It is important that such behaviours and presentations are properly understood if the Act is to be used appropriately.

35.5 Especially in times of crisis, decisions about the use of the Act for people with personality disorders will often have to be made by professionals who are not specialists in the field. It is therefore important that approved mental health professionals and doctors carrying out initial assessments have a sufficient understanding of personality disorders as well as other forms of mental disorder.

35.6 Individuals who have historically been labelled by various local agencies as having a personality disorder may never, in fact, have had a thorough clinical assessment and formulation. A number of validated assessment tools enable a more precise identification to be made. Professionals will need to ensure that any treatment and after-care plans are shaped by appropriate clinical assessments conducted by suitably trained practitioners.

35.7 In emergency or very high-risk situations, where such an assessment has not already been carried out and an application for detention under the Act is being considered, then responding to the immediate risk to the health or safety of the patient or to other people is the first priority. However, achieving an appropriate clinical assessment and formulation should be an immediate aim of detention.

Appropriate medical treatment

35.8 What constitutes appropriate medical treatment for a particular patient with a personality disorder will depend very much on their individual circumstances. First and foremost, that calls for a clinical judgement by the clinicians responsible for their assessment or treatment.

35.9 A proposed care plan will not, of course, meet the Act's definition of appropriate medical treatment unless it is for the purpose of alleviating or preventing a worsening of the patient's mental disorder, its symptoms or manifestations (see **chapter 6**).

35.10 Generally, treatment approaches for personality disorders need to be relatively intense and long term, structured and coherent. Sustainable long-term change is more likely to be achieved with the voluntary engagement of the patient.

35.11 People with personality disorders may take time to engage and develop motivation for such longer-term treatment. But even patients who are not engaged in that kind of treatment may need other forms of treatment, including nurse and specialist care, to manage the continuing risks posed by their disorders, and this may constitute appropriate medical treatment.

35.12 In the majority of cases, the primary model of intervention for personality disorders is rooted in a psycho-social model.

35.13 Patients who have been detained may often need to continue treatment in a community setting on discharge. Where there are continuing risks that cannot otherwise be managed safely, supervised community treatment, guardianship or (for restricted patients) conditional discharge may provide a framework within which such patients can continue their treatment in the community.

35.14 In deciding whether treatment under the Act can be delivered safely in the community, account should be taken of:

- where the specific model of treatment intervention can be delivered most effectively and safely;

- if management of personal and social relationships is a factor in the intervention, how the appropriate day-to-day support and monitoring of the patient's social as well as psychological needs can be provided;

- to what degree the psycho-social model of intervention requires the active participation of the patient for an effective and safe outcome;

- the degree to which the patient has the ability to take part in a psycho-social intervention that protects their own and others' safety;

- the degree to which 24-hour access to support will be required; and

- the need for the intervention plan to be supervised by a professional who is appropriately qualified in the model of intervention and in risk assessment and management in the community.

35.15 In the case of personality disordered offenders who may already have received long-term treatment programmes within secure or prison settings, treatment in the community may well still be required while they resettle in the community.

Related material

- *Personality disorder: No longer a diagnosis of exclusion. Policy implementation guidance for the development of services for people with personality disorder*, Department of Health, January 2003.

This material does not form part of the Code. It is provided for assistance only.

CHAPTER 36
CHILDREN AND YOUNG PEOPLE UNDER THE AGE OF 18

36.1 This chapter provides guidance on particular issues arising in relation to children (less than 16 years old) and young people (16 or 17 years old). [Reference Guide chapter 36.]

36.2 This chapter sets out some of the key factors that need to be borne in mind and their interconnections, including:

- some of the main concepts that need to be considered when dealing with patients who are under 18, such as who has parental responsibility, and the parental zone of control;

- when the Mental Health Act should be used and when the Children Act should be used;

- what it means for children and young people to be capable of consent;

- how to make decisions about admission or treatment of informal patients of 16 or 17 year olds;

- how to deal with informal patients under 16 years old;

- how treatment for under 18s is regulated by the Mental Health Act;

- when an application to the court should be made;

- the need to provide age-appropriate services;

- applications and references to the Tribunal; and

- general duties concerning, for example, local authorities visiting children and young people in hospital.

General considerations

36.3 The legal framework governing the admission to hospital and treatment of children is complex, and it is important to remember a number of factors. Those responsible for the care of children and young people in hospital should be familiar with other relevant legislation, including the Children Acts 1989 and 2004, Mental Capacity Act 2005 (MCA), Family Law Reform Act 1969, Human Rights Act 1998 and the United Nations Convention on the Rights of the Child, as well as relevant case law, common law principles and relevant codes of practice.

36.4 When taking decisions under the Act about children and young people, the following should always be borne in mind:

- the best interests of the child or young person must always be a significant consideration;
- children and young people should always be kept as fully informed as possible, just as an adult would be, and should receive clear and detailed information concerning their care and treatment, explained in a way they can understand and in a format that is appropriate to their age;
- the child or young person's views, wishes and feelings should always be considered;
- any intervention in the life of a child or young person that is considered necessary by reason of their mental disorder should be the option that is least restrictive and least likely to expose them to the risk of any stigmatisation, consistent with effective care and treatment, and it should also result in the least possible separation from family, carers, friends and community or interruption of their education, as is consistent with their wellbeing;
- all children and young people should receive the same access to educational provision as their peers;
- children and young people have as much right to expect their dignity to be respected as anyone else; and
- children and young people have as much right to privacy and confidentiality as anyone else.

People with parental responsibility

36.5 Those with parental responsibility will usually, but not always, be the parents of the child or young person. Legally, under the Children Act 1989, consent to treat a child or young person is needed from only one person with parental responsibility, although it is good practice to involve both parents and others close to the child or young person in the decision-making process. However, if one person with parental responsibility strongly disagreed with the decision to treat and was likely to challenge it in court, it might be appropriate to seek authorisation from the court before relying on the consent of another person with parental responsibility.

36.6 It is essential that those taking decisions under the Mental Health Act are clear about who has parental responsibility and that they always request copies of any court orders for reference on the child or young person's medical or social service file. These orders may include care orders, residence orders, contact orders, evidence of appointment as the child or young person's guardian, parental responsibility agreements or orders under section 4 of the Children Act and any order under wardship. If the parents of a child or young person are separated, and the child or young person is living with one parent, the person responsible for the care and treatment of the patient should try to establish whether there is a residence order and, if so, in whose favour.

36.7 Once it is established who has parental responsibility for the child or young person, the person responsible for the care and treatment of the patient must determine whether a person with parental responsibility has the capacity, within the meaning of the MCA, to take a decision about the child or young person's treatment and whether the decision is within the zone of parental control (see **paragraphs 36.9–36.15**).

Children looked after by the local authority

36.8 Where children or young people are looked after by the local authority (see section 22 of the Children Act 1989), treatment decisions should usually be discussed with the parent or other person with parental responsibility who continues to have parental responsibility for the child. If a child or young person is voluntarily accommodated by the local authority, parents or other people with parental responsibility have the same rights and responsibilities in relation to treatment as they would otherwise. If the child or young person is subject to a care order, the parents (or others with parental responsibility) share parental responsibility with the local authority, and it will be a matter for negotiation and agreement between them as to who should be consulted about treatment decisions. However, local authorities can, in the exercise of their powers under section 33(3)(b) of the Children Act 1989, limit the extent to which parents (or others) may exercise their parental responsibility. (See also **paragraphs 36.80–36.82** for the duties of local authorities in relation to hospital patients.)

Zone of parental control

36.9 People with parental responsibility may in certain circumstances (see below) consent on behalf of a child under 16 to them being given medical treatment or being admitted informally for such treatment. Even in these circumstances, mental health professionals can rely on such consent only where it is within what in this guidance is called the 'zone of parental control'. This may also apply to young people of 16 or 17 years of age who are given medical treatment for mental disorder and who lack the ability to consent for themselves, and to decisions about such young people being admitted for such treatment informally if they lack capacity. The concept of the zone of parental control derives largely from case law from the European Court of Human Rights in Strasbourg.[17] It is difficult to have clear rules about what may fall in the zone, when so much depends on the particular facts of each case. Certain guidelines are set out below, but where there is doubt professionals should take legal advice so that account may be taken of the most recent case-law.

---

[17] For example *Nielsen v Denmark* (1989) 11 EHRR 175.

36.10 In assessing whether a particular decision falls within the parameters of the zone of parental control, two key questions must be considered:

- firstly, is the decision one that a parent would be expected to make, having regard both to what is considered to be normal practice in our society and to any relevant human rights decisions made by the courts?; and
- secondly, are there no indications that the parent might not act in the best interests of the child or young person?

36.11 The less confident a professional is that they can answer both questions in the affirmative, the more likely it will be that the decision in question falls outside the zone.

36.12 The parameters of the zone will vary from one case to the next: they are determined not only by social norms, but also by the circumstances and dynamics of a specific parent and child or young person. In assessing where the boundaries lie in any particular case, and so whether a parent's consent may be relied upon, mental health professionals might find it helpful to consider the following factors:

- the nature and invasiveness of what is to be done to the patient (including the extent to which their liberty will be curtailed) – the more extreme the intervention, the more likely it will be that it falls outside the zone;
- whether the patient is resisting – treating a child or young person who is resisting needs more justification;
- the general social standards in force at the time concerning the sorts of decisions it is acceptable for parents to make – anything that goes beyond the kind of decisions parents routinely make will be more suspect;
- the age, maturity and understanding of the child or young person – the greater these are, the more likely it will be that it should be the child or young person who takes the decision; and
- the extent to which a parent's interests may conflict with those of the child or young person – this may suggest that the parent will not act in the child or young person's best interests.

36.13 For example, in a case where the parents had gone through a particularly acrimonious divorce, it might not be possible to separate the decision about whether to admit the child to hospital from the parents' own hostilities, and it might not be possible to treat the parents as able to make an impartial decision. It might also not be appropriate to rely on the consent of a parent in circumstances where the mental health of the child or young person has led to chronic battles over control in the home. In another case, there might be concerns about the mental capacity of the person with parental responsibility, and whether they have capacity to take a decision about the child's treatment.

36.14 It is also possible that a decision on treatment could be outside the zone of parental control simply because of the nature of the proposed treatment, eg where, like electro-convulsive therapy (ECT), it could be considered particularly invasive or controversial.

36.15 In any case where reliance could not be placed on the consent of a person with parental responsibility, or on that of the child or young person, consideration should be given to alternative ways to treat them. One way would be to apply to have the child or young person detained under the Mental Health Act, but this is available only where they meet all the criteria for such detention. In cases where they do not meet the criteria, it may be appropriate to seek authorisation from the court.

Care for children whose liberty must be restricted – when might the Mental Health Act or the Children Act be appropriate?

36.16 There is no minimum age limit for detention in hospital under the Mental Health Act. It may be used to detain children or young people where that is justified by the risk posed by their mental disorder and all the relevant criteria are met.

36.17 However, where the child or young person with a mental disorder needs to be detained, but the primary purpose is not to provide medical treatment for mental disorder, consideration should be given to using section 25 of the Children Act 1989.

36.18 For example, if a child or young person is seriously mentally ill, they may require to be admitted for treatment under the Mental Health Act. But if they are behaviourally disturbed, and there is no need for them to be hospitalised, their needs might be more appropriately met within secure accommodation under the Children Act. Professionals who address these questions should:

- be aware of the relevant statutory provisions and have easy access to competent legal advice;
- keep in mind the importance of ensuring that the care and treatment of the child or young person are managed with clarity and consistency and within a recognisable framework (such as the child and adolescent mental health services (CAMHS) Care Programme Approach); and
- attempt to select the option that reflects the predominant needs of the child or young person at that time, whether that is to provide specific mental healthcare and treatment or to achieve a measure of safety and protection. In any event, the least restrictive option consistent with the care and treatment objectives for the child or young person should be adopted.

Decisions on admission and treatment of under 18s

36.19 The decision to admit a child or young person to hospital is inextricably linked to the decision to treat them once they have been admitted. But they may need to be considered separately in light of the different provisions that are relevant to each decision.

36.20 At least one of the people involved in the assessment of a person who is under 18 years old, ie one of the two medical practitioners or the approved mental health professional (AMHP), should be a clinician specialising in CAMHS. Where this is not possible, a CAMHS clinician should be consulted as soon as possible. In cases where the child or young person has complex or multiple needs, other clinicians may need to be involved, eg a learning disability CAMHS consultant where the child or young person has a learning disability. See **chapter 4** for fuller information on the assessment process.

Informal admission and treatment of 16 or 17 year olds

36.21 The law about admission and treatment of young people aged 16 or 17 differs from that for children under 16. But in both cases, whether they are capable of consenting to what is proposed is of central importance.

Informal admission of 16 and 17 year olds with capacity to consent

36.22 A decision about admission for informal treatment of a 16 or 17 year old who has capacity must be made in accordance with section 131 of the Mental Health Act. Section 131 of the Act provides that where a patient who is 16 or 17 years old has capacity (as defined in the MCA) to consent to being admitted to hospital for treatment of a mental disorder, they themselves may consent or not consent to being admitted, regardless of the views of a person with parental responsibility. This means that if a young person who is 16 or 17 years old, and who has the capacity to make such a decision, consents to being admitted for treatment, they can be treated as an informal patient in accordance with section 131, even if a person with parental responsibility is refusing consent.

36.23 Section 131 also applies to a patient who is 16 or 17 years old and has capacity but does not consent (for whatever reason, including being overwhelmed by the implications of the decision) or who refuses consent, so in these circumstances a person with parental responsibility cannot consent on their behalf. In such cases, consideration should be given to whether the patient satisfies all the criteria for detention under the Act. If those criteria are not satisfied, but treatment in hospital is thought to be in the patient's best interests, it may be necessary to seek authorisation from the court instead.

36.24 If the young person is admitted informally, the considerations set out from **paragraph 36.27** onwards will apply to their treatment.

Informal admission of 16 and 17 year olds who lack capacity to consent

36.25 Different considerations apply to a decision to informally admit a young person aged 16 or 17 where the young person lacks capacity. Section 131 of the Act does not apply. The MCA may apply in the same way as it does to those who are aged 18 or over, unless the admission and treatment amounts to a deprivation of liberty. If there is a deprivation of liberty, admission of a 16 or 17 year old cannot be authorised under the MCA, and the legality of any such admission should be assessed under common law principles.

36.26 Common law principles allow a person with parental responsibility in these circumstances to consent, but only if the matter is within the zone of parental control. If it is outside the zone, then consideration should be given to whether the young person meets all the criteria for detention under the Mental Health Act. If the Act is not applicable, it may be necessary to seek authorisation from the court.

Informal treatment of 16 and 17 year olds who are capable of consenting

36.27 Special provision is made for the treatment of young people. By virtue of section 8 of the Family Law Reform Act 1969, people who are 16 or 17 years old are presumed to be capable of consenting to their own medical treatment and to any ancillary procedures involved in that treatment, such as an anaesthetic.

36.28 This test is different from that in section 131 of the Mental Health Act. A young person who has capacity to consent (within the meaning of the MCA) may nonetheless not be capable of consenting in a particular case, for example because they are overwhelmed by the implications of the relevant decision.

36.29 As would apply in the case of an adult, consent will be valid only if it is given voluntarily by an appropriately informed patient capable of consenting to the particular intervention. However, unlike in the case of an adult, the refusal by a person aged 16 or 17 to consent may in certain circumstances be overridden by a court.

36.30 Section 8 of the Family Law Reform Act applies only to the young person's own treatment. It does not apply to an intervention that is not potentially of direct health benefit to the young person, such as non-therapeutic research into the causes of a disorder. However, a young person may be able to consent to such an intervention if they have the understanding and ability to do so.

36.31 When assessing whether a young person is capable of consent, the same criteria should be used as for adults.

36.32 If the young person is capable of giving valid consent and does so, then it is not legally necessary to obtain consent from a person with parental responsibility as well. It is, however, good practice to involve the young person's family in the decision-making process, if the young person consents to their information being shared.

36.33 When a young person refuses consent, the courts in the past have found that a person with parental responsibility can overrule their refusal in non-emergency cases. However, there is no post-Human Rights Act decision on this, and the trend in recent cases is to reflect greater autonomy for under 18s in law. In the Department of Health's view, it is not wise to rely on the consent of a person with parental responsibility to treat a young person who refuses in these circumstances. Consideration should be given to whether the young person meets all the criteria for detention under the Mental Health Act. If they do not, it may be necessary to seek authorisation from the court.

36.34 In an emergency, where a 16 or 17 year old who is capable of consenting refuses to have treatment, it is likely that the young person's decision could be overruled and the clinician could act without anyone's consent if the refusal would in all likelihood lead to their death or to severe permanent injury.

Informal treatment of 16 and 17 year olds who are not capable of consenting

36.35 Different considerations also apply to a decision to treat a young person aged 16 or 17 informally where the young person lacks capacity or is otherwise not capable of consenting. Where the young person lacks capacity, the MCA will apply in the same way as it does to those aged 18 and over, unless the treatment amounts to a deprivation of liberty.

36.36 If the treatment amounts to a deprivation of liberty, it cannot be authorised under the MCA for a 16 or 17 year old, and the legality of any such treatment should be assessed under common law principles.

36.37 Common law principles will also apply if the young person has capacity to consent (as defined in the MCA) but for some other reason is not capable of consenting, for example because they are overwhelmed by the implications of the decision. This means that a person with parental responsibility could consent on their behalf if the matter is within the zone of parental control. If it is not, then consideration should be given to whether the young person meets all the criteria for detention under the Mental Health Act. If they do not, it may be necessary to seek authorisation from the court.

Under 16s

What is Gillick competence?

36.38 In the case of *Gillick*,[18] the court held that children who have sufficient understanding and intelligence to enable them to understand fully what is involved in a proposed intervention will also have the competence to consent to that intervention. This is sometimes described as being '*Gillick* competent'. A child may be *Gillick* competent to consent to admission to hospital, medical treatment, research or any other activity that requires their consent.

36.39 The concept of *Gillick* competence is said to reflect the child's increasing development to maturity. The understanding required for different interventions will vary considerably. A child may have the competence to consent to some interventions but not others. The child's competence to consent should be assessed carefully in relation to each decision that needs to be made.

36.40 In some cases, for example because of a mental disorder, a child's mental state may fluctuate significantly, so that on some occasions the child appears to be *Gillick* competent in respect of a particular decision and on other occasions does not. In cases such as these, careful consideration should be given to whether the child is truly *Gillick* competent at any time to take a relevant decision.

36.41 If the child is *Gillick* competent and is able to give voluntary consent after receiving appropriate information, that consent will be valid and additional consent by a person with parental responsibility will not be required. It is, however, good practice to involve the child's parents, guardian or carers in the decision-making process, if the child consents to their information being shared.

Informal admission and treatment of under 16s who are Gillick competent

36.42 Where a child who is *Gillick* competent consents, they may be admitted to hospital as an informal patient. Where a child who is *Gillick* competent to do so has

---

[18] *Gillick v West Norfolk and Wisbech Area Health Authority* [1986] AC 112.

consented to being admitted informally, they may be given treatment if they are competent to consent to it and do consent. Consent should be sought for each aspect of the child's care and treatment as it arises. 'Blanket' consent forms should not be used.

36.43 Where a child who is *Gillick* competent refuses to be admitted for treatment, in the past the courts have held that a person with parental responsibility can overrule their refusal. However, there is no post-Human Rights Act decision on this. The trend in recent cases is to reflect greater autonomy for competent under 18s, so it may be unwise to rely on the consent of a person with parental responsibility.

36.44 Consideration should be given to whether the child meets all the criteria for detention under the Mental Health Act. If they do not, it may be appropriate to seek authorisation from the court, except in cases where the child's refusal would be likely to lead to their death or to severe permanent injury, in which case the child could be admitted to hospital and treated without consent.

Informal admission and treatment of under 16s who are not Gillick competent

36.45 Where a child is not *Gillick* competent, it will usually be possible for a person with parental responsibility to consent on their behalf to their informal admission to hospital for treatment for mental disorder.

36.46 Before relying on parental consent in relation to a child who is under 16 years old and who is not *Gillick* competent, an assessment should be made of whether the matter is within the zone of parental control.

36.47 A child's views should be taken into account, even if they are not *Gillick* competent. How much weight the child's views should be given will depend on how mature the child is. Where a child has been *Gillick* competent to make a decision but then loses competence, any views they expressed before losing competence should be taken into account and may act as parameters limiting the zone of parental control. For example, if a child has expressed willingness to receive one form of treatment but not another while *Gillick* competent but then loses competence, it might not be appropriate to give the treatment to the child as an informal patient where the child has previously refused it, even if a person with parental responsibility consents.

36.48 If the decision regarding the admission and treatment of a child (including how the child is to be kept safely in one place) is within the zone of parental control, and consent is given by a person with parental responsibility, then the clinician may rely on that consent and admit and treat the child as an informal patient on that basis.

36.49 The fact that a parent or other person with parental responsibility has informally admitted a child should not lead professionals to assume that consent has been given to all components of a treatment programme regarded as 'necessary'. Consent should be sought for each aspect of the child's care and treatment as it arises. 'Blanket' consent forms should not be used.

36.50 If the decision is not within the zone of parental control, or the consent of a person with parental responsibility is not given, the child cannot be admitted and treated informally on the basis of the parent's consent. An application can be made under the Mental Health Act if the child meets all the criteria for detention under the Act. If the criteria are not met, it may be necessary to seek authorisation from the court.

Emergency treatment

36.51 A life-threatening emergency may arise when a patient who is under 18 is capable of consenting to a treatment but refuses to do so, or where a person with parental responsibility could consent but there is no time to seek their consent, or where they are refusing consent and there is no time to seek authorisation from the court. In such cases, the courts have stated that doubt should be resolved in favour of the preservation of life, and it will be acceptable to undertake treatment to preserve life or prevent irreversible serious deterioration of the patient's condition.

Treatments for under 18s regulated by the Mental Health Act

36.52 Treatment for mental disorder for under 18s is regulated by the Act when the patient is:

- detained;
- on supervised community treatment (SCT); or
- for some treatments, an informal patient.

36.53 Even where treatment under the Act does not require consent, the safeguards differ depending on whether the patient is able to and does consent, so it is important to know whether the patient is able to and does consent.

Treatment requiring the patient's consent (section 57)

36.54 Treatment covered by section 57 of the Act (primarily neurosurgery for mental disorder) cannot be given to a child or young person who does not personally consent to it, whether they are detained or not. These treatments cannot, therefore, be given to any young person or child who is not capable of consenting, even if a person with parental responsibility consents.

Electro-convulsive therapy (section 58A)

36.55 There is provision in the Act about treatment with ECT of patients who are under 18 which applies whether they are being informally treated or are detained under the Act.

36.56 Detained patients cannot be given ECT without their consent, if they are capable of consenting to the treatment, unless it is an emergency. If they are not capable of consenting, or if it is an emergency, they may be given ECT without their consent in accordance with rules described in **chapter 24**.

36.57 The same applies to SCT patients, except that, even in emergencies, if they have capacity or competence they may be given ECT without consent only if they have been recalled to hospital.

36.58 In addition, no child or young person under the age of 18 may be given ECT without the approval of a second opinion appointed doctor (SOAD), unless it is an emergency, even if they consent to it.

36.59 There is nothing in the Act itself to prevent a person with parental responsibility consenting to ECT on behalf of a child or young person who lacks the ability to consent for themselves and who is neither detained nor an SCT patient.

36.60 However, although there is no case law at present directly on this point, it would not be prudent to rely on such consent, because it is likely to lie outside the parental zone of control. Therefore, if a child under 16 who is not detained or an SCT patient needs ECT, court authorisation should be sought, unless it is an emergency. This should be done before a SOAD is asked to approve the treatment. In practice, the issues the court is likely to address will mirror those that the SOAD is required to consider.

36.61 This will also be the case for young people of 16 or 17 who are not detained or SCT patients and who lack the ability to consent for themselves, except where the MCA could be used to provide the necessary authority. The MCA can be used for this only where it is not necessary to deprive the young person of liberty.[19] As in cases where court authorisation is obtained, a SOAD certificate will still be needed, unless it is an emergency.

36.62 Children and young people who are not detained under the Act but may require ECT are eligible for access to independent mental health advocates.[20]

Other treatment under the Act – detained and SCT patients only

36.63 The Act itself sets out when detained and SCT patients (of all ages) can be given other types of treatment for mental disorder, such as the requirement in section 58 for consent or a second opinion before medication can be given to detained patients after the initial period of three months. People with parental responsibility are not required to consent to such treatment on behalf of children and young people in this position.

Supervised community treatment

36.64 There is no lower age limit for SCT. The number of children and young people whose clinical and family circumstances make them suitable to move from being detained to having SCT is likely to be small, but it should be used where appropriate.

36.65 Parents (or other people with parental responsibility) may not consent on a child's behalf to treatment for mental disorder (or refuse it) while the child is on SCT. However, if SCT patients under the age of 18 are living with one or both parents, the person giving the treatment should consult with the parent(s) about the particular treatment (subject to the normal considerations of patient confidentiality), bearing in mind that if there is something that the parents would not accept, it would make it very difficult for the patient to live with their parents while on SCT. This dialogue should continue throughout the patient's treatment on SCT. If a parent is unhappy with the

---

[19] The word 'not' was accidently omitted from the version of the code presented to Parliament, making the sentence factually incorrect. The MCA cannot be used to authorise deprivation of liberty of a person under 18.

[20] Independent mental health advocacy services under the Act were introduced in April 2009.

particular treatment or conditions attached to SCT, and the child is not competent to consent, a review by the patient's team should take place to consider whether the treatment and care plan, and SCT in general, are still appropriate for the child.

Applications to the High Court

36.66 In certain situations where decisions about admitting a child or young person informally or giving treatment need to be made, but the action cannot be taken under the MCA and it is not appropriate to use the Mental Health Act, the assistance of the High Court may be sought. Consideration will need to be given to whether an application should be made under the inherent jurisdiction or for a section 8 order under the Children Act 1989. This will depend on the facts of each case. Where a child is under 16, an application should be considered, in particular where the child:

- is not *Gillick* competent and where the person with parental responsibility cannot be identified or is incapacitated;
- is not *Gillick* competent and where one person with parental responsibility consents but another strongly disagrees and is likely to take the matter to court themselves;
- is not *Gillick* competent and where there is concern that the person with parental responsibility may not be acting in the best interests of the child in making treatment decisions on behalf of the child, eg where hostility between parents is a factor in any decision making or where there are concerns as to whether a person with parental responsibility is capable of making a decision in the best interests of the child;
- is not *Gillick* competent and where a person with parental responsibility consents but the decision is not within the zone of parental control, eg where the treatment in question is ECT; or
- is *Gillick* competent or is a young person who is capable of making a decision on their treatment and is refusing treatment.

Age-appropriate services[21]

36.67 Section 131A of the Act says that children and young people admitted to hospital for the treatment of mental disorder should be accommodated in an environment that is suitable for their age (subject to their needs).

36.68 This means that children and young people should have:

- appropriate physical facilities;
- staff with the right training, skills and knowledge to understand and address their specific needs as children and young people;

---

21 This duty is expected to be in force from April 2010, but hospital managers should take all the steps they reasonably can to comply with the duty even before it comes into force. The Secretary of State recognises that some hospitals will not be able to do so fully immediately.

- a hospital routine that will allow their personal, social and educational development to continue as normally as possible; and

- equal access to educational opportunities as their peers, in so far as that is consistent with their ability to make use of them, considering their mental state.

36.69 Hospital managers should ensure that the environment is suitable, and in reaching their determination they must consult a person whom they consider to be suitable because they are experienced in CAMHS cases.

36.70 If, exceptionally, a patient cannot be accommodated in a dedicated child or adolescent ward, then discrete accommodation in an adult ward, with facilities, security and staffing appropriate to the needs of the child, might provide the most satisfactory solution, eg young female patients should be placed in single-sex accommodation. Where possible, all those involved in the care and treatment of children and young people should be child specialists. Anyone who looks after them must always have enhanced disclosure clearance from the Criminal Records Bureau and that clearance must be kept up to date.

36.71 In a small number of cases, the patient's need to be accommodated in a safe environment could, in the short term, take precedence over the suitability of that environment for their age. Furthermore, it is also important to recognise that there is a clear difference between what is a suitable environment for a child or young person in an emergency situation and what is a suitable environment for a child or young person on a longer-term basis. In an emergency, such as when the patient is in crisis, the important thing is that the patient is in a safe environment. Once the initial emergency situation is over, hospital managers, in determining whether the environment continues to be suitable, would need to consider issues such as whether the patient can mix with individuals of their own age, can receive visitors of all ages and has access to education. Hospital managers have a duty to consider whether a patient should be transferred to more appropriate accommodation and, if so, to arrange this as soon as possible.

36.72 There will be times when the assessment concludes that the best place for an under 18 year old is an adult ward. This may happen when the young person is very close to their 18th birthday, and placing the young person on a CAMHS ward for a matter of weeks or days and then transferring them to an adult ward would be counter-therapeutic. In some cases the young person may express a preference to be on an adult ward, such as when they are under the care of the early intervention psychosis team and they wish to go to the ward when the team rotates rather than to a unit with much younger children.

36.73 Where a young patient's presence on a ward with other children and young people might have a detrimental effect on the other young patients, the hospital managers need to ensure that the interests of other patients are protected. However, the needs of other patients should not override the need to provide accommodation in an environment that is suitable for the patient's age (subject to their needs) for an individual patient aged under 18.

36.74 Children and young people aged under 18 should also have access to age-appropriate leisure activities and facilities for visits from parents, guardians, siblings or carers.

The responsible clinician and others caring for and treating under 18s

36.75 Where possible, those responsible for the care and treatment of children and young people should be child specialists. Where this is not possible, it is good practice for the clinical staff to have regular access to and make use of a CAMHS specialist for advice and consultation.

Rights to apply to the Tribunal

36.76 Children and young people who are detained under the Mental Health Act have the same rights as other patients to apply to the Tribunal. It is important that children and young people are given assistance so that they get access to legal representation at an early stage. In addition, hospital managers should bear in mind that their duties to refer patients to the Tribunal are different in respect of patients who are under 18 years old. Where older patients must be referred after a three-year period without a Tribunal hearing, children and young people must be referred after one year.

Education

36.77 No child or young person below the school leaving age should be denied access to learning merely because they are receiving medical treatment for a mental disorder. Young people over school leaving age should be encouraged to continue learning.

Confidentiality

36.78 All children and young people have a right to confidentiality. Under 16s who are *Gillick* competent and young people aged 16 or 17 are entitled to make decisions about the use and disclosure of information they have provided in confidence in the same way as adults. For example, they may be receiving treatment or counselling that they do not want their parents to know about. However, there are circumstances when the duty of care to the patient might require confidentiality to be breached to the extent of informing those with parental responsibility.

36.79 The decision to disclose information to parents and others with parental responsibility is complex for this age group and depends on a range of factors, including:

- the child or young person's age and developmental level;
- their maturity;
- their ability to take into account the future as well as the present;
- the severity of the mental disorder and the risks posed to themselves and to others;
- the degree of care and protection required;
- the degree of the parents' involvement in the care of the child or young person;
- the closeness of the relationship with the parents; and

- the current competence of the child or young person to make a decision about confidentiality.

In addition, it should be noted that competence to take a decision about information sharing, as with treatment, may change over time.

Duties of local authorities in relation to hospital patients

36.80 Local authorities should ensure that they arrange for visits to be made to:

- children and young people looked after by them who are in hospital, whether or not they are under a care order; and
- children and young people accommodated or intended to be accommodated for three months or more by NHS bodies, local education authorities or care homes.[22] This is in addition to their duty in respect of children and young people in their care in hospitals or nursing homes in England and Wales as required by section 116 of the Act. Local authorities should take such other steps in relation to the patient while they are in hospital or a nursing home as would be expected to be taken by the patient's parent(s).

36.81 Local authorities are under a duty in the Children Act 1989 to:

- promote contact between children and young people who are in need and their families, if they live away from home, and to help them get back together (paragraphs 10 and 15 of Schedule 2 to the Children Act); and
- arrange for people (independent visitors) to visit and befriend children and young people looked after by the authority, wherever they are, if they have not been regularly visited by their parents (paragraph 17 of Schedule 2 to the Act).

36.82 Local authorities should be alerted if the whereabouts of the person with parental responsibility is not known or if that person has not visited the child or young person for a significant period of time. When alerted to this situation, the local authority should consider whether visits should be arranged.

Related material

- Children Act 1989 and guidance (particularly volumes 1, 4, 6 and 7).
- National Service Framework for Children, Young People and Maternity Services – Standard 9 (The Mental Health and Psychological Well-being of Children and Young People) issued by the Department for Education and Skills and the Department of Health in October 2004.
- *Every Child Matters: Change for Children*, Department for Education and Skills, 2004.

---

22 See the Review of Children's Cases Regulations 1991 (Statutory Instrument 1991/895 as amended) and sections 85 and 86 of the Children Act 1989.

- *NHS Confidentiality Code of Practice*, Department of Health, 2003.
- *Working Together to Safeguard Children*, HM Government, 2006.

This material does not form part of the Code. It is provided for assistance only.

The following flow charts are for information only and do not form part of the Code, and they should be read in conjunction with the text in this chapter.

Informal admission and treatment of under 16s

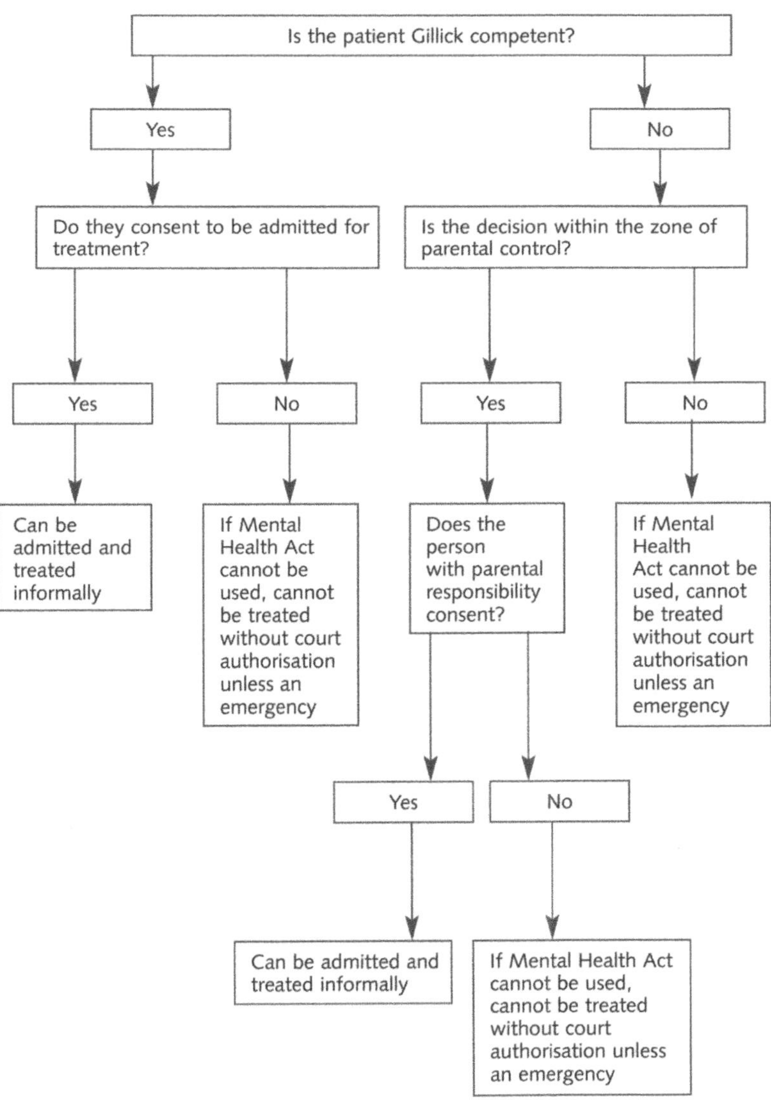
Is the patient Gillick competent?
Yes
No
Do they consent to be admitted for treatment?
Is the decision within the zone of parental control?
Yes
No
Yes
No
Can be admitted and treated informally
If Mental Health Act cannot be used, cannot be treated without court authorisation unless an emergency
Does the person with parental responsibility consent?
If Mental Health Act cannot be used, cannot be treated without court authorisation unless an emergency
Yes
No
Can be admitted and treated informally
If Mental Health Act cannot be used, cannot be treated without court authorisation unless an emergency

Informal admission of 16 and 17 year olds

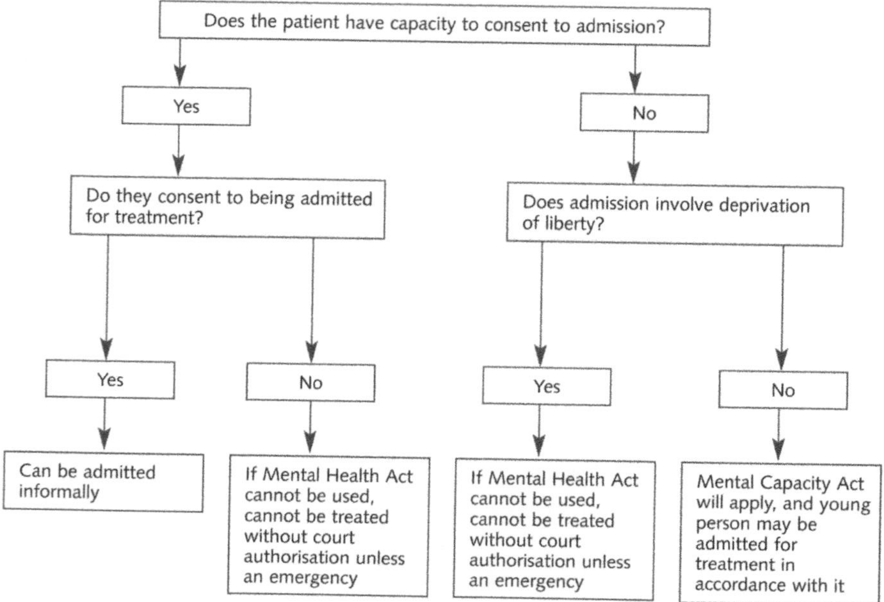
Does the patient have capacity to consent to admission?
Yes
No
Do they consent to being admitted for treatment?
Does admission involve deprivation of liberty?
Yes
No
Yes
No
Can be admitted informally
If Mental Health Act cannot be used, cannot be treated without court authorisation unless an emergency
If Mental Health Act cannot be used, cannot be treated without court authorisation unless an emergency
Mental Capacity Act will apply, and young person may be admitted for treatment in accordance with it

Informal treatment of 16 and 17 year olds

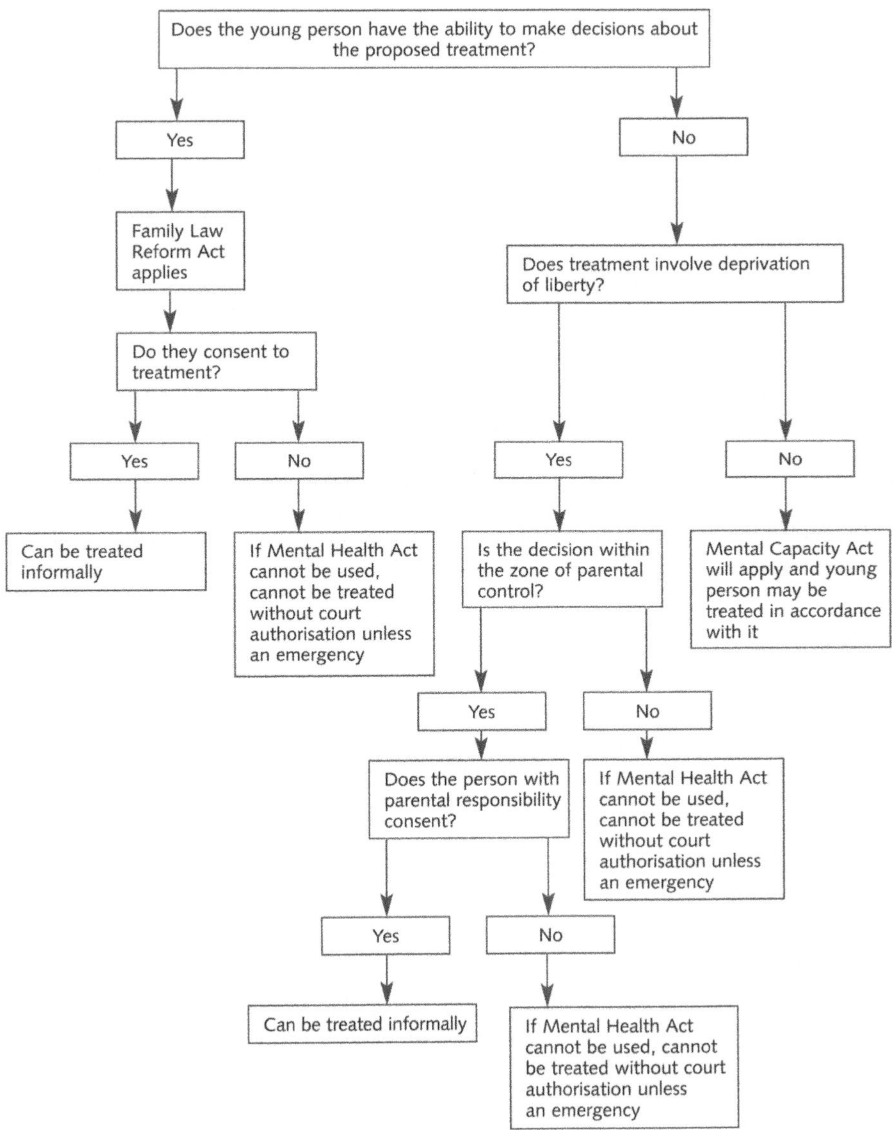
Does the young person have the ability to make decisions about the proposed treatment?
Yes
No
Family Law Reform Act applies
Do they consent to treatment?
Yes
No
Can be treated informally
If Mental Health Act cannot be used, cannot be treated without court authorisation unless an emergency
Does treatment involve deprivation of liberty?
Yes
No
Is the decision within the zone of parental control?
Mental Capacity Act will apply and young person may be treated in accordance with it
Yes
No
Does the person with parental responsibility consent?
If Mental Health Act cannot be used, cannot be treated without court authorisation unless an emergency
Yes
No
Can be treated informally
If Mental Health Act cannot be used, cannot be treated without court authorisation unless an emergency

Note: A decision on treatment could be outside the zone of parental control simply because of the nature of the proposed treatment, eg where, like ECT, it could be considered particularly invasive or controversial (see **paragraphs 36.9-36.15**)

Examples

36.83 The following examples should be read in conjunction with the preceding flow charts.

Example A

A 13 year old child is assessed as not being *Gillick* competent. The primary purpose of the intervention is to provide medical treatment for mental disorder. The decision to authorise treatment falls within the zone of parental control, as what is proposed is fairly standard, but no person with parental responsibility consents. The child cannot be admitted informally under section 131(1) of the Mental Health Act. If the child meets the relevant criteria, the child could be admitted to hospital for assessment (section 2) or for treatment (section 3) under the Act.

Example B

A 14 year old girl is assessed as not being *Gillick* competent. The primary purpose of the intervention is to provide medical treatment for mental disorder, but she is severely anorexic and this will involve force feeding. This is likely to take it outside the zone of parental control, so even though a person with parental responsibility consents, it is unlikely that the child can be admitted informally under section 131(1). If the child meets the relevant criteria, she could be admitted to hospital for assessment (section 2) or for treatment (section 3) under the Act.

Example C

A 15 year old child is assessed as being *Gillick* competent. The primary purpose of the intervention is to provide medical treatment for mental disorder. The child does not consent to treatment in hospital. The child's parents are keen for the child to be admitted to hospital and give their consent. However, it is not considered safe to rely on the parents' consent where a *Gillick*-competent child is refusing. The child cannot be admitted informally under section 131(1). If the child meets the relevant criteria, the child could be admitted to hospital for assessment (section 2) or for treatment (section 3) under the Act.

Example D

A 16 year old young person is assessed as being able to make decisions about the proposed intervention. The primary purpose of the intervention is to provide medical treatment for mental disorder. The young person consents to treatment in hospital (and they do not need to be detained). The young person should be treated as an informal patient.

Example E

A 17 year old young person is assessed as not having the capacity to make decisions about the proposed intervention. The MCA could be used to authorise treatment if the criteria for its use are met.

Example F

A 15 year old is assessed as not being able to make decisions about the proposed intervention. The primary purpose of the intervention is not to provide medical treatment for mental disorder but to provide safety and protection. Consideration should be given to using section 25 of the Children Act.

Part F

STATUTORY MATERIALS (INCLUDING TRIBUNAL RULES AND PRACTICE DIRECTION)

F1

F1

MENTAL HEALTH ACT 1983

ARRANGEMENT OF SECTIONS

PART II
COMPULSORY ADMISSION TO HOSPITAL AND GUARDIANSHIP

Guardianship

Hospital and guardianship orders

Restriction orders

PART 4A

TREATMENT OF COMMUNITY PATIENTS NOT RECALLED TO HOSPITAL

PART V

MENTAL HEALTH REVIEW TRIBUNALS

Constitution etc.

Applications and references concerning Part II patients

Applications and references concerning Part III patients

Discharge of patients

General

PART VIII

MISCELLANEOUS FUNCTIONS OF LOCAL AUTHORITIES AND THE SECRETARY OF STATE

Visiting patients

After-care

PART X
MISCELLANEOUS AND SUPPLEMENTARY

*****

PART II
COMPULSORY ADMISSION TO HOSPITAL AND GUARDIANSHIP

*****

Guardianship

7 Application for guardianship

(1) A patient who has attained the age of 16 years may be received into guardianship, for the period allowed by the following provisions of this Act, in pursuance of an application (in this Act referred to as "a guardianship application") made in accordance with this section.

(2) A guardianship application may be made in respect of a patient on the grounds that –

(a) he is suffering from mental disorder of a nature or degree which warrants his reception into guardianship under this section; and
(b) it is necessary in the interests of the welfare of the patient or for the protection of other persons that the patient should be so received.

(3) A guardianship application shall be founded on the written recommendations in the prescribed form of two registered medical practitioners, including in each case a statement that in the opinion of the practitioner the conditions set out in subsection (2) above are complied with; and each such recommendation shall include –

(a) such particulars as may be prescribed of the grounds for that opinion so far as it relates to the conditions set out in paragraph (a) of that subsection; and
(b) a statement of the reasons for that opinion so far as it relates to the conditions set out in paragraph (b) of that subsection.

(4) A guardianship application shall state the age of the patient or, if his exact age is not known to the applicant, shall state (if it be the fact) that the patient is believed to have attained the age of 16 years.

(5) The person named as guardian in a guardianship application may be either a local social services authority or any other person (including the applicant himself); but a guardianship application in which a person other than a local social services authority is named as guardian shall be of no effect unless it is accepted on behalf of that person by

the local social services authority for the area in which he resides, and shall be accompanied by a statement in writing by that person that he is willing to act as guardian.

Amendments—Mental Health Act 2007, ss 1(4), 55, Sch 1, Pt 1, paras 1, 3, Sch 11, Pt 1.

8 Effect of guardianship application, etc

(1) Where a guardianship application, duly made under the provisions of this Part of this Act and forwarded to the local social services authority within the period allowed by subsection (2) below is accepted by that authority, the application shall, subject to regulations made by the Secretary of State, confer on the authority or person named in the application as guardian, to the exclusion of any other person –

- (a) the power to require the patient to reside at a place specified by the authority or person named as guardian;
- (b) the power to require the patient to attend at places and times so specified for the purpose of medical treatment, occupation, education or training;
- (c) the power to require access to the patient to be given, at any place where the patient is residing, to any registered medical practitioner, approved mental health professional or other person so specified.

(2) The period within which a guardianship application is required for the purposes of this section to be forwarded to the local social services authority is the period of 14 days beginning with the date on which the patient was last examined by a registered medical practitioner before giving a medical recommendation for the purposes of the application.

(3) A guardianship application which appears to be duly made and to be founded on the necessary medical recommendations may be acted upon without further proof of the signature or qualification of the person by whom the application or any such medical recommendation is made or given, or of any matter of fact or opinion stated in the application.

(4) If within the period of 14 days beginning with the day on which a guardianship application has been accepted by the local social services authority the application, or any medical recommendation given for the purposes of the application, is found to be in any respect incorrect or defective, the application or recommendation may, within that period and with the consent of that authority, be amended by the person by whom it was signed; and upon such amendment being made the application or recommendation shall have effect and shall be deemed to have had effect as if it had been originally made as so amended.

(5) Where a patient is received into guardianship in pursuance of a guardianship application, any previous application under this Part of this Act by virtue of which he was subject to guardianship or liable to be detained in a hospital shall cease to have effect.

Amendments—Mental Health Act 2007, s 21, Sch 2, paras 1, 2(b).

*****

General provisions as to applications and recommendations

11 General provisions as to applications

(1) Subject to the provisions of this section, an application for admission for assessment, an application for admission for treatment and a guardianship application may be made either by the nearest relative of the patient or by an approved mental health professional; and every such application shall specify the qualification of the applicant to make the application.

(1A) No application mentioned in subsection (1) above shall be made by an approved mental health professional if the circumstances are such that there would be a potential conflict of interest for the purposes of regulations under section 12A below.

(2) Every application for admission shall be addressed to the managers of the hospital to which admission is sought and every guardianship application shall be forwarded to the local social services authority named in the application as guardian, or, as the case may be, to the local social services authority for the area in which the person so named resides.

(3) Before or within a reasonable time after an application for the admission of a patient for assessment is made by an approved mental health professional, that professional shall take such steps as are practicable to inform the person (if any) appearing to be the nearest relative of the patient that the application is to be or has been made and of the power of the nearest relative under section 23(2)(a) below.

(4) An approved mental health professional may not make an application for admission for treatment or a guardianship application in respect of a patient in either of the following cases –

(a) the nearest relative of the patient has notified that professional, or the local social services authority on whose behalf the professional is acting, that he objects to the application being made; or

(b) that professional has not consulted the person (if any) appearing to be the nearest relative of the patient, but the requirement to consult that person does not apply if it appears to the professional that in the circumstances such consultation is not reasonably practicable or would involve unreasonable delay.

(5) None of the applications mentioned in subsection (1) above shall be made by any person in respect of a patient unless that person has personally seen the patient within the period of 14 days ending with the date of the application.

(6) (*repealed*)

(7) Each of the applications mentioned in subsection (1) above shall be sufficient if the recommendations on which it is founded are given either as separate recommendations, each signed by a registered medical practitioner, or as a joint recommendation signed by two such practitioners.

Amendments—Mental Health Act 2007, ss 21, 22(1), (2), 55, Sch 2, paras 1, 4, Sch 11, Pt 1.

*****

13 Duty of approved mental health professionals to make applications for admission or guardianship

(1) If a local social services authority have reason to think that an application for admission to hospital or a guardianship application may need to be made in respect of a

patient within their area, they shall make arrangements for an approved mental health professional to consider the patient's case on their behalf.

(1A) If that professional is –

(a) satisfied that such an application ought to be made in respect of the patient; and

(b) of the opinion, having regard to any wishes expressed by relatives of the patient or any other relevant circumstances, that it is necessary or proper for the application to be made by him,

he shall make the application.

(1B) Subsection (1C) below applies where –

(a) a local social services authority makes arrangements under subsection (1) above in respect of a patient;

(b) an application for admission for assessment is made under subsection (1A) above in respect of the patient;

(c) while the patient is liable to be detained in pursuance of that application, the authority have reason to think that an application for admission for treatment may need to be made in respect of the patient; and

(d) the patient is not within the area of the authority.

(1C) Where this subsection applies, subsection (1) above shall be construed as requiring the authority to make arrangements under that subsection in place of the authority mentioned there.

(2) Before making an application for the admission of a patient to hospital an approved mental health professional shall interview the patient in a suitable manner and satisfy himself that detention in a hospital is in all the circumstances of the case the most appropriate way of providing the care and medical treatment of which the patient stands in need.

(3) An application under subsection (1A) above may be made outside the area of the local social services authority on whose behalf the approved mental health professional is considering the patient's case.

(4) It shall be the duty of a local social services authority, if so required by the nearest relative of a patient residing in their area, to make arrangements under subsection (1) above for an approved mental health professional to consider the patient's case with a view to making an application for his admission to hospital; and if in any such case that professional decides not to make an application he shall inform the nearest relative of his reasons in writing.

(5) Nothing in this section shall be construed as authorising or requiring an application to be made by an approved mental health professional in contravention of the provisions of section 11(4) above or of regulations under section 12A above, or as restricting the power of a local social services authority to make arrangements with an approved mental health professional to consider a patient's case or of an approved mental health professional to make any application under this Act.

Amendments—Mental Health Act 2007, ss 21, 22(1), (6), Sch 2, paras 1, 5.

14 Social Reports

Where a patient is admitted to a hospital in pursuance of an application (other than an emergency application) made under this Part of this Act by his nearest relative, the managers of the hospital shall as soon as practicable give notice of that fact to the local social services authority for the area in which the patient resided immediately before his admission; and that authority shall as soon as practicable arrange for an approved mental health professional to interview the patient and provide the managers with a report on his social circumstances.

Amendments—Children Act 2004, s 64, Sch 5, Pt 4; Mental Health Act 2007, s 21, Sch 2, paras 1, 6.

*****

17A Community treatment orders

(1) The responsible clinician may by order in writing discharge a detained patient from hospital subject to his being liable to recall in accordance with section 17E below.

(2) A detained patient is a patient who is liable to be detained in a hospital in pursuance of an application for admission for treatment.

(3) An order under subsection (1) above is referred to in this Act as a "community treatment order".

(4) The responsible clinician may not make a community treatment order unless –

- (a) in his opinion, the relevant criteria are met; and
- (b) an approved mental health professional states in writing –
  - (i) that he agrees with that opinion; and
  - (ii) that it is appropriate to make the order.

(5) The relevant criteria are –

- (a) the patient is suffering from mental disorder of a nature or degree which makes it appropriate for him to receive medical treatment;
- (b) it is necessary for his health or safety or for the protection of other persons that he should receive such treatment;
- (c) subject to his being liable to be recalled as mentioned in paragraph (d) below, such treatment can be provided without his continuing to be detained in a hospital;
- (d) it is necessary that the responsible clinician should be able to exercise the power under section 17E(1) below to recall the patient to hospital; and
- (e) appropriate medical treatment is available for him.

(6) In determining whether the criterion in subsection (5)(d) above is met, the responsible clinician shall, in particular, consider, having regard to the patient's history of mental disorder and any other relevant factors, what risk there would be of a deterioration of the patient's condition if he were not detained in a hospital (as a result, for example, of his refusing or neglecting to receive the medical treatment he requires for his mental disorder).

(7) In this Act –

"community patient" means a patient in respect of whom a community treatment order is in force;

"the community treatment order", in relation to such a patient, means the community treatment order in force in respect of him; and

"the responsible hospital", in relation to such a patient, means the hospital in which he was liable to be detained immediately before the community treatment order was made, subject to section 19A below.

Amendments—Inserted by the Mental Health Act 2007, s 32(1), (2).

17B Conditions

(1) A community treatment order shall specify conditions to which the patient is to be subject while the order remains in force.

(2) But, subject to subsection (3) below, the order may specify conditions only if the responsible clinician, with the agreement of the approved mental health professional mentioned in section 17A(4)(b) above, thinks them necessary or appropriate for one or more of the following purposes –

- (a) ensuring that the patient receives medical treatment;
- (b) preventing risk of harm to the patient's health or safety;
- (c) protecting other persons.

(3) The order shall specify –

- (a) a condition that the patient make himself available for examination under section 20A below; and
- (b) a condition that, if it is proposed to give a certificate under Part 4A of this Act that falls within section 64C(4) below in his case, he make himself available for examination so as to enable the certificate to be given.

(4) The responsible clinician may from time to time by order in writing vary the conditions specified in a community treatment order.

(5) He may also suspend any conditions specified in a community treatment order.

(6) If a community patient fails to comply with a condition specified in the community treatment order by virtue of subsection (2) above, that fact may be taken into account for the purposes of exercising the power of recall under section 17E(1) below.

(7) But nothing in this section restricts the exercise of that power to cases where there is such a failure.

Amendments—Inserted by the Mental Health Act 2007, s 32(1), (2); Health and Social Care Act 2012, s 299(1), (6).

17C Duration of community treatment order

A community treatment order shall remain in force until

- (a) the period mentioned in section 20A(1) below (as extended under any provision of this Act) expires, but this is subject to sections 21 and 22 below;
- (b) the patient is discharged in pursuance of an order under section 23 below or a direction under section 72 below;
- (c) the application for admission for treatment in respect of the patient otherwise ceases to have effect; or
- (d) the order is revoked under section 17F below, whichever occurs first.

Amendments—Inserted by the Mental Health Act 2007, s 32(1), (2); for transitional provisions and savings see SI 2008/1900, art 3, Schedule, paras 1, 12, Mental Health Act 2007, s 53, Sch 10, paras 1, 5.

17D Effect of community treatment order

(1) The application for admission for treatment in respect of a patient shall not cease to have effect by virtue of his becoming a community patient.

(2) But while he remains a community patient –

(a) the authority of the managers to detain him under section 6(2) above in pursuance of that application shall be suspended; and

(b) reference (however expressed) in this or any other Act, or in any subordinate legislation (within the meaning of the Interpretation Act 1978), to patients liable to be detained, or detained, under this Act shall not include him.

(3) And section 20 below shall not apply to him while he remains a community patient.

(4) Accordingly, authority for his detention shall not expire during any period in which that authority is suspended by virtue of subsection (2)(a) above.

Amendments—Inserted by the Mental Health Act 2007, s 32(1), (2); for transitional provisions and savings see SI 2008/1900, art 3, Schedule, paras 1, 12, Mental Health Act 2007, s 53, Sch 10, paras 1, 5.

17E Power to recall to hospital

(1) The responsible clinician may recall a community patient to hospital if in his opinion –

(a) the patient requires medical treatment in hospital for his mental disorder; and

(b) there would be a risk of harm to the health or safety of the patient or to other persons if the patient were not recalled to hospital for that purpose.

(2) The responsible clinician may also recall a community patient to hospital if the patient fails to comply with a condition specified under section 17B(3) above.

(3) The hospital to which a patient is recalled need not be the responsible hospital.

(4) Nothing in this section prevents a patient from being recalled to a hospital even though he is already in the hospital at the time when the power of recall is exercised; references to recalling him shall be construed accordingly.

(5) The power of recall under subsections (1) and (2) above shall be exercisable by notice in writing to the patient.

(6) A notice under this section recalling a patient to hospital shall be sufficient authority for the managers of that hospital to detain the patient there in accordance with the provisions of this Act.

Amendments—Inserted by the Mental Health Act 2007, s 32(1), (2); for transitional provisions and savings see SI 2008/1900, art 3, Schedule, paras 1, 12, Mental Health Act 2007, s 53, Sch 10, paras 1, 5.

17F Powers in respect of recalled patients

(1) This section applies to a community patient who is detained in a hospital by virtue of a notice recalling him there under section 17E above.

(2) The patient may be transferred to another hospital in such circumstances and subject to such conditions as may be prescribed in regulations made by the Secretary of State (if the hospital in which the patient is detained is in England) or the Welsh Ministers (if that hospital is in Wales).

(3) If he is so transferred to another hospital, he shall be treated for the purposes of this section (and section 17E above) as if the notice under that section were a notice recalling him to that other hospital and as if he had been detained there from the time when his detention in hospital by virtue of the notice first began.

(4) The responsible clinician may by order in writing revoke the community treatment order if –

(a) in his opinion, the conditions mentioned in section 3(2) above are satisfied in respect of the patient; and
(b) an approved mental health professional states in writing –
  (i) that he agrees with that opinion; and
  (ii) that it is appropriate to revoke the order.

(5) The responsible clinician may at any time release the patient under this section, but not after the community treatment order has been revoked.

(6) If the patient has not been released, nor the community treatment order revoked, by the end of the period of 72 hours, he shall then be released.

(7) But a patient who is released under this section remains subject to the community treatment order.

(8) In this section –

(a) "the period of 72 hours" means the period of 72 hours beginning with the time when the patient's detention in hospital by virtue of the notice under section 17E above begins; and
(b) references to being released shall be construed as references to being released from that detention (and accordingly from being recalled to hospital).

Amendments—Inserted by the Mental Health Act 2007, s 32(1), (2); for transitional provisions and savings see SI 2008/1900, art 3, Schedule, paras 1, 12, Mental Health Act 2007, s 53, Sch 10, paras 1, 5.

17G Effect of revoking community treatment order

(1) This section applies if a community treatment order is revoked under section 17F above in respect of a patient.

(2) Section 6(2) above shall have effect as if the patient had never been discharged from hospital by virtue of the community treatment order.

(3) The provisions of this or any other Act relating to patients liable to be detained (or detained) in pursuance of an application for admission for treatment shall apply to the patient as they did before the community treatment order was made, unless otherwise provided.

(4) If, when the order is revoked, the patient is being detained in a hospital other than the responsible hospital, the provisions of this Part of this Act shall have effect as if –

(a) the application for admission for treatment in respect of him were an application for admission to that other hospital; and
(b) he had been admitted to that other hospital at the time when he was originally admitted in pursuance of the application.

(5) But, in any case, section 20 below shall have effect as if the patient had been admitted to hospital in pursuance of the application for admission for treatment on the day on which the order is revoked.

Amendments—Inserted by the Mental Health Act 2007, s 32(1), (2); for transitional provisions and savings see SI 2008/1900, art 3, Schedule, paras 1, 12, Mental Health Act 2007, s 53, Sch 10, paras 1, 5.

18 Return and readmission of patients absent without leave

(1) Where a patient who is for the time being liable to be detained under this Part of this Act in a hospital –

(a) absents himself from the hospital without leave granted under section 17 above; or
(b) fails to return to the hospital on any occasion on which, or at the expiration of any period for which, leave of absence was granted to him under that section, or upon being recalled under that section; or
(c) absents himself without permission from any place where he is required to reside in accordance with conditions imposed on the grant of leave of absence under that section,

he may, subject to the provisions of this section, be taken into custody and returned to the hospital or place by any approved mental health professional, by any officer on the staff of the hospital, by any constable, or by any person authorised in writing by the managers of the hospital.

(2) Where the place referred to in paragraph (c) of subsection (1) above is a hospital other than the one in which the patient is for the time being liable to be detained, the references in that subsection to an officer on the staff of the hospital and the managers of the hospital shall respectively include references to an officer on the staff of the first-mentioned hospital and the managers of that hospital.

(2A) Where a community patient is at any time absent from a hospital to which he is recalled under section 17E above, he may, subject to the provisions of this section, be taken into custody and returned to the hospital by any approved mental health professional, by any officer on the staff of the hospital, by any constable, or by any person authorised in writing by the responsible clinician or the managers of the hospital.

(3) Where a patient who is for the time being subject to guardianship under this Part of this Act absents himself without the leave of the guardian from the place at which he is required by the guardian to reside, he may, subject to the provisions of this section, be taken into custody and returned to that place by any officer on the staff of a local social services authority, by any constable, or by any person authorised in writing by the guardian or a local social services authority.

(4) patient shall not be taken into custody under this section after the later of –

(a) the end of the period of six months beginning with the first day of his absence without leave; and
(b) the end of the period for which (apart from section 21 below) he is liable to be detained or subject to guardianship or, in the case of a community patient, the community treatment order is in force.

(4A) In determining for the purposes of subsection (4)(b) above or any other provision of this Act whether a person who is or has been absent without leave is at any time liable to be detained or subject to guardianship, a report furnished under section 20 or 21B below before the first day of his absence without leave shall not be taken to have renewed the authority for his detention or guardianship unless the period of renewal began before that day.

(4B) Similarly, in determining for those purposes whether a community treatment order is at any time in force in respect of a person who is or has been absent without leave, a report furnished under section 20A or 21B below before the first day of his absence without leave shall not be taken to have extended the community treatment period unless the extension began before that day.

(5) A patient shall not be taken into custody under this section if the period for which he is liable to be detained is that specified in section 2(4), 4(4) or 5(2) or (4) above and that period has expired.

(6) In this Act "absent without leave" means absent from any hospital or other place and liable to be taken into custody and returned under this section, and related expressions shall be construed accordingly.

(7) In relation to a patient who has yet to comply with a requirement imposed by virtue of this Act to be in a hospital or place, references in this Act to his liability to be returned to the hospital or place shall include his liability to be taken to that hospital or place; and related expressions shall be construed accordingly.

Amendments—Mental Health Act 2007, ss 21, 32(4), 55, Sch 2, paras 1, 7(a), Sch 3, paras 1, 3(1), (2), (3)(a), (3)(b), (5), Sch 11, Pt 5; Mental Health (Patients in the Community) Act 1995, s 2(1).

Duration of authority and discharge

20 Duration of authority

(1) Subject to the following provisions of this Part of this Act, a patient admitted to hospital in pursuance of an application for admission for treatment, and a patient placed under guardianship in pursuance of a guardianship application, may be detained in a hospital or kept under guardianship for a period not exceeding six months beginning with the day on which he was so admitted, or the day on which the guardianship application was accepted, as the case may be, but shall not be so detained or kept for any longer period unless the authority for his detention or guardianship is renewed under this section.

(2) Authority for the detention or guardianship of a patient may, unless the patient has previously been discharged under section 23 below, be renewed –

(a) from the expiration of the period referred to in subsection (1) above, for a further period of six months;

(b) from the expiration of any period of renewal under paragraph (a) above, for a further period of one year,

and so on for periods of one year at a time.

(3) Within the period of two months ending on the day on which a patient who is liable to be detained in pursuance of an application for admission for treatment would cease under this section to be so liable in default of the renewal of the authority for his detention, it shall be the duty of the responsible clinician –

(a) to examine the patient; and

(b) if it appears to him that the conditions set out in subsection (4) below are satisfied, to furnish to the managers of the hospital where the patient is detained a report to that effect in the prescribed form;

and where such a report is furnished in respect of a patient the managers shall, unless they discharge the patient under section 23 below, cause him to be informed.

(4) The conditions referred to in subsection (3) above are that –

(a) the patient is suffering from mental disorder of a nature or degree which makes it appropriate for him to receive medical treatment in a hospital; and

(b) (*repealed*)

(c) it is necessary for the health or safety of the patient or for the protection of other persons that he should receive such treatment and that it cannot be provided unless he continues to be detained; and
(d) appropriate medical treatment is available for him.

(5) Before furnishing a report under subsection (3) above the responsible clinician shall consult one or more other persons who have been professionally concerned with the patient's medical treatment.

(5A) But the responsible clinician may not furnish a report under subsection (3) above unless a person –

(a) who has been professionally concerned with the patient's medical treatment; but
(b) who belongs to a profession other than that to which the responsible clinician belongs,

states in writing that he agrees that the conditions set out in subsection (4) above are satisfied.

(6) Within the period of two months ending with the day on which a patient who is subject to guardianship under this Part of this Act would cease under this section to be so liable in default of the renewal of the authority for his guardianship, it shall be the duty of the appropriate practitioner –

(a) to examine the patient; and
(b) if it appears to him that the conditions set out in subsection (7) below are satisfied, to furnish to the guardian and, where the guardian is a person other than a local social services authority, to the responsible local social services authority a report to that effect in the prescribed form;

and where such a report is furnished in respect of a patient, the local social services authority shall, unless they discharge the patient under section 23 below, cause him to be informed.

(7) The conditions referred to in subsection (6) above are that –

(a) the patient is suffering from mental disorder of a nature or degree which warrants his reception into guardianship; and
(b) it is necessary in the interests of the welfare of the patient or for the protection of other persons that the patient should remain under guardianship.

(8) Where a report is duly furnished under subsection (3) or (6) above, the authority for the detention or guardianship of the patient shall be thereby renewed for the period prescribed in that case by subsection (2) above.

(9) (*repealed*)

(10) (*repealed*)

Amendments—Mental Health Act 2007, ss 1(4), 4(1), (4), 9(1), (4), 32(3), (4), 55, Sch 1, para 4, Sch 3, paras 1, 5, Sch 11, Pts 1, 2, 3.

20A Community treatment period

(1) Subject to the provisions of this Part of this Act, a community treatment order shall cease to be in force on expiry of the period of six months beginning with the day on which it was made.

(2) That period is referred to in this Act as 'the community treatment period'.

(3) The community treatment period may, unless the order has previously ceased to be in force, be extended –

(a) from its expiration for a period of six months;
(b) from the expiration of any period of extension under paragraph (a) above for a further period of one year,

and so on for periods of one year at a time.

(4) Within the period of two months ending on the day on which the order would cease to be in force in default of an extension under this section, it shall be the duty of the responsible clinician –

(a) to examine the patient; and
(b) if it appears to him that the conditions set out in subsection (6) below are satisfied and if a statement under subsection (8) below is made, to furnish to the managers of the responsible hospital a report to that effect in the prescribed form.

(5) Where such a report is furnished in respect of the patient, the managers shall, unless they discharge him under section 23 below, cause him to be informed.

(6) The conditions referred to in subsection (4) above are that –

(a) the patient is suffering from mental disorder of a nature or degree which makes it appropriate for him to receive medical treatment;
(b) it is necessary for his health or safety or for the protection of other persons that he should receive such treatment;
(c) subject to his continuing to be liable to be recalled as mentioned in paragraph (d) below, such treatment can be provided without his being detained in a hospital;
(d) it is necessary that the responsible clinician should continue to be able to exercise the power under section 17E(1) above to recall the patient to hospital; and
(e) appropriate medical treatment is available for him.

(7) In determining whether the criterion in subsection (6)(d) above is met, the responsible clinician shall, in particular, consider, having regard to the patient's history of mental disorder and any other relevant factors, what risk there would be of a deterioration of the patient's condition if he were to continue not to be detained in a hospital (as a result, for example, of his refusing or neglecting to receive the medical treatment he requires for his mental disorder).

(8) The statement referred to in subsection (4) above is a statement in writing by an approved mental health professional –

(a) that it appears to him that the conditions set out in subsection (6) above are satisfied; and
(b) that it is appropriate to extend the community treatment period.

(9) Before furnishing a report under subsection (4) above the responsible clinician shall consult one or more other persons who have been professionally concerned with the patient's medical treatment.

(10) Where a report is duly furnished under subsection (4) above, the community treatment period shall be thereby extended for the period prescribed in that case by subsection (3) above.

Amendments—Inserted by Mental Health Act 2007, s 32(1), (3).

20B Effect of expiry of community treatment order

(1) A community patient shall be deemed to be discharged absolutely from liability to recall under this Part of this Act, and the application for admission for treatment cease to have effect, on expiry of the community treatment order, if the order has not previously ceased to be in force.

(2) For the purposes of subsection (1) above, a community treatment order expires on expiry of the community treatment period as extended under this Part of this Act, but this is subject to sections 21 and 22 below.

Amendments—Inserted by Mental Health Act 2007, s 32(1), (3).

*****

23 Discharge of patients

(1) Subject to the provisions of this section and section 25 below, a patient who is for the time being liable to be detained or subject to guardianship under this Part of this Act shall cease to be so liable or subject if an order in writing discharging him absolutely from detention or guardianship is made in accordance with this section.

(1A) Subject to the provisions of this section and section 25 below, a community patient shall cease to be liable to recall under this Part of this Act, and the application for admission for treatment cease to have effect, if an order in writing discharging him from such liability is made in accordance with this section.

(1B) An order under subsection (1) or (1A) above shall be referred to in this Act as 'an order for discharge'.

(2) An order for discharge may be made in respect of a patient –

- (a) where the patient is liable to be detained in a hospital in pursuance of an application for admission for assessment or for treatment by the responsible clinician, by the managers or by the nearest relative of the patient;
- (b) where the patient is subject to guardianship, by the responsible clinician, by the responsible local social services authority or by the nearest relative of the patient;
- (c) where the patient is a community patient, by the responsible clinician, by the managers of the responsible hospital or by the nearest relative of the patient.

(3) (*repealed*)

(3A) (*repealed*)

(4) The powers conferred by this section on any authority trust, board (other than an NHS foundation trust, board) or body of persons may be exercised subject to subsection (5) below by any three or more members of that authority trust, board or body authorised by them in that behalf or by three or more members of a committee or sub-committee of that authority trust, board or body which has been authorised by them in that behalf.

(5) The reference in subsection (4) above to the members of an authority, *trust*, board or body or the members of a committee or sub-committee of an authority, trust, board or body –

(a) in the case of a Local Health Board, *Special Health Authority* [or Special Heath Authority] *or Primary Care Trust* or a committee or sub-committee of a Local Health Board, *Special Health Authority* [or Special Heath Authority] *or Primary Care Trust,* is a reference only to the chairman of the authority, *trust* or board and such members (of the authority, *trust*, board, committee or sub-committee, as the case may be) as are not also officers of the authority, *trust* or board, within the meaning of the National Health Service Act 2006 or the National Health Service (Wales) Act 2006; and

(b) in the case of a National Health Service trust or a committee or sub-committee of such a trust, is a reference only to the chairman of the trust and such directors or (in the case of a committee or sub-committee) members as are not also employees of the trust.

(6) The powers conferred by this section on any NHS foundation trust may be exercised by any three or more persons authorised by the board of the trust in that behalf each of whom is neither an executive director of the board nor an employee of the trust.

Amendments—National Health Service and Community Care Act 1990, s 66(1), Sch 9, para 24(3); Health Authorities Act 1995, s 2(1), Sch 1, para 107(1), (2); Health Act 1999 (Supplementary, Consequential etc. Provisions) Order 2000, SI 2000/90, art 3(1), Sch 1, para 16(1), (4); Health and Social Care (Community Health and Standards) Act 2003, s 34, Sch 4, paras 50, 53; National Health Service (Consequential Provisions) Act 2006, s 2, Sch 1, paras 62, 65; Mental Health Act 2007, ss 9(1), (6), 32(4), 45(1), Sch 3, paras 1, 10; References to Health Authorities Order 2007, SI 2007/961, art 3, Sch, para 13; Health and Social Care Act 2012, s 39(1).

Prospective Amendments—Sub-s (5): in para (a) words ", Special Health Authority" in italics in both places they occur repealed and subsequent words in square brackets substituted by the Health and Social Care Act 2012, s 55(2), Sch 5, paras 24, 26(a); Date in force (in so far as is necessary for enabling the exercise of any power to make an order or regulations or to give directions): 27 March 2012; Date in force (for remaining purposes): to be appointed; Sub-s (5): in para (a) words "or Primary Care Trust" in italics in both places they occur repealed by the Health and Social Care Act 2012, s 55(2), Sch 5, paras 24, 26(b); with effect from a date to be appointed; Sub-s (5): in para (a) word ", trust" in italics in each place it occurs repealed by the Health and Social Care Act 2012, s 55(2), Sch 5, paras 24, 26(c) with effect from a date to be appointed.

*****

Functions of relatives of patients

26 Definitions of 'relative' and 'nearest relative'

(1) In this Part of this Act 'relative' means any of the following persons –

(a) husband or wife or civil partner;
(b) son or daughter;
(c) father or mother
(d) brother or sister;
(e) grandparent;
(f) grandchild;
(g) uncle or aunt;
(h) nephew or niece.

(2) In deducing relationships for the purposes of this section, any relationship of the half-blood shall be treated as a relationship of the whole blood, and an illegitimate person shall be treated as the legitimate child of –

(a) his mother, and

(b) if his father has parental responsibility for him within the meaning of section 3 of the Children Act 1989, his father.

(3) In this Part of this Act, subject to the provisions of this section and to the following provisions of this Part of this Act, the 'nearest relative' means the person first described in subsection (1) above who is for the time being surviving, relatives of the whole blood being preferred to relatives of the same description of the half-blood and the elder or eldest of two or more relatives described in any paragraph of that subsection being preferred to the other or others of those relatives, regardless of sex.

(4) Subject to the provisions of this section and to the following provisions of this Part of this Act, where the patient ordinarily resides with or is cared for by one or more of his relatives (or, if he is for the time being an in-patient in a hospital, he last ordinarily resided with or was cared for by one or more of his relatives) his nearest relative shall be determined –

(a) by giving preference to that relative or those relatives over the other or others; and

(b) as between two or more such relatives, in accordance with subsection (3) above.

(5) Where the person who, under subsection (3) or (4) above, would be the nearest relative of a patient –

(a) in the case of a patient ordinarily resident in the United Kingdom, the Channel Islands or the Isle of Man, is not so resident; or

(b) is the husband or wife or civil partner of the patient, but is permanently separated from the patient, either by agreement or under an order of a court, or has deserted or has been deserted by the patient for a period which has not come to an end; or

(c) is a person other than the husband, wife, civil partner, father or mother of the patient, and is for the time being under 18 years of age;

(d) (*repealed*)

the nearest relative of the patient shall be ascertained as if that person were dead.

(6) In this section 'husband', 'wife' and 'civil partner' include a person who is living with the patient as the patient's husband or wife or as if they were civil partners, as the case may be (or, if the patient is for the time being an in-patient in a hospital, was so living until the patient was admitted), and has been or had been so living for a period of not less than six months; but a person shall not be treated by virtue of this subsection as the nearest relative of a married patient or a patient in a civil partnership unless the husband, wife or civil partner of the patient is disregarded by virtue of paragraph (b) of subsection (5) above.

(7) A person, other than a relative, with whom the patient ordinarily resides (or, if the patient is for the time being an in-patient in a hospital, last ordinarily resided before he was admitted), and with whom he has or had been ordinarily residing for a period of not less than five years, shall be treated for the purposes of this Part of this Act as if he were a relative but –

(a) shall be treated for the purposes of subsection (3) above as if mentioned last in subsection (1) above; and

(b) shall not be treated by virtue of this subsection as the nearest relative of a married patient or a patient in a civil partnership unless the husband, wife or civil partner of the patient is disregarded by virtue of paragraph (b) of subsection (5) above.

Amendments—Children Act 1989, s 108(7), Sch 15; SI 1991/1881, art 3; Mental Health Act 2007, s 26(1)–(5).

27 Children and young persons in care

Where –

(a) a patient who is a child or young person is in the care of a local authority by virtue of a care order within the meaning of the Children Act 1989; or

(b) the rights and powers of a parent of a patient who is a child or young person are vested in a local authority by virtue of section 16 of the Social Work (Scotland) Act 1968,

the authority shall be deemed to be the nearest relative of the patient in preference to any person except the patient's husband or wife or civil partner (if any).

Amendments—Children Act 1989, s 108(5), Sch 13, para 48(1); Mental Health Act 2007, s 26(6).

28 Nearest relative of minor under guardianship etc

(1) Where –

(a) a guardian has been appointed for a person who has not attained the age of eighteen years; or

(b) a residence order (as defined by section 8 of the Children Act 1989) is in force with respect to such a person,

the guardian (or guardians, where there is more than one) or the person named in the residence order shall, to the exclusion of any other person, be deemed to be his nearest relative.

(2) Subsection (5) of section 26 above shall apply in relation to a person who is, or who is one of the persons, deemed to be the nearest relative of a patient by virtue of this section as it applies in relation to a person who would be the nearest relative under subsection (3) of that section.

(3) In this section 'guardian' includes a special guardian (within the meaning of the Children Act 1989), but does not include a guardian under this Part of this Act.

(4) In this section 'court' includes a court in Scotland or Northern Ireland, and 'enactment' includes an enactment of the Parliament of Northern Ireland, a Measure of the Northern Ireland Assembly and an Order in Council under Schedule 1 of the Northern Ireland Act 1974.

Amendments—Children Act 1989, s 108(5), Sch 13, para 48(2)–(4); Adoption and Children Act 2002, s 139(1), Sch 3, para 41.

29 Appointment by court of acting nearest relative

(1) The county court may, upon application made in accordance with the provisions of this section in respect of a patient, by order direct that the functions of the nearest relative of the patient under this Part of this Act and sections 66 and 69 below shall, during the continuance in force of the order, be exercisable by the person specified in the order.

(1A) If the court decides to make an order on an application under subsection (1) above, the following rules have effect for the purposes of specifying a person in the order –

(a) if a person is nominated in the application to act as the patient's nearest relative and that person is, in the opinion of the court, a suitable person to act as such and is willing to do so, the court shall specify that person (or, if there are two or more such persons, such one of them as the court thinks fit);

(b) otherwise, the court shall specify such person as is, in its opinion, a suitable person to act as the patient's nearest relative and is willing to do so.

(2) An order under this section may be made on the application of –

(za) the patient;

(a) any relative of the patient;

(b) any other person with whom the patient is residing (or, if the patient is then an in-patient in a hospital, was last residing before he was admitted); or

(c) an approved mental health professional;

(3) An application for an order under this section may be made upon any of the following grounds, that is to say –

(a) that the patient has no nearest relative within the meaning of this Act, or that it is not reasonably practicable to ascertain whether he has such a relative, or who that relative is;

(b) that the nearest relative of the patient is incapable of acting as such by reason of mental disorder or other illness;

(c) that the nearest relative of the patient unreasonably objects to the making of an application for admission for treatment or a guardianship application in respect of the patient;

(d) that the nearest relative of the patient has exercised without due regard to the welfare of the patient or the interests of the public his power to discharge the patient under this Part of this Act, or is likely to do so; or

(e) that the nearest relative of the patient is otherwise not a suitable person to act as such.

(4) If, immediately before the expiration of the period for which a patient is liable to be detained by virtue of an application for admission for assessment, an application under this section, which is an application made on the ground specified in subsection (3)(c) or (d) above, is pending in respect of the patient, that period shall be extended –

(a) in any case, until the application under this section has been finally disposed of; and

(b) if an order is made in pursuance of the application under this section, for a further period of seven days;

and for the purposes of this subsection an application under this section shall be deemed to have been finally disposed of at the expiration of the time allowed for appealing from the decision of the court or, if notice of appeal has been given within that time, when the appeal has been heard or withdrawn, and 'pending' shall be construed accordingly.

(5) An order made on the ground specified in subsection (3)(a), (b) or (e) above may specify a period for which it is to continue in force unless previously discharged under section 30 below.

(6) While an order made under this section is in force, the provisions of this Part of this Act (other than this section and section 30 below) and sections 66, 69, 132(4) and 133 below shall apply in relation to the patient as if for any reference to the nearest relative of the patient there were substituted a reference to the person having the functions of that relative and (without prejudice to section 30 below) shall so apply notwithstanding that the person who was the patient's nearest relative when the order was made is no

longer his nearest relative; but this subsection shall not apply to section 66 below in the case mentioned in paragraph (h) of subsection (1) of that section.

Amendments—Mental Health Act 2007, ss 21, 23, 32, 55, Sch 2, paras 1, 7(c), Sch 3, paras 1, 13, Sch 11, Pts 4, 5.

*****

Supplemental

*****

33 Special provisions as to wards of court

(1) An application for the admission to hospital of a minor who is a ward of court may be made under this Part of this Act with the leave of the court; and section 11(4) above shall not apply in relation to an application so made.

(2) Where a minor who is a ward of court is liable to be detained in a hospital by virtue of an application for admission under this Part of this Act or is a community patient, any power exercisable under this Part of this Act or under section 66 below in relation to the patient by his nearest relative shall be exercisable by or with the leave of the court.

(3) Nothing in this Part of this Act shall be construed as authorising the making of a guardianship application in respect of a minor who is a ward of court, or the transfer into guardianship of any such minor.

(4) Where a community treatment order has been made in respect of a minor who is a ward of court, the provisions of this Part of this Act relating to community treatment orders and community patients have effect in relation to the minor subject to any order which the court makes in the exercise of its wardship jurisdiction; but this does not apply as regards any period when the minor is recalled to hospital under section 17E above.

Amendments—Mental Health (Patients in the Community) Act 1995, s 1(2), Sch 1, para 3; Mental Health Act 2007, s 32, Sch 3, paras 1, 16.

*****

PART III
PATIENTS CONCERNED IN CRIMINAL PROCEEDINGS OR UNDER SENTENCE

Remands to hospital

35 Remand to hospital for report on accused's mental condition

(1) Subject to the provisions of this section, the Crown Court or a magistrates' court may remand an accused person to a hospital specified by the court for a report on his mental condition.

(2) For the purposes of this section an accused person is –

(a) in relation to the Crown Court, any person who is awaiting trial before the court for an offence punishable with imprisonment or who has been arraigned before the court for such an offence and has not yet been sentenced or otherwise dealt with for the offence on which he has been arraigned;

(b) in relation to a magistrates' court, any person who has been convicted by the court of an offence punishable on summary conviction with imprisonment and any person charged with such an offence if the court is satisfied that he did the act or made the omission charged or he has consented to the exercise by the court of the powers conferred by this section.

(3) Subject to subsection (4) below, the powers conferred by this section may be exercised if –

(a) the court is satisfied, on the written or oral evidence of a registered medical practitioner, that there is reason to suspect that the accused person is suffering from mental disorder; and

(b) the court is of the opinion that it would be impracticable for a report on his mental condition to be made if he were remanded on bail;

but those powers shall not be exercised by the Crown Court in respect of a person who has been convicted before the court if the sentence for the offence of which he has been convicted is fixed by law.

(4) The court shall not remand an accused person to a hospital under this section unless satisfied, on the written or oral evidence of the approved clinician who would be responsible for making the report or of some other person representing the managers of the hospital, that arrangements have been made for his admission to that hospital and for his admission to it within the period of seven days beginning with the date of the remand; and if the court is so satisfied it may, pending his admission, give directions for his conveyance to and detention in a place of safety.

(5) Where a court has remanded an accused person under this section it may further remand him if it appears to the court, on the written or oral evidence of the approved clinician responsible for making the report, that a further remand is necessary for completing the assessment of the accused person's mental condition.

(6) The power of further remanding an accused person under this section may be exercised by the court without his being brought before the court if he is represented by an authorised person who is given an opportunity of being heard.

(7) An accused person shall not be remanded or further remanded under this section for more than 28 days at a time or for more than 12 weeks in all; and the court may at any time terminate the remand if it appears to the court that it is appropriate to do so.

(8) An accused person remanded to hospital under this section shall be entitled to obtain at his own expense an independent report on his mental condition from a registered medical practitioner or approved clinician chosen by him and to apply to the court on the basis of it for his remand to be terminated under subsection (7) above.

(9) Where an accused person is remanded under this section –

(a) a constable or any other person directed to do so by the court shall convey the accused person to the hospital specified by the court within the period mentioned in subsection (4) above; and

(b) the managers of the hospital shall admit him within that period and thereafter detain him in accordance with the provisions of this section.

(10) If an accused person absconds from a hospital to which he has been remanded under this section, or while being conveyed to or from that hospital, he may be arrested without warrant by any constable and shall, after being arrested, be brought as soon as practicable before the court that remanded him; and the court may thereupon terminate the remand and deal with him in any way in which it could have dealt with him if he had not been remanded under this section.

Amendments—Mental Health Act 2007, ss 1(4), 10(1), (2); Sch 1, Pt 1, paras 1, 5; Legal Services Act 2007, s 208(1), Sch 21, paras 53, 54.

36 Remand of accused person to hospital for treatment

(1) Subject to the provisions of this section, the Crown Court may, instead of remanding an accused person in custody, remand him to a hospital specified by the court if satisfied, on the written or oral evidence of two registered medical practitioners, that –

(a) he is suffering from mental disorder of a nature or degree which makes it appropriate for him to be detained in a hospital for medical treatment; and
(b) appropriate medical treatment is available for him.

(2) For the purposes of this section an accused person is any person who is in custody awaiting trial before the Crown Court for an offence punishable with imprisonment (other than an offence the sentence for which is fixed by law) or who at any time before sentence is in custody in the course of a trial before that court for such an offence.

(3) The court shall not remand an accused person under this section to a hospital unless it is satisfied, on the written or oral evidence of the approved clinician who would have overall responsibility for his case or of some other person representing the managers of the hospital, that arrangements have been made for his admission to that hospital and for his admission to it within the period of seven days beginning with the date of the remand; and if the court is so satisfied it may, pending his admission, give directions for his conveyance to and detention in a place of safety.

(4) Where a court has remanded an accused person under this section it may further remand him if it appears to the court, on the written or oral evidence of the responsible clinician, that a further remand is warranted.

(5) The power of further remanding an accused person under this section may be exercised by the court without his being brought before the court if he is represented by an authorised person who is given an opportunity of being heard.

(6) An accused person shall not be remanded or further remanded under this section for more than 28 days at a time or for more than 12 weeks in all; and the court may at any time terminate the remand if it appears to the court that it is appropriate to do so.

(7) An accused person remanded to hospital under this section shall be entitled to obtain at his own expense an independent report on his mental condition from a registered medical practitioner or approved clinician chosen by him and to apply to the court on the basis of it for his remand to be terminated under subsection (6) above.

(8) Subsections (9) and (10) of section 35 above shall have effect in relation to a remand under this section as they have effect in relation to a remand under that section.

Amendments—Mental Health Act 2007, ss 1(4), 5(1), (2), 10(1), (3), Sch 1, Pt 1, paras 1, 6; Legal Services Act 2007, s 208(1), 78 21, paras 53, 55.

Hospital and guardianship orders

37 Powers of courts to order hospital admission or guardianship

(1) Where a person is convicted before the Crown Court of an offence punishable with imprisonment other than an offence the sentence for which is fixed by law, or is convicted by a magistrates' court of an offence punishable on summary conviction with imprisonment, and the conditions mentioned in subsection (2) below are satisfied, the

court may by order authorise his admission to and detention in such hospital as may be specified in the order or, as the case may be, place him under the guardianship of a local social services authority or of such other person approved by a local social services authority as may be so specified.

(1A) In the case of an offence the sentence for which would otherwise fall to be imposed –

- (za) under section 1A(5) of the Prevention of Crime Act 1953,
- (a) under section 51A(2) of the Firearms Act 1968,
- (aa) under section 139AA(7) of the Criminal Justice Act 1988,
- (b) under section 110(2) or 111(2) of the Powers of Criminal Courts (Sentencing) Act 2000,
- (ba) under section 224A of the Criminal Justice Act 2003,
- (c) *under any of sections 225 to 228* [section 225(2) or 226(2)] of the Criminal Justice Act 2003, or
- (d) under section 29(4) or (6) of the Violent Crime Reduction Act 2006 (minimum sentences in certain cases of using someone to mind a weapon),

nothing in those provisions shall prevent a court from making an order under subsection (1) above for the admission of the offender to a hospital.

(1B) References in subsection (1A) above to a sentence falling to be imposed under any of the provisions mentioned in that subsection are to be read in accordance with section 305(4) of the Criminal Justice Act 2003.

(2) The conditions referred to in subsection (1) above are that –

- (a) the court is satisfied, on the written or oral evidence of two registered medical practitioners, that the offender is suffering from mental disorder and that either –
  - (i) the mental disorder from which the offender is suffering is of a nature or degree which makes it appropriate for him to be detained in a hospital for medical treatment and appropriate medical treatment is available for him; or
  - (ii) in the case of an offender who has attained the age of 16 years, the mental disorder is of a nature or degree which warrants his reception into guardianship under this Act; and
- (b) the court is of the opinion, having regard to all the circumstances including the nature of the offence and the character and antecedents of the offender, and to the other available methods of dealing with him, that the most suitable method of disposing of the case is by means of an order under this section.

(3) Where a person is charged before a magistrates' court with any act or omission as an offence and the court would have power, on convicting him of that offence, to make an order under subsection (1) above in his case then, if the court is satisfied that the accused did the act or made the omission charged, the court may, if it thinks fit, make such an order without convicting him.

(4) An order for the admission of an offender to a hospital (in this Act referred to as "a hospital order") shall not be made under this section unless the court is satisfied on the written or oral evidence of the approved clinician who would have overall responsibility for his case or of some other person representing the managers of the hospital that arrangements have been made for his admission to that hospital and for his admission to it within the period of 28 days beginning with the date of the making of such an order;

and the court may, pending his admission within that period, give such directions as it thinks fit for his conveyance to and detention in a place of safety.

(5) If within the said period of 28 days it appears to the Secretary of State that by reason of an emergency or other special circumstances it is not practicable for the patient to be received into the hospital specified in the order, he may give directions for the admission of the patient to such other hospital as appears to be appropriate instead of the hospital so specified; and where such directions are given –

(a) the Secretary of State shall cause the person having the custody of the patient to be informed, and
(b) the hospital order shall have effect as if the hospital specified in the directions were substituted for the hospital specified in the order.

(6) An order placing an offender under the guardianship of a local social services authority or of any other person (in this Act referred to as "a guardianship order") shall not be made under this section unless the court is satisfied that that authority or person is willing to receive the offender into guardianship.

(7) (*repealed*)

(8) Where an order is made under this section, the court shall not –

(a) pass sentence of imprisonment or impose a fine or make a community order (within the meaning of Part 12 of the Criminal Justice Act 2003) or a youth rehabilitation order (within the meaning of Part 1 of the Criminal Justice and Immigration Act 2008) in respect of the offence,
(b) if the order under this section is a hospital order, make a referral order (within the meaning of the Powers of Criminal Courts (Sentencing) Act 2000) in respect of the offence, or
(c) make in respect of the offender or an order under section 150 of that Act (binding over of parent or guardian),

but the court may make any other order which it has power to make apart from this section; and for the purposes of this subsection "sentence of imprisonment" includes any sentence or order for detention.

Amendments—Criminal Justice and Immigration Act 2008, ss 6(2), 149, Sch 4, Pt 1, para 30(a) (b); Crime (Sentences) Act 1997, ss 55, 56(2), Sch 4, para 12(1) (3), Sch 6; Criminal Justice Act 2003, s 304, Sch 32, Pt 1, paras 37, 38(a) (b) (c); Legal Aid, Sentencing and Punishment of Offenders Act 2012, ss 122(3), 142(3), Sch 19, Pt 1, para 1, Sch 26, para 2(1), (2), (3); Violent Crime Reduction Act 2006, ss 49, 65, Sch 1, para 2, Sch 5; Mental Health Act 2007, ss 1(4), 4(1), (5), 10(1), (4), 55, Sch 1, Pt 1, paras 1, 7(a) (b), Sch 11, Pt 1; Powers of Criminal Courts (Sentencing) Act 2000, Sch 9, paras 90(1), (6)(a) (b); Youth Justice and Criminal Evidence Act 1999, s 67, Sch 4, para 11.

Prospective Amendments—Subsection (1A), para (c) words 'any of sections 225 to 228' in italics repealed and subsequent words in square brackets substituted by the Criminal Justice and Immigration Act 2008, s 148, Sch 26, Pt 2, para 8.

38 Interim hospital orders

(1) Where a person is convicted before the Crown Court of an offence punishable with imprisonment (other than an offence the sentence for which is fixed by law) or is convicted by a magistrates' court of an offence punishable on summary conviction with imprisonment and the court before or by which he is convicted is satisfied, on the written or oral evidence of two registered medical practitioners –

(a) that the offender is suffering from mental disorder; and

(b) that there is reason to suppose that the mental disorder from which the offender is suffering is such that it may be appropriate for a hospital order to be made in his case,

the court may, before making a hospital order or dealing with him in some other way, make an order (in this Act referred to as 'an interim hospital order') authorising his admission to such hospital as may be specified in the order and his detention there in accordance with this section.

(2) In the case of an offender who is subject to an interim hospital order the court may make a hospital order without his being brought before the court if he is represented by an authorised person who is given an opportunity of being heard.

(3) At least one of the registered medical practitioners whose evidence is taken into account under subsection (1) above shall be employed at the hospital which is to be specified in the order.

(4) An interim hospital order shall not be made for the admission of an offender to a hospital unless the court is satisfied, on the written or oral evidence of the approved clinician who would have overall responsibility for his case or of some other person representing the managers of the hospital, that arrangements have been made for his admission to that hospital and for his admission to it within the period of 28 days beginning with the date of the order; and if the court is so satisfied the court may, pending his admission, give directions for his conveyance to and detention in a place of safety.

(5) An interim hospital order –

(a) shall be in force for such period, not exceeding 12 weeks, as the court may specify when making the order; but
(b) may be renewed for further periods of not more than 28 days at a time if it appears to the court, on the written or oral evidence of the responsible clinician, that the continuation of the order is warranted;

but no such order shall continue in force for more than twelve months in all and the court shall terminate the order if it makes a hospital order in respect of the offender or decides after considering the written or oral evidence of the responsible clinician to deal with the offender in some other way.

(6) The power of renewing an interim hospital order may be exercised without the offender being brought before the court if he is represented by counsel or a solicitor and his counsel or solicitor is given an opportunity of being heard.

(7) If an offender absconds from a hospital in which he is detained in pursuance of an interim hospital order, or while being conveyed to or from such a hospital, he may be arrested without warrant by a constable and shall, after being arrested, be brought as soon as practicable before the court that made the order; and the court may thereupon terminate the order and deal with him in any way in which it could have dealt with him if no such order had been made.

Amendments—Crime (Sentences) Act 1997, s 49(1); Mental Health Act 2007, ss 1(4), 10(1), (5), Sch 1, Pt 1, paras 1, 8; Legal Services Act 2007, s 208(1), Sch 21, paras 53, 56.

*****

40 Effect of hospital orders, guardianship orders and interim hospital orders

(1) A hospital order shall be sufficient authority –

(a) for a constable, an approved mental health professional or any other person directed to do so by the court to convey the patient to the hospital specified in the order within a period of 28 days; and
(b) for the managers of the hospital to admit him at any time within that period and thereafter detain him in accordance with the provisions of this Act.

(2) A guardianship order shall confer on the authority or person named in the order as guardian the same powers as a guardianship application made and accepted under Part II of this Act.

(3) Where an interim hospital order is made in respect of an offender –

(a) a constable or any other person directed to do so by the court shall convey the offender to the hospital specified in the order within the period mentioned in section 38(4) above; and
(b) the managers of the hospital shall admit him within that period and thereafter detain him in accordance with the provisions of section 38 above.

(4) A patient who is admitted to a hospital in pursuance of a hospital order, or placed under guardianship by a guardianship order, shall, subject to the provisions of this subsection, be treated for the purposes of the provisions of this Act mentioned in Part I of Schedule 1 to this Act as if he had been so admitted or placed on the date of the order in pursuance of an application for admission for treatment or a guardianship application, as the case may be, duly made under Part II of this Act, but subject to any modifications of those provisions specified in that Part of that Schedule.

(5) Where a patient is admitted to a hospital in pursuance of a hospital order, or placed under guardianship by a guardianship order, any previous application, hospital order or guardianship order by virtue of which he was liable to be detained in a hospital or subject to guardianship shall cease to have effect; but if the first-mentioned order, or the conviction on which it was made, is quashed on appeal, this subsection shall not apply and section 22 above shall have effect as if during any period for which the patient was liable to be detained or subject to guardianship under the order, he had been detained in custody as mentioned in that section.

(6) Where –

(a) a patient admitted to a hospital in pursuance of a hospital order is absent without leave;
(b) a warrant to arrest him has been issued under section 72 of the Criminal Justice Act 1967; and
(c) he is held pursuant to the warrant in any country or territory other than the United Kingdom, any of the Channel Islands and the Isle of Man,

he shall be treated as having been taken into custody under section 18 above on first being so held.

Amendments—Mental Health (Patients in the Community) Act 1995, s 2(4); Mental Health Act 2007, s 21, Sch 2, paras 1, 7(e).

Restriction orders

*****

42 Powers of Secretary of State in respect of patients subject to restriction orders

(1) If the Secretary of State is satisfied that in the case of any patient a. restriction order is no longer required for the protection of the public from serious harm, he may direct

that the patient shall cease to be subject to the special restrictions set out in section 41(3) above; and where the Secretary of State so directs, the restriction order shall cease to have effect, and section 41(5) above shall apply accordingly.

(2) At any time while a restriction order is in force in respect of a patient, the Secretary of State may, if he thinks fit, by warrant discharge the patient from hospital, either absolutely or subject to conditions; and where a person is absolutely discharged under this subsection, he shall thereupon cease to be liable to be detained by virtue of the relevant hospital order, and the restriction order shall cease to have effect accordingly.

(3) The Secretary of State may at any time during the continuance in force of a restriction order in respect of a patient who has been conditionally discharged under subsection (2) above by warrant recall the patient to such hospital as may be specified in the warrant.

(4) Where a patient is recalled as mentioned in subsection (3) above –

- (a) if the hospital specified in the warrant is not the hospital from which the patient was conditionally discharged, the hospital order and the restriction order shall have effect as if the hospital specified in the warrant were substituted for the hospital specified in the hospital order;
- (b) in any case, the patient shall be treated for the purposes of section 18 above as if he had absented himself without leave from the hospital specified in the warrant.

(5) If a restriction order in respect of a patient ceases to have effect after the patient has been conditionally discharged under this section, the patient shall, unless previously recalled under subsection (3) above, be deemed to be absolutely discharged on the date when the order ceases to have effect, and shall cease to be liable to be detained by virtue of the relevant hospital order accordingly.

(6) The Secretary of State may, if satisfied that the attendance at any place in Great Britain of a patient who is subject to a restriction order is desirable in the interests of justice or for the purposes of any public inquiry, direct him to be taken to that place; and where a patient is directed under this subsection to be taken to any place he shall, unless the Secretary of State otherwise directs, be kept in custody while being so taken, while at that place and while being taken back to the hospital in which he is liable to be detained.

Amendments—Mental Health Act 2007, ss 40(2), 55, Sch 11, Pt 8.

*****

PART 4A
TREATMENT OF COMMUNITY PATIENTS NOT RECALLED TO HOSPITAL

*****

64E Child community patients

(1) This section applies to the giving of relevant treatment to a community patient who –

- (a) is not recalled to hospital under section 17E above; and
- (b) has not attained the age of 16 years.

(2) The treatment may not be given to the patient unless –

(a) there is authority to give it to him; and
(b) if it is section 58 type treatment or section 58A type treatment, the certificate requirement is met.

(3) But the certificate requirement does not apply if –

(a) giving the treatment to the patient is authorised in accordance with section 64G below; or
(b) in a case where the patient is competent to consent to the treatment and does consent to it, the treatment is immediately necessary.

(4) Nor does the certificate requirement apply in so far as the administration of medicine to the patient at any time during the period of one month beginning with the day on which the community treatment order is made is section 58 type treatment.

(5) The reference in subsection (4) above to the administration of medicine does not include any form of treatment specified under section 58(1)(a) above and for the purpose of this subsection, subsection (4A) of section 64C above has effect as if—

(6) For the purposes of subsection (2)(a) above, there is authority to give treatment to a patient if –

(a) he is competent to consent to it and he does consent to it; or
(b) giving it to him is authorised in accordance with section 64F or 64G below.

(7) Subsections (3) to (4A) and (5) to (9) of section 64C above have effect for the purposes of this section as they have effect for the purposes of section 64B above; and for the purpose of this subsection, subsection (4A) of section 64C above has effect as if –

(a) the references to treatment were references only to section 58 type treatment,
(b) the reference to subsection (2)(a) of section 64C were a reference to subsection (6)(a) of this section, and
(c) the reference to capacity to consent were a reference to competence to consent.

(8) Regulations made by virtue of section 32(2)(d) above apply for the purposes of this section as they apply for the purposes of Part 2 of this Act.

Amendments—Inserted by Mental Health Act 2007, s 35(1); Health and Social Care Act 2012, s 299(1), (3)(a); (b).

64F Child community patients lacking competence

(1) A person is authorised to give relevant treatment to a patient as mentioned in section 64E(6)(b) above if the conditions in subsections (2) to (5) below are met.

(2) The first condition is that, before giving the treatment, the person takes reasonable steps to establish whether the patient is competent to consent to the treatment.

(3) The second condition is that, when giving the treatment, he reasonably believes that the patient is not competent to consent to it.

(4) The third condition is that –

(a) he has no reason to believe that the patient objects to being given the treatment; or
(b) he does have reason to believe that the patient so objects, but it is not necessary to use force against the patient in order to give the treatment.

(5) The fourth condition is that –

(a) he is the person in charge of the treatment and an approved clinician; or

(b) the treatment is given under the direction of that clinician.

Amendments—Inserted by Mental Health Act 2007, s 35(1).

64FA Withdrawal of consent

(1) Where the consent of a patient to any treatment has been given as mentioned in section 64C(2)(a) above for the purposes of section 64B or 64E above, the patient may at any time before the completion of the treatment withdraw his consent, and those sections shall then apply as if the remainder of the treatment were a separate form of treatment.

(2) Subsection (3) below applies where

(a) the consent of a patient to any treatment has been given as mentioned in section 64C(2)(a) above for the purposes of section 64B or 64E above; but
(b) before the completion of the treatment, the patient loses capacity or (as the case may be) competence to consent to the treatment.

(3) The patient shall be treated as having withdrawn his consent and section 64B or (as the case may be) section 64E above shall then apply as if the remainder of the treatment were a separate form of treatment.

(4) Without prejudice to the application of subsections (1) to (3) above to any treatment given under the plan of treatment to which a patient has consented, a patient who has consented to such a plan may at any time withdraw his consent to further treatment, or to further treatment of any description, under the plan.

(5) This section shall not preclude the continuation of any treatment, or of treatment under any plan, pending compliance with section 58, 58A, 64B or 64E above if the approved clinician in charge of the treatment considers that the discontinuance of the treatment, or of treatment under the plan, would cause serious suffering to the patient.

Amendments—Inserted by the Health and Social Care Act 2012, s 299(1), (4).

*****

PART V
MENTAL HEALTH REVIEW TRIBUNALS

Constitution etc.

65 Mental Health Review Tribunal for Wales

(1) There shall be a Mental Health Tribunal for Wales.

(1A) The purpose of that tribunal is to deal with applications and references by and in respect of patients under the provisions of this Act.

(2) The provisions of Schedule 2 to this Act shall have effect with respect to the constitution of Mental Health Review Tribunal for Wales.

(3) Subject to the provisions of Schedule 2 to this Act, and to rules made by the Lord Chancellor under this Act, the jurisdiction of a Mental Health Review Tribunal for Wales may be exercised by any three or more of its members, and references in this Act to a Mental Health Review Tribunal for Wales shall be construed accordingly.

(4) The Welsh Ministers may pay to the members of the Mental Health Review Tribunal for Wales such remuneration and allowances as they may determine, and

defray the expenses of that tribunal to such amount as they may determine, and may provide for that tribunal such officers and servants, and such accommodation, as that tribunal may require.

Amendments—Health Authorities Act 1995, s 2(1), Sch 1, para 107(1), (6); Mental Health Act 2007, s 38(1), (2); SI 2008/2833.

Applications and references concerning Part II patients

66 Applications to tribunals

(1) Where –

- (a) a patient is admitted to a hospital in pursuance of an application for admission for assessment; or
- (b) a patient is admitted to a hospital in pursuance of an application for admission for treatment; or
- (c) a patient is received into guardianship in pursuance of a guardianship application; or
- (ca) a community treatment order is made in respect of a patient; or
- (cb) a community treatment order is revoked under section 17F above in respect of a patient; or
- (d) *(repealed)*
- (e) a patient is transferred from guardianship to a hospital in pursuance of regulations made under section 19 above; or
- (f) a report is furnished under section 20 above in respect of a patient and the patient is not discharged under section 23 above; or
- (fza) a report is furnished under section 20A above in respect of a patient and the patient is not discharged under section 23 above; or
- (fa) a report is furnished under subsection (2) of section 21B above in respect of a patient and subsection (5) of that section applies (or subsections (5) and (6)(b) of that section apply) in the case of the report; or
- (faa) a report is furnished under subsection (2) of section 21B above in respect of a community patient and subsection (6A) of that section applies (or subsections (6A) and (6B)(b) of that section apply) in the case of the report; or
- (fb) *(repealed)*
- (g) a report is furnished under section 25 above in respect of a patient who is detained in pursuance of an application for admission for treatment or a community patient; or
- (ga)–(gc) *(repealed)*
- (h) an order is made under section 29 above on the ground specified in paragraph (c) or (d) of subsection (3) of that section in respect of a patient who is or subsequently becomes liable to be detained or subject to guardianship under Part II of this Act or who is a community patient,

an application may be made to a the appropriate tribunal within the relevant period –

- (i) by the patient (except in the cases mentioned in paragraphs (g) and (h) above), and
- (ii) in the cases mentioned in paragraphs (g) and (h) above, by his nearest relative.

(2) In subsection (1) above 'the relevant period' means –

- (a) in the case mentioned in paragraph (a) of that subsection, 14 days beginning with the day on which the patient is admitted as so mentioned;

(b) in the case mentioned in paragraph (b) of that subsection, six months beginning with the day on which the patient is admitted as so mentioned;

(c) in the case mentioned in paragraph (c) of that subsection, six months beginning with the day on which the application is accepted;

(ca) in the case mentioned in paragraph (ca) of that subsection, six months beginning with the day on which the community treatment order is made;

(cb) in the case mentioned in paragraph (cb) of that subsection, six months beginning with the day on which the community treatment order is revoked;

(d) in the case mentioned in paragraph (g) of that subsection, 28 days beginning with the day on which the applicant is informed that the report has been furnished;

(e) in the case mentioned in paragraph (e) of that subsection, six months beginning with the day on which the patient is transferred;

(f) in the case mentioned in paragraph (f) or (fa) of that subsection, the period or periods for which authority for the patient's detention or guardianship is renewed by virtue of the report;

(fza) in the cases mentioned in paragraphs (fza) and (faa) of that subsection, the period or periods for which the community treatment period is extended by virtue of the report;

(fa) (*repealed*)

(g) in the case mentioned in paragraph (h) of that subsection, 12 months beginning with the date of the order, and in any subsequent period of 12 months during which the order continues in force.

(2A) Nothing in subsection (1)(b) above entitles a community patient to make an application by virtue of that provision even if he is admitted to a hospital on being recalled there under section 17E above.

(3) Section 32 above shall apply for the purposes of this section as it applies for the purposes of Part II of this Act.

(4) In this Act 'the appropriate tribunal' means the First-tier Tribunal or the Mental Health Review Tribunal for Wales.

(5) For provision determining to which of those tribunals applications by or in respect of a patient under this Act shall be made, see section 77(3) and (4) below.

Amendments—Mental Health (Patients in the Community) Act 1995, ss 1(2), 2(6), Sch 1, para 7; Mental Health Act 2007, ss 1(4), 25, 32(4), 36(1), (3), 55, Sch 1, Pt 1, paras 1, 13, Sch 3, paras 1, 18, Sch 11, Pts 1, 5; SI 2008/2833.

67 References to tribunals by Secretary of State concerning Part II patients

(1) The Secretary of State may, if he thinks fit, at any time refer to a the appropriate tribunal the case of any patient who is liable to be detained or subject to guardianship under Part II of this Act or of any community patient.

(2) For the purpose of furnishing information for the purposes of a reference under subsection (1) above any registered medical practitioner or approved clinician authorised by or on behalf of the patient may, at any reasonable time, visit the patient and examine him in private and require the production of and inspect any records relating to the detention or treatment of the patient in any hospital or to any after-care services provided for the patient under section 117 below.

(3) Section 32 above shall apply for the purposes of this section as it applies for the purposes of Part II of this Act.

Amendments—Mental Health (Patients in the Community) Act 1995, ss 1(2), Sch 1, para 8; Mental Health Act 2007, ss 13(1), (2)(a), 32(4), 55, Sch 3, paras 1, 19, Sch 11, Pt 5; SI 2008/2833.

68 Duty of managers of hospitals to refer cases to tribunal

(1) This section applies in respect of the following patients –

- (a) a patient who is admitted to a hospital in pursuance of an application for admission for assessment;
- (b) a patient who is admitted to a hospital in pursuance of an application for admission for treatment;
- (c) a community patient;
- (d) a patient whose community treatment order is revoked under section 17F above;
- (e) a patient who is transferred from guardianship to a hospital in pursuance of regulations made under section 19 above.

(2) On expiry of the period of six months beginning with the applicable day, the managers of the hospital shall refer the patient's case to the appropriate tribunal.

(3) But they shall not do so if during that period –

- (a) any right has been exercised by or in respect of the patient by virtue of any of paragraphs (b), (ca), (cb), (e), (g) and (h) of section 66(1) above;
- (b) a reference has been made in respect of the patient under section 67(1) above, not being a reference made while the patient is or was liable to be detained in pursuance of an application for admission for assessment; or
- (c) a reference has been made in respect of the patient under subsection (7) below.

(4) A person who applies to a tribunal but subsequently withdraws his application shall be treated for these purposes as not having exercised his right to apply, and if he withdraws his application on a date after expiry of the period mentioned in subsection (2) above, the managers shall refer the patient's case as soon as possible after that date.

(5) In subsection (2) above, 'the applicable day' means –

- (a) in the case of a patient who is admitted to a hospital in pursuance of an application for admission for assessment, the day on which the patient was so admitted;
- (b) in the case of a patient who is admitted to a hospital in pursuance of an application for admission for treatment –
  - (i) the day on which the patient was so admitted; or
  - (ii) if, when he was so admitted, he was already liable to be detained in pursuance of an application for admission for assessment, the day on which he was originally admitted in pursuance of the application for admission for assessment;
- (c) in the case of a community patient or a patient whose community treatment order is revoked under section 17F above, the day mentioned in sub-paragraph (i) or (ii), as the case may be, of paragraph (b) above;
- (d) in the case of a patient who is transferred from guardianship to a hospital, the day on which he was so transferred.

(6) The managers of the hospital shall also refer the patient's case to the appropriate tribunal if a period of more than three years (or, if the patient has not attained the age of 18 years, one year) has elapsed since his case was last considered by such a tribunal, whether on his own application or otherwise.

(7) If, in the case of a community patient, the community treatment order is revoked under section 17F above, the managers of the hospital shall also refer the patient's case to the appropriate tribunal as soon as possible after the order is revoked.

(8) For the purposes of furnishing information for the purposes of a reference under this section, a registered medical practitioner or approved clinician authorised by or on behalf of the patient may at any reasonable time –

- (a) visit and examine the patient in private; and
- (b) require the production of and inspect any records relating to the detention or treatment of the patient in any hospital or any after-care services provided for him under section 117 below.

(9) Reference in this section to the managers of the hospital –

- (a) in relation to a community patient, is to the managers of the responsible hospital;
- (b) in relation to any other patient, is to the managers of the hospital in which he is liable to be detained.

Amendments—Substituted by Mental Health Act 2007, s 37(1), (3); SI 2008/2833.

Applications and references concerning Part III patients

69 Applications to tribunals concerning patients subject to hospitals and guardianship orders

(1) Without prejudice to any provision of section 66(1) above as applied by section 40(4) above, an application to the appropriate tribunal may also be made –

- (a) in respect of a patient liable to be detained in pursuance of a hospital order or a community patient who was so liable immediately before he became a community patient, by the nearest relative of the patient in any period in which an application may be made by the patient under any such provision as so applied; and
- (b) in respect of a patient placed under guardianship by a guardianship order –
  - (i) by the patient, within the period of six months beginning with the date of the order;
  - (ii) by the nearest relative of the patient, within the period of 12 months beginning with the date of the order and in any subsequent period of 12 months.

(2) Where a person detained in a hospital –

- (a) is treated as subject to a hospital order, hospital direction or transfer direction by virtue of section 41(5) above or section 80B(2), 82(2) or 85(2) below; or
- (b) is subject to a direction having the same effect as a hospital order by virtue of section 47(3) or 48(3) above,

then, without prejudice to any provision of Part II of this Act as applied by section 40 above, that person may make an application to the appropriate tribunal in the period of six months beginning with the date of the order or direction mentioned in paragraph (a) above or, as the case may be, the date of the direction mentioned in paragraph (b) above.

(3) The provisions of section 66 above as applied by section 40(4) above are subject to subsection (4) below.

(4) If the initial detention period has not elapsed when the relevant application period begins, the right of a hospital order patient to make an application by virtue of paragraph (ca) or (cb) of section 66(1) above shall be exercisable only during whatever remains of the relevant application period after the initial detention period has elapsed.

(5) In subsection (4) above –

(a) 'hospital order patient' means a patient who is subject to a hospital order, excluding a patient of a kind mentioned in paragraph (a) or (b) of subsection (2) above;
(b) 'the initial detention period', in relation to a hospital order patient, means the period of six months beginning with the date of the hospital order; and
(c) 'the relevant application period' means the relevant period mentioned in paragraph (ca) or (cb), as the case may be, of section 66(2) above.

Amendments—Crime (Sentences) Act 1997, s 55, Sch 4, para 12(8); Mental Health Act 2007, ss 32(4), 39(2), 55, Sch 3, paras 1, 20, Sch 5, Pt 2, para 18, Sch 11, Pt 5; SI 2008/2833.

70 Applications to tribunals concerning restricted patients

A patient who is a restricted patient within the meaning of section 79 below and is detained in a hospital may apply to the appropriate tribunal –

(a) in the period between the expiration of six months and the expiration of 12 months beginning with the date of the relevant hospital order, hospital direction or transfer direction; and
(b) in any subsequent period of 12 months.

Amendments—Crime (Sentences) Act 1997, s 55, Sch 4, para 12(9); SI 2008/2833.

71 References by Secretary of State concerning restricted patients

(1) The Secretary of State may at any time refer the case of a restricted patient to the appropriate tribunal.

(2) The Secretary of State shall refer to the appropriate tribunal the case of any restricted patient detained in a hospital whose case has not been considered by such a tribunal, whether on his own application or otherwise, within the last three years.

(3) The Secretary of State may by order vary the length of the period mentioned in subsection (2) above.

(3A) An order under subsection (3) above may include such transitional, consequential, incidental or supplemental provision as the Secretary of State thinks fit.

(4) Any reference under subsection (1) above in respect of a patient who has been conditionally discharged and not recalled to hospital shall be made to the tribunal for the area in which the patient resides.

(5), (6) (*repealed*)

Amendments—Domestic Violence, Crime and Victims Act 2005, s 58, Sch 10, para 20, Sch 11; Mental Health Act 2007, s 37(1), (4); SI 2008/2833.

Discharge of patients

72 Powers of tribunals

(1) Where application is made to the appropriate tribunal by or in respect of a patient who is liable to be detained under this Act or is a community patient, the tribunal may in any case direct that the patient be discharged, and –

- (a) the tribunal shall direct the discharge of a patient liable to be detained under section 2 above if it is not satisfied –
  - (i) that he is then suffering from mental disorder or from mental disorder of a nature or degree which warrants his detention in a hospital for assessment (or for assessment followed by medical treatment) for at least a limited period; or
  - (ii) that his detention as aforesaid is justified in the interests of his own health or safety or with a view to the protection of other persons;
- (b) the tribunal shall direct the discharge of a patient liable to be detained otherwise than under section 2 above if it is not satisfied –
  - (i) that he is then suffering from mental disorder or from mental disorder of a nature or degree which makes it appropriate for him to be liable to be detained in a hospital for medical treatment; or
  - (ii) that it is necessary for the health of safety of the patient or for the protection of other persons that he should receive such treatment; or
  - (iia) that appropriate medical treatment is available for him; or
  - (iii) in the case of an application by virtue of paragraph (g) of section 66(1) above, that the patient, if released, would be likely to act in a manner dangerous to other persons or to himself;
- (c) the tribunal shall direct the discharge of a community patient if it is not satisfied –
  - (i) that he is then suffering from mental disorder or mental disorder of a nature or degree which makes it appropriate for him to receive medical treatment; or
  - (ii) that it is necessary for his health or safety or for the protection of other persons that he should receive such treatment; or
  - (iii) that it is necessary that the responsible clinician should be able to exercise the power under section 17E(1) above to recall the patient to hospital; or
  - (iv) that appropriate medical treatment is available for him; or
  - (v) in the case of an application by virtue of paragraph (g) of section 66(1) above, that the patient, if discharged, would be likely to act in a manner dangerous to other persons or to himself.

(1A) In determining whether the criterion in subsection (1)(c)(iii) above is met, the tribunal shall, in particular, consider, having regard to the patient's history of mental disorder and any other relevant factors, what risk there would be of a deterioration of the patient's condition if he were to continue not to be detained in a hospital (as a result, for example, of his refusing or neglecting to receive the medical treatment he requires for his mental disorder).

(2) (*repealed*)

(3) A tribunal may under subsection (1) above direct the discharge of a patient on a future date specified in the direction; and where a tribunal does not direct the discharge of a patient under that subsection the tribunal may –

(a) with a view to facilitating his discharge on a future date, recommend that he be granted leave of absence or transferred to another hospital or into guardianship; and
(b) further consider his case in the event of any such recommendation not being complied with.

(3A) Subsection (1) above does not require a tribunal to direct the discharge of a patient just because it thinks it might be appropriate for the patient to be discharged (subject to the possibility of recall) under a community treatment order; and a tribunal –

(a) may recommend that the responsible clinician consider whether to make a community treatment order; and
(b) may (but need not) further consider the patient's case if the responsible clinician does not make an order.

(4) Where application is made to the appropriate tribunal by or in respect of a patient who is subject to guardianship under this Act, the tribunal may in any case direct that the patient be discharged, and shall so direct if it is satisfied –

(a) that he is not then suffering from mental disorder; or
(b) that it is not necessary in the interests of the welfare of the patient, or for the protection of other persons, that the patient should remain under such guardianship.

(4A) (*repealed*)

(5) (*repealed*)

(6) Subsections (1) to (4) above apply in relation to references to a the appropriate tribunal as they apply in relation to applications made to the appropriate tribunal by or in respect of a patient.

(7) Subsection (1) above shall not apply in the case of a restricted patient except as provided in sections 73 and 74 below.

Amendments—Mental Health Act 2007, ss 1(4), 4(1), (8) (a) (b), 32(4), 55, Sch 1, Pt 1, paras 1, 14(a), (b), (c), Sch 3, paras 1, 21 (1), (2)(a) (b), (3), (4), Sch 11, Pt 2, 5; Mental Health (Patients in the Community) Act 1995, s 1(2), Sch 1, para 10(1), (2), (3); SI 2001/3712; SI 2008/2833.

73 Power to discharge restricted patients

(1) Where an application to the appropriate tribunal is made by a restricted patient who is subject to a restriction order, or where the case of such a patient is referred to the appropriate tribunal, the tribunal shall direct the absolute discharge of the patient if

(a) the tribunal is not satisfied as to the matters mentioned in paragraph (b)(i), (ii) or (iia) of section 72(1) above; and
(b) the tribunal is satisfied that it is not appropriate for the patient to remain liable to be recalled to hospital for further treatment.

(2) Where in the case of any such patient as is mentioned in subsection (1) above –

(a) paragraph (a) of that subsection applies; but
(b) paragraph (b) of that subsection does not apply,

the tribunal shall direct the conditional discharge of the patient.

(3) Where a patient is absolutely discharged under this section he shall thereupon cease to be liable to be detained by virtue of the relevant hospital order, and the restriction order shall cease to have effect accordingly.

(4) Where a patient is conditionally discharged under this section –

- (a) he may be recalled by the Secretary of State under subsection (3) of section 42 above as if he had been conditionally discharged under subsection (2) of that section; and
- (b) the patient shall comply with such conditions (if any) as may be imposed at the time of discharge by the tribunal or at any subsequent time by the Secretary of State.

(5) The Secretary of State may from time to time vary any condition imposed (whether by the tribunal or by him) under subsection (4) above.

(6) Where a restriction order in respect of a patient ceases to have effect after he has been conditionally discharged under this section the patient shall, unless previously recalled, be deemed to be absolutely discharged on the date when the order ceases to have effect and shall cease to be liable to be detained by virtue of the relevant hospital order.

(7) A tribunal may defer a direction for the conditional discharge of a patient until such arrangements as appear to the tribunal to be necessary for that purpose have been made to its satisfaction; and where by virtue of any such deferment no direction has been given on an application or reference before the time when the patient's case comes before the tribunal on a subsequent application or reference, the previous application or reference shall be treated as one on which no direction under this section can be given.

(8) This section is without prejudice to section 42 above.

Amendments—Mental Health Act 2007, ss 4(1), (9), 53, Sch 10, paras 1, 2; SI 2001/3712, SI 2008/2833.

74 Restricted patients subject to restriction directions

(1) Where an application to the appropriate tribunal is made by a restricted patient who is subject to a limitation direction or restriction direction, or where the case of such a patient is referred to the appropriate tribunal the tribunal –

- (a) shall notify the Secretary of State whether, in its opinion, the patient would, if subject to a restriction order, be entitled to be absolutely or conditionally discharged under section 73 above; and
- (b) if the tribunal notifies him that the patient would be entitled to be conditionally discharged, may recommend that in the event of his not being discharged under this section he should continue to be detained in hospital.

(2) If in the case of a patient not falling within subsection (4) below –

- (a) the tribunal notifies the Secretary of State that the patient would be entitled to be absolutely or conditionally discharged; and
- (b) within the period of 90 days beginning with the date of that notification the Secretary of State gives notice to the tribunal that the patient may be so discharged,

the tribunal shall direct the absolute or, as the case may be, the conditional discharge of the patient.

(3) Where a patient continues to be liable to be detained in a hospital at the end of the period referred to in subsection (2)(b) above because the Secretary of State has not given the notice there mentioned, the managers of the hospital shall, unless the tribunal has made a recommendation under subsection (1)(b) above, transfer the patient to a prison

or other institution in which he might have been detained if he had not been removed to hospital, there to be dealt with as if he had not been so removed.

(4) If, in the case of a patient who is subject to a transfer direction under section 48 above, the tribunal notifies the Secretary of State that the patient would be entitled to be absolutely or conditionally discharged, the Secretary of State shall, unless the tribunal has made a recommendation under subsection (1)(b) above, by warrant direct that the patient be remitted to a prison or other institution in which he might have been detained if he had not been removed to hospital, there to be dealt with as if he had not been so removed.

(5) Where a patient is transferred or remitted under subsection (3) or (4) above the relevant hospital direction and the limitation direction or, as the case may be, the relevant transfer direction and the restriction direction shall cease to have effect on his arrival in the prison or other institution.

(5A) Where the tribunal has made a recommendation under subsection (1)(b) above in the case of a patient who is subject to a restriction direction or a limitation direction –

(a) the fact that the restriction direction or limitation direction remains in force does not prevent the making of any application or reference to the Parole Board by or in respect of him or the exercise by him of any power to require the Secretary of State to refer his case to the Parole Board, and
(b) if the Parole Board make a direction or recommendation by virtue of which the patient would become entitled to be released (whether unconditionally or on licence) from any prison or other institution in which he might have been detained if he had not been removed to hospital, the restriction direction or limitation direction shall cease to have effect at the time when he would become entitled to be so released.

(6) Subsections (3) to (8) of section 73 above shall have effect in relation to this section as they have effect in relation to that section, taking references to the relevant hospital order and the restriction order as references to the hospital direction and the limitation direction or, as the case may be, to the transfer direction and the restriction direction.

(7) This section is without prejudice to sections 50 to 53 above in their application to patients who are not discharged under this section.

This section derived from the Mental Health (Amendment) Act 1982, Sch 1, para 6.

Amendments—Criminal Justice Act 2003, s 295; Crime (Sentences) Act 1997, s 55, Sch 4, para 12(10), (11), (12); SI 2008/2833.

75 Applications and references concerning conditionally discharged restricted patients

(1) Where a restricted patient has been conditionally discharged under section 42(2), 73 or 74 above and is subsequently recalled to hospital –

(a) the Secretary of State shall, within one month of the day on which the patient returns or is returned to hospital, refer his case to the appropriate tribunal; and
(b) section 70 above shall apply to the patient as if the relevant hospital order, hospital direction or transfer direction had been made on that day.

(2) Where a restricted patient has been conditionally discharged as aforesaid but has not been recalled to hospital he may apply to the appropriate tribunal –

(a) in the period between the expiration of 12 months and the expiration of two years beginning with the date on which he was conditionally discharged; and

(b) in any subsequent period of two years.

(3) Sections 73 and 74 above shall not apply to an application under subsection (2) above but on any such application the tribunal may –

(a) vary any condition to which the patient is subject in connection with his discharge or impose any condition which might have been imposed in connection therewith; or
(b) direct that the restriction order, limitation direction or restriction direction to which he is subject shall cease to have effect;

and if the tribunal gives a direction under paragraph (b) above the patient shall cease to be liable to be detained by virtue of the relevant hospital order, hospital direction or transfer direction.

Amendments—Crime (Sentences) Act 1997, s 55, Sch 4, para 12(13); Mental Health Act 2007, s 41(a), (b); SI 2008/2833.

General

*****

77 General provisions concerning tribunal applications

(1) No application shall be made to the appropriate tribunal by or in respect of a patient under this Act.

(2) Where under this Act any person is authorised to make an application to the appropriate tribunal within a specified period, not more than one such application shall be made by that person within that period but for that purpose there shall be disregarded any application which is withdrawn in accordance with Tribunal Procedure Rules or rules made under section 78 below.

(3) Subject to subsection (4) below an application to a tribunal authorised to be made by or in respect of a patient under this Act shall be made by notice in writing addressed –

(a) in the case of a patient who is liable to be detained in a hospital, to the First-tier Tribunal where that hospital is in England and to the Mental Health Review Tribunal for Wales where that hospital is in Wales;
(b) in the case of a community patient, to the First-tier Tribunal where the responsible hospital is in England and to the Mental Health Review Tribunal for Wales where that hospital is in Wales;
(c) in the case of a patient subject to guardianship, to the First-tier Tribunal where the patient resides in England and to the Mental Health Review Tribunal for Wales if the patient resides in Wales.

(4) Any application under section 75(2) above shall be made to the First-tier Tribunal where the patient resides in England and to the Mental Health Review Tribunal for Wales where the patient resides in Wales.

Amendments—Mental Health Act 2007, s 32(4), Sch 3, paras 1, 23; SI 2008/2833; SI 2009/1307.

78 Procedure of Mental Health Review Tribunal for Wales

(1) The Lord Chancellor may make rules with respect to the making of applications to the Mental Health Review Tribunal for Wales and with respect to the proceedings of that tribunal and matters incidental to or consequential on such proceedings.

(2) Rules made under this section may in particular make provision –

(a) for enabling the tribunal, or the *chairman* [President] of the tribunal, to postpone the consideration of any application by or in respect of a patient, or of any such application of any specified class, until the expiration of such period (not exceeding 12 months) as may be specified in the rules from the date on which an application by or in respect of the same patient was last considered and determined under this Act by the tribunal or First-tier Tribunal

(b) for the transfer of proceedings to or from the Mental Health Review Tribunal for Wales in any case where, after the making of the application, the patient is moved into or out of Wales;

(c) for restricting the persons qualified to serve as members of the tribunal for the consideration of any application, or of an application of any specified class;

(d) for enabling the tribunal to dispose of an application without a formal hearing where such a hearing is not requested by the applicant or it appears to the tribunal that such a hearing would be detrimental to the health of the patient;

(e) for enabling a tribunal to exclude members of the public, or any specified class of members of the public, from any proceedings of the tribunal, or to prohibit the publication of reports of any such proceedings or the names of any persons concerned in such proceedings;

(f) for regulating the circumstances in which, and the persons by whom, applicants and patients in respect of whom applications are made to the tribunal may, if not desiring to conduct their own case, be represented for the purposes of those applications;

(g) for regulating the methods by which information relevant to an application may be obtained by or furnished to the tribunal, and in particular for authorising the members of the tribunal, or any one or more of them, to visit and interview in private any patient by or in respect of whom an application has been made;

(h) for making available to any applicant, and to any patient in respect of whom an application is made to a tribunal, copies of any documents obtained by or furnished to the tribunal in connection with the application, and a statement of the substance of any oral information so obtained or furnished except where the tribunal considers it undesirable in the interests of the patient or for other special reasons;

(i) for requiring the tribunal, if so requested in accordance with the rules, to furnish such statements of the reasons for any decision given by the tribunal as may be prescribed by the rules, subject to any provision made by the rules for withholding such a statement from a patient or any other person in cases where the tribunal considers that furnishing it would be undesirable in the interests of the patient or for other special reasons;

(j) for conferring on the tribunal such ancillary powers as the Lord Chancellor thinks necessary for the purposes of the exercise of its functions under this Act;

(k) for enabling any functions of the tribunal which relate to matters preliminary or incidental to an application to be performed by the *chairman* [President] of the tribunal.

(3) Subsections (1) and (2) above apply in relation to references to the Mental Health Review Tribunal for Wales as they apply in relation to applications to that tribunal by or in respect of patients.

(4) Rules under this section may make provision as to the procedure to be adopted in cases concerning restricted patients and, in particular –

(a) for restricting the persons qualified to serve as *president* [chairman]of the tribunal for the consideration of an application or reference relating to a restricted patient;

(b) for the transfer of proceedings to or from the tribunal in any case where, after the making of a reference or application in accordance with section 71(4) or 77(4) above, the patient begins or ceases to reside in Wales.

(5) Rules under this section may be so framed as to apply to all applications or references or to applications or references of any specified class and may make different provision in relation to different cases.

(6) Any functions conferred on the *chairman* [President] of the Mental Health Review Tribunal for Wales by rules under this section may be exercised by another member of that tribunal appointed by him for the purpose.

(7) The Mental Health Review Tribunal for Wales may pay allowances in respect of travelling expenses, subsistence and loss of earnings to any person attending the tribunal as an applicant or witness, to the patient who is the subject of the proceedings if he attends otherwise than as the applicant or a witness and to any person (other than an authorised person (within the meaning of Part 3)) who attends as the representative of an applicant.

(8) (*repealed*)

(9) Part I of the Arbitration Act 1996 shall not apply to any proceedings before the Mental Health Review Tribunal for Wales except so far as any provisions of that Act may be applied, with or without modifications, by rules made under this section.

Amendments—Arbitration Act 1996, s 107(1), Sch 3, para 40; Mental Health Act 2007, ss 38(1), (3), 55, Sch 11, Pt 6; Legal Services Act 2007, s 208(1), Sch 21, paras 53, 60; SI 2008/2833.

Prospective Amendments—Sub-s (2): in para (a), (k), word "chairman" in italics repealed and subsequent word in square brackets substituted by the Mental Health Act 2007, s 38(1), (3)(a); Sub-s (4): in para (a) word "president" in italics repealed and subsequent word in square brackets substituted by the Mental Health Act 2007, s 38(1), (3)(d), as from a date to be appointed; word "chairman" in italics repealed and subsequent word in square brackets substituted by the Mental Health Act 2007, s 38(1), (3)(a) as from a date to be appointed.

78A Appeal from the Mental Health Review Tribunal for Wales to the Upper Tribunal

(1) A party to any proceedings before the Mental Health Review Tribunal for Wales may appeal to the Upper Tribunal on any point of law arising from a decision made by the Mental Health Review Tribunal for Wales in those proceedings.

2 An appeal may be brought under subsection (1) above only if, on an application made by the party concerned, the Mental Health Review Tribunal for Wales or the Upper Tribunal has given its permission for the appeal to be brought.

3 Section 12 of the Tribunals, Courts and Enforcement Act 2007 (proceedings on appeal to the Upper Tribunal) applies in relation to appeals to the Upper Tribunal under this section as it applies in relation to appeals to it under section 11 of that Act, but as if references to the Mental Health Review Tribunal for Wales.

Amendment—Inserted by SI 2008/2833.

*****

PART VIII
MISCELLANEOUS FUNCTIONS OF LOCAL AUTHORITIES AND THE SECRETARY OF STATE

*****

Visiting patients

116 Welfare of certain hospital patients

(1) Where a patient to whom this section applies is admitted to a hospital, independent hospital or care home in England and Wales (whether for treatment for mental disorder or for any other reason) then, without prejudice to their duties in relation to the patient apart from the provisions of this section, the authority shall arrange for visits to be made to him on behalf of the authority, and shall take such other steps in relation to the patient while in the hospital, independent hospital or care home as would be expected to be taken by his parents.

(2) This section applies to –

- (a) a child or young person –
  - (i) who is in the care of a local authority by virtue of a care order within the meaning of the Children Act 1989, or
  - (ii) in respect of whom the rights and powers of a parent are vested in a local authority by virtue of section 16 of the Social Work (Scotland) Act 1968;
- (b) a person who is subject to the guardianship of a local social services authority under the provisions of this Act; or
- (c) a person the functions of whose nearest relative under this Act are for the time being transferred to a local social services authority.

Amendments—Mental Health (Scotland) Act 1984, s 127, Sch 3, para 55; Courts and Legal Services Act 1990, s 116, Sch 16, para 42; Care Standards Act 2000, s 116, Sch 4, para 9(1), (5); Mental Health (Care and Treatment) (Scotland) Act 2003 (Consequential Provisions) Order 2005, SI 2005/2078, art 16(1), Sch 3; Mental Health (Care and Treatment) (Scotland) Act 2003 (Modification of Enactments) Order 2005, SSI 2005/465, art 3, Sch 2.

After-care

117 After-care

(1) This section applies to persons who are detained under section 3 above, or admitted to a hospital in pursuance of a hospital order made under section 37 above, or transferred to a hospital in pursuance of a hospital direction made under section 45A above or a transfer direction made under section 47 or 48 above, and then cease to be detained and (whether or not immediately after so ceasing) leave hospital.

(2) It shall be the duty of the clinical commissioning group or Local Health Board and of the local social services authority to provide, in co-operation with relevant voluntary agencies, after-care services for any person to whom this section applies until such time as the clinical commissioning group or Local Health Board and the local social services authority are satisfied that the person concerned is no longer in need of such services; but they shall not be so satisfied in the case of a community patient while he remains such a patient.

(2A) (*repealed*)

(2B) Section 32 above shall apply for the purposes of this section as it applies for the purposes of Part II of this Act.

(2C) References in this Act to after-care services provided for a patient under this section include references to services provided for the patient –

(a) in respect of which direct payments are made under regulations under section 57 of the Health and Social Care Act 2001 or section 12A(4) of the National Health Service Act 2006, and

(b) which would be provided under this section apart from the regulations.

(2D) Subsection (2), in its application to the clinical commissioning group, has effect as if for "to provide" there were substituted "to arrange for the provision of".

(2E) The Secretary of State may by regulations provide that the duty imposed on the clinical commissioning group by subsection (2) is, in the circumstances or to the extent prescribed by the regulations, to be imposed instead on another clinical commissioning group or the National Health Service Commissioning Board.

(2F) Where regulations under subsection (2E) provide that the duty imposed by subsection (2) is to be imposed on the National Health Service Commissioning Board, subsection (2D) has effect as if the reference to the clinical commissioning group were a reference to the National Health Service Commissioning Board.

(2G) Section 272(7) and (8) of the National Health Service Act 2006 applies to the power to make regulations under subsection (2E) as it applies to a power to make regulations under that Act.

(3) In this section "the clinical commissioning group or Local Health Board" means the clinical commissioning group or Local Health Board, and "the local social services authority" means the local social services authority, for the area in which the person concerned is resident or to which he is sent on discharge by the hospital in which he was detained.

Amendments—Mental Health (Patients in the Community) Act 1995, s 1(2), Sch 1, para 15(1), (2), (3), (4); Health Authorities Act 1995, s 2(1), Sch 1, para 107(1), (8)(b); Crime (Sentences) Act 1997, s 55, Sch 4, para 12(17); National Health Service Reform and Health Care Professions Act 2002, s 2(5), Sch 2, Pt 2, paras 42, 47; Mental Health Act 2007, ss 53, 55, Sch 10, paras 1, 5, Sch 11, Pt 5; Health Act 2009, s 13, Sch 1, para 3; Health and Social Care Act 2012, s 40(1), (2)(a), (b), (c), (3), (4)(a), (b), (c); SI 2007/961.

****

PART X
MISCELLANEOUS AND SUPPLEMENTARY

Miscellaneous provisions

131 Informal admission of patients

(1) Nothing in this Act shall be construed as preventing a patient who requires treatment for mental disorder from being admitted to any hospital or registered establishment in pursuance of arrangements made in that behalf and without any application, order or direction rendering him liable to be detained under this Act, or from remaining in any hospital or registered establishment in pursuance of such arrangements after he has ceased to be so liable to be detained.

(2) Subsections (3) and (4) below apply in the case of a patient aged 16 or 17 years who has capacity to consent to the making of such arrangements as are mentioned in subsection (1) above.

(3) If the patient consents to the making of the arrangements, they may be made, carried out and determined on the basis of that consent even though there are one or more persons who have parental responsibility for him.

(4) If the patient does not consent to the making of the arrangements, they may not be made, carried out or determined on the basis of the consent of a person who has parental responsibility for him.

(5) In this section –

(a) the reference to a patient who has capacity is to be read in accordance with the Mental Capacity Act 2005; and
(b) 'parental responsibility' has the same meaning as in the Children Act 1989.

Amendments—Children Act 1989, s 108(5), Sch 13, para 48(5); Care Standards Act 2000, s 116, Sch 4, para 9(1), (2); Mental Health Act 2007, s 43.

131A Accommodation, etc. for children

(1) This section applies in respect of any patient who has not attained the age of 18 years and who –

(a) is liable to be detained in a hospital under this Act; or
(b) is admitted to, or remains in, a hospital in pursuance of such arrangements as are mentioned in section 131(1) above.

(2) The managers of the hospital shall ensure that the patient's environment in the hospital is suitable having regard to his age (subject to his needs).

(3) For the purpose of deciding how to fulfil the duty under subsection (2) above, the managers shall consult a person who appears to them to have knowledge or experience of cases involving patients who have not attained the age of 18 years which makes him suitable to be consulted.

(4) In this section, 'hospital' includes a registered establishment.

Amendments—Inserted by Mental Health Act 2007, s 31(1), (3).

132 Duty of managers of hospitals to give information to detained patients

(1) The managers of a hospital or registered establishment in which a patient is detained under this Act shall take such steps as are practicable to ensure that the patient understands –

(a) under which of the provisions of this Act he is for the time being detained and the effect of that provision; and
(b) what rights of applying to a tribunal are available to him in respect of his detention under that provision;

and those steps shall be taken as soon as practicable after the commencement of the patient's detention under the provision in question.

(2) The managers of a hospital or registered establishment in which a patient is detained as aforesaid shall also take such steps as are practicable to ensure that the patient understands the effect, so far as relevant in his case, of sections 23, 25, 56 to 64, 66(1)(g), 118 and 120 above and section 134 below; and those steps shall be taken as soon as practicable after the commencement of the patient's detention in the hospital or establishment.

(3) The steps to be taken under subsections (1) and (2) above shall include giving the requisite information both orally and in writing.

(4) The managers of a hospital or registered establishment in which a patient is detained as aforesaid shall, except where the patient otherwise requests, take such steps as are practicable to furnish the person (if any) appearing to them to be his nearest relative with a copy of any information given to him in writing under subsections (1) and (2) above; and those steps shall be taken when the information is given to the patient or within a reasonable time thereafter.

Amendments—Care Standards Act 2000, s 116, Sch 4, para 9(1), (2); Mental Health Act 2007, s 32(4), Sch 3, paras 1, 29; SI 2008/2833.

132A Duty of managers of hospitals to give information to community patients

(1) The managers of the responsible hospital shall take such steps as are practicable to ensure that a community patient understands –

(a) the effect of the provisions of this Act applying to community patients; and
(b) what rights of applying to a tribunal are available to him in that capacity;

and those steps shall be taken as soon as practicable after the patient becomes a community patient.

(2) The steps to be taken under subsection (1) above shall include giving the requisite information both orally and in writing.

(3) The managers of the responsible hospital shall, except where the community patient otherwise requests, take such steps as are practicable to furnish the person (if any) appearing to them to be his nearest relative with a copy of any information given to him in writing under subsection (1) above; and those steps shall be taken when the information is given to the patient or within a reasonable time thereafter.

Amendments—Inserted by Mental Health Act 2007, s 32(4), Sch 3, paras 1, 30; SI 2008/2833.

133 Duty of managers of hospitals to inform nearest relatives of discharge

(1) Where a patient liable to be detained under this Act in a hospital or registered establishment is to be discharged otherwise than by virtue of an order for discharge made by his nearest relative, the managers of the hospital or registered establishment shall, subject to subsection (2) below, take such steps as are practicable to inform the person (if any) appearing to them to be the nearest relative of the patient; and that information shall, if practicable, be given at least seven days before the date of discharge.

(1A) The reference in subsection (1) above to a patient who is to be discharged includes a patient who is to be discharged from hospital under section 17A above.

(1B) Subsection (1) above shall also apply in a case where a community patient is discharged under section 23 or 72 above (otherwise than by virtue of an order for discharge made by his nearest relative), but with the reference in that subsection to the managers of the hospital or registered establishment being read as a reference to the managers of the responsible hospital.

(2) Subsection (1) above shall not apply if the patient or his nearest relative has requested that information about the patient's discharge should not be given under this section.

Amendments—Care Standards Act 2000, s 116, Sch 4, para 9(1), (2); Mental Health Act 2007, s 32(4), Sch 3, paras 1, 31.

*****

135 Warrant to search for and remove patients

(1) If it appears to a justice of the peace, on information on oath laid by an approved mental health professional, that there is reasonable cause to suspect that a person believed to be suffering from mental disorder –

(a) has been, or is being, ill-treated, neglected or kept otherwise than under proper control, in any place within the jurisdiction of the justice, or
(b) being unable to care for himself, is living alone in any such place,

the justice may issue a warrant authorising any constable to enter, if need be by force, any premises specified in the warrant in which that person is believed to be, and, if thought fit, to remove him to a place of safety with a view to the making of an application in respect of him under Part II of this Act, or of other arrangements for his treatment or care.

(2) If it appears to a justice of the peace, on information on oath laid by any constable or other person who is authorised by or under this Act or under article 8 of the Mental Health (Care and Treatment) (Scotland) Act 2003 (Consequential Provisions) Order 2005 to take a patient to any place, or to take into custody or retake a patient who is liable under this Act or under the said article 8 to be so taken or retaken –

(a) that there is reasonable cause to believe that the patient is to be found on premises within the jurisdiction of the justice; and
(b) that admission to the premises has been refused or that a refusal of such admission is apprehended,

the justice may issue a warrant authorising any constable to enter the premises, if need be by force, and remove the patient.

(3) A patient who is removed to a place of safety in the execution of a warrant issued under this section may be detained there for a period not exceeding 72 hours.

(3A) A constable, an approved mental health professional or a person authorised by either of them for the purposes of this subsection may, before the end of the period of 72 hours mentioned in subsection (3) above, take a person detained in a place of safety under that subsection to one or more other places of safety.

(3B) A person taken to a place of safety under subsection (3A) above may be detained there for a period ending no later than the end of the period of 72 hours mentioned in subsection (3) above.

(4) In the execution of a warrant issued under subsection (1) above, a constable shall be accompanied by an approved mental health professional and by a registered medical practitioner, and in the execution of a warrant issued under subsection (2) above a constable may be accompanied –

(a) by a registered medical practitioner;
(b) by any person authorised by or under this Act or under article 8 of the Mental Health (Care and Treatment) (Scotland) Act 2003 (Consequential Provisions) Order 2005 to take or retake the patient.

(5) It shall not be necessary in any information or warrant under subsection (1) above to name the patient concerned.

(6) In this section 'place of safety' means residential accommodation provided by a local social services authority under Part III of the National Assistance Act 1948, a hospital as defined by this Act, a police station, an independent hospital or care home for mentally disordered persons or any other suitable place the occupier of which is willing temporarily to receive the patient.

Amendments—Mental Health (Scotland) Act 1984, s 127(1), Sch 3, para 56; Police and Criminal Evidence Act 1984, s 119, Sch 6, Pt I, para 26, Sch 7, Pt I; National Health Service and Community Care Act 1990, s 66(2), Sch 10; Care Standards Act 2000, s 116, Sch 4, para 9(1), (9); Mental Health (Care and Treatment) (Scotland) Act 2003 (Consequential Provisions) Order 2005, SI 2005/2078, art 15, Sch 1, para 2(1), (9); Mental Health Act 2007, ss 21, 44(1), (2), Sch 2, paras 1, 10.

136 Mentally disordered persons found in public places

(1) If a constable finds in a place to which the public have access a person who appears to him to be suffering from mental disorder and to be in immediate need of care or control, the constable may, if he thinks it necessary to do so in the interests of that person or for the protection of other persons, remove that person to a place of safety within the meaning of section 135 above.

(2) A person removed to a place of safety under this section may be detained there for a period not exceeding 72 hours for the purpose of enabling him to be examined by a registered medical practitioner and to be interviewed by an approved mental health professional and of making any necessary arrangements for his treatment or care.

(3) A constable, an approved mental health professional or a person authorised by either of them for the purposes of this subsection may, before the end of the period of 72 hours mentioned in subsection (2) above, take a person detained in a place of safety under that subsection to one or more other places of safety.

(4) A person taken to a place of a safety under subsection (3) above may be detained there for a purpose mentioned in subsection (2) above for a period ending no later than the end of the period of 72 hours mentioned in that subsection.

Amendments—Mental Health Act 2007, ss 21, 44(1), (3), Sch 2, paras 1, 10.

*****

Supplemental

*****

145 Interpretation

(1) In this Act, unless the context otherwise requires –

'absent without leave' has the meaning given to it by section 18 above and related expressions (including expressions relating to a patient's liability to be returned to a hospital or other place) shall be construed accordingly;

'application for admission for assessment' has the meaning given in section 2 above;

'application for admission for treatment' has the meaning given in section 3 above;

'the appropriate tribunal' has the meaning given by section 66(4) above

'approved clinician' means a person approved by the Secretary of State [or another person by virtue of section 12ZA or 12ZB above] (in relation to England) or by the Welsh Ministers (in relation to Wales) to act as an approved clinician for the purposes of this Act;

'approved mental health professional' has the meaning given in section 114 above;

'care home' has the same meaning as in the Care Standards Act 2000;

'community patient' has the meaning given in section 17A above;
'community treatment order' and 'the community treatment order' have the meanings given in section 17A above;
'the community treatment period' has the meaning given in section 20A above;
'high security psychiatric services' has the same meaning as in section 4 of the National Health Service Act 2006 or section 4 of the National Health Service (Wales) Act 2006,
'hospital' means –

(a) any health service hospital within the meaning of the National Health Service Act 2006 or the National Health Service (Wales) Act 2006; and
(b) any accommodation provided by a local authority and used as a hospital by or on behalf of the Secretary of State under that Act; and
(c) any hospital as defined by section 206 of the National Health Service (Wales) Act 2006 which is vested in a Local Health Board;

and 'hospital within the meaning of Part II of this Act' has the meaning given in section 34 above;
'hospital direction' has the meaning given in section 45A(3)(a) above;
'hospital order' and 'guardianship order' have the meanings respectively given in section 37 above;
'independent hospital' –

(a) in relation to England, means a hospital as defined by section 275 of the National Health Service Act 2006 that is not a health service hospital as defined by that section, and
(b) in relation to Wales, has the same meaning as in the Care Standards Act 2000;]

'interim hospital order' has the meaning given in section 38 above;
'limitation direction' has the meaning given in section 45A(3)(b) above;
'Local Health Board' means a Local Health Board established under section 11 of the National Health Services (Wales) Act 2006;
'local social services authority' means a council which is a local authority for the purpose of the Local Authority Social Services Act 1970;
'the managers' means –

(a) in relation to a hospital vested in the Secretary of State for the purposes of his functions under the National Health Service Act 2006, or in the Welsh Ministers for the purposes of their functions under the National Health Service (Wales) Act 2006, and in relation to any accommodation provided by a local authority and used as a hospital by or on behalf of the Secretary of State under the National Health Service Act 2006, or of the Welsh Ministers under the National Health Service (Wales) Act 2006, the Secretary of State where the Secretary is responsible for the administration of the hospital or] the *Primary Care Trust, Strategic Health Authority*, Local Health Board or Special Health Authority responsible for the administration of the hospital;
(b) (*repealed*)
(bb) in relation to a hospital vested in a Primary Care Trust or a National Health Service trust, the trust
(bc) in relation to a hospital vested in an NHS foundation trust, the trust;
(bd) in relation to a hospital vested in a Local Health Board, the Board;
(c) in relation to a registered establishment –
    (i) if the establishment is in England, the person or persons registered as a service provider under Chapter 2 of Part 1 of the Health and Social Care Act 2008 in respect of the regulated activity (within the meaning of

that Part) relating to the assessment or medical treatment of mental disorder that is carried out in the establishment, and

(ii) if the establishment is in Wales, the person or persons registered in respect of the establishment under Part 2 of the Care Standards Act 2000;]

and in this definition 'hospital' means a hospital within the meaning of Part II of this Act;

'medical treatment' includes nursing, psychological intervention and specialist mental health habilitation, rehabilitation and care (but see also subsection (4) below);

'mental disorder' has the meaning given in section 1 above (subject to sections 86(4) and 141(6B));

'nearest relative', in relation to a patient, has the meaning given in Part II of this Act;

'patient' means a person suffering or appearing to be suffering from mental disorder;

'Primary Care Trust' means a Primary Care Trust established under section 18 of the National Health Service Act 2006;

'registered establishment' has the meaning given in section 34 above;

'the regulatory authority' means –

(a) in relation to England, the Care Quality Commission;

(b) in relation to Wales, the Welsh Ministers;

'the responsible hospital' has the meaning given in section 17A above;

'restriction direction' has the meaning given to it by section 49 above;

'restriction order' has the meaning given to it by section 41 above;

'Special Health Authority' means a Special Health Authority established under section 28 of the National Health Service Act 2006, or section 22 of the National Health Service (Wales) Act 2006;

'Strategic Health Authority' means a Strategic Health Authority established under section 13 of the National Health Service Act 2006;

'transfer direction' has the meaning given to it by section 47 above.

(1AA) Where high security psychiatric services and other services are provided at a hospital, the part of the hospital at which high security psychiatric services are provided and the other part shall be treated as separate hospitals for the purposes of this Act.

(1AB) References in this Act to appropriate medical treatment shall be construed in accordance with section 3(4) above.

(1AC) References in this Act to an approved mental health professional shall be construed as references to an approved mental health professional acting on behalf of a local social services authority, unless the context otherwise requires.

(1A) *(repealed)*

(2) *(repealed)*

(3) In relation to a person who is liable to be detained or subject to guardianship or a community patient by virtue of an order or direction under Part III of this Act (other than under section 35, 36 or 38), any reference in this Act to any enactment contained in Part II of this Act or in section 66 or 67 above shall be construed as a reference to that enactment as it applies to that person by virtue of Part III of this Act.

(4) Any reference in this Act to medical treatment, in relation to mental disorder, shall be construed as a reference to medical treatment the purpose of which is to alleviate, or prevent a worsening of, the disorder or one or more of its symptoms or manifestations.

Amendments—National Health Service and Community Care Act 1990, s 66(1), Sch 9, para 24(9); Statute Law (Repeals) Act 1993; Mental Health (Amendment) Act 1994, s 1; Health Authorities Act 1995, s 2, Sch 1, Pt III, para 107(14); Mental Health (Patients in the Community) Act 1995, s 1(2), Sch 1, para 20; Crime (Sentences) Act 1997, s 55, Sch 4, para 12(19); Health Act 1999, ss 41(2), 65, Sch 4, paras 65, 69, Sch 5; Care Standards Act 2000, ss 116, 117(2), Sch 4, para 9(1), (10), Sch 6; Health Act 1999 (Supplementary, Consequential etc. Provisions) Order 2000, SI 2000/90, art 3(1), Sch 1, para 16(1), (9); National Health Service Reform and Health Care Professions Act 2002, s 2(5), Sch 2, Pt 2, paras 42, 49; National Health Service Reform and Health Care Professions Act 2002 (Supplementary, Consequential etc. Provisions) Regulations 2002, SI 2002/2469, reg 4, Sch 1, Pt 1, para 10(1), (4); Health and Social Care (Community Health and Standards) Act 2003, s 34, Sch 4, paras 50, 57; Mental Capacity Act 2005, s 67(1), (2), Sch 6, para 29(1), (7), Sch 7; National Health Service (Consequential Provisions) Act 2006, s 2, Sch 1, paras 62, 70; Mental Health Act 2007, ss 1(4), 4(1), (10), 7, 14(1), (5), 21, 32(4), 46(1), (3), 55, Sch 1, Pt 1, paras 1, 17, Sch 2, paras 1, 11, Sch 3, paras 1, 34, Sch 11, Pt 5; References to Health Authorities Order 2007, SI 2007/961, art 3, Sch 1, para 13(1), (13); SI 2008/2833; Health and Social Care Act 2008, s 52(5), Sch 3, paras 1, 13; SI 2010/813; Sub-s (1): in definition "the managers" in para (a) words from "the Secretary of" to "the hospital or" in square brackets inserted by the Health and Social Care Act 2012, s 55(2), Sch 5, paras 24, 31(1)(a)(i), Date in force (in so far as is necessary for enabling the exercise of any power to make an order or regulations or to give directions): 27 March 2012: see the Health and Social Care Act 2012, s 306(1)(d); Date in force (for remaining purposes): to be appointed: see the Health and Social Care Act 2012, s 306(4).

Prospective Amendments—Sub-s (1): in definition "approved clinician" words "or another person by virtue of section 12ZA or 12ZB above" in square brackets inserted by the Health and Social Care Act 2012, s 38(4); Sub-s (1): in definition "the managers" in para (a) words "Strategic Health Authority," in italics repealed by the Health and Social Care Act 2012, s 55(2), Sch 5, paras 24, 31(1)(a)(iii), as from a date to be appointed; Sub-s (1): definition "Primary Care Trust" repealed by the Health and Social Care Act 2012, s 55(2), Sch 5, paras 24, 31(1)(c); Date in force: to be appointed; Sub-s (1): definition "Strategic Health Authority" repealed by the Health and Social Care Act 2012, s 55(2), Sch 5, paras 24, 31(1)(d); as from a date to be appointed.

*****

F2

F2

TRIBUNALS, COURTS AND ENFORCEMENT ACT 2007

(2007 c. 15)

ARRANGEMENT OF SECTIONS

PART 1

TRIBUNALS AND INQUIRIES

Chapter 1

Tribunal Judiciary: Independence and Senior President

Review of decisions and appeals

PART 1
TRIBUNALS AND INQUIRIES

Chapter 1
Tribunal Judiciary: Independence and Senior President

Review of decisions and appeals

****

9 Review of decision of First-tier Tribunal

(1) The First-tier Tribunal may review a decision made by it on a matter in a case, other than a decision that is an excluded decision for the purposes of section 11(1) (but see subsection (9)).

(2) The First-tier Tribunal's power under subsection (1) in relation to a decision is exercisable –

(a) of its own initiative, or
(b) on application by a person who for the purposes of section 11(2) has a right of appeal in respect of the decision.

(3) Tribunal Procedure Rules may –

(a) provide that the First-tier Tribunal may not under subsection (1) review (whether of its own initiative or on application under subsection (2)(b)) a decision of a description specified for the purposes of this paragraph in Tribunal Procedure Rules;
(b) provide that the First-tier Tribunal's power under subsection (1) to review a decision of a description specified for the purposes of this paragraph in Tribunal Procedure Rules is exercisable only of the tribunal's own initiative;
(c) provide that an application under subsection (2)(b) that is of a description specified for the purposes of this paragraph in Tribunal Procedure Rules may be made only on grounds specified for the purposes of this paragraph in Tribunal Procedure Rules;
(d) provide, in relation to a decision of a description specified for the purposes of this paragraph in Tribunal Procedure Rules, that the First-tier Tribunal's power under subsection (1) to review the decision of its own initiative is exercisable only on grounds specified for the purposes of this paragraph in Tribunal Procedure Rules.

(4) Where the First-tier Tribunal has under subsection (1) reviewed a decision, the First-tier Tribunal may in the light of the review do any of the following –

(a) correct accidental errors in the decision or in a record of the decision;
(b) amend reasons given for the decision;
(c) set the decision aside.

(5) Where under subsection (4)(c) the First-tier Tribunal sets a decision aside, the First-tier Tribunal must either –

(a) re-decide the matter concerned, or
(b) refer that matter to the Upper Tribunal.

(6) Where a matter is referred to the Upper Tribunal under subsection (5)(b), the Upper Tribunal must re-decide the matter.

(7) Where the Upper Tribunal is under subsection (6) re-deciding a matter, it may make any decision which the First-tier Tribunal could make if the First-tier Tribunal were re-deciding the matter.

(8) Where a tribunal is acting under subsection (5)(a) or (6), it may make such findings of fact as it considers appropriate.

(9) This section has effect as if a decision under subsection (4)(c) to set aside an earlier decision were not an excluded decision for the purposes of section 11(1), but the First-tier Tribunal's only power in the light of a review under subsection (1) of a decision under subsection (4)(c) is the power under subsection (4)(a).

(10) A decision of the First-tier Tribunal may not be reviewed under subsection (1) more than once, and once the First-tier Tribunal has decided that an earlier decision should not be reviewed under subsection (1) it may not then decide to review that earlier decision under that subsection.

(11) Where under this section a decision is set aside and the matter concerned is then re-decided, the decision set aside and the decision made in re-deciding the matter are for the purposes of subsection (10) to be taken to be different decisions.

10 Review of decision of Upper Tribunal

(1) The Upper Tribunal may review a decision made by it on a matter in a case, other than a decision that is an excluded decision for the purposes of section 13(1) (but see subsection (7)).

(2) The Upper Tribunal's power under subsection (1) in relation to a decision is exercisable –

(a) of its own initiative, or
(b) on application by a person who for the purposes of section 13(2) has a right of appeal in respect of the decision.

(3) Tribunal Procedure Rules may –

(a) provide that the Upper Tribunal may not under subsection (1) review (whether of its own initiative or on application under subsection (2)(b)) a decision of a description specified for the purposes of this paragraph in Tribunal Procedure Rules;
(b) provide that the Upper Tribunal's power under subsection (1) to review a decision of a description specified for the purposes of this paragraph in Tribunal Procedure Rules is exercisable only of the tribunal's own initiative;
(c) provide that an application under subsection (2)(b) that is of a description specified for the purposes of this paragraph in Tribunal Procedure Rules may be made only on grounds specified for the purposes of this paragraph in Tribunal Procedure Rules;
(d) provide, in relation to a decision of a description specified for the purposes of this paragraph in Tribunal Procedure Rules, that the Upper Tribunal's power under subsection (1) to review the decision of its own initiative is exercisable only on grounds specified for the purposes of this paragraph in Tribunal Procedure Rules.

(4) Where the Upper Tribunal has under subsection (1) reviewed a decision, the Upper Tribunal may in the light of the review do any of the following –

(a) correct accidental errors in the decision or in a record of the decision;
(b) amend reasons given for the decision;
(c) set the decision aside.

(5) Where under subsection (4)(c) the Upper Tribunal sets a decision aside, the Upper Tribunal must re-decide the matter concerned.

(6) Where the Upper Tribunal is acting under subsection (5), it may make such findings of fact as it considers appropriate.

(7) This section has effect as if a decision under subsection (4)(c) to set aside an earlier decision were not an excluded decision for the purposes of section 13(1), but the Upper Tribunal's only power in the light of a review under subsection (1) of a decision under subsection (4)(c) is the power under subsection (4)(a).

(8) A decision of the Upper Tribunal may not be reviewed under subsection (1) more than once, and once the Upper Tribunal has decided that an earlier decision should not be reviewed under subsection (1) it may not then decide to review that earlier decision under that subsection.

(9) Where under this section a decision is set aside and the matter concerned is then re-decided, the decision set aside and the decision made in re-deciding the matter are for the purposes of subsection (8) to be taken to be different decisions.

11 Right to appeal to Upper Tribunal

(1) For the purposes of subsection (2), the reference to a right of appeal is to a right to appeal to the Upper Tribunal on any point of law arising from a decision made by the First-tier Tribunal other than an excluded decision.

(2) Any party to a case has a right of appeal, subject to subsection (8).

(3) That right may be exercised only with permission (or, in Northern Ireland, leave).

(4) Permission (or leave) may be given by –

- (a) the First-tier Tribunal, or
- (b) the Upper Tribunal,

on an application by the party.

(5) For the purposes of subsection (1), an 'excluded decision' is –

- (a) any decision of the First-tier Tribunal on an appeal made in exercise of a right conferred by the Criminal Injuries Compensation Scheme in compliance with section 5(1)(a) of the Criminal Injuries Compensation Act 1995 (c 53) (appeals against decisions on reviews),
- (aa) any decision of the First-tier Tribunal on an appeal made in exercise of a right conferred by the Victims of Overseas Terrorism Compensation Scheme in compliance with section 52(3) of the Crime and Security Act 2010,
- (b) any decision of the First-tier Tribunal on an appeal under section 28(4) or (6) of the Data Protection Act 1998 (c 29) (appeals against national security certificate),
- (c) any decision of the First-tier Tribunal on an appeal under section 60(1) or (4) of the Freedom of Information Act 2000 (c 36) (appeals against national security certificate),
- (d) a decision of the First-tier Tribunal under section 9 –
  - (i) to review, or not to review, an earlier decision of the tribunal,
  - (ii) to take no action, or not to take any particular action, in the light of a review of an earlier decision of the tribunal,
  - (iii) to set aside an earlier decision of the tribunal, or
  - (iv) to refer, or not to refer, a matter to the Upper Tribunal,
- (e) a decision of the First-tier Tribunal that is set aside under section 9 (including a decision set aside after proceedings on an appeal under this section have been begun), or
- (f) any decision of the First-tier Tribunal that is of a description specified in an order made by the Lord Chancellor.

(6) A description may be specified under subsection (5)(f) only if –

- (a) in the case of a decision of that description, there is a right to appeal to a court, the Upper Tribunal or any other tribunal from the decision and that right is, or includes, something other than a right (however expressed) to appeal on any point of law arising from the decision, or

(b) decisions of that description are made in carrying out a function transferred under section 30 and prior to the transfer of the function under section 30(1) there was no right to appeal from decisions of that description.

(7) Where –

(a) an order under subsection (5)(f) specifies a description of decisions, and
(b) decisions of that description are made in carrying out a function transferred under section 30,

the order must be framed so as to come into force no later than the time when the transfer under section 30 of the function takes effect (but power to revoke the order continues to be exercisable after that time, and power to amend the order continues to be exercisable after that time for the purpose of narrowing the description for the time being specified).

(8) The Lord Chancellor may by order make provision for a person to be treated as being, or to be treated as not being, a party to a case for the purposes of subsection (2).

Amendments—Crime and Security Act 2010, s 59(2)(b).

12 Proceedings on appeal to Upper Tribunal

(1) Subsection (2) applies if the Upper Tribunal, in deciding an appeal under section 11, finds that the making of the decision concerned involved the making of an error on a point of law.

(2) The Upper Tribunal –

(a) may (but need not) set aside the decision of the First-tier Tribunal, and
(b) if it does, must either –
 (i) remit the case to the First-tier Tribunal with directions for its reconsideration, or
 (ii) re-make the decision.

(3) In acting under subsection (2)(b)(i), the Upper Tribunal may also –

(a) direct that the members of the First-tier Tribunal who are chosen to reconsider the case are not to be the same as those who made the decision that has been set aside;
(b) give procedural directions in connection with the reconsideration of the case by the First-tier Tribunal.

(4) In acting under subsection (2)(b)(ii), the Upper Tribunal –

(a) may make any decision which the First-tier Tribunal could make if the First-tier Tribunal were re-making the decision, and
(b) may make such findings of fact as it considers appropriate.

13 Right to appeal to Court of Appeal etc

(1) For the purposes of subsection (2), the reference to a right of appeal is to a right to appeal to the relevant appellate court on any point of law arising from a decision made by the Upper Tribunal other than an excluded decision.

(2) Any party to a case has a right of appeal, subject to subsection (14).

(3) That right may be exercised only with permission (or, in Northern Ireland, leave).

(4) Permission (or leave) may be given by –

(a) the Upper Tribunal, or
(b) the relevant appellate court, on an application by the party.

(5) An application may be made under subsection (4) to the relevant appellate court only if permission (or leave) has been refused by the Upper Tribunal.

(6) The Lord Chancellor may, as respects an application under subsection (4) that falls within subsection (7) and for which the relevant appellate court is the Court of Appeal in England and Wales or the Court of Appeal in Northern Ireland, by order make provision for permission (or leave) not to be granted on the application unless the Upper Tribunal or (as the case may be) the relevant appellate court considers –

(a) that the proposed appeal would raise some important point of principle or practice, or
(b) that there is some other compelling reason for the relevant appellate court to hear the appeal.

(7) An application falls within this subsection if the application is for permission (or leave) to appeal from any decision of the Upper Tribunal on an appeal under section 11.

(8) For the purposes of subsection (1), an "excluded decision" is –

(a) any decision of the Upper Tribunal on an appeal under section 28(4) or (6) of the Data Protection Act 1998 (c 29) (appeals against national security certificate),
(b) any decision of the Upper Tribunal on an appeal under section 60(1) or (4) of the Freedom of Information Act 2000 (c 36) (appeals against national security certificate),
(c) any decision of the Upper Tribunal on an application under section 11(4)(b) (application for permission or leave to appeal),
(d) a decision of the Upper Tribunal under section 10 –
    (i) to review, or not to review, an earlier decision of the tribunal,
    (ii) to take no action, or not to take any particular action, in the light of a review of an earlier decision of the tribunal, or
    (iii) to set aside an earlier decision of the tribunal,
(e) a decision of the Upper Tribunal that is set aside under section 10 (including a decision set aside after proceedings on an appeal under this section have been begun), or
(f) any decision of the Upper Tribunal that is of a description specified in an order made by the Lord Chancellor.

(9) A description may be specified under subsection (8)(f) only if –

(a) in the case of a decision of that description, there is a right to appeal to a court from the decision and that right is, or includes, something other than a right (however expressed) to appeal on any point of law arising from the decision, or
(b) decisions of that description are made in carrying out a function transferred under section 30 and prior to the transfer of the function under section 30(1) there was no right to appeal from decisions of that description.

(10) Where –

(a) an order under subsection (8)(f) specifies a description of decisions, and

(b) decisions of that description are made in carrying out a function transferred under section 30, the order must be framed so as to come into force no later than the time when the transfer under section 30 of the function takes effect (but power to revoke the order continues to be exercisable after that time, and power to amend the order continues to be exercisable after that time for the purpose of narrowing the description for the time being specified).

(11) Before the Upper Tribunal decides an application made to it under subsection (4), the Upper Tribunal must specify the court that is to be the relevant appellate court as respects the proposed appeal.

(12) The court to be specified under subsection (11) in relation to a proposed appeal is whichever of the following courts appears to the Upper Tribunal to be the most appropriate –

(a) the Court of Appeal in England and Wales;
(b) the Court of Session;
(c) the Court of Appeal in Northern Ireland.

(13) In this section except subsection (11), "the relevant appellate court", as respects an appeal, means the court specified as respects that appeal by the Upper Tribunal under subsection (11).

(14) The Lord Chancellor may by order make provision for a person to be treated as being, or to be treated as not being, a party to a case for the purposes of subsection (2).

(15) Rules of court may make provision as to the time within which an application under subsection (4) to the relevant appellate court must be made.

14 Proceedings on appeal to Court of Appeal etc

(1) Subsection (2) applies if the relevant appellate court, in deciding an appeal under section 13, finds that the making of the decision concerned involved the making of an error on a point of law.

(2) The relevant appellate court –

(a) may (but need not) set aside the decision of the Upper Tribunal, and
(b) if it does, must either –
    (i) remit the case to the Upper Tribunal or, where the decision of the Upper Tribunal was on an appeal or reference from another tribunal or some other person, to the Upper Tribunal or that other tribunal or person, with directions for its reconsideration, or
    (ii) re-make the decision.

(3) In acting under subsection (2)(b)(i), the relevant appellate court may also –

(a) direct that the persons who are chosen to reconsider the case are not to be the same as those who –
    (i) where the case is remitted to the Upper Tribunal, made the decision of the Upper Tribunal that has been set aside, or
    (ii) where the case is remitted to another tribunal or person, made the decision in respect of which the appeal or reference to the Upper Tribunal was made;
(b) give procedural directions in connection with the reconsideration of the case by the Upper Tribunal or other tribunal or person.

(4) In acting under subsection (2)(b)(ii), the relevant appellate court –

(a) may make any decision which the Upper Tribunal could make if the Upper Tribunal were re-making the decision or (as the case may be) which the other tribunal or person could make if that other tribunal or person were re-making the decision, and
(b) may make such findings of fact as it considers appropriate.

(5) Where –

(a) under subsection (2)(b)(i) the relevant appellate court remits a case to the Upper Tribunal, and
(b) the decision set aside under subsection (2)(a) was made by the Upper Tribunal on an appeal or reference from another tribunal or some other person,

the Upper Tribunal may (instead of reconsidering the case itself) remit the case to that other tribunal or person, with the directions given by the relevant appellate court for its reconsideration.

(6) In acting under subsection (5), the Upper Tribunal may also –

(a) direct that the persons who are chosen to reconsider the case are not to be the same as those who made the decision in respect of which the appeal or reference to the Upper Tribunal was made;
(b) give procedural directions in connection with the reconsideration of the case by the other tribunal or person.

(7) In this section 'the relevant appellate court', as respects an appeal under section 13, means the court specified as respects that appeal by the Upper Tribunal under section 13(11).

'Judicial review'

15 Upper Tribunal's 'judicial review' jurisdiction

(1) The Upper Tribunal has power, in cases arising under the law of England and Wales or under the law of Northern Ireland, to grant the following kinds of relief –

(a) a mandatory order;
(b) a prohibiting order;
(c) a quashing order;
(d) a declaration;
(e) an injunction.

(2) The power under subsection (1) may be exercised by the Upper Tribunal if –

(a) certain conditions are met (see section 18), or
(b) the tribunal is authorised to proceed even though not all of those conditions are met (see section 19(3) and (4)).

(3) Relief under subsection (1) granted by the Upper Tribunal –

(a) has the same effect as the corresponding relief granted by the High Court on an application for judicial review, and
(b) is enforceable as if it were relief granted by the High Court on an application for judicial review.

(4) In deciding whether to grant relief under subsection (1)(a), (b) or (c), the Upper Tribunal must apply the principles that the High Court would apply in deciding whether to grant that relief on an application for judicial review.

(5) In deciding whether to grant relief under subsection (1)(d) or (e), the Upper Tribunal must –

(a) in cases arising under the law of England and Wales apply the principles that the High Court would apply in deciding whether to grant that relief under section 31(2) of the Senior Courts Act 1981 (c 54) on an application for judicial review, and
(b) in cases arising under the law of Northern Ireland apply the principles that the High Court would apply in deciding whether to grant that relief on an application for judicial review.

(6) For the purposes of the application of subsection (3)(a) in relation to cases arising under the law of Northern Ireland –

(a) a mandatory order under subsection (1)(a) shall be taken to correspond to an order of mandamus,
(b) a prohibiting order under subsection (1)(b) shall be taken to correspond to an order of prohibition, and
(c) a quashing order under subsection (1)(c) shall be taken to correspond to an order of certiorari.

Amendments—Constitutional Reform Act 2005, s 59(5), Sch 11, Pt 1, para 1(2).

16 Application for relief under section 15(1)

(1) This section applies in relation to an application to the Upper Tribunal for relief under section 15(1).

(2) The application may be made only if permission (or, in a case arising under the law of Northern Ireland, leave) to make it has been obtained from the tribunal.

(3) The tribunal may not grant permission (or leave) to make the application unless it considers that the applicant has a sufficient interest in the matter to which the application relates.

(4) Subsection (5) applies where the tribunal considers –

(a) that there has been undue delay in making the application, and
(b) that granting the relief sought on the application would be likely to cause substantial hardship to, or substantially prejudice the rights of, any person or would be detrimental to good administration.

(5) The tribunal may –

(a) refuse to grant permission (or leave) for the making of the application;
(b) refuse to grant any relief sought on the application.

(6) The tribunal may award to the applicant damages, restitution or the recovery of a sum due if –

(a) the application includes a claim for such an award arising from any matter to which the application relates, and
(b) the tribunal is satisfied that such an award would have been made by the High Court if the claim had been made in an action begun in the High Court by the applicant at the time of making the application.

(7) An award under subsection (6) may be enforced as if it were an award of the High Court.

(8) Where –

(a) the tribunal refuses to grant permission (or leave) to apply for relief under section 15(1),
(b) the applicant appeals against that refusal, and
(c) the Court of Appeal grants the permission (or leave),

the Court of Appeal may go on to decide the application for relief under section 15(1).

(9) Subsections (4) and (5) do not prevent Tribunal Procedure Rules from limiting the time within which applications may be made.

17 Quashing orders under section 15(1): supplementary provision

(1) If the Upper Tribunal makes a quashing order under section 15(1)(c) in respect of a decision, it may in addition –

(a) remit the matter concerned to the court, tribunal or authority that made the decision, with a direction to reconsider the matter and reach a decision in accordance with the findings of the Upper Tribunal, or
(b) substitute its own decision for the decision in question.

(2) The power conferred by subsection (1)(b) is exercisable only if –

(a) the decision in question was made by a court or tribunal,
(b) the decision is quashed on the ground that there has been an error of law, and
(c) without the error, there would have been only one decision that the court or tribunal could have reached.

(3) Unless the Upper Tribunal otherwise directs, a decision substituted by it under subsection (1)(b) has effect as if it were a decision of the relevant court or tribunal.

18 Limits of jurisdiction under section 15(1)

(1) This section applies where an application made to the Upper Tribunal seeks (whether or not alone) –

(a) relief under section 15(1), or
(b) permission (or, in a case arising under the law of Northern Ireland, leave) to apply for relief under section 15(1).

(2) If Conditions 1 to 4 are met, the tribunal has the function of deciding the application.

(3) If the tribunal does not have the function of deciding the application, it must by order transfer the application to the High Court.

(4) Condition 1 is that the application does not seek anything other than –

(a) relief under section 15(1);
(b) permission (or, in a case arising under the law of Northern Ireland, leave) to apply for relief under section 15(1);
(c) an award under section 16(6);
(d) interest;
(e) costs.

(5) Condition 2 is that the application does not call into question anything done by the Crown Court.

(6) Condition 3 is that the application falls within a class specified for the purposes of this subsection in a direction given in accordance with Part 1 of Schedule 2 to the Constitutional Reform Act 2005 (c 4).

(7) The power to give directions under subsection (6) includes –

(a) power to vary or revoke directions made in exercise of the power, and
(b) power to make different provision for different purposes.

(8) Condition 4 is that the judge presiding at the hearing of the application is either –

(a) a judge of the High Court or the Court of Appeal in England and Wales or Northern Ireland, or a judge of the Court of Session, or
(b) such other persons as may be agreed from time to time between the Lord Chief Justice, the Lord President, or the Lord Chief Justice of Northern Ireland, as the case may be, and the Senior President of Tribunals.

(9) Where the application is transferred to the High Court under subsection (3) –

(a) the application is to be treated for all purposes as if it –
  (i) had been made to the High Court, and
  (ii) sought things corresponding to those sought from the tribunal, and
(b) any steps taken, permission (or leave) given or orders made by the tribunal in relation to the application are to be treated as taken, given or made by the High Court.

(10) Rules of court may make provision for the purpose of supplementing subsection (9).

(11) The provision that may be made by Tribunal Procedure Rules about amendment of an application for relief under section 15(1) includes, in particular, provision about amendments that would cause the application to become transferrable under subsection (3).

(12) For the purposes of subsection (9)(a)(ii), in relation to an application transferred to the High Court in Northern Ireland –

(a) an order of mandamus shall be taken to correspond to a mandatory order under section 15(1)(a),
(b) an order of prohibition shall be taken to correspond to a prohibiting order under section 15(1)(b), and
(c) an order of certiorari shall be taken to correspond to a quashing order under section 15(1)(c).

19 Transfer of judicial review applications from High Court

(1) In the Senior Courts Act 1981 (c 54), after section 31 insert –

'31A Transfer of judicial review applications to Upper Tribunal

(1) This section applies where an application is made to the High Court –

(a) for judicial review, or
(b) for permission to apply for judicial review.

(2) If Conditions 1, 2, 3 and 4 are met, the High Court must by order transfer the application to the Upper Tribunal.

(3) If Conditions 1, 2 and 4 are met, but Condition 3 is not, the High Court may by order transfer the application to the Upper Tribunal if it appears to the High Court to be just and convenient to do so.

(4) Condition 1 is that the application does not seek anything other than –

(a) relief under section 31(1)(a) and (b);
(b) permission to apply for relief under section 31(1)(a) and (b);
(c) an award under section 31(4);
(d) interest;
(e) costs.

(5) Condition 2 is that the application does not call into question anything done by the Crown Court.

(6) Condition 3 is that the application falls within a class specified under section 18(6) of the Tribunals, Courts and Enforcement Act 2007.

(7) Condition 4 is that the application does not call into question any decision made under –

(a) the Immigration Acts,
(b) the British Nationality Act 1981 (c 61),
(c) any instrument having effect under an enactment within paragraph (a) or (b), or
(d) any other provision of law for the time being in force which determines British citizenship, British overseas territories citizenship, the status of a British National (Overseas) or British Overseas citizenship.'

(2) In the Judicature (Northern Ireland) Act 1978 (c 23), after section 25 insert –

'25A Transfer of judicial review applications to Upper Tribunal

(1) This section applies where an application is made to the High Court –

(a) for judicial review, or
(b) for leave to apply for judicial review.

(2) If Conditions 1, 2, 3 and 4 are met, the High Court must by order transfer the application to the Upper Tribunal.

(3) If Conditions 1, 2 and 4 are met, but Condition 3 is not, the High Court may by order transfer the application to the Upper Tribunal if it appears to the High Court to be just and convenient to do so.

(4) Condition 1 is that the application does not seek anything other than –

(a) relief under section 18(1)(a) to (e);
(b) leave to apply for relief under section 18(1)(a) to (e);
(c) an award under section 20;
(d) interest;
(e) costs.

(5) Condition 2 is that the application does not call into question anything done by the Crown Court.

(6) Condition 3 is that the application falls within a class specified under section 18(6) of the Tribunals, Courts and Enforcement Act 2007.

(7) Condition 4 is that the application does not call into question any decision made under –

(a) the Immigration Acts,
(b) the British Nationality Act 1981,
(c) any instrument having effect under an enactment within paragraph (a) or (b), or

(d) any other provision of law for the time being in force which determines British citizenship, British overseas territories citizenship, the status of a British National (Overseas) or British Overseas citizenship.'

(3) Where an application is transferred to the Upper Tribunal under 31A of the Senior Courts Act 1981 (c 54) or section 25A of the Judicature (Northern Ireland) Act 1978 (transfer from the High Court of judicial review applications) –

(a) the application is to be treated for all purposes as if it –
  (i) had been made to the tribunal, and
  (ii) sought things corresponding to those sought from the High Court,
(b) the tribunal has the function of deciding the application, even if it does not fall within a class specified under section 18(6), and
(c) any steps taken, permission given, leave given or orders made by the High Court in relation to the application are to be treated as taken, given or made by the tribunal.

(4) Where –

(a) an application for permission is transferred to the Upper Tribunal under section 31A of the Senior Courts Act 1981 (c 54) and the tribunal grants permission, or

(b) an application for leave is transferred to the Upper Tribunal under section 25A of the Judicature (Northern Ireland) Act 1978 (c 23) and the tribunal grants leave,

the tribunal has the function of deciding any subsequent application brought under the permission or leave, even if the subsequent application does not fall within a class specified under section 18(6).

(5) Tribunal Procedure Rules may make further provision for the purposes of supplementing subsections (3) and (4).

(6) For the purposes of subsection (3)(a)(ii), in relation to an application transferred to the Upper Tribunal under section 25A of the Judicature (Northern Ireland) Act 1978 –

(a) a mandatory order under section 15(1)(a) shall be taken to correspond to an order of mandamus,
(b) a prohibiting order under section 15(1)(b) shall be taken to correspond to an order of prohibition, and
(c) a quashing order under section 15(1)(c) shall be taken to correspond to an order of certiorari.

Amendments—Constitutional Reform Act 2005, s 59(5), Sch 11, Pt 1, para 1(2).

****

27 Enforcement

(1) A sum payable in pursuance of a decision of the First-tier Tribunal or Upper Tribunal made in England and Wales –

(a) shall be recoverable as if it were payable under an order of a county court in England and Wales;
(b) shall be recoverable as if it were payable under an order of the High Court in England and Wales.

(2) An order for the payment of a sum payable in pursuance of a decision of the First-tier Tribunal or Upper Tribunal made in Scotland (or a copy of such an order

certified in accordance with Tribunal Procedure Rules) may be enforced as if it were an extract registered decree arbitral bearing a warrant for execution issued by the sheriff court of any sheriffdom in Scotland.

(3) A sum payable in pursuance of a decision of the First-tier Tribunal or Upper Tribunal made in Northern Ireland –

(a) shall be recoverable as if it were payable under an order of a county court in Northern Ireland;
(b) shall be recoverable as if it were payable under an order of the High Court in Northern Ireland.

(4) This section does not apply to a sum payable in pursuance of –

(a) an award under section 16(6), or
(b) an order by virtue of section 21(1).

(5) The Lord Chancellor may by order make provision for subsection (1) or (3) to apply in relation to a sum of a description specified in the order with the omission of one (but not both) of paragraphs (a) and (b).

(6) Tribunal Procedure Rules –

(a) may make provision as to where, for purposes of this section, a decision is to be taken to be made;
(b) may provide for all or any of subsections (1) to (3) to apply only, or not to apply except, in relation to sums of a description specified in Tribunal Procedure Rules.

****

29 Costs or expenses

(1) The costs of and incidental to –

(a) all proceedings in the First-tier Tribunal, and
(b) all proceedings in the Upper Tribunal,

shall be in the discretion of the Tribunal in which the proceedings take place.

(2) The relevant Tribunal shall have full power to determine by whom and to what extent the costs are to be paid.

(3) Subsections (1) and (2) have effect subject to Tribunal Procedure Rules.

(4) In any proceedings mentioned in subsection (1), the relevant Tribunal may –

(a) disallow, or
(b) (as the case may be) order the legal or other representative concerned to meet,

the whole of any wasted costs or such part of them as may be determined in accordance with Tribunal Procedure Rules.

(5) In subsection (4) 'wasted costs' means any costs incurred by a party –

(a) as a result of any improper, unreasonable or negligent act or omission on the part of any legal or other representative or any employee of such a representative, or
(b) which, in the light of any such act or omission occurring after they were incurred, the relevant Tribunal considers it is unreasonable to expect that party to pay.

(6) In this section 'legal or other representative', in relation to a party to proceedings, means any person exercising a right of audience or right to conduct the proceedings on his behalf.

(7) In the application of this section in relation to Scotland, any reference in this section to costs is to be read as a reference to expenses.

****

F3

F3

PRACTICE DIRECTION FIRST-TIER TRIBUNAL

6 APRIL 2012

Health Education and Social Care Chamber Statements and Reports in Mental Health Cases

1 This practice direction is made by the Senior President of Tribunals with the agreement of the Lord Chancellor in the exercise of powers conferred by section 23 of the Tribunals, Courts and Enforcement Act 2007. It applies to a "mental health case" as defined in rule 1(3) the Tribunal Procedure (First-tier Tribunal) (Health, Education and Social Care Chamber) Rules 2008. Rule 32 requires that certain documents are to be sent or delivered to the tribunal (and, in restricted cases, to the Secretary of State) by the responsible authority, the responsible clinician and any social supervisor (as the case may be). This practice direction specifies the contents of the statements and the reports that are to be sent or delivered in accordance with rule 32. It replaces the previous Practice Direction on mental health cases dated 30 October 2008 with effect from 06 April 2012.

2 In this practice direction "the Act" refers to the Mental Health Act 1983, as amended.

A In-Patients

3 For the purposes of this practice direction, a patient is an in-patient if they are in hospital to be assessed or treated for a mental disorder, even if treatment is being provided informally, or under a provision other than that to which the application or reference to the tribunal relates.

4 A patient is also an in-patient if they are detained in hospital through the criminal justice system, or if they have been transferred to hospital from a custodial establishment. This includes patients detained under a hospital order or removed to hospital from prison -whether or not the patient is also a restricted patient.

5 In the case of a restricted patient detained in hospital, the tribunal may make a provisional decision to order a conditional discharge. Before it finally grants a conditional discharge, the tribunal may defer its decision so that arrangements to its satisfaction can be put in place. Unless and until the tribunal finally grants a conditional discharge, the patient remains an in-patient, and so this part of the practice direction applies.

6 If the patient is an in-patient, the responsible authority must send or deliver to the tribunal the following documents containing the specified information in accordance with paragraphs 7 or 8 below, as appropriate:

(i) Statement of Information about the Patient
(ii) Responsible Clinician's Report

(iii) In-Patient Nursing Report [A copy of the patient's current nursing plan must be appended to the report.]
(iv) Social Circumstances Report

7 In all cases except where a patient is detained under section 2 of the Act, the responsible authority must send or deliver to the tribunal the required documents, containing the specified information, so that the documents are received by the tribunal as soon as practicable and in any event within 3 weeks after the responsible authority made the reference or received a copy of the application or reference. If the patient is a restricted patient, the responsible authority must also, at the same time, send copies of the documents to the Secretary of State.

8 Where a patient is detained under section 2 of the Act, the responsible authority must prepare the required documents as soon as practicable after receipt of a copy of the application or a request from the tribunal. It may be that some of the specified information will not be immediately available. The responsible authority must balance the need for speed with the need to provide as much of the specified information as possible within the time available. If information is omitted because it is not available, then that should be mentioned in the relevant document. These documents must be made available to the tribunal panel and representative at least one hour ahead of the hearing.

(i) Statement of Information about the Patient

9 The statement provided to the tribunal must, in so far as it is within the knowledge of the responsible authority, include the following up-to-date information:

(a) the patient's full name (and any alternative names used in their patient records);
(b) the patient's date of birth, age and usual place of residence;
(c) the patient's first language and, if it is not English, whether an interpreter is required and, if so, in which language;
(d) if the patient is deaf, whether the patient will require the services of a British Sign Language interpreter or a Relay Interpreter;
(e) the date of admission or transfer of the patient to the hospital in which the patient is detained or liable to be detained, together with details of the application, order or direction that is the original authority for the detention of the patient, and details of any subsequent renewal of, or change in, the authority for detention;
(f) details of the hospital at which the patient is detained;
(g) details of any transfers between hospitals since the original application,order or direction was made;
(h) where the patient is detained in an independent hospital, details of any NHS body that funds, or will fund, the placement;
(i) the name of the patient's responsible clinician and the date when the patient'/came under the care of that clinician;
(j) the name and address of the local social services authority and NHS body which, were the patient to leave hospital, would have the duty to provide aftercare services for the patient under section 117 of the Act;
(k) the name of any care co-ordinator appointed for the patient;
(l) except in the case of a restricted patient, the name and address of the patient's nearest relative or of the person exercising that function, whether the patient has made any specific requests that their nearest relative should not be consulted or should not be kept informed about the patient's care or treatment

and, if so, the detail of any such requests and whether the responsible authority believes that the patient has capacity to make such requests;

(m) the name and address of any person who plays a significant part in the care of the patient but who is not professionally concerned with that care;

(n) the name and address of any deputy or attorney appointed for the patient under the Mental Capacity Act 2005;

(o) details of any registered lasting or enduring power of attorney made by the patient;

(p) details of any existing advance decisions made by the patient to refuse treatment for mental disorder.

(ii) Responsible Clinician's Report

10 This report must be up-to-date and specifically prepared for the use of the tribunal. Unless it is not reasonably practicable, the report must be written or countersigned by the patient's responsible clinician and must describe the patient's relevant medical history and current presentation, including:

(a) full details of the patient's mental state, behaviour and treatment for mental disorder;

(b) so far as it is within the knowledge of the person writing the report, a statement as to whether, at a time when the patient was mentally disordered, the patient has neglected or harmed themselves or threatened themselves with harm, or has harmed other persons or threatened them with harm, or damaged property or threatened to damage property, together with details of any neglect, harm, damage or threats;

(c) an assessment of the extent to which the patient or other persons would be likely to be at risk if the patient were to be discharged by the tribunal, and how any such risks could be managed effectively;

(d) an assessment of the patient's strengths and any other positive factors of which the tribunal should be aware;

(e) whether the patient has a learning disability that may adversely affect their understanding or ability to cope with the tribunal hearing, and whether there are any approaches or adjustments that the panel may consider in order to deal with the case fairly and justly.

(iii) In-Patient Nursing Report

11 This report must be up-to-date and specifically prepared for the use of the tribunal. In relation to the patient's current in-patient episode it must include full details of the following:

(a) the patient's understanding of, and willingness to accept, the current treatment for mental disorder provided or offered;

(b) the level of observation to which the patient is subject;

(c) any occasions on which the patient has been secluded or restrained, including the reasons why seclusion or restraint was considered to be necessary;

(d) any occasions on which the patient has been absent without leave whilst liable to be detained, or occasions when the patient has failed to return when required, after having been granted leave of absence;

(e) any incidents where the patient has harmed themselves or others or threatened such harm, or damaged property or threatened such damage.

(iv) Social Circumstances Report

12 This report must be up-to-date and specifically prepared for the use of the tribunal. It must include full details of the following:

(a) the patient's home and family circumstances, and the housing facilities available;
(b) so far as it is practicable, and except in restricted cases, a summary of the views of the patient's nearest relative unless (having consulted the patient) the person compiling the report considers that it would be inappropriate to consult the nearest relative;
(c) so far as it is practicable, the views of any person who plays a significant part in the care of the patient but is not professionally concerned with it;
(d) the views of the patient, including the patient's concerns, hopes and beliefs;
(e) the opportunities for employment available to the patient;
(f) what (if any) community support or after-care is being, or would be, made available to the patient, and the author's views as to its likely effectiveness were the patient to be discharged from hospital;
(g) the patient's financial circumstances (including entitlement to benefits);
(h) an assessment of the patient's strengths and any other positive factors of which the tribunal should be aware;
(i) an assessment of the extent to which the patient or other persons would be likely to be at risk if the patient were to be discharged from hospital, and how any such risks could be managed effectively.

B Community patients

13 If the patient is a community patient under section 17A of the Act the responsible authority must send or deliver to the tribunal the following documents, containing the specified information, so that the documents are received by the tribunal as soon as practicable and in any event within 3 weeks after the responsible authority made the reference or received a copy of the application or reference:

(i) Statement of Information about the Patient
(ii) Responsible Clinician's Report
(iii) Social Circumstances Report

(i) Statement of Information about the Patient

14 The statement provided to the tribunal must, in so far as it is within the knowledge of the responsible authority, include the following up-to-date information:

(a) the patient's full name (and any alternative names used in their patient records);
(b) the patient's date of birth, age and usual place of residence;
(c) the patient's first language and, if it is not English, whether an interpreter is required and, if so, in which language;
(d) if the patient is deaf, whether the patient will require the services of a British Sign Language interpreter or a relay interpreter;
(e) details of the place where the patient is living;
(f) the name of the patient's responsible clinician and the date when the patient came under the care of that clinician;
(g) the name and address of the local social services authority and NHS body having a duty to provide after-care services for the patient under section 117 of the Act;
(h) the name of any care co-ordinator appointed for the patient;

(i) the name and address of the patient's nearest relative or of the person exercising that function, whether the patient has made any specific requests that their nearest relative should not be consulted or should not be kept informed about the patient's care or treatment and, if so, the detail of any such requests and whether the responsible authority believes that the patient has capacity to make such requests;
(j) the name and address of any deputy or attorney appointed for the patient under the Mental Capacity Act 2005;
(k) details of any registered lasting or enduring power of attorney made by the patient;
(l) details of any existing advance decisions made by the patient to refuse treatment for mental disorder.

(ii) Responsible Clinician's Report

15 This report must be up-to-date and specifically prepared for the use of the tribunal. Unless it is not reasonably practicable, the report must be written or countersigned by the patient's responsible clinician and must describe the patient's relevant medical history and current presentation, including:

(a) where the case is a reference to the tribunal, an assessment of the patient's capacity to decide whether or not to attend, or be representedat, a hearing of the reference;
(b) whether the patient has a learning disability that may adversely affect their understanding or ability to cope with the tribunal hearing, and whether there are any approaches or adjustments that the panel may consider in order to deal with the case fairly and justly.
(c) details of the date of, and circumstances leading up to, the patient's underlying section 3 order, and a brief account of when, and why, the patient then came to be subject to a community treatment order;
(d) full details of the patient's mental state, behaviour and treatment for mental disorder, and relevant medical history;
(e) so far as it is within the knowledge of the person writing the report, a statement as to whether, at a time when the patient was mentally disordered, the patient has neglected or harmed themselves or threatened themselves with harm, or has harmed other persons or threatened them with harm, or damaged property or threatened to damage property, together with details of any neglect, harm, damage or threats;
(f) an assessment of the extent to which the patient or other persons would be likely to be at risk if the patient were to be discharged by the tribunal, and how any such risks could be managed effectively;
(g) an assessment of the patient's strengths and any other positive factors of which the tribunal should be aware;
(h) the reasons why it is necessary that the responsible clinician should be able to exercise the power under section 17E(1) of the Act to recall the patient to hospital;
(i) any conditions to which the patient is subject under section 17B of the Act.

(iii) Social Circumstances Report

16 This report must be up-to-date and specifically prepared for the use of the tribunal. It must include full details of the following:

- (a) the patient's home and family circumstances, and the housing facilities available;
- (b) so far as it is practicable a summary of the views of the patient's nearest relative, unless (having consulted the patient) the person compiling the report considers that it would inappropriate to consult the nearest relative;
- (c) the views of any person who plays a significant part in the care of the patient but is not professionally concerned with that care;
- (d) the views of the patient, including their concerns, hopes and beliefs;
- (e) the opportunities for employment available to the patient;
- (f) what (if any) community support or after-care is being, or would be, made available to the patient, and the author's views as to its likely effectiveness were the community treatment order to continue, or were it to be discharged;
- (g) the patient's financial circumstances (including entitlement to benefits);
- (h) an assessment of the patient's strengths and any other positive factors of which the tribunal should be aware;
- (i) an account of the patient's progress whilst a community patient, details of any conditions or requirements to which the patient is subject under the community treatment order, and details of any behaviour that has put the patient or others at risk;
- (j) an assessment of the extent to which the patient or other persons would be likely to be at risk if the tribunal were to discharge the community treatment order.

C Guardianship patients

17 If the patient has been received into guardianship under section 7 of the Act, the responsible authority must send or deliver to the tribunal the following documents, containing the specified information, so that the documents are received by the tribunal as soon as practicable and in any event within 3 weeks after the responsible authority made the reference or received a copy of the application or reference:

- (i) Statement of Information about the Patient
- (ii) Responsible Clinician's Report
- (iii) Social Circumstances Report

(i) Statement of Information about the Patient

18 The statement provided to the tribunal must, in so far as it is within the knowledge of the responsible authority, include the following up-to-date information:

- (a) the patient's full name (and any alternative names used in their patient records);
- (b) the patient's date of birth, age and usual place of residence;
- (c) the patient's first language and, if it is not English, whether an interpreter is required and, if so, in which language;
- (d) if the patient is deaf, whether the patient will require the services of a British Sign Language interpreter or a Relay Interpreter;
- (e) the date of the reception of the patient into guardianship, together with details of the application, order or direction that constitutes the original authority for the guardianship of the patient;
- (f) where the patient is subject to the guardianship of a private guardian, the name and address of that guardian;
- (g) the name of the patient's responsible clinician and the date when the patient came under the care of that clinician;
- (h) details of the place where the patient is living;

(i) the name of any care co-ordinator appointed for the patient;
(j) the name and address of the patient's nearest relative or of the person exercising that function, whether the patient has made any specific requests that their nearest relative should not be consulted or should not be kept informed about the patient's care or treatment and, if so, the detail of any such requests and whether the responsible authority believes that the patient has capacity to make such requests;
(k) the name and address of any person who plays a significant part in the care of the patient but who is not professionally concerned with that care;
(l) the name and address of any deputy or attorney appointed for the patient under the Mental Capacity Act 2005;
(m) details of any registered lasting or enduring power of attorney made by the patient;
(n) details of any existing advance decisions made by the patient to refuse treatment for mental disorder.

(ii) Responsible Clinician's Report

19 This report must be up-to-date and specifically prepared for the use of the tribunal. Unless it is not reasonably practicable, the report must be written or countersigned by the patient's responsible clinician and must describe the patient's relevant medical history and current presentation, including:

(a) full details of the patient's mental state, behaviour and treatment for mental disorder;
(b) so far as it is within the knowledge of the person writing the report, a statement as to whether, at a time when the patient was mentally disordered, the patient has neglected or harmed themselves or threatened themselves with harm, or has harmed other persons or threatened them with harm, or damaged property or threatened to damage property, together with details of any neglect, harm, damage or threats;
(c) an assessment of the extent to which the patient or other persons would be likely to be at risk if the patient were to be discharged from guardianship, and how any such risks could be managed effectively;
(d) an assessment of the patient's strengths and any other positive factors of which the tribunal should be aware;
(e) whether the patient has a learning disability that may adversely affect their understanding or ability to cope with the tribunal hearing, and whether there are any approaches or adjustments that the panel may consider in order to deal with the case fairly and justly.

(iii) Social Circumstances Report

20 This report must be up-to-date and specifically prepared for the use of the tribunal. It must include full details of the following:

(a) the patient's home and family circumstances, and the housing facilities available;
(b) so far as it is practicable, a summary of the views of the patient's nearest relative, unless (having consulted the patient) the person compiling the report considers that it would be inappropriate to consult the nearest relative;
(c) so far as it is practicable, the views of any person who plays a significant part in the care of the patient but is not professionally concerned with that care;
(d) the views of the patient, including their concerns, hopes and beliefs;

(e) the opportunities for employment available to the patient;
(f) what (if any) community support is being, or would be, made available to the patient, and the author's views as to its likely effectiveness were the guardianship order to continue, or were it to be discharged;
(g) the patient's financial circumstances (including entitlement to benefits);
(h) an assessment of the patient's strengths and any other positive factors of which the tribunal should be aware;
(i) an assessment of the extent to which the patient or other persons would be likely to be at risk if the patient were to be discharged by the tribunal, and how any such risks could be managed effectively.

D Conditionally discharged patients

21 A conditionally discharged patient is a restricted patient who has been discharged from hospital into the community, subject to a condition that the patient will remain liable to be recalled to hospital for further treatment, should it become necessary.

22 In the case of a restricted patient in hospital, the tribunal may make a provisional decision to order a conditional discharge. Before it finally grants a conditional discharge, the tribunal may defer its decision so that arrangements to its satisfaction can be put in place. Unless and until the tribunal finally grants a conditional discharge, the patient remains an in-patient, and so the in-patient part of the practice direction (and not this part) applies.

23 Upon being notified by the tribunal of an application or reference, the responsible clinician must send or deliver a responsible clinician's report, and any social supervisor must send or deliver a social circumstances report. The reports must contain the specified information and must be sent or delivered to the tribunal as soon as practicable, and in any event within 3 weeks after the responsible clinician or social supervisor (as the case may be) received the notification.

24 The responsible clinician and any social supervisor must also, at the same time, send copies of their reports to the Secretary of State.

(i) Responsible Clinician's Report

25 This report must be up-to-date and specifically prepared for the use of the tribunal. Unless it is not reasonably practicable, the report must be written or countersigned by the patient's Responsible Clinician and must describe the patient's relevant medical history and current presentation, including:

(a) full details of the patient's mental state, behaviour and treatment for mental disorder;
(b) so far as it is within the knowledge of the person writing the report, a statement as to whether, at a time when the patient was mentally disordered, the patient has neglected or harmed themselves or threatened themselves with harm, or has harmed other persons or threatened them with harm, or damaged property or threatened to damage property, together with details of any neglect, harm, damage or threats;
(c) an assessment of the extent to which the patient or other persons would be likely to be at risk if the patient were to be absolutely discharged by the tribunal, and how any such risks could be managed effectively;
(d) an assessment of the patient's strengths and any other positive factors of which the tribunal should be aware;

(e) details of any existing advance decisions to refuse treatment for mental disorder made by the patient;
(f) whether the patient has a learning disability that may adversely affect their understanding or ability to cope with the tribunal hearing, and whether there are any approaches or adjustments that the panel may consider in order to deal with the case fairly and justly;
(g) If the patient does not have a social supervisor, the responsible clinician must also provide, or arrange to be provided, as much of thesocial circumstances information below as can reasonably be obtained in the time available.

(ii) Social Circumstances Report

26 This report must be up-to-date and specifically prepared for the use of the tribunal. It must include full details of the following:

(a) the patient's full name (and any alternative names used in their patient records);
(b) the patient's date of birth, age and usual place of residence;
(c) the patient's first language and, if it is not English, whether an interpreter is required and, if so, in which language;
(d) if the patient is deaf, whether the patient will require the services of a British Sign Language interpreter or a Relay Interpreter;
(e) the patient's home and family circumstances, and the housing facilities available;
(f) so far as it is practicable, the views of any person who plays a significant part in the care of the patient but is not professionally concerned with that care;
(g) the views of the patient, including their concerns, hopes and beliefs;
(h) the opportunities for employment available to the patient;
(i) what (if any) community support or after-care is being, or would be, made available to the patient, and the author's views as to its likely effectiveness were the conditional discharge to continue, or were the patient to be absolutely discharged;
(j) the patient's financial circumstances (including entitlement to benefits);
(k) an assessment of the patient's strengths and any other positive factors of which the tribunal should be aware;
(l) an assessment of the extent to which the patient or other persons would be likely to be at risk if the patient were to be absolutely discharged by the tribunal, and how any such risks could be managed effectively;
(m) the name and address of any deputy or attorney appointed for the patient under the Mental Capacity Act 2005;
(n) details of any registered lasting or enduring power of attorney made by the patient.

E Patients under the age of 18

27 All the above requirements apply, as appropriate, depending upon the type of case.

28 In addition, for all patients under the age of 18, the **Social Circumstances Report** must state:

(a) the names and addresses of any persons with parental responsibility, and how they acquired parental responsibility;
(b) which public bodies either have liaised or need to liaise in relation to aftercare services that may be provided under section 117 of the Act;
(c) the outcome of any liaison that has taken place;

(d) if liaison has not taken place, why not – and when liaison will take place;
(e) the details of any multi-agency care plan in place or proposed;
(f) whether there are any issues as to funding the care plan and, if so, the date by which it is intended that those issues will be resolved;
(g) who will be the patient's care coordinator following discharge;
(h) whether the patient's needs have been assessed under the Chronically Sick and Disabled Persons Act 1970 (as amended) and, if not, the reasons why such an assessment has not been carried out and whether it is proposed to carry out such an assessment;
(i) if there has been an assessment under the Chronically Sick and Disabled Persons Act 1970, what needs have been identified and how those needs will be met;
(j) if the patient is subject to or has been the subject of a care order or an interim care order, the date and duration of any such order, the identity of the relevant local authority, any person(s) with whom the local authority shares parental responsibility, whether the patient is the subject of any care proceedings which have yet to be concluded and, if so, the court in which such proceedings are taking place and the date of the next hearing, whether the patient comes under the Children (Leaving Care) Act 2000, whether there has been any liaison between, on the one hand, social workers responsible for mental health services to children and adolescents and, on the other hand, those responsible for such services to adults, and the name of the social worker within the relevant local authority who is discharging the function of the nearest relative under section 27 of the Act;
(k) if the patient is subject to guardianship under section 7 of the Act, whether any orders have been made under the Children Act 1989 in respect of the patient, and what consultation there has been with the guardian;
(l) if the patient is a ward of court, when the patient was made a ward of court and what steps have been taken to notify the court that made the order of any significant steps taken, or to be taken, in respect of the patient;
(m) whether any orders under the Children Act 1989 are in existence in respect of the patient and, if so, the details of those orders, together with the date on which such orders were made, and whether they are final or interim orders;
(n) if a patient has been or is a looked after child under section 20 of the Children Act 1989, when the child became looked after, why the child became looked after, what steps have been taken to discharge the obligations of the local authority under paragraph 17(1) of Schedule 2 of the Children Act 1989, and what steps are being taken (if required) to discharge the obligations of the local authority under paragraph 10 (b) of Schedule 2 of the Children Act 1989;
(o) if a patient has been treated by a local authority as a child in need (which includes children who have a mental disorder) under section 17(11) of the Children Act 1989, the period or periods for which they have been so treated, why they were considered to be a child in need, what services were or are being made available to the child by virtue of that status, and details of any assessment of the child;
(p) if a patient has been the subject of a secure accommodation order (under section 25 of the Children Act 1989), the date on which the order was made, the reasons it was made, and the date it expired.

Lord Justice Carnwath
Senior President of Tribunals, 06 April 2012

F4

PRACTICE GUIDANCE ON PROCEDURES CONCERNING HANDLING REPRESENTATIONS FROM VICTIMS IN THE FIRST-TIER TRIBUNAL (MENTAL HEALTH)[1]

1 JULY 2011

The Tribunal Procedure (First-tier Tribunal) (Health, Education and Social Care Chamber) Rules 2008

Background

1 This Guidance Note is drafted to assist judges and members of the First-tier Tribunal, Mental Health – (the tribunal) – in handling relevant representations from the victims of patients, where such patients have applications or referrals before the tribunal. This guidance has been issued by the Chamber President of the Health, Education and Social Care Chamber and it is intended to promote consistent and high standards in making judicial decisions, particularly in relation to Rule 5 (Case management powers); Rule 15 (Evidence and submissions), Rule 33 (Notice of proceedings to interested persons); Rule 36 (Entitlement to attend a hearing), and Rule 38 (Public and private hearings).

2 The definition of "victim" is taken to include any person in relation to the patient's index offence or offences who appears to the relevant local probation board to be the victim of the offence or offences. This includes a victim's family in a case where the offence has resulted in the victim's death or incapacity and in other cases where the victim's age or circumstances make it more sensible to approach a family member.

Part A: Cases covered by the Domestic Violence, Crime and Victims Act 2004

3 The Domestic Violence, Crime and Victims Act 2004 (DVCVA) made provision for a number of measures improving services and support to victims of sexual or violent offences (see *Definitions*, below). This includes offences committed by people sent from prison to hospital for psychiatric treatment, as well as offenders subject to hospital orders. Under Schedule 6 of the Mental Health Act 2007, which amends the 2004 Act, these rights are extended to the victims of a sexual or violent offence committed by offenders who are detained in hospital but are not subject to special restrictions (unrestricted patients).

---

1 Issued by the Chamber President under Schedule 4 of the Tribunals, Courts and Enforcement Act 2007.

4 This Guidance Note suggests how the judiciary should approach requests from victims to make written representations, or to attend a hearing in person or through a representative. The Guidance Note does not address in detail the duty of the tribunal to notify the relevant local probation board if relevant applications or referrals or made, and the Guidance Note does not address in detail the duty of the tribunal to notify the local probation board of certain aspects of the outcome of the proceedings.

The Statutory Regime

A victim is not a party to the proceedings. However, where the court sentenced the patient to certain disposals the tribunal has a statutory duty to permit a victim to make certain representations to the tribunal, so long as sentencing occurred on or after 1 July 2005 or, for non-restricted patients, after 3 November 2008.[2] This duty is not retrospective, and applies only to victims.

The disposals include the following:

- those convicted of a sexual or violent offence who are then made subject of a hospital order;
- those found to be
  - a) unfit to plead and to have committed the act or made the omission charged as the offence; or
  - b) not guilty by reason of insanity, under the Criminal Procedure (Insanity) Act 1964 as amended by the DVCVA in respect of a sexual or violent offence; and are then made subject to a hospital order;
- those convicted of a sexual or violent offence, who are then made subject of a hospital direction and limitation direction (if the associated prison sentence is for 12 months or more); and
- those sentenced to 12 months imprisonment or more, for a sexual or violent offence, and transferred from prison to hospital, under a transfer direction.

The representations must only relate to the following questions:

- whether the patient should, in the event of his or her discharge or release from detention, be subject to any conditions and, if so,
- what particular conditions should be imposed.

5 These arrangements also apply to those patients in the above categories who have subsequently been made the subject of Conditional Discharge (restricted patients) or a Community Treatment Order (unrestricted patients). If an offender was subject to a hospital order with restrictions but had those restrictions removed on or after 3 November 2008, or was made subject to a transfer direction without restrictions being made, the victim will continue to enjoy the rights offered by the DVCVA, as long as the offender was sentenced after 1 July 2005.

Restricted Cases

6 The Ministry of Justice (MoJ) Mental Health Casework Section (MHCS) carries out the Secretary of State's responsibilities under the Mental Health Act 1983, and related legislation. It directs the admission to hospital of patients transferred from prison, and considers recommendations from Responsible Clinicians (RCs) in hospitals for leave, transfer or discharge of restricted patients. MHCS also prepares documentation for the tribunal and monitors patients who are conditionally discharged. Each restricted patient has a caseworker at MHCS.

---

2 Note: PART B below deals with the position regarding disposals prior to these dates.

7 For each new restricted case, including transferred prisoners, the Victim Liaison Officer (VLO), who is a Probation Officer with special responsibility for liaising with victims of sexual or violent offences, will contact the MHCS caseworker. MHCS will then inform the VLO of the details for the care team or RC, where this is known.

8 A detained patient may apply to have his or her case heard by a tribunal once each year. If the patient does not apply, his or her case will be referred to a tribunal every three years. In addition, after a conditionally discharged patient has been recalled, the Secretary of State must refer the case to a tribunal within one month of recall. The tribunal will then consider whether the individual needs to be detained in hospital for the purposes of appropriate and available mental health medical treatment.

9 When the Secretary of State refers a patient to the tribunal, MHCS will forward the details of the relevant VLO to the tribunal office. When an application is made to the tribunal, the tribunal office will obtain the details of the relevant VLO from MHCS. In both circumstances, the tribunal office will then inform the VLO of the date **(but not the venue)** of the tribunal hearing, once it has been set, and also advise of the date by which any written information, representations or submissions from the victim must be received. Note that a victim is not permitted to see the reports prepared for the tribunal by the witnesses in the case.

10 VLOs should consult victims about the information or submissions that they may wish to submit relating to possible discharge conditions, and forward them to the tribunal office by the specified date. VLOs should not encourage victims to make a general 'impact statement' because the tribunal is unable to take account of any representations from victims except those relating to the matters set out above.

11 If a restricted patient ceases to be subject to a restriction order, limitation direction or restriction direction on or after 3 November 2008, the arrangements below for unrestricted cases, involving hospital managers, will apply from the time when the restrictions are removed.

Unrestricted Cases

12 Unrestricted patients whose victims may make relevant written representations are those patients who are convicted of a sexual or violent offence on or after 1 July 2005 and are made subject to an unrestricted hospital order or transfer direction on or after 3 November 2008. In addition, they also include patients (whose victims fall within the scope of the statutory scheme) who were initially subject to a hospital order with restrictions, but in relation to whom restrictions were removed on or after 3 November 2008, whilst they remained detained in hospital.

13 For unrestricted patients, the role of probation services (Area or Trust) is limited to identifying the victim(s) and, if they consent, to passing on their details to hospital managers. For these cases, hospital managers (or staff to whom the function has been delegated) have the statutory duty to liaise with victims. Therefore, it is the hospital managers' responsibility to ensure that the victim is aware of the proceedings and to ascertain whether the victim wishes to make representations. The managers are required to pass any such representations to the RC, who should then forward them to the tribunal office.

14 Victims continue to fall under the new arrangements even if the relevant patient is subsequently discharged onto a Community Treatment Order (CTO). Note, however, that the tribunal has no power to attach conditions to a CTO or to amend conditions imposed under S.17(B) of the Mental Health Act 1983 (as amended). The tribunal may, however, summarise any relevant representations from a victim in its decision.

Provision of documents, written information or submissions to the tribunal.

15 Where a victim wishes to do so, and having submitted a written request to be advised of the date fixed for any hearing concerning that patient in advance of the hearing, a victim shall have the right to provide to the tribunal any relevant documents, written information or submissions that he or she wishes the tribunal to consider. Documents, information or submissions should only be regarded as relevant if they are capable of amounting to persuasive and cogent evidence, upon which the tribunal would be entitled to rely, relating to the following questions:

- whether the patient should, in the event of his or her discharge or release from detention, be subject to any conditions and, if so,
- what particular conditions should be imposed.

16 Conditions relevant to victims could, for example, relate to 'no contact' conditions or limited and carefully defined exclusion zones.

17 In the event of any difficulty, the tribunal will consider exercising its case management powers. In particular, under Rules 5 & 15, the tribunal may give directions as to the manner in which any representations are to be provided, which may include a direction for them to be given by written submissions or statement. Alternatively (and exceptionally), the tribunal may take the view that the victim should have an opportunity of being heard in person, or through a representative.

Application to Attend the Hearing

18 Rule 33(e) of the Tribunal Procedure (First-tier Tribunal) (Health, Education and Social Care Chamber) Rules 2008 ("the Rules") compels the tribunal to give notice of the proceedings (i.e. date, time and place) to any person who in the opinion of the tribunal: 'should have an opportunity of *being heard*'.

19 Representations made by a victim can only cover only a limited range of issues (see above) and the victim is not a party to the proceedings. In most cases, therefore, a written statement will be the most satisfactory way for the victim to express his/her views because direct involvement in the proceedings, or a procedure that brings the victim into direct conflict with the patient, is unlikely to be helpful to the victim, to the patient, or to the tribunal. However there may be some cases in which the victim believes that this is not sufficient and may decide to ask to attend the hearing. Any such requests will be treated on a case by case basis applying the principles in the overriding objective as set out in Rule 2. The victim will have to demonstrate that the opportunity to make written representations is insufficient and that he or she needs an opportunity to *be heard* in relation to relevant matters (see paragraphs 4 & 15 above).

20 If a victim wishes to contend that he or she needs an opportunity to give oral evidence in relation to relevant matters, they must make a written application to the tribunal in advance of the hearing. The application must explain why the right to provide relevant documents, or relevant information or submissions in writing is not sufficient to enable the tribunal to deal with the case fairly and justly.

21 The victim should understand that the tribunal will be required to consider a large amount of information from different sources, including confidential medical reports which the victim will not be permitted to see. A victim's representations, whilst potentially relevant and helpful, are only part of a constellation of factors that will inform the tribunal's final decision.

22 If the tribunal determines that a victim should have an opportunity of being heard, then the tribunal will advise the victim of the date, time and place of the hearing.

Rule 36(2) then permits such a person to attend and take part in the hearing to such extent as the tribunal considers proper. This gives the tribunal a wide discretion to regulate its own procedure, taking account of all the relevant circumstances.

23 Rule 38(4) and (5) may be particularly helpful when a tribunal is deciding what approach to take when dealing with the oral evidence of a victim who is permitted to attend a hearing. In particular, the tribunal has power under Rule 38(5) to exclude a victim from a hearing until the time comes for the victim to give his or her evidence. However, notwithstanding Rule 38(4), the tribunal will be reluctant to exclude a patient from a hearing relating to that patient's liberty, unless there are strong and evidentially supported reasons for doing so. Rule 5 empowers a tribunal judge to consider these matters at any time up to the hearing. Consequently, the manner and format in which the victim's oral evidence is presented to the tribunal (e.g. whether it is in the presence or absence of the other parties to the hearing) can be determined either by the judge dealing with the management of the case in advance of the hearing, or by the panel at the hearing itself.

Disclosure of the Victim's Evidence to the Patient.

24 Rule 15 (2) provides that the tribunal may admit in evidence any document or written material, whether or not that such document or material would be admissible in a civil trial. However, the tribunal will generally wish to copy such information or written material to the patient, unless it is satisfied that there are grounds to prohibit disclosure under Rule 14. If the tribunal decides to prohibit disclosure to the patient, it will usually send a copy of the material to the patient's legal representatives. In such circumstances, the representatives will not be permitted to disclose material, or the information contained within it, to the patient.

25 Victims should be made aware that no guarantees can be given that any representations they make will not be disclosed to the patient. The expectation is that all documents will be disclosed to the patient, and the circumstances in which documents can be withheld are very limited. Rule 14 allows the tribunal to withhold any document from the patient if they are satisfied that:

a) disclosure would be likely to cause that person or some other person serious harm, and
b) having regard to the interests of justice, it is proportionate not to disclose.

26 Rule 14 requires compliance with some important procedural steps. Further guidance is available in the tribunal's Reports Guidance Booklet "*Reports for Mental Health Tribunals*", available on the tribunal's website.

27 When deciding whether it is in the interests of justice to direct that the material must be withheld from the patient, the tribunal must ask itself whether non-disclosure would prevent the patient from participating effectively in all aspects of the proceedings (see RM v St Andrew's Healthcare [2010] UKUT 119 (AAC)).

Decision of the Tribunal

In restricted cases, the tribunal office should be able to inform the VLO of the relevant aspects of the tribunal's decision, in writing within seven days. In particular, the victim is entitled to know

- whether the patient is to be discharged and, if so, when the discharge will take effect;

- if a restricted patient is to be discharged, whether the discharge is to be absolute, or subject to conditions;
- if a restricted patient is to be discharged subject to conditions, what the conditions are;
- if a restricted patient has previously been discharged subject to conditions, of any variation of these conditions by the tribunal; and
- if the restriction order is to cease to have effect by virtue of action to be taken by the tribunal, of the date on which the restriction order is to cease to have effect.

28 With regard to prisoners who have been transferred to hospital, the tribunal may make recommendations on how they would have acted had the patient not been a transferred prisoner. Therefore, VLOs may forward the victim's representations about possible conditions in these cases, and the tribunal's conclusions in relation to possible discharge and conditions will be forwarded to the Parole Board where appropriate.

29 In unrestricted cases, the hospital managers are responsible for notifying the victim of the relevant aspects of the outcome of the hearing. The managers will have their own arrangements to ensure that they have the information they need to comply with this duty.

30 A victim is not permitted to make an application for permission to appeal on point of law to the Upper Tribunal under S.11 of the Tribunal Courts and Enforcement Act 2007, because this right is limited to parties to the proceedings, and a victim is not a party.

Part B: Cases not covered by the Domestic Violence, Crime and Victims Act 2004

31 As outlined at Part A above, The Domestic Violence, Crime and Victims Act 2004 ('DVCVA') came into force on 1 July 2005, but it does not apply to victims of incidents involving restricted patients where sentencing occurred prior to that date, as the DVCVA is not retrospective. For non-restricted patients, the relevant date is 3 November 2008.

32 The tribunal has given careful consideration to the position of persons who have been subject to a sexual or violent offences committed by persons who were subsequently detained under the provisions of the Mental Health Act 1983, where such offences occurred prior to the introduction of the DVCVA.

33 The tribunal has determined that where a patient's victim wishes to be advised of the date of any pending tribunal proceedings concerning that patient they shall, upon written request, be informed in advance of the date **(but not the venue)** fixed for any hearing concerning that patient. Such request must be in writing, and addressed to Tribunal Service Mental Health, PO Box 8793, 5th Floor, Leicester, LE1 8BN.

34 The tribunal will log and acknowledge in writing all such requests. The victim will subsequently be informed of the date **(but not the venue)** fixed for the hearing. Note, however, that this is not a notification under Rule 33(e), but merely a practice to be adopted in order to allow a victim to know when a tribunal hearing is taking place in order that the victim may have an opportunity of providing written information or submissions to the tribunal, under Rule 5(3)(d) and Rule 15(1)(e)(ii).

Definitions

A "**Sexual or Violent Offence**" falls within one of the following descriptions:

- Murder, attempted murder or conspiracy to murder and any offence in Schedule 15 Criminal Justice Act 2003 (c.44). This includes: manslaughter; kidnapping; false imprisonment; assaults under sections 18, 20 or 47 Offences Against the Person Act 1861 (as amended); child cruelty; possession of a firearm with intent; burglary; robbery; affray; death by dangerous driving; and a wide range of sexual offences;
- An offence which requires that a patient complies with the notification requirements of Part 2 of the Sexual Offenders Act 2003 (c.42). This refers to a large number of offences set out at schedule 3 which includes: rape; indecent assault; sexual offences involving children; and possession of indecent photographs of children;
- An offence against a child within the meaning of Part 2 of the Criminal Justice & Courts Services Act 2000.

Restricted Patients are those patients who were given:

- a restricted hospital order (i.e. a hospital order accompanied by a restriction order) (Section 37 and section 41 orders); or
- hospital and limitation directions (Section 45A); or
- a sentence of imprisonment for a qualifying offence but were subsequently transferred to hospital by a restricted transfer direction (i.e. a transfer direction accompanied by a restriction order) (Section 47 and 49 orders).

His Honour Judge Sycamore,
Chamber President,
Health, Education and Social Care Chamber,
First-tier Tribunal (Mental Health)

1 July 2011

F5

F5

THE TRIBUNAL PROCEDURE (FIRST-TIER TRIBUNAL) (HEALTH, EDUCATION AND SOCIAL CARE CHAMBER) RULES 2008

SI 2008/2699

ARRANGEMENT OF RULES

PART 1

INTRODUCTION

PART 2

GENERAL POWERS AND PROVISIONS

PART 4

PROCEEDINGS BEFORE THE TRIBUNAL IN MENTAL HEALTH CASES

Chapter 1

Before the hearing

Chapter 2

Hearings

Chapter 3

Decisions

PART 5

CORRECTING, SETTING ASIDE, REVIEWING AND APPEALING TRIBUNAL DECISIONS

PART 1

INTRODUCTION

1 Citation, commencement, application and interpretation

(1) These Rules may be cited as the Tribunal Procedure (First-tier Tribunal) (Health, Education and Social Care Chamber) Rules 2008 and come into force on 3rd November 2008.

(2) These Rules apply to proceedings before the Health, Education and Social Care Chamber of the First-tier Tribunal.

(3) In these Rules –

'the 2007 Act' means the Tribunals, Courts and Enforcement Act 2007;

'applicant' means a person who –

- (a) starts Tribunal proceedings, whether by making an application, an appeal, a claim or a reference;
- (b) makes an application to the Tribunal for leave to start such proceedings; or
- (c) is substituted as an applicant under rule 9(1) (substitution and addition of parties);

'childcare provider' means a person who is a child minder or provides day care as defined section 19 of the Children and Families (Wales) Measure 2010, or a person who provides childcare as defined in section 18 of the Childcare Act 2006;

'disability discrimination in schools case' means proceedings concerning disability discrimination in the education of a child or related matters;

'dispose of proceedings' includes, unless indicated otherwise, disposing of a part of the proceedings;

'document' means anything in which information is recorded in any form, and an obligation under these Rules or any practice direction or direction to provide or allow access to a document or a copy of a document for any purpose means, unless the Tribunal directs otherwise, an obligation to provide or allow access to such document or copy in a legible form or in a form which can be readily made into a legible form;

"health service case" means a case under the National Health Service Act 2006, the National Health Service (Wales) Act 2006, regulations made under either of those Acts, or regulations having effect as if made under either of those Acts by reason of section 4 of and Schedule 2 to the National Health Service (Consequential Provisions) Act 2006;

'hearing' means an oral hearing and includes a hearing conducted in whole or in part by video link, telephone or other means of instantaneous two-way electronic communication;

'legal representative' means a person who, for the purposes of the Legal Services Act 2007, is an authorised person in relation to an activity which constitutes the exercise of a right of audience or the conduct of litigation within the meaning of that Act;

'mental health case' means proceedings brought under the Mental Health Act 1983 or paragraph 5(2) of the Schedule to the Repatriation of Prisoners Act 1984;

'nearest relative' has the meaning set out in section 26 of the Mental Health Act 1983;

'party' means –

(a) in a mental health case, the patient, the responsible authority, the Secretary of State (if the patient is a restricted patient or in a reference under rule 32(8) (seeking approval under section 86 of the Mental Health Act 1983)), and any other person who starts a mental health case by making an application;

(b) in any other case, a person who is an applicant or respondent in proceedings before the Tribunal or, if the proceedings have been concluded, a person who was an applicant or respondent when the Tribunal finally disposed of all issues in the proceedings;

'patient' means the person who is the subject of a mental health case;

'practice direction' means a direction given under section 23 of the 2007 Act;

'respondent' means –

(a) in an appeal against an order made by a justice of the peace under section 79K of the Children Act 1989 section 34 of the Children and Families (Wales) Measure 2010, section 20 of the Care Standards Act 2000 or section 72 of the Childcare Act 2006, the person who applied to the justice of the peace for the order;

(b) in an appeal against any other decision, the person who made the decision;

(c) in proceedings on a claim under section 28I of the Disability Discrimination Act 1995, the body responsible for the school as determined in accordance with paragraph 1 of Schedule 4A to that Act or, if the claim concerns the residual duties of a local education authority under section 28F of that Act, that local education authority;

(d) in proceedings on an application under section 4(2) of the Protection of Children Act 1999 or section 86(2) of the Care Standards Act 2000, the Secretary of State; or

(da) in an application for, or for a review of, a stop order under the National Health Service (Optical Charges and Payments) Regulations 1997 –
  (i) the supplier, where the Secretary of State is the applicant;
  (ii) the Secretary of State, where the supplier is the applicant;

(db) in any other health service case –
  (i) the practitioner, performer or person against whom the application is made, where a Primary Care Trust or a Local Health Board is, or is deemed to be, the applicant;
  (ii) the Primary Care Trust or Local Health Board that served the notice, obtained the order or confirmation of the order, where any other person is the applicant; or

(e) a person substituted or added as a respondent under rule 9 (substitution and addition of parties);

'responsible authority' means –

(a) in relation to a patient detained under the Mental Health Act 1983 in a hospital within the meaning of Part 2 of that Act, the managers (as defined in section 145 of that Act);

(b) in relation to a patient subject to guardianship, the responsible local social services authority (as defined in section 34(3) of the Mental Health Act 1983);

(c) in relation to a community patient, the managers of the responsible hospital (as defined in section 145 of the Mental Health Act 1983);

(d) in relation to a patient subject to after-care under supervision, the Primary Care Trust or Local Health Board which has the duty to provide after-care for the patient.

'restricted patient' has the meaning set out in section 79(1) of the Mental Health Act 1983;

'special educational needs case' means proceedings concerning the education of a child who has or may have special educational needs;

'Suspension Regulations' means regulations which provide for a right of appeal against a decision to suspend, or not to lift the suspension of, a person's registration as a childcare provider;

'Tribunal' means the First-tier Tribunal;

'working day' means any day except a Saturday or Sunday, Christmas Day, Good Friday or a bank holiday under section 1 of the Banking and Financial Dealings Act 1971.

Amendments—SI 2012/43; SI 2010/2653; SI 2011/651.

2 Overriding objective and parties' obligation to co-operate with the Tribunal

(1) The overriding objective of these Rules is to enable the Tribunal to deal with cases fairly and justly.

(2) Dealing with a case fairly and justly includes –

(a) dealing with the case in ways which are proportionate to the importance of the case, the complexity of the issues, the anticipated costs and the resources of the parties;

(b) avoiding unnecessary formality and seeking flexibility in the proceedings;

(c) ensuring, so far as practicable, that the parties are able to participate fully in the proceedings;
(d) using any special expertise of the Tribunal effectively; and
(e) avoiding delay, so far as compatible with proper consideration of the issues.

(3) The Tribunal must seek to give effect to the overriding objective when it –

(a) exercises any power under these Rules; or
(b) interprets any rule or practice direction.

(4) Parties must –

(a) help the Tribunal to further the overriding objective; and
(b) co-operate with the Tribunal generally.

3 Alternative dispute resolution and arbitration

(1) The Tribunal should seek, where appropriate –

(a) to bring to the attention of the parties the availability of any appropriate alternative procedure for the resolution of the dispute; and
(b) if the parties wish and provided that it is compatible with the overriding objective, to facilitate the use of the procedure.

(2) Part 1 of the Arbitration Act 1996 does not apply to proceedings before the Tribunal.

PART 2
GENERAL POWERS AND PROVISIONS

4 Delegation to staff

(1) Staff appointed under section 40(1) of the 2007 Act (tribunal staff and services) may, with the approval of the Senior President of Tribunals, carry out functions of a judicial nature permitted or required to be done by the Tribunal.

(2) The approval referred to at paragraph (1) may apply generally to the carrying out of specified functions by members of staff of a specified description in specified circumstances.

(3) Within 14 days after the date on which the Tribunal sends notice of a decision made by a member of staff under paragraph (1) to a party, that party may apply in writing to the Tribunal for that decision to be considered afresh by a judge.

5 Case management powers

(1) Subject to the provisions of the 2007 Act and any other enactment, the Tribunal may regulate its own procedure.

(2) The Tribunal may give a direction in relation to the conduct or disposal of proceedings at any time, including a direction amending, suspending or setting aside an earlier direction.

(3) In particular, and without restricting the general powers in paragraphs (1) and (2), the Tribunal may –

(a) extend or shorten the time for complying with any rule, practice direction or direction, unless such extension or shortening would conflict with a provision of another enactment containing a time limit;

(b) consolidate or hear together two or more sets of proceedings or parts of proceedings raising common issues, or treat a case as a lead case;
(c) permit or require a party to amend a document;
(d) permit or require a party or another person to provide documents, information or submissions to the Tribunal or a party;
(e) deal with an issue in the proceedings as a preliminary issue;
(f) hold a hearing to consider any matter, including a case management issue;
(g) decide the form of any hearing;
(h) adjourn or postpone a hearing;
(i) require a party to produce a bundle for a hearing;
(j) stay proceedings;
(k) transfer proceedings to another court or tribunal if that other court or tribunal has jurisdiction in relation to the proceedings and –
  (i) because of a change of circumstances since the proceedings were started, the Tribunal no longer has jurisdiction in relation to the proceedings; or
  (ii) the Tribunal considers that the other court or tribunal is a more appropriate forum for the determination of the case; or
(l) suspend the effect of its own decision pending the determination by the Tribunal or the Upper Tribunal of an application for permission to appeal against, and any appeal or review of, that decision.

6 Procedure for applying for and giving directions

(1) The Tribunal may give a direction on the application of one or more of the parties or on its own initiative.

(2) An application for a direction may be made –

(a) by sending or delivering a written application to the Tribunal; or
(b) orally during the course of a hearing.

(3) An application for a direction must include the reason for making that application.

(4) Unless the Tribunal considers that there is good reason not to do so, the Tribunal must send written notice of any direction to every party and to any other person affected by the direction.

(5) If a party, or any other person given notice of the direction under paragraph (4), wishes to challenge a direction which the Tribunal has given, they may do so by applying for another direction which amends, suspends or sets aside the first direction.

7 Failure to comply with rules etc.

(1) An irregularity resulting from a failure to comply with any requirement in these Rules, a practice direction or a direction, does not of itself render void the proceedings or any step taken in the proceedings.

(2) If a party has failed to comply with a requirement in these Rules, a practice direction or a direction, the Tribunal may take such action as it considers just, which may include –

(a) waiving the requirement;
(b) requiring the failure to be remedied;
(c) exercising its power under rule 8 (striking out a party's case);
(d) exercising its power under paragraph (3); or

(e) except in mental health cases, restricting a party's participation in the proceedings.

(3) The Tribunal may refer to the Upper Tribunal, and ask the Upper Tribunal to exercise its power under section 25 of the 2007 Act in relation to, any failure by a person to comply with a requirement imposed by the Tribunal –

(a) to attend at any place for the purpose of giving evidence;
(b) otherwise to make themselves available to give evidence;
(c) to swear an oath in connection with the giving of evidence;
(d) to give evidence as a witness;
(e) to produce a document; or
(f) to facilitate the inspection of a document or any other thing (including any premises).

8 Striking out a party's case

(1) With the exception of paragraph (3), this rule does not apply to mental health cases.

(2) The proceedings, or the appropriate part of them, will automatically be struck out if the applicant has failed to comply with a direction that stated that failure by the applicant to comply with the direction would lead to the striking out of the proceedings or that part of them.

(3) The Tribunal must strike out the whole or a part of the proceedings if the Tribunal –

(a) does not have jurisdiction in relation to the proceedings or that part of them; and
(b) does not exercise its power under rule 5(3)(k)(i) (transfer to another court or tribunal) in relation to the proceedings or that part of them.

(4) The Tribunal may strike out the whole or a part of the proceedings if –

(a) the applicant has failed to comply with a direction which stated that failure by the applicant to comply with the direction could lead to the striking out of the proceedings or part of them;
(b) the applicant has failed to co-operate with the Tribunal to such an extent that the Tribunal cannot deal with the proceedings fairly and justly; or
(c) the Tribunal considers there is no reasonable prospect of the applicant's case, or part of it, succeeding.

(5) The Tribunal may not strike out the whole or a part of the proceedings under paragraph (3) or (4)(b) or (c) without first giving the applicant an opportunity to make representations in relation to the proposed striking out.

(6) If the proceedings, or part of them, have been struck out under paragraph (2) or (4)(a), the applicant may apply for the proceedings, or part of them, to be reinstated.

(7) An application under paragraph (6) must be made in writing and received by the Tribunal within 28 days after the date on which the Tribunal sent notification of the striking out to that party.

(8) This rule applies to a respondent as it applies to an applicant except that –

(a) a reference to the striking out of the proceedings is to be read as a reference to the barring of the respondent from taking further part in the proceedings; and

(b) a reference to an application for the reinstatement of proceedings which have been struck out is to be read as a reference to an application for the lifting of the bar on the respondent from taking further part in the proceedings.

(9) If a respondent has been barred from taking further part in proceedings under this rule and that bar has not been lifted, the Tribunal need not consider any response or other submission made by that respondent and may summarily determine any or all issues against that respondent.

Amendments—SI 2010/2653.

9 Substitution and addition of parties

(1) The Tribunal may give a direction substituting a party if –

(a) the wrong person has been named as a party; or
(b) the substitution has become necessary because of a change in circumstances since the start of proceedings.

(2) The Tribunal may give a direction adding a person to the proceedings as a respondent.

(3) If the Tribunal gives a direction under paragraph (1) or (2) it may give such consequential directions as it considers appropriate.

10 Orders for costs

(1) Subject to paragraph (2), the Tribunal may make an order in respect of costs only –

(a) under section 29(4) of the 2007 Act (wasted costs); or
(b) if the Tribunal considers that a party or its representative has acted unreasonably in bringing, defending or conducting the proceedings.

(2) The Tribunal may not make an order under paragraph (1)(b) in mental health cases.

(3) The Tribunal may make an order in respect of costs on an application or on its own initiative.

(4) A person making an application for an order under this rule must –

(a) send or deliver a written application to the Tribunal and to the person against whom it is proposed that the order be made; and
(b) send or deliver a schedule of the costs claimed with the application.

(5) An application for an order under paragraph (1) may be made at any time during the proceedings but may not be made later than 14 days after the date on which the Tribunal sends the decision notice recording the decision which finally disposes of all issues in the proceedings.

(6) The Tribunal may not make an order under paragraph (1) against a person (the 'paying person') without first –

(a) giving that person an opportunity to make representations; and
(b) if the paying person is an individual, considering that person's financial means.

(7) The amount of costs to be paid under an order under paragraph (1) may be ascertained by –

(a) summary assessment by the Tribunal;

(b) agreement of a specified sum by the paying person and the person entitled to receive the costs ('the receiving person'); or
(c) assessment of the whole or a specified part of the costs incurred by the receiving person, if not agreed.

(8) Following an order for assessment under paragraph (7)(c), the paying person or the receiving person may apply to a county court for a detailed assessment of costs in accordance with the Civil Procedure Rules 1998 on the standard basis or, if specified in the order, on the indemnity basis.

11 Representatives

(1) A party may appoint a representative (whether a legal representative or not) to represent that party in the proceedings.

(2) If a party appoints a representative, that party (or the representative if the representative is a legal representative) must send or deliver to the Tribunal and to each other party written notice of the representative's name and address.

(3) Anything permitted or required to be done by a party under these Rules, a practice direction or a direction may be done by the representative of that party, except –

(a) signing a witness statement; or
(b) signing an application notice under rule 20 (the application notice) if the representative is not a legal representative.

(4) A person who receives due notice of the appointment of a representative –

(a) must provide to the representative any document which is required to be provided to the represented party, and need not provide that document to the represented party; and
(b) may assume that the representative is and remains authorised as such until they receive written notification that this is not so from the representative or the represented party.

(5) At a hearing a party may be accompanied by another person whose name and address has not been notified under paragraph (2) but who, subject to paragraph (8) and with the permission of the Tribunal, may act as a representative or otherwise assist in presenting the party's case at the hearing.

(6) Paragraphs (2) to (4) do not apply to a person who accompanies a party under paragraph (5).

(7) In a mental health case, if the patient has not appointed a representative, the Tribunal may appoint a legal representative for the patient where –

(a) the patient has stated that they do not wish to conduct their own case or that they wish to be represented; or
(b) the patient lacks the capacity to appoint a representative but the Tribunal believes that it is in the patient's best interests for the patient to be represented.

(8) In a mental health case a party may not appoint as a representative, or be represented or assisted at a hearing by –

(a) a person liable to be detained or subject to guardianship or after-care under supervision, or who is a community patient, under the Mental Health Act 1983; or

(b) a person receiving treatment for mental disorder at the same hospital as the patient.

12 Calculating time

(1) An act required by these Rules, a practice direction or a direction to be done on or by a particular day must be done by 5pm on that day.

(2) If the time specified by these Rules, a practice direction or a direction for doing any act ends on a day other than a working day, the act is done in time if it is done on the next working day.

(3) In a special educational needs case or a disability discrimination in schools case –

(a) if the time for starting proceedings by providing the application notice to the Tribunal under rule 20 (the application notice) ends on a day from 25th December to 1st January inclusive, or on any day in August, the application notice is provided in time if it is provided to the Tribunal on the first working day after 1st January or 31st August, as appropriate; and
(b) the days from 25th December to 1st January inclusive and any day in August must not be counted when calculating the time by which any other act must be done.

(4) Paragraph (3)(b) does not apply where the Tribunal directs that an act must be done by or on a specified date.

13 Sending and delivery of documents

(1) Any document to be provided to the Tribunal under these Rules, a practice direction or a direction must be –

(a) sent by pre-paid post or delivered by hand to the address specified for the proceedings;
(b) sent by fax to the number specified for the proceedings; or
(c) sent or delivered by such other method as the Tribunal may permit or direct.

(1A) If the Tribunal permits or directs documents to be provided to it by email, the requirement for a signature on applications or references under rules 20(2), 22(4)(a) or 32(1)(b) may be satisfied by a typed instead of a handwritten signature.

(2) Subject to paragraph (3), if a party provides a fax number, email address or other details for the electronic transmission of documents to them, that party must accept delivery of documents by that method.

(3) If a party informs the Tribunal and all other parties that a particular form of communication, other than pre-paid post or delivery by hand, should not be used to provide documents to that party, that form of communication must not be so used.

(4) If the Tribunal or a party sends a document to a party or the Tribunal by email or any other electronic means of communication, the recipient may request that the sender provide a hard copy of the document to the recipient. The recipient must make such a request as soon as reasonably practicable after receiving the document electronically.

(5) The Tribunal and each party may assume that the address provided by a party or its representative is and remains the address to which documents should be sent or delivered until receiving written notification to the contrary.

Amendments—SI 2011/651.

14 Use of documents and information

(1) The Tribunal may make an order prohibiting the disclosure or publicatic

(a) specified documents or information relating to the proceedings; or
(b) any matter likely to lead members of the public to identify any person whom the Tribunal considers should not be identified.

(2) The Tribunal may give a direction prohibiting the disclosure of a document or information to a person if –

(a) the Tribunal is satisfied that such disclosure would be likely to cause that person or some other person serious harm; and
(b) the Tribunal is satisfied, having regard to the interests of justice, that it is proportionate to give such a direction.

(3) If a party ('the first party') considers that the Tribunal should give a direction under paragraph (2) prohibiting the disclosure of a document or information to another party ('the second party'), the first party must –

(a) exclude the relevant document or information from any documents that will be provided to the second party; and
(b) provide to the Tribunal the excluded document or information, and the reason for its exclusion, so that the Tribunal may decide whether the document or information should be disclosed to the second party or should be the subject of a direction under paragraph (2).

(4) The Tribunal must conduct proceedings as appropriate in order to give effect to a direction given under paragraph (2).

(5) If the Tribunal gives a direction under paragraph (2) which prevents disclosure to a party who has appointed a representative, the Tribunal may give a direction that the documents or information be disclosed to that representative if the Tribunal is satisfied that –

(a) disclosure to the representative would be in the interests of the party; and
(b) the representative will act in accordance with paragraph (6).

(6) Documents or information disclosed to a representative in accordance with a direction under paragraph (5) must not be disclosed either directly or indirectly to any other person without the Tribunal's consent.

(7) Unless the Tribunal gives a direction to the contrary, information about mental health cases and the names of any persons concerned in such cases must not be made public.

15 Evidence and submissions

(1) Without restriction on the general powers in rule 5(1) and (2) (case management powers), the Tribunal may give directions as to –

(a) issues on which it requires evidence or submissions;
(b) the nature of the evidence or submissions it requires;
(c) whether the parties are permitted or required to provide expert evidence, and if so whether the parties must jointly appoint a single expert to provide such evidence;
(d) any limit on the number of witnesses whose evidence a party may put forward, whether in relation to a particular issue or generally;

(e) the manner in which any evidence or submissions are to be provided, which may include a direction for them to be given –
  (i) orally at a hearing; or
  (ii) by written submissions or witness statement; and
(f) the time at which any evidence or submissions are to be provided.

(2) The Tribunal may –

(a) admit evidence whether or not –
  (i) the evidence would be admissible in a civil trial in England and Wales; or
  (ii) the evidence was available to a previous decision maker; or
(b) exclude evidence that would otherwise be admissible where –
  (i) the evidence was not provided within the time allowed by a direction or a practice direction;
  (ii) the evidence was otherwise provided in a manner that did not comply with a direction or a practice direction; or
  (iii) it would otherwise be unfair to admit the evidence.

(3) The Tribunal may consent to a witness giving, or require any witness to give, evidence on oath, and may administer an oath for that purpose.

(4) In a special educational needs case the Tribunal may require –

(a) the parents of the child, or any other person with care of the child or parental responsibility for the child (as defined in section 3 of the Children Act 1989), to make the child available for examination or assessment by a suitably qualified professional person; or
(b) the person responsible for a school or educational setting to allow a suitably qualified professional person to have access to the school or educational setting for the purpose of assessing the child or the provision made, or to be made, for the child.

(5) The Tribunal may consider a failure by a party to comply with a requirement made under paragraph (4), in the absence of any good reason for such failure, as a failure to co-operate with the Tribunal, which could lead to a result which is adverse to that party's case.

16 Summoning of witnesses and orders to answer questions or produce documents

(1) On the application of a party or on its own initiative, the Tribunal may –

(a) by summons require any person to attend as a witness at a hearing at the time and place specified in the summons; or
(b) order any person to answer any questions or produce any documents in that person's possession or control which relate to any issue in the proceedings.

(2) A summons under paragraph (1)(a) must –

(a) give the person required to attend 14 days' notice of the hearing, or such shorter period as the Tribunal may direct; and
(b) where the person is not a party, make provision for the person's necessary expenses of attendance to be paid, and state who is to pay them.

(3) No person may be compelled to give any evidence or produce any document that the person could not be compelled to give or produce on a trial of an action in a court of law.

(4) A summons or order under this rule must –

(a) state that the person on whom the requirement is imposed may apply to the Tribunal to vary or set aside the summons or order, if they have not had an opportunity to object to it; and
(b) state the consequences of failure to comply with the summons or order.

17 Withdrawal

(1) Subject to paragraphs (2) and (3), a party may give notice of the withdrawal of its case, or any part of it –

(a) at any time before a hearing to consider the disposal of the proceedings (or, if the Tribunal disposes of the proceedings without a hearing, before that disposal), by sending or delivering to the Tribunal a written notice of withdrawal; or
(b) orally at a hearing.

(2) Notice of withdrawal will not take effect unless the Tribunal consents to the withdrawal except –

(a) in proceedings concerning the suitability of a person to work with children or vulnerable adults; or
(b) in proceedings started by a reference under section 67 or 71(1) of the Mental Health Act 1983.

(3) A party which started a mental health case by making a reference to the Tribunal under section 68, 71(2) or 75(1) of the Mental Health Act 1983 may not withdraw its case.

(4) A party which has withdrawn its case may apply to the Tribunal for the case to be reinstated.

(5) An application under paragraph (4) must be made in writing and be received by the Tribunal within 28 days after –

(a) the date on which the Tribunal received the notice under paragraph (1)(a); or
(b) the date of the hearing at which the case was withdrawn orally under paragraph (1)(b).

(6) The Tribunal must notify each party in writing of a withdrawal under this rule.

*****

PART 4
PROCEEDINGS BEFORE THE TRIBUNAL IN MENTAL HEALTH CASES

Chapter 1
Before the hearing

31 Application of Part 4

This Part applies only to mental health cases.

32 Procedure in mental health cases

(1) An application or reference must be –

(a) made in writing;

(b) signed (in the case of an application, by the applicant or any person authorised by the applicant to do so); and
(c) sent or delivered to the Tribunal so that it is received within the time specified in the Mental Health Act 1983 or the Repatriation of Prisoners Act 1984.

(2) An application must, if possible, include –

(a) the name, address and date or birth of the patient;
(b) if the application is made by the patient's nearest relative, the name, address and relationship to the patient of the patient's nearest relative;
(c) the provision under which the patient is detained, liable to be detained, subject to guardianship, or a community patient;
(d) whether the person making the application has appointed a representative or intends to do so, and the name and address of any representative appointed;
(e) the name and address of the responsible authority in relation to the patient.

(2A) A reference must, if possible, include –

(a) the name and address of the person or body making the reference;
(b) the name, address and date of birth of the patient;
(c) the name and address of any representative of the patient;
(d) the provision under which the patient is detained, liable to be detained, subject to guardianship or a community patient (as the case may be);
(e) whether the person or body making the reference has appointed a representative or intends to do so, and the name and address of any representative appointed;
(f) if the reference is made by the Secretary of State, the name and address of the responsible authority in relation to the patient, or, in the case of a conditionally discharged patient, the name and address of the responsible clinician and any social supervisor in relation to the patient.

(3) Subject to rule 14(2) (withholding evidence likely to cause harm), when the Tribunal receives a document from any party it must send a copy of that document to each other party.

(4) If the patient is a conditionally discharged patient –

(a) upon being notified by the Tribunal of an application, the Secretary of State must immediately provide to the Tribunal the names and addresses of the responsible clinician and any social supervisor in relation to the patient; and
(b) upon being notified by the Tribunal of an application or reference, the responsible clinician and any social supervisor named by the Secretary of State under this rule must send or deliver the documents specified in the relevant practice direction to the Tribunal so that they are received by the Tribunal as soon as practicable and in any event within 3 weeks after the notification.

(5) In proceedings under section 66(1)(a) of the Mental Health Act 1983 (application in respect of an admission for assessment), on the earlier of receipt of the copy of the application or a request from the Tribunal, the responsible authority must immediately send or deliver to the Tribunal a copy of –

(a) the application for admission; and
(b) the written medical recommendations on which that application was founded;

and must as soon as practicable send or deliver to the Tribunal the documents specified in the relevant practice direction.

(6) If neither paragraph (4) nor (5) applies, the responsible authority must send or deliver the documents specified in the relevant practice direction to the Tribunal so that they are received by the Tribunal as soon as practicable and in any event within 3 weeks after the responsible authority made the reference or received a copy of the application or reference.

(7) If the patient is a restricted patient, a person or body providing a document to the Tribunal in accordance with paragraph (4)(b) or (6) must also send or deliver a copy of the document to the Secretary of State.

(7A) The Secretary of State must send the information specified in paragraph (7B) and any observations the Secretary of State wishes to make to the Tribunal as soon as practicable and in any event –

(a) in proceedings under section 75(1) of the Mental Health Act 1983 (reference concerning a conditionally discharged restricted patient who has been recalled to hospital), within 2 weeks after the Secretary of State received the documents sent or delivered in accordance with paragraph (7);
(b) otherwise, within 3 weeks after the Secretary of State received the documents sent or delivered in accordance with paragraph (7).

(7B) The information specified in this paragraph is –

(a) a summary of the offence or alleged offence that resulted in the patient being detained in hospital subject to a restriction order or, in the case of a patient subject to a restriction or limitation direction, that resulted in the patient being remanded in custody, kept in custody or sentenced to imprisonment;
(b) a record of any other criminal convictions or findings recorded against the patient;
(c) full details of the history of the patient's liability to detention under the Mental Health Act 1983 since the restrictions were imposed;
(d) any further information in the Secretary of State's possession that the Secretary of State considers relevant to the proceedings.

(8) If the Secretary of State wishes to seek the approval of the Tribunal under section 86(3) of the Mental Health Act 1983 (removal of alien patients), the Secretary of State must refer the patient's case to the Tribunal and the provisions of these Rules applicable to references under that Act apply to the proceedings.

Amendments—SI 2012/500.

33 Notice of proceedings to interested persons

When the Tribunal receives the information required by rule 32(4), (5) or (6) (procedure in mental health cases) the Tribunal must give notice of the proceedings –

(a) where the patient is subject to the guardianship of a private guardian, to the guardian;
(b) where there is an extant order of the Court of Protection, to that court;
(c) subject to a patient with capacity to do so requesting otherwise, where any person other than the applicant is named by the authority as exercising the functions of the nearest relative, to that person;
(d) where a health authority, Primary Care Trust, National Health Service trust or NHS foundation trust has a right to discharge the patient under the provisions of section 23(3) of the Mental Health Act 1983, to that authority or trust; and
(e) to any other person who, in the opinion of the Tribunal, should have an opportunity of being heard.

34 Medical examination of the patient

(1) Before a hearing to consider the disposal of a mental health case, an appropriate member of the Tribunal must, so far as practicable –

(a) examine the patient; and
(b) take such other steps as that member considers necessary to form an opinion of the patient's mental condition.

(2) For the purposes of paragraph (1) that member may –

(a) examine the patient in private;
(b) examine records relating to the detention or treatment of the patient and any after-care services;
(c) take notes and copies of records for use in connection with the proceedings.

Chapter 2
Hearings

35 Restrictions on disposal of proceedings without a hearing

(1) Subject to the following paragraphs, the Tribunal must hold a hearing before making a decision which disposes of proceedings.

(2) This rule does not apply to a decision under Part 5.

(3) The Tribunal may make a decision on a reference under section 68 of the Mental Health Act 1983 (duty of managers of hospitals to refer cases to tribunal) without a hearing if the patient is a community patient aged 18 or over and either –

(a) the patient has stated in writing that the patient does not wish to attend or be represented at a hearing of the reference and the Tribunal is satisfied that the patient has the capacity to decide whether or not to make that decision; or
(b) the patient's representative has stated in writing that the patient does not wish to attend or be represented at a hearing of the reference.

(4) The Tribunal may dispose of proceedings without a hearing under rule 8(3) (striking out a party's case).

Amendments—SI 2012/500.

36 Entitlement to attend a hearing

(1) Subject to rule 38(4) (exclusion of a person from a hearing), each party to proceedings is entitled to attend a hearing.

(2) Any person notified of the proceedings under rule 33 (notice of proceedings to interested persons) may –

(a) attend and take part in a hearing to such extent as the Tribunal considers proper; or
(b) provide written submissions to the Tribunal.

37 Time and place of hearings

(1) In proceedings under section 66(1)(a) of the Mental Health Act 1983 the hearing of the case must start within 7 days after the date on which the Tribunal received the application notice.

(2) In proceedings under section 75(1) of that Act, the hearing of the case must start at least 5 weeks but no more than 8 weeks after the date on which the Tribunal received the reference.

(3) The Tribunal must give reasonable notice of the time and place of the hearing (including any adjourned or postponed hearing), and any changes to the time and place of the hearing, to –

- (a) each party entitled to attend a hearing; and
- (b) any person who has been notified of the proceedings under rule 33 (notice of proceedings to interested persons).

(4) The period of notice under paragraph (3) must be at least 14 days, except that –

- (a) in proceedings under section 66(1)(a) of the Mental Health Act 1983 the period must be at least 3 working days; and
- (b) the Tribunal may give shorter notice –
  - (i) with the parties' consent; or
  - (ii) in urgent or exceptional circumstances.

38 Public and private hearings

(1) All hearings must be held in private unless the Tribunal considers that it is in the interests of justice for the hearing to be held in public.

(2) If a hearing is held in public, the Tribunal may give a direction that part of the hearing is to be held in private.

(3) Where a hearing, or part of it, is to be held in private, the Tribunal may determine who is permitted to attend the hearing or part of it.

(4) Tribunal may give a direction excluding from any hearing, or part of it –

- (a) any person whose conduct the Tribunal considers is disrupting or is likely to disrupt the hearing;
- (b) any person whose presence the Tribunal considers is likely to prevent another person from giving evidence or making submissions freely;
- (c) any person who the Tribunal considers should be excluded in order to give effect to a direction under rule 14(2) (withholding information likely to cause harm); or
- (d) any person where the purpose of the hearing would be defeated by the attendance of that person.

(5) The Tribunal may give a direction excluding a witness from a hearing until that witness gives evidence.

39 Hearings in a party's absence

(1) Subject to paragraph (2), if a party fails to attend a hearing the Tribunal may proceed with the hearing if the Tribunal –

- (a) is satisfied that the party has been notified of the hearing or that reasonable steps have been taken to notify the party of the hearing; and
- (b) considers that it is in the interests of justice to proceed with the hearing.

(2) The Tribunal may not proceed with a hearing in the absence of the patient unless –

- (a) the requirements of rule 34 (medical examination of the patient) have been satisfied; and

(b) the Tribunal is satisfied that –
  (i) the patient has decided not to attend the hearing; or
  (ii) the patient is unable to attend the hearing for reasons of ill health.

40 Power to pay allowances

The Tribunal may pay allowances in respect of travelling expenses, subsistence and loss of earnings to –

(a) any person who attends a hearing as an applicant or a witness;
(b) a patient who attends a hearing otherwise than as the applicant or a witness; and
(c) any person (other than a legal representative) who attends as the representative of an applicant.

Chapter 3
Decisions

41 Decisions

(1) The Tribunal may give a decision orally at a hearing.

(2) Subject to rule 14(2) (withholding information likely to cause harm), the Tribunal must provide to each party as soon as reasonably practicable after making a decision which finally disposes of all issues in the proceedings (except a decision under Part 5) –

(a) a decision notice stating the Tribunal's decision;
(b) written reasons for the decision; and
(c) notification of any right of appeal against the decision and the time within which, and the manner in which, such right of appeal may be exercised.

(3) The documents and information referred to in paragraph (2) must –

(a) in proceedings under section 66(1)(a) of the Mental Health Act 1983, be provided at the hearing or sent within 3 working days after the hearing; and
(b) in other cases, be provided at the hearing or sent within 7 days after the hearing.

(4) The Tribunal may provide written reasons for any decision to which paragraph (2) does not apply.

42 Provisional decisions

For the purposes of this Part and Parts 1, 2 and 5, a decision with recommendations under section 72(3)(a) or (3A)(a) of the Mental Health Act 1983 or a deferred direction for conditional discharge under section 73(7) of that Act is a decision which disposes of the proceedings.

PART 5
CORRECTING, SETTING ASIDE, REVIEWING AND APPEALING TRIBUNAL DECISIONS

43 Interpretation

In this Part –

'appeal' means the exercise of a right of appeal on a point of law under section 11 of the 2007 Act; and 'review' means the review of a decision by the Tribunal under section 9 of the 2007 Act.

44 Clerical mistakes and accidental slips or omissions

The Tribunal may at any time correct any clerical mistake or other accidental slip or omission in a decision, direction or any document produced by it, by –

(a) sending notification of the amended decision or direction, or a copy of the amended document, to all parties; and
(b) making any necessary amendment to any information published in relation to the decision, direction or document.

Setting aside a decision which disposes of proceedings

45 (1) The Tribunal may set aside a decision which disposes of proceedings, or part of such a decision, and re-make the decision or the relevant part of it, if –

(a) the Tribunal considers that it is in the interests of justice to do so; and
(b) one or more of the conditions in paragraph (2) are satisfied.

(2) The conditions are –

(a) a document relating to the proceedings was not sent to, or was not received at an appropriate time by, a party or a party's representative;
(b) a document relating to the proceedings was not sent to the Tribunal at an appropriate time;
(c) a party, or a party's representative, was not present at a hearing related to the proceedings; or
(d) there has been some other procedural irregularity in the proceedings.

(3) A party applying for a decision, or part of a decision, to be set aside under paragraph (1) must make a written application to the Tribunal so that it is received no later than 28 days after the date on which the Tribunal sent notice of the decision to the party.

46 Application for permission to appeal

(1) A person seeking permission to appeal must make a written application to the Tribunal for permission to appeal.

(2) An application under paragraph (1) must be sent or delivered to the Tribunal so that it is received no later than 28 days after the latest of the dates that the Tribunal sends to the person making the application –

(a) written reasons for the decision;
(b) notification of amended reasons for, or correction of, the decision following a review; or
(c) notification that an application for the decision to be set aside has been unsuccessful.

(3) The date in paragraph (2)(c) applies only if the application for the decision to be set aside was made within the time stipulated in rule 45 (setting aside a decision which disposes of proceedings) or any extension of that time granted by the Tribunal.

(4) If the person seeking permission to appeal sends or delivers the application to the Tribunal later than the time required by paragraph (2) or by any extension of time under rule 5(3)(a) (power to extend time) –

(a) the application must include a request for an extension of time and the reason why the application was not provided in time; and
(b) unless the Tribunal extends time for the application under rule 5(3)(a) (power to extend time) the Tribunal must not admit the application.

(5) An application under paragraph (1) must –

(a) identify the decision of the Tribunal to which it relates;
(b) identify the alleged error or errors of law in the decision; and
(c) state the result the party making the application is seeking.

47 Tribunal's consideration of application for permission to appeal

(1) On receiving an application for permission to appeal the Tribunal must first consider, taking into account the overriding objective in rule 2, whether to review the decision in accordance with rule 49 (review of a decision).

(2) If the Tribunal decides not to review the decision, or reviews the decision and decides to take no action in relation to the decision, or part of it, the Tribunal must consider whether to give permission to appeal in relation to the decision or that part of it.

(3) The Tribunal must send a record of its decision to the parties as soon as practicable.

(4) If the Tribunal refuses permission to appeal it must send with the record of its decision –

(a) a statement of its reasons for such refusal; and
(b) notification of the right to make an application to the Upper Tribunal for permission to appeal and the time within which, and the method by which, such application must be made.

(5) The Tribunal may give permission to appeal on limited grounds, but must comply with paragraph (4) in relation to any grounds on which it has refused permission.

48 Application for review in special educational needs cases

(1) This rule applies to decisions which dispose of proceedings in special educational needs cases, but not to decisions under this Part.

(2) A party may make a written application to the Tribunal for a review of a decision if circumstances relevant to the decision have changed since the decision was made.

(3) An application under paragraph (2) must be sent or delivered to the Tribunal so that it is received within 28 days after the date on which the Tribunal sent the decision notice recording the Tribunal's decision to the party making the application.

(4) If a party sends or delivers an application to the Tribunal later than the time required by paragraph (3) or by any extension of time under rule 5(3)(a) (power to extend time) –

(a) the application must include a request for an extension of time and the reason why the application was not provided in time; and
(b) unless the Tribunal extends time for the application under rule 5(3)(a) (power to extend time) the Tribunal must not admit the application.

49 Review of a decision

(1) The Tribunal may only undertake a review of a decision –

(a) pursuant to rule 47(1) (review on an application for permission to appeal) if it is satisfied that there was an error of law in the decision; or

(b) pursuant to rule 48 (application for review in special educational needs cases).

(2) The Tribunal must notify the parties in writing of the outcome of any review, and of any right of appeal in relation to the outcome.

(3) If the Tribunal takes any action in relation to a decision following a review without first giving every party an opportunity to make representations, the notice under paragraph (2) must state that any party that did not have an opportunity to make representations may apply for such action to be set aside and for the decision to be reviewed again.

50 Power to treat an application as a different type of application

The Tribunal may treat an application for a decision to be corrected, set aside or reviewed, or for permission to appeal against a decision, as an application for any other one of those things.

Schedule
Cases in which the Time for Providing the Application Notice is Within 3 Months After Written Notice of the Decision Being Challenged was Sent to the Applicant

Rule 20(1)(d)

Amendments—Substituted by SI 2011/651.

An appeal under section 65A of the Children Act 1989 (appeal against a refusal to give consent for a person who is disqualified from fostering a child privately to carry on, or be otherwise concerned in the management of, or have any financial interest in, or be employed in, a children's home)

An appeal, an application for permission to appeal or an application for permission to have an issue determined under section 4 of the Protection of Children Act 1999 (appeal against inclusion of a person on the list of individuals who are considered unsuitable to work with children or a refusal to remove a person from the list)

An appeal under section 68 of the Care Standards Act 2000 against a refusal to register a person as a social worker under section 58 of that Act (grant or refusal of registration)

An appeal, an application for permission to appeal or an application for permission to have an issue determined under section 86 of the Care Standards Act 2000 (appeal against inclusion of a person on the list of individuals who are considered unsuitable to work with vulnerable adults or a refusal to remove a person from the list)

An appeal under section 74(1)(a) of the Childcare Act 2006 (appeal against a refusal of registration as a childcare provider)

An appeal under section 37(1)(a) of the Children and Families (Wales) Measure 2010 (appeal against a refusal of an application for registration for child minding or providing day care for children)

An appeal under regulation 12 of the Education (Prohibition from Teaching or Working with Children) Regulations 2003 (appeal against a direction, or a refusal to revoke a direction, prohibiting or restricting a person from working in education or in a job which brings them regularly into contact with children).

Amendments—Substituted by SI 2011/651.

F6

F6

THE TRIBUNAL PROCEDURE (UPPER TRIBUNAL) RULES 2008

SI 2008/2698

ARRANGEMENT OF RULES

PART 1
INTRODUCTION

PART 2
GENERAL POWERS AND PROVISIONS

PART3
PROCEDURE FOR CASES IN THE UPPER TRIBUNAL

PART 1
INTRODUCTION

1 Citation, commencement, application and interpretation

(1) These Rules may be cited as the Tribunal Procedure (Upper Tribunal) Rules 2008 and come into force on 3rd November 2008.

(2) These Rules apply to proceedings before the Upper Tribunal except proceedings in the Lands Chamber.

(3) In these Rules –

'the 2007 Act' means the Tribunals, Courts and Enforcement Act 2007;

'appellant' means
- (a) a person who makes an appeal, or applies for permission to appeal, to the Upper Tribunal;
- (b) in proceedings transferred or referred to the Upper Tribunal from the First-tier Tribunal, a person who started the proceedings in the First-tier Tribunal; or
- (c) a person substituted as an appellant under rule 9(1) (substitution and addition of parties);

'applicant' means –
- (a) a person who applies for permission to bring, or does bring, judicial review proceedings before the Upper Tribunal and, in judicial review proceedings transferred to the Upper Tribunal from a court, includes a person who was a claimant or petitioner in the proceedings immediately before they were transferred; or
- (b) a person who refers a financial services case to the Upper Tribunal;

"appropriate national authority" means, in relation to an appeal, the Secretary of State, the Scottish Ministers, the Department of the Environment in Northern Ireland or the Welsh Ministers, as the case may be;

"asylum case" means proceedings before the Upper Tribunal on appeal against a decision in proceedings under section 82, 83 or 83A of the Nationality, Immigration and Asylum Act 2002 in which a person claims that removal from, or a requirement to leave, the United Kingdom would breach the United Kingdom's obligations under the Convention relating to the Status of Refugees done at Geneva on 28 July 1951 and the Protocol to the Convention;

"authorised person" means –
- (a) an examiner appointed by the Secretary of State under section 66A of the Road Traffic Act 1988;
- (b) an examiner appointed by the Department of the Environment in Northern Ireland under Article 74 of the Road Traffic (Northern Ireland) Order 1995; or
- (c) any person authorised in writing by the Department of the Environment in Northern Ireland for the purposes of the Goods Vehicles (Licensing of Operators) Act (Northern Ireland) 2010;

and includes a person acting under the direction of such an examiner or other authorised person, who has detained the vehicle to which an appeal relates;

'dispose of proceedings' includes, unless indicated otherwise, disposing of a part of the proceedings;

'document' means anything in which information is recorded in any form, and an obligation under these Rules or any practice direction or direction to provide or allow access to a document or a copy of a document for any purpose means, unless the Upper Tribunal directs otherwise, an obligation to provide or allow access to such document or copy in a legible form or in a form which can be readily made into a legible form;

"fast-track case" means an asylum case or an immigration case where the person who appealed to the First-tier Tribunal –
- (a) was detained under the Immigration Acts at a place specified in Schedule 2 to the Asylum and Immigration Tribunal (Fast Track Procedure) Rules 2005 when the notice of decision that was the subject of the appeal to the First-tier Tribunal was served on the appellant;
- (b) remains so detained; and

(c) the First-tier Tribunal or the Upper Tribunal has not directed that the case cease to be treated as a fast-track case;

"financial services case" means a reference to the Upper Tribunal in respect of –

(a) a decision of the Financial Services Authority;
(b) a decision of the Bank of England;
(c) a decision of the Pensions Regulator; or
(d) a decision of a person relating to the assessment of any compensation or consideration under the Banking (Special Provisions) Act 2008 or the Banking Act 2009; or
(e) any determination, calculation or dispute which may be referred to the Upper Tribunal under the Financial Services and Markets Act 2000 (Contribution to Costs of Special Resolution Regime) Regulations 2010 (and in these Rules a decision in respect of which a reference has been made to the Upper Tribunal in a financial services case includes any such determination, calculation or, except for the purposes of rule 5(5), dispute relating to the making of payments under the Regulations)

"fresh claim proceedings" means judicial review proceedings which call into question a decision of the Secretary of State not to treat submissions as an asylum claim or a human rights claim within the meaning of Part 5 of the Nationality, Immigration and Asylum Act 2002 wholly or partly on the basis that they are not significantly different from material that has previously been considered, and which have been begun in or transferred to the Upper Tribunal pursuant to a direction made by the Lord Chief Justice of England and Wales for the purposes of section 18(6) of the 2007 Act;

'hearing' means an oral hearing and includes a hearing conducted in whole or in part by video link, telephone or other means of instantaneous two-way electronic communication;

"immigration case" means proceedings before the Upper Tribunal on appeal against a decision in proceedings under section 40A of the British Nationality Act 1981, section 82 of the Nationality, Immigration and Asylum Act 2002, or regulation 26 of the Immigration (European Economic Area) Regulations 2006 that are not an asylum case;

'interested party' means –

(a) a person who is directly affected by the outcome sought in judicial review proceedings, and has been named as an interested party under rule 28 or 29 (judicial review), or has been substituted or added as an interested party under rule 9 (substitution and addition of parties);
(b) in judicial review proceedings transferred to the Upper Tribunal under section 25A(2) or (3) of the Judicature (Northern Ireland) Act 1978(2) or section 31A(2) or (3) of the Senior Court Act 1981(3), a person who was an interested party in the proceedings immediately before they were transferred to the Upper Tribunal; and
(c) in a financial services case, any person other than the applicant who could have referred the case to the Upper Tribunal and who has been added or substituted as an interested party under rule 9 (addition, substitution and removal of parties);

'judicial review proceedings' means proceedings within the jurisdiction of the Upper Tribunal pursuant to section 15 or 21 of the 2007 Act, whether such proceedings are started in the Upper Tribunal or transferred to the Upper Tribunal;

'mental health case' means proceedings before the Upper Tribunal on appeal against a decision in proceedings under the Mental Health Act 1983(5) or paragraph 5(2) of the Schedule to the Repatriation of Prisoners Act 1984(6);

"national security certificate appeal" means an appeal under section 28 of the Data Protection Act 1998 or section 60 of the Freedom of Information Act 2000 (including that section as applied and modified by regulation 18 of the Environmental Information Regulations 2004);

'party' means a person who is an appellant, an applicant, a respondent or an interested party in proceedings before the Upper Tribunal, a person who has referred a question or matter to the Upper Tribunal or, if the proceedings have been concluded, a person who was an appellant, an applicant, a respondent or an interested party when the Tribunal finally disposed of all issues in the proceedings;

'permission' includes leave in cases arising under the law of Northern Ireland;

'practice direction' means a direction given under section 23 of the 2007 Act;

"reference", in a financial services case, includes an appeal;

"relevant minister" means the Minister or designated person responsible for the signing of the certificate to which a national security certificate appeal relates;

'respondent' means –

- (a) in an appeal, or application for permission to appeal, against a decision of another tribunal, any person other than the appellant who –
  - (i) was a party before that other tribunal;
  - (ii) (*revoked*)
  - (iii) otherwise has a right of appeal against the decision of the other tribunal and has given notice to the Upper Tribunal that they wish to be a party to the appeal;
- (b) in an appeal other than a road transport case, the person who made the decision;
- (c) in judicial review proceedings –
  - (i) in proceedings started in the Upper Tribunal, the person named by the applicant as the respondent;
  - (ii) in proceedings transferred to the Upper Tribunal under section 25A(2) or (3) of the Judicature (Northern Ireland) Act 1978 or section 31A(2) or (3) of the Senior Courts Act 1981, a person who was a defendant in the proceedings immediately before they were transferred;
  - (iii) in proceedings transferred to the Upper Tribunal under section 20(1) of the 2007 Act, a person to whom intimation of the petition was made before the proceedings were transferred, or to whom the Upper Tribunal has required intimation to be made.
- (ca) in proceedings transferred or referred to the Upper Tribunal from the First-tier Tribunal, a person who was a respondent in the proceedings in the First-tier Tribunal;
- (d) in a reference under the Forfeiture Act 1982(7), the person whose eligibility for a benefit or advantage is in issue; or
- (da) in a financial services case, the maker of the decision in respect of which a reference has been made; or
- (e) a person substituted or added as a respondent under rule 9 (substitution and addition of parties);

"road transport case" means an appeal against a decision of a traffic commissioner or the Department of the Environment in Northern Ireland;

"tribunal" does not include a traffic commissioner;

'working day' means any day except a Saturday or Sunday, Christmas Day, Good Friday or a bank holiday under section 1 of the Banking and Financial Dealings Act 1971.

Amendments—Constitutional Reform Act 2005, s 59(5), Sch 11, Pt 1, para 1(2); SI 2009/274; SI 2009/1975; SI 2010/44; SI 2010/747; SI 2011/651; SI 2011/2343; SI 2012/1363.

2 Overriding objective and parties' obligation to co-operate with the Upper Tribunal

(1) The overriding objective of these Rules is to enable the Upper Tribunal to deal with cases fairly and justly.

(2) Dealing with a case fairly and justly includes –

(a) dealing with the case in ways which are proportionate to the importance of the case, the complexity of the issues, the anticipated costs and the resources of the parties;
(b) avoiding unnecessary formality and seeking flexibility in the proceedings;
(c) ensuring, so far as practicable, that the parties are able to participate fully in the proceedings;
(d) using any special expertise of the Upper Tribunal effectively; and
(e) avoiding delay, so far as compatible with proper consideration of the issues.

(3) The Upper Tribunal must seek to give effect to the overriding objective when it –

(a) exercises any power under these Rules; or
(b) interprets any rule or practice direction.

(4) Parties must –

(a) help the Upper Tribunal to further the overriding objective; and
(b) co-operate with the Upper Tribunal generally.

3 Alternative dispute resolution and arbitration

(1) The Upper Tribunal should seek, where appropriate –

(a) to bring to the attention of the parties the availability of any appropriate alternative procedure for the resolution of the dispute; and
(b) if the parties wish and provided that it is compatible with the overriding objective, to facilitate the use of the procedure.

(2) Part 1 of the Arbitration Act 1996(9) does:' not apply to proceedings before the Upper Tribunal.

PART 2
GENERAL POWERS AND PROVISIONS

4 Delegation to staff

(1) Staff appointed under section 40(1) of the 2007 Act (tribunal staff and services) may, with the approval of the Senior President of Tribunals, carry out functions of a judicial nature permitted or required to be done by the Upper Tribunal.

(2) The approval referred to at paragraph (1) may apply generally to the carrying out of specified functions by members of staff of a specified description in specified circumstances.

(3) Within 14 days after the date on which the Upper Tribunal sends notice of a decision made by a member of staff under paragraph (1) to a party, that party may apply in writing to the Upper Tribunal for that decision to be considered afresh by a judge.

5 Case management powers

(1) Subject to the provisions of the 2007 Act and any other enactment, the Upper Tribunal may regulate its own procedure.

(2) The Upper Tribunal may give a direction in relation to the conduct or disposal of proceedings at any time, including a direction amending, suspending or setting aside an earlier direction.

(3) In particular, and without restricting the general powers in paragraphs (1) and (2), the Upper Tribunal may –

- (a) extend or shorten the time for complying with any rule, practice direction or direction;
- (b) consolidate or hear together two or more sets of proceedings or parts of proceedings raising common issues, or treat a case as a lead case;
- (c) permit or require a party to amend a document;
- (d) permit or require a party or another person to provide documents, information, evidence or submissions to the Upper Tribunal or a party;
- (e) deal with an issue in the proceedings as a preliminary issue;
- (f) hold a hearing to consider any matter, including a case management issue;
- (g) decide the form of any hearing;
- (h) adjourn or postpone a hearing;
- (i) require a party to produce a bundle for a hearing;
- (j) stay (or, in Scotland, sist) proceedings;
- (k) transfer proceedings to another court or tribunal if that other court or tribunal has jurisdiction in relation to the proceedings and –
    - (i) because of a change of circumstances since the proceedings were started, the Upper Tribunal no longer has jurisdiction in relation to the proceedings; or
    - (ii) the Upper Tribunal considers that the other court or tribunal is a more appropriate forum for the determination of the case;
- (l) suspend the effect of its own decision pending an appeal or review of that decision;
- (m) in an appeal, or an application for permission to appeal, against the decision of another tribunal, suspend the effect of that decision pending the determination of the application for permission to appeal, and any appeal;
- (n) require any person, body or other tribunal whose decision is the subject of proceedings before the Upper Tribunal to provide reasons for the decision, or other information or documents in relation to the decision or any proceedings before that person, body or tribunal.

(4) The Upper Tribunal may direct that a fast-track case cease to be treated as a fast-track case if –

- (a) all the parties consent;
- (b) the Upper Tribunal is satisfied that there are exceptional circumstances which suggest that the appeal or application could not be justly determined if it were treated as a fast-track case; or
- (c) the Secretary of State for the Home Department has failed to comply with a provision of these Rules or a direction of the First-tier Tribunal or the Upper

Tribunal, and the Upper Tribunal is satisfied that the other party would be prejudiced if the appeal or application were treated as a fast-track case.

(5) In a financial services case, the Upper Tribunal may direct that the effect of the decision in respect of which the reference has been made is to be suspended pending the determination of the reference, if it is satisfied that to do so would not prejudice –

- (a) the interests of any persons (whether consumers, investors or otherwise) intended to be protected by that notice; or
- (b) the smooth operation or integrity of any market intended to be protected by that notice.

(6) Paragraph (5) does not apply in the case of a reference in respect of a decision of the Pensions Regulator.

Amendments—SI 2009/1975; SI 2010/44; SI 2010/747.

6 Procedure for applying for and giving directions

(1) The Upper Tribunal may give a direction on the application of one or more of the parties or on its own initiative.

(2) An application for a direction may be made –

- (a) by sending or delivering a written application to the Upper Tribunal; or
- (b) orally during the course of a hearing.

(3) An application for a direction must include the reason for making that application.

(4) Unless the Upper Tribunal considers that there is good reason not to do so, the Upper Tribunal must send written notice of any direction to every party and to any other person affected by the direction.

(5) If a party or any other person sent notice of the direction under paragraph (4) wishes to challenge a direction which the Upper Tribunal has given, they may do so by applying for another direction which amends, suspends or sets aside the first direction.

7 Failure to comply with rules etc.

(1) An irregularity resulting from a failure to comply with any requirement in these Rules, a practice direction or a direction, does not of itself render void the proceedings or any step taken in the proceedings.

(2) If a party has failed to comply with a requirement in these Rules, a practice direction or a direction, the Upper Tribunal may take such action as it considers just, which may include –

- (a) waiving the requirement;
- (b) requiring the failure to be remedied;
- (c) exercising its power under rule 8 (striking out a party's case); or
- (d) except in a mental health case, an asylum case or an immigration case restricting a party's participation in the proceedings.

(3) Paragraph (4) applies where the First-tier Tribunal has referred to the Upper Tribunal a failure by a person to comply with a requirement imposed by the First-tier Tribunal –

- (a) to attend at any place for the purpose of giving evidence;
- (b) otherwise to make themselves available to give evidence;

(c) to swear an oath in connection with the giving of evidence;
(d) to give evidence as a witness;
(e) to produce a document; or
(f) to facilitate the inspection of a document or any other thing (including any premises).

(4) The Upper Tribunal may exercise its power under section 25 of the 2007 Act (supplementary powers of the Upper Tribunal) in relation to such non-compliance as if the requirement had been imposed by the Upper Tribunal.

Amendments—SI 2010/44.

8 Striking out a party's case

(1A) Except for paragraph (2), this rule does not apply to an asylum case or an immigration case.

(1) The proceedings, or the appropriate part of them, will automatically be struck out –

(a) if the appellant or applicant has failed to comply with a direction that stated that failure by the appellant or applicant to comply with the direction would lead to the striking out of the proceedings or part of them; or
(b) when a fee has not been paid upon the grant of permission in fresh claim proceedings as required.

(2) The Upper Tribunal must strike out the whole or a part of the proceedings if the Upper Tribunal –

(a) does not have jurisdiction in relation to the proceedings or that part of them; and
(b) does not exercise its power under rule 5(3)(k)(i) (transfer to another court or tribunal) in relation to the proceedings or that part of them.

(3) The Upper Tribunal may strike out the whole or a part of the proceedings if –

(a) the appellant or applicant has failed to comply with a direction which stated that failure by the appellant or applicant to comply with the direction could lead to the striking out of the proceedings or part of them;
(b) the appellant or applicant has failed to co-operate with the Upper Tribunal to such an extent that the Upper Tribunal cannot deal with the proceedings fairly and justly; or
(c) in proceedings which are not an appeal from the decision of another tribunal or judicial review proceedings, the Upper Tribunal considers there is no reasonable prospect of the appellant's or the applicant's case, or part of it, succeeding.

(4) The Upper Tribunal may not strike out the whole or a part of the proceedings under paragraph (2) or (3)(b) or (c) without first giving the appellant or applicant an opportunity to make representations in relation to the proposed striking out.

(5) If the proceedings have been struck out under paragraph (1) or (3)(a), the appellant or applicant may apply for the proceedings, or part of them, to be reinstated.

(6) An application under paragraph (5) must be made in writing and received by the Upper Tribunal within 1 month after the date on which the Upper Tribunal sent notification of the striking out to the appellant or applicant.

(7) This rule applies to a respondent or an interested party as it applies to an appellant or applicant except that –

(a) a reference to the striking out of the proceedings is to be read as a reference to the barring of the respondent or an interested party from taking further part in the proceedings; and

(b) a reference to an application for the reinstatement of proceedings which have been struck out is to be read as a reference to an application for the lifting of the bar on the respondent or interested party taking further part in the proceedings.

(8) If a respondent or an interested party has been barred from taking further part in proceedings under this rule and that bar has not been lifted, the Upper Tribunal need not consider any response or other submission made by that respondent or interested party, and may summarily determine any or all issues against the respondent or interested party.

Amendments—SI 2009/274; SI 2010/44; SI 2011/2343.

9 Addition, substitution and removal of parties

(1) The Upper Tribunal may give a direction adding, substituting or removing a party as an appellant, a respondent or an interested party.

(2) The Upper Tribunal gives a direction under paragraph (1) it may give such consequential directions as it considers appropriate.

(3) A person who is not a party may apply to the Upper Tribunal to be added or substituted as a party.

(4) If a person who is entitled to be a party to proceedings by virtue of another enactment applies to be added as a party, and any conditions applicable to that entitlement have been satisfied, the Upper Tribunal must give a direction adding that person as a respondent or, if appropriate, as an appellant.

(5) In an asylum case, the United Kingdom Representative of the United Nations High Commissioner for Refugees ("the United Kingdom Representative") may give notice to the Upper Tribunal that the United Kingdom Representative wishes to participate in the proceedings.

(6) If the United Kingdom Representative gives notice under paragraph (5) –

(i) the United Kingdom Representative is entitled to participate in any hearing; and

(ii) all documents which are required to be sent or delivered to parties must be sent or delivered to the United Kingdom Representative.

Amendments—SI 2009/274; SI 2010/44.

10 Orders for costs

(1) The Upper Tribunal may not make an order in respect of costs (or, in Scotland, expenses) in proceedings transferred or referred by, or on appeal from, another tribunal except –

(aa) in a national security certificate appeal, to the extent permitted by paragraph (1A);

(a) in proceedings transferred by, or on appeal from, the Tax Chamber of the First-tier Tribunal; or

(b) to the extent and in the circumstances that the other tribunal had the power to make an order in respect of costs (or, in Scotland, expenses).

(1A) In a national security certificate appeal –

(a) the Upper Tribunal may make an order in respect of costs or expenses in the circumstances described at paragraph (3)(c) and (d);
(b) if the appeal is against a certificate, the Upper Tribunal may make an order in respect of costs or expenses against the relevant Minister and in favour of the appellant if the Upper Tribunal allows the appeal and quashes the certificate to any extent or the Minister withdraws the certificate;
(c) if the appeal is against the application of a certificate, the Upper Tribunal may make an order in respect of costs or expenses –
  (i) against the appellant and in favour of any other party if the Upper Tribunal dismisses the appeal to any extent; or
  (ii) in favour of the appellant and against any other party if the Upper Tribunal allows the appeal to any extent.

(2) The Upper Tribunal may not make an order in respect of costs or expenses under section 4 of the Forfeiture Act 1982.

(3) In other proceedings, the Upper Tribunal may not make an order in respect of costs or expenses except –

(a) in judicial review proceedings;
(b) (*revoked*)
(c) under section 29(4) of the 2007 Act (wasted costs);
(d) If the Upper Tribunal considers that a party or its representative has acted unreasonably in bringing, defending or conducting the proceedings; or
(e) if, in a financial services case, the Upper Tribunal considers that the decision in respect of which the reference was made was unreasonable.

(4) The Upper Tribunal may make an order for costs (or, in Scotland, expenses) on an application or on its own initiative.

(5) A person making an application for an order for costs or expenses must –

(a) send or deliver a written application to the Upper Tribunal and to the person against whom it is proposed that the order be made; and
(b) send or deliver with the application a schedule of the costs or expenses claimed sufficient to allow summary assessment of such costs or expenses by the Upper Tribunal.

(6) An application for an order for costs or expenses may be made at any time during the proceedings but may not be made later than 1 month after the date on which the Upper Tribunal sends –

(a) a decision notice recording the decision which finally disposes of all issues in the proceedings; or
(b) notice of a withdrawal under rule 17 which ends the proceedings.

(7) The Upper Tribunal may not make an order for costs or expenses against a person (the "paying person") without first –

(a) giving that person an opportunity to make representations; and
(b) if the paying person is an individual and the order is to be made under paragraph (3)(a), (b) or (d), considering that person's financial means.

(8) The amount of costs or expenses to be paid under an order under this rule may be ascertained by –

(a) summary assessment by the Upper Tribunal;
(b) agreement of a specified sum by the paying person and the person entitled to receive the costs or expenses ("the receiving person"); or
(c) assessment of the whole or a specified part of the costs or expenses incurred by the receiving person, if not agreed.

(9) Following an order for assessment under paragraph (8)(c), the paying person or the receiving person may apply –

(a) in England and Wales, to the High Court or the Costs Office of the Supreme Court (as specified in the order) for a detailed assessment of the costs on the standard basis or, if specified in the order, on the indemnity basis; and the Civil Procedure Rules 1998 shall apply, with necessary modifications, to that application and assessment as if the proceedings in the tribunal had been proceedings in a court to which the Civil Procedure Rules 1998 apply;
(b) in Scotland, to the Auditor of the Court of Session for the taxation of the expenses according to the fees payable in that court; or
(c) in Northern Ireland, to the Taxing Office of the High Court of Northern Ireland for taxation on the standard basis or, if specified in the order, on the indemnity basis.

Amendments—SI 2009/274; SI 2009/1975; SI 2010/43; SI 2010/747.

11 Representatives

(1) Subject to pargraph (5A), a party may appoint a representative (whether a legal representative or not) to represent that party in the proceedings save that a party in an asylum or immigration case may not be represented by any person prohibited from representing by section 84 of the Immigration and Asylum Act 1999.

(2) If a party appoints a representative, that party (or the representative if the representative is a legal representative) must send or deliver to the Upper Tribunal written notice of the representative's name and address.

(2A) If the Upper Tribunal receives notice that a party has appointed a representative under paragraph (2), it must send a copy of that notice to each other party.

(3) Anything permitted or required to be done by a party under these Rules, a practice direction or a direction may be done by the representative of that party, except signing a witness statement.

(4) A person who receives due notice of the appointment of a representative –

(a) must provide to the representative any document which is required to be provided to the represented party, and need not provide that document to the represented party; and
(b) may assume that the representative is and remains authorised as such until they receive written notification that this is not so from the representative or the represented party.

(5) Subject to paragraph (5B), at a hearing a party may be accompanied by another person whose name and address has not been notified under paragraph (2) but who, subject to paragraph (8) and with the permission of the Upper Tribunal, may act as a representative or otherwise assist in presenting the party's case at the hearing.

(5A) In fresh claim proceedings, a party may appoint as a representative only a person authorised under the Legal Services Act 2007 to undertake the conduct of litigation in the High Court.

(5B) At a hearing of fresh claim proceedings, rights of audience before the Upper Tribunal are restricted to persons authorised to exercise those rights in the High Court under the Legal Services Act 2007.

(6) Paragraphs (2) to (4) do not apply to a person who accompanies a party under paragraph (5).

(7) In a mental health case if the patient has not appointed a representative the Upper Tribunal may appoint a legal representative for the patient where –

(a) the patient has stated that they do not wish to conduct their own case or that they wish to be represented; or
(b) the patient lacks the capacity to appoint a representative but the Upper Tribunal believes that it is in the patient's best interests for the patient to be represented.

(8) In a mental health case a party may not appoint as a representative, or be represented or assisted at a hearing by –

(a) a person liable to be detained or subject to guardianship or after-care under supervision, or who is a community patient, under the Mental Health Act 1983; or
(b) a person receiving treatment for mental disorder at the same hospital home as the patient.

(9) In this rule 'legal representative' means a person who, for the purposes of the Legal Services Act 2007, is an authorised person in relation to an activity which constitutes the exercise of a right of audience or the conduct of litigation within the meaning of that Act, a qualified person as defined in section 84(2) of the Immigration and Asylum Act 1999, an advocate or solicitor in Scotland or a barrister or solicitor in Northern Ireland.

(10) In an asylum case or an immigration case, an appellant's representative before the First-tier Tribunal will be treated as that party's representative before the Upper Tribunal, unless the Upper Tribunal receives notice –

(a) of a new representative under paragraph (2) of this rule; or
(b) from the appellant stating that they are no longer represented.

Amendments—SI 2009/274; SI 2010/43; SI 2010/44; SI 2011/2343.

12 Calculating time

(1) An act required by these Rules, a practice direction or a direction to be done on or by a particular day must be done by 5pm on that day.

(2) If the time specified by these Rules, a practice direction or a direction for doing any act ends on a day other than a working day, the act is done in time if it is done on the next working day.

(3) In a special educational needs case or a disability discrimination in schools case, the following days must not be counted when calculating the time by which an act must be done –

(a) 25th December to 1st January inclusive; and

(b) any day in August.

(3A) In an asylum case or an immigration case, when calculating the time by which an act must be done, in addition to the days specified in the definition of "working days" in rule 1 (interpretation), the following days must also not be counted as working days –

(a) 27th to 31st December inclusive; and
(b) in a fast-track case, 24th December, Maundy Thursday, or the Tuesday after the last Monday in May.

(4) Paragraph (3) or (3A) does not apply where the Upper Tribunal directs that an act must be done by or on a specified date.

(5) In this rule –

'disability discrimination in schools case' means proceedings concerning disability discrimination in the education of a child or related matters; and
'special educational needs case 'means proceedings concerning the education of a child who has or may have special educational needs.'

Amendments—SI 2009/274; SI 2010/44.

13 Sending and delivery of documents

(1) Any document to be provided to the Upper Tribunal under these Rules, a practice direction or a direction must be –

(a) sent by pre-paid post or by document exchange or delivered by hand, to the address specified for the proceedings;
(b) sent by fax to the number specified for the proceedings; or
(c) sent or delivered by such other method as the Upper Tribunal may permit or direct.

(2) Subject to paragraph (3), if a party provides a fax number, email address or other details for the electronic transmission of documents to them, that party must accept delivery of documents by that method.

(3) If a party informs the Upper Tribunal and all other parties that a particular form of communication, other than pre-paid post or delivery by hand, should not be used to provide documents to that party, that form of communication must not be so used.

(4) If the Upper Tribunal or a party sends a document to a party or the Upper Tribunal by email or any other electronic means of communication, the recipient may request that the sender provide a hard copy of the document to the recipient. The recipient must make such a request as soon as reasonably practicable after receiving the document electronically.

(5) The Upper Tribunal and each party may assume that the address provided by a party or its representative is and remains the address to which documents should be sent or delivered until receiving written notification to the contrary.

(6) Subject to paragraph (7), if a document submitted to the Upper Tribunal is not written in English, it must be accompanied by an English translation.

(7) In proceedings that are in Wales or have a connection with Wales, a document or translation may be submitted to the Tribunal in Welsh.

Amendments—SI 2009/274; SI 2010/44.

14 Use of documents and information

(1) The Upper Tribunal may make an order prohibiting the disclosure or publication of –

(a) specified documents or information relating to the proceedings; or
(b) any matter likely to lead members of the public to identify any person whom the Upper Tribunal considers should not be identified.

(2) The Upper Tribunal may give a direction prohibiting the disclosure of a document or information to a person if –

(a) the Upper Tribunal is satisfied that such disclosure would be likely to cause that person or some other person serious harm; and
(b) the Upper Tribunal is satisfied, having regard to the interests of justice, that it is proportionate to give such a direction.

(3) If a party ('the first party') considers that the Upper Tribunal should give a direction under paragraph (2) prohibiting the disclosure of a document or information to another party ('the second party'), the first party must –

(a) exclude the relevant document or information from any documents that will be provided to the second party; and
(b) provide to the Upper Tribunal the excluded document or information, and the reason for its exclusion, so that the Upper Tribunal may decide whether the document or information should be disclosed to the second party or should be the subject of a direction under paragraph (2).

(4) (*revoked*)

(5) If the Upper Tribunal gives a direction under paragraph (2) which prevents disclosure to a party who has appointed a representative, the Upper Tribunal may give a direction that the documents or information be disclosed to that representative if the Upper Tribunal is satisfied that –

(a) disclosure to the representative would be in the interests of the party; and
(b) the representative will act in accordance with paragraph (6).

(6) Documents or information disclosed to a representative in accordance with a direction under paragraph (5) must not be disclosed either directly or indirectly to any other person without the Upper Tribunal's consent.

(7) Unless the Upper Tribunal gives a direction to the contrary, information about mental health cases and the names of any persons concerned in such cases must not be made public.

(8) The Upper Tribunal may, on its own initiative or on the application of a party, give a direction that certain documents or information must or may be disclosed to the Upper Tribunal on the basis that the Upper Tribunal will not disclose such documents or information to other persons, or specified other persons.

(9) A party making an application for a direction under paragraph (8) may withhold the relevant documents or information from other parties until the Upper Tribunal has granted or refused the application.

(10) In a case involving matters relating to national security, the Upper Tribunal must ensure that information is not disclosed contrary to the interests of national security.

(11) The Upper Tribunal must conduct proceedings and record its decision and reasons appropriately so as not to undermine the effect of an order made under paragraph (1), a direction given under paragraph (2) or (8) or the duty imposed by paragraph (10).

Amendments—SI 2009/1975.

15 Evidence and submissions

(1) Without restriction on the general powers in rule 5(1) and (2) (case management powers), the Upper Tribunal may give directions as to –

- (a) issues on which it requires evidence or submissions;
- (b) the nature of the evidence or submissions it requires;
- (c) whether the parties are permitted or required to provide expert evidence, and if so whether the parties must jointly appoint a single expert to provide such evidence;
- (d) any limit on the number of witnesses whose evidence a party may put forward, whether in relation to a particular issue or generally;
- (e) the manner in which any evidence or submissions are to be provided, which may include a direction for them to be given –
  - (i) orally at a hearing; or
  - (ii) by written submissions or witness statement; and
- (f) the time at which any evidence or submissions are to be provided.

(2) The Upper Tribunal may –

- (a) admit evidence whether or not –
  - (i) the evidence would be admissible in a civil trial in the United Kingdom; or
  - (ii) the evidence was available to a previous decision maker; or
- (b) exclude evidence that would otherwise be admissible where –
  - (i) the evidence was not provided within the time allowed by a direction or a practice direction;
  - (ii) the evidence was otherwise provided in a manner that did not comply with a direction or a practice direction; or
  - (iii) it would otherwise be unfair to admit the evidence.

(2A) In an asylum case or an immigration case –

- (a) if a party wishes the Upper Tribunal to consider evidence that was not before the First-tier Tribunal, that party must send or deliver a notice to the Upper Tribunal and any other party—
  - (i) indicating the nature of the evidence; and
  - (ii) explaining why it was not submitted to the First-tier Tribunal; and
- (b) when considering whether to admit evidence that was not before the First-tier Tribunal, the Upper Tribunal must have regard to whether there has been unreasonable delay in producing that evidence.

Amendments—SI 2010/44.

(3) The Upper Tribunal may consent to a witness giving, or require any witness to give, evidence on oath, and may administer an oath for that purpose.

16 Summoning or citation of witnesses and orders to answer questions or produce documents

(1) On the application of a party or on its own initiative, the Upper Tribunal may –

(a) by summons (or, in Scotland, citation) require any person to attend as a witness at a hearing at the time and place specified in the summons or citation; or

(b) order any person to answer any questions or produce any documents in that person's possession or control which relate to any issue in the proceedings.

(2) A summons or citation under paragraph (1)(a) must –

(a) give the person required to attend 14 days' notice of the hearing or such shorter period as the Upper Tribunal may direct; and

(b) where the person is not a party, make provision for the person's necessary expenses of attendance to be paid, and state who is to pay them.

(3) No person may be compelled to give any evidence or produce any document that the person could not be compelled to give or produce on a trial of an action in a court of law in the part of the United Kingdom where the proceedings are due to be determined.

(4) A person who receives a summons, citation or order may apply to the Upper Tribunal for it to be varied or set aside if they did not have an opportunity to object to it before it was made or issued.

(5) A person making an application under paragraph (4) must do so as soon as reasonably practicable after receiving notice of the summons, citation or order.

(6) A summons, citation or order under this rule must –

(a) state that the person on whom the requirement is imposed may apply to the Upper Tribunal to vary or set aside the summons, citation or order, if they did not have an opportunity to object to it before it was made or issued; and

(b) state the consequences of failure to comply with the summons, citation or order.

Amendments—SI 2009/274.

17 Withdrawal

(1) Subject to paragraph (2), a party may give notice of the withdrawal of its case, or any part of it –

(a) at any time before a hearing to consider the disposal of the proceedings (or, if the Upper Tribunal disposes of the proceedings without a hearing, before that disposal), by sending or delivering to the Upper Tribunal a written notice of withdrawal; or

(b) orally at a hearing.

(2) Notice of withdrawal will not take effect unless the Upper Tribunal consents to the withdrawal except in relation to an application for permission to appeal.

(3) A party which has withdrawn its case may apply to the Upper Tribunal for the case to be reinstated.

(4) An application under paragraph (3) must be made in writing and be received by the Upper Tribunal within 1 month after –

(a) the date on which the Upper Tribunal received the notice under paragraph (1)(a); or

(b) the date of the hearing at which the case was withdrawn orally under paragraph (1)(b).

(5) The Upper Tribunal must notify each party in writing of a withdrawal under this rule.

(6) Paragraph (3) does not apply to a financial services case other than a reference against a penalty.

Amendments—SI 2010/747.

17A Appeal treated as abandoned or finally determined in an asylum case or an immigration case

(1) A party to an asylum case or an immigration case before the Upper Tribunal must notify the Tribunal if they are aware that –

- (a) the appellant has left the United Kingdom;
- (b) the appellant has been granted leave to enter or remain in the United Kingdom;
- (c) a deportation order has been made against the appellant; or
- (d) a document listed in paragraph 4(2) of Schedule 2 to the Immigration (European Economic Area) Regulations 2006 has been issued to the appellant.

(2) Where an appeal is treated as abandoned pursuant to section 104(4) or (4A) of the Nationality, Immigration and Asylum Act 2002 or paragraph 4(2) of Schedule 2 to the Immigration (European Economic Area) Regulations 2006, or as finally determined pursuant to section 104(5) of the Nationality, Immigration and Asylum Act 2002, the Upper Tribunal must send the parties a notice informing them that the appeal is being treated as abandoned or finally determined.

(3) Where an appeal would otherwise fall to be treated as abandoned pursuant to section 104(4A) of the Nationality, Immigration and Asylum Act 2002, but the appellant wishes to pursue their appeal, the appellant must send or deliver a notice, which must comply with any relevant practice directions, to the Upper Tribunal and the respondent so that it is received within thirty days of the date on which the notice of the grant of leave to enter or remain in the United Kingdom was sent to the appellant.

(4) Where a notice of grant of leave to enter or remain is sent electronically or delivered personally, the time limit in paragraph (3) is twenty eight days.

(5) Notwithstanding rule 5(3)(a) (case management powers) and rule 7(2) (failure to comply with rules etc), the Upper Tribunal must not extend the time limits in paragraph (3) and (4).

Amendments—SI 2010/44.

18 Notice of funding of legal services

If a party is granted funding of legal services at any time, that party must as soon as practicable –

- (a)
  - (i) if funding is granted by the Legal Services Commission or the Northern Ireland Legal Services Commission, send a copy of the funding notice to the Upper Tribunal; or
  - (ii) if funding is granted by the Scottish Legal Aid Board, send a copy of the legal aid certificate to the Upper Tribunal; and
- (b) notify every other party in writing that funding has been granted.

19 Confidentiality in child support or child trust fund cases

(1) Paragraph (3) applies to an appeal against a decision of the First-tier Tribunal in proceedings under the Child Support Act 1991(12) in the circumstances described in paragraph (2), other than an appeal against a reduced benefit decision (as defined in section 46(10)(b) of the Child Support Act 1991, as that section had effect prior to the commencement of section 15(b) of the Child Maintenance and Other Payments Act 2008(13)).

(2) The circumstances referred to in paragraph (1) are that –

- (a) in the proceedings in the First-tier Tribunal in respect of which the appeal has been brought, there was an obligation to keep a person's address confidential; or
- (b) a person whose circumstances are relevant to the proceedings would like their address (or, in the case of the person with care of the child, the child's address) to be kept confidential and has given notice to that effect –
  - (i) to the Upper Tribunal in an application for permission to appeal or notice of appeal;
  - (ii) to the Upper Tribunal within 1 month after an enquiry by the Upper Tribunal; or
  - (iii) to the Secretary of State or the Upper Tribunal when notifying a change of address after proceedings have been started.

(3) Where this paragraph applies, the Secretary of State and the Upper Tribunal must take appropriate steps to secure the confidentiality of the address, and of any information which could reasonably be expected to enable a person to identify the address, to the extent that the address or that information is not already known to each other party.

(4) Paragraph (6) applies to an appeal against a decision of the First-tier Tribunal in proceedings under the Child Trust Funds Act 2004(14) in the circumstances described in paragraph (5).

(5) The circumstances referred to in paragraph (4) are that –

- (a) in the proceedings in the First-tier Tribunal in respect of which the appeal has been brought, there was an obligation to keep a person's address confidential; or
- (b) a person whose circumstances are relevant to the proceedings would like their address (or, in the case of the person with care of the eligible child, the child's address) to be kept confidential and has given notice to that effect –
  - (i) to the Upper Tribunal in an application for permission to appeal or notice of appeal;
  - (ii) to the Upper Tribunal within 1 month after an enquiry by the Upper Tribunal; or
  - (iii) to HMRC or the Upper Tribunal when notifying a change of address after proceedings have been started.

(6) Where this paragraph applies, HMRC and the Upper Tribunal must take appropriate steps to secure the confidentiality of the address, and of any information which could reasonably be expected to enable a person to identify the address, to the extent that the address or that information is not already known to each other party.

(7) This rule –

'eligible child' has the meaning set out in section 2 of the Child Trust Funds Act 2004; and

'HMRC' means Her Majesty's Revenue and Customs.

Amendments—SI 2012/2007.

20 Power to pay expenses and allowances

(1) Proceedings brought under section 4 of the Safeguarding Vulnerable Groups Act 2006, the Secretary of State may pay such allowances for the purpose of or in connection with the attendance of persons at hearings as the Secretary of State may, with the consent of the Treasury, determine.

(2) Paragraph (3) applies to proceedings on appeal from a decision of –

(a) the First-tier Tribunal in proceedings under the Child Support Act 1991, section 12 of the Social Security Act 1998(16) or paragraph 6 of Schedule 7 to the Child Support, Pensions and Social Security Act 2000(17);

(b) the First-tier Tribunal in a war pensions and armed forces case (as defined in the Tribunal Procedure (First-tier Tribunal) (War Pensions and Armed Forces Compensation Chamber) Rules 2008(18)); or

(c) a Pensions Appeal Tribunal for Scotland or Northern Ireland.

(3) The Lord Chancellor (or, in Scotland, the Secretary of State) may pay to any person who attends any hearing such travelling and other allowances, including compensation for loss of remunerative time, as the Lord Chancellor (or, in Scotland, the Secretary of State) may determine.

Amendments—SI 2009/274.

20A Procedure for applying for a stay of a decision pending an appeal

(1) This rule applies where another enactment provides in any terms for the Upper Tribunal to stay or suspend, or to lift a stay or suspension of, a decision which is or may be the subject of an appeal to the Upper Tribunal ("the substantive decision") pending such appeal.

(2) A person who wishes the Upper Tribunal to decide whether the substantive decision should be stayed or suspended must make a written application to the Upper Tribunal which must include –

(a) the name and address of the person making the application;

(b) the name and address of any representative of that person;

(c) the address to which documents for that person should be sent or delivered;

(d) the name and address of any person who will be a respondent to the appeal;

(e) details of the substantive decision and any decision as to when that decision is to take effect, and copies of any written record of, or reasons for, those decisions; and

(f) the grounds on which the person making the application relies.

(3) In the case of an application under paragraph (2) in a road transport case –

(a) the person making the application must notify the decision maker when making the application;

(b) within 7 days of receiving notification of the application the decision maker must send or deliver written reasons for refusing or withdrawing the stay –

(i) to the Upper Tribunal; and

(ii) to the person making the application, if the decision maker has not already done so.

(4) If the Upper Tribunal grants a stay or suspension following an application under this rule –

(a) the Upper Tribunal may give directions as to the conduct of the appeal of the substantive decision; and
(b) the Upper Tribunal may, where appropriate, grant the stay or suspension subject to conditions.

(5) Unless the Upper Tribunal considers that there is good reason not to do so, the Upper Tribunal must send written notice of any decision made under this rule to each party.

Amendments—SI 2009/1975; SI 2010/1363.

PART3
PROCEDURE FOR CASES IN THE UPPER TRIBUNAL

21 Application to the Upper Tribunal for permission to appeal

(1) (*revoked*)

(2) A person may apply to the Upper Tribunal for permission to appeal to the Upper Tribunal against a decision of another tribunal only if –

(a) they have made an application for permission to appeal to the tribunal which made the decision challenged; and
(b) that application has been refused or has not been admitted.

(3) An application for permission to appeal must be made in writing and received by the Upper Tribunal no later than –

(a) in the case of an application under section 4 of the Safeguarding Vulnerable Groups Act 2006, 3 months after the date on which written notice of the decision being challenged was sent to the appellant;
(aa) subject to paragraph (3A), in an asylum case or an immigration case where the appellant is in the United Kingdom at the time that the application is made –
  (i) seven working days after the date on which notice of the First-tier Tribunal's refusal of permission was sent to the appellant; or
  (ii) if the case is a fast-track case, four working days after the date on which notice of the First-tier Tribunal's refusal of permission was sent to the appellant;
(ab) subject to paragraph (3A), in an asylum case or an immigration case where the appellant is outside the United Kingdom at the time that the application is made, fifty six days after the date on which notice of the First-tier Tribunal's refusal of permission was sent to the appellant; or
(b) otherwise, a month after the date on which the tribunal that made the decision under challenge sent notice of its refusal of permission to appeal, or refusal to admit the application for permission to appeal, to the appellant.

(3A) Where a notice of decision is sent electronically or delivered personally, the time limits in paragraph (3)(aa) and (ab) are –

(a) in sub-paragraph (aa)(i), five working days;
(b) in sub-paragraph (aa)(ii), two working days; and

(c) in sub-paragraph (ab), twenty eight days.

(4) The application must state –

(a) the name and address of the appellant;
(b) the name and address of the representative (if any) of the appellant;
(c) an address where documents for the appellant may be sent or delivered;
(d) details (including the full reference) of the decision challenged;
(e) the grounds on which the appellant relies; and
(f) whether the appellant wants the application to be dealt with at a hearing.

(5) The appellant must provide with the application a copy of –

(a) any written record of the decision being challenged;
(b) any separate written statement of reasons for that decision; and
(c) if the application is for permission to appeal against a decision of another tribunal, the notice of refusal of permission to appeal, or notice of refusal to admit the application for permission to appeal, from that other tribunal.

(6) If the appellant provides the application to the Upper Tribunal later than the time required by paragraph (3) or by an extension of time allowed under rule 5(3)(a) (power to extend time) –

(a) the application must include a request for an extension of time and the reason why the application was not provided in time; and
(b) unless the Upper Tribunal extends time for the application under rule 5(3)(a) (power to extend time) the Upper Tribunal must not admit the application.

(7) If the appellant makes an application to the Upper Tribunal for permission to appeal against the decision of another tribunal, and that other tribunal refused to admit the appellant's application for permission to appeal because the application for permission or for a written statement of reasons was not made in time –

(a) the application to the Upper Tribunal for permission to appeal must include the reason why the application to the other tribunal for permission to appeal or for a written statement of reasons, as the case may be, was not made in time; and
(b) the Upper Tribunal must only admit the application if the Upper Tribunal considers that it is in the interests of justice for it to do so.

Amendments—SI 2009/274; SI 2009/1975; SI 2010/44.

22 Decision in relation to permission to appeal

(1) If the Upper Tribunal refuses permission to appeal, it must send written notice of the refusal and of the reasons for the refusal to the appellant.

(2) the Upper Tribunal gives permission to appeal –

(a) the Upper Tribunal must send written notice of the permission, and of the reasons for any limitations or conditions on such permission, to each party;
(b) subject to any direction by the Upper Tribunal, the application for permission to appeal stands as the notice of appeal and the Upper Tribunal must send to each respondent a copy of the application for permission to appeal and any documents provided with it by the appellant; and
(c) the Upper Tribunal may, with the consent of the appellant and each respondent, determine the appeal without obtaining any further response.

(3) Paragraph (4) applies where the Upper Tribunal, without a hearing, determines an application for permission to appeal –

to appeal under section 4 of the Safeguarding Vulnerable Groups Act 2006.

- (a) against a decision of –
  - (i) the Tax Chamber of the First-tier Tribunal;
  - (ii) the Health, Education and Social Care Chamber of the First-tier Tribunal;
  - (iia) the General Regulatory Chamber of the First-tier Tribunal;
  - (iii) the Mental Health Review Tribunal for Wales; or
  - (iv) the Special Educational Needs Tribunal for Wales; or
- (b) under section 4 of the Safeguarding Vulnerable Groups Act 2006.

(4) In the circumstances set out at paragraph (3) the appellant may apply for the decision to be reconsidered at a hearing if the Upper Tribunal –

- (a) refuses permission to appeal; or
- (b) gives permission to appeal on limited grounds or subject to conditions.

(5) An application under paragraph (4) must be made in writing and received by the Upper Tribunal within 14 days after the date on which the Upper Tribunal sent written notice of its decision regarding the application to the appellant.

Amendments—SI 2009/274; SI 2009/1975.

23 Notice of appeal

(1) This rule applies –

- (a) to proceedings on appeal to the Upper Tribunal for which permission to appeal is not required, except proceedings to which rule 26A or 26B applies;
- (b) if another tribunal has given permission for a party to appeal to the Upper Tribunal; or
- (c) subject to any other direction by the Upper Tribunal, if the Upper Tribunal has given permission to appeal and has given a direction that the application for permission to appeal does not stand as the notice of appeal.

(1A) In an asylum case or an immigration case in which the First-tier Tribunal has given permission to appeal, subject to any direction of the First-tier Tribunal or the Upper Tribunal, the application for permission to appeal sent or delivered to the First-tier Tribunal stands as the notice of appeal and accordingly paragraphs (2) to (6) of this rule do not apply.

(2) The appellant must provide a notice of appeal to the Upper Tribunal so that it is received within 1 month after –

- (a) the date that the tribunal that gave permission to appeal sent notice of such permission to the appellant; or
- (b) if permission to appeal is not required, the date on which notice of decision to which the appeal relates was sent to the appellant.

(3) The notice of appeal must include the information listed in rule 21(4)(a) to (e) (content of the application for permission to appeal) and, where the Upper Tribunal has given permission to appeal, the Upper Tribunal's case reference.

(4) If another tribunal has granted permission to appeal, the appellant must provide with the notice of appeal a copy of –

(a) any written record of the decision being challenged;
(b) any separate written statement of reasons for that decision; and
(c) the notice of permission to appeal.

(5) If the appellant provides the notice of appeal to the Upper Tribunal later than the time required by paragraph (2) or by an extension of time allowed under rule 5(3)(a) (power to extend time) –

(a) the notice of appeal must include a request for an extension of time and the reason why the notice was not provided in time; and
(b) unless the Upper Tribunal extends time for the notice of appeal under rule 5(3)(a) (power to extend time) the Upper Tribunal must not admit the notice of appeal.

(6) When the Upper Tribunal receives the notice of appeal it must send a copy of the notice and any accompanying documents –

(a) to each respondent; or
(b) in a road transport case, to –
  (i) the decision maker;
  (ii) the appropriate national authority; and
  (iii) in a case relating to the detention of a vehicle, the authorised person.

Amendments—SI 2009/1975; SI 2010/44; SI 2010/747; SI 2012/1363.

24 Response to the notice of appeal

(1) This rule and rule 25 do not apply to a road transport case, in respect of which Schedule 1 makes alternative provision.

(1A) Subject to any direction given by the Upper Tribunal, a respondent may provide a response to a notice of appeal.

(2) Any response provided under paragraph (1A) must be in writing and must be sent or delivered to the Upper Tribunal so that it is received –

(a) if an application for permission to appeal stands as the notice of appeal, no later than one month after the date on which the respondent was sent notice that permission to appeal had been granted;
(aa) in a fast-track case, one day before the hearing of the appeal; or
(b) in any other case, no later than 1 month after the date on which the Upper Tribunal sent a copy of the notice of appeal to the respondent.

(3) The response must state –

(a) the name and address of the respondent;
(b) the name and address of the representative (if any) of the respondent;
(c) an address where documents for the respondent may be sent or delivered;
(d) whether the respondent opposes the appeal;
(e) the grounds on which the respondent relies, including (in the case of an appeal against the decision of another tribunal) any grounds on which the respondent was unsuccessful in the proceedings which are the subject of the appeal, but intends to rely in the appeal; and
(f) whether the respondent wants the case to be dealt with at a hearing.

(4) If the respondent provides the response to the Upper Tribunal later than the time required by paragraph (2) or by an extension of time allowed under rule 5(3)(a) (power

to extend time), the response must include a request for an extension of time and the reason why the response was not provided in time.

(5) When the Upper Tribunal receives the response it must send a copy of the response and any accompanying documents to the appellant and each other party.

Amendments—SI 2009/274; SI 2009/1975; SI 2010/43; SI 2010/44; SI 2012/1363.

25 Appellant's reply

(1) Subject to any direction given by the Upper Tribunal, the appellant may provide a reply to any response provided under rule 24 (response to the notice of appeal).

(2) Subject to paragraph (2A), any reply provided under paragraph (1) must be in writing and must be sent or delivered to the Upper Tribunal so that it is received within one month after the date on which the Upper Tribunal sent a copy of the response to the appellant.

(2A) In an asylum case or an immigration case, the time limit in paragraph (2) is –

- (a) one month after the date on which the Upper Tribunal sent a copy of the response to the appellant, or five days before the hearing of the appeal, whichever is the earlier; and
- (b) in a fast-track case, the day of the hearing.

(3) When the Upper Tribunal receives the reply it must send a copy of the reply and any accompanying documents to each respondent.

Amendments—SI 2010/44.

26 References under the Forfeiture Act 1982

(1) If a question arises which is required to be determined by the Upper Tribunal under section 4 of the Forfeiture Act 1982, the person to whom the application for the relevant benefit or advantage has been made must refer the question to the Upper Tribunal.

(2) The reference must be in writing and must include –

- (a) a statement of the question for determination;
- (b) a statement of the relevant facts;
- (c) the grounds upon which the reference is made; and
- (d) an address for sending documents to the person making the reference and each respondent.

(3) When the Upper Tribunal receives the reference it must send a copy of the reference and any accompanying documents to each respondent.

(4) Rules 24 (response to the notice of appeal) and 25 (appellant's reply) apply to a reference made under this rule as if it were a notice of appeal.

26A Cases transferred or referred to the Upper Tribunal, applications made directly to the Upper Tribunal and proceedings without notice to a respondent

(1) Paragraphs (2) and (3) apply to –

- (a) a case transferred or referred to the Upper Tribunal from the First-tier Tribunal; or

(b) a case, other than an appeal or a case to which rule 26 (references under the Forfeiture Act 1982) applies, which is started by an application made directly to the Upper Tribunal.

(2) In a case to which this paragraph applies –

(a) the Upper Tribunal must give directions as to the procedure to be followed in the consideration and disposal of the proceedings;

(aa) in a reference under Schedule 1D of the Charities Act 1993, the Upper Tribunal may give directions providing for an application to join the proceedings as a party and the time within which it may be made; and

(b) the preceding rules in this Part will only apply to the proceedings to the extent provided for by such directions.

(3) If a case or matter to which this paragraph applies is to be determined without notice to or the involvement of a respondent –

(a) any provision in these Rules requiring a document to be provided by or to a respondent; and

(b) any other provision in these Rules permitting a respondent to participate in the proceedings

does not apply to that case or matter.

(4) Schedule 2 makes further provision for national security certificate appeals transferred to the Upper Tribunal.

Amendments—SI 2009/274; SI 2010/43; SI 2012/500.

26B Financial services cases

Schedule 3 makes provision for financial services cases.

Amendments—SI 2010/747.

PART 4
JUDICIAL REVIEW PROCEEDINGS IN THE UPPER TRIBUNAL

27 Application of this Part to judicial review proceedings transferred to the Upper Tribunal

(1) When a court transfers judicial review proceedings to the Upper Tribunal, the Upper Tribunal –

(a) must notify each party in writing that the proceedings have been transferred to the Upper Tribunal; and

(b) must give directions as to the future conduct of the proceedings.

(2) The directions given under paragraph (1)(b) may modify or disapply for the purposes of the proceedings any of the provisions of the following rules in this Part.

(3) In proceedings transferred from the Court of Session under section 20(1) of the 2007 Act, the directions given under paragraph (1)(b) must –

(a) if the Court of Session did not make a first order specifying the required intimation, service and advertisement of the petition, state the Upper Tribunal's requirements in relation to those matters;

(b) state whether the Upper Tribunal will consider summary dismissal of the proceedings; and

(c) where necessary, modify or disapply provisions relating to permission in the following rules in this Part.

28 Applications for permission to bring judicial review proceedings

(1) A person seeking permission to bring judicial review proceedings before the Upper Tribunal under section 16 of the 2007 Act must make a written application to the Upper Tribunal for such permission.

(2) Subject to paragraph (3), an application under paragraph (1) must be made promptly and, unless any other enactment specifies a shorter time limit, must be sent or delivered to the Upper Tribunal so that it is received no later than 3 months after the date of the decision, action or omission to which the application relates.

(3) An application for permission to bring judicial review proceedings challenging a decision of the First-tier Tribunal may be made later than the time required by paragraph (2) if it is made within 1 month after the date on which the First-tier Tribunal sent –

(a) written reasons for the decision; or
(b) notification that an application for the decision to be set aside has been unsuccessful, provided that that application was made in time.

(4) The application must state –

(a) the name and address of the applicant, the respondent and any other person whom the applicant considers to be an interested party;
(b) the name and address of the applicant's representative (if any);
(c) an address where documents for the applicant may be sent or delivered;
(d) details of the decision challenged (including the date, the full reference and the identity of the decision maker);
(e) that the application is for permission to bring judicial review proceedings;
(f) the outcome that the applicant is seeking; and
(g) the facts and grounds on which the applicant relies.

(5) If the application relates to proceedings in a court or tribunal, the application must name as an interested party each party to those proceedings who is not the applicant or a respondent.

(6) The applicant must send with the application –

(a) a copy of any written record of the decision in the applicant's possession or control; and
(b) copies of any other documents in the applicant's possession or control on which the applicant intends to rely.

(7) If the applicant provides the application to the Upper Tribunal later than the time required by paragraph (2) or (3) or by an extension of time allowed under rule 5(3)(a) (power to extend time) –

(a) the application must include a request for an extension of time and the reason why the application was not provided in time; and
(b) unless the Upper Tribunal extends time for the application under rule 5(3)(a) (power to extend time) the Upper Tribunal must not admit the application.

(8) Except where rule 28A(2)(a) (special provisions for fresh claim proceedings) applies, when the Upper Tribunal receives the application it must send a copy of the application and any accompanying documents to each person named in the application as a respondent or interested party.

Amendments—SI 2009/274; SI 2011/2343.

28A Special provisions for fresh claim proceedings

(1) The Upper Tribunal must not accept an application for permission to bring fresh claim proceedings unless it is either accompanied by any required fee or the Upper Tribunal accepts an undertaking that the fee will be paid.

(2) Within 9 days of making an application referred to in paragraph (1), an applicant must provide –

(a) a copy of the application and any accompanying documents to each person named in the application as a respondent or an interested party; and
(b) the Upper Tribunal with a written statement of when and how this was done.

Amendments—SI 2011/2343.

29 Acknowledgment of service

(1) A person who is sent or provided with a copy of an application for permission under rule 28(8) (application for permission to bring judicial review proceedings) or rule 28A (2) (a) (special provisions for fresh claim proceedings) and wishes to take part in the proceedings must provide to the Upper Tribunal an acknowledgment of service so that it is received no later than 21 days after the date on which the Upper Tribunal sent or in fresh claim proceedings the applicant provided, a copy of the application to that person.

(2) An acknowledgment of service under paragraph (1) must be in writing and state –

(a) whether the person intends to support or oppose the application for permission;
(b) their grounds for any support or opposition under sub-paragraph (a), or any other submission or information which it considers may assist the Upper Tribunal; and
(c) the name and address of any other person not named in the application as a respondent or interested party whom the person providing the acknowledgment considers to be an interested party.

(2A) In fresh claim proceedings, a person who provides an acknowledgement of service under paragraph (1) must also provide a copy to –

(a) the applicant; and
(b) any other person named in the application under rule 28(4)(a) or acknowledgement of service under paragraph (2)(c) no later than the time specified in paragraph (1).

(3) A person who is provided with a copy of an application for permission under rule 28(8) or 28A (2) (a) but does not provide an acknowledgment of service to the Upper Tribunal may not take part in the application for permission unless allowed to do so by the Upper Tribunal, but may take part in the subsequent proceedings if the application is successful.

Amendments—SI 2009/274; SI 2011/651; SI 2011/2343.

30 Decision on permission or summary dismissal, and reconsideration of permission or summary dismissal at a hearing

(1) The Upper Tribunal must send to the applicant, each respondent and any other person who provided an acknowledgment of service to the Upper Tribunal, and may send to any other person who may have an interest in the proceedings, written notice of –

(a) its decision in relation to the application for permission; and
(b) the reasons for any refusal of the application, or any limitations or conditions on permission.

(2) In proceedings transferred from the Court of Session under section 20(1) of the 2007 Act, where the Upper Tribunal has considered whether summarily to dismiss of the proceedings, the Upper Tribunal must send to the applicant and each respondent, and may send to any other person who may have an interest in the proceedings, written notice of –

(a) its decision in relation to the summary dismissal of proceedings; and
(b) the reasons for any decision summarily to dismiss part or all of the proceedings, or any limitations or conditions on the continuation of such proceedings.

(3) Paragraph (4) applies where the Upper Tribunal, without a hearing –

(a) determines an application for permission to bring judicial review proceedings and either refuses permission, or gives permission on limited grounds or subject to conditions; or
(b) in proceedings transferred from the Court of Session, summarily dismisses part or all of the proceedings, or imposes any limitations or conditions on the continuation of such proceedings.

(4) In the circumstances specified in paragraph (3) the applicant may apply for the decision to be reconsidered at a hearing.

(5) An application under paragraph (4) must be made in writing and must be sent or delivered to the Upper Tribunal so that it is received within 14 days, or in fresh claim proceedings 9 day, after the date on which the Upper Tribunal sent written notice of its decision regarding the application to the applicant.

Amendments—SI 2011/2343.

31 Responses

(1) Any person to whom the Upper Tribunal has sent notice of the grant of permission under rule 30(1) (notification of decision on permission), and who wishes to contest the application or support it on additional grounds, must provide detailed grounds for contesting or supporting the application to the Upper Tribunal.

(2) Any detailed grounds must be provided in writing and must be sent or delivered to the Upper Tribunal so that they are received not more than 35 days after the Upper Tribunal sent notice of the grant of permission under rule 30(1).

32 Applicant seeking to rely on additional grounds

The applicant may not rely on any grounds, other than those grounds on which the applicant obtained permission for the judicial review proceedings, without the consent of the Upper Tribunal.

33 Right to make representations

Each party and, with the permission of the Upper Tribunal, any other person, may –

(a) submit evidence, except at the hearing of an application for permission;
(b) make representations at any hearing which they are entitled to attend; and
(c) make written representations in relation to a decision to be made without a hearing.

33A Amendments and additional grounds resulting in transfer of proceedings to the High Court in England and Wales

(1) This rule applies only to judicial review proceedings arising under the law of England and Wales.

(2) In relation to such proceedings –

(a) the powers of the Upper Tribunal to permit or require amendments under rule 5(3)(c) extend to amendments which would, once in place, give rise to an obligation or power to transfer the proceedings to the High Court in England and Wales under section 18(3) of the 2007 Act or paragraph (3);
(b) except with the permission of the Upper Tribunal, additional grounds may not be advanced, whether by an applicant or otherwise, if they would give rise to an obligation or power to transfer the proceedings to the High Court in England and Wales under section 18(3) of the 2007 Act or paragraph (3).

(3) Where the High Court in England and Wales has transferred judicial review proceedings to the Upper Tribunal under any power or duty and subsequently the proceedings are amended or any party advances additional grounds –

(a) if the proceedings in their present form could not have been transferred to the Upper Tribunal under the relevant power or duty had they been in that form at the time of the transfer, the Upper Tribunal must transfer the proceedings back to the High Court in England and Wales;
(b) subject to sub-paragraph (a), where the proceedings were transferred to the Upper Tribunal under section 31A(3) of the Senior Courts Act 1981(power to transfer judicial review proceedings to the Upper Tribunal), the Upper Tribunal may transfer proceedings back to the High Court in England and Wales if it appears just and convenient to do so.

Amendments—SI 2011/2343.

PART 5
HEARINGS

34 Decision with or without a hearing

(1) Subject to paragraph (2), the Upper Tribunal may make any decision without a hearing.

(2) The Upper Tribunal must have regard to any view expressed by a party when deciding whether to hold a hearing to consider any matter, and the form of any such hearing.

35 Entitlement to attend a hearing

(1) Subject to rule 37(4) (exclusion of a person from a hearing), each party is entitled to attend a hearing.

(2) In a national security certificate appeal the relevant Minister is entitled to attend any hearing.

Amendments—SI 2010/43.

36 Notice of hearings

(1) The Upper Tribunal must give each party entitled to attend a hearing reasonable notice of the time and place of the hearing (including any adjourned or postponed hearing) and any change to the time and place of the hearing.

(2) The period of notice under paragraph (1) must be at least 14 days except that –

- (a) in applications for permission to bring judicial review proceedings, the period of notice must be at least 2 working days;
- (aa) in a fast-track case the period of notice must be at least one working day; and
- (b) in any case other than a fast-track case the Upper Tribunal may give shorter notice –
  - (i) with the parties' consent; or
  - (ii) in urgent or exceptional cases.

Amendments—SI 2010/44.

36A Special time limits for hearing an appeal in a fast-track case

(1) Subject to rule 36(2)(aa)(notice of hearings) and paragraph (2) of this rule, where permission to appeal to the Upper Tribunal has been given in a fast-track case, the Upper Tribunal must start the hearing of the appeal not later than –

- (a) four working days after the date on which the First-tier Tribunal or the Upper Tribunal sent notice of its grant of permission to appeal to the appellant; or
- (b) where the notice of its grant of permission to appeal is sent electronically or delivered personally, two working days after the date on which the First-tier Tribunal or the Upper Tribunal sent notice of its grant of permission to appeal to the appellant.

(2) If the Upper Tribunal is unable to arrange for the hearing to start within the time specified in paragraph (1), it must set a date for the hearing as soon as is reasonably practicable.

Amendments—SI 2010/44.

37 Public and private hearings

(1) Subject to the following paragraphs, all hearings must be held in public.

(2) The Upper Tribunal may give a direction that a hearing, or part of it, is to be held in private.

(2A) In a national security certificate appeal, the Upper Tribunal must have regard to its duty under rule 14(10) (no disclosure or information contrary to the interests of national security) when considering whether to give a direction that a hearing, or part of it , is to be held in private.

(3) Where a hearing, or part of it, is to be held in private, the Upper Tribunal may determine who is entitled to attend the hearing or part of it.

(4) The Upper Tribunal may give a direction excluding from any hearing, or part of it –

- (a) any person whose conduct the Upper Tribunal considers is disrupting or is likely to disrupt the hearing;
- (b) any person whose presence the Upper Tribunal considers is likely to prevent another person from giving evidence or making submissions freely;
- (c) any person who the Upper Tribunal considers should be excluded in order to give effect to the requirement at rule 14(11) (prevention of disclosure or publication of documents and information);
- (d) any person where the purpose of the hearing would be defeated by the attendance of that person; or
- (e) a person under the age of eighteen years.

(5) The Upper Tribunal may give a direction excluding a witness from a hearing until that witness gives evidence.

Amendments—SI 2009/274; SI 2009/1975; SI 2010/43.

38 Hearings in a party's absence

If a party fails to attend a hearing, the Upper Tribunal may proceed with the hearing if the Upper Tribunal –

- (a) is satisfied that the party has been notified of the hearing or that reasonable steps have been taken to notify the party of the hearing; and
- (b) considers that it is in the interests of justice to proceed with the hearing.

PART 6
DECISIONS

39 Consent orders

(1) The Upper Tribunal may, at the request of the parties but only if it considers it appropriate, make a consent order disposing of the proceedings and making such other appropriate provision as the parties have agreed.

(2) Notwithstanding any other provision of these Rules, the Tribunal need not hold a hearing before making an order under paragraph (1).

Amendments—SI 2009/274.

40 Decisions

(1) The Upper Tribunal may give a decision orally at a hearing.

(2) Except where rule 40A (special procedure for providing notice of a decision relating to an asylum case) applies, the Upper Tribunal must provide to each party as soon as reasonably practicable after making a decision which finally disposes of all issues in the proceedings (except a decision under Part 7) –

- (a) a decision notice stating the Tribunal's decision; and
- (b) notification of any rights of review or appeal against the decision and the time and manner in which such rights of review or appeal may be exercised.

(3) Subject to rule 14(11) (prevention of disclosure or publication of documents and information), the Upper Tribunal must provide written reasons for its decision with a decision notice provided under paragraph (2)(a) unless –

(a) the decision was made with the consent of the parties; or
(b) the parties have consented to the Upper Tribunal not giving written reasons.

(4) The Upper Tribunal may provide written reasons for any decision to which paragraph (2) does not apply.

(5) In a national security certificate appeal, when the Upper Tribunal provides a notice or reasons to the parties under this rule, it must also provide the notice or reasons to the relevant Minister and the Information Commissioner, if they are not parties.

Amendments—SI 2009/274; SI 2009/1975; SI 2010/43; SI 2010/44.

40A Special procedure for providing notice of a decision relating to an asylum case

(1) This rule applies to an appeal before the Upper Tribunal under section 11 of the 2007 Act in an asylum case where –

(a) the person who appealed to the First-tier Tribunal is in the United Kingdom; and
(b) the case is not a fast-track case.

(2) The Upper Tribunal must provide to the Secretary of State for the Home Department as soon as reasonably practicable –

(a) a decision notice stating the Upper Tribunal's decision; and
(b) a statement of any right of appeal against the decision and the time and manner in which such a right of appeal may be exercised.

(3) The Secretary of State must, subject to paragraph (5) –

(a) send the documents listed in paragraph (2) to the other party not later than 30 days after the Upper Tribunal sent them to the Secretary of State for the Home Department; and
(b) as soon as practicable after sending the documents listed in paragraph (2), notify the Upper Tribunal on what date and by what means they were sent.

(4) If the Secretary of State does not notify the Upper Tribunal under paragraph (3)(b) within 31 days after the documents listed in paragraph (2) were sent, the Upper Tribunal must send the notice of decision to the other party as soon as reasonably practicable.

(5) If the Secretary of State applies for permission to appeal under section 13 of the 2007 Act, the Secretary of State must send the documents listed in paragraph (2) to the other party no later than the date on which the application for permission is sent to the Upper Tribunal.

Amendments—SI 2010/44.

PART 7
CORRECTING, SETTING ASIDE, REVIEWING AND APPEALING DECISIONS OF THE UPPER TRIBUNAL

41 Interpretation

In this Part –

"appeal" except in rule 44(2) (application for permission to appeal), means the exercise of a right of appeal under section 13 of the 2007 Act; and

"review" means the review of a decision by the Upper Tribunal under section 10 of the 2007 Act.

Amendments—SI 2009/274.

42 Clerical mistakes and accidental slips or omissions

The Upper Tribunal may at any time correct any clerical mistake or other accidental slip or omission in a decision or record of a decision by –

(a) sending notification of the amended decision, or a copy of the amended record, to all parties; and

(b) making any necessary amendment to any information published in relation to the decision or record.

43 Setting aside a decision which disposes of proceedings

(1) The Upper Tribunal may set aside a decision which disposes of proceedings, or part of such a decision, and re-make the decision or the relevant part of it, if –

(a) the Upper Tribunal considers that it is in the interests of justice to do so; and

(b) one or more of the conditions in paragraph (2) are satisfied.

(2) The conditions are –

(a) a document relating to the proceedings was not sent to, or was not received at an appropriate time by, a party or a party's representative;

(b) a document relating to the proceedings was not sent to the Upper Tribunal at an appropriate time;

(c) a party, or a party's representative, was not present at a hearing related to the proceedings; or

(d) there has been some other procedural irregularity in the proceedings.

(3) Except where paragraph (4) applies, a party applying for a decision, or part of a decision, to be set aside under paragraph (1) must make a written application to the Upper Tribunal so that it is received no later than 1 month after the date on which the Tribunal sent notice of the decision to the party.

(4) In an asylum case or an immigration case, the written application referred to in paragraph (3) must be sent or delivered so that it is received by the Upper Tribunal –

(a) where the person who appealed to the First-tier Tribunal is in the United Kingdom at the time that the application is made, no later than twelve days after the date on which the Upper Tribunal or, as the case may be in an asylum case, the Secretary of State for the Home Department, sent notice of the decision to the party making the application; or

(b) where the person who appealed to the First-tier Tribunal is outside the United Kingdom at the time that the application is made, no later than thirty eight days after the date on which the Upper Tribunal sent notice of the decision to the party making the application.

(5) Where a notice of decision is sent electronically or delivered personally, the time limits in paragraph (4) are ten working days.

Amendments—SI 2010/44.

44 Application for permission to appeal

(1) Subject to paragraph (4A), A person seeking permission to appeal must make a written application to the Upper Tribunal for permission to appeal.

(2) Paragraph (3) applies to an application under paragraph (1) in respect of a decision –

(a) on an appeal against a decision in a social security and child support case (as defined in the Tribunal Procedure (First-tier Tribunal) (Social Entitlement Chamber) Rules 2008);
(b) on an appeal against a decision in proceedings in the War Pensions and Armed Forces Compensation Chamber of the First-tier Tribunal;
(ba) on an appeal against a decision of a Pensions Appeal Tribunal for Scotland or Northern Ireland; or
(c) in proceedings under the Forfeiture Act 1982.

(3) Where this paragraph applies, the application must be sent or delivered to the Upper Tribunal so that it is received within 3 months after the date on which the Upper Tribunal sent to the person making the application –

(a) written notice of the decision;
(b) notification of amended reasons for, or correction of, the decision following a review; or
(c) notification that an application for the decision to be set aside has been unsuccessful.

(3A) An application under paragraph (1) in respect of a decision in an asylum case or an immigration case must be sent or delivered to the Upper Tribunal so that it is received within the appropriate period after the Upper Tribunal or, as the case may be in an asylum case, the Secretary of State for the Home Department, sent any of the documents in paragraph (3) to the party making the application.

(3B) The appropriate period referred to in paragraph (3A) is as follows –

(a) where the person who appealed to the First-tier Tribunal is in the United Kingdom at the time that the application is made –
    (i) twelve working days; or
    (ii) if the party making the application is in detention under the Immigration Acts, seven working days; and
(b) where the person who appealed to the First-tier Tribunal is outside the United Kingdom at the time that the application is made, thirty eight days.

(3C) Where a notice of decision is sent electronically or delivered personally, the time limits in paragraph (3B) are –

(a) in sub-paragraph (a)(i), ten working days;
(b) in sub-paragraph (a)(ii), five working days; and
(c) in sub-paragraph (b), ten working days.

(3D) An application under paragraph (1) in respect of a decision in a financial services case must be sent or delivered to the Upper Tribunal so that it is received within 14 days after the date on which the Upper Tribunal sent to the person making the application –

(a) written notice of the decision;
(b) notification of amended reasons for, or correction of, the decision following a review; or

(c) notification that an application for the decision to be set aside has been unsuccessful.

(4) Where paragraph (3), (3A) or (3D) does not apply, an application under paragraph (1) must be sent or delivered to the Upper Tribunal so that it is received within 1 month after the latest of the dates on which the Upper Tribunal sent to the person making the application –

(a) written reasons for the decision;
(b) notification of amended reasons for, or correction of, the decision following a review; or
(c) notification that an application for the decision to be set aside has been unsuccessful.

(4A) Where, in judicial review proceedings in the Immigration and Asylum Chamber of the Upper Tribunal, a decision is given orally at a hearing, a person may apply to the Tribunal for permission to appeal –

(a) orally at that hearing; or
(b) in writing, before the commencement or the expiry of the relevant period determined by reference to paragraph (4).

(5) The date in paragraph (3)(c) or (4)(c) applies only if the application for the decision to be set aside was made within the time stipulated in rule 43 (setting aside a decision which disposes of proceedings) or any extension of that time granted by the Upper Tribunal.

(6) If the person seeking permission to appeal provides the application to the Upper Tribunal later than the time required by paragraph (3), (3A), (3D) or (4), or by any extension of time under rule 5(3)(a) (power to extend time) –

(a) the application must include a request for an extension of time and the reason why the application notice was not provided in time; and
(b) unless the Upper Tribunal extends time for the application under rule 5(3)(a) (power to extend time) the Upper Tribunal must refuse the application.

(7) An application under paragraph (1) or (4A)(a) must –

(a) identify the decision of the Tribunal to which it relates;
(b) identify the alleged error or errors of law in the decision; and
(c) state the result the party making the application is seeking.

Amendments—SI 2009/274; 2010/44; SI 2010/747; SI 2011/651; SI 2012/2890.

45 Upper Tribunal's consideration of application for permission to appeal

(1) On receiving an application for permission to appeal the Upper Tribunal may review the decision in accordance with rule 46 (review of a decision), but may only do so if –

(a) when making the decision the Upper Tribunal overlooked a legislative provision or binding authority which could have had a material effect on the decision; or
(b) since the Upper Tribunal's decision, a court has made a decision which is binding on the Upper Tribunal and which, had it been made before the Upper Tribunal's decision, could have had a material effect on the decision.

(2) If the Upper Tribunal decides not to review the decision, or reviews the decision and decides to take no action in relation to the decision or part of it, the Upper Tribunal must consider whether to give permission to appeal in relation to the decision or that part of it.

(3) The Upper Tribunal must send a record of its decision to the parties as soon as practicable.

(4) If the Upper Tribunal refuses permission to appeal it must send with the record of its decision –

(a) a statement of its reasons for such refusal; and
(b) notification of the right to make an application to the relevant appellate court for permission to appeal and the time within which, and the method by which, such application must be made.

(5) The Upper Tribunal may give permission to appeal on limited grounds, but must comply with paragraph (4) in relation to any grounds on which it has refused permission.

46 Review of a decision

(1) The Upper Tribunal may only undertake a review of a decision pursuant to rule 45(1) (review on an application for permission to appeal) –

(a) pursuant to rule 45(1) (review on an application for permission to appeal); or
(b) pursuant to rule 47 (reviews of decisions in proceedings under the Forfeiture Act 1982).

(2) The Upper Tribunal must notify the parties in writing of the outcome of any review and of any rights of review or appeal in relation to the outcome.

(3) If the Upper Tribunal decides to take any action in relation to a decision following a review without first giving every party an opportunity to make representations, the notice under paragraph

(2) must state that any party that did not have an opportunity to make representations may apply for such action to be set aside and for the decision to be reviewed again.

Amendments—SI2011/2343.

47 Setting aside a decision in proceedings under the Forfeiture Act 1982

(1) A person who referred a question to the Upper Tribunal under rule 26 (references under the Forfeiture Act 1982) must refer the Upper Tribunal's previous decision in relation to the question to the Upper Tribunal if they –

(a) consider that the decision should be set aside and re-made under this rule; or
(b) have received a written application for the decision to be set aside and re-made under this rule from the person to whom the decision related.

(2) The Upper Tribunal may set aside the decision, either in whole or in part, and re-make it if –

(a) (*revoked*)
(b) the decision was made in ignorance of, or was based on a mistake as to, some material fact; or
(c) there has been a relevant change in circumstances since the decision was made.

(3) When a person makes the reference to the Upper Tribunal, they must also notify the person to whom the question relates that the reference has been made.

(3) Rule 26(2) to (4), Parts 5 and 6 and this Part apply to a reference under this rule as they apply to a reference under rule 26(1).

Amendments—SI 2011/2343.

48 Power to treat an application as a different type of application

The Tribunal may treat an application for a decision to be corrected, set aside or reviewed, or for permission to appeal against a decision, as an application for any other one of those things.

Amendments—SI 2010/2653.

F6.1

F6.1

TABULAR SUMMARY OF FIRST-TIER RULES; UPPER TRIBUNAL RULES

THE TRIBUNAL PROCEDURE (UPPER TRIBUNAL) RULES 2008

Upper Tribunal rule (and similarity to equivalent First-tier Tribunal rule)	CPR Part 54
Part 1: Introduction Rule 1: Citation, commencement, application and interpretation	
The new Rules define the following: • The 2007 Act (TCEA 2007) • Appellant • Applicant • Disability discrimination in schools case • Dispose of proceedings • Document • Hearing • Legal representative • Mental health case • Party • Permission • Practice direction • Respondent • Special educational needs case • Working day With the exception of the following terms, none of the above are defined within Part 54 of the CPR. The following terms are defined in both sets of rules but their definitions are different: • Interested party	CPR, r 54.1 defined the following terms which are not defined within the new Rules: • A claim for judicial review • Court

<table>
<tr><td>• Judicial review proceedings/the judicial review procedure</td><td></td></tr>
<tr><td colspan="2">Part 1: Introduction
Rule 2: Overriding objective and parties' obligation to co-operate with the Tribunal</td></tr>
<tr><td>Rule 2(1) states that the overriding objective of these Rules is to enable the Upper Tribunal to deal with cases fairly and justly. Rule 2(2) provides a non-exhaustive list of how this can be done. This rule is identical to r 2 of the First-tier Tribunal Rules.</td><td>CPR, r 1.1 states: 'These Rules are a new procedural code with the overriding objective of enabling the court to deal with cases justly.'</td></tr>
<tr><td colspan="2">Part 1: Introduction
Rule 3: Alternative dispute resolution and arbitration</td></tr>
<tr><td>This rule is identical to r 3 of the First-tier Tribunal Rules.</td><td>CPR Part 54 does not specify any rule relating to alternative dispute resolution and arbitration.</td></tr>
<tr><td colspan="2">Part 2: General powers and provisions
Rule 4: Delegation to staff</td></tr>
<tr><td>This rule is identical to r 4 of the First-tier Tribunal Rules.</td><td>CPR Part 54 does not set out powers to delegate to staff.</td></tr>
<tr><td colspan="2">Part 2: General powers and provisions
Rule 5: Case management powers</td></tr>
<tr><td>This rule is similar to r 5 of the First-tier Tribunal Rules and to CPR, r 54.10.

5(3) provides a non-exhaustive list of the case management powers of the Upper Tribunal and, in addition to the list provided in the First-tier Tribunal Rules, it provides two further examples ((m) and (n)) which relate to the fact that the Upper Tribunal may be used for an appeal from another Tribunal. 5(3)(j) is also slightly different from the example given in the First-tier Tribunal Rules as it states 'stay (or in Scotland, sist) proceedings'.</td><td>CPR, r 54.10(1) states that where permission is given to proceed the court may also 'give directions'. Rule 54.10(2) states that these may include a stay of proceedings to which the claim relates. The case management powers of the court therefore appear to be very similar to the powers of the Upper Tribunal.
CPR Part 54 does not further provide examples of how these powers may be used.</td></tr>
<tr><td colspan="2">Part 2: General powers and provisions
Rule 6: Procedure for applying for and giving directions</td></tr>
</table>

Rule 6 is identical to r 6 of the First-tier Tribunal Rules and states that the Tribunal may give a direction on the application of one or more of the parties or on its own initiative. The remainder of r 6 sets out the procedure.	CPR, r 54.10(1) states that where permission to proceed is given the court may also give directions. CPR, r 54.11 states that any directions should be served upon the claimant, the defendant and any other person who has filed an acknowledgement of service. The only provision Part 54 gives for directions specifically requested by a party is CPR, r 54.17 which states that any person may apply for permission to file evidence or make representations at the hearing of judicial review.
Part 2: General powers and provisions Rule 7: Failure to comply with Rules etc	
7(1) and 7(2) are identical to the rules under the First-tier Tribunal Rules. 7(3) sets out what the Upper Tribunal may do where the First-tier Tribunal has referred a matter to it and 7(4) states that the Upper Tribunal may exercise its power under TCEA 2007, s 25 in relation to non-compliance.	The CPR appears to be much stricter in relation to a failure to comply and it would seem that a failure may render void the proceedings or any step taken in the proceedings. For example, CPR, r 54.5(1) states that the claim form must be filed promptly and in any event not later than 3 months after the grounds to make the claim first arose. CPR, r 54.5(2) states that the time-limit in this rule may not be extended by agreement between the parties.
Part 2: General powers and provisions Rule 8: Striking out a party's case	
In contrast to the First-tier Tribunal Rules, the whole of this rule appears to relate to mental health cases. The rule lists when the Upper Tribunal must strike out the whole or part of proceedings and when it may do so. A caveat has been placed on 8(3)(c) so that it reads: 'The Upper Tribunal may strike out the whole or part of the proceedings if, in proceedings which are not an appeal from the decision of another Tribunal or judicial review proceedings, the Upper Tribunal considers there is no reasonable prospect of the appellant's or the applicant's case, or part of it, succeeding.'	Part 54 makes no specific reference to striking out a party's case.

An application for reinstatement of proceedings that have been struck out must be made within one month after the date the Upper Tribunal sent notification of the striking out to the appellant or applicant. This differs from the First-tier Tribunal Rules, which specify 28 days.	
Part 2: General powers and provisions Rule 9: Substitution and addition of parties	
This rule is similar to the rule under the First-tier Tribunal Rules but that the Upper Tribunal may, in judicial review proceedings, give a direction adding a person as an interested party.	There is no equivalent provision within CPR Part 54.
Part 2: General powers and provisions Rule 10: Orders for costs	
This rule is similar to the rule under the First-tier Tribunal Rules. 10(3)(d) allows for a wasted costs order to be made if the Upper Tribunal considers that a party or its representative has acted unreasonably in bringing, defending or conducting the proceedings. Although this is also provided for in the First-tier Tribunal Rules it is not applicable to mental health cases. On an appeal, the Upper Tribunal is limited in that it may only make an order for costs under the rules governing the other Tribunal, although those rules in the First-tier Tribunal Rules are very similar to the rule governing proceedings other than appeals or under s 4 of the Forfeiture Act 1982.	There is no provision relating to costs under CPR Part 54 other than at CPR, r 54.9(2) in relation to failure to file an acknowledgement of service. In this instance, and where that person takes part in the hearing of the judicial review, the court may take his or her failure to file an acknowledgement of service into account when deciding what order to make about costs.
Part 2: General powers and provisions Rule 11: Representatives	

This rule is very similar to r 11 of the First-tier Tribunal Rules. 11(3) states: 'Anything permitted or required to be done by a party under these Rules … may be done by the representative of that party, except signing a witness statement.' It does not give the second exception of the application notice, for obvious reasons. It also defines 'legal representative' as this is not included in the list of definitions at r 1.	There is no equivalent provision within CPR Part 54.
Part 2: General powers and provisions Rule 12: Calculating time	
This rule is similar to r 12 of the First-tier Tribunal Rules except that there is no reference to the date the application notice is to be filed, as that is a not necessary requirement under these Rules. It also defines 'disability discrimination in schools case' and 'special educational needs case' as these are not defined at r 1.	There is no equivalent provision within CPR Part 54.
Part 2: General powers and provisions Rule 13: Sending and delivery of documents	
This rule is identical to the rule under the First-tier Tribunal Rules other than it also refers to document exchange.	There is no provision within CPR Part 54 relating to the sending and delivery of documents.
Part 2: General powers and provisions Rule 14: Use of documents and information	
This rule is identical to the rule under the First-tier Tribunal Rules.	There is no equivalent provision within CPR Part 54.
Part 2: General powers and provisions Rule 15: Evidence and submissions	
This rule is identical to the rule under the First-tier Tribunal Rules other than those Rules make further provision for special educational needs cases. However, see r 28 (Upper Tribunal Rules) and also s 16 of TCEA 2007.	CPR, r 54.12 allows the court to make a permission decision without a hearing. CPR, r 54.12(3) states that the claimant may not appeal but may request the decision to be reconsidered at a hearing. CPR, r 54.16(2) states that no written

	evidence may be relied upon unless it has been served in accordance with a rule under this section, a direction of the court or the court gives permission. CPR, r 54.17 states that any person may apply for permission to file evidence or make representations at the hearing of the judicial review but CPR, r 54.17(2) states that any such application should be made promptly.
Part 2: General powers and provisions Rule 16: Summoning or citation of witnesses and orders to answer questions or produce documents	
16(1), (2) and (6) are identical to the rule under the First-tier Tribunal Rules other than 16(1)(a) specifies that in Scotland a citation, rather than a summons, is used. 16(4) and (5) are not cited within the First-tier Tribunal Rules. 16(4) expressly states that a person may apply to the Upper Tribunal for a summons to be varied or set aside if they did not have the opportunity to object to it before it was made or issued and 16(5) states that this must be done as soon as reasonably practicable after receiving it.	There is no equivalent provision within CPR Part 54.
Part 2: General powers and provisions Rule 17: Withdrawal	
This rule is similar to the rule under the First-tier Tribunal Rules. 17(2) is slightly different in that there is only one exception in relation to an application for permission to appeal where, generally, notice of withdrawal will not take effect unless the Upper Tribunal consents to it. There are no exceptions to a party being able to withdraw its case where it relates to a mental health case (as under r 17(3) of the First-tier Tribunal Rules) and any application must be made within one month after the date the Upper Tribunal received the notice or the date the case was withdrawn orally, as opposed to 28 days under the other Rules.	There is no equivalent provision within CPR Part 54.
Part 2: General powers and provisions Rule 18: Notice of funding of legal services	

This rule provides that if funding of legal services is granted, a copy of the funding notice/legal aid certificate must be sent to the Upper Tribunal as soon as is practicable and should notify every other party in writing. There is no similar provision in the First-tier Tribunal Rules.	There is no equivalent provision within CPR Part 54.
Part 2: General powers and provisions Rule 19: Confidentiality in child support or child trust fund cases	
This rule sets out where the Upper Tribunal, Secretary of State, the Child Maintenance and Enforcement Commission and HMRC must take appropriate steps to secure the confidentiality of an address, and of any information which could reasonably be expected to enable a person to identify the address, to the extent that the address or that information is not already known to each other party. This is not provided for in the First-tier Tribunal Rules.	There is no equivalent provision within CPR Part 54.
Part 2: General powers and provisions Rule 20: Power to pay expenses and allowances	
This rule sets out circumstances where the Secretary of State or Lord Chancellor may pay allowances where proceedings are brought under s 4 of the Safeguarding Vulnerable Groups Act 2006 which are not an appeal from the decision of another tribunal or judicial review, the Child Support Act 1991, s 12 of the Social Security Act 1998, para 6 of Sch 7 to the Child Support, Pensions and Social Security Act 2000, a war pensions and armed forces case and in a Pensions Appeal Tribunal for Scotland or Northern Ireland.	There is no equivalent provision within CPR Part 54.
Part 3: Procedure for Cases in the Upper Tribunal Rule 21: Application to the Upper Tribunal for permission to appeal	

21(2) states that a person may apply to the Upper Tribunal for permission to appeal against a decision of another tribunal only if they have made an application for permission to appeal to the tribunal which made the decision challenged and that application has been refused or not admitted. The application must be made no later than one month after the date the other tribunal sent notice of its refusal to the appellant or, in the case of an application under s 4 of the Safeguarding Vulnerable Groups Act 2006, 3 months after the date on which written notice of the decision was sent to the appellant. 21(4) sets out what must be included on the application and does not specify that any name and address should be provided other than the appellant's, his or her representative's and any address where documents for the appellant may be sent or delivered. 21(5) sets out a list of documents which must accompany the claim form. 21(6) allows for an application for an extension of time, under r 5(3)(a). Rule 46 of the First-tier Tribunal Rules sets out the provisions for 'Application for permission to appeal'. However, the provisions and requirements in that rule are very different from those included in r 21.	CPR Part 54 specifically relates to judicial review and statutory review. It does not deal with appeals in general and therefore cannot be compared to rr 21–26 of the Upper Tribunal Rules.

Part 3: Procedure for Cases in the Upper Tribunal
Rule 22: Decision in relation to permission to appeal

Although it is not explicitly stated that the Upper Tribunal can deal with an application for permission to appeal without a hearing, it is clear from this rule (in particular 22(3)) that this is the case. The Rules do not specify that any respondent should file an acknowledgement of service, or indeed that they should be served with a copy of the application until a decision is made. Once the Upper Tribunal has made a decision in relation to permission to appeal, it must send written notice and reasons for the decision to the appellant and, in the case of giving permission, each party. If permission is granted, the Upper Tribunal should also, at this stage, send to each respondent a copy of the application and any accompanying documents. In some circumstances where a decision is made without a hearing (set out at 22(3)) the appellant may apply for the decision to be reconsidered (not appealed) at a hearing if the Upper Tribunal refuses permission or gives it on limited grounds. Any application must be made in writing within 14 days after the date the Upper Tribunal sent written notice to the appellant. Rule 47 of the First-tier Tribunal Rules deals with 'Tribunal's consideration of application for permission to appeal'. Again, the provisions in this rule are quite different. If, in the First-tier Tribunal, an application for permission is refused, the Tribunal must send to the parties a record of its decision, written reasons and notification of the right to appeal to the Upper Tribunal, setting out the time-limits and method for doing so.	

Part 3: Procedure for Cases in the Upper Tribunal
Rule 23: Notice of appeal

Under r 22(2)(b) where the Upper Tribunal gives permission to appeal, subject to any direction, the application for permission stands as the notice of appeal and the Upper Tribunal must send to each respondent a copy of it with accompanying documentation. Rule 23 applies where another tribunal has given permission to appeal or the Upper Tribunal has given permission but has given a direction that the application does not stand as the notice of appeal. 23(2) states that a notice of appeal must be provided to the Upper Tribunal within one month after the tribunal sent notice of the permission to the appellant and should include information as listed in 23(4). If the notice of appeal is provided later than one month after the tribunal notified the appellant of the decision to grant permission the Upper Tribunal can only extend the time under r 5(3)(a).	
Part 3: Procedure for Cases in the Upper Tribunal Rule 24: Response to the notice of appeal	
Rule 24 allows for a respondent to respond to a notice of appeal within one month after the Upper Tribunal sent notice it had granted permission to the appellant or sent a copy of the notice of appeal. 24(3) sets out what should be included in the response and an extension of time can only be allowed under r 5(3)(a).	
Part 3: Procedure for Cases in the Upper Tribunal Rule 25: Appellant's reply	
Rule 25 allows for the appellant to reply to any response received under r 24. Any reply should be made in writing within one month after the Upper Tribunal sent the response to the appellant and, upon receipt, the Upper Tribunal must send a copy of the reply and any accompanying documents to each respondent.	
Rule 26 relates to References under the Forfeiture Act 1982.	

Part 3: Procedure for Cases in the Upper Tribunal Rule 26A: Cases transferred or referred to the Upper Tribunal, applications made directly to the Upper Tribunal and proceedings without notice to a respondent	
Rule 26A sets out the procedure for cases that have been transferred or referred to the Upper Tribunal from the First-tier Tribunal and for cases, other than an appeal or a case to which r 26 (references under the Forfeiture Act 1982) applies, which is started by an application made directly to the Upper Tribunal. 26A(3) expressly states that if a case or matter is to be determined without notice or involvement of a respondent, any provision in the Rules requiring a document to be provided to a respondent or permitting a respondent to participate in the proceedings does not apply to that case or matter.	CPR Part 54 does not make provision for proceedings without notice to a respondent.
Part 4: Judicial review proceedings in the Upper Tribunal Rule 27: Application of this Part to judicial review proceedings transferred to the Upper Tribunal	
Rule 27 sets out what the Upper Tribunal must do where judicial review proceedings have been transferred to them by a court. Part 4 (rr 27–33) specifically relates to judicial review proceedings and there is therefore no equivalent rules under the First-tier Tribunal Rules.	There is no equivalent provision within CPR Part 54.
Part 4: Judicial review proceedings in the Upper Tribunal Rule 28: Applications for permission to bring judicial review proceedings	

Rule 28 specifies that any application for permission to bring judicial review proceedings should be made in writing and no later than 3 months after the date the decision, act or omission was made or within one month after the First-tier Tribunal sent its written reasons or notification that an application for the decision to be set aside had been unsuccessful, whichever date is later. 28(4) sets out what the application must state within it and what should accompany the application. These requirements are very similar to those under CPR, r 54. 28(7), and provide the Upper Tribunal with the power to extend time under r 5(3)(a). There does not appear to be any discretion for this under CPR Part 54.	In relation to permission to bring judicial review proceedings, CPR Part 54 does not provide any conditions as to who may apply. CPR, r 54.4 merely states: 'The court's permission to proceed is required in a claim for judicial review …' The CPR also allows 3 months for the application to be made – r 54.5 states that the claim form must be filed promptly and in any event not later than 3 months after the grounds to make the claim first arose. CPR, r 54.6 sets out what a person must state on the claim form in addition to the information requested in r 8.2. This further information is the name and address of any party he or she considers to be an interested party, that he or she is requesting permission to proceed with a claim for judicial review and any remedy (including any interim remedy) he or she is seeking. CPR, r 54.6(2) states that the claim form must be accompanied by the documents required by the relevant practice direction. Neither under CPR, r 8.2 nor 54.6 is it explicitly stated that the claim form should state the name and address of the appellant and/or his or her representative or an address where documents for the appellant may be sent or delivered. Within Part 54, there appears to be no power for a court to extend the period of time for making the application (r 54.5).

Part 4: Judicial review proceedings in the Upper Tribunal
Rule 29: Acknowledgement of service

This requirement for the filing of an acknowledgement of service is not included in Part 3 of the Rules – Appeals and references to the Upper Tribunal. Within judicial review proceedings, a person who is sent an application seeking permission under r 28(8) and who wishes to take part in them must send or deliver an acknowledgement of service no later than 21 days after the date the Upper Tribunal sent a copy to them. It must be in writing and state whether the person supports or opposes the application, the grounds for this support or opposition and the name and address of any other person they consider to be an interested person. 29(3) states that where someone fails to send an acknowledgement of service, they may not take part in the application for permission but may take part in subsequent proceedings.	The provisions within CPR Part 54 are extremely similar to those contained in r 29. CPR, r 54.8(2) also specifies a 21-day period and r 54.8(4) sets out what should be included in the acknowledgement of service, which are the same things as should be included under r 29. CPR, r 54.9 deals with a failure to file an acknowledgement of service and this too is very similar to r 29. It provides a further condition, that a person who has failed to file an acknowledgement of service may take part in the hearing of the judicial review provided he or she complies with CPR, r 54.14 or any other direction of the court regarding the filing and service of detailed grounds for contesting the claim or supporting it on additional grounds and any written evidence.

Part 4: Judicial review proceedings in the Upper Tribunal
Rule 30: Decision on permission or summary dismissal, and reconsideration of permission or summary dismissal at a hearing

Rule 30(1) states that the Upper Tribunal should send its decision and the reasons for it, including any conditions or limitations, to the applicant, each respondent, each person who filed an acknowledgement of service and any other interest party. A decision made without a hearing can be 'reconsidered' at a hearing. An application should be made and sent so that the Upper Tribunal receives it within 14 days after the date it sent notice of the decision.	Similarly, under CPR, r 54.11, where the court refuses permission, it should serve the order, reasons and any directions on the claimant, defendant and any other person who filed an acknowledgement of service. Where a court, without a hearing, refuses permission or gives it on limited grounds, the claimant may request that the decision be reconsidered at a hearing. This request must be filed within 7 days after service of the reasons (CPR, r 54.12). This is a shorter period than that specified within the Upper Tribunal Rules.

Part 4: Judicial review proceedings in the Upper Tribunal
Rule 31: Responses

Rule 31 states that any person who has been sent notice of the grant of permission and who wishes to contest the application or support it on additional grounds must provide detailed written grounds, which should be sent so that they are received no later than 35 days after the notice was sent.	CPR, r 54.14 is almost identical to r 31. It provides that a defendant and any other person served with a claim form who wishes to contest or support it on additional grounds must file and serve detailed grounds and any written evidence within 35 days after service of the order giving permission.

Part 4: Judicial review proceedings in the Upper Tribunal Rule 32: Applicant seeking to rely on additional grounds	
Rule 32 states that the applicant may not rely on additional grounds without the consent of the Upper Tribunal.	Similarly, CPR, r 54.15 states that the court's permission is required if a claimant seeks to rely on grounds other than those for which he or she has been given permission to proceed.
Part 4: Judicial review proceedings in the Upper Tribunal Rule 33: Right to make representations	
Rule 33 allows for each party and any other person who has the permission of the Upper Tribunal to submit evidence, except at the hearing relating to permission, to make representations at a hearing they are entitled to attend and make written representations in relation to a decision being made without a hearing.	CPR, r 54.16 states that no written evidence may be relied on unless it has been served in accordance with any rule under this section, direction of the court or the Court gives permission. CPR, r 54.17 states that any person may apply for permission to file evidence or make representations at the hearing for judicial review. Any application should be made promptly.
Part 5: Hearings Rule 34: Decision with or without a hearing	
Rule 34 simply states that the Upper Tribunal may make any decision without a hearing but it must have regard to any view expressed by a party when deciding whether to hold a hearing to consider any matter and the form of any hearing. Rule 23 of the First-tier Tribunal Rules is different and is more similar to CPR Part 54, requiring the consent of the parties and that the Tribunal should consider it is able to deal with the matter without a hearing.	CPR, r 54.18 is slightly different from r 34. It states that the court may decide the claim for judicial review without a hearing where all the parties agree. Presumably, therefore, if one party were not in agreement the court would have to have a hearing.
Part 5: Hearings Rule 35: Entitlement to attend a hearing	
Rule 35 states that subject to r 37(4) (exclusion of a person from a hearing) each party is entitled to attend. Rule 4 of the First-tier Tribunal Rules is very similar.	CPR Part 54 does not explicitly say that each party is entitled to attend the judicial review hearing and only gives limitations on persons allowed to make representations.
Part 5: Hearings Rule 36: Notice of hearings	

Under r 36, the Upper Tribunal must give each party 14 days' notice of the time and place for a hearing. It specifies some exceptions to this rule, which are in applications for permission to bring judicial review proceedings where the period of notice is 2 working days and where shorter notice is given with the parties' consent or in urgent or exceptional cases. The same 14-day time period is specified in r 25 of the First-tier Tribunal Rules, also with certain exceptions.	Under CPR, r 54.12(5) the claimant, defendant and any other person who has filed an acknowledgement of service should be given 2 days' notice of a hearing relating to a permission hearing. There is no specific provision relating to the hearing of the judicial review.
Part 5: Hearings Rule 37: Public and private hearings	
Rule 37 states that all hearings must be held in public unless the Upper Tribunal makes a direction that a hearing or part of it is to be held in private. 36(4) allows the Upper Tribunal to exclude from a hearing anyone whose conduct the Upper Tribunal considers is disrupting or is likely to disrupt the hearing, anyone whose presence the Upper Tribunal considers is likely to prevent another person giving evidence or making submissions freely, anyone who should be excluded to give effect to a direction under r 14(2) (withholding information likely to cause any harm), anyone where the purpose of the hearing would be defeated by the attendance of him and anyone under the age of 18. The Upper Tribunal may also exclude a witness until that person gives evidence. This rule is very similar to r 26 of the First-tier Tribunal Rules; the only difference being that those rules specify particular rules relating to special educational needs and disability discrimination in schools cases.	CPR Part 54 does not specifically state that a hearing should be held in public unless otherwise decided.
Part 5: Hearings Rule 38: Hearing in a party's absence	

This rule is identical to r 27 of the First-tier Tribunal Rules. If a party fails to attend a hearing, the hearing may proceed where the Upper Tribunal is satisfied that the party has been notified or that reasonable steps have been taken to notify the party and it is in the interests of justice to proceed.	CPR Part 54 does not specify where a court may proceed with a hearing in the absence of a party.
Part 6: Decisions Rule 39: Consent orders	
Rule 39 is identical to r 29 of the First-tier Tribunal Rules. It allows the Upper Tribunal to make consent orders and in such cases it does not have to hold a hearing or provide reasons for the order.	CPR Part 54 does not specifically state that a court may make a consent order.
Part 6: Decisions Rule 40: Decisions	
This rule is similar to r 30 of the First-tier Tribunal Rules. However, under the Upper Tribunal Rules, written reasons for a decision do not need to be provided where a decision was made with the consent of all parties and where the parties have consented to the Upper Tribunal not giving reasons.	The only provisions of CPR Part 54 which relate to 'Decisions' are in relation to the court's decision about whether permission is granted to proceed with an application for judicial review.
Part 7 of the Tribunal Procedure (Upper Tribunal) Rules 2008 relates to 'Correcting, setting aside, reviewing and appealing decisions of the Upper Tribunal'. CPR Part 54 does not allow for any appeal of a decision. Rules 41–47 of the Upper Tribunal Rules are similar to rr 43–49 of the First-tier Rules, although some of the time limits are different.	

F7

F7

CIVIL PROCEDURE RULES 1998

SI 1998/3132

****

PART 54
JUDICIAL REVIEW AND STATUTORY REVIEW

ARRANGEMENT OF RULES

PART 54

JUDICIAL REVIEW AND STATUTORY REVIEW

Section I – Judicial Review

Section I – Judicial Review

54.1 Scope and interpretation

(1) This Section of this Part contains rules about judicial review.

(2) In this Section –

(a) a 'claim for judicial review' means a claim to review the lawfulness of –
  (i) an enactment; or

(ii) a decision, action or failure to act in relation to the exercise of a public function.

(b)–(d)(*revoked*)

(e) 'the judicial review procedure' means the Part 8 procedure as modified by this Section;

(f) 'interested party' means any person (other than the claimant and defendant) who is directly affected by the claim; and

(g) 'court' means the High Court, unless otherwise stated.

(Rule 8.1(6)(b) provides that a rule or practice direction may, in relation to a specified type of proceedings, disapply or modify any of these rules set out in Part 8 as they apply to those proceedings)

Amendments—SI 2000/2092; SI 2003/364; SI 2003/3361.

54.1A Who may exercise the powers of the High Court

(1) A court officer assigned to the Administrative Court office who is –

(a) a barrister; or

(b) a solicitor, may exercise the jurisdiction of the High Court with regard to the matters set out in paragraph (2) with the consent of the President of the Queen's Bench Division.

(2) The matters referred to in paragraph (1) are –

(a) any matter incidental to any proceedings in the High Court;

(b) any other matter where there is no substantial dispute between the parties; and

(c) the dismissal of an appeal or application where a party has failed to comply with any order, rule or practice direction.

(3) A court officer may not decide an application for –

(a) permission to bring judicial review proceedings;

(b) an injunction;

(c) a stay of any proceedings, other than a temporary stay of any order or decision of the lower court over a period when the High Court is not sitting or cannot conveniently be convened, unless the parties seek a stay by consent.

(4) Decisions of a court officer may be made without a hearing.

(5) A party may request any decision of a court officer to be reviewed by a judge of the High Court.

(6) At the request of a party, a hearing will be held to reconsider a decision of a court officer, made without a hearing.

(7) A request under paragraph (5) or (6) must be filed within 7 days after the party is served with notice of the decision.

Amendments—Inserted by SI 2012/2208.

54.2 When this Section must be used

The judicial review procedure must be used in a claim for judicial review where the claimant is seeking –

(a) a mandatory order;

(b) a prohibiting order;

(c) a quashing order; or
(d) an injunction under section 30 of the Senior Court Act 1981 (restraining a person from acting in any office in which he is not entitled to act).

Amendments—SI 2000/2092; SI 2003/364.

54.3 When this Section may be used

(1) The judicial review procedure may be used in a claim for judicial review where the claimant is seeking –

(a) a declaration; or
(b) an injunction.

(Section 31(2) of the Senior Court Act 1981 sets out the circumstances in which the court may grant a declaration or injunction in a claim for judicial review)

(Where the claimant is seeking a declaration or injunction in addition to one of the remedies listed in rule 54.2, the judicial review procedure must be used)

(2) A claim for judicial review may include a claim for damages, restitution or the recovery of a sum due but may not seek such a remedy alone.

(Section 31(4) of the Senior Court Act 1981 sets out the circumstances in which the court may award damages, restitution or the recovery of a sum due on a claim for judicial review)

Amendments—SI 2000/2092; SI 2003/364; Constitutional Reform Act 2005, Sch 11, para 1(2).

54.4 Permission required

The court's permission to proceed is required in a claim for judicial review whether started under this Section or transferred to the Administrative Court.

Amendments—SI 2000/2092; SI 2003/364.

54.5 Time limit for filing claim form

(1) The claim form must be filed –

(a) promptly; and
(b) in any event not later than 3 months after the grounds to make the claim first arose.

(2) The time limit in this rule may not be extended by agreement between the parties.

(3) This rule does not apply when any other enactment specifies a shorter time limit for making the claim for judicial review.

Amendments—SI 2000/2092.

54.6 Claim form

(1) In addition to the matters set out in rule 8.2 (contents of the claim form) the claimant must also state –

(a) the name and address of any person he considers to be an interested party;
(b) that he is requesting permission to proceed with a claim for judicial review;
(c) any remedy (including any interim remedy) he is claiming; and
(d) where appropriate, the grounds on which it is contended that the claim is an Aarhus Convention claim.

(Rules 45.41 to 45.44 make provision about costs in Aarhus Convention claims)

(2) The claim form must be accompanied by the documents required by practice direction 54A.

Amendments—SI 2000/2092; SI 2009/3309; SI 2013/262.

54.7 Service of claim form

The claim form must be served on –

(a) the defendant; and
(b) unless the court otherwise directs, any person the claimant considers to be an interested party, within 7 days after the date of issue.

Amendments—SI 2000/2092.

54.7A Judicial review of decisions of the Upper Tribunal

(1) This rule applies where an application is made, following refusal by the Upper Tribunal of permission to appeal against a decision of the First-tier Tribunal, for

judicial review –

(a) of the decision of the Upper Tribunal refusing permission to appeal; or
(b) which relates to the decision of the First-tier Tribunal which was the subject of the application for permission to appeal.

(2) Where this rule applies –

(a) the application may not include any other claim, whether against the Upper Tribunal or not; and
(b) any such other claim must be the subject of a separate application.

(3) The claim form and the supporting documents required by paragraph (4) must be filed no later than 16 days after the date on which notice of the Upper Tribunal's decision was sent to the applicant.

(4) The supporting documents are –

(a) the decision of the Upper Tribunal to which the application relates, and any document giving reasons for the decision;
(b) the grounds of appeal to the Upper Tribunal and any documents which were sent with them;
(c) the decision of the First-tier Tribunal, the application to that Tribunal for permission to appeal and its reasons for refusing permission; and
(d) any other documents essential to the claim.

(5) The claim form and supporting documents must be served on the Upper Tribunal and any other interested party no later than 7 days after the date of issue.

(6) The Upper Tribunal and any person served with the claim form who wishes to take part in the proceedings for judicial review must, no later than 21 days after service of the claim form, file and serve on the applicant and any other party an acknowledgment of service in the relevant practice form.

(7) The court will give permission to proceed only if it considers –

(a) that there is an arguable case, which has a reasonable prospect of success, that both the decision of the Upper Tribunal refusing permission to appeal and the decision of the First-tier Tribunal against which permission to appeal was sought are wrong in law; and

(b) that either –

(i) the claim raises an important point of principle or practice; or

(ii) there is some other compelling reason to hear it.

(8) If the application for permission is refused on paper without an oral hearing, rule 54.12(3) (request for reconsideration at a hearing) does not apply.

(9) If permission to apply for judicial review is granted –

(a) if the Upper Tribunal or any interested party wishes there to be a hearing of the substantive application, it must make its request for such a hearing no later than 14 days after service of the order granting permission; and

(b) if no request for a hearing is made within that period, the court will make a final order quashing the refusal of permission without a further hearing.

(10) The power to make a final order under paragraph (9)(b) may be exercised by the Master of the Crown Office or a Master of the Administrative Court.

Amendments—Inserted by SI 2012/2208.

54.8 Acknowledgment of service

(1) Any person served with the claim form who wishes to take part in the judicial review must file an acknowledgment of service in the relevant practice form in accordance with the following provisions of this rule.

(2) Any acknowledgment of service must be –

(a) filed not more than 21 days after service of the claim form; and

(b) served on –

(i) the claimant; and

(ii) subject to any direction under rule 54.7(b), any other person named in the claim form, as soon as practicable and, in any event, not later than 7 days after it is filed.

(3) The time limits under this rule may not be extended by agreement between the parties.

(4) The acknowledgment of service –

(a) must –

(i) where the person filing it intends to contest the claim, set out a summary of his grounds for doing so; and

(ii) state the name and address of any person the person filing it considers to be an interested party; and

(b) may include or be accompanied by an application for directions.

(5) Rule 10.3(2) does not apply.

Amendments—Inserted by SI 2000/2092.

54.9 Failure to file acknowledgment of service

(1) Where a person served with the claim form has failed to file an acknowledgment of service in accordance with rule 54.8, he –

(a) may not take part in a hearing to decide whether permission should be given unless the court allows him to do so; but
(b) provided he complies with rule 54.14 or any other direction of the court regarding the filing and service of –
    (i) detailed grounds for contesting the claim or supporting it on additional grounds; and
    (ii) any written evidence,
may take part in the hearing of the judicial review.

(2) Where that person takes part in the hearing of the judicial review, the court may take his failure to file an acknowledgment of service into account when deciding what order to make about costs.

(3) Rule 8.4 does not apply.

54.10 Permission given

(1) Where permission to proceed is given the court may also give directions.

(2) Directions under paragraph (1) may include

(a) a stay of proceedings to which the claim relates;
(b) directions requiring the proceedings to be heard by a Divisional Court

(Rule 3.7 provides a sanction for the non-payment of the fee payable when permission to proceed has been given)

Amendments—SI 2000/2092; SI 2010/2577.

54.11 Service of order giving or refusing permission

The court will serve –

(a) the order giving or refusing permission; and
(b) any directions,

on –

(i) the claimant;
(ii) the defendant; and
(iii) any other person who filed an acknowledgment of service.

54.12 Permission decision without a hearing

(1) This rule applies where the court, without a hearing –

(a) refuses permission to proceed; or
(b) gives permission to proceed –
    (i) subject to conditions; or
    (ii) on certain grounds only.

(2) The court will serve its reasons for making the decision when it serves the order giving or refusing permission in accordance with rule 54.11.

(3) The claimant may not appeal but may request the decision to be reconsidered at a hearing.

(4) A request under paragraph (3) must be filed within 7 days after service of the reasons under paragraph (2).

(5) The claimant, defendant and any other person who has filed an acknowledgment of service will be given at least 2 days' notice of the hearing date.

(6) The court may give directions requiring the proceedings to be heard by a Divisional Court.

Amendments—SI 2000/2092; SI 2010/2577.

54.13 Defendant etc may not apply to set aside

Neither the defendant nor any other person served with the claim form may apply to set aside an order giving permission to proceed.

Amendments—SI 2000/2092.

54.14 Response

(1) A defendant and any other person saved with the claim form who wishes to contest the claim or support it on additional grounds must file and serve –

(a) detailed grounds for contesting the claim or supporting it on additional grounds; and
(b) any written evidence,

within 35 days after service of the order giving permission.

(2) The following rules do not apply –

(a) rule 8.5(3) and 8.5(4) (defendant to file and serve written evidence at the same time as acknowledgment of service); and
(b) rule 8.5(5) and 8.5(6) (claimant to file and serve reply within 14 days).

Amendments—Inserted by SI 2000/2092.

54.15 Where claimant seeks to rely on additional grounds

The court's permission is required if a claimant seeks to rely on grounds other than those for which he has been given permission to proceed.

Amendments—Inserted by SI 2000/2092.

54.16 Evidence

(1) Rule 8.6(1) does not apply.

(2) No written evidence may be relied on unless –

(a) it has been served in accordance with any –
  (i) rule under this Section; or
  (ii) direction of the court; or
(b) the court gives permission.

Amendments—Inserted by SI 2000/2092; amended by SI 2002/2058; SI 2003/364.

54.17 Court's powers to hear any person

(1) Any person may apply for permission –

(a) to file evidence; or
(b) make representations at the hearing of the judicial review.

(2) An application under paragraph (1) should be made promptly.

Amendments—Inserted by SI 2000/2092.

54.18 Judicial review may be decided without a hearing

The court may decide the claim for judicial review without a hearing where all the parties agree.

Amendments—Inserted by SI 2000/2092.

54.19 Court's powers in respect of quashing orders

(1) This rule applies where the court makes a quashing order in respect of the decision to which the claim relates.

(2) The court may –

(a) (i) remit the matter to the decision-maker; and
(ii) direct it to reconsider the matter and reach a decision in accordance with the judgment of the court; or

(b) in so far as any enactment permits, substitute its own decision for the decision to which the claim relates.

(Section 31 of the Senior Court Act 1981 enables the High Court, subject to certain conditions, to substitute its own decision for the decision in question.)

Amendments—SI 2000/2092; SI 2007/3543 (in force from 6 April 2008); Constitutional Reform Act 2005, Sch 11, para 1(2).

54.20 Transfer

The court may –

(a) order a claim to continue as if it had not been started under this Section; and
(b) where it does so, give directions about the future management of the claim.

(Part 30 (transfer) applies to transfers to and from the Administrative Court)

Amendments—Inserted by SI 2000/2092; amended by SI 2003/364.

****

F7

F7

CLAIMS FOR JUDICIAL REVIEW

LEGAL BACKGROUND

Claims for judicial review are governed by CPR Pt 54.

A claim for judicial review is a means of vindicating rights in public law. It is defined in the CPR as 'a claim to review the lawfulness of (i) an enactment; or (ii) a decision, action or failure to act in relation to the exercise of a public function'. It is sometimes difficult to tell whether a particular complaint involves a matter of public law or of private law. Frequently, the complaint involves elements of both; where it does, the courts are allowing claimants greater flexibility in choosing their forum. But the distinction between public and private law remains important for a number of purposes.

There are a number of respects in which claims for judicial review differ from private law claims –

There are short time-limits.
The claimant requires the permission of the court to bring the proceedings.
The proceedings are generally conducted without oral evidence.
There is rarely disclosure of documents.
Relief is discretionary.

A Practice Direction on Judicial Review accompanies Pt 54. In addition, there is available from the Administrative Court Office a helpful booklet entitled *Notes for Guidance on Applying for Judicial Review*. The Pre-Action Protocol – Judicial Review – is set out in Section 4 of this work.

PROCEDURE[1]

Availability	Where the substance of the claim is a matter of public law and the remedy sought is as stated above. Proceedings for judicial review are generally not appropriate where an alternative remedy is available, such as a statutory appeal	Judicial Review Protocol, paras 2–4 SCA, ss 29–31 Rules 54.2, 54.3

1 Reproduced from *Civil Court Service* (Jordan Publishing, 2013).

	Judicial review is available in criminal proceedings save in matters relating to trial on indictment	SCA, s 29(3)
Letters before action	The prospective claimant should write a detailed letter before action, allowing 14 days for the prospective defendant to respond, save where the nature of the claim precludes this. The prospective defendant should write a similarly detailed response. The letters should be copied to any interested parties	Judicial Review Protocol, paras 8–17, Annexes A and B
Venue	Proceedings must be issued in the High Court. A claim for judicial review cannot be transferred to a county court	CLSA 1990, s 1(10); CCA 1984, s 38(3)
	Proceedings should be issued in the Administrative Court Office in the Royal Courts of Justice, London or in the Administrative Court Office at Birmingham, Cardiff, Leeds or Manchester High Courts	PD54D
	The claimant or defendant can make an application to transfer the claim to a more convenient venue if the criteria set out in the Practice Direction 54D are met. Similarly the court can transfer a case to a different court centre of its own volition if it appears that the case is more conveniently heard at a different court centre	
Permission	A claimant needs the permission of the court to bring a claim for judicial review	SCA, s 31(3) Rule 54.4
	The application for permission is generally made on the papers in the first instance	PD54A, para 8.4
	If permission is refused, or is granted subject to conditions or on certain grounds only, the application may be renewed to a judge orally but only if the initial refusal was on the papers	Rule 54.12

	Where a person served with the claim form has not filed an acknowledgment of service in accordance with the rules (see below), he will not be permitted to take part in the renewed permission hearing unless the court allows him to do so, but the defendant may take part in the substantive hearing, providing that he complies with any directions about filing his grounds and evidence	Rule 54.9
	If permission is refused at the oral hearing, the claimant may apply for permission to appeal to the Court of Appeal. Such application must be filed within 7 days of the decision of the High Court. If the Court of Appeal grants permission to apply for judicial review, the case will proceed in the High Court unless the Court of Appeal orders otherwise	Rule 52.15
	If the Court of Appeal refuses permission to appeal, no further appeal lies to the Supreme Court	AJA 1999, s 54
	Where permission is given, the court may give directions. The court will serve the order giving permission, and any directions, on the claimant, the defendant and on any interested party who has acknowledged service	Rule 54.10 Rule 54.11
	Neither the defendant nor any other party served with the claim form may apply to set aside the grant of permission to apply for judicial review	Rule 54.13
Time-limits	The proceedings must be brought promptly and in any event within 3 months from the date when the grounds for the application first arose	Rule 54.5
	Where the claimant seeks the quashing of a judgment, order or conviction, time begins to run from the date of that judgment, order or conviction	PD54A, para 4.1
	If there is undue delay by the claimant, the court may refuse to grant permission or any relief	SCA, s 31(6)
	The claimant must serve the claim form on the defendant and on any interested party within 7 days after the date of issue	Rule 54.7

	An interested party is any other person who is directly affected by the claim	Rule 54.1(2)(f)
	The defendant and any interested party served with the claim form who wishes to take part in the judicial review must file an acknowledgment of service not more than 21 days after the claim form is served on him; and must serve his acknowledgment on the other parties within 7 days after it is filed. It is not served by the court	Rule 54.8
	If the application for permission is refused, or is granted subject to conditions or on certain grounds only, the application to renew the request for permission at an oral hearing must be made within 7 days after the court serves on the claimant its reasons for not (simply) granting permission	Rule 54.12(4)
	An application for permission to appeal to the Court of Appeal against the refusal of permission must be made within 7 days of the decision of the High Court	Rule 52.15
Contents of claim form	The claim form must specify the relief claimed and must include –	Rule 54.6
	the name and address of any interested party;	
	a detailed statement of the claimant's grounds for bringing the claim for judicial review;	
	a statement of the facts relied on;	
	any application to extend the time-limit for filing the claim form;	
	any application for directions; and	PD54A, para 5.6
	It should be accompanied by –	
	any written evidence relied on;	
	a copy of any order that the claimant seeks to have quashed;	
	where the claim relates to a decision of a court or tribunal, an approved copy of the reasons for reaching that decision;	
	copies of any documents on which the claimant proposes to rely;	
	copies of any relevant statutory material;	

	a list of essential documents for advance reading by the court (with page references to the passages relied on); and,	
	insofar as any of the above are not available, reasons why they are unavailable	PD54A, paras 5.7, 5.8
	The claim form should also give details of the claimant's solicitors.	
	Where the claimant seeks to raise any issue under HRA 1998, the claim form must give the particulars required by PD16, para 16.1	PD54A, para 5.3
	Where the claimant seeks to raise a devolution issue, the claim form must say so and must specify the relevant statutory provision and the relevant facts	PD54A, para 5.4
Acknowledgment of service	The acknowledgment of service should state whether the defendant contests the claim and, if so, summarise his grounds for doing so	Rule 54.8(4)
Opposing the claim	The defendant, and any interested party who wishes to oppose or be heard on the claim, must serve detailed grounds and any evidence within 35 days after service of the order giving permission	Rule 54.14(1)
	The claimant must serve any reply within 14 days of service of the defendant's or interested party's evidence	Rule 54.14(2)
	No other evidence is admissible without the court's permission	Rule 54.16
Preparation for hearing	The claimant requires the court's permission to rely on any grounds other than those for which he has been given permission	Rule 54.15
	The claimant must give the other parties 7 clear days' notice of an application to rely on additional grounds	PD54A, para 11.1
	Any person wishing to apply to the court for permission to file evidence or to make representations at the hearing of the claim for judicial review should do so promptly	Rule 54.17

	The court may allow such an intervention and may do so subject to conditions	PD54A, paras 13.1, 13.2
	Disclosure is not required unless the court orders otherwise	PD54A, para 12.1
	The court may order cross-examination but this is rare	
	The claimant must file two copies of a paginated and indexed bundle	PD54A, paras 5.9, 5.10
	The bundle, and the claimant's skeleton argument, must be filed 21 working days before the hearing	PD54A, para 15.1
	The defendant and any interested party wishing to make representations must file skeleton arguments 14 working days before the hearing date	PD54A, para 15.2
	Skeleton arguments must contain – a time estimate for the complete hearing, including judgment; a list of issues; a list of the legal points to be taken (together with any relevant authorities with page references to the passages relied on); a chronology of events (with page references to the bundle of documents); a list of essential documents for the advance reading of the court (with page references to the passages relied on) (if different from that filed with the claim form); a time estimate for that reading; and a list of persons referred to.	PD54A, para 15.3
Transfer	Proceedings which commenced as a claim for judicial review may be ordered to continue as if they had not been commenced under Pt 54	Rule 54.20
	Proceedings which were commenced other than under Pt 54 may be transferred to the Administrative Court	PD54A, paras 14.1, 14.2 Rule 30.5

Agreed final orders	Where the parties agree about the final order to be made in a claim for judicial review, the claimant should file a document (with two copies) signed by all the parties setting out the terms of the proposed order, together with a short statement of the matters relied on as justifying the proposed order and copies of any authorities and provisions relied on	PD54A, para 17.1
	If the court is satisfied that the proposed order should be made, it may make it without a hearing	Rule 54.18
	If the court is not so satisfied, a hearing date will be set	PD54A, para 17.3
Forms	Claim Form N461	
	Application for urgent consideration N463	
	Acknowledgment of service N462	
	Form N464 Application for directions as to venue for administration and determination	
	Form N465 Response to application for directions as to venue for administration and determination	
	Application for permission to appeal a refusal of permission to bring claim for judicial review N161	

INDEX

References are to paragraph numbers.